Dunbar the Makar

Dunbar the Makar

PRISCILLA BAWCUTT

CLARENDON PRESS · OXFORD
1992

Oxford University Press, Walton Street, Oxford OX2 6DP
Oxford New York Toronto
Delhi Bombay Calcutta Madras Karachi
Petaling Jaya Singapore Hong Kong Tokyo
Nairobi Dar es Salaam Cape Town
Melbourne Auckland
and associated companies in
Berlin Ibadan

Oxford is a trade mark of Oxford University Press

Published in the United States
by Oxford University Press, New York

© Priscilla Bawcutt 1992

All rights reserved. No part of this publication may be reproduced,
stored in a retrieval system, or transmitted, in any form or by any means,
electronic, mechanical, photocopying, recording or otherwise, without
the prior permission of Oxford University Press

British Library Cataloguing in Publication Data
Data available

Library of Congress Cataloging in Publication Data
Bawcutt, Priscilla J.
Dunbar the makar / Priscilla Bawcutt.
Includes bibliographical references and index.
1. Dunbar, William, 1460?–1520?—Criticism and interpretation.
I. Title.
PR2269.B37 1992   821'.2—dc20
ISBN 0-19-812963-7

Typeset by Cambridge Composing (UK) Ltd
Printed and bound in
Great Britain by Bookcraft Ltd
Midsomer Norton, Bath

Than cam in Dunbar the mackar,
On all the flure thair was nane frackar.

Preface

WILLIAM DUNBAR is a poet whose virtuosity is often praised, but rarely analysed. This book, as its title implies, is largely a study of the way his poems are *made*. What particularly interests me is Dunbar's adroit and sensitive handling of language, and of extremely varied modes and genres. I have sought also to illuminate the complex literary context in which he flourished. Although I do not neglect much-discussed poems, such as *The Goldyn Targe*, I have given particular attention to the comic poems, the petitions, and other works that seem, by comparison, critically neglected or undervalued.

I have been assisted by the staff of many libraries, especially the Sydney Jones Library, University of Liverpool, and the National Library of Scotland. I am grateful for the award of two Fellowships, at the Institute for Advanced Study in the Humanities, Edinburgh University, and at the Humanities Research Centre, the Australian National University, Canberra; both provided extremely congenial environments in which to study. I owe much to the triennial international conferences in Medieval and Renaissance Scottish Literature, which gave me an opportunity to try out in lecture-form some sections of this book. I am also grateful to many friends and fellow-scholars, particularly A. J. Aitken, John Durkan, Douglas Gray, Bridget Henisch, Emily Lyle, Alasdair MacDonald, and Felicity Riddy. But my greatest debt, as always, is to my dear husband, Nigel.

Contents

Texts and Abbreviations	x
1. Introduction	1
2. Dunbar's World	39
3. Court Poems: Praise and Petition	78
4. 'Moralitee and Hoolynesse'	131
5. 'Sportis and Jocositeis'	185
6. Flyting	220
7. 'Elrich Fantasyis'	257
8. 'Ladeis Bewtie . . . Luiffis Blys'	293
9. Language at Large	347
Select Bibliography	383
Index	387

Texts and Abbreviations

I have used James Kinsley's edition of *The Poems of William Dunbar* (Oxford, 1979). Quotations are from this work, except when otherwise indicated, and the numbering of poems also follows Kinsley (in the form K 5, etc.). I do not, however, always observe his punctuation or somewhat inconsistent lay-out of stanzas. Past editors have given Dunbar's poems many different titles; yet few have any claim to originate with the poet, and several are misleading. I here adopt the practice that will be followed in my own forthcoming edition of Dunbar, and use first-line titles, with the exception of a few that are particularly well-established or derive from the earliest witnesses—instances are *The Goldyn Targe*, *The Flyting*, and *The Tua Mariit Wemen and the Wedo*. References to the Bannatyne Manuscript are by folio, to facilitate use either of the facsimile or the STS edition. No place of publication is given for works published in London.

Asloan Manuscript	*The Asloan Manuscript*, ed. W. A. Craigie (STS, 1923–5)
AUJ	*Aberdeen University Journal*
Bannatyne Facsimile	*The Bannatyne Manuscript*, introd. D. Fox and W. A. Ringler (1980)
Bannatyne Manuscript	*The Bannatyne Manuscript*, ed. W. Tod Ritchie (STS, 1928–34)
Bawcutt, *Douglas*	P. Bawcutt, *Gavin Douglas: A Critical Study* (Edinburgh, 1976)
Bawcutt, 'Dunbar: New Light'	P. Bawcutt, 'Dunbar: New Light on Old Words', in *The Nuttis Schell: Essays on the Scots Language*, ed. C. Macafee and I. Macleod (Aberdeen, 1987), 83–95
Baxter	J. W. Baxter, *William Dunbar: A Biographical Study* (Edinburgh, 1952)
Blanchot and Graf, *Actes*	J.-J. Blanchot and C. Graf, *Actes du 2ᵉ colloque de langue et de littérature écossaises* (Strasbourg, 1978)
Bruce	*Barbour's Bruce*, ed. M. P. McDiarmid and J. A. C. Stevenson (STS, 1980–4)
CB XIII	*English Lyrics of the Thirteenth Century*, ed. Carleton Brown (Oxford, 1932)
CB XIV	*Religious Lyrics of the Fourteenth Century*, ed. Carleton Brown (Oxford, rev. edn. 1957)

CB XV	*Religious Lyrics of the Fifteenth Century*, ed. Carleton Brown (Oxford, 1939)
Chaucer	*The Riverside Chaucer*, ed. L. D. Benson (Oxford, 1988)
Chau R	*Chaucer Review*
CT	*The Canterbury Tales*
CUL	Cambridge University Library
DOST	*A Dictionary of the Older Scottish Tongue from the Twelfth Century to the End of the Seventeenth*
Douglas, *Eneados*	*Virgil's Aeneid Translated by Gavin Douglas*, ed. D. F. C. Coldwell (STS, 1957–64)
Douglas, *The Palice of Honour*	in *The Shorter Poems of Gavin Douglas*, ed. P. J. Bawcutt (STS, 1967)
EC	*Essays in Criticism*
EETS	Early English Text Society (ES: Extra Series; OS: Original Series)
ELH	*ELH, A Journal of English Literary History*
ES	*English Studies*
Greene, *Carols*	*The Early English Carols*, ed. R. L. Greene (Oxford, 1935; rev. edn. 1977)
Henryson	*The Poems of Robert Henryson*, ed. D. Fox (Oxford, 1981)
Holland, *The Howlat*	in *Longer Scottish Poems I: 1375–1650*, ed. P. Bawcutt and F. Riddy (Edinburgh, 1987)
IMEV	C. Brown and R. H. Robbins, *The Index of Middle English Verse* (New York, 1943); *Supplement* (Lexington Ky., 1965)
JEGP	*Journal of English and Germanic Philology*
Kingis Quair	*The Kingis Quair*, ed. J. Norton-Smith (Oxford, 1971; rev. 1981)
Lindsay	*The Works of Sir David Lindsay*, ed. D. Hamer (STS, 1931–6)
Lyall and Riddy	*Proceedings of the Third International Conference on Scottish Language and Literature (Medieval and Renaissance)*, ed. R. J. Lyall and F. Riddy (Stirling, 1981)
Mackenzie	*The Poems of William Dunbar*, ed. W. Mackay Mackenzie (1932; rev. 1960)
MÆ	*Medium Ævum*

Maitland Folio	*The Maitland Folio Manuscript*, ed. W. A. Craigie (STS, 1919–27)
MED	*Middle English Dictionary*
Mill	A. J. Mill, *Mediaeval Plays in Scotland* (Edinburgh, 1927)
MLR	*Modern Language Review*
Montgomerie	*The Poems of Alexander Montgomerie*, ed. J. Cranstoun (STS, 1887)
MP	*Modern Philology*
NLS	National Library of Scotland
N&Q	*Notes and Queries*
OED	*The Oxford English Dictionary*
PBA	*Proceedings of the British Academy*
PMLA	*Publications of the Modern Language Association of America*
PQ	*Philological Quarterly*
Rauf Coilyear	in *Longer Scottish Poems I: 1375–1650*, ed. P. Bawcutt and F. Riddy (Edinburgh, 1987)
Reiss	E. Reiss, *William Dunbar* (Boston, Mass., 1979)
RES	*Review of English Studies*
ROSC	*Review of Scottish Culture*
Ross	I. S. Ross, *William Dunbar* (Leiden, 1981)
SATF	Société des anciens textes français
SBRS	Scottish Burgh Record Society
Schipper	*The Poems of William Dunbar*, ed. J. Schipper (Vienna, 1892–4)
Scott	T. Scott, *Dunbar: A Critical Exposition of the Poems* (Edinburgh, 1966)
Scott, *Poems*	*The Poems of Alexander Scott*, ed. J. Cranstoun (STS, 1896)
SHS	Scottish History Society
SHR	*Scottish Historical Review*
Skelton	*John Skelton: The Complete English Poems*, ed. J. Scattergood (1983)
SL	*Secular Lyrics of the XIVth and XVth Centuries*, ed. R. H. Robbins (Oxford, 1952)
SLJ	*Scottish Literary Journal*
Small	*The Poems of William Dunbar*, ed. J. Small, with W. Gregor and Æ. J. G. Mackay (STS, 1884–93)

SND	*The Scottish National Dictionary*
SP	*Studies in Philology*
SRS	Scottish Record Society
SSL	*Studies in Scottish Literature*
Strauss and Drescher	*Scottish Language and Literature, Medieval and Renaissance*, ed. D. Strauss and H. W. Drescher (Frankfurt, 1986)
STS	Scottish Text Society
Tilley	M. P. Tilley, *A Dictionary of Proverbs in England in the Sixteenth and Seventeenth Centuries* (Ann Arbor, 1950)
TA	*Accounts of the Lord High Treasurer of Scotland*, ed. T. Dickson and Sir J. Balfour Paul, vols. i–iv (Edinburgh, 1877–1902)
Utley	F. L. Utley, *The Crooked Rib: An Analytical Index to the Argument about Women in English and Scots Literature* (Columbus, Ohio, 1944)
UTQ	*University of Toronto Quarterly*
Wallace	*Hary's Wallace*, ed. M. P. McDiarmid, 2 vols. (STS, 1968–9)
Whiting	B. J. Whiting, *Proverbs, Sentences and Proverbial Phrases from English Writings Mainly before 1500* (Cambridge, Mass., 1968)
Whiting, 'Scottish Proverbs'	B. J. Whiting, 'Proverbs from Scottish Writings before 1600', *Mediaeval Studies*, 11 (1969), 123–205; 13 (1951), 87–164
Woolf	R. Woolf, *The English Religious Lyric in the Middle Ages* (Oxford, 1968)
YES	*Yearbook of English Studies*

1

Introduction

> It is, to a large extent, through his letters that Burns is known, through his short, careless, pithy sayings, which imbedded themselves in the memories of his hearers ... these fill up interstices between works, bring apparent opposition into intimate relationship, and make wholeness out of confusion. Not on the stage alone, in the world also, a man's real character comes out best in his asides. With Dunbar there is nothing of this. He is a name, and little more. He exists in a region to which rumour and conjecture have never penetrated. He was long neglected by his countrymen, and was brought to light as if by accident. He is the Pompeii of British poetry.[1]

ALEXANDER SMITH, the nineteenth-century poet and essayist, here expresses a view of Dunbar that is remarkably familiar. The details of his life are still scanty. We know that Dunbar was a graduate and a priest, associated with the court of James IV of Scotland, but are uncertain when he was born and when he died. Dunbar's 'real character' is equally elusive. 'Pompeii' too is a brilliant and suggestive image. It is historically apt, since Dunbar's poems were rediscovered in the eighteenth century, after a long period of neglect. It also well conveys the sense of shock and excitement that many readers experience when first encountering Dunbar, akin to discovering a vivid but long-buried world. Dunbar is a poet of enormous variety. He speaks with almost too many voices. One poem idealizes women, another makes fun of them. Many poems reject the vanities of this world, but one flippantly concludes:

> Now quhill thair is gude wyne to sell,
> He that dois on dry breid wirry
> I gif him to the Devill of hell. (K 70)

In addition to striking alternations of mood, Dunbar displays a remarkable range of style and language. Metrically too he has great versatility, writing carols, refrain-poems, rhyme royal, and the archaic, unrhymed alliterative verse. W. H. Auden said of him:

---

[1] 'William Dunbar', in *Dreamthorp* (1863; 1907), 109.

INTRODUCTION

Whatever your taste, pious, gay, melancholy, bawdy, he will write a poem for you, apt and elegant. The first gift of such a poet is verse technique, and Dunbar is unfailingly brilliant. His poems never fail to do what he intends them to do. He knows exactly the kind of verse which will suit any given subject, exactly what can be got out of a metre or a stanza form.[2]

Yet it is paradoxical that the very qualities which give his readers pleasure seem to constitute a problem for Dunbar's critics.

John Speirs located 'the core of his living achievement' in Dunbar's 'saturnine poems that give his work as a whole its dark cast'.[3] Yet it is not easy to see Dunbar 'as a whole', or to form a coherent image of him as a poet. We cannot say of Dunbar, as does Douglas Gray of his great contemporary, Robert Henryson, that there is 'a unity and a coherence about his *œuvre*'.[4] Some critics indeed sharpen and over-simplify the various strains in his poetry into polarities and dichotomies: they contrast the 'aureate' with the 'eldritch', or the 'pasquinade' with the 'panegyric'. One detects in Dunbar 'that "antithetical mind" which Byron later found in Burns'.[5] At the moment, however, two approaches to Dunbar are particularly popular. Several recent critics have laid great stress on the moral significance of apparently light-hearted and humorous poems. But the most consistent exponent of this approach is Edmund Reiss. Puzzled by the discrepant viewpoints in Dunbar, he seeks for something to reconcile seeming contradictions, and finds an underlying continuity in 'morality': 'at the heart of his poems—no matter whether they are in the form of humorous banterings, grotesqueries, celebrations, or allegories—lies a moral sense that ultimately views everything human in terms of eternal values and ultimate truths'.[6] Reiss denies that any difference exists between Dunbar 'the court entertainer' and Dunbar 'the moralist', and asserts that his humour is superficial, merely a 'way of arriving at doctrinal truth'. This stems from the simplistic conception of medieval literature, associated with D. W. Robertson, which finds no place in it for what the troubadour Peire d'Alvernhe called 'sport and laughter'.[7] No

---

[2] Reviewing Mackenzie in *The Criterion*, 12 (1933), 677.

[3] *The Scots Literary Tradition* (1940), 36.

[4] *Robert Henryson* (Leiden, 1979), 1; cf. D. Fox, 'The Coherence of Henryson's Work', in *Fifteenth-Century Studies*, ed. R. F. Yeager (Hamden, Conn., 1984), 275–81.

[5] Reiss, 19; J. Leyerle, 'The Two Voices of William Dunbar', 31 (1962), 316; Ross, 49.

[6] Reiss, 69. See also Ross, 159 ff.; and E. A. Tilley, 'The Meaning of Dunbar's "The Golden Targe"', *SSL* 10 (1973), 220–31; B. S. Hay, 'William Dunbar's Flying Abbot: Apocalypse Made to Order', *SSL* 11 (1974), 217–25; and R. J. Lyall, 'Moral Allegory in Dunbar's "Goldyn Targe"', *SSL* 11 (1974), 47–65.

[7] 'Cantarai d'agestz trobadors'; see *Songs of the Troubadours*, ed. A. Bonner (1973), 78. On the theoretical justifications of non-didactic literature, see G. Olson, 'The Medieval Theory of Literature for Refreshment and its use in the Fabliau Tradition', *SP* 71 (1974), 291–313, and his *Literature as Recreation in the Later Middle Ages* (Ithaca, New York, 1982).

INTRODUCTION

reader could deny that Dunbar wrote many serious poems, some of very high quality. But to see morality as the key to all of Dunbar entails in practice perverse misreadings of some of his finest and wittiest poems. What is more, the very search for unity extinguishes Dunbar's variety, flattening the peaks and valleys of his poetic landscape into a monotonous, featureless plain. 'Dunbar moralized' is as much a travesty as the medieval 'Ovide moralisé'; both are poets misunderstood.

The view of Dunbar most prevalent today, however, is that which represents him as, above all, the brilliant craftsman. In an influential essay Denton Fox said:

> Dunbar wrote happily and skilfully in almost any genre ... The stylistic virtuosity of the Middle Scots poets is a result of their attitude towards poetry: they regard it less as a means of self-expression than as a craft which has to be learned. And just as a good carpenter can build either a house or a chair, so a competent poet should be able to work in any genre. Dunbar, who seems the most representative of the Middle Scots poets, the one who carries their characteristic qualities to the furthest extreme, is only the most conspicuous of a number of virtuosos.[8]

There is much truth in this. Dunbar is not an autobiographical poet, nor a profound and original thinker; he is a maker. He excels in the shaping of his poems, in the vitality of his language, and in the matching of theme to metre. (This was something to which Auden was clearly responsive.) It is suggestive that several of Dunbar's poems contain parodic features; delight in parody seems characteristic of poets acutely aware of the formal aspects of poetry. This kind of critical approach can be helpful in explaining some of the differences between Dunbar's poems. Why, for instance, does he speak so differently about women? Part, though by no means the whole, of the answer lies in the genres adopted, each of which possessed its own conventions, topoi, and imagery. This aspect of Dunbar is still comparatively unexplored; yet it is rewarding both to identify the 'kind' to which his poems belong and to compare them with others in the same genre. Although there has been much critical praise of Dunbar's 'craft' and the 'energy' of his language, here too there has been surprisingly little analysis of the way Dunbar's poems are put together, or of their verbal texture.

Yet this approach to Dunbar is often curiously reductive. Dunbar is a virtuoso, or 'a highly conscious technician'; his poetry displays

---

[8] 'The Scottish Chaucerians', in *Chaucer and Chaucerians*, ed. D. S. Brewer (1966), 180.

3

'unparalleled technical virtuosity', but remains 'a poetry of surfaces'.[9] Criticism of this kind seems to reduce Dunbar's poems to a collection of brilliant but unrelated artefacts. Dunbar is seen as a craftsman who supplies a demand, a poet governed by external pressures; his poems framed in accordance with the rules of a genre, and prompted by the requirements of his patrons, either in the court (Auden called him 'the servant of a court society') or the Church. But this is far from the truth. Some of Dunbar's poems are indeed largely shaped by the conventions of a particular literary kind, but many defy easy categorization; they break the rules, and transcend the conventions. Again, although some poems are likely to have been commissioned (those celebrating Bernard Stewart, for instance), there are many others for which no such explanation can be devised. Their origin may well lie in Dunbar's spontaneous response to some experience, trivial or profound. It is wholly mistaken to treat Dunbar's poems as if all are exactly alike—all equally moral, or equally generic, or indeed equally successful artistically.

John Burrow questions the 'modern opposition between the conventional and the autobiographical'. He points out that three distinct schools of thought have converged, to bring into disrepute the biographical reading of medieval poems:

Historical criticism has stressed the conventional character of authorial self-reference in medieval times (the use of traditional topics, the influence of St Augustine, and so on); the New Criticism has discouraged biographical interest as a distraction from the words on the page; and formalist or structuralist criticism treats first-person discourse as part of the fictive world of 'le texte'.[10]

It is easy to make fun of earlier scholars who read all Dunbar's poems as if they were exact transcripts of reality, and from them constructed an imaginary autobiography. We are unlikely to believe, with the Scottish Text Society editor, that in *My hartis tresure* (K 12) 'Dunbar finally abandons love, and his hopes turn to the desire for a post or a pension', or that *The Tabill of Confessioun* (K 6) necessarily 'belongs to the close of Dunbar's life'.[11] No one today thinks that he was literally tempted by a devil in the shape of St Francis (K 55). Yet it is equally ludicrous to divorce Dunbar's poems totally from his own life. When he spoke of his 'pension', this was fact, not fiction; so too his oft-voiced desire for a benefice was unlikely to be wholly imaginary. In

---

[9] Scott, 306; D. Pearsall, *Old English and Middle English Poetry* (1977), 277; Fox, 'The Scottish Chaucerians', 186.
[10] 'Autobiographical Poetry in the Middle Ages: The Case of Thomas Hoccleve', *PBA* 68 (1982), 390.
[11] Small, i, pp. clxiv and clxx.

INTRODUCTION

I that in heill wes and gladnes (K 62) Dunbar referred to Stobo and Walter Kennedy; these were actual men, the one recently dead, the other on his deathbed. Dunbar probably knew them as well as Wordsworth knew the poets whom he mourned in his *Effusion on the Death of James Hogg*. The 'I' of *I that in heill wes* is not simply a persona, and the 'greit seiknes' mentioned in the first stanza is not, I think, mere fiction. Burrow challenged what he called 'the conventional fallacy', in connection with Thomas Hoccleve. In Dunbar's case it is no less desirable to discriminate between poems which are largely shaped by convention, and those which employ conventions to say something relating to his own experience. The 'I'-figure of some poems is little more than a mouthpiece for orthodox morality; the 'I' of *I that in heill wes* is in part an Everyman-figure, yet still speaks for Dunbar himself.

Yet 'the self' and 'the personality' are slippery concepts, not only in literature but in life. It is a commonplace that most of us act and talk differently, according to whether we are among friends or strangers; we are 'different people' in different circumstances, perhaps playing roles or striking poses. The diversity and occasional contradictions of Dunbar's poetry are in this respect no different from life. The 'real' Dunbar is ultimately unknowable. Yet we can distinguish between Dunbar's orthodox and public voice, and a more private and intimate-sounding voice. The petitionary poems, for instance, are firmly rooted in actuality, and are charged with powerful feeling, although the exact degree of self-expression in them will always be debatable. Dunbar clearly takes great delight in the formal aspects of poetry; he would perhaps have found congenial one of Auden's *obiter dicta*: 'if one plays a game, one needs rules, otherwise there is no fun'.[12] This 'game' element is very important in Dunbar: he plays with words, metres, and literary conventions, just as he plays with his audience, and their expectations. But his finest poems have something distinctive to say, and cannot be paralleled in any other poet. He is the most accomplished, not simply 'the most representative', of early Scottish poets.

Many readers experience the old-fashioned desire to know more of Dunbar's life, yet no biography in the usual sense can be written about him.[13] There is a disappointing paucity of facts, and more conjecture than Alexander Smith anticipated. The best evidence is furnished by

---

[12] Quoted by C. Osborne, *Auden: The Life of a Poet* (1980), 329.
[13] The most useful survey of the facts is J. W. Baxter's *William Dunbar* (1952). Cf. also M. P. McDiarmid, 'The Early William Dunbar and his Poems', *SHR* 59 (1980), 126–39.

the Scottish records in the reign of James IV, especially *The Treasurer's Accounts* from 1500 to 1513. In these Dunbar is regularly styled 'Maister William Dunbar', just as he is in the titles and colophons of several poems. This indicates that he was a university graduate, and it is very likely—though not absolutely certain—that the poet can be identified with the man of the same name who studied at St Andrews, 'determining' in 1477 and graduating in 1479. If so, a good case can be made for a birth-date about 1460.[14] We do not know who Dunbar's parents were, but his surname may link him with the family of the earls of Dunbar and March; yet there is no clear evidence that he was of noble birth—the reference to 'nobill strynd' (K 82. 17) is not necessarily autobiographical. We do not know precisely where Dunbar was born, but in *The Flyting* he associates himself with the Lothian area of Scotland. Between 1479 and 1500 there is a blank period, filled only with speculation as to Dunbar's activities. No external evidence confirms the long-held belief that he was a Franciscan friar, or the more recent suggestion that he might have been in France, as a member of the Scots Guard.[15]

From 1500 to 1513, however, Dunbar was a 'servitour' of James IV, receiving miscellaneous fees, and a 'pension', or annual salary. Dunbar's position at court, which was of crucial importance to his poetry, will be discussed later. Two other occurrences of his name, however, show him in less familiar contexts, and will be briefly mentioned here. On 15 February 1502 'Mastir Willyaim Dumbar' was one of several procurators and 'special erand beraris' appointed by Sir John Wemyss of Wemyss (1425–1502) to act on his behalf in a rancorous and complicated suit against his own son and other members of his family. Sir John died shortly afterwards, and the case presumably lapsed. Its interest, as far as Dunbar is concerned, is that it shows him as a 'lovitt', or trusted, associate and legal representative of this Fifeshire laird. His fellow-procurators included another St Andrews graduate, 'Mastir Henry Quhitt', parson of Rothes.[16] In a later legal transaction, of 13 March 1509, Dunbar was a witness to a transfer of property lying near the Market Cross; we here see Dunbar as an Edinburgh citizen, as perhaps himself a property-owner (since witnesses commonly had an interest in adjoining property), and, most

---

[14] The usual age for graduating was the twentieth year, but there were often exceptions. See Baxter, 9–10; and *Acta Facultatis Artium Universitatis Sanctiandree 1413–1588*, ed. A. I. Dunlop (SHS, 3rd ser. 54–5, 1964), lxxxi–lxxxii, 199, and 206.

[15] See Baxter, 26–40; and J.-J. Blanchot, 'William Dunbar in the Scottish Guard in France?', in Lyall and Riddy, 315–27; also his 'William Dunbar (1460?–1520?) rhetoriqueur écossais' (diss., Paris-Sorbonne, 1987), 111–22.

[16] Published by Sir W. Fraser in *Memorials of the Family of Wemyss of Wemyss* (Edinburgh, 1888), ii. 117–19.

significantly, as a chaplain.¹⁷ Yet Dunbar seems never to have received a benefice, and in this his career contrasts strikingly with that of his younger contemporary, Gavin Douglas, also a poet and graduate, but, unlike Dunbar, a member of a rich and powerful family. Dunbar is last mentioned on 14 May 1513, but the *Accounts* between August 1513 and June 1515 are not extant and he may have survived into James V's reign. There is no evidence, however, that he did so.

We have one vivid contemporary sketch of Dunbar. What Kennedy says of him in *The Flyting* (a verse quarrel between the two poets) is extremely interesting, yet difficult to assess. In the past scholars treated this work as a biographical quarry, uncritically reading every statement at its face-value. Recent opinion has swung to the opposite extreme—Kinsley thus tells us, 'we ought to believe little of what Kennedy says about Dunbar'.¹⁸ It would clearly be mistaken to treat *The Flyting* as a source of precise biographical data, yet there must be a factual substratum supporting the comic edifice. The *Flyting* portraits have much in common with caricature or cartoon; and successful caricatures, however much they distort, must be recognizable. They exaggerate the beaky nose or the wild mane of hair, yet sometimes have more truth to life than the respectful studio portrait. Kennedy's image of Dunbar, in *The Flyting*, is both comic and hostile, but it contains features that his contemporaries are likely to have recognized.

Clearly we must discard the filth and the fantasy—Dunbar was not perpetually being seasick, nor did his ancestors include a devil and a she-bear. But beneath the apparently random insults there exists a portrait more coherent than is usually acknowledged, and one that occasionally tallies with the few facts that we possess. Kennedy repeatedly alludes to Dunbar's small stature, and calls him a dwarf (33, 395, 408); we perhaps should not attach over-much weight to this—such taunts must sometimes be read in reverse—yet it is the sole clue to Dunbar's physical appearance. More important is Kennedy's mockery of Dunbar's education, saying he was given a degree in jest: 'maid maister bot in mows' (29). He implies Dunbar's desire for preferment in the Church:

> Ane benefice quha wald gyve sic ane beste?   (505)

Particularly striking is the way Kennedy presents Dunbar as ever on the move: crossing the Border, sailing to Denmark, contending with the rigours of Alpine passes. He jeers:

---

¹⁷ See *The Protocol Book of John Foular 1503–1513* (SRS, vol. 72, Edinburgh, 1940), no. 543. Cf. M. P. McDiarmid, reviewing Baxter in *SHR* 33 (1954), 46–52; see also Fox, 'The Chronology of William Dunbar', *PQ* 39 (1960), 417–18.

¹⁸ Kinsley, 286.

INTRODUCTION

> In Parise wyth the maister buriawe [hangman]
> Abyde, and be his prentice nere the bank. (437–8)

Beneath this lies an insulting stereotype: Dunbar is a member of the Goliardic *ordo vagorum*, wandering clerks who lived disreputably and dishonoured their calling.[19] Yet this too has its significance: Scottish students regularly studied in Paris, and clerics, like merchants, travelled to England, France, Denmark, and Rome, whether on the king's business or their own. Kennedy's allusions evoke this cosmopolitan world, to which both he and Dunbar belonged. Yet of Dunbar's travels outside Scotland there now survives but one documentary proof: the payment of his half-yearly pension in 1501, 'eftir he com furth of Ingland'.[20]

One problem facing those who try to form a coherent picture of Dunbar is the difficulty of dating any but a small fraction of his poems.[21] Another, rarely mentioned by critics, is our uncertainty as to the extent of his canon. Dunbar gives the impression of being a fluent writer: in one poem he mentions his 'sangis . . . undir the levis grene' (K 50. 28), and in another his 'ballattis under the byrkis' (K 42. 69). Some poems imply, admittedly in a jocular way, that he saw himself as a love poet:

> Lang heff I maed of ladyes quhytt (K 33. 1)

or was so seen by others:

> Thow that hes lang done Venus lawis teiche. (K 55. 13)

Yet few love poems are now attributed to Dunbar. It is most unlikely that *all* Dunbar's poems have survived, or, if extant, are invariably associated with his name. But it is also questionable whether all the poems today attributed to Dunbar are definitely of his composition. Neatly assembled in a scholarly edition, *The Poems of William Dunbar* present the modern reader with a spurious impression of completeness and finality. It is as well to remember the piecemeal way in which these poems have been preserved, over a long period of time ranging from the beginning of the sixteenth century to the early seventeenth. A few texts date from Dunbar's own lifetime, or not long after: three poems in the Aberdeen Burgh Sasine Register (*c.*1505–1511); six in the Chepman and Myllar prints (*c.*1508) and another undated but early print; four in the Asloan Manuscript (*c.*1515); and three in the Arundel Manuscript (?1540). But by far the largest number is

---

[19] Cf. Bawcutt, 'The Art of Flyting', *SLJ* 10, no. 2 (1983), 19–21.
[20] *TA* ii. 95.
[21] The chronology of Dunbar's poems will be discussed in the next chapter.

preserved in two great poetic miscellanies belonging to the second half of the sixteenth century, the Bannatyne Manuscript (*c.*1568) and the Maitland Folio (*c.*1570). Latest of all is the Reidpeth Manuscript (1622–3), a close transcript of part of the Maitland Folio.[22] No holograph of Dunbar's poems survives, as is the case with Thomas Hoccleve; no manuscript copied by a scribe close to him, such as the copy of Douglas's *Eneados* made by Matthew Geddes. Sir Richard Maitland's poems were lovingly copied and preserved by his own family, but this was not so with Dunbar.

This uncertainty as to the precise nature of his canon is not peculiar to Dunbar, although it is perhaps more characteristic of those who write short, popular, or humorous poems, which can be rapidly memorized and copied. In the sixteenth century, as for long before and after, it was common for readers to make their own copies of poems that they liked; it was also common to cull relatively self-contained extracts from longer works. Sententious passages from Lydgate's *The Fall of Princes* were often copied and treated as separate poems. The authorship of such pieces was then sometimes forgotten, or regarded as unimportant. They continued to lead an independent and anonymous existence; a good example is the eight-line piece of verse printed in Carleton Brown's *Religious Lyrics of the Fifteenth Century* (no. 164), which has since been identified as a stanza from John Walton's translation of Boethius.[23] The practice of excerpting was not confined to moral or devotional works. Chaucer's *Troilus and Criseyde* served as a quarry from which were hewn small, quotable pieces on love. The Devonshire Manuscript contains a number of 'poems', at first thought to have been composed by Sir Thomas Wyatt and his circle, but later identified as extracts not only from *Troilus* but also from *Anelida and Arcite,* Hoccleve's *Letter of Cupid* and Ross's *La Belle Dame Sans Merci.*[24] It is increasingly evident that a similar practice was followed in the making of the Bannatyne Manuscript. George Bannatyne included many extracts from longer works, some Scots, some English, some pious, some amorous. At times these are correctly identified (as with the Prologues to Douglas's *Eneados*); but many pieces give no hint as to their origin or their author—miscellaneous examples are the passages from Lydgate's *Life of Our*

---

[22] See Kinsley, xiii–xvi; and Bawcutt, 'The Earliest Texts of Dunbar', in *Regionalism in Late Medieval Manuscripts and Texts*, ed. F. Riddy (1991), 183–98.

[23] See A. S. G. Edwards, 'Selections from Lydgate's *Fall of Princes*: A Check-List', *Library*, 5th ser. 26 (1971), 337–42; R. H. Robbins, 'The Findern Anthology', *PMLA* 69 (1954), 610–42; and D. Gray, *A Selection of Religious Lyrics* (Oxford, 1975), no. 91.

[24] Cf. E. Seaton, '"The Devonshire Manuscript" and its Medieval Fragments', *RES*, NS 7 (1956), 55–6; R. Southall finds much of the received Wyatt corpus 'mere conjectural accretion' (*The Courtly Maker* (Oxford, 1964), 6).

Lady and *Fall of Princes*, and a stanza from Walton's *Boethius*. Another apparently independent poem is a stanza from Henryson's *Fables* which appears, also anonymously, in John Maxwell's unpublished Commonplace Book (*c*.1584).[25]

The complementary practice of 'fathering' works of uncertain authorship upon famous poets is much more familiar. In the fifteenth and sixteenth centuries Chaucer had such prestige that poem after poem was mistakenly ascribed to him; some were the work of Lydgate and Hoccleve, others, such as *The Floure and the Leafe*, still remain anonymous.[26] All but one of Bannatyne's attributions to Chaucer are erroneous; yet the error is not his but that of his source, Thynne's edition of Chaucer. Such a phenomenon has existed for a long time; many classical authors acquired a family of spurious works in the Middle Ages.[27] Douglas clearly believed that several verses he quoted or paraphrased were written by Virgil; but few modern scholars now accept them as Virgilian. Dunbar too has acquired an extended family. The eighteenth-century editor John Pinkerton attributed to him amusing poems, such as *The Freiris of Berwick*, which have long remained linked with his name, although there is not a shred of external evidence that they were written by Dunbar. Most of these later attributions have been firmly rejected by modern editors. But it is important to remember that this practice has long existed, and that to the compilers of the sixteenth-century anthologies Dunbar's was a very famous name. A cautionary tale concerns a poem attributed to Dunbar by Reidpeth, yet included in no modern edition. This is 'Eird uppoun eird wonderfull is wrocht', a Scottish version of a very popular English poem that dates from the fourteenth century. Reidpeth's attribution in this case is disregarded, but it should be recalled that Reidpeth is now the sole authority for the text and authorship of eight other poems attributed to Dunbar (K 18, 21, 36, 46, 47, 48, 51, and 75).[28]

A few of Dunbar's contemporaries did their best to ensure that their authorship would not be forgotten. Skelton listed a remarkable number of his poems in *The Garland of Laurel*. Douglas followed 'Virgilian' precedent in recording 'thre of hys pryncipall warkis', and

---

[25] See the Scolar Press Facsimile of *The Bannatyne Manuscript* (henceforth referred to as *Bannatyne Facsimile*), ed. D. Fox and W. A. Ringler (1980), nos. 28, 98, 106, and 117; and Bawcutt, 'The Commonplace Book of John Maxwell', in *A Day Estivall*, ed. A. Gardner-Medwin and J. H. Williams (Aberdeen, 1990), 59–68. On excerpts from Bellenden, see A. S. G. Edwards, *Bibliotheck*, 6 (1972), 89–90.

[26] F. W. Bonner, 'Genesis of the Chaucer Apocrypha', *SP* 48 (1951), 461–81.

[27] Cf. P. Lehmann, *Pseudo-Antike Literatur des Mittelalters* (1927; 2nd edn. Darmstadt, 1964).

[28] See Baxter, 225–8. On another poet called Dunbar, see Bawcutt, 'Dunbar and an Epigram', *SLJ* 13, no. 2 (1986), 16–19.

at the end of the *Eneados* devised a rebus 'to knaw the naym of the translatour'. Alexander Scott also incorporated his name in two poems.[29] There is no parallel to this in Dunbar. His name is most securely linked with *Schir lat it never in toune be tald* (K 43), which ends with a *Respontio Regis*:

> Efter our wrettingis, thesaurer,
> Tak in this gray hors, auld Dumbar . . .   (69–70)

But whether this is regarded as a kind of 'signature' depends on whether we think James IV or Dunbar wrote this final verse. Dunbar's authorship of approximately eighty poems is based for the most part, upon the testimony of those by whom they were copied or printed.[30]

It is surely important to scrutinize these attributions carefully, and to assess their respective authority. The testimony of the four earliest witnesses is extremely valuable, particularly that of the prints, which appeared in Dunbar's lifetime: these attribute to him *The Goldyn Targe* (K 10), *The Ballade of Bernard Stewart* (K 35), *The Tua Mariit Wemen and the Wedo* (K 14), and *I that in heill wes*. Dunbar's authorship of *The Goldyn Targe* is corroborated by Sir David Lindsay—one of the few references by a close contemporary to a specific poem. John Asloan's testimony is also of high value, since his lifetime overlapped with Dunbar's; both resided in Edinburgh, although there is no certainty that they knew each other. Asloan was a notary, and had a professional duty of scribal accuracy.[31] His attributions to Dunbar include poems still extant in his manuscript, such as *Ane Ballat of Our Lady* (K 2) and *The Passioun of Crist* (K 3); but his original list of contents provides valuable further evidence as to Dunbar's authorship of poems now missing from the manuscript—'the flyting betuix kennyde & dunbar' and 'Dunbarris derige of Edinburgh & striuling'. At the other extreme are the Bannatyne and Maitland anthologies, which were compiled long after Dunbar's death, and indeed reflect post-Reformation pressures in the Protestant 'editing' of some poems. The Bannatyne Manuscript has been carefully studied, and we now know much about its make-up, and arrangement according to subject and genre.[32] The Maitland Folio, unfortunately, has not received such close scrutiny. It is a composite manuscript, written in a number of

---

[29] See Bawcutt, *Douglas*, 48–9, 88–9; and Scott, *Poems*, nos. 1 and 34.

[30] The fluctuating number of poems attributed to Dunbar stems not only from editorial decisions to include (or reject) poems but also from concepts of 'unity'. Kinsley's no. 52 corresponds to three poems in Mackenzie.

[31] Cf. J. Durkan, 'The Early Scottish Notary', in *The Renaissance and Reformation in Scotland*, ed. I. B. Cowan and D. Shaw (Edinburgh, 1983), 28.

[32] See *Bannatyne Facsimile*; Fox, 'Manuscripts and Prints of Scots Poetry in the Sixteenth Century', in *Bards and Makars*, ed. A. J. Aitken *et al.* (Glasgow, 1977), 156–71; and W. Ramson, 'On Bannatyne's Editing', ibid. 172–83.

hands, and assembled for Sir Richard Maitland and his family over a number of years. It seems more author-centred than the Bannatyne Manuscript, and is dominated by two poets, Maitland himself and Dunbar; there are fifty attributions to Dunbar, nearly a third of the total number of items in the manuscript. It is thus the single most important repository of Dunbar's poems; and this does not take into account the eleven anonymous pieces it contains that are attributed to Dunbar elsewhere. Kinsley plausibly suggests that Maitland may have had access to 'a collection of relatively intimate and domestic verse' originating in the court, and unknown to Bannatyne.[33]

If these witnesses are examined, the attributions to Dunbar seem to fall into three main categories:

First, there is a small but distinctive group of poems which can be attributed to Dunbar with a high degree of confidence. The testimony to his authorship is early, reliable, and—where there are several witnesses—unanimous. This group includes *Ane Ballat of Our Lady*, *The Tabill of Confessioun*, *The Goldyn Targe*, *The Flyting*, *The Tua Mariit Wemen and the Wedo*, *I that in heill wes*, *The Ballade of Bernard Stewart*, *Schir lat it never in toune be tald*, and *The Dregy*. These display the thematic range and metrical versatility long associated with Dunbar, but the proportion of humorous poems should be noted.

There is a second class of poems, whose attribution to Dunbar also seems highly probable. There is no conflict between the witnesses as to his authorship; yet these witnesses are all late (Bannatyne, Maitland, and Reidpeth). (Often, of course, a poem survives only in a single text.) A very large number of poems falls into this category; it includes many of the petitions, chiefly (and perhaps significantly) preserved in the Maitland and Reidpeth manuscripts.

The third and most problematic group consists of poems, preserved chiefly in the three late manuscripts, which have conflicting attributions. A poem ascribed in one manuscript to Dunbar is elsewhere assigned to 'Stewart' (K 81) or 'Clerk' (K 13), or more often is anonymous. Proportionately, the number of the more debatable poems may seem surprisingly large (seventeen). Apart from four poems (K 3, 9, 13, and 38), their subject is moral-didactic. (In Kinsley's edition their numbers are 57, 61, 65, 67, 68, 70, 78, 79, 80, 81, and 83; to these should be added two poems excluded by Kinsley, but included by earlier editors.) It is hardly surprising, however, that there was uncertainty, even in Dunbar's own century, as to the authorship of these pieces, since their tone is impersonal and their style lacks individuality. They include the most conventional poems in the Dunbar canon. Dunbar may well have written all of them, but so too

---

[33] Kinsley, xv.

INTRODUCTION

could many of his contemporaries. This is not the place for detailed discussion, but two of the more interesting cases may be mentioned. *Quhat is this lyfe* (K 57) is attributed to Dunbar by Maitland, but not by Bannatyne; although its brevity sounds epigrammatic, it may well be a single rhyme-royal stanza extracted from a longer work. Perhaps the most puzzling problem is posed by *The Testament of Maister Andro Kennedy* (K 38), which most critics would be reluctant to see expelled from the Dunbar canon. Yet its attribution to Dunbar rests solely on Bannatyne's colophon; it is anonymous in the print, and curiously, though not inexplicably, ascribed to 'Kennedy' in Maitland and Reidpeth. The failure to mention Dunbar in the print is surprising; yet it could be argued that a satirical testament, in which the poet adopts the persona of the testator, might well, for best effect, circulate anonymously.

This discussion of the canon is in no way exhaustive; my object is not to effect a Homeric disintegration of Dunbar, but to remind readers how fragmentary and imperfect is the evidence for his authorship of many poems. If we possessed more exact information as to what he wrote, we might modify our image of Dunbar substantially. Awareness of the problems should inject caution into the discussion of some topics. Those critics, for instance, who find spiritual truths 'at the heart' of Dunbar's poetry lay a great deal of weight upon the poems which are most conventional and least certainly his.[34] I prefer to regard the remarkably varied poems, here placed in group 1, as constituting the 'heart' or core of Dunbar's poetry. But it also seems wise for editors not to be too categoric in rejecting from the canon any poem which has an early attribution. These witnesses are flawed and imperfect, yet they are all that exist. Kinsley may well be correct in excluding two poems, chiefly on stylistic and linguistic grounds; yet similar objections could be raised against other poems that he retains.[35] Interesting stylistic affinities can be discerned among some of the poems attributed most confidently to Dunbar; yet style alone is not a reliable criterion of authorship, particularly at this period and with a poet of Dunbar's versatility.

Dunbar's poems pose other questions that are difficult to answer precisely. What audience did he envisage? And in what sense were his poems 'published'? Some of his contemporaries dedicated their works to noblemen, or announced that they wrote at the prompting of friends—Douglas, for instance, says that he translated the *Aeneid* at the request of his kinsman, Henry, Lord Sinclair.[36] But there is no

---

[34] Cf. Reiss, ch. 4: 'The Christian Moralist'.
[35] Kinsley, 374–5; cf. his notes on K 67 and K 68.
[36] On the blend of truth and convention in the request-theme, cf. Bawcutt, *Douglas*, 92–4.

INTRODUCTION

evidence that any poem of Dunbar's was commissioned by a wealthy patron, presumably because he did not write ambitious, large-scale works. John Bellenden dedicated his translation of Hector Boece's *Scotorum Historiae* to James V, a work for which in 1531 he received a total of £66. Two years later he was paid a slightly smaller sum for his 'lauboris' in translating Livy.[37] Although Dunbar had a royal pension, there is no evidence that he was paid for being a poet; no record unmistakably links a fee with a poem, even though we may suspect that he sometimes received such reward, like Stephen Hawes, 'for a ballett that he gave to the Kinges grace'.[38]

Douglas carefully discriminates between different sections of the potential audience for his *Eneados*:

> Now salt thou with every gentill Scot be kend,
> And to onletterit folk be red on hight,
> That erst was bot with clerkis comprehend.[39]

There is no parallel to this in Dunbar, yet his poems give some clue as to their intended audience, usually in the opening lines. Poems addressed to *man*—

> O man, haif mynd that thow mon pas   (K 59)

or

> Man, sen thy lyfe is ay in weir   (K 67)

clearly envisage the most universal audience possible, Everyman. At the other extreme is the group of poems addressed to a single person, the king himself; these are usually signalled by the deferential *Schir*:

> Schir, I complane of injuris   (K 26)
> Schir, at this feist of benefice   (K 41)
> Schir, 3it remember as befoir.   (K 42)

A few are addressed explicitly to the queen, as 'Madam' (K 29), or 'gracious princes' (K 30). In between these extremes are poems addressed to a plural audience, such as a group of Edinburgh citizens (K 75). But we should not assume that any poem was designed solely for one person or one type of audience. The poem addressed to 'Illuster Lodovick, of France most Cristin king' (K 36) is a public lament for Bernard Stewart, most unlikely to have been destined simply for the attention of Louis XII. Those to James IV, although more intimate in tone, sound as if they were designed also to reach

---

[37] On Bellenden, see E. A. Sheppard's Appendix to *The Chronicles of Scotland*, ed. R. W. Chambers, E. C. Batho, and H. W. Husbands (STS, 1938–41); ii. 436 and 448.
[38] See R. F. Green, *Poets and Princepleasers* (Toronto, 1980), 126.
[39] 'Exclamatioun', 43–5; iv. 193.

the court. Many of Dunbar's most interesting poems seem to have been written for a small circle of people who knew each other well: the king and other members of the royal household, some of whom were 'clerkis' and also wrote poetry. Douglas hoped that his *Eneados* would be read throughout 'the ile yclepit Albyon', but Dunbar rarely betrays such far-reaching ambition.[40] After his death Dunbar continued to be read and admired in Scotland, but seems—unlike Henryson, Douglas, and Lindsay—to have been virtually unknown in England. The sole sixteenth-century English mention is John Bale's inclusion of his name in a list of *Scotici Scriptores*.[41]

A few of Dunbar's poems were published, almost in the modern sense, in small printed pamphlets, in the same way that the shorter pieces of Skelton were printed for the English market in miscellanies, such as *Agaynste a Comely Coystrowne* and *Dyvers Balettys and Dyties Solacyous*. The Chepman and Myllar prints survived only by a happy accident; it seems probable, as Fox argued, that there once existed similar prints, available to Bannatyne but now lost.[42] These small cheap tracts were typographically akin to the broadsides, and are likely to have been aimed at a similarly wide, fairly popular market.[43] They contain one interesting clue to Dunbar's readership that has been curiously neglected: on the title-page of *The Goldyn Targe* is the inscription, *Liber Florentini mertini*.[44] There are references to Florentine (or Florimund) Martin in the records between 1511 and 1518. He and his father Alexander were minor landowners in Fife, and possessed property at 'Gibletstoun' (modern Gibliston), about a mile from Colinsburgh.[45] This suggests that one of Dunbar's first readers was a literate layman, not a cleric, and not—so far as is known—prominent at court.

Other poems, such as the petitions, presumably first circulated in manuscript. Lindsay, writing of James V's court, mentions poets composing ballats, 'Quhilks tyll our Prince daylie thay do present'.[46] A carol by William Stewart (*c*.1527) hints amusingly at the multitude of such poems appearing on New Year's Day:

---

[40] 'Conclusio', 11; iv. 187.
[41] In notes that remained unpublished until edited by R. L. Poole as *John Bale's Index of British and Other Writers* (Oxford, 1902); see W. Geddie, *A Bibliography of Middle Scots Poets* (STS, 1912), xlv and 14.
[42] 'Manuscripts and Prints', 164.
[43] Cf. A. B. Friedman, *The Ballad Revival* (1961), 42–6.
[44] It is noted by W. Beattie, *The Chepman and Myllar Prints: A Facsimile* (Edinburgh, 1950), xxi; J. Durkan and A. Ross, *Early Scottish Libraries* (Glasgow, 1961), 129 and 136, suggest that Martin owned the early print of *Golagros and Gawane*.
[45] See *The Sheriff Court Book of Fife 1515–22*, ed. W. C. Dickinson (SHS, 1928), 1, 3, 130, 187, 193, and 259; and *Register of the Great Seal of Scotland 1424–1513*, ed. J. Balfour Paul (Edinburgh, 1882), i, no. 3709.
[46] *Papyngo*, 39.

INTRODUCTION

> Off Galloway the bischop new
> Furcht of my hand ane ballat drew . . .
>
> Of Halie Croce the abbot ying
> I did to him ane ballat bring.[47]

Dunbar's religious poems, such as those included in the Arundel Manuscript, were probably intended for solitary devotional reading. Others, of a satiric or didactic character, might have been put in a public place, where many could see them. Scurrilous verses were sometimes fixed to church doors or city gates; and moral verses were often inscribed on walls—Maitland's poem 'Dreid god and luif him faythfullie' has a heading, 'To be put in ony publict hous'.[48] Some of Dunbar's poems are short enough to be easily memorized, and to circulate by word of mouth. Whether any were designed to be read aloud is uncertain. *The Flyting* gives the impression of being suitable for public performance, and one piece opens with an abrupt command, in minstrel style—'Now lythis off ane gentill knycht' (K 27). *The Tua Mariit Wemen and the Wedo* ends with a question put to 'auditoris'. In each case, of course, these listeners may have been imaginary, not actual. Yet the recitation of complimentary poems occurred at royal entries and banquets, and tale-telling was a familiar entertainment at the Scottish court. Douglas hoped that his *Eneados* would be read aloud to the illiterate, and much later in the century James Melvill's sister read to him as a child in winter nights from 'David Lindsayes book'.[49] It is a reasonable, though unstartling, conclusion, that Dunbar's poems reached many different people, and circulated in a variety of ways.

It might seem a hopeless task to enquire what we can learn of Dunbar's attitude to poetry. He left no 'Apology for Poetry', nothing even as detailed and explicit as Douglas's Prologues to the *Eneados*. Yet *The Goldyn Targe* and *The Flyting* contain much that is critically interesting; and scattered throughout his poems are brief references to himself and other poets, from which it is possible to deduce more than might be expected of Dunbar's views on his art, and his literary affiliations. It is not always easy to gauge his exact tone, since he is often jocular and ironic, and his literary comments are usually incidental to other topics. Yet modern assessments of Dunbar's poetry

---

[47] Greene, *Carols*, no. 121.2.

[48] See *Maitland Folio*, no. xx; on the custom of posting verses in public places, see V. J. Scattergood, *Politics and Poetry in the Fifteenth Century* (1971), 25–6.

[49] On the recitation of poems, see below (Ch. 3); and *The Diary of Mr James Melvill 1556–1601* (Bannatyne Club, 34, Edinburgh, 1829), 15.

INTRODUCTION

and its place in literary history should take account of what he himself says.

Dunbar places himself at the very centre of *Sir Jhon Sinclair begowthe to dance* (K 28):

> Than cam in Dunbar the mackar;
> On all the flure thair was nane frackar [more nimble],
> And thair he dancet the dirrye dantoun;
> He hoppet lyk a pillie wanton
> For luff of Musgraeffe, men tellis me;
> He trippet quhill he tint his panton [slipper]:
> A mirrear dance mycht na man see. (22–8)

Dunbar here dances, hops, and trips; the self-portrayal is characteristically mocking, even bawdy.[50] Yet it is noteworthy that in a poem that introduces most of the dancers by their title or office—'Sir Jhon Sinclair', or 'Maistir Robert Schau', or 'the maister almaser'—Dunbar styles himself 'the mackar'. He does not call himself 'Maister Gilliam', as Kennedy does in *The Flyting* (497), and he identifies his court role not as chaplain but as poet. So too in *I that in heill wes* it is not the 'clerkis' with whom Dunbar aligns himself; it is the 'makaris' to whom he devotes most attention and whom he calls, in a double sense, his brothers:

> I se that makaris amang the laif
> Playis heir ther pageant, syne gois to graif;
> Sparit is nought ther faculte. (45–7)
>
> Sen he has all my brether tane
> He will naught lat me lif alane. (93–4)

Elsewhere Dunbar refers to himself as a 'ballet maker' (K 51. 90), and speaks of his poetry as 'making' (K 26. 3); he also applies the verb *mak* in an absolute sense to the writing of poetry:

> My heid did ȝak ȝester nicht
> This day to mak that I na micht. (K 21; cf. K 33. 1–2)

In modern critical usage the term *makar* has acquired a highly restricted sense: 'the makars' is a useful group label for Scottish poets of the fifteenth and sixteenth centuries, such as Henryson, Douglas, and Dunbar himself. Literary histories have chapter headings such as 'The Medieval Makars', and Tom Crawford, in his book on Burns, speaks of making 'a perfect work of art, in the sense which underlies the old Scots word, 'makar', or poet'.[51] Yet the use of 'makar' as

---

[50] *Pillie* seems to have an obscene sense (see *DOST*), despite editorial suggestions that it means 'colt' or 'turkey'.
[51] *Burns: A Study of the Poems and Songs* (1960), 75.

roughly synonymous with 'poet' was not peculiarly Scottish, nor, at this time, particularly common in Scotland. Henryson and Douglas do not use the term, either of themselves or of other poets. Dunbar praises Chaucer as flower of 'makaris' (K 62. 50), but Douglas calls him 'principall poet but peir' (*Eneados*, Prol. 1. 339), just as he calls Virgil 'of Latyn poetis prynce' (Prol. 1. 3). In *The Palice of Honour* (850 ff.) all the Muses' followers are termed poets, not *makars*, whatever language they speak. Lindsay speaks similarly of his Scottish predecessors as 'Poetis' (*Papyngo*, 29). *DOST* cites only three other Scots uses of *makar* in this literary sense, apart from Dunbar's; and other dictionaries give no evidence for its Scottish currency in the late sixteenth or seventeenth centuries.[52] In 1724, however, Allan Ramsay published *I that in heill wes* in his popular and influential *Ever Green*; and in 1770, in Lord Hailes's *Ancient Scottish Poems*, this poem received the title by which it is still best known, 'Lament for the Death of the Makkars'. It thus seems likely that it is Dunbar, aided by his eighteenth-century editors, who is largely responsible for the term's special Scottish vogue today.

Maker, as a near-synonym for poet, occurred frequently in Chaucer and late medieval English writers, and, although increasingly archaic, it continued in use throughout the sixteenth century. Puttenham reflected on its etymology, in *The Art of English Poesie*—'A poet is as much to say as a maker'—and also differentiated the poet, or 'courtly maker', from the minstrel and 'rude rayling rimer'.[53] Dunbar's preference for the term may have originated in his reading of Chaucer; his usage recalls the famous stanza in *Troilus and Criseyde* that begins

> Ther God thi makere yet, ere that he dye,
> So sende myght to make in som comedye!
> But litel book, no makyng thou n'envie,
> But subgit be to alle poesye . . .   (v. 1787–90)

In Chaucer, however, *maker* coexists and competes with *poet*; he fairly consistently applies *poet* to the ancients, like Virgil and Ovid, also to Dante and Petrarch; but he usually speaks of himself and other vernacular poets as makers. Although no precise distinction can be drawn between the terms, they seem contrasted in their implications. *Maker* and *making* are not undignified, yet they do not seem to have as high status as *poet* and *poetry*; these latter are associated with learned, humanistic compositions, classical subject-matter, and a high moral purpose. G. Olson, in 'Making and Poetry in the Age of

---

[52] One is the highly Chaucerian envoi to Hary's *Wallace*, xii. 1453. On Scottish usage I am indebted to *DOST*, *SND*, and *CSD*.
[53] I. i and II. x; in *Elizabethan Critical Essays*, ed. G. Gregory Smith (Oxford, 1904), ii. 3 and 87.

Chaucer', argues that *poet* is inherently laudatory, but *maker* is more neutral.[54] *Maker*, 'one who makes', seems self-evidently to lay stress on the poet as craftsman rather than *vates*; E. K. thus commented on Spenser's April Eclogue: 'In this woorde makyng our olde English poets were wont to comprehend all the skill of Poetrye.' Yet the term does not necessarily exclude the idea of inspired creativity, since God the Creator was termed 'the Maker'.

It may be fortuitous that Dunbar does not call himself a poet, yet his failure to use the term does suggest a disclaimer of its more lofty connotations. For Douglas the poet was clearly a figure of great dignity; poetry—and epic in particular—brought not only delight but profound wisdom, and gave fame to the poets themselves. Dunbar could not fail to be aware of this exalted conception of the poet but there is little sign that he had such large-scale ambitions for himself. Dunbar says little indeed of his intentions in writing. In one poem, however, he comments interestingly on an earlier one, which painted a comic portrait of a fellow-courtier (K 29). Addressing the queen, Dunbar says:

> Thocht I in ballet did with him bourde
> In malice spack I nevir ane woord
> Bot all, my dame, to do 3ow gam.[55]   (K 30. 5–7)

We should beware of reading too much into a fleeting comment, and of taking Dunbar over-literally, especially in his disavowal of 'malice'. Yet what is said of this one poem corresponds closely to the experience of reading many others. Dunbar here represents his poetry-making almost as an extension of conversation; it is social, playful, and recreative. It draws members of the court together into a relationship that is common enough in life—a *bourde*, or jest, at one person's expense provokes *gam*, or amusement, in others. The term *bourde* was applied to jests with a cruel edge, or to crude practical jokes. This element is certainly present in some of Dunbar's poems. The foul climax of *The Turnament* (K 52B) likewise causes 'solace', and is termed a good 'bourd' (220–1). *Gam* was a word with a wide range of implications, resembling those of *play* or *ludus*. As in modern usage, *game* implied playful rivalry or contest—there is a strong element of this in *The Flyting* and a few other poems. Its leading senses, however, were 'pleasure, entertainment', and more narrowly, 'fun, amusement'; there is a clear and sometimes explicit contrast with the serious aspects of life. Dunbar sometimes, like Chaucer, writes 'bitwixen game and

---

[54] In *Comparative Literature*, 31 (1979), 272–90. Olson notes that Eustache Deschamps applied *faiseur* to the lyric poet.

[55] In line 7 Kinsley reads 3*our*; I prefer Reidpeth's 3*ow*.

ernest', but the primary objective of many poems is to divert—to produce in his audience an equivalent to his New Year's wish for the king: 'Play, pleasance, myrth and mirrie cheir' (K 18).

The distinction between *makar* and *poet* may have been a fine one, but the difference between *makar* and *bard* was clear-cut and very important to Dunbar. Indeed in *The Flyting* he vehemently exclaims, 'wondir laith wer I to be ane baird' (17). *Baird* is, throughout *The Flyting*, a term of abuse, repeatedly hurled at his antagonist, Kennedy, and coupled with charges of begging, blasphemy, poverty, and theft (49, 63, 96, 120, 183, 208, 244). In this Dunbar was characteristic of most Scottish Lowlanders in the fifteenth and sixteenth centuries, to whom the bard was a rather low kind of Gaelic-speaking poet or scurrilous entertainer. Richard Holland, in *The Howlat* (795 ff.), painted an uncomplimentary portrait of 'a bard out of Irland', and put him in the company of fools, minstrels, and jugglers. Some references are neutral; we read of the king's gifts, when he was in the Highlands, to 'heland bardis', or to 'Duncane Campbellis bard'. But most of the citations in *DOST* are pejorative, and collocate bards with other undesirable members of society, such as scolds and flyters, beggars and feigned fools. Bellenden places 'juglaris, mynstralis, bardis and skafferis' in the category of idle people.[56] We are far removed from the vague veneration for the bard as a *vates*, associated with Blake and other Romantic poets:

> Hear the voice of the Bard,
> Who present, past and future sees.

But we are equally distant from the precise usage of Gaelic poetry, in which the bard was differentiated from other types of poet. Derrick Thomson suggests that in Gaelic tradition the properly accredited bard would have been distinguished from the strolling bard; and that it is this latter figure, classed with 'menstrallis, sangstaris and tail tellaris not avouit in speciall service be sum of the lordis of parliament or greit barronis', that attracted particular hostility, from legislators as well as poets.[57] Dunbar's proclaimed aversion to Highlanders may be partly a humorous ploy, but no evidence has been produced to show that it masks, in reality, a deep affection for Gaelic culture and an intimate acquaintance with its verse.[58] Beneath the rude and boisterous

---

[56] See *TA* ii. 119, and iii. 339; *DOST*, s.v. *bard, bairding, bairdrie*; and Bellenden, *Chronicles*, IX. xvii (i. 392).

[57] 'Scottish Gaelic Folk-Poetry ante 1650', *Scottish Gaelic Studies*, 8 (1958), 3 (1–17). The relevant Acts of Parliament (of 1449 and 1579) are excerpted in Mill, 294–6.

[58] Critics who assert Gaelic influence upon Dunbar usually speak vaguely of his Gaelic (or Celtic) 'blood', 'spirit', or 'temperament'. Cf. K. Wittig, *The Scottish Tradition in Literature* (1958), 61.

INTRODUCTION

language of flyting, Dunbar is making a serious point. He is dissociating himself from one poetic tradition, that of Gaelic-speaking Scotland, and proclaiming his allegiance to another, that of 'Inglis' speakers. He mocks Kennedy for presumptuously calling himself a 'rethory', and continues:

> Sic eloquence as thay in Erschry use,
> In sic is sett thy thraward appetyte.
> Thow hes full littill feill of fair indyte:
> I tak on me ane pair of Lowthiane hippis
> Sall fairar Inglis mak, and mair parfyte,
> Than thow can blabbar with thy Carrik lippis. (107–12)

Poetry and language-choice are here as closely intertwined as in *The Goldyn Targe*, which contains one of Dunbar's most important statements about poetry.

At two points in *The Goldyn Targe* Dunbar breaks off from his narrative to reflect about his poem, and its place in literary tradition. The two passages are contrasted but complementary. The first is designed to enhance the importance of his subject by proclaiming—in a variant of the inexpressibility topos—that it outstrips the power of even the greatest writers:

> Discrive I wald, bot quho coud wele endyte
> How all the feldis wyth thai lilies quhite
> Depaynt war brycht, quhilk to the hevyn did glete?
> Noucht thou, Omer, als fair as thou coud wryte,
> For all thine ornate stilis so perfyte;
> Nor yit thou, Tullius, quhois lippis suete
> Off rethorike did in to termes flete. (64–70)

The second is a traditional expression of authorial modesty; it too uses a common topos, to which the term 'outdoing' is sometimes applied (Dunbar's own word is 'surmounting'):[59]

> O reverend Chaucere, rose of rethoris all,
> As in oure tong ane flour imperiall
> That rais in Britane, evir quho redis rycht,
> Thow beris of makaris the tryumph riall;
> Thy fresch anamalit termes celicall
> This mater coud illumynit have full brycht:
> Was thou noucht of oure Inglisch all the lycht,
> Surmounting eviry tong terrestriall
> Alls fer as Mayes morow dois mydnycht?
>
> O morall Gower and Ludgate laureate,
> Your sugurit lippis and tongis aureate

[59] See E. R. Curtius, *European Literature and the Latin Middle Ages*, trans. W. R. Trask (1953), 159–65.

INTRODUCTION

> Bene to oure eris cause of grete delyte;
> Your angel mouthis most mellifluate
> Oure rude langage has clere illumynate,
> And fair ourgilt oure spech that imperfyte
> Stude or your goldyn pennis schupe to write;
> This ile before was bare and desolate
> Off rethorike, or lusty fresch endyte.   (253-70)

Both of these passages are extremely formal set-pieces, employing various rhetorical *termes*, or figures of speech, such as apostrophe, *interrogatio*, and *repetitio*. Both pay tribute to the past. The first, more briefly and distantly, mentions two great and contrasted figures from classical antiquity: Homer stands not only for the achievement of the Greeks, but for poetry at its most 'perfyte'; Cicero for the Latins, perhaps for prose, and certainly for the art of rhetoric. Nowhere else does Dunbar refer by name to Greek or Latin writers; all the poets mentioned in *I that in heill wes* are vernacular ones. There is nothing in Dunbar comparable to the long lists of classical authors in Skeltons's *Garland of Laurel* and Douglas's *Palice of Honour*. This suggests that the great tradition of classical poetry, as known to the Middle Ages—Chaucer's 'Virgile, Ovide, Omer, Lucan and Stace'— was of less significance for Dunbar than it was for Chaucer, Skelton, or Douglas. His poetry bears this out. There are occasional slight resemblances, not precise debts, to such poets as Horace and Martial; and the deities of the ancient world, though not completely absent, are confined to a small group of his poems (for example, K 10, 16, 35, 50, 53, and 54). The Latin tradition that was important to Dunbar was associated primarily with the Church—the Scriptures, the liturgy, hymns, prayers, and devotional works—and with the churchmen who wrote the witty, irreverent poems often termed 'Goliardic'. Although Dunbar does not tell us this explicitly, he leaves scattered clues, such as references to 'haly writ' (K 5), or 'haly legendis' (K 55), or the opening of a hymn to the Virgin, *gaude flore* (K 3), and his quotations, sometimes devout, sometimes parodic, from the Bible and liturgy.

The second passage, containing a eulogy of Chaucer, Gower, and Lydgate, is more detailed and more fervent. Dunbar here unequivocally embraces the language and poetic traditions associated with Chaucer. When he speaks of 'Britane' and 'this ile' he ignores the political boundaries between Scotland and England; he recognizes a single language-community, transcending local ones, speaking of *'oure* tong' and *'oure* Inglisch'. For Dunbar Chaucer and his followers were, in a sense, the classics of the vernacular; they represented a standard of literary excellence, familiar yet not oppressively close. Dunbar distinguishes a poem's *mater*, or subject, from its decorative expression, and implies a near-equation between poetry and rhetoric.

INTRODUCTION

Apart from a brief earlier reference to 'My lady Cleo that help of makaris bene' (77), he says nothing of the role of inspiration in poetry; he is here interested chiefly in technique and style. Such an approach to poetry springs from the long-established medieval stress on one branch of rhetoric, *elocutio*; many earlier poets consciously sought 'the eloquence off ornat rethorye' (K 76. 10). Much else in the passage is far from original, including the choice of three English poets, and the imagery, which can be paralleled in several fifteenth-century authors. The notion that the great poet *illuminates* both his subject and his native language has a long history, and may be found in Lydgate, Chaucer, and Dante.[60] Yet Dunbar voices these ideas memorably and concisely, and *The Goldyn Targe* itself brilliantly embodies the concept of poetry which this passage articulates.

Dunbar's imagery here has often been discussed, notably by Denton Fox:

Dunbar suggests several metaphors for good writing, a principal one being that of light ... Bareness is a symbol for bad writing ('Rude is thy wede, disteynit, bare and rent'), or for the absence of good writing ('This Ile before was bare and desolate'), while poetic beauty is characterized by flowers ... But the most revealing image and the one which connects all the others is 'anamalit'. Enamel is clear and brilliant, colourful, with a rich sweet beauty, and most particularly is a surface adornment, like illumination, flowers, and gold or sugar coating.[61]

His analysis is subtle and persuasive, although 'sugurit', like 'mellifluate', surely implies sweet and melodious sound, not icing on a cake. Dunbar here visualizes a poem as a work of art, an artefact. Yet some critics over-emphasize the art-images ('anamalit', 'ourgilt') at the expense of those from the natural world (Chaucer as 'rose of rethoris'); there is perhaps too much stress on their visual quality—Dunbar also says that poets delight the ear (264). This has led to one prevalent view of Dunbar as a poet of hard, brilliant surfaces, his style 'a verbal counterpart of the enameler's art'.[62] This well conveys the effect produced by some of Dunbar's most striking poems, notably *The Goldyn Targe* itself; but it seems an inadequate characterization of the many others in which he demonstrates his command of an easy, colloquial style, great sensitivity to nuances of meaning, and a remarkable flexibility of tone. Lois Ebin says that in these stanzas

---

[60] The 15th-century view of Chaucer has been much discussed: see Fox, 'The Scottish Chaucerians', 167–71, and A. C. Spearing, *Medieval to Renaissance in English Poetry* (Cambridge, 1985), 59–120.

[61] 'Dunbar's *The Golden Targe*', *ELH* 26 (1959), 332–3.

[62] L. Ebin, 'Poetics and Style in Late Medieval Literature', in *Vernacular Poetics in the Late Middle Ages*, ed. Ebin (Kalamazoo, Mich., 1984), 277; Fox, 'Dunbar's *Golden Targe*', 333–4.

Dunbar 'defines the relation between the poet and his matter which is central to most of his other poems'.[63] I see them rather as adumbrating a poetic ideal, to which he aspires in some but not all of his poems. This passage expresses ideas that were clearly important to Dunbar, but there seems a risk of exaggerating the extent to which he put them into practice.

Precisely how much Dunbar owed to Chaucer has long been debated. Some scholars disregard this glowing eulogy, or treat it as mere lip-service. Few would now apply to Dunbar the outmoded phrase 'Scottish Chaucerian'. Formations of this kind tend inevitably to acquire pejorative implications. What is more, it is easy to question the phrase's aptness to Dunbar. 'Chaucerian' qualities can be discerned in Henryson, but it has become a critical truism that 'no two medieval poets [are] more unlike than Chaucer and Dunbar'.[64] Yet the increasing distaste for the phrase is not wholly disinterested; it has clearly been fuelled by Scottish nationalism. When Hugh MacDiarmid put together a small volume of *Selections from Dunbar* (1952), he deliberately omitted the more courtly poems, in an avowed resolve 'to get rid of the absurd appellation, "Scottish Chaucerian"'. The reaction against Chaucer is excessive and misguided, particularly when it leads critics to substitute 'Lydgatian' for 'Chaucerian'. It is wholly mistaken to say that 'Dunbar's debt to Lydgate . . . is much more direct and extensive than his debt to Chaucer'.[65] Statements like this are common, yet have never been substantiated. The resemblances between Dunbar and Lydgate, for the most part, illustrate their common debt to a shared literary tradition—they usually consist in traditional phrases, images, and poetic kinds. It is suggested, for instance, that two of Dunbar's moral poems (K 81 and 82) are modelled on Lydgate's *A Wicked Tunge*; it is more accurate to say that all three belong to the same minor didactic genre.[66] Where Dunbar is undeniably close to Lydgate is in his stance towards Chaucer; the stanzas quoted earlier certainly recall passages in Lydgate. Yet if one reads Dunbar attentively, seeking evidence of specific literary influences, the poet of whom one is most conscious is Chaucer. It is not surprising that the two poems in which Dunbar names Chaucer, *The Goldyn Targe* and *I that in heill wes*, should contain allusions to poems

[63] 'Poetics and Style', 276.
[64] G. Kratzmann, *Anglo-Scottish Literary Relations 1430–1550* (Cambridge, 1980), 129; Fox, 'Scottish Chaucerians', 186.
[65] Pearsall, *Old English and Middle English Poetry*, 332–3. For discussion, see P. H. Nichols, 'William Dunbar as a Scottish Lydgatian', *PMLA* 46 (1931), 214–24; R. D. S. Jack, 'Dunbar and Lydgate', *SSL* 8 (1970–1), 215–27; and Bawcutt, 'Source-Hunting: Some Reulis and Cautelis', in Lyall and Riddy, *Proceedings*, 95–9.
[66] See below, 139.

by him, or that a courtly dream poem, *The Thrissill and the Rois*, sometimes echoes *The Knight's Tale* or *The Parliament of Fowls*. But there are other reminiscences of Chaucer in unexpected places: of *The Parson's Tale* in *The Tua Mariit Wemen and the Wedo*, for instance, and of *The Parliament of Fowls* in *The Abbot of Tungland* (K 54).[67] Critics grudgingly concede some similarity between the Widow in *The Tua Mariit Wemen and the Wedo* and the Wife of Bath; only rarely do they note the equally interesting relationship between that poem and *The Merchant's Tale*.

It is a mistake, however, to expect to find many 'direct and extensive' debts to earlier poets in Dunbar. Despite much scholarly investigation it has repeatedly proved easier to demonstrate the kinds or genres to which his poems belong than to identify sources or influences. The label 'Scottish Villon' has also been applied to Dunbar, and to see him in this light, as an illustration not of cultural subjection to the 'Auld Innemy' but of the fruitful working of the 'Auld Alliance', would clearly please many Scots.[68] Yet Dunbar, even in *The Testament of Maister Andro Kennedy*, is quite unlike Villon; and no unmistakable debt to Villon or any other French poet has so far been demonstrated. The French influence upon Dunbar consists chiefly in his adoption of poetic modes or styles that either originated in France, or found their most famous exemplars in French verse. The dream tradition to which *The Goldyn Targe* and *The Thrissill and the Rois* belong may be traced back to *Le Roman de la Rose*. But this is an ultimate ancestor, not a source. Dunbar is a remarkably different poet not only from Chaucer but from his contemporaries, such as Henryson, Skelton, and, above all, Douglas. Douglas abounds in references to other writers and their works; he translates, paraphrases, and quotes, sometimes giving precise references to chapter and verse in Boccaccio or the Bible. Almost the opposite is true of Dunbar. Janet Smith remarked that Dunbar 'never worked ... with a foreign book at his elbow';[69] one might extend this further—Dunbar rarely worked with *any* book at his elbow. Clearly Dunbar did not exist in some strange literary vacuum. He was well-read, and interested in many different kinds of poetry; but he was not a learned, intellectual, or 'bookish' poet.

To treat *I that in heill wes* simply as a poetic manifesto would be a profound misreading of a fine poem. Yet its list of Scottish poets, from the late fourteenth century to Dunbar's own time, is the first of

---

[67] See below, 277; also Bawcutt, *N&Q*, NS 1 (1964), 332-3.
[68] See J.-J. Blanchot, 'William Dunbar and François Villon', in Aitken, *Bards and Makars*, 72-87.
[69] *The French Background of Middle Scots Literature* (Edinburgh, 1934), 77.

INTRODUCTION

its kind and of great literary importance. It proclaims Dunbar's interest in poets as individuals, and his awareness of a distinctive tradition of Scottish poetry, 'of this cuntre' (55) and separate from that of England, yet not wholly cut off, since the Scottish procession is headed by the English trio of Chaucer, Gower, and Lydgate. 'This cuntre' is no abstraction—Dunbar gives several poets their local habitation, Eglinton, Tranent, Corstorphine, or Aberdeen. The sheer number of names conveys a sense of literary abundance—many minor, often forgotten, figures accompany the better-known poets, such as Barbour and Henryson. Dunbar also makes us aware, casually and unsystematically, of the diversity of these poets: an allegorist, such as Holland, mingles with chroniclers, such as Barbour and Wyntoun; 'balat making and trigide' (59) is followed by an unidentified Arthurian romance, 'the anteris of Gawane' (66). Some poets are recalled primarily as friends—'Two bettir fallowis did no man se' (79). Dunbar passes few critical comments, yet the bare mention of a name may have significance for his poetry. His inclusion of Holland, for instance, confirms that he was acquainted with one of the major Scottish alliterative poets. One poet is exceptional in having a stanza devoted to him:

> He has reft Merseir his endite
> That did in luf so lifly write,
> So schort, so quyk, of sentence hie:
> *Timor mortis conturbat me.* (73–6)

Mersar's few extant poems hardly justify this eulogy, which partly derives from Chaucer's portrait of the Clerk—also 'schort and quyk and ful of hy sentence'. Yet these lines interestingly complement *The Goldyn Targe*'s stress on rich ornamentation; they suggest that Dunbar also valued a style that was lively, vivid, and terse.

This poem, of its very nature, is concerned with named poets. But very occasionally Dunbar makes fleeting references to a less prestigious and usually anonymous body of literature: songs, ballads, romances, and ghost stories. He alludes to a time-honoured method of oral transmission: 'Wyvis ... Spynnand on rokkis' (K 34. 46–7). He reminds us that music-making and tale-telling were an important part of court entertainment: 'Sum singis, sum dances, sum tellis storyis' (K 20. 7). The names of some of the favourite tale-tellers at the Scottish court are known, 'Widderspune', for instance, and 'Wallass that tellis the geistis to the king'. Unfortunately the titles of their songs or tales are rarely mentioned—'Graysteill' is a rare exception. Dunbar himself casually names two songs (K 75. 29–30)— 'Now the day dawis', which seems to have been a contemporary 'hit', and 'Into Joun', of which nothing is now known.⁷⁰ Tapestries and wall-paintings also contained narratives—in one poem Dunbar mentions 'the nobill storyis, ald and new', depicted in his bedchamber (K 51. 4). In *The Flyting* he compares Kennedy to the 'spreit of Gy' (172), a revenant and central figure of a popular didactic tale about Purgatory.⁷¹ Dunbar's interest in other tales surfaces occasionally in throw-away allusions to 'Rauf Col3ard and Johnne the reif' (K 42. 33), 'Cokelbeis gryce' (K 44. 66), and the 'golk of Maryland' (K 13. 51). Most revealing, however, is the passage that refers to 'Sir Bevis the knycht off Southe Hamptowne' and other popular heroes:

> Was never wyld Robein under bewch
> Nor 3et Roger off Cleknisklewch
> So bauld a berne as he;
> Gy off Gysburne, na Allan Bell,
> Na Simonis sonnes off Quhynfell
> At schot war never so slie.   (K 27. 25–30)

The precise identity of all these figures is not known; the only other reference to 'Simonis sonnes off Quhynfell' treats it as the name of a dance.⁷² But these allusions are interesting, for several reasons. Dunbar ignores not only the geographical frontiers between England and Scotland, but other boundaries, drawn by modern scholars, between literary kinds, such as the ballad and the chivalric romance. He counts on his Scottish audience to be as familiar with John the reeve, upstart hero of an English comic tale, as with Rauf Coilyear, his Scottish equivalent. Figures from the ballads, such as Robin Hood, are linked with the knight, Sir Bevis of Southampton. Puttenham, later in the century, spoke superciliously of 'such stories of old time, as the tale of *Sir Topas*, the reportes of *Beuis of Southamton*, *Guy of Warwicke*, *Adam Bell*, and *Clymme of the Clough* . . . made purposely for recreation of the common people'.⁷³ Yet *Bevis* held its popularity for a long time, and in Scotland also, where the author of *The Complaynt of Scotland* named it, alongside *The Goldyn Targe*, in a list of stories and 'flet taylis'.⁷⁴

Critics tend to underestimate the extent of Dunbar's acquaintance with these and other kinds of popular writing. His humorous poems,

---

⁷⁰ For Widderspune, see *TA* i. 307, 330; ii. 102; for Wallass, ibid. i. 176, 183; for 'Graysteill', ibid. i. 330. Greene, *Carols*, no. 432, lists references to songs on the theme 'Now the day dawis'.
⁷¹ Cf. Lindsay, *The Dreme*, 16, and see below, 264.
⁷² *Colkelbie Sow*, ed. G. Kratzmann (New York, 1983), 381.
⁷³ *The Art of English Poesie*, II. xi; *Elizabethan Critical Essays*, ii. 87. Cf. J. A. Burrow, '*Sir Thopas* in the Sixteenth Century', in *Middle English Studies Presented to Norman Davis*, ed. D. Gray and E. G. Stanley (Oxford, 1983), 69–91.
⁷⁴ Ed. A. M. Stewart (STS, 1979), 50.

in particular, are often seen in curious isolation, unrelated to various long-lived forms, such as invectives and prophecies, or other light-hearted, convivial, indeed trivial writings, such as riddles and *demandes*, bawdy love poems, drinking songs, *facetiae*, and the vernacular jest books that succeeded them. It is true that Dunbar himself says almost nothing of this strain in his poetry. It is likely that he did not value it as highly as the more refined tradition that we now call 'Chaucerian', but he probably also felt it unnecessary to call attention to something that would have been clear and obvious to his contemporaries. The comparative neglect of this context for Dunbar seems to have various causes. Such writings were not respectable in a double sense, both moral and literary. Vulgar and bawdy poems often survived by accident, or in a furtive and subterranean way—witness the so-called 'Bradshaw carols'.[75] F. P. Wilson commented on the heavy mortality of the earliest jest books, pointing out that those who would consult them 'in the earliest editions must travel over half the world'.[76] Even today some of these writings are only available in limited editions, such as F. J. Furnivall's *Loose and Humorous Songs from Bishop Percy's Folio Manuscript* (1868). Lack of critical esteem is therefore intertwined with difficulty of access.

Modern neglect of this aspect of Dunbar also stems from the accepted view of him as a court poet, and from an over-rigid distinction between the 'courtly' and the 'popular' in literature. Certain writings are here termed popular, not because they were composed 'by the people', or were designed solely for the lower or less educated classes, but because they appealed to a wide and miscellaneous audience rather than to a small élite. Their popularity transcended barriers of class (and language), and sometimes lasted for centuries. Many of the jokes that appeared in Poggio's *Facetiae* had an international currency; they were repeatedly recycled, passing from speech to writing, and from one language to another.[77] Riddles and other verbal games are today associated chiefly with children; but in eighteenth-century Scotland, according to James Hogg, they were a common method, among countrymen, of passing the long winter evenings.[78] In Dunbar's time *The Demaundes Joyous*, a small collection printed by Wynkyn de Worde (1511), was not intended solely for children or rustics. 'Fair demaundis' are linked with interludes as a courtly pastime in Douglas's *Palice of Honour* (1181–2). The verse

---

[75] Cf. R. H. Robbins, 'The Bradshaw Carols', *PMLA* 81 (1966), 308–10; and P. J. Croft, 'The "Friar of Order Gray" and the Nun', *RES*, NS 32 (1981), 1–16.

[76] 'The English Jest-Books of the Sixteenth and Early Seventeenth Centuries', in *Shakespearian and Other Studies* (Oxford, 1969), 285–6.

[77] Ibid. 290 ff.

[78] Cf. D. Buchan, *Scottish Tradition* (1984), 2–4.

INTRODUCTION

prophecy too is now an unfamiliar genre, and if known at all usually treated with contempt. Yet its vogue lasted well into the seventeenth century; although sophisticated people derided 'diverse prophane propheseis of merlyne ... in rusty ryme', they were widely quoted and studied, by kings as well as peasants.[79] Such prophecies are put to comic use in *Lucina schynnyng in silence of the nicht* (K 53); and their 'rusty' verse, a debased version of the long alliterative line, shows that the metre chosen for *The Tua Mariit Wemen and the Wedo* may have seemed archaic, but was not unfamiliar, in the sixteenth century.

Dunbar does not speak of writing poems; he refers variously to his *sangis* (K 50. 28), *dyt* (K 47. 21), and *indyting* (K 26. 15), but the term he uses most often is *ballat* or *ballattis*:

> Quhen I wald blythlie ballattis breif
> Langour thairto givis me no leif.   (K 19. 6–7)
>
> Thocht I in ballet did with him bourde   (K 30. 5)
>
> Allace, I can bot ballattis breif.   (K 42. 48)

What does this word mean? Etymologically, it is the same as modern *ballad* or *ballade*—indeed, these spellings also occur in Scots, as in the contemporary title, 'the Ballade of . . . Barnard Stewart' (K 35). But in Dunbar's time the term did not necessarily signify a short, popular narrative poem (as in 'the Border Ballads'), nor was it restricted to a poem of a fixed form, consisting of three stanzas, using identical rhymes, and linked by a refrain (as in Chaucer's *Rosemound*). Late medieval usage, in Scots as in English, was far more free: a ballat could have any metrical shape, and deal with almost any subject. Asloan applied the term both to the devout 'Ballat of Our Lady' (K 2) and the comical 'Ballat of the Abbot of Tungland' (K 54). Bannatyne labelled one section of his manuscript 'Ballattis of Lufe', and another 'Ballattis full of Wisdome and Moralitie'.

The term may thus appear almost as vague and elastic as *poem*. Yet it seems to have had certain connotations. A ballat tends to be short. The last section of Bannatyne's anthology, chiefly containing longer poems, is entitled 'Fabillis Wyis and Sapient'. Douglas's *Palice of Honour* is termed by its printer, Charteris, 'this plesand and delectabill wark', but the small inset poems it contains are referred to as 'lays', and once as a 'ballat' (995). (When Henryson calls *The Testament of Cresseid* 'this ballet schort' (610), we have, I think, a slight shock of surprise.) *Ballat* also, rather like *lyric*, had associations with music. *DOST* defines it as 'a ballad or song, originally one accompanying a dance'. John Rolland, referring to 'Sum ballet or sang breuit of the

---
[79] *Complaynt of Scotland*, 65.

new', treated the term as synonymous with song. For Douglas one of the pleasures of the Elysian Fields was 'to syng ballatis, and go in karalyng' (*Eneados*, VI. x. 40). So too in *The Goldyn Targe* Dunbar refers to the singing of 'ballettis in lufe' (103), and later links the activity with music and dancing:

> On harp or lute full merily thai playit
> And sang ballettis with michty notis clere;
> Ladyes to dance full sobirly assayit.   (128–30)

Ballats, like sonnets later in the century, were frequently though not invariably associated with love and lovers' wooing. It was a common occupation of the lovesick 'to make balades or songes'.[80] Douglas speaks of the lover, who 'ballettis lyst endyte of hys lady' (*Eneados*, Prol. 12. 205).

Perhaps because of this there sometimes lurks a latent disapproval in the term. *The Gude and Godlie Ballatis* were designed, in part, to counter such 'lufe ballatis'. It might be argued that *ballat* itself was a neutral term, and that in phrases such as 'lewd baladis' or 'odious balletis' it is the epithet that conveys disapproval. But the word seems to have absorbed the associations of the pleasant but morally suspect activities with which it was so often linked—music, singing and dancing, and love. In *The Tua Mariit Wemen and the Wedo* the Widow envisages the reading of ballats as part of the amorous ritual, and links them damagingly with 'riatus' speech:

> And all my luffaris lele my lugeing persewis
> . . . .
> Sum rownis and sum raleis and sum redis ballatis,
> Sum raiffis furght rudly with riatus speche.   (478 ff.)

Another of Dunbar's poems opens

> In to thir dirk and drublie dayis
> Quhone sabill all the hevin arrayis,
> With mystie vapouris, cluddis and skyis,
> Nature all curage me denyis
> Off sangis, ballatis and of playis.   (K 69. 1–5)

The word's connotations here, sandwiched between 'sangis' and 'playis', are clearly pleasurable. But the syntax is ambiguous: Dunbar seems to say that he lacks *curage* ('heart') to compose such songs and poems, as well as to enjoy them. In two other poems he speaks similarly of the act of composition, stressing that his 'curage' must be 'glaid and blisfull' (K 50. 25–8), not 'dullit in dulnes and distres'

---

[80] This discussion is indebted to the articles (on *ballad*, *ballat*, etc.) in *OED*, *DOST*, and *MED*; full references will be found there. See also A. B. Friedman, 'The Late Mediaeval Ballade and the Origin of Broadside Balladry', *MÆ* 27 (1958), 95–110.

INTRODUCTION

(K 21. 10). For Dunbar and his contemporaries ballats were short and tuneful poems; and, unless the term is defined by some modifier, their subjects tended to be secular, light, and lacking in high seriousness. Whether Dunbar intended any of his poems to be sung, or set to music, is now impossible to say. He speaks warmly of 'musicianis, menstralis and mirrie singaris' in one poem (K 44. 9), although he criticizes the 'commone menstrallis' of Edinburgh (K 75. 29–35). He sometimes refers to his poetical activity as singing:

> Thane had my dyt beine all in duill,
> Had I my wage wantit quhill 3uill,
> Quhair now I sing with heart onsair. (K 47. 21–3)

But such phrasing is commonly no more than metaphorical. Two of Dunbar's poems are technically carols (K 17 and 43), and he has a striking fondness, like Wyatt, for the refrain, which he terms 'ouir word' (K 40. 4), and which he uses with great dexterity in some fifty poems. None the less no poem with an early attribution to Dunbar is accompanied by music—in this respect he contrasts with later poets with whom he has some affinity, such as Alexander Scott and Alexander Montgomerie. (The song *Now fayre, fayrest off every fayre* (K 24) was only attributed to Dunbar in the nineteenth century.[81])

Critics have disagreed as to whether Dunbar's poems should be called lyrical;[82] but there can be no argument that, by the standards of the time, they tend to be short. His longest work, *The Tua Mariit Wemen and the Wedo*, contains 530 lines; this the Maitland Folio interestingly calls a *tretis*, or 'narrative', not a ballat. Only two other poems have more than 200 lines, *The Goldyn Targe* and Dunbar's contribution to *The Flyting*. Sixteen have 100 lines or more—these are, in addition to the three just mentioned, *The Passioun of Crist* (K 3), *The Tabill of Confessioun* (K 6), *Sen that I am a presoneir* (K 9), *The Merle and the Nychtingall* (K 16), *The Dregy* (K 22), *The Testament of Maister Andro Kennedy* (K 38), *This waverand warldis wretchidnes* (K 39), *The Thrissill and the Rois* (K 50), *This hinder nycht halff sleiping as I lay* (K 51), the two linked poems that constitute *Fasternis Evin* (K 52), *The Abbot of Tungland* (K 54), and *I that in heill wes* (K 62). Dunbar's favourite length for a poem seems to be between thirty and seventy lines, but some pieces attributed to him are extremely short (K 7 and 57); a few poems have a very effective three-part structure of fifteen lines disposed in three stanzas, rhyming *aabba*: *Sweit rois of*

---

[81] See Baxter, 118 and 222.
[82] A. K. Moore, *The Secular Lyric in Middle English* (Lexington, Ky., 1951), 194, contests views that Dunbar is not lyrical.

31

INTRODUCTION

vertew (K 8), *My heid did ʒak ʒester nicht* (K 21), and *Schir at this feist of benefice* (K 41). Dunbar's liking for short lines, particularly those with four-stress rhythms, is also evident. In this he offers a striking contrast with the best-known Scottish poets of his day, Blind Hary, Henryson, and Douglas. Dunbar's section of *The Flyting* is far shorter than that of Kennedy; his poem on the Passion (144 lines) is also considerably shorter than Kennedy's poem on the same subject (1,715 lines). Dream-allegories, like Douglas's *Palice of Honour* or Skelton's *Garland of Laurel*, commonly run into thousands of lines; Dunbar's *Goldyn Targe* (279 lines) is on a much smaller scale. Satirical testaments are also often long—Villon's *Grand Testament* contains 2,023 lines—but *The Testament of Maister Andro Kennedy* (116 lines) is predictably brief. Again and again Dunbar's handling of a specific genre shows this taste for brevity, and contrasts with the leisurely manner of his contemporaries.

In two poems Dunbar vividly imagines how some of his fellow-courtiers respond to him. The first contrasts his lack of success at court with the rapid rise of others:

> Jok that wes wont to keip the stirkis
> Can now draw him ane cleik of kirkis
> With ane fals cairt in to his sleif
> Worthe all my ballattis under the byrkis.   (K 42. 66–9)

and earlier

> Quhone utheris dois flattir and feynʒe,
> Allace, I can bot ballattis breif.   (47–8)

'I can do nothing but write ballats'—the humility is not to be taken literally. It implies the scale of values that rewards flatterers more highly than poets. There is similar irony in *This hinder nycht halff sleiping as I lay* (K 51):

> Thane com anon ane callit Sir Johne Kirkpakar,
> Off many cures ane michtie undertaker;
> Quod he, I am possest in kirkis sevin,
> And ʒitt I think thai grow sall till ellevin
> Or he be servit in ane, ʒone ballet maker.   (86–90)

'ʒone ballet maker' is clearly contemptuous, but the contempt is imputed to the greedy, pluralist churchman, not Dunbar's own view of his calling. This pejorative use of *ballet maker* interestingly anticipates later uses, such as William Webbe's derisive reference to 'the vncountable rabble of ryming Ballet makers and compylers of sencelesse sonets'. By the end of the sixteenth century poets were regularly distinguished from vulgar ballad makers, and Ben Jonson told William

Drummond of Hawthornden: 'a Poet should detest a Ballet maker.'[83] Clearly the phrase would not have exactly the same force for Dunbar, writing a century earlier and before the proliferation of broadside ballads, yet the tone is similar. Dunbar here dramatizes not merely a philistine contempt for poetry in general but an undefined lack of esteem for 'ballats' in particular.

How highly did Dunbar value his own poetry? Two contrasted but not necessarily contradictory tendencies can be observed. The first apparently depreciative attitude is illustrated in the passages just quoted, and in the last stanza of *The Goldyn Targe*:

> Thou lytill quair, be evir obedient,
> Humble, subject, and symple of entent
> Before the face of eviry connyng wicht:
> I knaw quhat thou of rethorike hes spent;
> Off all hir lusty rosis redolent
> Is none in to thy gerland sett on hicht;
> Eschame thar of, and draw the out of sicht.
> Rude is thy wede, disteynit, bare and rent;
> Wele aucht thou be aferit of the licht.

In these poems Dunbar's stance is self-protective. In *The Goldyn Targe* he speaks with humility, not of all that he has written but of one poem only. The high degree of rhetorical skill 'spent' on *The Goldyn Targe*, however, should make one wary of accepting such disparagement at its face-value. Dunbar is here writing within the ancient tradition of the *captatio benevolentiae*—speaking modestly of his work so as to gain for it a favourable reception. (Douglas uses the same ploy, at the beginning and end of *The Palice of Honour*.) Dunbar's farewell to his 'quair' immediately follows the eulogy of Chaucer; he is speaking comparatively, not absolutely, placing his own poem within the most lofty tradition of English poetry known to him, rather as Chaucer himself had set the 'litel bok' of Troilus beside the tradition of classical poetry.[84] In such a context Dunbar's modesty might seem justified, if hyperbolical.

Elsewhere Dunbar offers a very different self-appraisal. *Schir I complane of injuris* (K 26) is a complaint about another poet, who has 'magellit' or mutilated, one of Dunbar's poems. His worst crime was to impute to Dunbar clumsy 'versis off his awin hand wryting':

---

[83] *Of English Poetry*, in *English Critical Essays*, i. 246. Jonson's remark is quoted by Hyder E. Rollins, together with others by Nashe and William Kemp, in 'The Black-Letter Broadside Ballad', *PMLA* 34 (1919), 301. He comments, 'to call a poet "balladmaker" was the deadliest of insults', and notes that, although few now survive, printed ballads were on sale in the early 16th century.

[84] *Troilus and Criseyde*, v. 1786–92; Dunbar probably had this passage in mind, although the farewell to one's book was common in 15th-century poets.

> That fulle dismemberit hes my meter
> And poysonid it with strang salpeter,
> With rycht defamows speiche off lordis
> Quhilk with my collouris all discordis,
> Quhois crewall sclander servis ded [deserves death];
> And in my name all leis recordis:
> ȝour grace beseik I of remeid.   (8–14)

There is a double purpose here. Dunbar, in the first place, disowns a slander entailing a punishment which might be inflicted on him. But what also emerges powerfully is Dunbar's strong sense of poetic identity, and pride in his own reputation—*my name*. The stance recalls Martial:

> vipereumque vomat nostro sub nomine virus.
>
> [under my name a man vomits his viperous venom][85]

For Dunbar the other poet is less of a knave than a fool, who is metrically and rhetorically maladroit, spoiling his 'collouris', or figures of speech. Dunbar here displays not only pride in craftsmanship, but a concern for the integrity of the finished work of art that recalls Chaucer's complaint to his scribe Adam, and anticipates Douglas's command to his copyists not to 'maggill nor mysmetyr my ryme'.[86] This protest implies that Dunbar was far from indifferent to what happened to his poems once they passed from their author's control.

Dunbar makes the highest claim for his poetry in *Schir ȝe have mony servitouris* (K 44). The opening section of this poem assembles what at first seems a miscellaneous list of those who serve the king—'Kirkmen, courtmen, and craftismen fyne'. But they form a coherent group because they possess a craft, practise it, and are therefore entitled to fair reward. Dunbar then turns to himself:

> And thocht that I amang the laif
> Unworthy be ane place to have
> Or in thair nummer to be tald,
> Als lang in mynd my work sall hald,
> Als haill in everie circumstance,
> In forme, in mater and substance,
> But wering or consumptioun,
> Roust, canker or corruptioun,
> As ony of thair werkis all—
> Suppois that my rewarde be small.   (25–34)

The basic claim of this passage is superficially modest: at its beginning Dunbar speaks of his unworthiness, and at its end he does no more

---

[85] *Epigrams*, vii. 12, ed. W. C. A. Ker (Loeb, 1919–20).
[86] 'Tyme, space and dait', 24; iv. 194.

than say that his poetry will last 'Als lang ... as' (not *longer than*) the products of printers, painters, and shipwrights. Yet most readers, rightly, I think, have interpreted this as understatement, and discerned in lines 28–32 a proud boast for the immortality of his poetry. Here indeed Dunbar views his poems as far more than ephemeral trifles. His choice of the word 'work' (28) is doubly significant: it links the poet's labours with the 'craft' (17) and 'werkis' (33) of the king's other servitors; and it has a much weightier ring than 'ballats'. It is the word chosen by Douglas, when he makes a similar claim for what he has accomplished in translating Virgil:

> Now is my wark all fynyst and compleit,
> Quham Iovis ire, nor fyris byrnand heit,
> Nor trynschand swerd sal defas ne doun thryng,
> Nor lang proces of age, consumys al thyng.[87]

Douglas is paraphrasing the conclusion of Ovid's *Metamorphoses*, and it is possible that Dunbar also recalls either Ovid or Horace's *Exegi monumentum aere perennius* (*Odes*, iii. 30).

Yet it should be noted that Dunbar's vocabulary here owes more to scholastic philosophy than to classical poetry. The four terms employed in lines 29–30—*circumstance, form, matter, substance*—belong to opposing pairs. The contrast between matter and form was common in medieval thought, and goes back ultimately to Aristotle: a substance is composed both of *matter*, 'which in itself is not a particular', and *form*, 'in virtue of which it is then spoken of as a particular'.[88] (See also *OED*, which defines *matter* as 'that component of the essence of anything ... which has bare existence, but requires the addition of a particular *form* to constitute it as a determinate species or kind of being'.) *Substance*, however, is also contrasted, philosophically, with *circumstance*: *substance* is 'that which underlies phenomena ... that in which attributes inhere'; these phenomenal attributes were commonly termed *accidents*, but sometimes received the name of *circumstance*, which had both plural and singular sense. Dunbar is not using this terminology in the rigorous manner of a philosopher, but jesting— rather like Chaucer, when he speaks of cooks turning 'substaunce into accident'.[89] What Dunbar seems to stress is that his poems are 'haill', whole and complete entities, and that this very wholeness challenges corruption and the normal processes of decay.

The second part of Dunbar's poem brings together a very different

---

[87] 'Conclusio', 1–4; iv. 187.
[88] *De Anima*, trans. D. W. Hamlyn (Oxford, 1968), II. i. 412a 6. See J. A. Burrow, in *Review*, 4 (1982), 113–14, who first noted the philosophical terminology. I am much indebted to his discussion, though I interpret the passage slightly differently.
[89] *CT* VI. 538–9.

group of idlers and parasites. It constitutes a protest at the injustices of court life, and ends:

> My mind so fer is set to flyt
> That of nocht ellis I can endyt,
> For owther man my hart to-breik[90]
> Or with my pen I man me wreik;
> And sen the tane most nedis be—
> In to malancolie to de
> Or lat the vennim ische all out—
> Be war anone, for it will spout
> Gif that the tryackill cum nocht tyt
> To swage the swalme of my dispyt.   (79–88)

Dunbar now displays his poetry in a different and aggressive light. His stance is vengeful—'I man me wreik'—and the threatening 'Be war' is addressed primarily to the king, though implicitly also to those regarded as unworthy favourites. Dunbar proclaims the destructive power of his 'pen', and of poetry itself, the power to harm one's enemies and to effect satiric exposure. Dunbar does not here call poetic language 'sugurit' or 'mellifluate'; his words are poisonous, dangerous as the 'vennim' of a snake. It was a medieval commonplace that malicious speech and writing was poisoned, or venomous. Yet the figure had classical precedent, particularly in Martial, who spoke not only of the 'viperous venom' vomited by one poet (vii. 12), but of other verses 'steeped in black venom': *atro . . . veneno* (vii. 72). Some ancient poets viewed the satirist's compulsion to voice his anger as a kind of 'personal catharsis'; Puttenham was aware of this notion when he said that epigrams were devised because of men's need to 'utter their splenes . . . or their bowels would burst'.[91] The further implications of this complex passage will be discussed later. What is evident is that one function of poetry, for Dunbar, is to express powerful emotions, however unworthy or painful these might be. Many of his poems do indeed voice 'dispyt', and reveal a mind 'set', or disposed, towards flyting. The concept of poetry as a 'craft' is not necessarily incompatible with self-expression.

There is an unfortunate dearth of early critical comment on Dunbar, yet that which survives seems to recognize something of his diversity. Those who refer to Douglas in the sixteenth century praise him,

---

[90] Editors usually read *to breik*; but *to* is grammatically more likely to be the intensive prefix.
[91] *Art of English Poesie*, I. xxvi; in *Elizabethan Critical Essays*, ii. 56. Cf. M. C. Randolph, 'The Medical Concept in English Renaissance Satiric Theory: Its Possible Relationships and Implications', *SP* 38 (1941), 125–57.

almost with one voice, for his learning and eloquence. Douglas himself was possibly the first to recognize Dunbar's genius; in *The Palice of Honour* (923) he is placed in the court of the Muses, one of the three poets 'of this natioun' worthy to rank with the English trio, Chaucer, Gower, and Lydgate. Lindsay saw him similarly as upholding the elevated tradition of poetry in the 'vulgare toung'—

> quho can now the workis cuntrafait
> Off Kennedie, with termes aureait?
> Or of Dunbar, quhilk language had at large,
> As maye be sene in tyll his golden targe?[92]

The printer, Henry Charteris, followed Lindsay, both in associating Dunbar with Kennedy and in commending his diction and 'rethorik'.[93]

But there is one dissenting voice. What Kennedy says of Dunbar in *The Flyting* is rarely taken seriously; yet there often lies a kernel of truth within the comic exaggeration. Kennedy, for instance, confirms Dunbar's self-avowed hostility towards those who speak Gaelic— 'thow lufis nane Irische' (345)—and his admiration for English poetry; he misconstrues both as proving a lack of patriotism. Kennedy also says:

> I perambalit of Pernaso the montayn,
> Enspirit wyth Mercury fra his goldyn spere,
> And dulcely drank of eloquence the fontayne
> Quhen it was purifit wyth frost and flowit clere;
> And thou come, fule, in Marche or Februere
> Thare till a pule, and drank the padok rod.
> That gerris the ryme in to thy termes glod
> And blaberis that noyis mennis eris to here. (337–44)

Kennedy here comically embroiders a famous rhetorical topos, deriving from the Prologue to Persius's *Satires*. But he uses it to boast, not—like Chaucer's Franklin or Douglas in *The Palice of Honour* (1143)—to convey modesty. He then pictures an uninspired Dunbar, drinking not from the clear spring of Hippocrene but from a pool turbid with frog-spawn. The precise sense of the epithet 'glod' is unknown, but, like 'blaberis', it is undoubtedly pejorative. When Kennedy later exclaims 'Tale tellare' (551), or commands, 'Tak the a fidill or a floyte, and geste' (507), the force of the insults is clear: Dunbar is ranked not with poets of the loftiest kind but with popular entertainers. Those, like Lindsay and some modern critics, who see Dunbar as predominantly the poet of *The Goldyn Targe*, would find

---

[92] *Papyngo*, 15–18.
[93] In his 'Adhortatioun' to the 1568 edition of Lindsay; Geddie, *Bibliography of Middle Scots Poets*, xx.

this view self-evidently absurd. But those prepared to acknowledge the full range and diversity of his poetry will concede the element of truth in Kennedy's charge. Dunbar clearly had pride in himself as a 'makar', yet he did not always take himself as seriously as he is taken in the present age. He had some aspiration to the high style, but this coexisted with less elevated and more playful objectives. It is arguable that his peculiar excellence as a poet—the verbal 'energy' so often remarked by critics—springs, in part, from the tension between these opposing forces. His comic poems are elegantly crafted, even when undeniably vulgar; and in his more refined poems he rarely loses sight of the basic, down-to-earth need to win and to retain the reader's attention. Again and again Dunbar defeats easy, simple formulations: he is both courtly and popular, literary but not bookish, intensely Scottish yet a master 'of oure Inglisch'.

2
Dunbar's World

> Nature never set forth the earth in so rich tapestry as divers poets have done . . . Her world is brazen, the poets only deliver a golden.[1]

THERE is no fixed and immutable relationship between the world in which Dunbar lived and the poetic world that he created. Gavin Douglas's poetry is characteristically timeless or set in the distant past, and peopled with figures from myth and legend, in grand evocative landscapes, such as Troy or Helicon. Dunbar, however, often selects the ingredients of his poems from the flux of actual life; he mentions real places, people, and events. His imaginative world is sometimes golden; more often it is low and undignified, constructed out of everyday and trivial activities. (It is striking how little affected Dunbar appears by the great intellectual currents of his time, such as humanism or scholasticism; one would hardly guess that he was a contemporary of John Major, Ficino, or Erasmus.) Because of this, paradoxically, his poetry is sometimes more difficult to interpret than Douglas's. It is often far from easy to determine the degree of literal truth in his poems. Dunfermline provides the location for a fable that Bannatyne entitled 'The wowing of the king quhen he wes in Dunfermeling' (K 37): Bannatyne may be correct in associating this poem with the king's visit to an important burgh, yet it is equally plausible to see this as a literary 'placing', a bow towards the tradition of Henryson, schoolmaster of Dunfermline. Names like 'Jok Fule' and 'Master Johne Clerk' (K 38) may belong to real people, but may perhaps be as fictional as the present-day 'Tom Fool' or the lawyer's 'John Doe'. Although a date like the ninth of May sounds precise, its significance may be primarily symbolic. The problem is compounded by the comparative paucity of information about early sixteenth-century Scotland. This chapter is concerned with Dunbar's use of place, people, and time; it does not, of course, examine every possible way in which his poems interrelate with the world around him.

---

[1] Sir Philip Sidney, *An Apology for Poetry*, ed. G. Shepherd (1965), 100.

'Heir at hame'

Dunbar's wide-ranging imagination spans heaven and hell. But a poem which audaciously opens 'We that ar heir in hevins glory' (K 22) is a comic celebration of Edinburgh; and another, containing a vision of hell (K 52), takes the shape of a contemporary court revels. Many of Dunbar's poems are located in *this* world, and—what is more—in 'this cuntre' or 'this regioun' of Scotland. He often refers to specific places, but only rarely are they literary, mythological, or Scriptural— one important exception is the symbolic use of Jerusalem (K 75). The localities that Dunbar mentions are actual, and many would be well known to his audience—Aberdeen, Ayr, Carrick, Dumfries, Edinburgh, Galloway, and Stirling. Other places, though more distant, would be familiar to well-travelled Scottish clerics, merchants, and courtiers, 'new cum owt of France' (K 28): Canterbury, Dover, Calais and Picardy (K 55), Angers and Orléans (K 22). Dunbar's poems are firmly grounded in his own experience, 'heir at hame' in Scotland, yet they are neither parochial nor insular.

Dunbar's awareness of the European context is evident in several poems, as in an *occupatio* about Bernard Stewart's military campaigns 'In France, in Bertan, in Naplis and Lumbardy' (K 35). At other times he is deliberately cryptic, as in this boast of his youthful loyalty to the king:

> I had beine bocht in realmes by
> Had I consentit to be sauld. (K 43. 53–4)

'Realmes by' implies nearby kingdoms, such as England, France, Denmark, or Spain. There is evidence, as we have seen, that Dunbar had travelled outside Scotland, and in *The Flyting* (90–6) he draws upon this experience for a brief account of a storm-tossed voyage along the headlands of eastern Scotland to Shetland and Norway, out into the 'sey desert' of the Atlantic.[2] But the keenness of Dunbar's interest is the wider world is best illustrated in *This waverand warldis wretchidnes* (K 39), where he complains of his long wait for a benefice:

> It [the benefice] micht have cuming in schortar quhyll
> Fra Cal3ecot and the new fund Yle,
> The partis of Transmeridiane;
> Quhilk to consider is ane pane.

---

[2] I interpret this passage differently from Kinsley; see Bawcutt, 'Dunbar: New Light', 85–7.

> It micht be this, had it bein kynd,
> Cuming out of the desertis of Ynde
> Our all the grit se oceane;
> Quhilk to considder is ane pane.
>
> It micht have cuming out of all ayrtis
> Fra Paris and the Orient partis,
> And fra the ylis of Aphrycane;
> Quhilk to consydder is ane pane.
>
> It is so lang in cuming me till,
> I dreid that it be quyt gane will—
> Or bakwart it is turnit agane;
> Quhilk to considder is ane pane.   (61–76)

This interesting passage has received strangely varied interpretations, even at the most factual level—*Cal3ecot*, for instance, was long taken to be Calcutta instead of the correct Calicut, on the south-east coast of India; and some scholars are reluctant to take *Paris* as the European city, preferring such emendations as *Persia* or *Paradise*. At a more imaginative level, most critics have read the passage as testimony to Dunbar's excited response to the great voyages of Discovery; Alasdair MacDonald, however, in a recent study, finds such an interpretation anachronistic, and questions D. B. Quinn's opinion that this is 'the first British reference to the New World in literature'.[3] Noting how slowly the significance of the Discoveries was understood, particularly in the British Isles, he argues that the geography that informs this passage is shaped by ancient views of the world, and is as traditional as the morality of the poem in which it is embedded. But *This waverand warldis wretchidnes* is far from being a stock complaint on the times, and it is precisely at this point that the poem begins to break the conventional mould.

Geographical excursuses were not uncommon in late-medieval poetry, but did not necessarily always have the same function. Douglas's description of his flight with the Muses, in *The Palice of Honour*, is a highly literary journey, packed with allusions to Ovid and other classical poets; Lindsay, in *The Dreme*, gives a more systematic exposition of ancient cosmography.[4] Dunbar's purpose is very different: this passage is not didactic, but a piece of comic hyperbole, designed to suggest the magnitude of the poet's wait for preferment in terms of the sheer remoteness of the places he enumerates. Time is measured through distance. The list is short,

---

[3] See 'William Dunbar, Mediaeval Cosmography, and the Alleged First Reference to the New World in English Literature', *ES* 68 (1987), 377–91. Quinn's opinion is quoted by Kinsley, 317.

[4] Cf. S. Cairns, '*The Palice of Honour* of Gavin Douglas, Ovid and Raffaello Regio's Commentary on Ovid's *Metamorphoses*', *Res Publica Litterarum*, 7 (1984), 17–38.

apparently casual and impressionistic, darting from named city to the vaguer 'partis' (62–3 and 70); the apparently topical 'new fund Yle' mixes with very ancient geographical terms, such as 'the grit se oceane' (Latin *magnum mare oceanum*). The logic that underlies the grouping of place-names is not easy to discover; but it should be noted that the conjunction *and*—as in 'Cal3ecot and the new fund Yle'—is ambiguous, and may signify distance, not proximity ('China and Peru'). Dunbar's arrangement of items sometimes seems largely determined by rhetoric, or by the demands of his rhyme-scheme. Yet the triple group of Paris, the Orient, and 'the ylis of Aphrycane' (70–1) is not necessarily arbitrary: it may possibly exemplify three *ayrtis*, or 'points of the compass, directions' (69), by mentioning locations in the north, east, and south or west. (The Atlantic islands of Madeira, the Canaries, and Cape Verdes were all known by 1460.) It would thus neatly symbolize the old threefold division of the world into Europe, Asia, and Africa.

Dunbar here translates his intense longing for a benefice into a merchant's anxiety as to the fate of a rich cargo: he fears that it is 'quyt gane will' (i.e. lost); or 'bakwart it is turnit agane'. It is striking that his list begins with Calicut, which is given this prime position not simply for its distance from Edinburgh, but because it was then famous as the richest port in India. Calicut was an entrepôt, a place 'where the eastern flow of trade met the western'—jewels, spices, and cloth (calico, Calicut cloth) were brought there from the Far East, and thence transported to Lisbon and Antwerp. It was a place that occasionally furnished the Scottish court with unusual animals, such as 'the mermuset of Cal3ecut', for which a green satin coat was made in May 1508.[5] Calicut must have been for Dunbar as potent a symbol of exotic wealth as Ormuz was for Milton. The significance of some of the other geographical terms is undoubtedly more puzzling. The learned-sounding 'partis of Transmeridiane' has still not been satisfactorily explained; I think that Dunbar is probably referring to the southern hemisphere, since Lindsay calls the equator 'the hote meridionall' and in other Scottish writers the terms *meridiane* and *meridionall* usually signify 'southerly'.[6] As for 'the new fund Yle', this was long taken to be modern Newfoundland, discovered by Cabot in 1497. But a phrase of such vagueness cannot be identified with certainty. It might, with equal plausibility, refer to the earlier and far

---

[5] *Treasurer's Accounts*, iv. 117. On Calicut, see Baxter, 147, and B. Penrose, *Travel and Discovery in the Renaissance 1420–1620* (Cambridge, Mass., 1952), 55–6, 59–60.

[6] Kinsley accepts *OED*'s explanation of *transmeridiane* (for which this is the only citation) as 'the region beyond the meridian in the Atlantic which separates the New from the Old World'; MacDonald suggests that the meridian is that of Jerusalem. See, however, *Papyngo*, 750, and *DOST*, s.v. *meridiane, meridionall*.

more famous discoveries made by Columbus in the Caribbean. These were reported in the well-known *Letter of Columbus* (1493); within four years at least eighteen editions of this had appeared, in Latin and other languages, whose titles contain phrases very similar to Dunbar's—*Epistola de insulis nuper inventis*, or *Epistola de insulis de novo repertis*, or *Paesi novamenti retrovati*.[7] The very structure of Dunbar's phrase 'new fund Yle' is redolent of the Age of Discoveries: *new found* does not seem to be recorded in Scots or English usage before the 1490s; and in the decade following 1497 the expression 'new found *island* [which interchanges with *land*]' figures repeatedly in English documents referring to North America.[8] Somewhat later, in 1532, a Scottish report on the Franciscans in Mexico refers to 'new spanye or hirketan [Yucatan] at we call the new fund yle in gret ynd in afrik'.[9] This writer sounds uncertain about the continent to which Yucatan belongs, and unaware that it is a peninsula. We shall never know if Dunbar had a more precise idea of where his 'new fund Yle' was located, but the phrase is none the less significant, implying an excited if vague awareness of the geographically 'new' that is very characteristic of this period.

Dunbar tends to write as a city dweller, with a marked contempt for the countryman and the rural areas he inhabits. In order to suggest the naïvety and unsophistication of a speaker (K 74) it is enough simply to introduce him as 'Ane murlandis man of uplandis mak'. *Uplandis*, 'in, or belonging to the country', is used of the country mouse in Henryson's *Fables*. For Dunbar it is a term that connotes boorish behaviour and rustic ignorance. He speaks, for instance, of 'uplandis Michell', who secures many benefices, 'Thocht he fra nolt [cattle] had new tane leif' (K 42. 71–3). His comic portrait of Kennedy, in *The Flyting*, is based, in part, on a stereotype of the impoverished country bumpkin:

> Now upaland thow leivis on rubbit quheit;
> Oft for ane caus thy burdclaith neidis no spredding,
> For thow hes nowthir for to drink nor eit . . .
>
> Thow bringis the Carrik clay to Edinburgh cors
> Upoun thy botingis [boots] hobland, hard as horne;
> Stra wispis hingis owt quhair that the wattis ar worne. (205 ff.)

---

[7] No English-language account of the Discoveries existed in Dunbar's time, but he could read Latin. On the importance of Columbus's *Letter*, see R. Hirsch, 'Printed Reports on the Early Discoveries and their Reception', in *First Images of America*, ed. F. Chiappelli (Berkeley, 1976), 537–58.

[8] See *DOST, new fund, OED, new-found*; and *New American World*, ed. D. B. Quinn, 5 vols. (1979), i, nos. 53, 55, 77, 78, 80, 83, 84, 87, and 88.

[9] Cited by A. Stewart, 'Adam Abell's "Roit or Quheill of Time"', *AUJ* 44 (1971–2), 386–93; see fol. 119a.

Dunbar also voices a Lowlander's dislike of the Highlander's speech, behaviour, and region of Scotland. A glen is described in *The Flyting* (153 ff.) as 'owt of repair'—unfrequented, except by lepers; there is similar repugnance in another reference to 'thay dully [gloomy] glennis' (K 27. 15). It would be anachronistic to expect Dunbar to respond to the majestic but wild landscape of the Highlands. For him, as for most medieval poets, ideal natural beauty was represented by a garden, the 'rosy garth' of *The Goldyn Targe*, or the 'gudlie grein garth full of gay flouris' that is the setting of *The Tua Mariit Wemen and the Wedo*. Nature here is cultivated, and peopled. In one of his moral poems Dunbar writes:

> Heir helth returnis in seiknes
> And mirth returnis in havines,
> Toun in desert, forrest in plane:
> All erdly joy returnis in pane. (K 59. 25–8)

The antithesis between *toun* and *desert* is revealing: the town is correlated with the good things of life, health and mirth; its opposite is seen not as the country, but as the desert, empty and unpeopled.[10] Yet Dunbar is not blind to the ugly features of the medieval town, and from it draws some of his most repellent imagery. A young wife compares her old husband's rheumy eyes to 'tua gutaris that war with glar [slime] stoppit' (K 14. 99). Dunbar often calls attention to the 'mydding', or rubbish dump (K 14. 355; K 38. 37; K 52. 68); the stocks (K 32. 28); and—above all—the gallows (K 80. 19); the procession accompanying the condemned man (K 74. 39); or the 'stark theif glowrand in ane tedder' (*Flyting*, 176 and *passim*).

Dunbar's name has been associated with various towns and cities. He is regularly linked with London, because of the persistent though dubious attribution to him of the poem *To London*.[11] Another belief, that he visited or studied at Oxford, has a slender basis, deriving solely from the colophon to one of the two copies of *To speik of science craft or sapience* (K 76): 'Quod Dumbar at Oxinfurd'. Baxter perhaps indulges in wishful thinking, when she says, 'the northerner scrutinized Oxford keenly, and was not enthusiastic'.[12] Yet we know that Dunbar visited England on at least one occasion. Aberdeen is celebrated in a poem (K 48) recording the queen's visit in 1511; this describes pageants, streets hung with tapestry, and wine running abundantly at the market cross. Dunbar's report, like that of some modern journalist accompanying a royal tour, is dutiful but pedestrian. Dunbar is believed to

---

[10] On the medieval reactions to 'le désert-forêt', cf. J. Le Goff, *L'Imaginaire médiéval* (Paris, 1985), 59–75.
[11] See below, 82.
[12] Baxter, 84.

have spent his formative years as a student at the university of St Andrews, yet it is striking that St Andrews plays no part in his poetry. Some scholars have detected an allusion to the college of St Salvator in the opening of one poem: 'Sanct salvatour, send silver sorrow!' (K 19). But this misconstrues Dunbar's irreverent use, in an imprecation, of a pious title for Christ.

Edinburgh is the place where Dunbar spent at least thirteen years (1500–13), and possibly longer; and it is Edinburgh and its environs that figure most significantly in his poems. Sometimes there is merely a passing allusion—to the Tollbooth (K 44. 60), or 'Leith sandis' (K 51. 114), or St Anthony's hospital at Leith (K 38. 60). But in four poems Edinburgh plays a very important part. In *The Dregy* (K 22) 'Edinburgh, the mirry toun' is celebrated affectionately, its good cheer contrasted in friendly rivalry with the austerity of Stirling. Yet it is Edinburgh also that furnishes the location for a satirical account of the vice associated with the 'Sessioun' (K 74); and for the vivid cityscape in *The Flyting*, which depicts Kennedy as pursued by a mob:

> Off Edinburch the boyis as beis owt thrawis [swarms]
> And cryis owt ay, Heir cumis our awin queir clerk!
> Than fleis thow lyk ane howlat chest with crawis,
> Quhill all the bichis at thy botingis dois bark.
> Than carlingis cryis, Keip curches [head-dresses] in the merk—
> Our gallowis gaipis—lo! quhair ane greceles gais!
> Ane uthir sayis, I se him want ane sark—
> I reid 3ow, cummer, tak in 3our lynning clais. (217–24)

Most famous probably is the poem explicitly addressed to the merchants of Edinburgh (K 75): in it their 'nobill toun' is viewed through the critical eyes of one who knows it well, but also knows other countries:

> 3our foirstair makis 3our housis mirk
> Lyk na cuntray bot heir at hame. (17–18)

Dunbar elsewhere refers to the 'toune' (K 43), or 'this court' (K 27, K 45, K 51), and here too the vantage-point is likely to be that of an Edinburgh resident. Although James IV made frequent journeys, with members of his household, all over the kingdom, Holyrood was his principal palace.

Little now survives of medieval Edinburgh, yet it is not wholly inaccessible to the imagination. Those who know the handsome modern city must first mentally strip away such later developments as the neoclassical New Town, the massive North and George IV bridges, and the suburbs of the twentieth century. The medieval burgh of Edinburgh, together with the adjacent burgh of Canongate, consisted essentially of what we now call the Old Town, lying on the narrow ridge that descends, west to east, from the Castle to Holyrood. To the north—instead of Waverley Gardens and the railway station—was the North Loch; to the south, where the Meadows now lie, were the Burgh Loch (or South Loch) and the Burgh Muir. Some natural features obviously remain—Arthur's Seat, for instance, on which Kennedy threatened to have Dunbar burnt, 'Wyth pik, fire, ter, gunpuldre or lynt' (*Flyting*, 335). The Castle also remains, which Douglas (after his imprisonment there) called 'wyndy and richt unplesand'.[13] But the church of St Giles is now much altered from what it was in Dunbar's time, because of damage inflicted by the Reformers, later reconstruction by the Presbyterians, and restoration in the nineteenth century. Sadly little survives of the medieval abbey and palace of Holyrood. Even the picturesque buildings in the High Street are mostly post-medieval, and rise several storeys higher than those of the early sixteenth century; yet the Widow's reference to her husband's 'biggingis . . . and hie burrow landis' (K 14. 338) clearly implies the existence of some high-rise tenements. The houses were then mostly built of wood not stone, and had the characteristic forestairs that Dunbar mentions—external flights of steps, rising to the first storey.[14]

A seventeenth-century writer, Thomas Morer, remarked that 'Edinburgh is by some liken'd to an ivory comb, whose teeth on both sides are very foul, though the space between 'em is clean and sightly'.[15] He, like many visitors, was impressed both by the beauty of the High Street, and the contrast offered by the 'nasty' wynds and vennels on either side. Dunbar's image of Edinburgh is equally mixed. He singles out one notorious landmark, the 'Stinkand Styll' (38): this was a covered passage that pierced the Buith Raw (or Luckenbooths), a row of shops and stalls parallel to the north front of St Giles. Later writers complained, as does Dunbar, of the overcrowding in these buildings and the way they encroached both on St Giles and the High Street. He refers contemptuously to the misuse of the two central features of a burgh, the Mercat Cross and the Tron, or public weigh-house:

> At 3our hie croce quhar gold and silk
> Sould be, thair is bot crudis and milk;

[13] Bawcutt, *Douglas*, 13.
[14] Cf. P. Robinson, 'Tenements: A Pre-Industrial Urban Tradition', *ROSC* 1 (1984), 52–64. On early Edinburgh, see M. Lynch, *Edinburgh and the Reformation* (1981), especially ch. 1; also *The Scottish Medieval Town*, ed. M. Lynch, M. Spearman, and G. Stell (Edinburgh, 1988). See also G. Stell, 'Destruction, Damage and Decay: The Collapse of Scottish Medieval Buildings', *ROSC* 2 (1986), 59–69.
[15] *Early Travellers in Scotland*, ed. P. Hume Brown (Edinburgh, 1891), 280.

And at 30ur trone bot cokill and wilk,
Pansches, pudingis of Jok and Jame. (22-5)

The contemporary Burgh Records confirm Dunbar's picture of streets offensive to eye, ear, and nose. Repeated attempts were made to regulate the markets, and to 'clenge' the streets. On 4 July 1505, for instance, an ordinance was made 'for purgeing and clengeing of the hie streitt ... of all maner of mwk, filth of fische and flesche, and fulzie weit and dry'. Dunbar speaks robustly of the 'stink of haddockis and of scaittis' (9); the Council speaks more periphrastically of the 'euil disposit savour' resulting from the melting of tallow, and instructs furriers and skinners not to 'dicht nor schaik their skynis on the hie gaitt, nor hing thame on the forestairis, for till eschew the evil sawour thairof'.[16]

Yet Dunbar also presents Edinburgh as a 'nobill toun', to which visitors make 'great repair' (58). As early as the fourteenth century Froissart regarded Edinburgh as the capital of Scotland, and John Major similarly called it the chief city.[17] As a royal burgh, only two miles from the port of Leith, it was a busy trading centre. It was also, even before James V's establishment of the College of Justice, increasingly important as a place where lawsuits were heard and Parliament met. Edinburgh had at this time no university, and was not a centre of learning, yet it was there, in 1507, that the first Scottish printers, Walter Chepman and Andro Myllar, were licensed to establish a press in the Southgait (now the Cowgate). It was not the seat of a bishop—St Giles was a collegiate church (not a cathedral) and Dunbar terms it simply the 'parroche kirk' (16)—yet most of the religious orders had houses in Edinburgh, and bishops of remote dioceses, like Dunkeld, had homes there. Above all, it was the chief residence of the king. In comparison with Paris, London, or Venice, Edinburgh was neither rich nor large; but it seems to have been busy, prosperous, and cultured—'the lampe and A per se / Of this regioun'.[18]

'Servitouris and Officiaris'

Some of the most famous works of medieval literature, such as *Le Roman de la Rose* or *Piers Plowman*, are peopled almost entirely with

---

[16] *Extracts from the Records of the Burgh of Edinburgh*, ed. J. D. Marwick (SBRS, 1869), i. 105 and 107.
[17] See Hume Brown, *Early Travellers*, 9–10; and *Scotland Before 1700 from Contemporary Documents*, ed. P. Hume Brown (Edinburgh, 1893), 42.
[18] *The Crying of ane Play*, 133–4; in Mackenzie's Dunbar.

personified abstractions. Many of Dunbar's finest poems belong to this category; indeed C. S. Lewis commented, 'no one knows better than Dunbar how to touch a personification into life'.[19] Yet a surprising number of his poems are studded with ordinary and genuine-sounding names, like Andro Kennedy, Thomas Norny, Curry, John Bute, Master Robert Schaw, Sandy Traill, Patrick Johnston, and Quintyne Schaw. Many of these people were, like Dunbar himself, members of the royal household; the remarkable diversity of their occupations is suggested in the poem that begins,

> Schir, 3e have mony servitouris
> And officiaris of dyvers curis;
> Kirkmen, courtmen and craftismen fyne,
> Doctouris in jure and medicyne,
> Divinouris, rethoris and philosophouris,
> Astrologis, artistis and oratouris,
> Men of armes and vail3eand knychtis
> And mony uther gudlie wichtis . . .   (K 44)

James IV, to whom this was addressed, formed the apex of the court, and will be discussed in the next chapter. Here I am chiefly concerned with Dunbar's fellow-servitors, who furnished material—and probably an audience—for some of his most distinctive poems. They mixed with him in life, just as their names accompanied his on the same pages of *The Treasurer's Accounts*.

The Treasurer, or 'Lord Thesaurair' (K 46 and K 47), was one of the highest officers of state, responsible for the collection and administration of various Crown revenues. A list of merely a few of his many responsibilities provides some hint of the complexity of the Scottish court:

The Treasurer made provision for the miscellaneous expenses of the king and queen . . . as well as for everything that related to their apparel, together with the liveries of the henchmen, pages, yeomen, huntsmen, falconers, and other officers and servants of the king's house, the state dresses of the heralds, pursuivants and trumpeters, and the frequent gifts of dress which the king was accustomed to bestow on ambassadors and foreign visitors to his court, or on his favourite servants. To these are to be added the expenses of the royal stable . . . the purchase of horses and the furnishing of their equipments . . . [In addition] the sums required for the erection and repair of the king's castles . . . for the alms disbursed by his almoner . . . for his largess and gifts to heralds, minstrels, servants and others at Easter, Christmas and New Year's Day, for rewards to those who came to him as bearers of gifts or messages, for pensions and the fees of certain officers of state and the clerks of the exchequer, for the lodging and entertainment of foreign ambassadors and

---

[19] *English Literature in the Sixteenth Century* (Oxford, 1954), 92.

other strangers, and for various other miscellaneous outlays, were all provided out of the revenue intrusted to the Treasurer.[20]

In James IV's reign the Treasurer was usually a churchman of high rank, and educated 'kirkmen' were prominent at all levels of administration, as members of the king's Council, and as envoys, scribes, clerks, or what would now be called civil servants. Several of the poets whom Dunbar mentions were churchmen, who served the king in a variety of ways. Walter Kennedy claimed to be the king's 'trew speciall clerk' (*Flyting*, 417); John Reid, called 'Stobo' both by Dunbar (K 62. 86) and by the public records, was a priest, notary, and secretary to James II, James III, and James IV; Patrick Johnston (K 62. 71) devised court entertainments, but was also a notary, and the official receiver of revenues for West Lothian. Such a multiplicity of roles seems to have been common. One of Dunbar's fellow-servitors, Thomas Galbraith, was a clerk in the Chapel Royal and also an artist, who illuminated books, coats of arms, and the ratification of the marriage contract between James and Margaret Tudor. The most important officers were usually wealthy nobles or churchmen, financed by the revenues of their benefices. More lowly members of the royal household were remunerated by a pension, or yearly salary; they also received board and lodging, and a clothing allowance, usually twice a year at Christmas and Whitsun.[21]

For Dunbar the Scottish court at the opening of the sixteenth century had something of the importance that eighteenth-century London society had for Alexander Pope. Yet the rich and abundant documentation that characterizes the eighteenth century is sadly lacking for Dunbar's Scotland: few portraits, diaries, memoirs, or personal letters survive, and even the public records are scantier than those for contemporary England. Undoubtedly the most valuable source of information is the work known as *The Treasurer's Accounts*; the first four volumes contain detailed, usually dated, records of the expenditure of the king, queen, and royal household throughout the reign of James IV. They provide an insight into many aspects of everyday life in the court; they also confirm the real existence of many persons named by Dunbar, and give valuable clues as to their status and occupation, as well as the approximate period when they were in the household. Yet it is well to remember the limitations of *The*

---

[20] *TA* i, pp. xxii–xxiv. For the rest of the chapter, references to this work are incorporated in the text.
[21] Baxter, 229–34, gives the most detailed account of the poets known to Dunbar; on Galbraith, see M. R. Apted and S. Hannabuss, *Painters in Scotland 1301–1700* (Edinburgh, 1978), 40–1; on court life, see R. F. Green, *Poets and Princepleasers* (Toronto, 1980).

Treasurer's Accounts. They were intended for the use of contemporary auditors, not for historians and biographers centuries later. Their evidence is sometimes difficult to interpret, confusing, and tantalizingly scrappy. A given person may at one time be called by his full name, and at another by his surname alone, or by his title or office, or even by what sounds like a nickname. Antoine d'Arce, seigneur de la Bastie, as he was styled in France, appears variously as 'Anthoun Darsee' (iii. 364), 'Schir Anthon Darse' (iii. 416), and 'the Franch knycht' (iii. 365). Andrew Forman, bishop of Moray, is styled sometimes 'Beschop of Murray' (iii. 364), sometimes 'the prothonotar' (ii. 104). Bernard Stewart (iv. 110) appears more frequently as 'my lord Owbyn3e' (iv. 118). This variety of nomenclature is compounded by the vagaries of Scottish spelling. The surname of the 'Maesteres Musgraeffe' who figures in one poem (K 28) sometimes has similar spellings in *The Treasurer's Accounts* (iv. 401, 410), but is also spelt 'Musgray' (iv. 324). Some persons, even when located in the records, remain mysterious; 'Strait Gibboun' (*Flyting*, 209) is mentioned in the accounts (ii. 378 and 395), but we are still uncertain who he was or what he did.

The Treasurer's Accounts must be handled with caution, yet they illuminate some aspects of Dunbar's poems, such as their subject, date, and even tone. The death of persons named in a poem may help to establish its approximate dating. *I that in heill wes*, for instance, is thought to have been written shortly after July 1505; this is when Stobo died, and Dunbar's reference to Death having taken him 'now ... last of aw' (85) suggests a recent occurrence. Contrariwise a reference to Stobo as if he were still living supplies a *terminus ad quem* of 1505 for *The Flyting*. The mention of the fool Curry, who died in 1506, supplies a later limit of 1506 for *Schir Thomas Norny* (K 27).[22] Yet the great care that must be used in drawing inferences from these records is illustrated by the case of *Sir Jhon Sinclair begowthe to dance* (K 28). It is usually dated in 1506, largely because of the stanza devoted to 'the maister almaser', whose clumsy dancing resembles 'a stirk stackarand in the ry' (15–21). According to Kinsley, the *maister almaser* 'may have been the Englishman Dr Babington who was concerned in the queen's marriage arrangements in 1503, remained in Scotland as her almoner, was nominated Dean of Aberdeen in December 1505, and had died by May 1507'.[23] But the argument seems fallacious: individuals die, but there is no evidence that the office of this unnamed *almaser* was discontinued. Furthermore the

---

[22] Stobo was sick in May 1505 (*TA* iii. 138, 142), and dead by July 1505 (*Exchequer Rolls*, xii. 372). Curry had died by 2 June 1506 (*TA* iii. 197).

[23] Kinsley, 302; Baxter, 161–2.

term *maister almaser* (principal almoner) commonly referred not to the queen's but to the king's almoner, who throughout the reign of James IV was the Scotsman, Sir Andrew McBrek. *The Treasurer's Accounts* abound in payments to him, to 'dispone' to the poor.[24] This passage shows Dunbar making fun of a high official, but unfortunately affords no clue as to the date of composition; indeed it is possible that the poem belongs closer to the end of the reign.[25]

Several poems have as their subject a single individual. It is clearly important to identify these figures correctly, and in many cases there is no problem. The French knight, Bernard (or Béraud) Stewart, seigneur d'Aubigny, to whom two poems are devoted (K 35 and 36), had an international reputation; the praise which Dunbar showers on his military prowess seems well justified. Stewart illustrates the close relationship that then existed between France and Scotland, not only diplomatically—he had come on an 'embassat'—but also through ties of blood. He was of Scottish ancestry, as Dunbar emphasizes, calling him 'our Scottis chiftane most dughti' (K 35. 21).[26] James Dog, who figures in three poems (K 28–30), was far less distinguished, yet he too is well documented. Dunbar calls him the queen's 'wardraipper', or keeper of the wardrobe (K 30), yet he is first recorded as serving the king in a variety of roles, and only in 1511 is he specifically listed among the *servitores regine* (iv. 265). It is unlikely, however, that the subject of another poem, 'the refing sonne off rakyng Muris' (K 26. 2), will ever be identified. This is not because he is fictitious, but because of Dunbar's contemptuous vagueness, and because Mure was then (as now) a common Scottish name.

The identity of the testator in *The Testament of Maister Andro Kennedy* (K 38) is also problematical. Yet it makes a great deal of difference to the interpretation of a mock-testament to know precisely who is its subject; the victim's state of health affects the tone—callous, if he is indeed dead or dying, more jocular, if he is alive and flourishing. Most readings of *The Testament* are based on the belief that Kennedy was a physician; there is a long-established editorial tradition to this effect. Ross, for instance, states that Kennedy was 'a drunken, quack physician at the court of James IV', and concludes by suggesting that 'we may see in him also the anti-type of Christ, the false healer'.[27] Yet the evidence, whether internal or external, for

---

[24] On the almoner's duties, see i, p. ccxxxv.

[25] Of the persons mentioned in this poem, Bute and Musgrave figure in late entries (1508–12); Dog is not known to be in the queen's household till 1511; and Sinclair is specifically associated with the queen only in 1513.

[26] Cf. D. Gray, 'A Scottish "Flower of Chivalry" and his Book', *Words*, 4 (1974), 22–34.

[27] Ross, 121; cf. also Kinsley, 313, Mackenzie, 213, Baxter, 31, and Reiss, 58.

regarding Kennedy as a doctor is remarkably flimsy. We are usually referred, puzzlingly, to the opening lines:

> I maister Andro Kennedy
> Curro quando sum vocatus.

But the second line simply means that the testator is at everyone's beck and call; it might imply that he was a 'currour', or messenger. Again, *solacia* (57) has been glossed too specifically as 'quack remedies', when it means 'pleasures, worldly joys'. These *solacia* are bequeathed to 'the maister of Sanct Antane' (60), the preceptor of St Anthony's Hospital, Leith. But the canons of St Anthony's did more than tend the sick; one of their duties, in collaboration with Edinburgh Council, was to regulate the distribution of wine as it entered the port of Leith.[28] There seems a covert joke at their expense, which hinges on cheating practices and possibly drunkenness. No convincing evidence that there existed a court physician called Andrew Kennedy has so far been produced. A man of this name figures in *The Treasurer's Accounts* between 1502 and 1503; but his occupation is unspecified, and he might well be a messenger, in view of the payment to him 'to pas to Wigtoun to the King with ane relique of Sanct Niniane' (ii. 393). In this respect there is a contrast with Master Robert Schaw, mentioned in *Sir Jhon Sinclair begowthe to dance* (K 28. 8): in the records he is associated with apothecaries (ii. 445) and prescribes a 'ressait' for the queen's nose-bleed (ii. 477); elsewhere he is definitely styled a Bachelor of Medicine.[29] The name Andrew Kennedy was not uncommon—Andrew was, after all, the patron saint of Scotland. The testator in this poem might equally plausibly be identified with another Andrew Kennedy, who in 1501 received the gift of lands 'liand in the erldome of Carrik and schirefdom of Are' (cf. line 36); or, even more satisfyingly, in view of his proclaimed ignorance of his parentage (5–6), with the Andrew Kennedy who died at Edinburgh in 1491, *bastardus absque legitimis heredibus*.[30] One defect, however, of all these identifications is that in none does the real-life Kennedy receive the style 'Master'.

The *Testament* itself, if read carefully, supplies plenty of hints for a

---

[28] Out of every tun of wine entering Leith the canons were apparently entitled to a Scottish quart; see Charles Rogers, *Historical Notices of St Anthony's Monastery, Leith* (Grampian Club, Edinburgh, 1877); and Marwick, *Edinburgh Burgh Records*, i. 119 (Dec. 1508) and 201–2 (Oct. 1520).

[29] A. I. Dunlop, *Scots Abroad in the Fifteenth Century* (Historical Association Pamphlet, 124, 1942) 15. In 1492 Shaw was elected to represent the German nation at Paris university.

[30] *The Register of the Privy Seal of Scotland*, ed. M. Livingstone (Edinburgh, 1908), i, no. 693; *The Register of the Great Seal of Scotland*, ed. J. Balfour Paul (Edinburgh, 1882), i, no. 2070.

self-drawn satiric portrait, not of a 'quack physician' but of what Lord Hailes shrewdly called 'a drunken graceless scholar'.[31] If we give due weight to the poem's first line, we find that Kennedy is a university graduate, although he seems to have profited little from his education. He may have a right to the title 'maister', but acknowledges later that he is more stupid than the official fool—'I am mair fule than he' (75). The repeated references to 'my lord' (20, 32, 53, 79) suggest that he is in the household either of the king or of a nobleman or prelate. He is the sort of man who likes to boast of noble connections to which he is not entitled:

> I callit my lord my heid, but hiddill,
> *Sed nulli alii hoc dixerunt*;
> We weir als sib as seve and riddill
> *In una silva que creverunt.*   (53–6)

Line 54 clearly nullifies the one that precedes it; and a comment by Kelly, the eighteenth-century proverb collector, illuminates lines 55–6: 'Spoken of them who groundlessly pretend kindred to great persons'.[32] The Kennedys were associated particularly with the south-west of Scotland; different branches held lands in Galloway, Carrick, and also Ayr—the place where the testator's drunken body is to be ignominiously buried (36). This area was still largely Gaelic-speaking, and indeed Kennedy at one point uses the Gaelic word *caupe* (50), which was a kind of combined death-duty and protection money, paid to one's chief. *The Testament* in some respects resembles Dunbar's *Flyting*, which is directed against another Kennedy, the poet Walter Kennedy. Perhaps we should regard 'Andro' not as an individual but as the fictitious representative of a surname. The satirical testament was a flexible genre: its targets included patent fictions, such as the English drunkard, Colin Blowbol, but also notorious historical figures, such as the Highlander, Duncan MacGregor.[33] The drunken 'Andro Kennedy' belongs to the same literary type as Colin Blowbol, yet the many specific details in the poem, difficult though they are to interpret, suggest that he was modelled on some real-life rogue.

Another poem opens:

> Lang heff I maed of ladyes quhytt;
> Nou of ane blak I will indytt
> That landet furth of the last schippis . . .   (K 33)

---

[31] *Ancient Scottish Poems* (Edinburgh, 1770), 243.
[32] *A Complete Collection of Scottish Proverbs* (1721), 31.
[33] See *Colyn Blowbols Testament*, ed. F. Lehmeyer (Erlangen, 1907); for Duncan MacGregor's *Testament*, see *The Black Book of Taymouth*, introd. C. Innes (Bannatyne Club, 1855), 151–73.

James IV's household included a number of black people, who served chiefly as musicians and entertainers. A black trumpeter was employed, at about the same time, in the English court, and is portrayed in the 1511 Great Tournament Roll.[34] Dunbar's phrase 'furth of the last schippis' suggests an almost journalistic response to a very recent phenomenon. The ships were possibly those of the piratical Barton brothers, who made repeated attempts to capture Portuguese vessels and their rich cargoes.[35] Dunbar's description of the black lady conveys something more than mockery—fascination with the novelty of her appearance. In his history of black people in Britain, Peter Fryer pointed out that the British were far less familiar than the Spaniards and Portuguese with dark-skinned people, and that it was a severe culture shock when they first encountered Africans.[36]

This poem has long been linked with one of the most brilliant festivals of James IV's reign, the Tournament of the Black Lady. There seem indeed to have been two such tournaments: the first took place in June 1507, and is probably the one to which Dunbar alludes; it was repeated in almost identical form in May 1508. The later sixteenth-century Scottish historians, John Leslie and Lindsay of Pitscottie, give vivid but rather confused accounts of what happened. *The Treasurer's Accounts* correct and supplement their evidence, supplying many small but fascinating details of expenditure: on the attendants dressed as Wild Men, who wore harts' horns and goatskins (iii. 386); on the tree of Esperance, from which the shields of the combatants were suspended, together with flowers, leaves, and thirty-seven pears (iii. 394); and, above all, on the Black Lady herself. She sat in a 'chair triumphale', accompanied by richly dressed squires and ladies, and wore a gown of damask, 'floured with gold' (iii. 258–9). According to Pitscottie, the culminating event was a 'triumphe and bancat' at Holyrood:

thair come ane clwdd out of the rwffe of the hall as appeirit to men and opnit and cleikkit vp the blak lady in presence of thame all that scho was no moir sene bot this was done be the art of Igramancie for the kingis plesour [by] ane callit bischope Andrew forman quha was ane Igramancier ...[37]

Dunbar's poem and the event that occasioned it tend to excite embarrassment in modern critics. One says that Dunbar 'pokes dubious fun at the appearance of the Mooress', and another exclaims at the 'barbarity' of the Scottish court, 'apparent not only in the fact

---

[34] S. Anglo, *The Great Tournament Roll of Westminster* (Oxford, 1968), i. 85.
[35] See R. L. Mackie, *King James IV of Scotland* (Edinburgh, 1958), 207–13.
[36] *Staying Power: The History of Black People in Britain* (1984), 2–4 and 136 ff.
[37] *The Historie and Cronicles of Scotland*, ed. Æ. J. G. Mackay (STS, 1899), i. 243–4; for Leslie's brief account, see *The History of Scotland* (Bannatyne Club, 1830), 78.

of the cruel enslaving of a negress as an object of amusement, but in the fact that Dunbar could write such a poem about her for a court audience'.³⁸ But this leaps from one poem, to a generalization about contemporary society that lacks firm foundation. There is not a shred of evidence extant to suggest that the Black Lady of the Tournament was enslaved, or subjected to public ridicule. The idea that the tournaments were devised as a mockery, or caused a 'scandal' is a modern myth.³⁹ It receives no support from the records or from Leslie and Pitscottie. The documentary evidence is admittedly scanty, but suggests that black people at the Scottish court were treated much like the other 'servitouris'. The 'More taubronar' (Moorish drummer), who often figures in *The Treasurer's Accounts*, received a horse, lodging, and clothing of a similar value to those of other entertainers.⁴⁰ On New Year's Day 1513 gifts of ten French crowns were given to several ladies, including 'Maistres Musgraif'; the same amount was also given to 'the twa blak ladeis' (iv. 401). Similar gifts had been made in 1512, when 'Elene Moire' received five crowns, and 'Mastres Musgray' received eight (iv. 324). Dunbar's description of the black lady is clearly unflattering; he was far from thinking that 'black is beautiful', and his attitude would be reinforced by the traditional negative associations of that colour with death, mourning, and the devil. But Dunbar penned sketches of white men that are more repellent than this black woman. It is difficult also to know how representative of public feeling this poem is. No doubt the mockery met with a response from many in Dunbar's audience; yet there survives at least one appreciative comment about an unnamed 'Mour'—Marion, Lady Home, in a letter of 1549, requested Mary of Lorraine to be good to him, saying 'He is als scharp ane man as rydis'.⁴¹

The names of only a few black ladies at the Scottish court have been preserved—'blak Margaret' (iv. 436), for instance, and 'Elene Moire', who was perhaps the same as 'blak Elene' (iv. 404, 434). Dunbar's black lady is unnamed, yet his first audience probably identified her easily. His poems may well contain allusions to other court figures, whom we now fail to recognize. The gibe at an ambitious churchman, unsatisfied with a bishopric, who 'Wald clym to be ane cardinall' (K 39. 50), may have had a specific target. Another sarcastic

---

³⁸ Ross, 182; Scott, 68.
³⁹ Cf. R. Nicholson, *Scotland: The Later Middle Ages* (Edinburgh, 1974) 576; and G. Hunter, 'Othello and Colour Prejudice', *PBA* 53 (1967), 142.
⁴⁰ See *TA* ii. 427, 430, 439, 444, 451, 459, and 472; vol. iii records many similar payments.
⁴¹ *The Scottish Correspondence of Mary of Lorraine*, ed. A. I. Cameron (SHS, 1927), 297.

sketch of an upstart 'in a prelottis clais' (K 45. 53) perhaps contains clues that we can no longer decipher. Another person to whom Dunbar alludes in this more covert manner is John Damian, one of the most prominent yet mysterious figures at the court. Scholars have varied strikingly in their assessment of him: Baxter thought that his attempt to fly should be included in 'the history of aeronautics', even comparing him to Leonardo da Vinci; others have adopted a viewpoint closer to Dunbar's, calling him a 'charlatan' and comparing him to the adventurer and confidence-trickster Cagliostro.[42]

Damian's precise origin is not known: in *The Treasurer's Accounts* he is regularly called French, but he seems to have come originally from Italy—a letter to the pope on his behalf calls him *Damianus de Falcutiis*.[43] In his career two strands are apparent, both clearly attractive to James IV. The first is his reputation as doctor and alchemist. At his earliest appearance in the records, in January 1502, he is called 'leich' (ii. 133), and in later entries he is similarly styled 'the Franch leich' (ii. 390, 395) or 'Maister Johne the Franch medicinar' (ii. 419). Purchases of drugs are made on his behalf, and of a pestle and mortar (ii. 142 and 148); and there are numerous payments for the apparatus, or 'stuf' required for alchemical experiments—cakes of glass, saltpetre, or coals for the furnace. The king's interest in medicine and alchemy is well known.[44] But Damian was also popular with James because he was a lively and entertaining companion. He often played at cards with the king (iv. 83, 89, and 101), or 'at the hasard of dis' (iv. 89); on one occasion they played mysteriously 'eftir soupir at the Irische game' (iv. 104). Damian also organized dances. The morris that took place at Epiphany 1504 is explicitly called 'Maister Johnis dans', and many payments to him are recorded for his purchase of belts, headgear, and coats for the dancers (ii. 414). The king's favour to Damian was shown not solely in repeated fees and payments for alchemical 'stuf', but by the bestowal of a benefice. An entry dated March 1504 (ii. 423) refers to 'Maister Johne, the new Abbot of Tungland'. It is unlikely that he resided at this abbey of Premonstratensian canons in Kirkcudbrightshire, but he seems to have drawn its revenues until 1509. In that year he apparently resigned, and the king requested Julius II to bestow the abbey on

---

[42] Baxter, 171, Scott, 127; also J. Wormald, *Court, Kirk and Community: Scotland 1470–1625* (1981), 56. For a different view, see Small, i, p. ccxv, and Mackie, *James IV*, 181. On the background, see. J. Read, 'Alchemy under James IV of Scotland', *Ambix*, 2 (1938–46), 60–7.

[43] *Letters of James IV 1505–1513*, ed. R. K. Hannay and R. L. Mackie (SHS, 1953), nos. 289 and 290.

[44] Cf. Nicholson, *Scotland: Later Middle Ages*, 591; and *TA* ii, pp. lxxiii–lxxix.

David, bishop of Candida Casa, so that he might 'reform its discipline and repair the ruins'.[45]

There may possibly be veiled allusions to Damian in Dunbar's sardonic comment on those who win reward less by long service than by skill at entertaining:

> Sum lait at evin bringis in the moryis.   (K 20. 8)

or by their alchemical ventures:

> In quintiscence eik, ingynouris joly
> That far can multiplie in folie.   (K 44. 55–6)

Dunbar here puns on the technical alchemical sense of *multiplie*—'to increase the precious metals, by transmutation of baser metals'—as in the matter-of-fact record of a payment to 'the leich [probably Damian], to multiply' (ii. 138). But one of Dunbar's poems is wholly devoted to the exploits of Damian. The earliest though incomplete text is found in the Asloan Manuscript, which describes it as 'a ballat of the abbot of tungland' (K 54). The anti-hero of this poem, who also figures in *Lucina schynnyng in silence of the nicht* (K 53), has much in common with the real-life Damian: suspiciously foreign, and linked with France and 'Lumbardy'; specifically an 'abbot', and in *The Abbot of Tungland* playing a variety of roles, including 'religious man', 'leich', alchemist, and 'new maid channoun'—this latter phrase recalls the reference in *The Treasurer's Accounts* to 'the new Abbot of tungland', and suggests that the poem's date of composition was not far distant from March 1504. Yet for the central event of both poems—the abbot's flight, and his ignominious fall—there is a striking lack of contemporary evidence. Only the historian, Leslie, provides two differing accounts of the incident: the first and briefest, in Scots, is dated 1568–70; the second, in Latin, is fuller and rhetorically embroidered (1578), and this latter was freely translated back into Scots by Dalrymple (*c.*1596).[46] It is Leslie—not Dunbar—who says that Damian broke his thigh in the fall, locates the incident at Stirling Castle, and also vaguely links it with a Scottish embassy to France, headed by the earl of Arran.

This embassy took place in September 1507, yet the references to Damian in *The Treasurer's Accounts* continue unabated till 1508; in

---

[45] See I. Cowan and D. E. Easson, *Medieval Religious Houses: Scotland* (1957; rev. 1976), 103. According to N. Backmund, the Scottish Premonstratensians were lax in observing the order's rules and suffered from the system of commendatory abbots: 'The Premonstratensian Order in Scotland', *Innes Review*, 4 (1953), 25–41.

[46] See respectively *The History of Scotland* (Bannatyne Club), 76; *De Origine Moribus et Rebus Gestis Scotorum* (Rome, 1578), 345–6; and *The Historie of Scotland*, ed. E. G. Cody (STS, 1888–95), ii. 124–6.

September of that year he received permission to leave the realm to study, for a period of five years, without prejudice to his abbacy at Tongland.[47] *The Treasurer's Accounts* furnish no evidence of any diminution in his alchemical experiments—on 13 October 1507 there is an entry 'for ane punschioun of wyne to the Abbot of Tungland to mak quinta essencia' (iv. 79)—and, what is more surprising, no sign of Damian's fall or injury. He was able to vie with the king in the shooting matches that occurred at Holyrood in February 1508 (iv. 103), and at Stirling in April 1508—twenty-eight shillings were paid out 'that nycht the King schot in the hall of Strivelin and tynt with the Abbot of Tungland' (iv. 111). The tales narrated by Dunbar and Leslie sound rather like different versions of a 'tall story', in which an unpopular royal favourite gets his come-uppance. One cause of Damian's unpopularity is implicit in an entry that mentions money lent to him, 'and can nocht be gottin fra him' (iii. 406). Yet the story of the flying abbot probably had some foundation; it perhaps originated in Damian's attempt to entertain the king by some mechanically contrived feat of levitation, similar to that which Bishop Forman devised for the Tournament of the Black Lady. The machinery for achieving such spectacular ascents was no novelty—it had been employed in miracle plays since the fourteenth century—but the astonishment it may have aroused in naïve spectators is suggested by Pitscottie's calling Forman 'ane Igramanciar', or necromancer.

At the court of James IV the entertainers were of many kinds, amateur and professional, native and foreign: Alexander Kers, the cook, sometimes played the Abbot of Unreason (ii. 320; iii. 127), and James Widderspune was a fowler as well as a 'fithelar and tellar of tales' (ii. 102). There were numerous luters, harpers, jugglers, and minstrels from France and Italy. Most European courts at this time also contained fools. Indeed, according to Sydney Anglo, in the Accounts of Henry VII they are the most frequently mentioned entertainers.[48] Fools, like other entertainers, often passed from one country to another: at the English court in December 1508 payment was made to John, 'late the king of Castelles fole', and in the Scottish court there was an English fool, variously called 'Inglis Johne the fwle' (i. 95) or 'Joly Johne the fule of Inglande' (i. 112). Some of the great Scottish nobles also had fools in their households. There is a reference to the fool of Lord Hamilton (iv. 109), and in 1505 Sir William Murray's fool, 'Swaggar', received a kersey coat from James IV. But it is the king's own fools in whom Dunbar displays particular interest.

[47] *Register of the Privy Seal*, ed. Livingstone, i, no. 1727.
[48] 'The Court Festivals of Henry VII: A Study Based upon the Account Books of John Heron, Treasurer of the Chamber', *Bulletin of John Rylands Library*, 43 (1960–1), 12–45 (15–16).

'Cuddy Rug the Drumfres fuill' (K 26, 24) was no fiction. His first mention in *The Treasurer's Accounts* occurs in September 1504, when James visited Dumfries, and he seems to have stolen a drum from a 'taubronar' (ii. 457). His name figures in the records from 1504 to 1512, and he should be distinguished from another entertainer, 'English Cuddy', who played the lute. We know a little more about 'Curry' (K 27. 43-8), who often appears in the records, along with several members of his family from 1495 onwards; he accompanied James on his travels around Scotland, and died shortly before June 1506. Dunbar also speaks of 'Curris kneff', who was the lad, or 'child', who regularly escorted Curry. The exact status of a fool's attendants is often uncertain; as Enid Welsford says, 'the terminology does not necessarily enable us to distinguish the body-servant from the warder'.[49] In this case it looks as if Curry was not considered responsible for his actions. There are repeated payments to Curry's man to conduct him round the country—'to haf him to Arbroth agane 3ule' (ii. 351), 'to haf him to Edinburgh fra Dunde' (ii. 354), or 'to haf him to Strivelin' (ii. 369). Curry was probably what would then have been termed a 'natural' fool; this suspicion is strengthened by the fact that his wife is called 'daft Anne' (iii. 369). John Bute (K 28, 19-20) was possibly also a fool of this kind. He too had a man, called 'Spark', who regularly accompanied him, and in March 1512 had to 'turs the said Johne of Edinburgh to Linlithgow' (iv. 263). There survive detailed accounts of John Bute's costly clothing—a hood of red leather, for instance, 'of the best fassone' (iv. 436), and a particoloured coat of red and yellow, patterned 'of the fassoun of the sey wawis [waves]' (iv. 263). 'Jok Fule' (K 38. 73) is slightly more problematical: this may be a type-name, yet there is evidence that a man of this name really existed—the payments made to 'Jok fule', when the king was at Dundee in January 1503 (ii. 354), and again 'to daft Jok the fule' in September 1505 (iii. 160).

Scholars still disagree as to whether the subject of the poem usually entitled *Schir Thomas Norny* (K 27) was a knight—as the poem repeatedly styles him—or a fool. Ross and Baxter regard Norny as a 'court braggart' or *miles gloriosus*; but Elizabeth Eddy argues convincingly that he was a fool.[50] She calls attention to one crucial piece of evidence: in March 1511, when he was about to go on pilgrimage to St James of Compostella, four French crowns were paid 'to Thomas Norny, fule, in elimose [alms, charity] at his passage to Sanct James' (iv. 184). Although there are no other references to Norny's being a

---

[49] *The Fool: His Social and Literary History* (1935), 119.
[50] Ross, 182; Baxter, 129; Eddy, 'Sir Thopas and Sir Thomas Norny: Romance Parody in Chaucer and Dunbar', *RES*, NS 22 (1971), 401-9.

fool in *The Treasurer's Accounts*, it is noticeable that he is regularly listed with other fools or entertainers (e.g. iv. 82, 100, and 116). Yet the records, like Dunbar, occasionally give him the title 'Schir'—'ane ribane to Schir Thomas Norneis bonet' (iii. 155), or 'to schir Thomas Nornee, at the kingis command' (iii. 166). These entries belong to 1505; and as Dunbar's poem is thought to have been composed not later than 1506 (see above, p. 50), Kinsley suggests that Norny's title 'was probably a short-lived joke initiated by Dunbar's poem'.[51] But the title—whether 'joke' or not—was still in use as late as 1512 (iv. 358). The evidence is scanty and confusing, and it seems equally possible that some real-life incident provoked Dunbar's poem. Several hypotheses might be devised. It is by no means impossible that Norny was a knight *and* a fool. Alternatively, if two men shared the same name, the joke might lie in deliberately confusing one with the other. But perhaps the most attractive possibility is that Norny the fool acted the part of a knight in some entertainment, or was knighted in a mock-ceremony, such as the burlesque investiture of buffoon knights that occurred at Ferrara in 1490. At the same court Isabella d'Este's favourite fool, *Il Matello*, was referred to as 'His Majesty'.[52] Scotland was familiar with the 'Lord of Misrule' tradition. In the last stanza Dunbar says of Norny:

> Quhairfoir ever at Pesche [Easter] and 3ull
> I cry him lord of evere full
>   That in this regeone duellis. (49–51)

This is an equivocation. If Norny were a knight, he might well retain fools in his household, and thus be their 'lord'; but he is also proclaimed chief of fools, in a very different sense—a superlative specimen of a fool.

The ambiguous nature of Dunbar's 'Schir Thomas Norny' seems as characteristic of its own time as is the present desire for clear-cut distinctions. A similar haze of ambiguity enshrouds many fools in the fifteenth and sixteenth centuries. Again and again there is uncertainty as to their exact mental state: a fool might be a simpleton, a madman, or a person of mildly eccentric behaviour. The word was also applied to someone of normal intelligence, who assumed the role of fool in order to gain a livelihood. Epithets sometimes make distinctions between the 'daft' or 'natural' fool, on the one hand, and the 'witty' or 'artificial' fool, on the other. When Dunbar speaks of 'wod' fools (K 14. 298; K 26. 18) he implies extreme madness; when he refers to 'fantastik fulis' (K 44. 57) the phrase seems to signify those subject to delusions. There is an ambiguity also about the fool's social status that

---

[51] p. 300.   [52] Welsford, *The Fool*, 18 and 132.

we find difficult to comprehend. At James IV's court, as elsewhere in Europe, fools had a privileged life, close to the king and often accompanying him on his travels; they were richly clothed, and well tended when ill. Yet the evidence suggests that they ran the risk of being subjected to practical jokes, verbal mockery, and harsh punishment. Outside the court environment, 'feigned fools' excited considerable hostility in Scotland. The phrase had connotations similar to modern 'layabouts', referring to those thought to find idleness more profitable than work. Several acts of parliament criticized those 'that makis thaim fulis that ar nocht', and proclaimed severe punishments— 'that thar eris be nalyt to the trone or to ane vthir tre and cuttit of and bannyst the cuntre. Ande gif thareftir thai be fundyn again at thai be hangit.'[53] Yet, paradoxically, moralists regarded another kind of 'feigned fool' with great reverence; this was the wise or sage fool, whose apparent folly covered profound wisdom. The Fool in *King Lear* is well known, but there is a good Scottish example of the theme in Fictus of *The Thre Prestis of Peblis*.[54]

For Dunbar, however, the fool seems always the object of contempt and a vehicle for derision. There are no sage fools in his poetry, no celebration of the higher wisdom that seems folly in the eyes of the world. The actual fools in his poems are introduced chiefly to degrade those with whom they are juxtaposed. The fool is sometimes a privileged and mocking onlooker: John Bute thus coarsely mocks a dancer in *Sir Jhon Sinclair begowthe to dance*; and Scorn, the 'bourdour in the hall', shakes his bauble at the narrator in *Sen that I am a presoneir* (K 9. 35–6). But Scorn is later punished cruelly—'a prik' put through his nose, as if he were an animal. In *Schir I complane of injuris* (K 26) Dunbar protests at another poet's behaviour, and requests a punishment to fit his crime. Mure's lack of 'wit and ressoun' demonstrates that he is a 'wod fuill' (18–20), and he should be treated accordingly:

> gar deliver him a babile
> That Cuddy Rug the Drumfres fuill
> May him resave agane this 3uill,
> All roundit in to 3allow and reid,
> That ladis may bait him lyk a buill.   (23–7)

He is to carry the fool's mock-sceptre, have his hair cropped, and wear motley. The implicit indignity becomes fully explicit in line 27, which suggests both the torture of an animal and the group-rejection

---

[53] For the year 1449; quoted by Mill, 295.
[54] Cf. Welsford, *The Fool*, 122 and 127, and S. Wenzel, 'The Wisdom of the Fool', in *The Wisdom of Poetry*, ed. L. D. Benson and S. Wenzel (Kalamazoo, 1982), 225–40.

of an individual. Kennedy, in *The Flyting*, envisages similar social and physical humiliation for Dunbar himself:

> I sall ger crop thy tong
> . . . .
> I sall degrade the, graceles, of thy greis,
> Scaile the for scorne and shere the of the scule,
> Ger round the hede, transforme the till a fule. (393 ff.)

A whole stanza is devoted to the fool in *The Testament of Maister Andro Kennedy*:

> To Jok Fule my foly fre
> *Lego post corpus sepultum*;
> In faith I am mair fule than he,
> *Licet ostendit bonum vultum*:
> Of corne and catall, gold and fe,
> *Ipse habet valde multum*,
> And ȝit he bleris my lordis e
> *Fingendo eum fore stultum*. (73–80)

This draws an obvious ironic contrast between the professed scholar and the professional fool; the one penniless, the other rich. But the contempt is evenly balanced: the usual hostility to the feigned fool is matched by derision of the testator's own innate 'foly'. Dunbar elsewhere depicts the court as a place where folly flourishes, thronged with 'fulis' of all kinds (K 44. 55–66); it is his most characteristic stance towards his environment.

'Tyme, space and dait'

The chronology of Dunbar's poems is notoriously difficult to establish, and only a handful can be dated with certainty.[55] The most precisely dated are two poems that welcome Bernard Stewart to Scotland (K 35) and lament his death (K 36): we know that Stewart arrived in May 1508, and died in June of the same year. The topic similarly fixes the approximate date of a few other poems: the wedding of James IV and Margaret Tudor in 1503 is celebrated in *The Thrissill and the Rois* (K 50); and the queen's visit to Aberdeen in 1511 is commemorated in *Blyth Aberdeane thow beriall of all tounis* (K 48). Limits for the composition of other poems can be established by their reference to contemporaries, whose date of death is known (see above, p. 50). *The Goldyn Targe* was composed before 1508, the likely date of the print

---

[55] See D. Fox, 'The Chronology of William Dunbar', *PQ* 39 (1960), 413–25; and M. P. McDiarmid, 'The Early William Dunbar and his Poems', *SHR* 59 (1980), 126–39.

in which it appears. The print containing *The Tua Mariit Wemen and the Wedo*, however, is undated, and provides no such *terminus ad quem*. There are a few scattered clues to the dating of some of Dunbar's petitions; and poems addressed to the queen presumably post-date 1503. But this evidence is both scanty and difficult to interpret; all too often scholars have pushed conjecture too far, or resorted to the widely held but unproven assumption that comic and bawdy poems are likely to belong to a poet's youth, and grave, moral ones to his old age. It is virtually impossible to arrange Dunbar's poems in order of composition; impossible therefore to distinguish juvenilia from works of maturity, or to trace his growth and development as a poet.

Yet a different kind of dating was very important to Dunbar. Like many medieval poets, he often includes some reference to the hour, day, month, or season in his poems, usually at the beginning, sometimes at the end. But his use of such time-references varies considerably. Some poems are introduced by the formulaic phrase 'this hindir nicht':

> In secreit place this hindir nycht
> I hard ane bern say till a bricht . . . (K 13)
>
> This hindir nycht in Dumfermeling
> To me wes tawld ane windir thing . . . (K 37)
>
> This hinder nycht halff sleiping as I lay
> Me thocht . . . (K 51)
>
> Musing allone this hinder nicht . . . (K 81)

Hindir literally means 'recently past', but here it is far from being so specific. This poetic and ritualized phrase resembles, in its deliberate vagueness, the fairy-tale opening 'Once upon a time'. It corresponds to Middle English 'this endres day' and medieval French *lautrier*, and is regularly associated with the opening of the *chansons d'aventure*. In English usage it is not tied to specific themes or subjects.[56] For Dunbar it seems primarily a device for distancing himself from what follows—the poet overhears a conversation (K 13) or a disembodied voice (K 81), or a strange tale is reported to him (K 37). It is also a useful way of leading into the ambiguous experience of dreams (K 51); the apparently precise but equally vague 'this nycht' introduces other vision poems (K 55 and 56).

At the other extreme are the poems in which Dunbar seems concerned with actual time, or what happens 'daylie in court befoir myn e' (K 44. 72). His poem about a 'magryme' has a matter-of-fact beginning:

---

[56] Cf. *DOST*, hender, a.1, and *hinder*, a.1; and H. E. Sandison, *The Chanson d'Aventure in Middle English* (Bryn Mawr, Penn., 1913).

> My heid did 3ak 3ester nicht,
> This day to mak that I na micht . . . (K 21)

Other poems are preoccupied, sometimes quite literally, with the 'here and now'. Lamenting Stewart's death, Dunbar writes, 'Pray *now* for him all that him loveit heir' (K 36. 25). Addressing Kennedy, he says, 'Bot *now* in winter for purteth [poverty] thow art traikit' (K 23. 118). Elsewhere he assumes in his audience an awareness of current events in the Highlands, when he remarks, 'As in the ilis / Is *now* a preiff' (K 34. 17–18). The topicality of such phrases as 'the new fund Yle' and 'furth of the last schippis' has already been noted. In the eulogy of Stewart Dunbar undertakes to write more fully of his exploits, at some later stage:

> As I think eftir withe all my diligence,
> Or thow departe, at lenthe for to discry. (K35. 86–7)

This may be viewed as an *occupatio*. Yet nothing could be more up to the minute than the phrase 'Or [before] thow departe', and nothing more rapidly out-of-date, since Stewart died soon after he reached Scotland. Such immediacy has other penalties. We are often puzzled by Dunbar's topical allusions, which tied his poems closely to a particular event, and were readily understood by his first audience.

Time may be perceived as linear, an irrevocable sequence of moments, days, and years; it may also be seen as cyclic, viewed in terms of the natural revolution of the seasons, or the partly overlapping religious cycle of the Christian Church. For medieval people, far more powerfully than for us, the year had a pattern to it. It was punctuated by saints' days, the 'hie feistis of sanctis in glorie' (K 40. 11), by the alternation of fast and feast, and by the distinctive rituals associated with different festivals. Even the basic contrast between winter and summer must have been felt more keenly by a society without electric light or central heating. (Visitors to Scotland from southern latitudes, such as Aeneas Sylvius or Pierre Brantôme, regularly commented on its wintry coldness and gloomy skies.[57]) One of Dunbar's finest poems, *In to thir dirk and drublie dayis* (K 69), is in part a meditation on time: melancholy reflections on mutability are prompted, yet assuaged, by the alternation of the seasons. This is reflected in the poem's own circular structure: it begins when 'the nycht dois lenth in houris', and closes with an anticipation of that time, 'quhone the nycht begynnis to schort'. Medieval calendars frequently specified the exact proportion of day-hours to night-hours in a given month; in December, for instance, the night had eighteen hours and the day six. Several of Dunbar's poems are linked in some way or other with the cycle of the

[57] P. Hume Brown, *Early Travellers*, xvi and 25–6.

year: some are designed quite straightforwardly to celebrate the great liturgical feasts, and are thus 'occasional' in a far from trivial sense; others make a rich use of the traditional associations of a specific season. A few, such as *The Tua Mariit Wemen and the Wedo*, exploit the tensions between holy day and holiday, between the sacred significance of a feast and its secular celebration.

The birth of Christ, in Dunbar's time as in our own, was simultaneously a religious and a secular festival. It was marked by special services, and by the king's attendance at mass on Christmas Day. But for the Scottish court Yule was a season of extended revelry, lasting approximately a month, from St Nicholas's Day (6 December) to 'Uphaliday', or Epiphany (6 January). Invitations were sent to the great lords, to call them to 'the king's Yule', minstrels and other entertainers flocked to court, and received rich rewards. We have no detailed accounts of the entertainments, but they included dancing, and various rites of inversion, such as the election of the King of the Bean, the Abbot of Unreason, and 'Sanct Nicholas bischoppis', or boy-bishops.[58] It was a time for lavish display and consumption. Vast sums were expended on new clothing for the king, queen, and their households; and on New Year's Day it was the custom to present gifts to the king, who in turn gave gifts to the household. The court may have delighted in such 'magnificence', but critical voices were also heard. It was not only the Protestants who—much later in the century—objected to the way Christmas was observed, castigating James VI for its 'greit abus'. Hector Boece (as translated by Bellenden) held King Arthur ultimately responsible for 'the surfaitt chere' of Christmas, and complained:

> Nochttheles, how euir that schaymfull glutony began, it hes corruppit the ingyne sa of Inglismen & Scottis that in the dayis of Cristis Natiuite callit Cristmes thai ar gevin mair to voracite than vertu, and mair to thair wame than to divyne seruice.[59]

Boece's misgivings are not expressed by Dunbar, but his poems reflect this season's duality. *Rorate celi desuper* (K 1) is designed to celebrate Christ's birth; the opening line and other phrases are liturgical in origin—the refrain, for instance, derives from the introit for the mass on Christmas Day. It has been suggested that the poem might have been sung on Christmas morning, at the door of the king's chamber; but this, although an attractive possibility, is no more than speculation.[60] It is the secular aspects of Yule, however, that are most

---

[58] *TA* i. 239; see i, pp. ccxxxvii-ccxliv, for Yule in the Scottish court.
[59] *The Chronicles of Scotland*, ed. R. W. Chambers, E. Batho, and H. W. Husbands (STS, 1938–41), i. 369. On the Reformers' objections, see Mill, 91 and 109.
[60] Ross, 64.

prominent in Dunbar. Yule, like Easter, is a time to be 'glaid' (K 67), and a time for largess (K 83), when fools, like other entertainers, assemble at the court (K 26 and 27). Two of Dunbar's poems are unambiguously linked with New Year. The custom of sending friends and patrons verses at this season occurred in Roman antiquity, and was common in medieval Europe. Sometimes they accompanied gifts; a contemporary instance is the Latin poem that Skelton sent, together with a book, to Henry VIII (*c.*1512).[61] But poems were often sent on their own, like Christmas cards today, to express good wishes for the coming year. This is clearly the primary purpose of Dunbar's *My prince in god gif the guid grace* (K 18). Such poems often deliver moral exhortation—something very evident in Alexander Scott's New Year address to Mary Queen of Scots—and many are explicitly petitionary, requesting 'Lerges of this New Yeir day'.[62] Dunbar thus prays that the king will be endowed both with grace to govern justly and with generosity—a 'liberall heart and handis not sweir'. *This hinder nycht halff sleiping as I lay* (K 51) similarly associates hope of reward with 'this guid new 3eir' (54–5).

Of all Dunbar's poems the one most firmly though most tantalizingly linked with Yule is the petition that opens

> Schir, lat it never in toune be tald
> That I suld be ane 3owllis 3ald. (K 43)

A 3*ald* was a pejorative term for an old horse, but there is evidence (from later Scottish usage) that figuratively it signified a person who had nothing new to wear either at Easter (a 'Pays yad') or at Christmas (a 'Yule's yaud' or 'Yeel's jaad').[63] Such a person was likely to be unlucky for the rest of the year, and was also the object of derision— Dunbar's phrase 'in toune be tald' implies public mockery of the Yule '3ald'. Using this persona of an old horse, he humorously reminds the king that he has not received his Christmas livery. Allowances of clothing were not then given simply to lowly flunkeys. Some sections of *The Treasurer's Accounts* contain detailed itemization of the rich liveries given to the lords and ladies of the court. 'Maesteres Musgraeffe' has two pages devoted to the clothes bought for her between 1511 and 1512, including her 'leveray goune agane 3ule' (iv. 230). In 1511 an entry records the payment of £12. 10*s*. for Dunbar's own

---

[61] See R. S. Kinsman and T. Yonge, *John Skelton: Canon and Census* (Renaissance Soc. of America, Bibliographies and Indexes, 4, 1967), C 31. For French New Year poems, see J. M. Smith, *French Background of Middle Scots Literature* (1934), 65.
[62] Scott, *Poems*, no. 1; Greene, *Carols*, no. 121.2.
[63] See M. Macleod Banks, *British Calendar Customs: Scotland* (1937–41), i. 39, and iii. 216; W. Gregor, *Notes on the Folklore of the North-East of Scotland* (1881), 157; and *SND*, *Yule*.

'3ule leveray' (iv. 249). But it is an earlier entry that provides the most likely clue to the approximate date of this poem: on 27 January 1506 Dunbar was paid £5, 'be the kingis command, for caus he wantit his goun at 3ule' (iii. 181).

Scholars long failed to realize that this poem is a Christmas carol. But it has the carol's distinguishing feature: a burden, which, like a refrain, is repeated after every stanza, but, unlike a refrain, is quasi-independent and regularly placed at the beginning of the piece. It also has what seems the most common metrical shape for carols: the burden is a four-beat couplet, and is linked wih a stanza rhyming *aaab*.[64] Carols were often associated with 'holiday feasting' in large households and particularly though not exclusively with Christmas revelry. In Scotland the Reformers later fulminated against such customs. On 30 December 1574, in Aberdeen, fourteen women were charged with 'dansin, and singin off fylthe carrolles on Yeull Day'. But moral disapproval was not confined to Protestants; one of the pieces in the pre-Reformation manuscript, Arundel 285, considered it a sin to listen to carols on holy days.[65] The carol perhaps retained its link with the round dance longer in Scotland than in England. At the opening of the sixteenth century Douglas described children 'syngand karrellis and dansand in a ryng'; and at its very end (1595) six parishioners of Errol confessed to 'going about in ringis and carrelling vpon the day callit 3oull Day'.[66] Unfortunately very few texts of Scottish carols now survive, but several—like this one—were evidently associated either with Yule or New Year. One, an anonymous riddling piece in praise of beer, possibly refers to the custom of calling for a song from each member of the company: 'In 3ule quhen ilk man singis his carrel'.[67] Many English carols are accompanied by music, and some contain internal evidence that in performance there was a division between a soloist who sang the stanzas and a chorus who sang the burden. Dunbar's carol has no music, yet it is not inconceivable that it was sung, although the sense of the burden would seem to rule out choral singing. The poem is specific and personal, yet well within the carol tradition: a poem for a social and convivial occasion.

There is a further interesting possibility, that Dunbar may allude to some lost Christmas custom or game. Although it has no known source, the poem has a curious analogue. This is a folk-song, commonly known as 'Poor Old Horse', recorded centuries after Dunbar, and from widely separate areas of England. It was a favourite

---

[64] See Greene, *Carols*, especially xxxii–xxxiii and liii.
[65] Cf. Mill, 162; and *Devotional Pieces in Verse and Prose*, ed. J. A. W. Bennett (STS, 1955), 234.
[66] For these and other citations, see Greene, *Carols*, lxiii and lxxiv.
[67] Bannatyne, fol. 107b.

of Edward Thomas, who quoted a version beginning 'My clothing was once of the linsey woolsey fine', in chapter 36 of *The Heart of England*. Although the wording differs, all have a similar refrain—'Poor old horse, poor old horse'. The singer, in all of them, identifies with the horse, and laments his vanished youth; and all use motifs that occur in Dunbar—the horse is neglected and badly fed, or anticipates his approaching death.[68] These 'Old Horse' songs did not exist in a vacuum, but were performed in a social context. They formed the verbal and musical component in a regular Christmas observance: in it a group of performers, accompanied by a 'horse' (in some shape or other), paid house-to-house visits, and usually requested payment or reward. Similar calendar customs, such as 'the Old Tup' (involving a sheep's head), and the Welsh *Mari Lwyd*, have been recorded in many parts of the British Isles.[69] Dunbar's carol resembles the folk-songs in three respects: the speaker or singer identifies with an old, neglected animal; the occasion is convivial, and the season either Christmas or New Year; and the function tends to be petitionary—a *quête* on behalf of an individual or a group.

Between Dunbar's poem and these calendar customs lies an enormous gap—both literary and chronological. Dunbar is complex and witty, whereas the 'Old Horse' songs are unsophisticated, rich chiefly in pathos. Dunbar lived in the reign of James IV, yet few of these ceremonies can be dated earlier than the nineteenth century. What is more, the 'Old Horse' songs are English, and it is usually said that there is no evidence for similar Scottish songs and customs, despite their wide distribution elsewhere in England, Wales, and Ireland.[70] Yet there survives at least one Scottish folk song about an ill-treated 'jade', or mare, recorded in 1805; although fragmentary and obscure, it displays characteristic sympathy with the horse, and has a Christmas setting.[71] The New Year custom of paying visits and singing begging-songs or 'hagmonayis' has also long existed in Scotland. It seems possible—though this is speculation—that there existed in Dunbar's time 'Old Horse' songs and customs similar to those that have been preserved in England, but the Reformers found them so obnoxious that they were ruthlessly extirpated, like much else 'superstitious observation of auld reitis and ceremoneis expresly

---

[68] Several versions are found in J. Reeves's *The Everlasting Circle* (1960), and *Cecil Sharp's Collection of English Folk Songs*, ed. M. Karpeles (1974). See, more fully, Bawcutt, 'Dunbar's Christmas Carol', in Strauss and Drescher, 381–92.

[69] Cf. E. C. Cawte, *Ritual Animal Disguise* (Cambridge, 1978), and R. Greig, 'We Have a Poor Old Horse', *Lore and Language*, 9 (1973), 7–10.

[70] Cawte, op. cit. 222.

[71] *Scottish Tradition*, ed. D. Buchan (1984), no. 30: 'In Brechin did a Webster dwell'.

forbidden during the tyme callit Yool'.⁷² It is suggestive that Dunbar's use of '3owllis 3ald' is the only occurrence recorded until the nineteenth century—as if the phrase only survived orally—and that it clearly belongs to the realm of folklore and popular superstition.

One of Dunbar's best-known poems begins

> Off Februar the fyiftene nycht
> Full lang befoir the dayis lycht
>   I lay in till a trance;
> And than I saw baith hevin and hell:
> Me thocht amangis the feyndis fell
>   Mahoun gart cry ane dance
> Off schrewis that wer nevir schrevin
> Aganis the feist of Fasternis evin
>   To mak thair observance... (K 52. 1–9)

It has long been considered that Dunbar, in this passage, dates his poem with great precision; yet there is no unanimity as to the year of composition. Some early scholars thought that Dunbar says not only that his vision occurred on 15 February, but that this was also the date of 'Fasternis evin' (Shrove Tuesday). But the usual opinion today seems to be that the opening phrase, 'Off Februar the fyiftene nycht', refers not to Shrove Tuesday itself but to the preceding night. During this period Fasternis Evin fell on 16 February in three years, 1496, 1507, and 1518. Baxter, who believes that 1496 is 'much too early' and 1518 'much too late', therefore attributes the poem to 1507.⁷³ I am not convinced, however, that we can date this poem so precisely. The phrase 'Aganis the feist of Fasternis evin' is extremely vague: *aganis* means 'in preparation for', and is not identical with *on* or *upon*. The usage contrasts strikingly with that employed in the opening of one poem—'Apon the midsummer evin' (K 14)—and the penultimate line of another—'Quhat me befell on Gud Fryday' (K 3). It also contrasts with the way another poem begins:

> Madam, 3our men said thai wald ryd
> And latt this Fasterennis evin ower slyd. (K 32)

There is much that is puzzling about this second piece, apparently addressed to the queen, which mixes piety and bawdy; but '*this* Fasterennis evin' has a remarkably topical ring. Dunbar's vision of hell has a wholly different character. Its time references seem designed to locate the poem not in a specific year but in a specific season of the Church calendar, for which February was the most common month and 'the fyiftene nycht' pleasingly alliterative.

---

⁷² See Banks, *Calendar Customs: Scotland*, ii. 61–6; *DOST, hagmane*; and Mill, 242.
⁷³ For the fullest discussion, see Baxter, 154–6.

Dunbar is here less concerned with actual time than with symbolic time, and with the imaginative significance of 'Fasternis evin'. Continental folklorists have a wealth of evidence concerning Carnival; the Scottish testimony is scanty, yet what survives suggests that medieval Scotland, like the rest of Europe, celebrated the eve of Lent as a festival, attended by revelry of many kinds. It is usually said that Carnival was less common in north-west Europe, and that there is no pre-Reformation evidence for the cock-fighting and football that later became common Shrovetide sports in Scotland.[74] Yet one of the earliest pieces of legislation undertaken by the St Andrews Faculty of Arts (1415) was to limit the time spent in cock-fighting at Carnival; and in 1537 an inter-college football match at the same time of year caused a breach of the peace.[75] The poem *Colkelbie Sow* refers to the heavy gambling on one 'battalous' fighting-cock 'at Schriftis Evin'.[76] John Barbour alludes to the custom of dancing, singing, and revelling 'apon Fastryn evyn'; and one of the poets known to Dunbar, Patrick Johnston, devised *ludi*, unfortunately unspecified, for the court of James III, both at Yule and Carnival (*tempore . . . Carnisprivii*).[77] In James IV's reign two activities were particularly popular. The first, dancing and *gysing*, 'masking', was a forerunner of the later Shrovetide masques, such as that associated with the wedding of Mary Livingstone in 1565. One elaborate dance of this kind was devised in February 1505: *The Treasurer's Accounts* (ii. 477) record payments 'for xii cotis and xii pair hos half Scottis blak half quhit to xii dansaris be the More taubronaris devis agane Fasteringis Evin, be the kingis command'. Another seasonal pastime, as on the Continent, was jousting. There are numerous references in *The Accounts*, especially from 1503 to 1507, to the preparation of armour and weapons 'for tournaying at Fasternis Evin'. Many payments are recorded to armourers and 'cultellaris', concerning long swords for the 'barres', and short swords for tournaying, and diamonds and 'virales' for spears. One citation, for 1 February 1505 (ii. 476) must suffice: 'to James Hog, for dighting of viii suordis, binding of thair handis [handles] agane Fasteringis Evin to the tournaying, dighting of thre steil sadilles with ymree, tua tre axes and tua spere hedis'.

These seasonal activities of the court are mirrored in the structure of Dunbar's poem: the first part is both dance and 'gyis' (10), and the

---

[74] Cf. J. Bossy, *Christianity in the West 1400–1700* (Oxford, 1985), 44–5; Banks, *Calendar Customs: Scotland*, i. 16.
[75] *Acta Facultatis Artium Universitatis Sanctiandree 1413–1588*, ed. A. I. Dunlop (SHS, 3rd ser. 54–5, 1964), cxxxii.
[76] *Colkelbie Sow*, ed. G. Kratzmann (New York, 1983), 943–5.
[77] *Bruce*, x. 422–6; *Exchequer Rolls*, ed. G. Burnett (Edinburgh, 1855), viii. 333; Mill, 57 and 311.

second is a 'turnament' (121). Court life is also reflected in tiny details—the modish dances, 'That last came out of France' (12), and the 'lovery' (102), an allowance of food and drink served to courtiers. Yet the mirror is grotesquely distorting. This court is located in hell, and presided over by the devil; the dancing 'gallandis' include the Seven Deadly Sins, and the jousters are not knights but cowardly craftsmen. Dunbar evokes the strange ambivalence of 'the feist of Fasternis evin', in which feast commonly triumphed over fast. It was associated with gargantuan eating and drinking; with the indecency of the German *Fastnachtspiele* (of which one scholar remarked, 'every speech is a vulgarity, every joke an obscenity'[78]); with public riot and strife; and with the temporary suspension of normal rules of behaviour, when men wore masks, or dressed as women or demons. If Dunbar's poem is set in the context of Carnival there is much that is familiar: the procession that is half-dance, half-battle; the devils who mix with personified vices; the theme of role-reversal in the tournament; and the prevailing tone of grotesque comedy.[79]

Carnival's spiritual opponent was Lent; *Mardi Gras* battled against a thin and repulsive *Carême* not only in Bruegel's famous painting but in medieval poetry and pageants.[80] Lent was a time of prohibition, associated not only with fasting but also with sexual abstinence—marriages were prohibited during this period. It was also a time for the annual ritual of penance, since the Church required people to confess their sins before receiving the eucharist at Easter: 'Men ar haldin to mak confessioun anys in the 3ere at Pasche becaus of the resauing of the haly sacrament of the body and noble persoun of Ihesu'.[81] *The Maner of Passing to Confessioun* was designed primarily for this season:

> O synfull man, thir ar the fourty dayis
> That every man sulde wilfull pennence dre:
> Oure Lorde Jesu as haly writ sayis
> Fastit himself, oure exampill to be.   (K 5. 1–4)

Dunbar here draws the orthodox parallel between Lent and Jesus's forty days in the wilderness. Possibly *The Tabill of Confessioun* (K 6) was also intended for Lenten contemplation. But the common critical

---

[78] Cf. M. J. Rudwin, 'The Origin of the German Carnival Comedy', *JEGP* 18 (1919), 402–54, quoting H. Goedecke (444).
[79] There is much detail in B. Googe's *The Popish Kingdome* (1570), book 4; see also M. Bakhtin, *Rabelais and his World*, trans. H. Iswolski (1968), *passim*; and P. Burke, *Popular Culture in Early Modern Europe* (1978), 178–204.
[80] Cf. the poem *La Bataille de Caresme et de Charnage*, ed. G. Lozinski (Paris, 1933), and the tournament in Bologna (1506) between Carnival, on a fat horse, and Lent, on a thin one (Burke, *Popular Culture*, 185).
[81] 'Of Penance and Confession', in *Asloan Manuscript*, i. 19.

assumption that *The Dregy* (K 22) was composed during Lent rests on a shaky foundation; the belief that the poem alludes to James IV's custom of going on Lenten retreat to Stirling. Yet its one seasonal reference is to Yule:

> And thairfoir tak in patience
> 3our pennaunce and 3our abstinence,
> And 3e sall cum or 3ule begyn
> Into the blis that we ar in.   (87–90)

If this is read literally, the poem is more plausibly associated with Advent, which was also a period of abstinence. Dunbar's humorous tone recalls the Advent carols that complain of the rigours of fasting, and joyfully proclaim, 'Farewele, Advent; Cristemas is cum!'[82]

Three other poems are associated specifically with the first day of Lent, Ash Wednesday. Two are wholly didactic, in the manner of a Lenten sermon. One opens:

> Off Lentren in the first mornyng
> Airly as did the day up spring
> Thus sang ane bird with voce upplane:
> All erdly joy returnis in pane.
>
> O man, haif mynd that thow mon pas;
> Remembir that thow art bot as [ash] . . .   (K 59. 1–6)

This draws upon the liturgy for Ash Wednesday, recalling the ritual distribution of ashes, and the priest's words, *Memento quia cinis es et in cinerem reverteris*. The same words (which derive ultimately from Genesis 3: 19) are half-quoted in a second poem:

> *Memento homo quod cinis es—*
> Think, man, thow art bot erd and as;
> . . . . . .
> Think, thocht thy bodye ware of bras,
> *Quod tu in cinerem reverteris*.   (K 61. 1 ff.)

This solemnity contrasts with Dunbar's other Ash Wednesday poem:

> Rycht airlie on Ask Weddinsday
> Drynkand the wyne satt cumeris tway;
> The tane cowth to the tother complene:
> Graneand and suppand cowd scho say,
> This lang Lentern makis me lene.   (K 73. 1–5)

Abstinence, particularly from meat, was required of all, except for children and the sick; but it was long accepted that drinking, in moderation, did not break the fast. John Ireland thus says, 'Dragy

---

[82] Greene, *Carols*, no. 3.

[sweetmeats] na sic thing brekis nocht fasting, na drink sa it be sobirly tane'.[83] But there is nothing 'sobir' about Dunbar's two 'cumeris', who are clearly habitual tipplers. With their 'fatt' figures they reverse the popular stereotype of Lent, often personified as an emaciated woman. Their dialogue vividly embodies popular dislike of Lent, and the topsy-turvy logic and ingenious quibbles devised to evade its restrictions. A fifteenth-century homilist complained that few people abstained from drinking in Lent: 'on the contrary, they go to the taverns, and some imbibe and get drunk more than they do out of Lent, thinking and saying "fishes *must* swim"'. The same joke recurs in one of *The Mery Tales of the Mad Men of Gotham*, which is set, like Dunbar's poem, on Ash Wednesday: a priest tells an alehouse-keeper to abstain from drink—'Not so, said the fellow for it is an old Prouerbe that fish must swim. Yea, said the Priest, it must swim in water. I cry you mercy ... I thought it should have swom in good ale.'[84]

Good Friday and Easter are two of the most important seasons of the Christian year: the one a time of sorrow, commemorating the Crucifixion, the other a time of joy, celebrating the Resurrection. Dunbar's two poems on these great events are fully orthodox, voicing the response of a devout Christian. *The Passioun of Crist* has much in common with other devotional writings on the Crucifixion; where it is unusual is in taking the form of a vision experienced when the poet kneels before a crucifix. It ends:

> Than wrayt I all without delay
> Richt heir as I have schawin to 30w,
> Quhat me befell on Gud Fryday
> Befoir the crose of sweit Jesu.   (K 3. 141–4)

This is unlikely to be literally true. The author of the contemporary *Contemplacioun of Synnaris* chose Friday, with similar decorum, as the day for a meditation on the Passion.[85] But it is a bold and imaginative device, suggesting the intensity of the dreamer's devotion, who re-enacts in his mind what happened long ago. Dunbar, rather like Donne in *Good Friday 1613 Riding Westward*, shows how vividly 'that spectacle of too much weight' is 'present' to his memory. Dunbar's poem on the Resurrection (K 4) is also linked clearly, though not so explicitly, with the Church calendar. Its theme proclaims it to be an Easter poem, and its refrain—*Surrexit dominus de sepulchro*—derives from the mass for Easter Day.

---

[83] 'Of Penance and Confession'; op. cit. i. 41.
[84] Cf. B. A. Henisch, *Fast and Feast: Food in Medieval Society* (1976), 41; *Shakespeare Jest Books*, ed. W. C. Hazlitt, 3 vols. (1864), iii. 25.
[85] See *Devotional Pieces*, ed. Bennett, 125–41.

One poem, *The Thrissill and the Rois*, is apparently dated very precisely. It celebrates the wedding of James IV and Margaret Tudor on 8 August 1503, and ends:

> And thus I wret, as 3e haif hard to forrow,
> Off lusty May upone the nynte morrow.   (K 50. 188–9)

Many scholars interpret these lines literally, and consider that the poem was composed well in advance of the wedding, in May 1503. This may indeed be so, yet it seems more likely that the choice of month has a primarily imaginative significance. *The Goldyn Targe* and *The Merle and the Nychtingall*, like countless medieval poems, are likewise set in May; they, like *The Thrissill and the Rois*, draw upon the traditional idyllic view of the month and associate it both with love and with Nature's cyclic renewal. In Malory's words,

> lyke as trees and erbys burgenyth and florisshyth in May, in lyke wyse every lusty harte that ys ony maner of lover spryngith, burgenyth, buddyth, and florysshyth in lusty dedis. For hit gyvyth unto all lovers corrayge, that lusty moneth of May...[86]

May is personified in *The Thrissill and the Rois*. She chides the sleeping poet for his sluggardy and lack of 'curage'—less as lover than as poet—and bids him 'Uprys and do thy observance' (37). In *The Goldyn Targe* the month of May is associated with 'mirth', mirthful activities, and seasonal 'observance' by youthful green-clad figures:

> Endlang the lusty ryvir so thai mayit
> Thair observance rycht hevynly was to here.   (131–2)

Malory describes a similar 'maying' by Guinevere and her knights, dressed in green and decorated with flowers. Such customs were no literary fiction, divorced from life. There is abundant Scottish evidence for May games, and the sports associated with 'the bringin in' of summer. The intense hostility displayed by the Reformers to 'the auld superstitioun... commonlie vsit in the tyme of May' implies the strength of popular attachment to such customs.[87]

But why does Dunbar refer so precisely to 9 May? That it had some special significance is suggested by the fact that two contemporary Scottish poems are also linked with this date: the anonymous *Quare of Jelusy* is set on the seventh Ide of May,[88] and Douglas associates his Twelfth Prologue with 'the nynt morow of fresch temperit May' (268). In the Church calendar this day was associated

---

[86] *Works of Sir Thomas Malory*, ed. E. Vinaver (Oxford, 1954), 790.
[87] Mill, 20, 224, and 228–9; on scholars' bringing in *Mayum seu estatem*, see Dunlop, *Acta*, 37; and for other customs, cf. Scott, *Poems*, no 5.
[88] Ed. J. Norton-Smith and I. Pravda (Heidelberg, 1976), 7.

principally with the Translation of St Nicholas. It was so identified in the records of Glasgow University (1462), when this date was chosen for the annual Faculty feast, at which there was a procession, banquet, and short play.[89] But what may be more relevant to *The Thrissill and the Rois* is that the date was sometimes regarded as the first day of summer. Historically, there have been many different methods of dividing the year into seasons. But the idea that summer begins on 9 May can be traced to a Greek tradition, which associated that season with the rising of the constellation of the Pleiades in the morning, as opposed to the night. In the Anglo-Saxon and early medieval period there are references to 9 May as marking *aetatis initium* or 'sumeres fruma' in Bede, calendars, the *Old English Martyrology*, and the *Menologium,* or *Calendar Poem*.[90] The tradition was known in Dunbar's time, since the work sometimes called *Arnold's Chronicle* (*c*.1502) contains a brief account of the four seasons, and observes, 'Somer ... beginnithe the vii ide of May'.[91] Although Douglas's Twelfth Prologue is commonly regarded as a 'spring poem', it is worth noting that in it the season is twice termed summer (93 and 204). Dunbar perhaps selected this date precisely because of its liminal qualities: 9 May marked the very beginning of the most joyous season of the year. *The Thrissill and the Rois* likewise celebrates a beginning, in both human and political terms: the fresh start implicit in any marriage, and the inauguration of a potentially happier relationship between England and Scotland. Leslie saw the marriage in this light: it promised 'perfyte peace and syncere amity keipit betwix the tua realmes'.[92]

There is nothing fortuitous in the setting of *The Tua Mariit Wemen and the Wedo* 'Apon the midsummer evin, mirriest of nichtis'. Midsummer Eve was celebrated on 23 June, although in this period it was no longer the actual solstice. The day had high religious significance, since it was St John's Eve, or the vigil of the Nativity of St John. On this day, according to Reginald Pecock, Londoners decorated their houses with flowers and branches, in remembrance of John the Baptist

---

[89] C. Innes, *Munimenta Alme Universitatis Glasguensis* (Maitland Club, Glasgow, 1854), ii. 39; in St Andrews too the *solempnitas* first held on the December feast of St Nicholas was transferred to his Translation (Dunlop, *Acta,* cxxxiii and 4). In some Scottish calendars, 9 May is linked with the Translation of St Andrew; cf. A. P. Forbes, *Kalendars of Scottish Saints* (Edinburgh, 1872), 100 and 152. But St Andrew was more usually associated either with 30 November or 6 February; on this new feast, see *The Medieval Church of St Andrews,* ed. D. McRoberts (Glasgow, 1976), 93.

[90] See *Bedae Opera de Temporibus,* ed. C. W. Jones (Cambridge, Mass., 1943), 247; R. T. Hampson, *Medii Aevi Kalendarium* (1841), i. 405, 426, and 439; *An Old English Martyrology,* ed. G. Herzfeld (EETS, OS 116, 1900), 80; and *Menologium,* 87–92, in *The Anglo-Saxon Minor Poems,* ed. E. V. K. Dobbie (New York, 1942).

[91] *The Customs of London, Otherwise Called Arnold's Chronicle* (1811), 171.

[92] Leslie, *History,* 72.

and the prophecy that many should rejoice in his birth. All over Europe it was celebrated with feasting, dancing, and the lighting of bonfires.[93] At the beginning of Dunbar's poem the narrator speaks as a weary reveller, who has withdrawn from the 'mirthis' to seek repose:

> I muvit furth allane in meid as midnicht wes past
> . . . .
> I drew in derne to the dyk to dirkin efter mirthis. (2 ff.)[94]

But he finds that for three ladies the Midsummer revelry continues, and their dancing, drinking, and, above all, talking last till dawn. The poem is devoted to this 'game amang the grene leiffis' (241), which the poet observes but does not join.

Many moralists condemned the Midsummer revels. One fifteenth-century preacher said that the feast should be celebrated with joy, but 'not with such merriment as is shown by the profane lovers of this world, who make great fires in the streets, and indulge themselves with filthy and unlawful games, to which they add gluttony and drunkenness, and the commission of many other shameful indecencies' (*turpibus et illicitis ludis, commessationibus et ebrietatibus, cubilibus et impudicitiis*).[95] The well-known carol 'Ladd y the daunce a Myssomer Day' illustrates one likely consequence of such revelry.[96] Midsummer Day also attracted the disapproval of preachers, because it was (and long continued to be) a focus for all sorts of non-Christian beliefs and practices; in Scotland after the Reformation St John's Eve and St Peter's Eve (29 June) were termed 'superstitious days'. Many rituals were concerned with fertility; their object was to ensure a good harvest, or to cure sterility in animals or impotence. There were also charms to find out whether a girl would be married in the coming year. Such practices, although unmentioned in the poem, suggest the associations that this date held for Dunbar, as centuries later for Strindberg, who set *Miss Julie* on this night—desires and fears about sexuality and the choice of marriage partners. These are leading themes of *The Tua Mariit Wemen and the Wedo*.

The Second Wife mentions another date in what Lydgate termed 'Cupydes Kalundere':[97]

> 3e speik of berdis one bewch; of blise may thai sing
> That one sanct Valentynis day ar vacandis ilk 3eir;

---

[93] *The Repressor of Over Much Blaming of the Clergy*, ed. C. Babington (1860), i. 28; cf. Burke, *Popular Culture*, 180–1; and J. G. Frazer, *The Golden Bough: Balder the Beautiful*, i (1930), 160 ff.

[94] *in meid*: my emendation of MS *meid*. On 'dirkin', see below, 331.

[95] The passage is quoted by A. K. Moore, 'The Setting of the Tua Mariit Wemen and the Wedo', *ES* 32 (1951), 56–62.

[96] Greene, *Carols*, no. 453.

[97] *Minor Poems I*, ed. H. N. MacCracken (EETS, ES 107, 1911), no. 64.

> Hed I that plesand prevelege to part quhen me likit,
> To change and ay to cheise agane—than chastite adew! (205–8)

St Valentine's Day is today far more familiar than St John's Eve; yet folklorists have found no evidence for St Valentine's Day customs before the fifteenth century. The association of St Valentine with the mating of birds and human courtship was primarily a literary and courtly cult, one which almost certainly originated in Chaucer's *Parliament of Fowls*, and was adopted by other poets, such as Gower, Lydgate, and Charles d'Orléans.[98] Late-medieval 'Valentine' poems tend to be highly idealistic: the day is one on which a lover makes a choice for life, or renews vows of constancy. In Chaucer's *Complaint of Mars*, on St Valentine's Day, a bird sings:

> Yet at the leste renoveleth your servyse;
> Confermeth hyt perpetuely to dure.

The Wife's words are thus, from the courtly point of view, heretical; they parallel the Widow's misuse of Scripture. Dunbar's stance in the poem, however, is that of the ironist. He speaks blandly of the 'mirthis' of Midsummer Eve, 'mirriest of nichtis', in the same manner that he refers to the ladies' 'game amang the grene leiffis' (241) and 'pastance most mery' (526). Only occasional hints, such as the word 'wantoun', applied to the Widow and later all three women (37, 529), remind us that the moralist might regard their 'game' as *turpibus ludis* and their uninhibited conversation as *impudicitiis*.

This chapter has been almost as much concerned with questions as with answers. Readers of Dunbar owe a great deal to his earliest editors, especially David Laing, yet many of their surmises and tentative suggestions have hardened, over the years, into definite 'facts', repeated somewhat uncritically again and again. It seems better, if less comfortable, to admit the limits of our knowledge than to continue retailing long-accepted but erroneous beliefs. To highlight a problem (such as Andro Kennedy's identity) may even, by promoting further enquiry, lead to its solution. This is particularly likely at the present time, when historians have made available a mass of new information (such as the records in the Vatican archives), and are reassessing many aspects of life in early modern Scotland.

[98] Cf. J. B. Oruch, 'St Valentine, and Spring in February', *Speculum*, 56 (1981), 534–65.

3
Court Poems: Praise and Petition

JAMES IV is one of Scotland's most popular kings. Despite the disastrous foreign policy that led to his death at Flodden, his reign is usually regarded as highly successful. Picturesque stories cluster about James's name: remorse for his implication in the death of James III led him to wear a heavy iron chain about his waist; and a mysterious apparition of St James is said to have warned him in Linlithgow church not to journey to the field of Flodden.[1] James is a complex figure, who evokes as mingled a response from modern historians as from contemporary chroniclers. One of these, Adam Abell, praised him for governing his kingdom 'pecebillie' and for his support of the Franciscans, yet also censured certain vices—notably his predisposition to lechery and 'plesour of the flesche'.[2] James's piety is undoubted; so too are his many love-affairs, even after his marriage. His treatment of the Scottish Church has been much criticized, particularly the 'scandalous successive nominations of his brother and then his illegitimate son to the archbishopric of St Andrews in 1497 and 1504'.[3] Yet James was a strong and effective ruler, who attempted to implement a uniform system of justice throughout Scotland, in the Borders and Highlands as well as the Lowlands. One of his most striking traits was a love of chivalry: Adam Abell said that in jousting 'he had few lik him in Scotland', and his court was famed throughout Europe for

> Tryumphand tornayis, iustyng, & knychtly game,
> With all pastyme accordyng for one kyng.
> He wes the glore of princelie gouernyng.[4]

James enjoyed other aristocratic sports, such as hunting and hawking, and was keenly interested in firearms. Yet his pursuit of princely 'glore' led him to live beyond his means. He expended vast sums on

---

[1] R. L. Mackie, *King James IV of Scotland* (Edinburgh, 1958), and N. Macdougall, *James IV* (Edinburgh, 1989).

[2] *The Roit or Quheill of Tyme* (NLS MS 1746), fol. 112a. See also Ch. 2, n. 9.

[3] L. Macfarlane, 'Was the Scottish Church Reformable by 1513?', in *Church, Politics and Society: Scotland 1408–1929*, ed. N. Macdougall (Edinburgh, 1983), 33. Cf. P. I. Kaufman, 'Piety and Proprietary Rights: James IV of Scotland', *Sixteenth Century Journal*, 13 (1982), 83–99.

[4] Lindsay, *Papyngo*, 502–4. On James's 'chivalric magnificence', cf. S. Anglo, *The Great Tournament Roll of Westminster* (Oxford, 1968), i. 9–11.

ships and artillery, as well as on the palaces at Stirling, Linlithgow, and Falkland. He seems to have seen himself as a 'Renaissance prince', and acted like one; yet 'the fortunes at the disposal of Henry VIII, Louis XII or the Medici were not his to command'.[5]

James is commonly regarded as a patron of the arts, and has received credit for the flowering of poetry in his reign.[6] But it is difficult to be sure how great was his interest in literature, or how much encouragement he gave contemporary poets. He was intelligent, and—according to the Spanish envoy, Pedro de Ayala—'well read in the Bible . . . and many Latin and French histories'.[7] But he does not seem to have been, like his great-grandson, James VI, an intellectual or bookish man. He did not emulate Henry VII in founding a royal library and appointing a librarian for its care; no inventory of his books has survived, such as that of the collection belonging to Mary, Queen of Scots.[8] The books whose purchase was recorded in *The Treasurer's Accounts* were chiefly legal and liturgical, and not necessarily bought for his own use; some, like the *Ars moriendi*, were explicitly purchased *pro fratribus de Strivelin*.[9] James was responsible for the introduction of printing to Scotland, but his motives were not to foster the reading of vernacular poetry. The royal patent, dated 1507, speaks rather of printing 'the bukis of our lawis, actis of parliament, croniclis, mes bukis and portuus [missals and breviaries] efter the use of our realme'.[10] The purchase of 'potingary bukis in Inglis' tallies with James's interest in medicine, yet might have had a merely practical purpose, like the buying of some keep-fit manual today. There is one tantalizing clue to his taste in the Exchequer Rolls; this mentions the pledging and redemption of a book belonging to the king, called *Gestorum de Gower*, and has been variously interpreted as either the works of John Gower or a Gawain-romance.[11]

The evidence for James's support of writers is sparse. Two ambitious works were dedicated to him: John Ireland's *The Meroure of Wysdome* (c.1490), and Gavin Douglas's *Palice of Honour* (c.1503).

---

[5] L. Macfarlane, *William Elphinstone and the Kingdom of Scotland 1431–1514* (Aberdeen, 1985), 419.
[6] Cf. A. Cherry, *Princes Poets and Patrons: The Stuarts and Scotland* (Edinburgh, 1987), 22–8.
[7] See G. Gregory Smith, *The Days of James IV* (1890), 54.
[8] Cf. G. Kipling, *The Triumph of Honour* (Leiden, 1977), 31–40; and J. Durkan, 'The Library of Mary, Queen of Scots', in *Mary Stewart: Queen in Three Kingdoms*, ed. M. Lynch (Oxford, 1988), 71–104.
[9] *TA* ii, pp. cxi–cxviii, and 359.
[10] *Register of the Privy Seal of Scotland*, ed. M. Livingstone (Edinburgh, 1908), no. 1546; on the king's motivation, see Macfarlane, *Elphinstone*, 236.
[11] *Exchequer Rolls*, ed. G. Burnett (Edinburgh, 1888), xi. 123; *Gower* is mistakenly read as *Gowane* in *TA* i, p. cclxxviii.

Ireland, a distinguished theologian, became James's chaplain and confessor; Douglas was more richly rewarded by the benefice of St Giles, which was in the king's patronage.[12] *The Treasurer's Accounts* record many payments to minstrels, musicians, and also—between 1490 and 1492—to 'Blind Harry', poet of *The Wallace*; there are rewards for the singing of 'ballats', but not their writing.[13] The Account Books of Henry VII record miscellaneous payments 'for making of balades', 'To a Walsheman for making a ryme', or 'To an Italian a poete';[14] there seems no equivalent in *The Treasurer's Accounts*, but it may be that in this respect, as so often, the Scottish records are neither complete nor sufficiently detailed.

Yet poetry undoubtedly flourished at this court; the number of poets who served in the household has already been noted. These men were not full-time poets; poetry was subordinate to their other duties, as chaplains, clerks, letter-writers, envoys, or notaries. Authorship at this time was—in R. F. Green's words—'very much a sparetime occupation, and its material rewards largely incidental ones'.[15] The Register of the Privy Seal records the granting of a 'pensioun' to Dunbar, but does not explain it.[16] *The Treasurer's Accounts* are similarly reticent, although they are sometimes informative about other recipients of pensions, listed in proximity to Dunbar: Thomas Marshall, described as the chaplain 'that singis for the king and queen in Cambuskenneth'; or David Lindsay, who in 1512 was termed usher to the Prince, the future James V; or Master Walter Ogilvy, who in March 1504 received a special fee 'for to pas to London'.[17] Ogilvy was a learned man, who possessed a copy of Livy, and Valla's version of Homer; his Latin account of the festivities at the wedding of Prince Arthur to Katherine of Aragon is still extant.[18] Yet the *Accounts* are non-informative about other figures of whom one would like to know more; all they tell us of the poet Quintin Shaw is that in 1504 he, like Dunbar, received a yearly pension of £10.[19] Dunbar certainly writes, at times, as if he regarded making poems as his chief occupation;

---

[12] See Introduction to *The Meroure of Wysdome*, ed. C. Macpherson (STS, 1926); and Bawcutt, *Douglas*, 47.
[13] Cf. *Wallace*, i, p. xxviii; for the singing of a ballat, see *TA* i. 184.
[14] See S. Anglo, 'The Court Festivals of Henry VII: A Study Based upon the Account Books of John Heron', *Bulletin of the John Rylands Library*, 43 (1960–1), 12–45.
[15] *Poets and Princepleasers* (Toronto, 1980), 203.
[16] *Register of Privy Seal*, ed. Livingstone, i, no. 563; cf. Baxter, 61.
[17] *TA* ii. 93 and 95, and iii. 327; iv. 441, and ii. 423.
[18] This untitled manuscript (NLS Adv. 33. 2. 24) contains a dedication to Henry VII. On Ogilvy's books, cf. Durkan and Ross, *Early Scottish Libraries*, 134; see also *Memorials of King Henry VII*, ed. James Gairdner (Rolls series, 1858), lxii–lxiii.
[19] *TA* ii. 92, 93, 445.

there may have been some recognition of his poetry in the award of a pension, but it is most likely that he was primarily rewarded for duties similar to those of the other poet-servitors. Some of the extra fees that Dunbar occasionally received from the *bursa regis* were possibly for the writing of ballats. But only one entry can be plausibly explained in this way: the payment of £3. 10s. on 26 June 1508, a date which suggests a connection with the two poems on Bernard Stewart.[20]

James IV was of great importance to Dunbar—as king, personal lord, and source of his livelihood—and he figures, often obliquely, in many poems. But the records, unfortunately, shed little light on the king's response to Dunbar—to what extent he recognized his poetic genius, or valued him for other, more mundane reasons. James was extremely sociable, and played cards, dice, and bowls, with companions of varied character and rank, from John Damian to the earl of Angus—but Dunbar is not recorded in such roles at court. We should not lay too much stress on this absence of external evidence. Dunbar's own poems suggest that his relationship with the king was friendly and intimate—their tone is teasing, mocking, or reproving, and sometimes verges on impertinence. We may attribute this to Dunbar's innate independence of spirit, and also to the toleration of plain speaking that marked the Scottish court—a similar tone is heard in Lindsay's poems addressed to James V. But we should also, I think, connect it with an aspect of James's personality, often noted by historians—his accessibility to people of all sorts, from great lords to the peasants who brought him gifts of cherries and strawberries. A king's personality powerfully affected the style of his court; Henry VII was characterized, in Bacon's phrase, by the 'keeping of distance... towards all'.[21] James's relations with his court were not marked by such 'distance' or aloofness.

One of the chief functions of a court poet was the writing of complimentary verse—eulogies, sometimes of places but more frequently of persons of high rank, on festive occasions or other important moments in their lives or the history of their countries. Only a handful of such poems by Dunbar survives, although he may well have written more. It should be stressed that none displays the gross adulation practised by court historiographers, such as Jean Molinet or Bernard André, who—in *Les Douze Triomphes de Henry VII*—pictured

---

[20] *TA* iv. 127; see Baxter, 181.
[21] Cf. *TA* iv. 126–7, 132–3, and G. Donaldson's estimate in *Scottish Kings* (1973). See also D. Starkey, 'Court History in Perspective', in *The English Court: From the Wars of the Roses to the Civil War*, ed. Starkey (1987), 7–8 and 73.

COURT POEMS: PRAISE AND PETITION

Henry as Hercules.[22] In other respects they are highly characteristic of the kind, adroit and elegant, but—with one exception—undistinguished. They are usually topical, celebrating such events as the wedding of James and Margaret Tudor, or the queen's visit to Aberdeen. Contemporary chronicles that preserve the poem *To London* illustrate the sort of occasion for which such poems were composed, and the context in which they might be delivered. Although there are no firm grounds for attributing it to Dunbar, the poem was certainly written by a Scot. What is interesting is the convivial context—a banquet given by the mayor of London to visiting Scottish envoys, the circumstantial detail, in one account, of the 'Scottysh preyst sytting at oon of the syde tablys', and the reference, in another, to remuneration—the 'Skotte hauyng much money of dyuers lordes for hys Indyting'.[23] On such occasions the poet is speaking on behalf of a group, in this case the Scottish visitors to London. In poems more securely attributed to Dunbar he is also a spokesman, sometimes for the court, sometimes more widely, for 'all this regioun' (K 31. 28) or the whole 'Scottis natioun' (K 36. 29). Again and again the choice of pronouns implies this shared, public voice—*we, us, our*: Queen Margaret is 'Our perle of price, our princes fair and gud' (K 31. 4); and Bernard Stewart is said to have helped 'our naceoun' and to be welcome to all—'to king, queyne, lord, clerk, knight and servatour' (K 35. 26, 7). Such poems do not display private or intimate feeling; indeed when Dunbar does use the first person singular, as in the penultimate stanza of the address to Stewart (K 35), it produces a slight awkwardness, like a clumsy change of gear. These poems voice a communal emotion, and some may have been designed to play a part in public ritual. Their style is appropriately elevated, but lacks individuality. They abound in rhetorical commonplaces, and such figures as apostrophe, *repetitio*, and hyperbole; and they employ long stanzas, either one of eight lines (*ababbcbC*) or rhyme royal.

Dunbar's poem to Bernard Stewart is a well-deserved tribute to a great soldier. We know that the praise lavished on his courage, military skill, and diplomacy was justified. Yet in the poem there are few details of his campaigns, apart from a brief reference to his victories in France, England, Naples, and Lombardy (84–5). We learn more facts from the elaborate title of this 'ballade' concerning, 'Barnard Stewart Lord of Aubigny . . . chamberlane ordinare to the maist hee, maist excellent, and maist Crystyn prince Loys king of France, knyght

---

[22] Cf. N. Dupire, *Jean Molinet: La Vie, les œuvres* (Paris, 1932), 105–6, and Kipling, *Triumph of Honour*, 16–20.

[23] Five copies exist of *To London*, none attributed to Dunbar. See C. Bühler, '*London thow art the Floure of Cytes all*', *RES* 13 (1937), 1–9; Baxter, 87–92; and Mackie, *James IV*, 95–6.

of his ordoure, Capitane of the kepyng of his body'. Dunbar places Stewart in a traditional mould: he is described in superlatives—'Most wyse, most valyand, moste laureat hie victour' (4)—and depicted as the ideal Christian knight, 'The prince of knightheyd and flour of chevalry' (18). This type of noun phrase, implying that the person described was a choice example of the specified virtue, was very common in panegyric. The poem is strikingly repetitious. In addition to the sustained *repetitio* on 'Welcum', there is a remarkable piling-up of near-synonyms, as in the refrain: 'With glorie and honour, lawde and reverence'.

Various eulogistic commonplaces occur. One stanza is wholly devoted to Stewart's fame, which has spread not only through Scotland and France, but 'our all cuntreis undirnethe the sky' (49-56). This a topos of great antiquity, which Curtius named 'the whole earth sings his/your praise'.[24] Another stanza magnifies Stewart by identifying him with great classical heroes, such as Achilles or Hector, and adds to them a British name of great potency—'O vailyeant Arthur in knyghtli vassalage' (59). One interesting passage envisages Stewart's reception by the Scottish parliament:

> Thi cristall helme withe lawry suld be crownyt,
> And in thy hand a branche of olyve greyn;
> The sueird of conquis and of knyghtheid keyn
> Be borne suld highe before the in presence,
> To represent sic man as thou has beyn. (67-71)

There is no record of such a ceremony, and it may be as imaginary as the horoscope that follows. But it is a vivid and symbolic scene.

The last stanza may remind readers of their introduction to the alphabet:

> B in thi name betaknis batalrus,
> A able in feild, R right renoune most hie;
> N nobilnes and A for aunterus,
> R ryall blude; for dughtines is D;
> V valyeantnes, S for strenewite:
> Quhoise knyghtli name so schynyng in clemence
> For wourthines in gold suld writtin be. (89-95)

Such ingenious games with letters were not then considered childish, but often found in serious poetry, such as Chaucer's poem to the Virgin, called an *ABC*, or *carmen secundum ordinem litterarum alphabeti*. It was not uncommon for poets to devise acrostics on their own names

---

[24] It figures in Theodulf's poem to Charlemagne, in *Poetry of the Carolingian Renaissance*, ed. P. Godman (1985), no. 15; cf. Curtius, *European Literature and the Latin Middle Ages*, 159-62.

or those of others: Humfrey Newton, an English contemporary of Dunbar's, introduced his own name and that of his wife Elena into his verses.[25] Acrostics were particularly common in eulogy. Alexander Barclay embedded in his translation of *The Ship of Fools* (*c.*1509) a tribute to James IV; this contains a stanza, beginning 'In prudence pereles is this most comely king', in which the first letters of each line together form the name IACOBVS.[26]

Perhaps the best parallel to Dunbar's practice occurs in Jean Molinet's *Le Trosne d'Honneur*, a tribute to Philip, Duke of Burgundy (died 1467). Towards the end of this long vision, in verse and prose, the dreamer sees nine ladies, nine 'preux', and 'noeuf lettres d'or, qui, coeullies ensembles, faisoient Philippus, propre nom de ceste tres haulte et precieuse fleur de noblesse'.[27] These nine golden letters symbolize appropriate moral virtues, such as 'Prudence', 'Hardiesse', 'Instruction Chevalereuse' and 'Largesse'. Similar acrostics figured in eulogies by other 'Grands Rhétoriqueurs', such as Chastelain and Lemaire.[28] The secondary notion, of inscribing a word in gold, had a factual basis—Dunbar's Widow owned a prayer book, 'With mony lusty letter ellummynit with gold' (K 14. 425). But this too was a late-medieval literary topos. Lydgate, for instance, said that the name of Marcus Manlius ought 'With goldene lettres to been enlumyned'; and when Douglas wished to praise his Twelfth Prologue, he too said it should be 'illumynit' with gold.[29] Dunbar thus brings his poem to a climax with a well-established topic of commendation. Stewart's 'name' is viewed both literally and symbolically, in terms of its constituent letters; gold is an appropriate medium for honouring his high moral worth.

Stewart died on 11 June 1508, shortly after his arrival in Scotland, and Dunbar wrote a second poem, now entitled *Elegy on Bernard Stewart Lord of Aubigny* (K 36). It might better be styled a complaint than an elegy, a term which may rouse unfulfilled expectations as to form and imagery. The poem belongs to a very common medieval genre: the formal lament for a person of great rank or distinction. Hundreds of French examples exist of such *complaintes*, *regretz*, *epitaphes*, and *déplorations*, especially from the fifteenth century; indeed

---

[25] R. H. Robbins, 'Poems of Humfrey Newton, Esq. 1466–1536', *PMLA* 65 (1950), 253.
[26] *The Ship of Fools*, ed. T. H. Jamieson (Edinburgh, 1884), ii. 208, stanza 1572.
[27] *Les Faictz et dictz*, ed. N. Dupire (SATF, 1936–9), i. 46.
[28] For Chastelain's *Rhythmes* on the death of Philip, and Lemaire's *La Couronne margaratique* (1505), see C. Martineau-Génieys, *Le Thème de la mort dans la poésie française de 1450 à 1550* (Paris, 1978), 303–4, 408–9.
[29] *The Fall of Princes*, ed. H. Bergen (EETS, ES 121–4, 1924–7), iv. 371; *Eneados*, Prol. 12. 309–10.

among French literary historians the genre has long had a bad reputation—'royaume du cliché, du topos ... d'une courtisanerie bassement intéressé'.³⁰ Recently it has received more sympathetic attention, notably from Christine Martineau-Génieys, who draws parallels between the increasing elaboration of the *déploration* and that of other forms of funeral art, such as the magnificent tombs for the dukes of Burgundy in Brou and Dijon.³¹ The earliest extant Scottish poem of this kind, the 'playnt' for Margaret, daughter of James I and briefly dauphine of France (died 1445), is directly based on a French work, the anonymous *Complainte pour la mort de madame Marguerite d'Ecosse*.³² But Dunbar's short sombre poem is simpler in structure than the 'playnt' for Margaret, and far removed from the full-blown *déplorations*, such as Molinet's *Trosne d'Honneur*. It has more in common with contemporary English pieces, such as the anonymous lament for Henry VII (died 1509),³³ or with French complaints of an earlier period, such as those by Eustache Deschamps and Christine de Pisan, many of which were *ballades*. Dunbar's poem has a shape somewhat resembling that of the *ballade*: three stanzas with a refrain, followed by an envoi-like fourth stanza.

The two poems on Stewart must have been written close together in time, and have much in common, including stanza form and eulogistic topoi. In this complaint, for instance, Stewart's fame is expressed geographically: 'to the Turkas sey all land did his name dreid' (13). This neatly magnifies his military exploits, implying that even the Turks, then at the zenith of their military power, knew and feared Stewart. His knighthood is repeatedly praised in the refrain: 'Sen he is gon, the flour of chevelrie'. It is often said that this deliberately echoes a line in Deschamps' lament for another great soldier, Bertrand du Guesclin:

> Plourez, plourez flour de chevalerie.³⁴

But it was then so common, among both French and English writers, to call a knight the flower of chivalry that it is impossible to say where

---

³⁰ C. Thiry, 'De la mort marâtre à la mort vaincue', in *Death in the Middle Ages*, ed. H. Braet and W. Verbeke (Louvain, 1983), 239.
³¹ *Le Thème de la mort*, 295–437.
³² Cf. Bawcutt, 'A Medieval Scottish Elegy and its French Original', *SLJ* 15, no. 1 (1988), 5–13.
³³ See G. V. Scammell and H. L. Rogers, 'An Elegy on Henry VII', *RES*, NS 8 (1957), 167–70.
³⁴ *Oeuvres complètes de Eustache Deschamps*, ed. Q. de Saint-Hilaire and G. Raynaud (SATF, Paris, 1878–1903), ii. 27–8; see C. Brookhouse, 'Deschamps and Dunbar: Two Elegies', *SSL* 7 (1969–70), 123; Helena Shire, *The Thrissil, the Rois, and the Flour-de-Lys* (Cambridge, 1962), 25–6; Ross, 152–3.

Dunbar first learnt the phrase.³⁵ It is more important to be aware that Dunbar's refrain recalls his own earlier commendation of the living Bernard Stewart as 'The prince of knightheyd and flour of chevalry' (K 35. 18). The first half of this line is also reused in the later poem: 'The prince of knychtheid, nobill and chevilrous' (19). Another eulogistic phrase similarly occurs, remarkably unchanged, in both poems:

> Welcum, in armis moste aunterous and able.   (K 35. 42)

and

> In deid of armes most anterous and abill.   (K 36. 4)

In complaint eulogy mingles with exhortations to express grief outwardly, in tears, sighs, and mourning garments:

> Illuster Lodovick, of France most Cristin king,
> Thow may complain with sighis lamentable
> The death of Bernard Stewart, nobill and ding,
>   .   .   .   .
> For him, allace, now may thow weir the sabill.   (1–3, 7)

Molinet, in his lament for Philip of Burgundy, similarly exhorts the French monarch, but his tone becomes far more hyperbolical:

> Pleure, pleure, tres noble roy franchois
>   .   .   .   .
> O Bourguignons, plourés par millions . . .³⁶

French poets commonly urged mourners to put on black garments; but Dunbar's figurative use of *sabill*, the heraldic term for black, seems to have been peculiar to users of English; indeed the best parallel to Dunbar's phrasing here is a line in Chaucer's *Complaint of Mars*, 284: 'Now have ye cause to clothe yow in sable'.³⁷ It was also common to hurl curses and execrations at Death, some poets devoting many stanzas to the topic; Dunbar's single line, 'O duilfull death, O dragon dolorous!', is extremely restrained.

One consolatory topic, the immortality of the subject's fame, often figures in Renaissance elegies, but is absent from Dunbar's poem. Instead it has a highly medieval ingredient, a final 'orisoun' for Stewart's soul:

> Pray now for him all that him loveit heir,
> And for his saull mak intercessioun
> Unto the Lord that hes him bocht so deir. . . . .   (25–7)

---

³⁵ For Chaucer's use, cf. *Knight's Tale*, I. 982; see also *OED*, *chivalry*, sense 7.
³⁶ *Faictz et dictz*, i. 40–1.
³⁷ See *OED*, *Sable*, sb. 2.

Midway through the lament for Henry VII his subjects are exhorted similarly:

> To god with our prayers make we exclamacion
> His soule forto guyde to his supernall toure. (27–8)

Dunbar's placing of the prayer at the poem's end seems more traditional. Christine de Pisan's *ballade* on the death of Philip the Bold (1404) concludes with an envoi: 'Princes royaulx, priez par bon talent / Pour le bon duc . . .'; and Chastelain's epitaph for Pierre de Brézé (1465) also ends with a prayer:

> Priez pour luy, tout peuple seculier;
> Noble et non noble et tout clerc regulier . . .[38]

Such passages remind us that these poems were not simply consolatory but had a very practical function. Prayers for the dead were considered efficacious in lessening the pains of those in Purgatory.

Verses of this kind sometimes functioned as epitaphs, and were exhibited on or near the tomb. Such a destination was explicitly envisaged for the poem on Henry VII—'aboute his herse / let this be grauyd for endeles memorie'. The French *Complainte* for the dauphine Margaret is said to have been placed upon her tomb.[39] But this was not necessarily the purpose of Dunbar's poem. Addressed to Louis XII, its tone is one of sympathetic commiseration for the loss of a great public servant. Stewart came to Scotland as an envoy, and this poem might be seen as an attempt to preserve good relations between France and Scotland, a poetic equivalent of the formal diplomatic letters sent between the two countries. Dunbar is punctilious in selecting the correct title for Louis in his opening line, 'Illuster Lodovick, of France most Cristin king'. In late medieval Europe the style 'le roi trés chrétien' was reserved solely for the king of France.[40] This poem does not express Dunbar's private grief, but speaks on behalf of the 'Scottis natioun' (29).

Among the various complimentary poems addressed to Margaret Tudor, the one most likely to be Dunbar's is *Gladethe, thoue queyne of Scottis regioun* (K 31).[41] It is a fairly conventional panegyric, whose most serious lines refer to national hopes for an heir to the throne:

---

[38] *Ballades, Rondeaux and Virelais*, ed. K. Varty (Leicester, 1965), no. 117; for Chastelain's epitaph, see Martineau-Génieys, *Thème de la mort*, 325.
[39] See Bawcutt, 'A Medieval Scottish Elegy', 6. Cf. a French epitaph for Richard, Duke of York, discussed by R. F. Green, *Studies in Bibliography*, 41 (1988), 218–24. See also D. Gray, *Themes and Images*, 202ff.
[40] Adam Loutfut's heraldic treatise (Harleian MS 6149, fol. 36b), dated 1494, notes that the pope addressed no other ruler in this way.
[41] See Baxter, 222–4; Dunbar's authorship of K 24 and K 49 is unlikely.

> Gret Gode us graunt that we have long desirit—
> A plaunt to spring of thi successioun. (29–30)

The 'successioun' is still of concern to hereditary monarchies, and in an age of high infant mortality must have caused genuine anxiety. None of Margaret's children by her first husband survived infancy, apart from the future James V. Sir Richard Maitland, in a poem on Mary, Queen of Scots, prayed similarly that God would 'send our Princes gud successioun'.[42] Dunbar's poem is likely to pre-date February 1507, when Margaret's first child was born. The thought is delicately expressed, in terms of the imagery first applied to Margaret herself, who is both 'our roys riale' (6) and 'Roys red and quhit, resplendent of colour' (25). This clearly alludes to the well-known Tudor badge. Dunbar's references to Margaret's youth, such as 'O ȝing and tendir flour' (27), are not empty phrases. She was thirteen when she married James, and seventeen when her first child was born. Margaret has been harshly treated by historians, ridiculed for her apparent lack of beauty, and termed a 'sullen child' by one biographer for writing a homesick letter to her father shortly after arrival in Scotland.[43]

No trace of human imperfection, however, appears in Dunbar's image of the queen; she is a paragon of beauty and wisdom, Nature's masterpiece:

> Of thi fair fegour Natur micht rejois
> That so the kervit withe all hir cur and slicht;[44]
> Scho has the maid this verray wairldis chois. (17–19)

Chaucer used the same hyperbole to suggest the extreme beauty of heroines such as Virginia and Blanche;[45] and the female eagle, in *The Parliament of Fowls*, is likewise the goodliest of Nature's 'werkes'—

> Nature hireself hadde blysse
> To loke on hire, and ofte hire bek to kysse. (377–8)

But the topos long antedated Chaucer, and was popular with many medieval poets.[46]

The most interesting feature of this poem is the pun on Margaret's name (Latin *margarita*). She is addressed both as 'Our perle of price' (4) and

---

[42] *Maitland Folio*, no. xvi.
[43] Agnes Strickland, *Lives of the Queens of Scotland*, i (1850), 67; cf. P. Hill Buchanan, *Margaret Tudor Queen of Scots* (Edinburgh, 1985), 34–6.
[44] Editors erroneously read *curiys slicht*.
[45] *Physician's Tale*, VI. 9–28; *Book of the Duchess*, 908–12.
[46] Cf. E. C. Knowlton, 'Nature in Old French', *MP* 20 (1922–3), 309–12.

COURT POEMS: PRAISE AND PETITION

> O precius Mergreit, plesand cleir and quhit,
> Moir blitht and bricht na is the beriall schene,
> Moir deir na is the diamaunt of delit,
> Moir semly na is the sapheir one to seyne,
> Moir gudely eik na is the emerant greyne,
> Moir riche na is the ruby of renowne,
> Fair gem of joy, Mergreit, of the I meyne:
> Gladethe, thoue queyne of Scottis regioun.   (33–40)

In 1502 Walter Ogilvy likewise called the princess a *margareta preciosissima*, but such word-play was almost inevitable in compliments to women with this name. Skelton praised Margaret Tilney as 'Margarite, / Perle orient, lodesterre of lyght, /Moche relucent'; and Lindsay, like Dunbar, called Queen Margaret 'that peirle preclare'. Later Scottish poets also employed the image in poems about girls named Margaret.[47] The medieval symbolism of the pearl owed its diffusion to the cult of St Margaret of Antioch, whose legend begins: 'Margaret is said of a precious gem . . .'[48] But it was much influenced by the Scriptural parable of the *pretiosa margarita* (Matthew 13; 46), or pearl of great price, to which Dunbar clearly alludes. The queen's name provides an excuse for a striking display of lapidary symbolism: the particular 'virtues' of the stones are here less significant than their beauty, brightness, and high value, and their part in a decorative metrical scheme. Dunbar's alliterative coupling of epithets with gems is traditional, and has many parallels: in *Annot and John* the lady is likewise 'ase beryl so bryht', 'ase saphyr in seluer semly on syht', and 'ase diamaund the dere'; a fifteenth-century compliment to a woman piles up very similar jewels and epithets.[49] The pell-mell quality of these poems, however, contrasts with the neatness of this one. The stanza is governed by the 'outdoing topos';[50] the pearl—both in beauty and virtue—transcends other jewels, even the ruby. Dunbar's compliment to the queen thus aptly recalls another Scriptural passage, in praise of the virtuous woman, whose price is 'above rubies' (Proverbs 31: 10).

Blyth Aberdeane, thow beriall of all tounis (K 48) is a highly topical poem. James IV visited Aberdeen frequently, on pilgrimage to St Duthac's shrine at Tain and in connection with the justice ayres;[51] but Queen Margaret's first visit did not occur until May 1511, and this is

---

[47] See *Garland of Laurel*, 947–50; *Papyngo*, 547; Montgomerie, *Poems*, 214–15; Drummond, *Poetical Works*, ed. L. E. Kastner (STS, 1913), ii. 184. For Ogilvy, see n. 18 above.
[48] Caxton, *Golden Legend*, ed. F. S. Ellis (n.d.), iv. 66.
[49] *Harley Lyrics*, ed. G. L. Brook (Manchester, 1954), no. 3; *SL*, no. 205.
[50] See Ch. 1, n. 59.
[51] Macfarlane, *Elphinstone*, 272–3.

the event which the poem celebrates. The burgh records mention advance preparations, the cleansing of the streets, the removal of swine, and the decorating of the forestairs with 'arres werk';[52] but Dunbar provides the sole eyewitness account of the processions, music, and firing of 'artel3ie', devised to welcome the queen. Such royal entries were common all over Europe, and were spectacular and highly ritualized entertainments. The pattern of events was partly determined by precedent. When Dunbar refers to the pall 'of velves cramase', carried above the queen's head, 'as the custome hes bein' (13–14), the latter phrase is not otiose but a compliment to the burgesses on their observance of tradition. When a later queen, Mary of Guise, visited Aberdeen, the citizens were concerned that she should be entertained 'as the ald ws [use] hes bene within the burght at the first cuming of princis'.[53] The records of later Scottish royal entries regularly refer to the velvet canopy, borne above the sovereign's head; they tell us, in words similar to Dunbar's, that 'at thair croce aboundantlie rane wyne' (58).[54] The very fixity of the pattern helps to explain obscurities in Dunbar's poem. He refers to a representation of Robert Bruce, 'rydand under croun' (34); but the subject of the next pageant is not known, since there is a lacuna at line 37. Almost certainly it was a family tree of Scottish kings, surmounted with an image of James IV, 'with branches new and greine' (38). Such genealogical plants and trees were fashionable, and figured in later Scottish entries. At the 1590 entry of James VI and Anne of Denmark into Edinburgh one spectator writes of seeing 'the kingis grace genelageie in the forme of a trie from the Bruce till himselff, quhair ane bairne at the root of the trie maid ane Oresoun in latyne discryvand the haill bairnes and brainches'.[55]

Such entertainments were intended to demonstrate loyalty and deference, as Dunbar notes: 'The legeis all did to thair lady loutt' (52). But they were also a manifestation of civic dignity and wealth. There is a clear sign of rivalry with other cities in the Aberdeen burgesses' decision 'to ressaue oure souerane lady the queyne als honorablie as ony burgh of Scotland, except Edinburgh allanerlie ... for the honour of the towne'.[56] The custom of the 'propyne' called for lavish expenditure—

> Ane riche present thai did till hir propyne,
> Ane costlie coup that large thing wald contene,
> Coverit and full of cun3eitt gold rycht fyne. (61–3)

It was common to present distinguished visitors with gifts: sometimes of wine and other luxuries, such as wax and spices, sometimes, as

---

[52] See Mill, 158.   [53] Ibid. 159.   [54] Ibid. 194 and 204.
[55] Ibid. 204.   [56] Ibid. 158.

here, with a goblet filled with coins.[57] But there seems to have been an ulterior motive in the 'propyne'—generosity was intended to provoke a return of some kind.

Blyth Aberdeane has an interesting structure, consisting of two apostrophes. The first, which occupies most of the poem, is addressed to the city itself. Dunbar begins with stock eulogistic figures—'beriall of all tounis' and 'lamp of bewtie'—and praises Aberdeen for its lavish hospitality and 'gud cheir'. The central section is largely devoted to describing the pageantry; yet the refrain—'Be blyth and blisfull, burgh of Aberdein'—and other direct addresses to Aberdeen—'And syne *thow* gart the orient kingis thrie . . .' (25)—remind us that this is not wholly straightforward third-person narrative. Throughout this part of the poem Margaret herself is spoken of in the third person. Only in the last stanza is she addressed directly:

> O potent princes, pleasant and preclair,
> Great caus thow hes to thank this nobill toun
> That for to do the honnour did not spair
> Thair geir, riches, substance and persoun,
> . . . .
> Thairfoir sa lang as quein thou beiris croun,
> Be thankfull to this burcht of Aberdein. (65ff.)

This second apostrophe is less a compliment than a piece of counsel. The queen is urged to take note of the citizens' generosity, and to act fittingly. She is twice recommended to thank the town, in line 66 and the significantly altered refrain—'Be thankfull to this burcht of Aberdein'. Royal favour was certainly important to a town's prosperity, but how 'potent' the queen was in this respect is unknown.

This twofold structure, in which Dunbar addresses first the citizens and then the queen, presumably reflects the poem's occasion. Since it mentions the conclusion of the pageantry and the queen's arrival at her 'ludgeing' (59), it cannot have been delivered in the midst of the proceedings—unlike the verses, addressed, on a later occasion, to Mary, Queen of Scots, by a small boy dressed as an angel.[58] Yet its purpose does not seem primarily commemorative—it does not give a straight historical account of the events, like Lydgate's poem on Henry VI's entry into London (1432), or John Burel's verses on Anne of Denmark's reception by Edinburgh (1590).[59] *Blyth Aberdeane* surveys the day's events from a point seemingly close in time; it suggests an occasion on which poet, queen, and leading citizens were together,

---

[57] James II, visiting Aberdeen in 1448, received two tuns of Gascony wine. See *DOST* s.v. *propine*, n.
[58] Mill, 190.
[59] Lydgate, *Minor Poems II*, ed. H. N. MacCracken (EETS, os 192, 1961), no. 32; for an extract from Burel's poem, see Mill, 201–2.

perhaps at an evening banquet after the pageantry had ended. If so, the poem may have been written in haste, and this perhaps accounts for its curious slackness, verbally and metrically, despite occasional vivid touches, like the procession of maidens, with embroidered white hats and 'hair detressit, as threidis of gold did hing' (43). Slapdash repetitions occur: the repeated use of 'Gryt was' (15, 50, 57) has no rhetorical point, and the proximity of 'rycht bravelie' and 'rycht sweitlie' (44–5) seems careless. Some of the stylistic weaknesses might be attributed to corruption in transmission; the solitary witness, Reidpeth, has several lacunae in the text. But the best explanation is that this poem was made rapidly, for a convivial occasion and for an audience judged to be undemanding.

The Thrissill and the Rois (K 50) is an arresting title, but it is not Dunbar's invention. It was coined by Allan Ramsay, who was the first to print the poem, in his *Ever Green* (1724). Although a more apt title is difficult to find, it none the less gives greater prominence to the dynastic alliance between the Thistle and Rose than Dunbar himself does. In the eighteenth century the poem was very popular, and often included in anthologies, one of which had the revealing title, *The Union: Or Select Scots and English Poems* (1753). *The Thrissill and the Rois* was then 'esteemed the most excellent' of Dunbar's poems, both for its smoothness of style and versification and because its occasion was 'an event of great political importance . . . productive of the union of the crowns, the union of the kingdoms, and the cause of the protestant succession'.[60] In the twentieth century, however, some critics, particularly those with nationalist beliefs, have been unimpressed by either style or subject—one writes, 'the thing is forced, contrived . . . spurious'.[61] But this does the poem an injustice. Dunbar undoubtedly celebrates the marriage of James and Margaret, but this, although a leading theme, is not the only one. Despite its short span—fewer than 200 lines—*The Thrissill and the Rois* has many strands, and a complexity that is masked by its elegant style. Structurally, it is a dream-vision, like Chaucer's *Parliament of Fowls*, and it also has elements of the *reverdie*, or poem in celebration of May. It partakes of several genres, and might be regarded both as a kind of epithalamium (like later poems honouring Mary, Queen of Scots' marriages[62]) and as a miniature *speculum principis*. Bannatyne placed it among his

---

[60] Sir Egerton Brydges, *Restituta; Or Titles, Extracts and Characters of Old Books in English Literature Revived* (1814–16), ii. 508.
[61] Scott, 48.
[62] Mary's marriage to the dauphin Francis was celebrated in a Latin epithalamium by Buchanan, and a Scots poem by Sir Richard Maitland (*Quarto*, no. vi); her marriage to Darnley was the subject of Latin verses by Thomas Craig (1565).

COURT POEMS: PRAISE AND PETITION

'fabillis wyse and sapient', immediately after Henryson's *The Lion and the Mouse*. Dunbar's poem contains moralized creatures that might well have stepped out of a beast fable; but it is also a fable in a further sense, a fictitious story with an underlying 'sentence', and deftly employs a remarkable repertoire of symbolic images.

A royal wedding is usually an occasion for rejoicing and a theme for compliment. The poem thus begins and ends by celebrating the Rose. At its beginning the personified month of May appears to the sleeping poet, and recalls his promise:

> For to discryve the Ros of most plesance. (39)

This is presented, initially, as part of a wider 'observance' of May customs, and May chides the dreamer for his sloth:

> Slugird, scho said, Awalk annone for schame,
> And in my honour sum thing thow go wryt;
> The lork hes done the mirry day proclame
> To rais up luvaris with confort and delyt . . . (22–5)

At this stage the precise significance of the Rose is not defined. It might well be an actual flower, like the daisy that Chaucer wished to observe, in the Prologue to *The Legend of Good Women*. Yet the poet, although not explicitly a lover, is twice associated somewhat vaguely with 'luvaris', and the scene recalls the spring opening of *The Romaunt of the Rose*, the archetypal medieval dream, in which a poet speaks of his beloved as one who should be 'cleped rose of every wight'. But in the early sixteenth century few could fail to be aware of the political symbolism of the Rose, and specifically the parti-coloured Rose, adopted by Henry VII, Margaret's father, as the emblem of the Tudors. Many contemporary English poems and songs made play with this imagery, and Skelton began a complimentary piece, addressed to Henry VIII, 'The rose both white and rede/In one rose now doth grow'.[63] The same figure was often applied to Margaret in Scottish poems. At the opening of *The Thrissill and the Rois* Dunbar hints at such a compliment to the young princess, but does not actually deliver it until the poem's climax.

This last section is largely devoted to the coronation of the Rose by Nature:

> A coistly croun with clarefeid stonis brycht
> This cumly quene did on hir heid inclois. (155–6)

Thereupon she is saluted by many birds, first singly, and then in unison:

---

[63] *Poems*, ed. Scattergood, no. ix. See also Greene, *Carols*, nos. 290, 294, and 295; and poem F 8 in J. Stevens, *Music and Poetry in the Early Tudor Court* (1961; 1979), 355.

> The merle scho sang, Haill Rois of most delyt,
> Haill of all flouris quene and soverane;
> The lark scho song, Haill Rois both reid and quhyt,
> Most plesand flour of michty cullouris twane;
> . . . .
> The commoun voce uprais of birdis small
> Apone this wys: O blissit be the hour
> That thow wes chosin to be our principall . . . (169–72; 176–8)

Dunbar may have had in mind the queen's actual coronation: according to the herald, Young, she wore a crown at the wedding, although Leslie said that she was not crowned until a later ceremony.[64] But Nature's action is accompanied by a speech that suggests a more exalted precedent. Nature praises the Rose's purity, 'But ony spot or macull doing spring', and continues:

> Cum, blowme of joy, with jemis to be cround,
> For our the laif thy bewty is renownd. (153–4)

These words directly echo two famous verses, addressed to the Bride in the Song of Songs (4: 7–8): *Tota pulchra es, amica mea, et macula non est in te. Veni de Libano, sponsa mea, veni; coronaberis.* In the Middle Ages these words were traditionally applied to the Virgin Mary; they were often quoted in poems and hymns written in her honour, including Dunbar's *Ballat of Our Lady*, which styles her 'moder and maide but makle' (22).[65] This Scriptural passage came to be particularly associated with the Assumption and Coronation of the Virgin—the York play of the Assumption, for instance, contains musical settings of texts such as *Veni de Libano*.[66] For Nature to address such words to one who was newly both a bride and a queen is evidently apt, if hyperbolical. Yet the fusion of religious and political imagery is more than just compliment; it implies that the Virgin should be the model for earthly queens.

The centre of Dunbar's poem, however, is occupied not by Margaret but by James—who is also crowned by Nature, in triple heraldic manifestation, as Lion, Eagle, and Thistle. The Lion is an ancient symbol of sovereignty, 'king of beistis' (103) in myth, fable, and folklore. But Dunbar unmistakably alludes to James by describing the key features of the Scottish royal arms, the rampant lion (*gules* upon *or*), within a border of fleur-de-lys:

> This awfull beist full terrible wes of cheir,
> . . . .
> Reid of his cullour as is the ruby glance:

---

[64] Young's description is printed in J. Leland, *De Rebus Britannicis Collectanea* (1774), iv. 291–4; see also Leslie, *History of Scotland* (Bannatyne Club, Edinburgh, 1830), 73.

[65] Cf. Greene, *Carols*, nos. 138 and 262, and *CB XV*, no. 37.

[66] *The York Plays*, ed. R. Beadle (1982), no. xlv. Cf. R. Muir Wright, 'The Iconography of the Coronation of the Virgin', *Cosmos*, 2 (1986), 53–82.

COURT POEMS: PRAISE AND PETITION

> On feild of gold he stude full mychtely
> With flour delycis sirculit lustely. (92ff.)

The Eagle appears, equally traditionally, as 'king of fowlis' (120), although its chief heraldic association was not with the Scottish monarch but with the German emperor. In Dunbar's trio the Eagle (with one stanza) has far less prominence than the Lion and the Thistle, which are allotted, respectively, five and two stanzas. In such a symmetrically patterned poem the bird kingdom had to be represented; the Eagle also serves as a focus for the many references to birds—their song accompanies the poem's opening, and wakes the dreamer at its end. The Thistle is today such a familiar symbol of all things Scottish that it is easy to forget how novel was its use by Dunbar. The legend that it was adopted as a national emblem early in the Middle Ages because Danish invaders trod upon thistles and revealed their presence by shrieks of pain is surprisingly recent; it belongs to the nineteenth century.[67] The emblematic Scottish thistle first occurred in the reign of James III, on certain silver coins; it only became common in the reign of James IV. James IV's Great Signet bore a rampant lion, surrounded by a collar of thistles, and decorative thistles occur in the surviving documents associated with his marriage, such as the contract, illuminated by Thomas Galbraith.[68] But Dunbar seems to have been the first Scot to put this largely visual symbol to literary use; what today may appear hackneyed was in his own time both topical and innovative. This section of the poem is decorative, ritualized, and highly eulogistic. All three images are handsome and 'awfull' (awe-inspiring) icons of royal power. But compliment is intertwined with instruction: Nature admonishes the kings as well as crowning them.

The personified figure of Nature has an important role in *The Thrissill and the Rois*—even more than in the two other poems where she is the focus for a similar cluster of ideas and images. As in *The Merle and the Nychtingall* (K 16) and *The Goldyn Targe* (K 10), she is a queen, and the companion of May, Flora, and Venus (or 'lufe'); as in *The Goldyn Targe*, she is rapturously saluted by the birds. In *The Goldyn Targe* she enamels the fields with flowers (251), and her most striking act is to present a many-coloured gown to May (88–90); May is clad in a similar 'weid' in *The Thrissill and the Rois*—

> In brycht atteir of flouris forgit new,
> Hevinly of color, quhyt, reid, broun and blew. (18–19)

---

[67] See J. H. Dickson and A. Walker, 'What is the Scottish Thistle?', *Journal of Glasgow Natural History Society*, 20 (1981), 1–21.

[68] For fuller documentation, see Bawcutt, 'Dunbar's Use of the Symbolic Lion and Thistle', *Cosmos*, 2 (1986), 83–95.

Only in *The Thrissill and the Rois*, however, does Dunbar give Nature a voice, and a voice of great authority—she is allotted the most thoughtful passages in the poem. There is nothing very original or recondite about Dunbar's ideas: throughout the Middle Ages Nature was a potent but ambiguous concept for philosophers, and a popular personification in poets. She plays a brief, decorative role in many medieval poems—few descriptions of a spring landscape fail to refer to her tapestries, painting, or embroidery.[69] One of the ultimate sources for Dunbar's conception of Nature, I think, was the famous passage in Alain de Lille's *Planctus Naturae* that stirred the imagination of many poets, including Chaucer and Spenser.[70] But two poems that Dunbar definitely knew were Chaucer's *Parliament of Fowls* and Holland's *Howlat*; their depiction of Nature as goddess and queen, as a kindly but authoritative figure presiding over an assembly of birds, has much in common with Dunbar's.

In *The Thrissill and the Rois* three aspects of Nature are stressed. First, she is explicitly the 'makar', or creator, of all living things— bird, beast, and flower; this is implicit also in the beautiful spring-setting. Such a view was a long-established commonplace. *Natura* is *princeps et creatrix* in Statius, and *genetrix rerum* in Alain de Lille; and the image of Nature busily working at her forge is familiar, not only from the text of *Le Roman de la Rose* but from its illustrations.[71] Dunbar does not say here, as does Chaucer, that Nature in her creative power is but 'the vicaire of th'almighty Lord';[72] but elsewhere, in *The Merle and the Nychtingall* (53), he stresses that God 'of Natur ... wirker wes and king'. More prominent in this poem is the ultimately Aristotelian notion of Nature as the principle of order in the sublunary world.[73] Nature is here ruler and lawgiver. She controls the sequence of the months (1–3), and other aspects of the weather:

> Dame Nature gaif ane inhibitioun thair
> To fers Neptunus and Eolus the bawld
> Nocht to perturb the wattir nor the air. (64–6)

She is conceived as a feudal magnate, who holds a court, rather like the Lion's parliament in Henryson's *Fables*, to which her subjects are summoned to do homage:

---

[69] See E. C. Knowlton, 'Nature in Old French', 309ff., and 'Nature in Middle English', *JEGP* 20 (1921), 186–207.

[70] This work was still popular in the 15th century; see G. Raynaud de Lage, *Alain de Lille: Poète du XIIe siècle* (Montreal, 1951).

[71] Cf. E. C. Knowlton, 'The Goddess Nature in Early Periods', *JEGP* 19 (1920), 214ff.; and J. A. W. Bennett, *The Parlement of Foules* (Oxford, 1957), 194–212 (for illustrations, 204n.).

[72] *Parliament of Fowls*, 379.

[73] Cf. G. Economou, *The Goddess Natura in Medieval Literature* (1971), 10.

COURT POEMS: PRAISE AND PETITION

> Scho ordand eik that every bird and beist
> Befoir hir hienes suld annone compeir,
> And every flour of vertew, most and leist,
> And every herb be feild, fer and neir,
> As thay had wont in May fro ȝeir to ȝeir,
> To hir thair makar to mak obediens,
> Full law inclynnand with all dew reverens. (71–7)

Much of this phrasing has a legal ring: *compeir* (which Henryson uses similarly) means 'to appear, especially in a court of justice, or before a person of authority'; and *mak obediens* means 'to do ceremonial homage to one's superior, particularly the king'. *Inhibitioun*, 'formal prohibition', also occurs chiefly in legal contexts. Neptune and Aeolus are viewed as potential malefactors, or disturbers of the peace. Nature represents, in part, the orderly recurrence of things. The phrase 'fro ȝeir to ȝeir' is no more superfluous here than in *The Parliament of Fowls*, where the birds assembled before Nature, 'As they were woned alwey fro yer to yeere' (321), and later sang her praise—'As yer by yer was alwey hir usaunce' (674).

Nature's most important role in this poem, however, is as an educator; Dunbar says, almost as explicitly as Wordsworth, 'Let nature be your teacher!' In *The Merle and the Nychtingall* Nature 'taucht' Flora to cover the earth with flowers. Here, speaking as the Adviser of Princes, she gives instruction in good government. She addresses those whose position of power within a kingdom parallels her own position in the world. The Lion inclines in reverence before her (90), along with other creatures; but these in turn fall down before the Lion's feet, and make him 'homege and fewte' (117). The Rose too is called 'Naturis suffragene' (173). *The Thrissill and the Rois* is an intensely feudal poem, celebrating hierarchy, rank, and degree. The animal world, which contains 'All kynd of beistis in to thair degre' (114), is ruled by the animal which is 'gretast of degre' (87). Sometimes these social differences take on a moral significance; in the plant kingdom, for instance, the 'wyld weid full of churlichenes' is opposed to the lily's 'nobilnes' (139–40). The poem embodies a view of the world as both orderly and pervaded by symbolic correspondences. It is no accident that bird-song is compared to 'the blisfull soun of cherarchy' (57), the music of the three hierarchies, or nine orders of angels. Cosmic harmony was sometimes represented, in medieval art, by celestial music-making.[74] In this poem Dunbar repeatedly draws such analogies not only between birds and angels, but between

---

[74] Poets often vaguely compared the song of birds to that of angels—cf. *Parliament of Fowls*, 91—but *cherarchy* is a learned and technical term.

beasts and flowers, and humans; and, above all, between the harmonious processes of nature and the well-governed kingdom.

Sir Gilbert Haye, in *The Governance of Princes*, says that 'justice is the fairest vertu that is in a prince'.[75] The king was traditionally regarded as the fount of justice, and Nature's speeches to the Lion and Eagle are wholly orthodox in their concern with fairness and impartiality in the administration of the law:

> Exerce justice with mercy and conscience,
> And lat no small beist suffir skaith na skornis
> Of greit beistis that bene of moir piscence;
> Do law elyk to aipis and unicornis,
> And lat no bowgle with his busteous hornis
> The meik pluch ox oppress for all his pryd,
> Bot in the 30k go peciable him besyd. (106–12)

Fifteenth-century Scottish kings were fully aware both of the ideal of justice and the practical difficulties of its implementation. Historians have noted James I's 'constant pre-occupation with law, justice, and the preservation of order'.[76] The same concern is voiced in numerous articles of James IV's parliament in March 1504: they complain of 'great abusioune of justice', and ordain that 'all our soverane lordis lieges . . . and in speceale all the Ilis be reulit be our soverane lordis awne lawis and the commoun lawis of the realme and be nain other lawis'.[77] Nature's exhortation of the Eagle—'And mak a law for wycht fowlis and for wrennis' (124)—puts similar stress on '*a* law', one law, for all alike.

Such oppositions, between 'greit beistis' and small, or between 'wycht fowlis' and weak wrens, are easily transposed into the rich and poor folk, so often mentioned in the Scottish statutes. It is debatable, however, whether we should invariably seek a precise class symbolism in the many different creatures whom Dunbar mentions. It is plausible that the lines referring to the plough ox and the 'bowgle' (ferocious wild ox) desiderate the peaceful coexistence of Lowlander and Highlander; there existed a long Scottish tradition of contrasting the 'domesticated' Lowlanders with the 'wild' Highlanders.[78] But the significance sometimes appears moral rather than social. Dunbar's coupling of 'aipis and unicornis' is more than a fantastic 'flight of imagination'. The unicorn, in medieval iconography, often figured as the virtuous anti-type of the ape: the unicorn commonly symbolized

---

[75] *Gilbert of the Haye's Prose Manuscript*, ed. J. H. Stevenson (STS, 1914), ii. 145.
[76] R. Nicholson, *Scotland: The Later Middle Ages* (Edinburgh, 1974), 309.
[77] *Acts of the Parliaments of Scotland*, ii. 244.
[78] Cf. John Major, in *Scottish Historical Documents*, ed. G. Donaldson (Edinburgh, 1970), 101–2; and Nicholson, op. cit., 206. See below, 256.

virginity or chastity; but the ape was proverbially lecherous, and signified carnality.[79] The distinction resembles that between the 'herb of vertew' and 'herb without vertew' (135–6), in the plant kingdom.

How far does Dunbar differentiate between Lion, Eagle, and Thistle? Critics are by no means agreed on their significance. Scott thought that they represented James in his triple role as head of government, lawgiver, and war-leader. For Spearing, on the other hand, Lion, Eagle, and Thistle symbolize royal mercy, liberality, and 'power and fidelity'.[80] *The Thrissill and the Rois* is a poem, not a treatise, and its symbolism is neither systematic nor clear-cut. Sometimes Dunbar is highly explicit, sometimes he is more veiled. But he usually gives readers clues that enable them to choose the most relevant of the many, often conflicting, *significationes* that animals and plants then possessed.

Today we are most aware of the lion as a type of courage and ferocity (Dunbar alludes to this in lines 89–91). But there was another long-standing belief, recorded in the bestiaries but dating from Pliny and Martial, that the lion possessed such magnanimity that it would spare those who prostrated themselves before it. Dunbar tells us that the Lion's subjects fell down at his feet:

> And he did thame ressaif with princely laitis,
> Quhois noble yre is *parcere prostratis*   (118–19)

Dunbar is half-paraphrasing, half-quoting the first line of a medieval Latin distich, a sententious maxim that was then very well known: *Parcere prostratis scit nobilis ira leonis*. It was often placed in the mouths of suppliants, addressing kings or powerful magnates, and combined flattery with moral exhortation.[81] It was associated with one particular virtue, held to distinguish the good ruler from the tyrant: clemency. This is the aspect of kingship that the Lion principally symbolizes— justice tempered by mercy. Dunbar's lines read like a compressed version of an incident in Henryson's *Trial of the Fox*; when the Lion calls a parliament, all beasts bow before him in feudal submission, 'flatlingis to his feit'. The Lion proclaims, in response, that he is 'merciabill' and injures none who are 'prostrait' before him (929–30). Submission in homage blends with the other image of fearful and prostrate animals. The Eagle does not, I think, symbolize royal liberality. Although this was indeed one of its attributes, there is no pointer to this interpretation here, such as occurs in another poem

---

[79] See further, H. W. Janson, *Apes and Ape Lore* (1952), 114ff. and 139–40.

[80] Scott, 50; A. C. Spearing, *Medieval to Renaissance in English Poetry* (Cambridge, 1985), 210.

[81] See Bawcutt, 'The Symbolic Lion and Thistle', 84–9. There is no evidence for the common belief that this maxim was the Scottish royal motto.

(below, p. 124). The Eagle indeed does not seem significantly differentiated from the Lion; the role of both is to enforce justice within the kingdom.

The Thistle, however, is strikingly different; its primary significance is defensive, symbolizing a king's duty to protect his realm from invasion. In a brief but vivid passage Nature inspects the varying properties of plants, and singles out the 'awfull Thrissill', guarded by 'a busche of speiris'—

> Concedring him so able for the weiris,
> A radius croun of rubeis scho him gaif
> And said, In feild go furth and fend the laif. (131-3)

In the early sixteenth century the Scottish royal motto was *In Defens*: it was regularly placed in a scroll surmounting the full form of the royal arms, and occurs, together with the thistle collar, in the 1503 Vienna Book of Hours.[82] Nature's exhortation to 'fend the laif' (defend the rest of the country) perhaps contains an allusion to this motto commonly associated with James IV. The thistle's prickly nature adequately accounts for its military symbolism. But—unlike the Lion and Eagle—its heraldic use was by no means common. It is interesting therefore that the thistle's adoption as a Scottish emblem is paralleled by its use, at almost the same time, in Lorraine, a small duchy in a vulnerable position on the eastern border of France, dividing the two provinces of Burgundy. The Thistle seems to have been adopted there as a symbol of heroic resistance to invasion, after René II's successful struggle to preserve Lorraine's independence from Burgundy. In Lorraine the Thistle was associated with defiant mottoes, such as *Non inultus premor*; in Scotland, at a later date, it was linked similarly with *Nemo me impune lacessit*, now the motto of the modern Order of the Thistle.[83] The Thistle's warlike yet protective significance was well understood a century later, at the Union of the Crowns (1603). One Scottish poet commented, 'The Thirsel now defends and guards the Red Rose and the White';[84] and Henry Peacham, in *Minerva Britanna* (1612), devised an emblem of a bush simultaneously bearing roses and thistles: accompanying verses referred to 'the Thistle arm'd with vengeance for his foe', now growing in 'perpetuall league' with the Rose.

---

[82] Cf. C. Burnett, 'The Development of the Royal Arms to 1603', *Journal of the Heraldry Society of Scotland*, 1 (1977-8), 9-19, and 'The Thistle as a Symbol', in *The Thistles of Scotland* (Glasgow, 1983), 8-13; L. Macfarlane, 'The Book of Hours of James IV and Margaret Tudor', *Innes Review*, 11 (1960), 3-21.

[83] Bawcutt, 'The Symbolic Lion and Thistle', 90-3; for Lorraine, see Léon Germain, 'Le Chardon Lorrain sous les ducs René II et Antoine', *Mémoires de l'académie de Stanislas* (1884), 207-36.

[84] *Poetical Works of Alexander Craig*, ed. D. Laing (Glasgow, 1873-4), i. 24.

COURT POEMS: PRAISE AND PETITION

Dunbar also imposes upon the Thistle a more paradoxical meaning. Nature counsels it:

> Herb without vertew thow hald nocht of sic pryce
> As herb of vertew and of odor sueit;
> And lat no nettill vyle and full of vyce
> Hir fallow to the gudly flour delyce,
> . . . .
> Nor hald non udir flour in sic denty
> As the fresche Ros of cullour reid and quhyt;
> For gife thow dois, hurt is thyne honesty. (135ff.)

It has long been recognized that Dunbar here exhorts the king to be faithful to his queen; *honesty*, as in other poems, means both 'honour' and more specifically 'chastity'.[85] But implicit in this passage is an analogy between the well-governed kingdom and a garden; brief though it is, it looks forward to the famous garden scene in *Richard II*. Dunbar possibly here drew upon the *speculum principis* tradition: the last chapter of Haye's *Governance of Princis* is entitled 'How the prince and peple ar comparit till a gardyn'; and according to *Le Rosier des guerres*, the prince must tend his people, as a good gardener.[86] But here, strangely, the good gardener is the Thistle, which in such contexts usually had an adverse significance, coupled with thorns and weeds.[87] The Thistle is exhorted to be 'discreit': to discriminate between herbs 'of vertew' and those 'without vertew', and to value the Rose above them all. The symbolism is both personal and political.

In its iconography *The Thrissill and the Rois* has affinities with contemporary civic pageantry, such as the royal entry. When Henry VII entered York in 1486, it was devised that he should be greeted by a pageant in which should be represented a red rose and a white, 'unto whome so being togedre all other floures shall lowte and evidentlie yeve suffrantie'.[88] Dunbar pays similar tribute to Henry's daughter: a red and white Rose, 'of michty cullouris twane', and 'soverane' over all flowers (168-70). When Margaret's sister, Mary, married Louis XII of France in 1514, Pierre Gringore arranged a series of pageants to welcome her to Paris; in one of these the Rose and the Lily were shown united, with tiny figures, representing the king and queen, rising from the foliage and flowers. The pageants were accompanied by explanatory speeches; these associated Mary (like Margaret in this poem) both with the Virgin—*Rose vermeille en*

---

[85] Cf. *Thir ladyis fair* (K 71), and see below, 217.
[86] The latter work was said to be composed for the son of Louis XI. Cf. C. Samaran, 'Pierre Choisnet: *Le Rosier des Guerres*', *L'École des chartes*, 87 (1926), 372-80.
[87] Scriptural references are usually adverse; cf. Gen. 3: 18; Matt. 7: 16.
[88] Quoted and discussed by S. Anglo, *Spectacle, Pageantry and Early Tudor Policy* (Oxford, 1969), 24.

iherico plantee—and with the Bride in the Song of Songs—*Veni . . . coronaberis*.[89] Vivid tableaux, accompanied by speeches, abound in *The Thrissill and the Rois*, and it is tempting to wonder whether it might have been enacted, or linked to some actual spectacle. Yet although Young gives a detailed account of the wedding festivities—dancing, banqueting, and a 'Moralite' performed by 'Master Inglische and hys companyons'[90]—there is nothing that resembles Dunbar's poem.

A parallel might be drawn, however, with the ceremonial gateway, of a type common in the sixteenth century, that greeted James and Margaret as they entered Edinburgh. On it were depicted the four cardinal virtues: Justice, holding a naked sword and pair of balances, with Nero lying beneath her feet; and Force, Temperance, and Prudence, each with their appropriate attributes.[91] *The Thrissill and the Rois*, like this gateway, has an ambivalent message; the compliments are clearly intertwined with admonition. Dunbar's object, in part, is to remind both king and queen of the virtues to which they should aspire.

The Thrissill and the Rois is, of course, a dream poem, not a pageant, and Dunbar distances the dreamer slightly from all the compliments and hyperbole. He is an observer, not a participant, recording 'the commoun voce' of the birds, when they sing their praise of 'our princes of honour', not uttering it in his own person, as in *Gladethe, thoue Queyne*. There is a striking contrast between the climate of the dream and that of the first, prologue-like stanzas, the only place where the poet speaks on his own behalf, humorously and somewhat tartly. He mentions March winds and April showers, and when May bids him awake, ripostes:

> Quhairto, quod I, Sall I uprys at morrow,
> For in this May few birdis herd I sing?
> Thai haif moir caus to weip and plane thair sorrow,
> Thy air it is nocht holsum nor benyng;
> Lord Eolus dois in thy sessone ring.   (29–33)

The setting for the dream is specifically a garden (44), and the dreamer follows his guide into it, rather like the poet in *The Parliament of Fowls*; it is an enclosure, demarcated, if somewhat vaguely, from the country outside, like the walled gardens of many dream poems. The brief but idyllic description of 'this garth, most dulce and redolent' (47) locates it firmly in the idealized tradition of the *locus amoenus* and the *hortus conclusus* of the Song of Songs.[92] A whole stanza is devoted

---

[89] See C. R. Baskervill, *Pierre Gringore's Pageants for the Entry of Mary Tudor into Paris* (Chicago, 1934), especially 6 and 8.
[90] Leland, *De Rebus Britannicis*, iv. 300.
[91] Ibid. 289–90.
[92] Cf. Curtius, *European Literature and the Latin Middle Ages*, 183–202; A. C. Spearing, *Medieval Dream Poetry* (Cambridge, 1976), 16–18.

COURT POEMS: PRAISE AND PETITION

to Nature's 'inhibitioun' to Neptune and Aeolus, and her command that the sky be 'amene and dry' (64–70); this suggests that Dunbar did not wish the climatic change that accompanies the dream to pass unnoticed. Yet how should it be interpreted?

Several critics have regarded the poem's opening as indicating a new realism in the description of the natural world—the voice of one who 'knows what the Scottish spring is really like'. Ross, however, interprets it differently, as the poet's 'acknowledgment of unhappy experience as a servant of love'.[93] I see the contrast in another way: the first landscape, weather and all, belongs to the imperfect world of waking experience—'things as they are'; but the idyllic landscape of the dream accompanies the image of a just and harmonious society— 'things as they should be'. Spearing justly comments that *The Thrissill and the Rois* is a vision that 'celebrates an ideal, while at the same time admitting, with poise and toughness, that reality often diverges from it'.[94] The dream form indeed enables Dunbar to juxtapose two poetic voices—that of the solitary, slightly recalcitrant, narrator, and the 'commoun voce' of public ritual. Each has its validity.

Approximately twenty poems—a large proportion of Dunbar's *œuvre*—have been variously labelled as precatory pieces, begging-poems, or petitions. In form and style they have much in common: most employ a four-stress line, and a short, simple stanza; many have witty refrains, and their diction is easy, colloquial, and informal. But it is their shared subject-matter that most justifies this grouping: a few contain requests for something tangible, a doublet (K 29) or a livery (K 43); others seek preferment in the Church, referring explicitly to a benefice (K 25. 6) or 'ane kirk scant coverit with hadder' (K 39. 86). Some adopt a slightly more veiled approach, and the petitionary strand is but one of many in the poem (K 53 and K 55). Other pieces that are not strictly petitions belong to the same social type—they might be described as verse apologies (K 21) or 'thank-you letters' (K 30 and K 47). The milieu to which they belong is evident in casual allusions—'Thocht I in courte be maid refuse' (K 42. 36) or 'The court hes done my curage cuill' (K 43. 39). All are addressed to persons of higher status than the poet—important officials (K 46 and K 47), the queen (K 29 and 30), or, most often, the king himself. These have a highly characteristic opening, which is intimate but deferential:

> Schir, 3e have mony servitouris. (K 44)

---

[93] Reiss, 49; Ross, 243.
[94] *Medieval to Renaissance*, 212.

COURT POEMS: PRAISE AND PETITION

Even poems that do not begin with *Schir* commonly sign off in what resembles an envoi, directly addressing 'the kingis grace' (K 20 and K 39), or 'prince maist honorable' (K 45). Most important of all, in these poems the speaker himself is prominent, speaking as an individual, not as a representative of the 'commoun voce'.

Many of these poems are amusing, and some are of exceptional interest. Yet they have received curiously little critical attention, and the response to the group as a whole has not been enthusiastic. Rachel Taylor, complaining of his 'persistent importunities', said, 'Dunbar is unfortunate in having so many begging-poems preserved. The reader feels that as a poet, and, much more, as a Scot, Dunbar should not have begged in so many tones, and so persistently.'[95] It is the genre, above all, that is disliked—even C. S. Lewis, usually a warm admirer of Dunbar, thus found these poems 'at first sight unattractive'.[96] Another critic, considering Dunbar's approach to the king 'tactless', thought that this explained his apparent failure to obtain a benefice: 'It is difficult not to feel that Dunbar was his own worst advocate—that if he had been able to control his feelings and his tongue more firmly, his petitions for preferment might have met with better success.'[97] Others, however, have questioned the petitions' degree of self-expression, stressing their conventionality and generic character. 'How much in these poems is "for real",' enquired Reiss, 'how much literary tradition, and how much standard moralizing?'[98]

Tradition and human experience are not mutually exclusive. But there is undoubtedly a precedent for Dunbar's petitions in medieval English poetry—Chaucer's *Complaint to his Purse*, Lydgate's *Letter to Gloucester*, and several of Hoccleve's ballades, addressed variously to the Lord Chancellor, Henry Somer, or Master Carpenter. There are more distant parallels also in the many European poets who petitioned bishops, princes, dukes, and kings—including the Archpoet, Eustache Deschamps, Politian, Guillaume Crétin, and Clément Marot.[99] Long after Dunbar's death Robert Maxwell, a schoolmaster, used Latin verse to request a benefice from the archbishop of Glasgow;[100] and later Scottish poets, such as Alexander Montgomerie and Alexander Craig, continued to seek favours from their kings. The tradition of the

---

[95] *Dunbar* (1931), 64.
[96] *English Literature in the Sixteenth Century* (Oxford, 1954), 93.
[97] T. S. Dorsch, 'Of Discretioun in Asking: Dunbar's Petitionary Poems', *Chaucer und seine Zeit*, ed. A. Esch (Tübingen, 1968), 292.
[98] Reiss, 36.
[99] Cf. K. J. Holzknecht, *Literary Patronage in the Middle Ages* (1923; 1966); Curtius, op. cit., 470–3.
[100] See J. Durkan, 'Education in the Century of the Reformation', in *Essays on the Scottish Reformation 1513–1625*, ed. D. McRoberts (Glasgow, 1962), 165–6.

witty begging-poem is very long indeed; among its exponents are Martial and Ben Jonson, poets with whom Dunbar has some affinity. But it is a literary kind that is difficult to define. What formal expectations are raised by the term 'begging-poem'? These poets rarely show much awareness of their predecessors, and little sense of writing within a tradition. There are no obvious rules, and few distinctive topoi, apart from those commonplaces that arise inevitably from the subject—disclaimers of flattery, professions of loyal service, and jokes about threadbare cloaks or empty purses. The resemblances between the many specimens of this poetic kind seem to me less striking than their differences. If they constitute a genre, it is one that is remarkably flexible, partaking both of the epigram and the verse epistle, and determined more by function than by literary form.

Petitionary verse was very much 'for real', and the social reality from which it sprang was patronage. In medieval and early modern Europe supplications to popes and petitions to kings and lesser magnates were an accepted means of self-advancement, and a necessary element in the administration of Church and State. Writing of England in the fourteenth century, J. A. Tuck says: 'The importance of the petition in medieval government can hardly be over-emphasised ... It was the subject's means of gaining access to government, [of] bringing local and particular grievances and requests to the notice of a government which was bound otherwise to remain ignorant and indifferent'.[101] Among the Paston papers are many drafts of such petitions and complaints. The position in Scotland was similar. William Elphinstone, founder of Aberdeen University, is one of the most distinguished of medieval Scottish churchmen. Yet at the beginning of his career, 'Elphinstone had the unenviable task of first seeking out patrons and suitable exchanges of benefices ... before supplicating the pope for the benefice or dignity concerned. He was not without friends who were themselves patrons ... and by 1476 the most powerful patron of all, the king, knew him personally.'[102] In Scotland as elsewhere, 'if you had friends at court, you used them'.[103]

Gavin Douglas well illustrates this. He had paid agents in Rome and allies at court, such as Margaret Tudor. In 1514 she wrote to the pope, requesting the archbishopric of St Andrews for Douglas, and

---

[101] 'Richard II's System of Patronage', in *The Reign of Richard II*, ed. F. R. H. Du Boulay (1971), 4. I am indebted to Green, *Poets and Princepleasers*, 22–3, 49–52; and two essays by J. A. Burrow, 'The Poet as Petitioner', *Studies in the Age of Chaucer*, 3 (1981), 61–75, and 'Autobiographical Poetry in the Middle Ages: The Case of Thomas Hoccleve', *PBA* 68 (1982), 389–412.

[102] Macfarlane, *Elphinstone*, 77.

[103] A. L. Brown, 'The Scottish "Establishment" in the Later Fifteenth Century', *Juridical Review* (1978), 105.

also induced Henry VIII to write on his behalf. A little later, after Douglas had become bishop of Dunkeld, it was the turn of his own agents to petition him. Alexander Turnbull wrote from Rome:

> Item, as for my simplenes, your Lordschip may remember and reward as your Lordschip thinkis tyme and caus. I sal be leile and traist to your Lordschip and your materis sa fer as I haue grace and knawlage. The Italianis has ane proverbe—*fidelis servus asinus perpetuus*. I waite that I serf na Italiane; I traist sickerlie that I serve ane noble, discret and kind Lord.[104]

Dunbar's poems often comment on the system. *Off every asking followis nocht* (K 78) in no way questions the morality of the petition, but carefully distinguishes legitimate 'asking' from begging:

> To ask but service hurtis gud fame;
> To ask for service is not to blame. (16–17)

But means 'without', *for* 'in return for'; the difference of prepositions is crucial. *Be divers wyis and operatiounes* (K 20) offers a more cynical analysis of the ways in which 'Men makis in court thair solistationes' [suits]. Three-quarters of the poem is devoted to itemizing these worthless suitors, among whom is the worldly churchman, who 'besy labouris for premocione' (18). Only at the end does the poet refer to himself, in a manner that recalls Turnbull:

> My sempillnes amang the laiff
> Wait off na way, sa God me saiff,
> Bot with ane humble cheir and face
> Refferis me to the kyngis grace. (21–4)

The poem's structure is deliberately asymmetrical: twenty lines are concerned with 'the laiff'—the rest of the court—six with the poet. The wit lies chiefly in this turn, contrasting the one with the many, the artless 'sempillnes' of the speaker with the busy scheming of others. He thus proclaims his moral superiority in the very act of self-depreciation: a stance not uncommon in Dunbar.

Petitions had the same practical function, whatever their medium. Hoccleve chose French prose, when he made a request to Henry VI for a corrody, or ecclesiastical annuity. But he chose English verse, when asking for the arrears of his pension:

> My lord the Chanceller with al humblesse
> I, your seruant at your commandement,

---

[104] See Douglas, *Works*, ed. J. Small (Edinburgh, 1874), i, pp. lvii–lviii; and Bawcutt, *Douglas*, 11–16.

COURT POEMS: PRAISE AND PETITION

> Byseeche vn-to your excellent noblesse
> . . . .
> That myn arrerages been granted me.[105]

Delays in the payment of fees and pensions were common, and it was often necessary to remind the authorities in this way. Hoccleve's wages for Michaelmas 1410 seem not to have been paid until July 1411. The Beggar, in *The Regement of Princes*, advises the poet that he must not keep his grievances to himself, but complain to the king 'As I haue herd the unto me compleyne'—

> Endite in frensch or latyn thi greef clere,
> And for to write it wel, do thi poweer.   (1849ff.)[106]

We should recall this background, when reading Dunbar's *I thocht lang quhill sum lord come hame* (K 47). Addressed to the Lord Treasurer, it thanks him for the promptness of his 'nobill payment' (9). The tone is exultant, yet an underlying anxiety is apparent in remarks such as 'I thocht lang' (waited impatiently), or 'Neidis nane ȝour payment till dispair' (15), or 'ȝett in a pairt I was agast' (17). Joy is heightened by awareness of 'duill'—

> Thane had my dyt beine all in duill,
> Had I my wage wantit quhill ȝuill,
> Quhair now I sing with heart onsair:
> Welcum, my awin lord thesaurair!   (21-4)

In 1512 Dunbar did indeed wait until Christmas Eve for his half-yearly 'Mertynmes fee'; but he was usually paid remarkably promptly, on either 11 or 12 November.[107] At the very end the greeting swells to a crescendo:

> Welcum, als heartlie as I can,
> My awin dear maister to ȝour man,
> And to ȝour servand singulair:
> Welcum, my awin lord thesaurair!   (29-32)

A similar *repetitio* on 'Welcum' occurs in the eulogy of Stewart (K 35), but there is far more vitality in these lines. In their gaiety they recall the medieval Christmas carols—

> Wolcum, Yol, thou mery man,
> In worschepe of this holy day.[108]

---

[105] *The Minor Poems*, ed. F. J. Furnivall and I. Gollancz, rev. J. Mitchell and A. I. Doyle (EETS, ES 61, 73, 1970), lxviii and 58.
[106] References are to *The Regement of Princes*, ed. F. J. Furnivall (EETS, ES 72, 1897).
[107] The evidence is discussed by Baxter, 122-3, 141-2, 181-4, and 187.
[108] Greene, *Carols*, no. 7B.

The Treasurer was not Dunbar's 'awin' lord, as far as we know; there is comic hyperbole in the way Dunbar appropriates him, as the immediate source of his 'pensioun most preclair' (27).

Literary critics commonly assume that Dunbar's petitions met with ill success, since there is no evidence that he was awarded a benefice.[109] But historians approach the matter differently; Mackie, for instance, is puzzled that Dunbar was 'unsatisfied' with his pension, and comments that it was 'more than twice the sum that Hector Boece received as Principal of Aberdeen University'.[110] Neither image of Dunbar seems attractive: he is shown either as complaining fruitlessly or as greedy and 'unsatisfied'. Yet what must be stressed, as so often, is the scantiness of the facts and the difficulty of relating the poems to them. There are few firm clues to date Dunbar's petitions. For some a relative dating may be inferred: *The wardraipper of Venus boure* (K 29) thus presumably precedes *O gracious princes, guid and fair* (K 30). These and other poems that mention the queen must post-date 1503. In several the poet speaks of himself as old—'my ʒouthe is done forloir' (K 42. 2), or 'I am ane auld hors, as ʒe knaw' (K 43. 9)—and these references to old age should not be dismissed as empty convention. No petition, however, can be firmly located in a specific year; nor can we be sure to what extent they should be grouped together, or whether they were written at intervals over a long period.

Any interpretation of such scanty data is necessarily conjectural. But I suggest that 1507 should be regarded as a key date in Dunbar's career in the royal household, and a turning-point in his finances. Up to that year he received an annual pension of £10. If this is compared with the sum of £26. 13s. 4d. that Boece received in 1505, his first year as Principal of Aberdeen, the comparison is hardly advantageous to Dunbar.[111] It seems, in any case, more pertinent to compare Dunbar's income with that of other members of the household; these were men whom Dunbar saw every day, and whose 'reward'—as is evident from *Schir ʒe have mony servitouris* (K 44)—he contrasted with his own. In 1505, as in other years, Patrick Paniter received £50 a year; the chapel clerks received £40; Walter Merlioun, the master mason, £40; Hans, the Danish 'gunnar', £19. 13s. 4d.; Hannay, the falconer, £20; even Nannik, the 'broudstar', or embroiderer, received £13. 4s. 8d.[112] Dunbar's pension, compared with these, may have been fair, but was not munificent; some sense of dissatisfaction is understandable. In 1507, however, Dunbar's pension was doubled; and in

---

[109] Cf. Dorsch, 'Discretioun in Asking'; and Scott, 109.
[110] *King James IV*, 177–8; Baxter, 181; Donaldson, *Scottish Kings*, 133, refers to Dunbar's 'querulousness'.
[111] Macfarlane, *Elphinstone*, 358.
[112] See the pensions listed in *TA* iii. 117–18; for 1501, see ii. 93–6.

COURT POEMS: PRAISE AND PETITION

1510 it was again raised, to the high sum of £80 a year. Only then did his pension overtake that of Boece. It seems likely that the poems displaying a strong sense of grievance (notably K 42, K 43, and K 44) were written within a short space of time, and before 1507. The poems that voice more trivial requests or complaints (K 29 and K 26) might have been written before or after this date. *I thocht lang quhill sum lord come hame*, however, suggests high contentment with Dunbar's 'pensioun most preclair', and it seems plausible to date this piece after 1510.[113]

Dunbar's petitions have a wide range of tone. Several are humorous and comparatively light-hearted, designed chiefly to entertain, and redeemed from ephemerality by their wit or neat construction. *My prince in God, gif the guid grace* (K 18) belongs to a common type of poem, designed—as the refrain indicates—'In hansill of this guid New 3eir'. A *hansill* was something given as a token of good luck, especially at New Year; in *Sir Gawain and the Green Knight* King Arthur's courtiers

> forth runnen to reche hondeselle,
> 3e3ed 3eres-3iftes on hi3, 3elde hem bi hond.   (66–7)[114]

Dunbar's poem has been entitled 'Presentation verses with a New Year's gift', but this seems misleading.[115] The poem itself is the gift, rather like a handmade greetings card. It has a simple shape, consisting of a series of prayers for the king's welfare, and syntactic repetition enforces awareness of this structure. One stanza after another begins 'God gif', 'God gif', and the poem ends:

> God gif the blis quharevir thow bownes,
> And send the many Fraunce crownes,
> Hie liberall heart and handis not sweir,
> In hansell of this guid New 3eir.   (17–20)

Hansel-giving was usually reciprocal, and there is a clear hint that the king should be generous to his servitors.

Schir for 3our grace bayth nicht and day (K 25) ostensibly also voices a prayer on the king's behalf, but is wittier and more audacious. It begins with a fine display of piety:

> Schir, for 3our grace bayth nicht and day
> Richt hartlie on my kneis I pray
> With all devotioun that I can . . .   (1–3)

---

[113] Cf. Baxter, 182–3.
[114] Cf. *DOST, handsel; MED, hanselle.*
[115] *SL*, no. 97.

These phrases imply the 'hartlie' intensity of the poet's 'devotioun'—
praying night and day—but the stanza ends with an extraordinary
anticlimax:

> God gif 3e war Johne Thomsounis man!

This is the poet's prayer and also the poem's refrain. Since the
expression 'Johne Thomsounis man' is no longer current, its piquancy
perhaps needs demonstration. It was recorded in Ferguson's proverb-
collection, under the heading *Of effeminate persons*. An anti-feminist
passage in John Rolland's *Sevin Seages* warns old men not to marry
young wives: '3e suld tak tent / Or efterwart 3e sall repent / Quhen
3e ar maid Iohne Thomsounis man.'[116] Although the saying's literal
sense is not wholly clear, there is no doubt as to its implications: it
was applied to men dominated by their wives, and had a contemptuous
ring. Some have thought that Dunbar's comic impertinence offended
James: 'no man likes it to be suggested that he should do as his wife
tells him'.[117]

But compliments to the queen balance apparent insults to the king:
she is 'that sweit meik rose', who has the power to soften the Thistle's
sharp 'pykis' (21–3). In *Be divers wyis and operatiounes* Dunbar scorned
those who had 'advocattis in chalmir' (19); here he rejoices in his own
'advocat' (25), and hopes for her influence in gaining the king's favour.
The poem reveals itself to be a prayer for the poet's own welfare, even
more than the king's:

> I wald gif all that ever I have
> To that conditioun, sa God me saif,
> That 3e had vowit to the swan
> Ane 3eir to be Johne Thomsounis man. (17–20)

The comic effect springs largely from the refrain, which evokes the
humdrum world of domineering wives and complaisant husbands. It
collides incongruously with the fantastic vows of medieval chivalry,
with the courtly symbolism of Rose and Thistle, and with the last
pious image of 'sweit sanct An' (31).

Another petition (K 19) opens explosively, with a curse:

> Sanct salvatour, send silver sorrow!

This is no denunciation of money as the root of all evil, but a
humorous grumble about the poet's 'penuritie'. The purse was an
obvious focus for such jests. In Chaucer's *Complaint to his Purse* the
basic conceit is to address the purse as the poet's mistress:

---

[116] See *DOST, John Thomson's man*; Whiting, J 53; and *The Seuin Seages*, ed. G. F.
Black (STS, 1932), 4823–5.
[117] Dorsch, 'Discretioun in Asking', 290.

> To yow, my purse, and to noon other wight
> Complayne I, for ye be my lady dere.
> I am so sory, now that ye been lyght.   (1–3)

Such puns on the double sense of *light* and *heavy* were common, as in the proverb 'Light purse, heavy heart'.[118] Dunbar's theme, however, is different: the emptiness of his purse brings him bodily distress— 'My verry corpis for cair wald cleif' (9). His purse torments him, since it is *full*, as the refrain reiterates, not of silver but of pain:

> My panefull purs so prikillis me.

This figure was not original. Hoccleve complains, 'My body and purs been at ones seeke'; and proverbs speak of the 'purse-sick' man needing a physician.[119] But the most elaborate development of the topic occurs in Lydgate's *Letter to Gloucester*, which abounds in comic images—the purse's guts are turned inside out, and it has grown slender from 'consumpcioun'.[120] Dunbar's tripping stanzas are quite unlike Lydgate's ponderous verse, and he does not embroider the figure so ingeniously. But both, at the end, make a slightly similar turn: Lydgate appeals to his patron, since he 'may al our soor recure', and Dunbar says likewise that the king alone knows the remedy for 'this malice' (malaise, malady).

Dunbar's allusive humour often requires careful unravelling. But suggestions that this refrain contains some sexual implication are unconvincing.[121] The relevance to the poem of such a sexual innuendo is unclear, and has never been demonstrated; nor does lexicographical evidence give much support to the notion. It is true that *purse* occasionally had the sense 'scrotum', but the use was rare, specialized, and contextual, and indicated by some modifier—as in 'nether purs' or 'ballok purs'.[122] Yet there is certainly other word-play:

> My purs is maid of sic ane skyn
> Thair will na cors byd it within—
> Fra it as fra the Feynd thay fle.
> . . . .
> Had I ane man of ony natioun
> Culd mak on it ane conjuratioun
> To gar silver ay in it be,
> The Devill suld haif no dominatioun
> With pyne to gar it prickill me.   (21–3, 26–30)

---

[118] Whiting, P 444 and P 454.
[119] *La Male Regle*, 409; *Minor Poems*, 38.
[120] *Minor Poems II*, no. 39.
[121] Cf. Reiss, 42; Scott, 94.
[122] *OED*, sense 8b; *MED*, sense 4; *DOST*, sense 3, does not include this use by Dunbar.

Dunbar makes a common pun on *cors* as (1) cross, and therefore a Christian symbol, and (2) a coin, with a cross stamped on one side. But he also alludes to another belief, that it was necessary to have some piece of money, however small, in one's purse to keep the devil away. In *The Regement of Princes* the Beggar thus reflects on his own empty purse:

> The feend, men seyn, may hoppen in a pouche
> Whan that no croys there-inne may a-pere. (684–5)

Although this is the first recorded occurrence, 'men seyn' implies that the saying was well known in Hoccleve's period. Similar notions were voiced for a very long time, usually making the same punning reference to the antagonism between the Cross and the Fiend: Robert Greene writes of an empty pocket—'well might the Divell daunce there, for ever a crosse to keepe him backe'.[123] But Dunbar playfully alters the stock idea; in this case the devil has such power over his purse that he can be expelled, or exorcised, only by a 'conjuratioun'. The king thus figures not only as physician but as exorcist: he alone has the remedy for the sick purse, and can 'gar silver ay in it be'.

Two other poems are commonly linked, because of the similarity of their opening lines—'Schir, at this feist of benefice' (K 41), and 'Off benefice, Sir, at everie feist' (K 40). Despite this, they develop very differently. *Schir, at this feist of benefice* is neat, witty, and audacious. Its argument is conducted entirely in metaphorical terms. The first stanza makes the case for a more equitable distribution of benefices through the analogy of a feast at which the guests receive equal portions. The second questions the merit of plying a man who is 'fow' (full, drunk) with still more drink, when his 'fallow' is dying of thirst. The third concludes:

> It is no glaid collatioun
> Quhair ane makis myrrie, ane uther lukis doun;
> Ane thristis, ane uther playis cop out;
> Lat anis the cop ga round about
> And wyn the covanis banesoun. (11–15)

Largess was a virtue much commended in a king; he was expected to provide rich feasts and lavish hospitality. But the Scottish king was also a patron, with the right to nominate to many ecclesiastical offices. The equation between benefices, with their valuable revenues, and the wines and delicacies of a banquet, is easily perceived—we still talk of 'plum jobs' and 'fat livings'. Dunbar's theme is 'equale distributioun' (3). He does not say that Church offices should go only to those

---

[123] See Tilley, D 233, who also cites Drant's 'The deuill may daunce in a crosslesse purse'. Cf. Whiting, D 191.

who are most deserving, spiritually or intellectually—apart from the use of the word 'worthie' (10)—but rather, 'let everyone have a fair share!' The tone is light, jesting, and amoral, very different from Lindsay's discussion of the same topic, which envisages a king receiving advice from scholars and theologians.[124] Dunbar is conversational, as if the king were in front of him—urging, 'Think', in the first stanza, and questioning him, 'Schir, quhidder is it mereit mair?', in the second. The diction is plain, but includes some ingenious word-play, notably on *collatioun*. The primary sense here is that of a meal, which often included wine and spices; for Henryson's Cresseid it symbolized lost pleasures and luxury. But Dunbar also refers wittily to its ecclesiastical sense, 'the formal appointment or admission of someone to a benefice'.[125] *The covanis banesoun* signifies 'the assembly's approval'; *banesoun* means 'blessing' and also refers, more specifically, to the grace or benediction likely to be said at the end of a feast.

Maitland's colophon to this poem reads: 'Quod Dunbar quhone mony benefices vakit'; a later editor cynically entitled *Off benefice, Sir, at everie feist* 'To the king after the benefices were filled up'.[126] But the relationship between the two poems is by no means so clear-cut, although they were possibly composed at about the same time. *Off benefice* is a longer and more solemn poem. Its first three stanzas employ the same image of the feast:

> Sum swelleis swan, sum swelleis duke [duck],
> And I stand fastand in a nuke
> Quhill the effect of all thai fang thame;
> Bot Lord! how petewouslie I luke
> Quhone all the pelfe thai pairt amang thame.   (6–10)

But the differences are apparent: Dunbar here identifies himself explicitly with the 'fastand' have-nots, whereas in the former poem an unnamed 'uther' thirsts, and 'lukis doun' miserably. The tone reveals more contempt than amusement. *Pelf*, 'plunder', is highly depreciative; churchmen divide benefices among themselves, as if they were robbers. The latter part of the poem is a fairly orthodox attack on those who wish for the emoluments of a church living, without its responsibilities:

> Swa thai the kirk have in thair cure—
> Thai fors bot litill how it fure.   (21–2)

[124] *Papyngo*, 1018–28.
[125] *Testament of Cresseid*, 418. See also *DOST*, sense 3, and *MED*, sense 5.
[126] Small, i, p. clxvi.

Perhaps the most striking feature is the refrain; slightly varying, its one fixed element is the final phrase, 'amang thame', which is matched with ingenious feminine rhymes—'wrang thame', 'stang thame'. Dunbar ends with thoughts of the Last Judgement:

> Quha maist hes than sall maist repent,
> With largest compt to pairt amang thame.   (29–30)

The substitution of *compt* for *pelf* neatly stresses the consequences of greed for 'this warldis rent'.

Among the petitions some stand out as exceptionally interesting: *My heid did ʒak ʒester nicht* (K 21), *This waverand warldis wretchidnes* (K 39), *Schir, ʒit remember as befoir* (K 42), *Schir, lat it never in toune be tald* (K 43), *Schir, ʒe have mony servitouris* (K 44), *Complane I wald* (K 45), and *This hinder nycht halff sleiping as I lay* (K 51). They are mostly longer than those so far discussed, and certainly more complex and substantial. They vary in form, yet share a distinctive tone, in which different strains mingle—humorous, sardonic, reflective, and melancholy. Some contain explicit moralizing; the poet becomes a preacher, proclaiming, 'With gredines I sie this world ourgane' (K 51. 99). What separates these poems from the simpler didactic ones, however, is their individualistic viewpoint, that of the keen-sighted but compromised observer of society. In *Schir, ʒe have mony servitouris* Dunbar may rail at 'this fals warld', but his is not the stance of the disinterested moralist. As he candidly acknowledges, indignation is partly fuelled by self-interest; when fools

> Ar all rewardit, and nocht I,
> Than on this fals warld I cry, Fy:
> My hart neir bristis than for teyne,
> Quhilk may nocht suffer nor sustene
> So grit abusioun for to se
> Daylie in court befoir myn e.   (67–72)

He confesses that he would overlook many faults—'Had I rewarde amang the laif' (74). Dunbar is indeed, in this recurrent phrase, 'amang the laif'.[127] He is 'one among the others', not detached from 'this warld', but very much involved in the society that he criticizes.

Dunbar evokes its uneasy and suspicious atmosphere with a repeated image, of covert, malicious whispering:

> Sum standis in a nuk and rownes.
> (K 20. 13; cf. K 52. 52–3 and K 63. 37)

The intense rivalries at court were likely to foster a sense of individuality. John Burrow has plausibly argued that the medieval

---

[127] See also K 20. 21; K 39. 53; and K 44. 25.

COURT POEMS: PRAISE AND PETITION

petition—whether in the form of prayers to God or pleas to princes—provided 'the chief matrix within which what we would call "autobiographical writing" first grows and develops in England'.[128] These poems of Dunbar's are not autobiographical, but they are certainly introspective. We are strongly conscious of the speaker's voice, which is not superhumanly righteous, but fallible, unhappy, and self-interested. It may be argued that what we are shown is not 'personality' but 'persona'—a mask to conceal rather than to reveal. Dunbar's self-depiction is no doubt carefully designed both to entertain and to arouse sympathy; and there is almost no external evidence to corroborate the impression these poems produce. Yet this is the face he turned towards the king and court, and the image has consistency. Not only are these petitions imaginatively coherent, there are links and interconnections with the most interesting of Dunbar's other poems—the satirical method in *Complane I wald*, for instance, recalls *The Flyting*, and their reflective and often sombre tone resembles that of the finest moralities. Here, if anywhere, is the core of Dunbar's poetry and that 'unifying consciousness' that some critics would deny him.[129]

The shortest is *My heid did ȝak ȝester nicht* (K 21). Its opening has a painful matter-of-factness:

> My heid did ȝak ȝester nicht,
> This day to mak that I na micht;
> So sair the magryme dois me menȝie,
> Perseing my brow as ony ganȝie,
> That scant I luik may on the licht. (1–5)

The first simple reference to an aching head is followed by the technicality of the *magryme* (migraine); this was then a learned word, used chiefly in medical contexts. Those who have experienced some form of migraine will recognize the symptoms that are here described with precision—the sharp pain, implied by the verbs *menȝie* (wound) and *perseing*, the localization in the brow, and, above all, the discomfort caused by looking at bright light. The poem's interpretation, unfortunately, is hampered by the obscurity of a few phrases, which may be attributable not to Dunbar but to Reidpeth, the only witness. An example occurs in line 2:

> This day to mak that I na micht.

Is *micht* verb or noun? If it is the modal auxiliary, 'was able', it should take the simple infinitive, not the infinitive with *to*. One might also expect the present tense, *may*, as in the lines that follow. To take *micht*

---
[128] *Medieval Writers and Their Work* (Oxford, 1982), 38.
[129] Cf. A. J. Smith, 'Incumbent Poets', *MLQ* 29 (1968), 341–50.

as the noun, 'powers, ability', is preferable, yet difficult syntactically; some emendation, perhaps to 'I nad micht' or 'I haue na micht', seems necessary. There is precedent for this usage in Chaucer's prayer that God would send him 'myght to make in som comedye'.[130] Yet, however the line is construed, Dunbar's drift seems clear. He is apologizing for failure to write a poem.

The second stanza elaborates on this: directly addressing the king, Dunbar speaks of his unsuccessful attempts to 'dyt'—'The sentence lay full evill to find' (8). There is an interesting parallel in *I seik about this warld unstabille* (K 58), where the poet likewise seeks 'To find ane sentence convenabille' (2). *Sentence* is not restricted to 'moral truth'; here it is perhaps better glossed as 'the right theme'. 'Writer's block' is a perennial problem, and Dunbar here voices, simply but poignantly, a sense of literary incapacity, 'Dullit in dulnes and distres'. *My heid did 3ak*, like the first sonnet of *Astrophil and Stella*, embodies a familiar literary paradox, a witty composition about one's inability to write. Dunbar's tone, however, is far less cheerful than Sidney's.

Some critics find other meanings in the poem. For one the headache is symbolic, not 'an actual headache to be taken literally', and the poet's 'dulnes' is a moral and spiritual malaise; another suggests that Dunbar's *magryme* may be interpreted as 'royal neglect, which is having the disastrous effect of preventing him write poetry'. But earlier poets bemoaned their gout or baldness, and I see no reason to doubt that the poem's starting-point is an actual headache; nor can I detect any suggestion of the king's neglect.[131] None the less in the third stanza the poem's scope certainly widens:

> Full oft at morrow I upryse
> Quhen that my curage sleipeing lyis;
> For mirth, for menstrallie and play,
> For din nor danceing nor deray,
> It will not walkin me no wise. (11–15)

Dunbar moves from one occasion to many—'This day' to 'Full oft'— and now is less concerned with his aching head than his sleeping 'curage'. He is generalizing, speaking of some recurrent state of mind, a kind of apathy or mental torpor. Pleasurable activities—'menstrallie and play'—contrast with this inner distress, but fail to alleviate it; the final double negative—'*not . . . no* wise'—enforces the sense of nullity. Yet no moral is drawn, and no explicit plea for help is made to the king. The mood of depression resembles the opening of *In to thir dirk*

---

[130] *Troilus and Criseyde*, v. 1788.
[131] Cf. Reiss, 27, and Ross, 156. For Guillaume Machaut's complaint of a gouty foot, see *One Hundred Ballades, Rondeaux and Virelais*, ed. N. Wilkins (Cambridge, 1969), no. 13; see also 127 below.

and drublie dayis, where Nature likewise denies the poet 'all curage . . . Off sangis, ballattis and of playis' (4–5).

Disease is often mentioned in Dunbar's petitions, but its significance varies. Sometimes it is a means of ridiculing others—'Mismaid mandragis' (mandrakes) (K 45. 21) or inferior 'scabbit' horses (K 43. 60). Sometimes the sickness is the poet's own, and is unmistakably figurative, forming part of a common train of thought, that the king alone can supply the cure, or 'best remeid for this malice' (K 19. 34). So in *Schir ʒit remember as befoir* he requests 'sum medecyne'—

> Nane can remeid my maledie
> Sa weill as ʒe, Sir, veralie. (56–7).

Twice, however, Dunbar is more specific. Discretion, in *This hinder nycht halff sleiping as I lay*, identifies the poet's 'malady':

> The strok he feillis of melancholie—
> And Nobilnes, his lecheing lyis in the. (49–50)

But the most vivid self-diagnosis occurs in *Schir ʒe have mony servitouris*:

> owther man my hart to-breik
> Or with my pen I man me wreik;
> And sen the tane most nedis be—
> In to malancolie to de
> Or lat the vennim ische all out—
> Be war anone, for it will spout
> Gif that the tryackill cum nocht tyt
> To swage the swalme of my dispyt. (81–8)

This resembles an outburst in *The Tua Mariit Wemen and the Wedo*:

> Now sall the byle all out brist that beild has so lang.
> For it to beir one my breist was berdin our hevy;
> I sall the venome devoid with a vent large
> And me assuage of the swalme that suellit wes gret. (164–7)

The sheer physicality of both passages shocks yet amuses; words like 'spout' and 'devoid' suggest an act of excretion or vomiting. Yet this is more than metaphor. Melancholy was a condition as much physiological as psychological. An imbalance of the bodily humours, resulting from a preponderance of black bile, was thought to be responsible for serious diseases. It was commonly believed that one could be suffocated by melancholy, and that it was dangerous not to unburden oneself of 'dispyt' or other painful emotions.[132] On the physical level, purgation was indeed one remedy advocated for

---

[132] See R. Klibansky, E. Panofsky, and F. Saxl, *Saturn and Melancholy* (1964), and B. G. Lyons, *Voices of Melancholy* (1971).

melancholy; but a 'tryackill'—or sweet-flavoured medicine, like Henryson's 'sugerit syrops for digestioun'—would clearly be more palatable.[133] The *venom*, mentioned in both passages, is doubly harmful, as noxious to those who harbour it as to their victims. If the poet does not receive the 'tryackill' of royal favour, the only alternative, he suggests, is to purge his anger, therapeutically, by flyting.

This poem contains one of Dunbar's most important claims for his poetry, and has been discussed earlier. But something should also be said of its structure, which consists of four sections. Two carefully balanced passages speak of the court in general: the king's 'profitable' servants (1–24) are contrasted with those of 'ane uthir sort', who are by no means so worthy or 'sa profitable' (35–60). These are juxtaposed with two passages, both introduced by a concessive clause—'And thocht that I' (25), 'And thocht this' (61)—which are devoted to the poet himself, his place 'amang the laif', and his treatment by the king. Dunbar's tone modulates interestingly: he is deferential to the king, and his manner, particularly at the beginning, is calm and rational, appealing to logic and 'reassoun' (63). But when he turns to the disorderly 'thrang' of court parasites, his tone becomes correspondingly impassioned, and at the end is distinctly menacing.

Several petitions move to their point gradually and covertly. *This waverand warldis wretchidnes* opens with stock generalizations about this world's iniquity, which may be observed 'In hall and bour, in burgh and plane' (23), and not only in 'this cuntre', but in 'France, Ingland, Ireland, Almanie' (17–18). The very air is 'infectit and prophane' (35). But approximately half-way through the focus narrows, and a wide-ranging complaint on the times turns into a complaint on behalf of the speaker:

> I knaw nocht how the Kirk is gydit,
> Bot beneficis ar nocht leill devydit:
> Sum men hes sevin and I nocht ane;
> Quhilk to considder is ane pane. (45–8)

The rest of the poem is devoted to this personal plea, not for a great abbey's revenues but simply for 'ane kirk' (54, 86). The last stanzas balance the despair, born of experience (93), with trust in the king's assistance (93–100).

In its overall strategy this poem resembles *Complane I wald, wist I quhome till*. The latter also begins as a general complaint, and purports to speak on behalf of those who have suffered injustice in their dealings with court and kirk. Only in its last ten lines does Dunbar

---

[133] Robert Burton included 'purging simples', or medicines 'purging upward or downward', among the cures for melancholy: *The Anatomy of Melancholy*, ed. Holbrook Jackson (Everyman's Library, 1932), ii. 225–34; cf. *Testament of Cresseid*, 247.

become more specific, addressing the king directly and identifying himself, if somewhat obliquely, as one of the 'auld servandis' (69) for whom the poem makes its plea. *This waverand warldis wretchidnes* seems, structurally, less successful. The poem virtually splits into two remarkably different sections: the first contains fairly conventional moralizing; the second is humorous, charged with feeling and vivid particularity. Some implications of the geographical excursus (61–76) have already been mentioned (pp. 41–3); the benefice for which the poet hopes seems as distant yet as desirable as a cargo from 'Cal3ecot and the new fund Yle' (62). Waiting for its arrival is 'sa done tyrsum . . . It breikis my hairt and birstis my brane' (82–3).

Some of Dunbar's early phrases—'The labour lost . . . And the litill rewarde agane' (13–15)—anticipate leading themes in the latter section. But what chiefly holds the poem together is the wittily handled refrain:

> Quhilk to considder is ane pane.[134]

Its implications change as it occurs in different contexts. The 'pane' of the first stanzas is vague and unfocused, an emotion that contemplation of the world's evils is likely to provoke in most right-thinking persons. But a change occurs at line 48: this 'pane' is peculiar to the speaker, a private misery, and thus it continues, virtually till the end. At 92 the refrain alters to 'Na for sic syn to suffer pane'—there is a wry joke here that at least the poet will not suffer punishment in Purgatory, on account of his pluralism. The refrain changes even more strikingly in the last stanza:

> The formest hoip 3it that I have
> In all this warld, sa God me save,
> Is in 3our grace, bayth crop and grayne,
> Quhilk is ane lessing of my pane. (97–100)

Only now does Dunbar speak explicitly of '*my* pane'. He plays too on the double sense of *grace*, which signifies 'favour' as well as forming part of an honorific title for the king. He also seems to pun on the two possible senses of *lessing*, 'alleviation' and 'lessening'.[135] Yet his tone is guarded—to lessen pain is not to remove it completely, nor is alleviation synonymous with a total cure.

Among the petitions *This hinder nycht halff sleiping as I lay* is unusual in its form. Although commonly known as *Ane Dreme*, Dunbar himself terms it, at the poem's beginning and end, a 'phary' (11, 111), a supernatural experience, perhaps of fairy origin. He briefly considers

---

[134] In the first 4 stanzas the refrain is 'For to considder is ane pane'.
[135] See *DOST*, *lessing*, 1 and 2; there is a similar semantic overlap between the verbs *les*, 1, 'diminish', and *les*, 2, 'alleviate'.

whether it might be diabolical—'ane feindlie fantasie' (14)—but does not pursue this line of thought.[136] The poem ends rapidly and explosively, with the shooting of a cannon, as does the dream in *The Goldyn Targe*. But the theme is quite unlike that of *The Goldyn Targe*: the melancholy dreamer lacks reward, and familiar petitionary phrases occur—his 'malady' (48), his long service (53), and need for 'grace' (30). The poet lies in bed, 'halff sleiping', as in *The Thrissill and the Rois* and many other dream poems, and is the passive observer of what goes on around him. But the dreamer's role is far more important than in *The Thrissill and the Rois*: the apparitions whom he sees are remarkably interested in the poet, and talk incessantly about him, sometimes with sympathy, sometimes with contempt. They do not talk *to* him, like the personifications in *In to thir dirk and drublie dayis*, but *about* him—one is fleetingly reminded of a group of hospital consultants discussing their patient in the third person. In his handling of the dream form Dunbar thus takes a comically detached view of himself, yet remains at the centre of our attention.

The personification allegory that the dream encloses belongs to a common type. It resembles the morality plays, and contemporary poems like *King Hart* or Skelton's *Bouge of Court*. It begins with the appearance of 'ane guidlie companie' (13), chiefly female, who sing, dance and make music. But this company rapidly splits into those, such as 'Twa sisteris callit Confort and Pleasance' (32), who try vainly to entertain the dreamer, and those, such as 'Langour', who embody his unhappiness:

> Scho playit sangis so duilfull to heir,
> Me thocht ane houre seimeit ay ane ȝeir. (23–4)

They speak of the poet's distress, its causes and possible remedy; and the poem's scope now widens into a satirical analysis of the ills of the court. It consists essentially of a debate between Vices and Virtues as to which of them is most influential, and most useful to the ambitious courtier. 'Blind Effectioun', or partiality towards friends and kin, boasts:

> Of all the court I have the governance. (60)

'Inoportunitie' likewise claims: 'I stand ay befoir the kingis face' (78). Human greed is vividly exemplified in two type characters, 'Sir Johne Kirkpakar' and 'Sir Bet-the-Kirk': these are pluralistic clerics, the first busily amassing 'cures', the second 'Ay still awaitting upoun kirkmenes deidis [deaths]' (94), and employing agents to inform him

[136] See below, 265.

COURT POEMS: PRAISE AND PETITION

of ecclesiastical vacancies. Reason, Discretion, and Temperance protest, but seem to concede defeat—

> With gredines I sie this world ourgane,
> And sufficience dwellis nocht bot in heavin.   (99–100)

Only at this point, almost at the poem's end, is the dreamer addressed directly. Patience advises him to 'mak guid cheir', and trust in his prince:

> For I full weill dois knaw his nobill intent:
> He wald not for ane bischopperikis rent
> That 3ow war unrewairdit half ane 3eir.   (108–10)

The effect is startling, as when a character in a play unexpectedly turns to speak to the audience.

Dunbar here makes well-founded, if obvious, generalizations: pluralism is rife in the Church, and royal patronage is sometimes misguided. But there is no doubt about the poem's self-reference. It speaks of Dunbar's own situation—he is the 'wicht' whose service is said to have been vain (53), and the man 'That lange hes bene ane servand to the king' (67). James may not be directly addressed, as elsewhere, but Dunbar is none the less arguing with him, and presenting a case through the mouths of 'Will' and Reason. The king is thus criticized: censured, as in the *speculum principis* tradition, for allowing himself to be swayed by evil counsellors. But he is also implicitly flattered, I think, in the figure 'Nobilnes', whose benign interest in the dreamer's welfare is stressed (26–30; 42); and who is singled out as able to provide the dreamer with 'lecheing' (a cure) for his malady, and help (50, 72). Patience refers also to the prince's 'nobill intent' (108). Dunbar seems to be calling upon James to demonstrate his inherent nobleness, of character as well as of birth; and to display it not only in his 'governance', in general, but in a generous treatment of one particular servant.

This hinder nycht consists almost entirely of talk—as allegory it stands at the opposite extreme from the highly visual *Dance of the Sevin Deidly Sinnis* (K 52). The personifications are hardly described at all, and reveal their significance in what they say. For this there is ample literary precedent. But Dunbar is, as so often, brief: his Virtues and Vices utter pithy proverbs and taunts, not the extended monologues that characterize the allegorical method of Jean de Meun, Lydgate, or Langland. The work is, in a rudimentary way, dramatic, and occasionally suggests the to-and-fro of speech. But the success of such a poem largely depends on the vivacity of the dialogue, and *This hinder nicht* is, in this respect, not nearly as impressive as *The Bouge of Court*. Words cascade from the mouths of Skelton's personifications, in pungent, slangy, idiomatic conversation. Dunbar's poem has a clearer structure than Skelton's, but lacks its verbal energy. This is surprising, yet there is much else that seems clumsy: hypermetric lines, such as

> Weill spokin, Ressoun my brother, quoth Discretioun; (73)

repetition of rhyme words (46, 50); and other apparently pointless repetitions. The simile 'sad as the leid' (20), for instance, is followed by 'wan and wallowed as the leid' (25). This is uncharacteristic of Dunbar, and suggests the possibility of textual corruption; the only copy, in Reidpeth, contains other undoubted errors.[137]

This poem has not pleased many critics, who usually attribute its 'lack of success' to its form, saying, 'The allegorical machinery is too cumbersome for the subject', or that Dunbar's 'narrow personal concern suits ill with the broad, general, and august associations of allegory'.[138] But the allegorical dream poem was a remarkably versatile form. Its 'associations', in Skelton, Holland, Chaucer, and many other English and French poets, are humorous and satiric, and by no means inevitably 'august'. *This hinder nycht* should perhaps be regarded as an interesting failure, but through weaknesses in its execution rather than an inherent unsuitability of form to content.

Schir ȝit remember as befoir (K 42) has as its refrain 'Exces of thocht dois me mischeif'. It is a poem dominated by *thought*, in a sense that now seems obsolete, of obsessive, morbid brooding over one's problems. Some of the word's implications are well illustrated in a passage from *The Regement of Princes*, where Hoccleve personifies 'Thoght' as a cruel foe, who chases away sleep, and brings one close to despair. The poet reflects:

> Who so that thoghty is, is wo-be-gon,
> The thoghtful wight is vessel of turment.

The Beggar counsels him to beware of 'thoght'—

> His violence is full outrageous;
> Vnwise is he that besy thoght ne dredeth.[139]

Thought, in this sense, vexes Dunbar at the opening of *In to thir dirk and drublie dayis*, depriving him of sleep, and also oppresses him in *Lucina schynnyng in silence of the nycht*. The refrain sums up the poet's anxious self-preoccupation. No other poem of Dunbar's is so explicitly or so painfully concerned with his worldly failure and apparent nullity:

> No thing I gett nor conqueis can ... (34)

---

[137] It is arguable that Discretion's words (73) originally were 'Weill spokin, Ressoun'; and that the simile was the more alliterative 'wallowed as the weid'.
[138] Scott, 153; Kinsley, 334.
[139] Ed. Furnivall, lines 80–1, 269–70; cf. *OED, thought*, sense 5.

COURT POEMS: PRAISE AND PETITION

> A sempill vicar I can not be . . . (64)
> He playis with totum and I with nychell . . . (74)

The court is presented satirically, chiefly as a foil to the speaker's misery. Repeatedly his own lot is contrasted with that of 'utheris' (39); repeatedly his argument is punctuated by direct appeals to the king. The penultimate stanza sums up his predicament:

> How sould I leif, and I not landit,
> Nor 3it withe benefice am blandit?
> I say not, Sir, 3ow to repreiff,
> Bot doutles I go rycht neir hand it:
> Exces of thocht dois me mischeiff. (76–80)

The tone is of someone thinking aloud: the bluntness of the first two lines is followed by apologetic correction.

One particularly interesting passage develops from Dunbar's comparison of himself to a hawk:

> 3our clarkis ar servit all aboute
> And I do lyke ane rid halk schout
> To cum to lure that hes na leif,
> Quhair my plumis begynnis to mowt. (6–9)

Precisely what type of bird is meant by a 'rid' (red) hawk is not certain; there is no evidence to support earlier conjectures that it refers either to a kestrel or a merlin. It is more probable that a red hawk, like a sore hawk, signifies a 'hawk of the first year that has not moulted and still has red plumage'.[140] According to Dunbar, his plumage is now beginning to moult, and he is calling loudly to his master, in order to return to the *lure*, the mock-up of a bird, containing pieces of meat, used in training hawks. This comical image of the poet resembles the way the old horse is used in *Schir lat it never in toune be tald* (K 43); there, however, the figure furnishes the structure of the whole poem, whereas here it is sustained for five stanzas and then dropped. The court is viewed as a bird assembly, and the passage culminates in this appeal:

> O gentill egill, how may this be?
> Quhilk of all foulis dois heast fle,
> 3our leggis [lieges] quhy do 3e not relcif
> And chirreis thame eftir thair degre? (26–34)

This alludes, humorously, to *The Thrissill and the Rois*, in which James figures also as 'the Egle king of fowlis'. Such imagery was well calculated to appeal to the king, whose most famous portrait shows

---

[140] Small, iii. 177; Kinsley, 319. See further *OED*, *red*, sense 17b; *sore*, a.2. Dunbar speaks elsewhere of merlins as 'marle3onis' and the kestrel as 'stanchel' (K 54. 90, 82).

him carrying a peregrine falcon on his left wrist, and a perch in his right hand.[141] James, like most contemporary kings and noblemen, was fascinated by hawking, and spent much money on acquiring and training birds. 'Facilities for the chase and falconry were the mark of a rich and hospitable court.'[142] But Dunbar is here speaking primarily of the eagle's symbolic properties, in heraldry and the bestiaries. He refers both to the bird's high flight and to its reputation for liberality. In Loutfut's heraldic treatise the eagle is a 'foull royall quhilk optenis the lordschip amang al foullis and is richt liberal, for bot gif he haue gret hunger, he eitis nocht him allane the pra [prey] that he takis. And his parte tane he deliuerys to othir foullis thair part.'[143] The king's exercise of patronage is here implicitly a feast, as in *Off benefice, Sir, at everie feist* and *Schir at this feist of benefice*. Dunbar reminds the king of his duty to cherish and support his lieges, just as the eagle distributes his prey to lesser birds. The stanza thus draws together earlier themes—the hawk wishing to return to the lure, and the goshawk that 'gois undynd', whereas the inferior kite is permitted to gorge itself on partridges (11–14).

Hawks and falcons were usually classed with the eagle. They were hunting birds, the noblest of the 'foules of ravyne', and contrasted with lesser birds of prey, such as the kite and the 'pyat', or magpie. Dunbar reinforces these distinctions by his epithets: the goshawk, like the eagle, is 'gentill', whereas the magpie's throat is 'carleche', producing a harsh, coarse sound, as befits a carl, or peasant. Dunbar makes no one-to-one equation between birds and specific ranks or occupations, such as occurs in *The Howlat*, where the falcon is an earl and the goshawks 'chosin chiftanis chevalrus' (321–8). His method is closer to that of Chaucer in *The Parliament of Fowls*, a vague but suggestive opposition between 'gentill and sempill' (32), both in birds and men. In asking the king to take account of 'degre', Dunbar clearly implies that those of noble origin are being passed over, and the low-born are being rewarded at their expense.

But the bird-allegory has a further dimension:

> The pyat withe the pairtie cote
> Feyn3eis to sing the nychtingale note,
> Bot scho can not the corchet cleiff
> For haskness of hir carleche throte.   (16–19)

Dunbar wittily alludes to the magpie's distinctive black and white plumage as well as its mimicry of other birds; he also contrasts the

---

[141] See J. M. Gilbert, *Hunting and Hunting Reserves in Medieval Scotland* (Edinburgh, 1979), 68 ff., and plate 13 (the Mytens portrait of James).
[142] Ibid. 74.
[143] Fol. 20a; see above, n. 40.

normal harshness of its voice with the legendary beauty of the nightingale's song. It cannot 'cleave the crotchet', apparently a reference to the rapid singing of many short notes in polyphonic vocal music. Jankin, in the medieval carol, somewhat similarly 'crakit notes . . . and yyt he hakkyt hem smallere than wortes to the pot.'[144] Here and in the next stanza Dunbar views birds as singers, and by implication as poets and entertainers. In classical legend the Pierides, who challenged the Muses in song, were metamorphosed into magpies; the magpie thus sometimes symbolized the bad poet or poetaster, not only because of its ugly song but because of its thieving ways. In an epigram attacking a plagiarist, Martial, like Dunbar, contrasted the 'worthless magpie' (*improba* . . . *pica*) with the 'varied tones of the Athenian nightingale'.[145]

Interwoven with this is a minor theme, summed up in the proverb, 'Ay fairast feddiris hes farrest foulis' (21). Exotic birds from distant lands, such as peacocks and parrots, have privileged status because of their brilliant plumage, though 'thai have na sang bot 30wlis' (22). But those of native origin are treated like owls—ugly, unmelodious birds, of ill repute. The animus against foreign favourites is clear. In this set of oppositions Dunbar does not align himself solely with one bird, but with those that are 'gentill' and 'native'. The poet, in his need for sustenance, 'cryis' for reward (4), just as the hawk must 'schout' to return to the lure (7); yet he also, if more covertly, identifies his own voice with the nightingale's as the authentic, inimitable 'note' of poetry; and he even hints that, in his apparent state of disfavour— 'refuse' (rejected) by the court (36)—he is 'odious as ane owle'.[146]

In the rest of the poem no single figure is developed so richly as this. Yet several themes recur. The indirect claim for the worth of Dunbar's poetry offsets his later ironic self-disparagement as a mere maker of 'ballattis' (48, 69). But Dunbar is now discursive, passing from one topic to another, with frequent unexpected changes of tack:

> 3it am I cum of Adame and Eve
> And fane wald leif as utheris dois. (38–9)

This proverb was often quoted in arguments for social equality, and was directed against the 'gentill' classes, not for them: 'A bonde man or a churle wyll say, all we be cummin of Adam'.[147] More character-

---

[144] Greene, *Carols*, no. 457.
[145] *Epigrams*, ed. W. C. A. Ker (Loeb, 1919–20), i. 53. 9–10. Persius, in the Prologue to his *Satires*, spoke sarcastically of 'raven poets' and 'magpie poetesses' (*poetridas picas*). On the Carolingian tradition, see Curtius, *European Literature and the Latin Middle Ages*, 95.
[146] See below, 254.
[147] Whiting, A 37.

istically, Dunbar restates his earlier theme that those of lowly origin fare better at court than he does. His reference to 'Rauf Col3ard and Johnne the reif' (33) is not sympathetic: these heroes of popular romance, both knighted by kings, serve as instances of the promotion of undeserving *carls*. His later attack on two pluralistic churchmen portrays them as peasants: 'Jok that wes wont to keip the stirkis' and 'uplandis Michell' (66–74). Dunbar's stance, as so often, is that of the impoverished aristocrat for whom low birth connotes 'odius ignorance'.

The poem's most audacious figure occurs at its end:

> As saule in to purgatorie
> Leifand in pane with hoip of glorie,
> So is my selffe 3e may beleiff
> In hoip, Sir, of 3our adjutorie:
> Exces of thocht dois me mischeiff.   (81–5)

Adjutorie, 'help, assistance', was rare in the vernacular, and had liturgical connotations, particularly for clerics and devout members of the laity. The versicle, *Deus in adiutorium meum intende*, and its response, *Domine ad adiuvandum me festina*, were said before each of the canonical hours; Lindsay addressed a plea for 'adjutory' to God.[148] Dunbar compares his present misery quite explicitly to that of a soul in purgatory; in hoping that James will grant release through his 'adjutorie', he implicitly compares the king to God. (The same figure receives humorous treatment in *The Dregy*.)

Some aspects of *Schir lat it never in toune be tald* (K 43) have been mentioned already, notably its metrical form and link with Yule festivities (pp. 66–9). The poem begins, in the traditional carol manner, with the burden:

> Schir, lat it never in toune be tald
> That I suld be ane 3owllis 3ald.

Dunbar asks that the king spare him the public humiliation of being a *3owllis 3ald*, a laughing-stock from the lack of a new livery for Christmas. But *3ald* was a highly pejorative term for a horse, and Dunbar reflects that even if he were an old draught-horse, he would be clothed and sheltered at Yule: 'Suppois I war ane auld 3aid aver . . . I wald at 3oull be housit and stald' (2 ff.) The tentative analogy is followed by bold assertion:

> I am ane auld hors, as 3e knaw,
> That ever in duill dois drug and draw;   (9–10)

---

[148] The Latin words are the first verse of Psalm 70; cf. Lindsay, *Monarche*, 6270.

COURT POEMS: PRAISE AND PETITION

and the rest of the poem humorously explores the implications of this metaphor. He is old, white-haired, poorly fed and ill-treated, unlike 'uthair hors' in the king's possession. The poem's structure is not tightly organized, and the sequence of stanzas has no obvious logic.[149] The effect is conversational, weaving to and fro in time. Sometimes the speaker reminisces—'Quhen I was 30ung' (51)—sometimes he anticipates death, and fearfully imagines the common fate of old horses—

> Lat nevir the soutteris have my skin,
> With uglie gumes to be gnawin. (35–6)

None the less the poem is intensely preoccupied with the present moment—'this Crysthinmes'. The last stanza wittily rephrases the first request for the poet's Yule clothing:

> Thocht in the stall I be not clappit
> As cursouris that in silk beine trappit,
> With ane new hous I wald be happit
> Aganis this Crysthinmes for the cald. (63–6)

This repeats the concessive syntax of the first stanza, and echoes the key words 'housit' and 'stald'.

But the poem has, in effect, a double ending, since there follow eight more lines, entitled *Respontio Regis*:

> Efter our wrettingis, thesaurer,
> Tak in this gray hors, auld Dumbar,
> . . . .
> Gar hows him new aganis this 3uill
> And busk him lyk ane bischopis muill . . . (69ff.)

Some have queried whether this piece of verse was written by Dunbar himself rather than James IV. Questions as to authorship regularly arise in such literary interchanges between poet and patron. Among Martial's epigrams is one that purports to be the emperor Domitian's reply to a poem by Martial; a recent scholar, however, considers that Martial put the poem in Domitian's mouth.[150] A literary precedent closer to Dunbar is supplied by two French poems. One, by Deschamps, is a 'supplicacion' to the duke of Orléans, requesting permission to keep his bald head covered in winter:

> Qu'il ait par vostre autorité
> Chaperon tant comme yver dure.

---

[149] Editors, until Kinsley, ordered the stanzas incorrectly, yet the poem's popularity was unaffected by this dislocation; see Kinsley, 320, and Bawcutt, 'Dunbar's Christmas Carol', in Strauss and Drescher, 181–92.

[150] *Epigrams*, i. 5; see P. Howell, *A Commentary on Book One of the Epigrams of Martial* (1980), 4 and 116.

The duke, in the next poem, graciously concedes this 'piteuse requeste':

> Nous plaist qu'en yver et esté
> Nous serve chaperon en teste.[151]

Deschamps' editors thought that he, not the duke, wrote this poem; but there is no conclusive proof of this.[152] Dunbar was audacious enough to devise a favourable coda to his poem, yet I am inclined to accept Baxter's arguments for the king's authorship of the *Respontio*: 'Reidpeth closes the petition itself with a definite attribution to Dunbar, but the *Responsio Regis* has no colophon . . . If Reidpeth had considered the reply to be also Dunbar's, he would have reserved his "Q: Dunbar" for the end.'[153] Other Scottish kings were poets, and James V is known to have engaged in a verse quarrel with Lindsay. It would fit the social, playful nature of Dunbar's poem and the season for which it was written, if the king did indeed reply in kind.

Schir lat it never in toune be tald starts with a play on words, and is replete with verbal jokes and humorous ambiguities. Some—such as the comparison of his hair to a horse's mane (21)—are obvious, even hackneyed, to modern readers, but were probably less so in Dunbar's time. The full piquancy of some words and phrases, however, may not always be appreciated today. Dunbar says that, when young, he 'wald cast gammaldis to the sky' (52): *gammaldis* was applied both to the bounds of a horse and to the vigorous skips and leaps of contemporary court dances.[154] He refers contemptuously to 'gillettis . . . That riddin ar baith with lord and lawd' (47–8): the sexual innuendo in the verb *ride* was then common, but *gillettis* also contains a *double entendre*, meaning both 'mares' and 'wanton young women'.[155] The punning use of other words is even closer to the heart of this poem. Yule is the time when 'lufferis cummis with larges lowd' (45). Dunbar here refers not to the presence of *lovers* at court, but to the ceremonial distribution of *liveries*, both in the primary sense, 'gratuity or bounty of various kinds, including food', and in the specialized secondary sense, 'clothing bestowed as a livery'. But he is also joking—in his animal persona—on a further sense of *livery*: 'an allowance of provender for a horse'. Edmund Spenser commented interestingly on the word's

---

[151] *Œuvres complètes* (see n. 34), vii, nos. 1378 and 1379.
[152] Ibid. xi. 26 and 257.
[153] Baxter, 151.
[154] Cf. French *gambade*, English *gambol*. *DOST*, *gambat*, does not record the application to a horse, but cf. 'gawmondis' in Bellenden, *The Chronicles of Scotland*, ed. R. W. Chambers, E. Batho, and H. W. Husbands (STS, 1938–41), ii. 243.
[155] Cf. Skelton, *The Ancient Acquaintance*, 21, and *Bouge of Court*, 402, 409; Whiting, P 102—'the fayrer woman, the more gylott'.

semantic range: 'what livery is we ... do know well enough, namely that it is allowance of horse-meat, as commonly they use the word in stabling ... And livery is also called the upper garment which a servingman weareth.'[156]

Dunbar puns also on two other words that figure importantly:

> I wald at ȝoull be housit and stald. (6)
> Gryt court hors puttis me fra the staw. (11)
> Thocht in the stall I be not clappit
> . . . .
> With ane new hous I wald be happit. (63 ff.)

In *hous* and the related verb *housit* Dunbar makes a passing allusion to the familiar, present-day word *house*, but this is not his primary meaning; he is using a second word (= French *house*), now obsolete, which signified a covering for horses: 'Horses would be housed in Summer season with canvas to defend the flies, and in Winter with a thicke woollen housing cloth, to keepe them warme.'[157] There is a different play in the case of *stald* and *staw*: Dunbar speaks primarily of the stabling of horses and other animals, but refers to his desire for a benefice, although this is not the poem's main theme. *Stall* had a recognized ecclesiastical sense—as Dunbar writes elsewhere,

> sum unworthy to browk ane stall
> Wald clym to be ane cardinall. (K 39. 49-50)

This poem does not tell a story or make a neat moral point, in the manner of fables, yet its sustained and often humorous equivalence between humans and animals is strongly reminiscent of the beast fable. Through the central image of the horse we are invited to consider various relationships: not only between the poet and the king but between the poet and his fellow-courtiers. In the ranking of horses there existed a hierarchy similar to that in human society. At the top of the equine pyramid—like the aristocrats who rode upon them— were the expensive warhorses and hunting horses—'cursouris that in silk beine trappit' (64); at the bottom were the beasts of burden, such as the humble *aver* (3, 59), that was always mentioned with contempt: 'A kindely aver will never become a good horse'.[158] Different types of horse had different riders—the palfrey was a swift horse, ridden by

---

[156] See *DOST*, *levery*, *liverye*, *luveray*, for the numerous variant spellings; and *A View of the Present State of Ireland*, ed. W. L. Renwick (Oxford, 1970), 34.

[157] Cited, from the treatise on horsemanship attributed to Blundevill, in *OED*, *house*, 2.

[158] Proverbial; cited (from James VI) in *DOST*, *aver*. On the cost of horses, see R. H. C. Davis, *The Medieval Warhorse* (1989), 67.

knights and ladies, whereas mules were particularly associated with clerics. Dunbar evokes this stratified society, as he plays with different self-images: as hard-working and despised as an *aver*, he is excluded from the company of 'court hors' (11) and 'gentill hors' (57) to which he rightfully belongs. Exhausted through long service, he is 'ane forriddin muill' (40).

Yet the poem has further implications: the lot of horses is contrasted with that of men, as well as paralleled. In *The Complaynt of Scotland* nobles are attacked for their 'prodig expensis' on horses and dogs; 'ane man is nocht reput for ane gentill man in Scotland', it is said, unless he spends more on them than on his wife and children.[159] James IV received much-appreciated gifts of horses from Louis XII and John of Denmark; and *The Treasurer's Accounts* document the splendid fabrics with which some of his horses were clad—'housit' not just with wool but with velvet, red crammesy, white damask and cloth of gold, and ornamented with fringes and 'knoppis'.[160] At James's wedding £63 was spent on a rich caparison for the king's horse; but the Yule gown that Dunbar received in 1505 cost £5.[161] Great churchmen kept equally lavish equipages. The *Respontio* promised to 'busk [the poet] lyk ane bischopis muill' (74); if this had been fulfilled literally, Dunbar might have been dressed, like a mule ridden by Cardinal Wolsey, in crimson velvet.[162] One of the poem's subsidiary themes is that the good king has a duty to care for his servitors as solicitously as his horses.

The image of the old horse unifies this poem, and is richly multivalent. It is both self-mocking and self-pitying, 'comical-pathetical'. By its means Dunbar transcends the small, limited matter of his Yule livery. We cannot, on the strength of this poem, enlist Dunbar into the Animal Rights Movement, nor depict him as a social reformer. But he shows, in speaking figuratively of his own 'duill' and 'miserabell' life, an imaginative awareness of the wretched lot of others, whether horses or men, that is rare in his poetry. He also voices, very powerfully, not only his private sense of exclusion from the king's favour but the perennial human fear of being outside in the cold, of rejection (for whatever cause) from a community to which one hopes or expects to belong.

[159] Ed. A. M. Stewart (STS, 1979), 123.
[160] *Letters of James IV 1505–1513*, ed. R. K. Hannay and R. L. Mackie (SHS, 1953), nos. 68 and 135; and Gilbert, *Hunting and Hunting Reserves*, 66–7. See also *TA* Indices, under *house*, *horses*, and the various fabrics.
[161] *TA*, ii. 214; iii. 181.
[162] See Cavendish's *Wolsey*, in *Two Early Tudor Lives*, ed. R. S. Sylvester and D. P. Harding (1962), 25; Lindsay makes the same point more explicitly in *Papyngo*, 1050–2.

4

'Moralitee and Hoolynesse'

MANY of Dunbar's poems are preserved in the first two sections of Bannatyne's anthology, called 'Ballatis of theoligie' and 'Ballatis . . . of moralitie'. Recent editors have adopted a similar categorization: the same seven poems are labelled 'Religious' by Mackenzie and 'Divine' by Kinsley; distinguished from these are the twelve poems that Mackenzie calls 'Moralisings' and the substantially larger number (twenty-seven) that Kinsley calls 'Moralities'. The 'Divine Poems' and 'Moralities' are placed at opposite ends of Kinsley's edition—a physical separation that reinforces one's sense that these are very different types of poem. To some extent the distinction is justified—poems offering practical advice on good conduct or the nature of life are likely to have a different tone and style from prayers, hymns, or meditations on the Crucifixion. Yet 'moralitee and hoolynesse', in Chaucer's phrase,[1] are often allied. In practice it is not always easy—or even desirable—to make a hard and fast distinction between these poems. Dunbar's *Maner of Passyng to Confessioun* (K 5) is placed in the Divine category, yet has little in common with the neighbouring *Done is a battell on the dragon blak* (K 4); it is much closer to the Moralities in its preoccupation with conduct and its hortatory tone: 'I reid the, man . . . Repent the, man, and kepe thi conscience clene' (64 ff.). Conversely, most of Dunbar's moral poems are strongly imbued with a sense of the mutability of 'this warld'. Their counsels for the good life are written *sub specie aeternitatis*, and framed by a Christian perspective of the four last things, death, judgement, heaven, and hell. Some of the Moralities are indeed fine religious poems; it is as well to stress this, since a reader new to Dunbar but aware that he was a churchman might be surprised at the scantiness of the Divine poems. It should also be remembered that Dunbar may well have written much more poetry of an overtly religious nature than has survived (see below, p. 164).

The response to these poems has been mixed. Critics have long concurred in regarding some, notably *Done is a battell* and *I that in heill wes and gladnes* (K 62), as unquestioned masterpieces. The eighteenth-century scholar John Pinkerton, who included many of Dunbar's poems in his pioneering *Ancient Scotish Poems* (1786), praised

---

[1] *CT* I. 3180.

Dunbar's power as a moralist: 'his short moral pieces have a terseness, elegance and force, only inferior to those of Horace'.[2] Yet when he spoke of specific poems, Pinkerton found *Quhat is this lyfe* (K 57) 'beneath notice', and called *The Passioun of Crist* (K 3) 'stupid', *O wreche be war* (K 60) 'very dull', and *Salviour, suppois my sensualite* (K 7) 'pious lines of no moment'. None of the comments on Dunbar, however, is quite so scathing as his dismissal of a poem by Sir Richard Maitland as 'another leaden lump of godliness'.[3] Pinkerton's phrasing is more pungent than that of twentieth-century critics, yet few of these have a good word for *Man sen thy lyfe is ay in weir* (K 67), even if they do not go as far as Scott in calling it 'the worst poem' that Dunbar wrote.[4] The characteristic response today, particularly to the moral poems, seems indifference rather than hostility. They are rarely anthologized, rarely discussed, and (I suspect) rarely read. Despite the recent spate of scholarly articles on Dunbar, few are devoted to the moral poems. Even critics who regard 'morality' as the key to Dunbar have, in practice, surprisingly little to say of them.[5]

There is no doubt that Dunbar's moral poems would have been popular in his own time, and for long afterwards. More than a quarter of Bannatyne's Main Manuscript is devoted to 'ballatis of moralitie'. According to Fox's reckoning it contains 109 separate items, some admittedly short; this number is exceeded only by 'the ballatis of lufe' (142), many of which are highly didactic. The commonplace book compiled by John Maxwell is crammed with pieces of useful knowledge, lists of proverbs, and short sententious verses.[6] Throughout *The Fables* Henryson repeatedly justifies poetry in terms of its truth-telling: he speaks of its 'morall sweit sentence' (12), 'gude moralitie' (366) and—with particular relish—'gude morall edificatioun' (1893). There clearly existed a widespread acceptance, indeed enjoyment, not just of veiled morality, couched in myth and fable, but of explicit didacticism. Dunbar and his readers encountered didactic verse in many forms and many places. Couplets and quatrains were embedded in sermons, serving as useful mnemonics.[7] Lessons on death's inevitability were inscribed on funeral monuments, sundials, and *memento*

---

[2] II. 412.
[3] Ibid. 455, 456, and 461; also 460.
[4] Scott, 258.
[5] See, however, W. Ramson, 'Lettres of Gold Writtin I Fand: A Defence of Moral Verse', *Parergon*, 23 (1979), 37–46, and Introduction to *Poetry of the Stewart Court*, ed. J. Hughes and W. Ramson (Canberra, 1982).
[6] See above, 10, and n. 25.
[7] See S. Wenzel, *Verses in Sermons: 'Fasciculus Morum' and its Middle English Poems* (Cambridge, Mass., 1978), and *Preachers, Poets and the Early English Lyric* (Princeton, 1986).

mori rings. Instructive verses, both in Latin and the vernacular, were placed on chimney-pieces, woven into tapestries, or accompanied wall-paintings. Our knowledge of such practices chiefly derives from England and the Continent; the medieval Scottish evidence has largely been destroyed. Yet Sir James Douglas of Dalkeith is unlikely to have been the only Scottish knight to possess rings bearing mottoes and inscriptions such as 'Vertu ne pus auoir conterpois'.[8] Early in the sixteenth century numerous moral verses and axioms were inscribed in the 'garret' and upon the ceiling of the library in the earl of Northumberland's two Yorkshire houses, at Leconfield and Wressel.[9] Dunbar may well have seen in the palaces of Holyrood and Linlithgow some parallel to these, or to the ceilings of Crathes Castle near Aberdeen, where descriptive verses accompany crude but brilliant paintings of the Nine Nobles and the Nine Muses.[10] When Henryson says, in *The Abbey Walk* (6), that he found 'this' (the poem) 'written upoun a wall', the fiction was based upon a social reality. In the twentieth century our eyes and ears are assaulted by exhortations to spend, to buy, and to consume. To recapture something of the world to which these poems belong we must substitute moral maxims for advertisements, the voice of the Preacher for that of Mammon.

Dunbar's moral poems are best understood if they are placed not only in this wider social milieu, but in an appropriate literary context: the other 'ballatis of moralitie' that surround them in Bannatyne; or Henryson's *The Abbey Walk* and the *Moralitates* to his *Fables*; or the numerous medieval English didactic pieces, many anonymous, some attributed to famous poets, such as Chaucer and Lydgate. Such poems are public and highly impersonal. Their speaker is rarely individualized, rather a representative of humanity in sober and reflective mood:

> Musing allone this hinder nicht
> Of mirry day quhen gone was licht
> Within ane garth undir a tre
> I hard ane voce . . . (K 81. 1-4)

What could be more devoid of personality than the listening poet or the disembodied voice that utters the rest of this poem? It is not surprising that there is some uncertainty as to its authorship—

---

[8] Cf. R. H. Robbins, 'Wall Verses at Launceston Priory', *Archiv*, 200 (1963-4), 338-9, and D. Gray, *Themes and Images in the Medieval English Religious Lyric* (1972), 45-55, on *tituli*-verses and 'speaking objects', such as the tankard which warned its user, 'Pense à ta mort'. For Sir James Douglas's testament (1390), see *Bannatyne Miscellany II*, ed. D. Laing (Bannatyne Club, 1836), 109.

[9] Printed by E. Flügel, *Anglia*, 14 (1891), 472-97.

[10] See H. Hargreaves, 'The Crathes Ceiling Inscriptions', in *Bryght Lanternis: Essays on the Language and Literature of Medieval and Renaissance Scotland*, ed. J. D. McClure and M. R. Spiller (Aberdeen, 1989), 373-86.

attributed to Dunbar in Bannatyne, to 'Stewart' in Maitland—or that many other pieces are anonymous. One of the best-known of Chaucer's moral poems, usually called *Truth*, is anonymous in more than half of the many manuscripts that contain copies of it, including two Scottish ones (Selden B. 24, and CUL Kk. 1. 5). Copies of *Lack of Steadfastness* occur in Bannatyne and Maitland, but in neither is the poem attributed to Chaucer, and in both the language is given a Scottish colouring.[11] Poems of this type were not closely attached to a particular poet or a particular locality. They usually voice sentiments of such a high degree of generality that they could pass easily from one country (and one language) to another. Most are without a setting; some, such as *Musing allone this hinder nicht*, refer vaguely to 'ane garth undir a tre' or similar *chanson d'aventure* location. There is usually, as with 'this hinder nicht', equal vagueness as to time; occasionally an appropriately symbolic date is mentioned, such as Ash Wednesday (K 59). The lack of topical references makes it difficult therefore to link such poems with particular epochs, or with stages in a poet's life.

There is a similar lack of specificity as to the envisaged audience. It is a trademark of this class of poems to contain, usually in the opening, an apostrophe to 'man' or *homo*:

> O man, haif mynd that thow mon pas; (K 59. 5)

or

> *Memento homo quod cinis es.* (K 61. 1)

When Dunbar writes in this way, he is addressing Everyman; these are not necessarily 'court poems'. No less generalized are the 'bredir' to whom the poet twice turns, like a preacher, in *Quho thinkis that he hes sufficence* (K 66):

> Thairfoir I pray 30w, bredir deir,
> Not to delyt in daynteis seir. (11–12)

The *moralitates* to Henryson's *Fables* are similarly scattered with appeals to 'man' (381, 1126), or 'freindis' (365), or 'gude folk' (613, 789). The tone tends to be highly admonitory; these poems, syntactically, often consist of a series of commands. This is particularly evident in *Memento homo quod cinis es*; here the opening exhortation is repeated in different forms, usually in the penultimate line of a stanza:

> Think, man, exceptioun thair is none . . . (15)
> Think, man, amang all uthir sport . . . (23)
> Thairfoir remembir at all houris . . . (31)

---

[11] *Bannatyne Manuscript*, fol. 67a; *Maitland Folio*, no. clvi.

The admonitory *think* punctuates the poem, and achieves the stated object—to 'impres' within the reader's heart the central topic, *Quod tu in cinerem reverteris* (39–40).

Late-medieval poets in England and Scotland favoured, for didactic purposes, the stanza used by Chaucer in *The Monk's Tale*, consisting of eight five-stress lines, rhyming *ababbcbc*. Dunbar also used this form (K 60, 65, 76, and 77), but his taste for a shorter, four-beat line is illustrated in the version of this stanza used in *Memento homo*. He had an evident preference for shorter and more lyrical stanzas, consisting of four or five lines. The most striking metrical feature of Dunbar's moral poems, however, is the use of a refrain, usually proverbial and sometimes Scriptural or liturgical in origin:

> All erdly joy returnis in pane. (K 59)
>
> Into this warld may none assure. (K 63)
>
> *Vanitas vanitatum et omnia vanitas.* (K 60)[12]

This too was a very well-established practice. It is frequent in other Scottish 'ballatis of moralitie', and in the poems attributed to Lydgate, which his editor called 'little homilies with proverbial refrains'.[13] It is a striking feature also of many pieces in the fourteenth-century Vernon Manuscript, which have refrains resembling Dunbar's—'Merci passeth alle thinges', or 'This worlde fareth as a fantasy'.[14] In many of these poems, Dunbar's included, the refrain functions rather like the text of a sermon—it indicates the central theme, which the rest of the poem amplifies. The technique is a simple one, imprinting an idea in the mind by insistent repetition.

In the moral poems, as elsewhere, Dunbar uses refrains adroitly and inventively. In some the refrain is a detached *sententia*, in others it is integrated, syntactically, with the rest of the stanza. Dunbar, like Wyatt, occasionally makes slight but telling adjustments to the wording of his refrains, often to signal the poem's conclusion. In *Quho thinkis that he hes sufficence* (K 66) each stanza ends with the proposition, 'He hes anewch that is content'; in the last two lines this is put in a negative form:

> For of all gudis no thing he hes
> That of no thing can be content. (34–5)

In *Fredome, honour and nobilnes* (K 68) the usual refrain is 'And all for caus of cuvetice'; but the poem ends with

---

[12] Whiting J 58, W 671, and A 92 (Eccles. 1: 2).
[13] *Minor Poems II*, ed. H. N. MacCracken (EETS, OS 192, 1934; rev. 1961), vii.
[14] Cf. *CB XIV*, nos. 95–120.

> Wirk for the place of paradyce,
> For thairin ringis na cuvettyce. (43–4)

In both cases the explanatory conjunction, *For*, gives an air of summing-up. Two poems on a similar theme, *Musing allone this hinder nicht* (K 81) and *How sould I rewill me or in quhat wys* (K 82), also change their refrains in the final stanza. In *Musing allone* the refrain is so varied that it is perhaps better to speak of repeated key-words, such as 'undemit' and 'demyng'; but at the very end the thought shifts from the secular to the spiritual plane, with the prayer,

> In hevin that I may haif ane place;
> For thair sall no man demit be. (54–5)

How sould I rewill me is punctuated by the anxious query: 'Lord God, how sould I governe me?' This is answered only at the end, with a striking turn in the refrain:

> Lat everie man say quhat he will,
> The gratious God mot governe me. (49–50)

Dunbar also makes a neat use of alternating refrains in *The Merle and the Nychtingall* (K 16). The two refrains—'A lusty lyfe in luves service bene' and 'All luve is lost bot upone God allone'—encapsulate the conflicting views of the speakers in this symmetrically patterned debate-poem.

Proverbs and other brief formulaic sayings—maxims, sententiae, stock similes—figure frequently in Dunbar's moral poems. Some virtually consist of a chain of proverbs (in this wider sense), although these often pass unnoticed, because they are now obsolete. A good illustration is provided by the first of a series of three poems, to which Kinsley gave the joint title *Of Discretioun* (K 78–80). Each of these has a refrain containing the word 'discretioun', or good judgement: the second is concerned with discretion in 'giving', whether this be 'almous deidis' (charity) or the reward of servants; the third attacks the greed and lack of discretion in most people's 'taking'. The first of the trio advocates discretion in 'asking', and is essentially a short essay on the art of presenting petitions. There exist other verses on this topic: a quatrain in the Blage Manuscript, for instance, beginning 'He that spares to speak hathe hardly his entent'; or some marginalia in a Hoccleve manuscript.[15] Dunbar's poem, like these, mostly consists of generalities, yet contains a passing rueful mention of himself:

> Sum schames to ask and braidis of [resembles] me,
> And all withowt reward he stervis. (13–14)[16]

---

[15] See *Sir Thomas Wyatt: Unpublished Poems*, ed. K. Muir (1961), xiii; and Whiting, D 166.
[16] In line 13 I adopt Maitland's reading.

'MORALITEE AND HOOLYNESSE'

Other references to 'man and maistir' (19) and servant and lord (41–2) are perhaps equally self-referential. The second stanza (quoted here from the better version in Maitland) runs:

> A fule, quhidder he haue caus or nane,
> Cryis gif me, gif me, in till a rane;
> And he that dronis on as ane be
> Suld haue ane herare dull as a stane:
> In asking suld discretioun be.   (5–10)

The proverbial character of the two similes is obvious, but the phrase 'gif me, gif me' perhaps needs comment. A Scottish homiletic treatise speaks similarly of greedy fools who want everything they see, 'And euir sais, gyf me, gif me'; the ultimate source is Scriptural (Proverbs 30: 15).[17] In Dunbar the snatch of speech exemplifies both greed and monotonous repetition, likely to bore the 'herare'.

A later passage is also partly built out of proverbs:

> He that dois all his best servyis
> May spill it all with crakkis and cryis—
> Be fowll inoportunitie;
> Few wordis may serve the wyis:
> . . . . . .
> Nocht neidfull is, men sowld be dum;
> Na thing is gottin but wordis sum;
> Nocht sped but diligence, we se;
> For nathing it allane will cum . . .   (21 ff.)

These two stanzas contrast two equally fruitless approaches: 'inoportunitie', or irritating persistence in begging, and total silence. The first is clinched by a version of the maxim *Sapienti pauca*, commonly rendered in English as 'few words to the wise suffice'.[18] The opening lines of the next stanza are also proverbial—a supplicant requesting Gavin Douglas's favour wrote similarly, 'A dum man gettis seldom land'. Line 29 is a version of *ex nihilo nihil fit*, which is probably best known today from Lear's words to Cordelia, 'Nothing will come of nothing'.[19] Dunbar ends with the wry reflection that, even if a petition is fruitless, it is useless to complain: 'To fecht with fortoun is no wit' (44). This too is axiomatic, but the usual Scottish form of the proverb supports Maitland's reading, *flyte*, rather than Bannatyne's *fecht*.[20] To

---

[17] *The Foly of Fulys*, in *Ratis Raving*, ed. R. Girvan (STS, 1939), 61.
[18] Whiting, W 588.
[19] Douglas, *Works*, ed. J. Small (Edinburgh, 1874), i, p. lix; Whiting, M 276 and N 151.
[20] Cf. Whiting, F 504 and F 545. For the version with *flyte*, see D 102, and Montgomerie's 'Invectione' against Fortune, in *Poems*, 129.

flyte is to 'fight' verbally, and the word is particularly apt in a poem whose theme is the effective use of language.

Attitudes to proverbs have shifted over the centuries. Today we tend to associate them with the rustic, the unlearned, and, above all, 'the folk'. G. R. Owst, discussing the use of proverbs in medieval homilies, called them 'quaint pessimistic folk-utterances', and David Buchan included proverbs in the 'Folksay' section of his *Scottish Tradition*.[21] But in Dunbar's time and for long afterwards they were much esteemed by the educated—T. A. Shippey neatly summarizes the change, when he speaks of 'the long slide which proverbs have taken from being the signs of the sage to being merely the mark of the vulgar'.[22] Whatever their ultimate origin, proverbs were often first encountered by children at school, in the process of learning Latin. They were quoted and collected by educated men. The *Adagia* was one of Erasmus's most successful books; it continued to be published throughout the sixteenth century, and the English translation by Taverner was equally popular. Proverbs were literally 'the signs of the sage', often being attributed to men famed for their wisdom, such as Cato, Seneca, and Solomon. The flippant or the foolish might show derision, like Chaucer's January: 'Straw for thy Senek and for thy proverbes'. But the advice of one anonymous Scottish writer—'Tak kep to prowerbis, quhare thou heris'—was more representative.[23] Proverbs today are often scorned for their triteness; Dunbar's contemporaries valued them precisely because they were 'old' and 'soth'— they enshrined a collective wisdom handed down from antiquity.

The attempt to find specific sources for Dunbar's moral poems seems fruitless. They draw upon a vast and amorphous didactic tradition—both oral and written, in Latin and the vernaculars, embodied sometimes in proverbs, sometimes in short verses of the type quoted in homilies, sometimes in the homilies themselves or other works of instruction. Characteristic examples from a fifteenth-century Scottish manuscript have titles that speak for themselves: *The Foly of Fulys and the Thewis [virtues] of Wysmen*, *The Thewis of Gud Women*, and *The Craft of Deying*.[24] The ultimate germ of many ideas and sayings can be found in the Wisdom books of the Bible, such as Proverbs, Ecclesiastes, and the non-canonical Ecclesiasticus, which were long believed to be the work of Solomon. Henryson, like other writers, thus buttresses some pronouncements in *The Fables* with references to Solomon (391, 1130). But the Scriptural origin of many

---

[21] *Literature and Pulpit in Medieval England* (1933; rev. Oxford, 1961), 43.
[22] 'Maxims in Old English Narrative: Literary Art or Traditional Wisdom?', in *Oral Tradition, Literary Tradition*, ed. P. Foote et al. (Odense, 1977), 44.
[23] *CT* IV. 1567; Girvan, *Ratis Raving*, 175.
[24] CUL Kk. 1. 5; printed by Girvan, op. cit.

sayings was forgotten, and they seem to have been absorbed into the common stock of popular, semi-proverbial wisdom. Dunbar rarely refers to authorities, apart from the occasional vague 'as haly writ sayis' (K 5. 3) or 'the psalme sayis' (K 77. 15). As far as his moral poems are concerned, it is better to speak of analogues than sources, and most profitable to identify stock themes and genres, and the degree of skill with which these are treated.

None the less it is repeatedly said that Dunbar is indebted to Lydgate, and two poems often cited as evidence are *Musing allone this hinder nicht* (K 81) and *How sould I rewill me or in quhat wys* (K 82). Kinsley says tentatively that they are 'perhaps modelled on Lydgate's *A wicked Tunge wille sey Amys*', but not all literary historians have been so cautious, and the assertion needs to be firmly rebutted.[25] Neither of these poems resembles Lydgate's *A Wicked Tunge* at all closely; the similarities are essentially generic. All three treat what Owst called a 'typical pulpit theme':[26] the impossibility of avoiding malicious criticism, or 'deming'. Preachers tended to place this topic under the larger heading of Envy, in its sub-branch of slander or backbiting; there are thus references, in *Musing allone*, to 'vicious wordis' and 'tratling tungis' (38–9), and, in *How sould I rewill me*, to 'malice and invy' and 'sklandir' (37–9). Gregory Kratzmann perceptively noted that Dunbar and Lydgate shared not only a subject but a technique, 'the use of a *pro* and *contra* arrangement' of their ideas.[27] He compared Dunbar's

> Be I bot littill of stature
> Thay call me catyve createure,
> And be I grit of quantetie
> Thay call me monstrowis of nature.
> (*Musing allone*, 26–9)

to Lydgate's

> 3if thow be fatte owther corpolent,
> Than wille folke seyn thow art a grete glotown
> . . . .
> 3if thow be lene or megre of fassioun,
> Calle the a negard yn ther oppynyoun.
> (*A Wicked Tunge*, 43 ff.)

This balancing of alternatives, however, was not peculiar to Lydgate, but a stock feature of the theme. Both the Dunbar poems, it is true,

---

[25] See *Minor Poems II*, no. 76, and Kinsley, 372. The notion can be traced to Lord Hailes, *Ancient Scottish Poems*, 263; cf. R. D. S. Jack, 'Dunbar and Lydgate', *SSL* 8 (1970–1), 222; and F. Ridley, in *A Manual of Writings in Middle English 1050–1500*, ed. A. E. Hartung, iv (1973), 1010.
[26] *Literature and Pulpit*, 457.
[27] *Anglo-Scottish Literary Relations 1430–1550* (Cambridge, 1980), 139–40.

have a similar pattern—a string of hypothetical clauses, often arranged in antithetical pairs, beginning 'Be I . . .' in *Musing allone*, and 'Gif I . . .' in *How sould I rewill me*. But exactly the same rhetorical pattern is found in two prose passages quoted by Owst: one is translated from the Latin of Nicholas Bozon, the other comes from a vernacular homily, depicting the malicious behaviour of a backbiter. If he hears a man saying his prayers,

he demeth hym ane ypocrite and would ben holden holy; and iff that he see hym not so, than he demeth hym undevoute and worldely; and 3iff that he see hym a pacient man . . . than he demeth [hym] herteles and dredefull; and 3iff he answere ageyn shortely he demeth hym prowde . . . so that what thinge a man doth, he demeth hym amysse.[28]

The same type of syntax occurs in a later poem, *Aganis Sklanderous Tungis*, attributed to John Maitland, and in a fifteenth-century carol.[29] This latter, although it cannot be termed Dunbar's 'source', is closer to him than is the Lydgate poem in three respects: it is written in the first person; it has a simple metre, the common carol form with a four-beat line; and the burden,

> Lord, how scholde I roule me
> Of al men to ipreysed be?

has a striking resemblance not only to the opening line of *How sould I rewill me* but also to its refrain, 'Lord God, how sall I governe me?'.

The two Dunbar poems are much the same length, and share the same metrical form; they also reach a similar conclusion, that the best course is to disregard malicious criticism, and to be virtuous—'Do weill, and sett not by demyng' (K 81. 49), and 'To do the best my mynd salbe' (K 82. 48). It is not impossible that Dunbar tackled the same theme twice, though one might expect him to have executed some ingenious variations, as in the two poems on the 'feist of benefyce' (K 40 and K 41). It should be recalled that Bannatyne is alone in attributing *Musing allone* to Dunbar, and it seems to me a less successful piece than *How sould I rewill me*. Its imagined speaker has no plausibility, but is simply a device to consider a number of figures, from 'crownit king' to 'lady fresche and fair'. Its tone is sometimes curiously threatening—'Bot God send thame a widdy wicht' (24)—and sometimes sycophantic, in its praise of 'Gude James the ferd, our nobill king' (46). *How sould I rewill me* is far better constructed, with its series of neatly paired antithetical stanzas, and effective use of *interrogatio*. Its speaker, although a stereotype of the anxious courtier, is psychologically more coherent. The poem does more than condemn

---

[28] Op. cit. 456–7.
[29] *Maitland Folio*, no. lxxxviii; Greene, *Carols*, no. 349.

backbiting and slander; it also incorporates short snatches of such speech—'3one man, out of his mynd is he' (8) or 'Evill gydit is 3on man, par de' (28)—as Dunbar does elsewhere, in *The Flyting* (K 23) and *This hinder nycht halff sleiping as I lay* (K 51).

Another highly generic poem, *To dwell in court, my freind, gife that thow list* (K 77), has had few admirers. Scott unkindly saw Dunbar as here playing the role of a 'prating avuncular Polonius'.[30] The poem is indeed indebted to the same tradition that informs Polonius's advice to Laertes—stock 'precepts' couched in the form of a parent addressing his son (see lines 6 and 30). Practical counsel on how to succeed in the world is interspersed with conventional moralizing. The most influential medieval example of this genre was the pseudo-Cato's *Disticha de Moribus ad Filium*, which was a common school text. But there were many vernacular works that, in some way or other, partook of the tradition; Scottish examples include *Ratis Raving*, and *The Consail and Teiching at the Vys Man gaif his Sone*, and an anonymous poem in the Maitland Folio, that begins 'My sone, gif thow to the court will ga' and has this colophon: 'How the fader teichit the sone'.[31] *To dwell in court* has the lack of logical development that seems characteristic of the kind; its leading theme is voiced by the refrain, 'He rewlis weill that weill him self can gyd'. This recalls lines in Chaucer's *Truth*: 'Reule wel thyself, that other folk canst rede ... Daunte thyself' (6, 13); and might be traced, ultimately, to Boethius's advice, in *The Consolation of Philosophy* (II. iv), to be 'mighty over thyself'. But by the late Middle Ages the thought was a commonplace, and had virtually proverbial status. Alexander Scott thus admonished Mary, Queen of Scots: 'Thai gyde [behave] nocht ill that governis weill thame sell'.[32]

Perhaps the most interesting fact about *To dwell in court* is that it was reworked by Maitland, in his poem beginning, 'My sone, in court gif thow pleisis remane'.[33] The relationship between these two poems goes beyond the usual generic similarity. Maitland uses the same eight-line stanza as Dunbar, and virtually the same refrain. He also takes over many lines, some almost verbatim:

> Behold and heir and lat thy tung tak rest.   (Dunbar, 3)
> Behald and heir and to thy tung tak tent.   (Maitland, 4)
> Be war quhome to thy counsale thow discure.   (Dunbar, 9)
> Be war quhamto thy counsale thow reveile.   (Maitland, 17)

---

[30] Scott, 154.
[31] *Maitland Folio*, no. xlvii. For a useful survey of the tradition, see *Hamlet*, ed. H. Jenkins (1982), 440–3.
[32] *Poems*, no. I. 99; cf. Whiting, G 407.
[33] *Maitland Folio*, no. xiv.

'MORALITEE AND HOOLYNESSE'

With wilfull men, son, argown thow no tyd. (Dunbar, 30)
With weilfull men to argoun is folie. (Maitland, 23)

We do not know whether Maitland was aware of Bannatyne's attribution of this poem to Dunbar—no other copy now survives—but he certainly used it as a starting-point for his own much longer piece. What is more, he makes it more specifically a court poem, significantly altering Dunbar's refrain, 'He rewlis weill that weill himself can gyd', to 'He reulis weill that weill in court can gyde'. Maitland is clearly addressing those likely to hold political office; later stanzas (which have no equivalent in Dunbar) speak of loyalty to one's prince and service to 'the common weill'. Despite its triteness, the poem may well have been intended for his sons' instruction; two of them, John and William, became well-known statesmen in the reigns of Mary and James VI. English aristocrats, such as Lord Burleigh and Sir Walter Ralegh, addressed their sons in this way. Dunbar's poem, despite one mention of the court in its first line, seems more concerned with conduct in society at large. It is not inconceivable that it was addressed 'to a young friend at court';[34] but, if so, there is no clue to identify him, and a total absence of the small satirical references to court life that characterize much of Dunbar's poetry.

A small number of these poems form a sub-group, treating such interrelated themes as the right use of worldly goods, the folly of avarice, and the virtue of contentment. *Quho thinkis that he hes sufficence* (K 66) counsels acceptance of one's lot, whether good or bad:

> Thank God of it is to the sent,
> And of it glaidlie mak gud cheir:
> Anewch he hes that is content. (13–15)

This poem has much in common with the *Moralitas* of Henryson's *Two Mice*. Its proverbial refrain resembles Henryson's 'Quha hes aneuch, of na mair hes he neid' (375). A later line, 'Gif we not clym we tak no fall' (29), recalls Henryson's reflection on the 'vexatioun' of those who climb too high (371); and the warning that a sour sauce accompanies the sweet pleasures of life (19) is similar to the words at the fable's end: 'Thy guse is gude, thy gansell sour as gall' (345). But stock themes tended to generate stock phrases and imagery. In *Be mery, man, and tak nocht fer in mynd* (K 65), occurs a line very similar to the passage just quoted:

> Mak gude cheir of it that God the sendis. (9)

The refrain to Henryson's *Abbey Walk* has the same ring:

---

[34] Kinsley, 369.

'MORALITEE AND HOOLYNESSE'

> Obey and thank thi God off all.

A similar cluster of ideas occurs in Lydgate:

> Be paied with litel, content with suffisaunce,
> Clymb nat to hih, thus biddith Socrates;
> Glad pouert is of tresours moost substaunce . . .[35]

For Chaucer the theme of 'glad poverty' was associated with 'Senec and othere clerkes', rather than Socrates.[36] But the notion of 'sufficence' also had a Scriptural basis. It derived from St Paul's praise of *sufficientia*, or contentment (1 Timothy 6: 6), and his words, 'I have learned, in whatsoever state I am, therewith to be content [Vulgate: *sufficiens esse*]' (Philippians 4: 11). Such beliefs inevitably promoted acceptance of the established social order.[37]

The right use of worldly goods does not rule out their proper enjoyment. These poems are strewn with exhortations to be glad and merry, and to 'mak gud cheir'. Such sentiments also possessed Scriptural sanction. In the fifteenth-century Scottish paraphrase of Ecclesiastes we are told that the wise man 'fand at thar was na-thing in erd sa gud fore manis sone as to hald hyme weill at es of the gudis thate god sendis hyme in this warld, and mak gud chere quhill he is here, and leiff weill'.[38] The same work renders the verse that begins *Laudavi igitur laetitiam* as 'Item he sais, et and drink and mak gud cheir'.[39] In the *Moralitas* to *The Two Mice* Henryson translated another verse from Ecclesiastes (3: 12) as

> Under the hevin thair can not better be
> Than ay be blyth and leif in honestie. (392–3)

Proverbs voiced similar counsel—'Men should make merry while they may' or 'Longer lives a glad man than a sorry'.[40] Maitland comforted himself with this train of thought in a real instance of adversity, the 'spulʒie' of his estates; he even punned on the word 'blyth' and the name of his barony of Blyth. But there was a dangerous ambiguity in the notion of 'gud cheir'. The moralist advocated a temperate enjoyment—Henryson thus coupled being 'blyth' with living 'in honestie'; and Maitland, in another poem, recommended 'leifsum', or

---

[35] *Minor Poems II*, no. 57.
[36] *Wife of Bath's Tale*, III. 1183 ff.
[37] Cf. the verse, quoted in Durkan and Ross, *Early Scottish Libraries*, 21: 'And quhat his majeste hes appointit / Thairof we ar richt weill contentit'.
[38] Girvan, *Ratis Raving*, 182. The Salernitan regimen of health recommended *mens laeta*; cf. Olson, *Literature as Recreation in the Later Middle Ages* (Ithaca, New York, 1982), 52.
[39] Girvan, 189; Eccles. 8: 15.
[40] Whiting, M 214 and M 131; cf. M 513.

legitimate, merriness.⁴¹ Some Scottish 'gud cheir' poems, however, approach the tone of *carpe diem*. The authorship of one is jocularly attributed to a pseudonymous 'Iohin Blyth'; it employs much the same saying as the paraphrase of Ecclesiastes—'Mak we gud cheir quhill we ar heir'—but turns it into a flippant incitement to drinking and revelry.⁴² Dunbar's *He that hes gold and grit riches* (K 70) is a poem of this type, and will be discussed later (p. 185).

One poem from this group, *Man, sen thy lyfe is ay in weir* (K 67), is rarely liked and often misunderstood.⁴³ Its theme is expressed in the refrain, 'Thyne awin gude spend quhill thow hes space'. To equate this with the familiar modern saying, 'Spend, spend, spend!' would be a misreading. This is no exhortation to selfish extravagance, but a practical counsel to use one's possessions in the best possible way while still alive. The poem contains a standard reproof of the miser, 'Ay gadderand geir with sorrow and pane' (18). It also recommends drawing up a will, to prevent quarrels, even bloodshed, after one's death:

> Quhill thow hes space see thow dispone
> That for thy geir, quhen thow art gone,
> No wicht ane uder slay nor chace. (13–15)

The commonsense of this is still evident today. The poem tends to be misunderstood, I think, because it is viewed in isolation, and taken to express the intimate feelings of Dunbar himself. Whether he wrote it, in fact, seems questionable; Bannatyne's attribution is not supported by Maitland, and there are several clumsy passages.

This poem is better understood if related to other writings on the theme, such as the tags and short verses often quoted in sermons and copied into commonplace books. The *Fasciculus Morum*, a popular Latin handbook for preachers, includes an English version of the well-known riddling saying, *Quod expendi habui, Quod donavi habeo*—'That y spende that y had. / That y ȝeue that y haue'.⁴⁴ These verses, and others, are embedded in a discussion of the importance of almsgiving while still alive; a man should not 'leave his goods after his death to his heirs, who will grasp them without care for their relative's eternal welfare'.⁴⁵ Dunbar seems to allude, obscurely, to such verses in line 29, and also mentions the heir's reluctance to say (or endow) prayers for the dead (21–22). He comments,

> Sum grit gud gadderis and ay it spairis,
> And efter him thair cumis ȝung airis
> That his auld thrift settis [gambles] on ane es [ace]. (25–7)

---

[41] *Maitland Folio*, nos. xxiii and cii. [42] *Bannatyne Manuscript*, fol. 113a.
[43] Cf. Scott, 258–60. [44] See Wenzel, *Verses in Sermons*, no. 50.
[45] Ibid. 190.

This does not voice warm-hearted trust in human nature, but the cynicism is not peculiar to Dunbar. Numerous medieval poems express similar distrust of children, wives, heirs, and also executors. One snatch of verse was copied again and again:

> Wyves be rekeles, chyldren be onkynd,
> Executurs be covetys and hold that thei fynd.[46]

The idea, as so often, can be traced to Ecclesiastes (2: 18–19).

The dominant theme of most medieval moralists is human mortality, and the mutability of all worldly things. It is not surprising that these are the central preoccupations of at least ten of Dunbar's poems. Such key phrases as 'this warld' and 'this life' occur frequently, often at a poem's beginning, and signal the homiletic approach:

> O wreche, be war: this warld will wend the fro. (K 60)

or

> this fals warld is ay on flocht. (K 64)

or

> Quhat is this lyfe bot ane straucht way to deid,
> Quhilk hes a tyme to pas and nane to duell;
> A slyding quheill us lent to seik remeid,
> A fre chois gevin to paradice or hell,
> A pray to deid, quhome vane is to repell;
> A schoirt torment for infineit glaidnes—
> Als schoirt ane joy for lestand hevynes. (K 57)

Quhat is this lyfe is Dunbar's shortest poem; it may possibly be a stanza excerpted, as was common, from some longer work, written in rhyme royal. Our attention is arrested by the opening question, and by the sequence of replies, that contain stark antitheses, often with a hint of paradox. The piece has an epigrammatic neatness and brevity. The opening idea, that life is nothing but a path to death, resembles a famous saying of Seneca: *hominis tota vita nihil aliud quam iter ad mortem*.[47] But both the thought and its formulation were very common; numerous proverbs and verses tell us that life is 'but a' journey or a pilgrimage; analogous images for its brevity are a dream or a puff of air:

---

[46] Quoted by Greene, *Carols*, no. 366 n.; see also *Colkelbie Sow*, ed. G. Kratzmann (New York, 1983), 254 ff., and the many citations in Whiting, M 59.
[47] Cf. Kinsley, 350 and Gray, *Themes and Images*, 176.

'MORALITEE AND HOOLYNESSE'

> Quhat ar we bot a puff of braith
> Quho live assurd of no thing bot of deth.[48]

The definition, sometimes of life but more commonly of love, forms a minor poetic topos. Many medieval poets attempted to define love, sometimes in independent poems, sometimes in brief sections of long works, such as the stanza in Henryson's *Orpheus and Eurydice* (401 ff.) that opens, 'Quhat art thow lufe? How sall I the dyffyne?'[49] Definition poems about life seem rarer, but *Quhat is this lyfe* has a parallel in the fifteenth-century *What is this worlde but oonly vanite?*, to which it is far superior. The most famous example of the kind is a sixteenth-century poem, *What is our life? A play of passion*, which is sometimes attributed to Ralegh.[50] The Elizabethan poem develops a detailed and ingenious analogy between the theatre and the life of man; Dunbar's poem is more succinct but less witty.

Quhat is this lyfe contains, in little, several of the leading themes of Dunbar's mortality lyrics: it presents uncompromising choices between 'this lyfe' and the next, and between paradise and hell. Man is a *viator*, a traveller or 'pilgrame' (K 60. 9),

> tending to ane uther place
> A journay going everie day.   (K 69. 29–30)

Preachers constantly made this point: everyone is a pilgrim, 'ilke day of hys lyf travayling a dayes jorne towarde the place where he shall dwelle ay without ende'.[51] In this poem man is Death's *prey*, as in *I that in heill wes* (95), and also in *Off Lentren in the first mornyng* (K 59), where

> Deth followis lyfe with gaipand mowth
> Devoring fruct and flowring grane.   (10–11)

In *Memento homo quod cinis es* the reader is admonished similarly:

> Thy lustye bewte and thy 3outh
> Sall feid as dois the somer flouris;
> Syne sall the swallow with his mouth
> The dragone death that all devouris.   (25–8)

Life is a game of chess that one cannot win; death will 'say to the than, Chakmait' (*To dwell in court*, 21). Dunbar's imagery for death and mutability is highly traditional, and often Scriptural in origin; but

---

[48] Attributed to Sir William Alexander, *Bannatyne Manuscript*, 54; see also Whiting, L 240, L 241, and L 242.
[49] See Bawcutt, 'Source-Hunting: Some Reulis and Cautelis', in Lyall and Riddy, 93–4.
[50] See *CB XV*, no. 168, and Ralegh, *Poems*, ed. A. Latham (1951), no. xxxi.
[51] Owst, *Literature and Pulpit*, 103.

it is also apt and effective.[52] It should also be noted that in these poems Dunbar rarely dwells on the corruption of the body after death, in the manner of many late-medieval writers. There is one brief reference, in *Memento homo* (20), to 'ane ugsum ugelye tramort'; Dunbar's reticence contrasts with the grisly description of the corpses in Henryson's *Thre Deid Pollis*.[53]

Change, paradoxically, is the one unchanging feature of 'this warld unstabille', ruled by the goddess Fortune. The ever-turning wheel is the traditional emblem of her 'fals change' (K 64. 7–9); and in *Quhat is this lyfe* (3) symbolizes life's different stages.[54] It is appropriate that the rhetorical devices most often employed in these poems are antithesis and some form of *repetitio*. *Off Lentren in the first mornyng* (K 59) is largely built from a combination of these two figures:

> Heir helth returnis in seiknes
> And mirth returnis in havines,
> Toun in desert, forrest in plane;
> All erdly joy returnis in pane. (25–8)

When this pattern is repeated for several stanzas, the message is clear but the effect monotonous. Bannatyne's attribution to Dunbar may be correct, but the poem does not show him at his best; it is anonymous in Maitland. Elsewhere, however, at the end of *O wreche be war* (K 60) Dunbar employs a similar technique very effectively:

> Heir nocht abydis, heir standis nothing stabill;
> This fals warld ay flittis to and fro;
> Now day up bricht, now nycht als blak as sabill,
> Now eb, now flude, now freynd, now cruell fo,
> Now glaid, now said, now weill, now in to wo,
> Now cled in gold, dissolvit now in as;
> So dois this warld transitorie go:
> *Vanitas vanitatum et omnia vanitas.* (17–24)

This is an instance of what might be called the 'Now this, now that' formula; it was so frequent in medieval writers that Whiting gave it proverbial status.[55] The topos was particularly associated with the reversals of Fortune, and often employed in formal Complaints against Fortune, such as that of the poet-dreamer in *The Palice of Honour*

---

[52] See I. Hyde, 'Primary Sources and Associations of Dunbar's Aureate Imagery', *MLR* 51 (1956), 481–92.

[53] On such imagery in *The Flyting*, however, see below, 194.

[54] See H. R. Patch, *The Goddess Fortuna in Mediaeval Literature* (Cambridge, Mass., 1927); on the wheel of *life*, see M. Dove, *The Perfect Age of Man's Life* (Cambridge, 1986), 80 ff.

[55] It is copiously documented in N 179; for Scottish uses, see *Wallace*, iv. 336–40; Henryson, *Fables*, 2941–7, and *Testament of Cresseid*, 237–8.

(174 ff.).⁵⁶ Dunbar's use is leisurely, but elegant. His list, which is an amplification of the statement in line 18, contains six antithetical pairs, several of which have the extra ornament of rhyme or alliteration. Most make a strong contrast between a good term and an adverse one, usually placed in emphatic final position. But the pattern of distribution within the line varies. Lines 20 and 21 thus contrast with lines 19 and 22 in containing two pairs, not one. The last line is particularly striking: the body of the richest man, 'cled in gold', must eventually dissolve into dust and ashes. The pomp of life is contrasted with the disintegration of the corpse, and leads fittingly to the poem's refrain, the famous words of Ecclesiastes—'Vanity, vanity, all is vanity'. This stanza is as carefully patterned, syntactically, as that which concludes *Done is a battell*. It also echoes themes and images used earlier in the poem—the friend-foe contrast (2), or the fear of approaching night (11)—and furnishes an excellent climax.

One of the most attractive of these poems is *I seik about this warld unstabille* (K 58). It starts not with the usual tone of cast-iron certainty as to the nature of life, but in the tentative, exploratory manner of someone searching for the right words:

> Bot I can nocht in all my wit
> Sa trew ane sentence fynd off it
> As say, it is dessaveabille.   (3–5)

This poem has no refrain, and its four stanzas convey a sense of logical progression that is often difficult to achieve in refrain-poems. Small grammatical pointers lightly guide our perception of this movement of ideas. The conjunction *For* introduces the two central stanzas that explain *why* the poet chooses this particular 'sentence'. The last stanza seems to sum up, in the manner of a theorem, twice prefixing conclusions with *So*—'So nixt to summer winter bein [is]', and 'Sa is this warld, and ay hes bein'. The central stanzas deftly suggest an imaginary debate, between the poet—'I did declair' (6)—and his antagonist, the weather, who out-argues him—'Concluding all in my contrair' (10).⁵⁷ These two stanzas are a vivid embodiment of the 'now this, now that' topos. The see-sawing between opposed states is translated into a highly circumstantial grumble about a change in the weather:

> 3isterday fair up sprang the flouris,
> This day thai ar all slane with schouris;

---

⁵⁶ Patch, op. cit. 55 ff.
⁵⁷ *DOST*, *conclude*, 2d, glosses this use as 'come to an end'. But both the verb and the related 'conclusionis' (K 62. 39) were applied to verbal argument and logical confutation: see *OED*, *conclude*, 4 and 8.

'MORALITEE AND HOOLYNESSE'

  And fowllis in forrest that sang cleir
  Now walkis with a drery cheir,
  Full caild ar baith thair beddis and bouris. (11–15)

Every detail contributes to one major image, that of a blighted spring, a 'seasoun' (7) in which winter seems to coexist with summer. There is the usual rhetorical patterning in the twice repeated antithesis between 'ʒisterday' and 'This day'; but the balance is tipped very much to the adverse side. Less space is devoted to the former 'cleir' song of the birds than to their present 'drery cheir'; yet there is a leavening wry humour in the anthropomorphic reference to their beds and bowers.

  Full oft I mus and hes in thocht (K 64) also suggests a man turning over in his mind familiar commonplaces, such as Fortune's revolving wheel. The poem opens in the first person: 'Full oft I mus ... and quhen I haif my mind all socht' (1–4). It has a proverbial-sounding refrain, 'For to be blyth me think it best', which resembles that of an anonymous Scottish poem: 'In baill be blyth for that is best'.[58] Dunbar's refrain is similarly alliterative, but the phrase *me think* is appropriate to his more tentative and intimate poem. The penultimate stanza voices remarkably raw and painful emotion:

    Had I for warldis unkyndnes
    In hairt tane ony havines
    Or fro my plesans bene opprest
    I had bene deid lang syne, dowtles. (31–4)

Yet this is followed by conventional moralizing:

    How evir this warld do change and vary,
    Lat us in hairt nevir moir be sary ... (36–7)

and there are other passages of third-person admonition:

    Wald man considdir in mynd rycht weill
    Or Fortoun on him turn hir quheill
    That erdly honour may nocht lest,
    His fall less panefull he suld feill. (11–14)

  The poem is an interesting, if not wholly successful, mixture of modes: personal and impersonal, reflective and hortatory. Its syntax is characterized by hypothetical conditional clauses—'Wald man considdir', or 'Had I for warldis unkyndnes ... bene opprest'. Dunbar looks now to the future, now back to a painful past—'I had bene deid lang syne, dowtles'. Such twists and turns suggest a mind 'in thocht', as in *I seik about this warld unstabille*. The poem is pervaded by awareness

---

[58] *Maitland Folio*, no. lxxxv.

that this life is, in the Scriptural phrase, 'bot twynklyng of ane e' (29), compared to eternity. Yet its theme is not *contemptus mundi*, but rather the best manner of living while in the world. One should not live 'in dolour' (17) or 'drowp' (26) because of adversity or 'unkyndnes'; one should take a fit pleasure in the good things of life (21-4), as in the 'gud cheir' poems mentioned earlier. The refrain admirably catches the poet's tone, a kind of dogged resolution to make the best of things: 'For to be blyth me think it best.'

Modern readers might well be surprised by Bannatyne's remark that the second section of his anthology contained 'verry singular ballattis'.[59] Singularity is precisely what seems missing from most late-medieval moral poems. Their poets do not seek to be original, either in theme or expression, but rather to express lasting truths as plainly as possible. They are characterized not by intimate personal feeling but by impersonality; stylistically, they tend to conform to the conventions of particular genres. The short moral poems attributed to Dunbar are largely of this kind, and it is not surprising that his authorship, as we have seen, is sometimes in doubt. Several are neat and adroit, and may well have been written by Dunbar; but they could also have been written by any reasonably competent poet of his time. A few of Dunbar's moral poems, however, are exceptional; they are singular in the usual modern sense as well as in Bannatyne's sense of 'morally excellent'. Although firmly rooted in the same traditions as the others, they stand out, for their urgency of tone, more daring use of language, and precision in the charting of emotion.

Quhy will ȝe merchantis of renoun (K 75) is a hortatory poem that undoubtedly derives much force from its specificity: the merchants belong not to 'N-town' but to Edinburgh. The reader is invited to 'pas throw' its 'principall gaittis' (streets) (8), and to observe well-known landmarks (above, p. 46); one's senses are assaulted by vivid details—street-cries, snatches of popular song, and 'the stink of haddockis' or 'pudingis of Jok and Jame' (9, 25). It is thus often regarded as a satire or descriptive piece, and valued for the murky light it casts on late-medieval Edinburgh. It is included in W. C. Dickinson's *A Source Book of Scottish History*, and other historians treat its testimony with respect.[60] Yet Kinsley is right to include it among the 'Moralities', and to suggest its affinity with the medieval *sermones ad status*, homilies addressed to different classes of society.[61] *To speik of science, craft or*

---

[59] Fol. 43b.
[60] Vol. 2 (1963), 226-8. Cf. P. Hume Brown, *Scotland before 1700* (Edinburgh, 1893), 109-12.
[61] Kinsley, 366-7.

sapience (K 76) might also be regarded as a poem of this type, since it is directed explicitly to 'clerkis', or scholars, and is concerned with the vanity of all forms of learning that are unaccompanied by 'guid lyff' (14). Yet the latter is a rather dull piece, and lacks local colour. Nothing in its text links the poem with 'Oxenford', mentioned in one colophon, or indeed with any other university.

Dunbar opens by addressing the merchants, the powerful and prosperous oligarchy that governed Edinburgh:[62]

> Quhy will 3e merchantis of renoun
> Lat Edinburgh 3our nobill toun
> For laik of reformatioun
> The commone proffeitt tyine, and fame?
>   Think 3e not schame,
> That onie uther regioun
> Sall with dishonour hurt 3our name?   (1-7)

Dunbar's principal concern is with Edinburgh's *name*, the word that occurs finally in this and every succeeding stanza. *Name* has the specialized sense of 'reputation'. Edinburgh possesses a 'great name' (63), but one that is all too often linked with dishonour or 'hurt and sklander' (21 and *passim*). The repeated coupling of 'name' and 'schame' in the fifth and seventh lines of each stanza is highly damaging. The poem is rhetorically striking, both for the *repetitio* on 3*our*—insisting that Edinburgh is the merchants' responsibility—and the effective use of *interrogatio*. But Dunbar shows greatest virtuosity in his handling of the unusual stanza. Its most obvious feature is the internal refrain, 'Think 3e nocht schame'; this gains prominence from its brevity, which contrasts with the four-stress pattern of other lines. It serves as the pivot of the stanza: the preceding quatrain usually contains the vivid particulars of the indictment, whereas the last three lines function like an expanded refrain, and often carry a more explicit comment. One slight change, from 'Think 3e nocht schame' to 'And eschew schame' (61), seems to signal a change of tone, from reproach to exhortation.

Dunbar appeals, in part, to the merchants' self-interest:

> Sen for the court and the sessioun
> The great repair of this regioun
> Is in 3our burgh, thairfoir be boun
> To mend all faultis that ar to blame,
>   And eschew schame;
> Gif thai pas to ane uther toun
> 3e will decay, and 3our great name.   (57-63)

---

[62] Cf. J. Wormald, *Court, Kirk and Community: Scotland 1470-1625* (1981), 46-9.

Edinburgh's predominance over other burghs 'as a royal, political and judicial centre was a phenomenon of the later fifteenth century', as R. J. Lyall has noted;[63] presumably, if it lost that position, the merchants' business would suffer. But Dunbar also appeals to their moral sense, in his first passing reference to 'the commone proffeitt' (4) and the later:

> Singular proffeit so dois 3ow blind
> The common proffeit gois behind. (71-2)

'Singular proffeit' signified a man's concern with his private (and usually selfish) interests; 'common proffeit', like the analogous 'common weill', referred to the public interest, the good of the community at large. The latter derived from the classical concept of *res publica*, and carried a weight of traditional thinking; by the fourteenth century it was a commonplace, especially in legal writing. In Dunbar's time both phrases were almost clichés—as familiar as 'private profit' or 'the community' are today—and were often juxtaposed. Sir Gilbert Haye, criticizing the king who spends lavishly on himself while his country is poor, says: 'than gais singulere prouffit before the commoun prouffit'.[64] Dunbar's stance here is wholly orthodox: the self-interest of a particular class should give way to the good of the community.

What this poem says would hardly be novel to the merchants; they themselves repeatedly complained 'anent the multitude of beggares', or proclaimed that flyting should be punished, and that butchers should not sell 'thair nolt heids, nowmyllis nor interallis [entrails]' in the open street.[65] Dunbar calls rather upon the merchants to practise what they preached. His phrasing is remarkably close to that used by contemporary Edinburgh councils. On 20 August 1500 the provost declared that he sought 'the worschip and polece of this burgh, and commoun proffitt of the nichtbouris thairof and all vtheris reparand thairto'.[66] Dunbar likewise urges the merchants to 'wirk polesie' (18): he asks them to implement *policy* both in its wider sense, 'good government or administration', and in its specifically Scottish sense, 'embellishment, improvement (of a town or building)'. Running throughout this poem is uneasy awareness of the comments of

---

[63] 'Complaint, Satire, and Invective in Middle Scots Literature', in *Church, Politics and Society: Scotland 1408–1929*, ed. N. Macdougall (Edinburgh, 1983), 48.

[64] *The Governance of Princes*, in *Gilbert of the Haye's Prose Manuscript*, ed. J. H. Stevenson (STS, 1914), ii. 80. Lindsay complains that James V's counsellors were less interested in the 'commoun weill' than 'singulare proffect': *Dreme*, 909–10.

[65] *Extracts from the Records of the Burgh of Edinburgh I: 1403–1528*, ed. J. D. Marwick (SBRS, Edinburgh, 1869), 137, 97, and 114.

[66] Ibid. 80.

'strangeris' (14, 27), and an implicit contrast with the rich and famous cities of other countries—Paris, Venice, Florence, and London, 'flour of cities alle'. None of these, however, is mentioned. The only city to be named, apart from Edinburgh itself, is Jerusalem, in a final pious reference to the Lord 'That deit into Jerusalem' (74). Historically, this city was the site of the Crucifixion; but most of Dunbar's readers would also be aware of Jerusalem's spiritual significance, as the eternal city, Augustine's City of God, and a model therefore for all imperfect temporal cities. Dunbar thus ends with a prayer and an invocation of spiritual values. But his poem appeals primarily to civic pride and civic standards, and also to sheer common sense (the 'witt' mentioned in line 40). The warning, '3e will decay' (63), envisages not the spiritual but the material decline of Edinburgh.

I that in heill wes and gladnes (K 62) is probably best known to many readers as 'The Lament for the Makars'. But this title, which derives not from Dunbar but Lord Hailes, is misleading. The poem is as much a meditation on Death the Leveller as an elegy for dead poets. Dunbar confronts us at once with the transitoriness of 'this fals warld' (6), and employs the familiar formula for man's mutability:

> Now sound, now seik, now blith, now sary,
> Now dansand mery, now like to dee. (10-11)

Equally traditional is his powerful and succinct refrain:

> *Timor mortis conturbat me.*

Today it is so closely associated with this poem that when the heroine of a novel by Barbara Pym murmurs it on her sick-bed there can be little doubt that she is alluding to Dunbar.[67] Yet Dunbar did not, of course, invent the expression; nor was it uncommon as a refrain, despite repeated assertions that he took the idea from Lydgate's *So as I lay this othir nyght*.[68] The phrase originated in the Office of the Dead, a service which was said daily by clerics and often read privately by laymen as a devotional exercise. It is quoted as a detached *sententia* in the long section on death in Bromyard's *Summa Praedicantium*, and also figures in epitaphs.[69] *Timor mortis conturbat me* thus voices a solemn, communal emotion, associated both with Church ritual and private meditation. In using it as a refrain Dunbar is closer to the

---

[67] *Some Tame Gazelle* (1950; 1981), 191.

[68] See Small, iii. 91; P. H. Nichols, 'Dunbar as a Scottish Lydgation', *PMLA* 46 (1931), 216; Kinsley, 352; and Kratzmann, *Anglo-Scottish Literary Relations*, 140. Yet this notion's invalidity was shown by F. A. Patterson, *The Middle English Penitential Lyric* (New York, 1911), 182–3.

[69] Woolf, 333–5. On epitaphs, see Gray, *Themes and Images*, 46, and 'In What Estate So Ever I Be', *N&Q* 205 (1960), 403–4.

poets of the so-called *Timor Mortis* carols than to Lydgate.[70] As in the burdens of these carols, Dunbar's refrain is free-standing, syntactically, but is metrically tied to the stanza both by rhyme and rhythm. The strong, four-stress beat of the Latin may have provided Dunbar with a model, especially for those lines that start with a stressed first syllable:

> Princis, prelotis and potestatis. (18)
> Victour he is at all melle. (23)

Scholars have called attention to other traditional features. One of these, the Dance of Death, was a remarkably popular theme in late-medieval art and literature. The fifteenth-century French poem *La Danse des morts* circulated both in manuscript and in the prints of Guyot Marchand and Vérard, where it was accompanied by gruesome woodcuts. In England it was familiar from the translation, attributed to Lydgate, and was painted on the walls of old St Paul's churchyard; images from the scheme are possibly represented in the church of Roslin, not far from Edinburgh.[71] Few people at this time could have failed to encounter the theme, in some form or other. Yet we should not exaggerate its influence upon *I that in heill wes*. The personified figure of Death certainly dominates both the Dance of Death and Dunbar's poem; in both there is the same stress on death's inexorable power; and there is a similar enumeration of his victims, ranging through 'all estatis', from powerful 'knychtis in to feild' (21) to the pathetic 'bab full of benignite' at its mother's breast (27). Yet some of the most piquant features of the Dance of Death are absent from Dunbar's poem. There may be a list of the different 'estatis', but there is little to suggest a dance.[72] There is no trace of dialogue—the nearest Dunbar comes to this is when Death whispers to Henryson (81–2). Yet the strength of the French poem (and its English translation), as Rosemary Woolf noted, largely lies in 'the successive pairs of stanzas in which Death satirically and harshly warns his victim', and the victim mournfully responds.[73] Nor, it should be noted, is Dunbar's poem strikingly pictorial; it would be misleading to term it a counterpart of Dance of Death paintings.

---

[70] See Patterson, op. cit.; Greene, *Carols*, nos. 369–72.
[71] Cf. R. D. Drexler, 'Dunbar's "Lament for the Makaris" and the Dance of Death Tradition', *SSL* 13 (1978), 144–58; J. M. Clark, *The Dance of Death in the Middle Ages and Renaissance* (Glasgow, 1950), 26; and *The Dance of Death*, ed. F. Warren (EETS, OS 181, 1930).
[72] In *The Ship of Fools*, ed. T. H. Jamieson (Edinburgh, 1884), ii. 119, Barclay refers explicitly to Death's 'cruell daunce'. Dunbar speaks of life as 'dansand mery', or as a brief pageant (46), but the latter was a common image (Gray, *Themes and Images*, 205).
[73] Woolf, 349.

Behind the Dance of Death and this poem lies another, more ancient tradition, that of the *Vado Mori* verses. These were a widely popular set of Latin verses, in which representative figures, such as king, knight, or physician, complain in turn that they must die. Each couplet begins and ends with *vado mori*, 'I go to die'. This phrase is possibly recalled in Dunbar's '*One to the ded gois* all estatis' (17). The logician says:

> Vado mori, logicus, aliis concludere novi;
> Conclusit breviter mors mihi; vado mori.[74]

The grim pun here on the two senses of *concludere*—'out-argue' and 'put an end to'—is not employed by Dunbar, yet it seems to lurk behind his own ironical remark that neither logicians nor theologians can outwit death:

> Thame helpis no conclusionis sle. (39)

I that in heill wes seems, at first, to have a remarkably simple structure. The stanzas proceed in a series of evenly-balanced sense-units, linked by the refrain and the insistent *repetitio*, chiefly on 'he' and 'takis'. Death picks off his victims, one after another:

> He takis the knychtis in to feild . . . (21)
> He takis the campion in the stour . . . (29)
> He sparis no lord for his piscence . . . (33)

The pattern is established early, and—with slight variations of verb—is maintained almost to the end. The chief danger of such a catalogue is monotony; it is striking that some of the poem's numerous anthologists have abridged it.[75] Woolf preferred what she called 'the first and stronger' part of the poem, saying that the second part was 'encumbered' by the proper names.[76] But to truncate *I that in heill wes* radically alters its meaning. It is a strength of the poem that this pattern of incessant repetition is complemented by a structure of a different kind—one that alters, develops, and reaches a climax. In the first part we are shown Death the Leveller, indifferent to distinctions of wealth, age, sex, and learning. With a slight play on words, Dunbar moves from the mutable 'stait of man' (9) to the different 'estatis' of society:

> One to the ded gois all estatis,
> Princis, prelotis and potestatis,
> Baith riche and pur of al degre. (17–19)

---

[74] For this tradition, see Woolf, 347–8; Gray, *Themes and Images*, 209–11.
[75] R. T. Davies, *Medieval English Lyrics* (1963), no. 146, omits 7 stanzas.
[76] Woolf, 335.

'MORALITEE AND HOOLYNESSE'

But in the second half the perspective alters: instead of reviewing the varied classes, the poet lingers on one in particular, that of poets; and instead of referring to representative social types—'*the* campion' or '*the* lady'—he names specific individuals. The turning-point occurs roughly midway:

> I se that makaris amang the laif
> Playis heir ther pageant, syne gois to graif.   (45–6)

The poet's own greater involvement here is implicit in his use of the first person, which briefly interrupts the prevailing syntactic pattern, and recalls the poem's opening. Place and time similarly become far more specific. Earlier Death took 'the knychtis *in to feild*' and 'the lady *in bour*'; now he takes Scottish poets 'out of this cuntre' (55) and

> In Dunfermelyne he has done roune
> With Maister Robert Henrisoun.   (81–2)

Although the list of poets does not observe a strict chronological sequence, it none the less creates a sense of moving through real time, closer and closer to the moment of writing. Chaucer is named first, both because he had died a century earlier and from a feeling for hierarchy—corresponding, in this, to the choice of princes and prelates to lead the 'estatis'. But the list draws to an end with Dunbar's friends and contemporaries:

> And he has now tane last of aw
> Gude gentill Stobo and Quintyne Schaw.   (85–6)

Here too syntax contributes. Throughout the first part of the poem Dunbar employs the simple present, the tense of eternal truths and recurrent events—'No stait in erd heir standis sickir' (13). But in this latter part he switches to the present perfect, a tense which commonly signals very recent actions. He returns to the simple present only with these lines:

> Gud Maister Walter Kennedy
> In poynt of dede lyis veraly—
> Gret reuth it wer that so suld be . . .   (89–91)

Here it would seem to mark a genuinely present moment, or 'poynt' in time. This duality of structure is important. The pattern of repetition enforces our sense not only of death's power and ubiquity, but also of its banality. But the steady onwards movement of the poem mirrors the way in which many experience the meaning of death. At first it is a familiar but distant commonplace; only after the death of one's 'fallowis' (79), friends or those close to one, does it become a personal, poignant, and experienced reality. *I that in heill wes* is partly about the stages by which we come to understand a general truth—at the poem's end death is perceived differently from the way in which it is regarded at the beginning. Dunbar confronts the thought that he may be Death's 'nyxt pray' (95). The poem has great psychological exactness. But if, as Woolf says, the aim of the traditional death lyric was to dispel 'the comforting remoteness' of death, it is also, morally, extremely effective.[77]

The colophon to the print reads, 'Quod Dunbar quhen he wes sek'. This may have been extrapolated from the first stanza, and is not necessarily authorial, but I see no reason to deny the literal reality of the poet's 'seiknes' (2). Scott found the poem 'sick' in a different and colloquial sense, embodying a morbid response to death.[78] This seems to misread it fundamentally. The tone is melancholy, but quite lacking in morbidity. There is no charnel-house imagery, no hysterical hurling of insults at death, rather grim understatement and irony of a perennial kind—as in the allusion to physicians who cannot heal themselves (41–3).[79] The most explicit expression of emotion occurs in the refrain—*conturbat* is a strong verb—and the response to Kennedy's imminent death—'Gret reuth it wer that so suld be'.

The last stanza is calm and practical:

> Sen for the ded remeid is none
> Best is that we for dede dispone
> Eftir our deid that lif may we:
> *Timor mortis conturbat me.* (97–100)

The 'I' of the previous stanza is now absorbed into the collective 'we', and the voice is no longer that of a single individual. The hortatory 'Best is that we . . .' recalls the self-admonishment of 'For to be blyth me think it best'. For medieval Christians the notion of a sudden, unprepared death was fearful to contemplate. To die without penance, in a state of sin, might entail the loss of salvation. The liturgical context of Dunbar's refrain should be recalled:

Peccantem me quotidie et non poenitentem timor mortis conturbat me. Quia in inferno nulla est redemptio miserere mei Deus et salva me.[80]

The fear of death was considered salutary, if it caused men to think of their souls and the future life. Many treatises, of varying length and character, were devoted to the *ars moriendi*; one short Scottish *Craft of*

---

[77] Ibid. 74.
[78] Scott, 251.
[79] Cf. Luke 4: 23; and Whiting, L 170–1.
[80] Response in 3rd Nocturn, Office of the Dead: *Sarum Breviary*, ed. F. Proctor and C. Wordsworth, 3 vols. (Cambridge, 1879–86), ii. 278.

Deying has already been mentioned.[81] Such works gave guidance on how to 'dispone', or prepare oneself for death, by appropriate contemplation. This is the practice to which Dunbar briefly alludes in his highly orthodox conclusion.

In to thir dirk and drublie dayis (K 69) is also a poem about mutability, yet its tone and structure are wholly different. The starting-point, as in the Harley lyric, *Wynter wakeneth al my care*, is the weather:

> In to thir dirk and drublie dayis
> Quhone sabill all the hevin arrayis,
> With mystie vapouris, cluddis and skyis,
> Nature all curage me denyis
> Of sangis, ballattis and of playis.
>
> Quhone that the nycht dois lenth in houris
> With wind, with haill and havy schouris,
> My dule spreit dois lurk for schoir;
> My hairt for langour dois forloir
> For laik of Symmer with his flouris.   (1–10)

Dunbar does not use the word 'winter'—titles, such as 'In Winter' or 'Meditation in Winter', are editorial. Yet he evokes the season by precise details, like the lengthening of the night, and by his stress on privation—the 'laik' of summer, and Nature's denial to the poet of 'curage' for enjoying or composing songs and 'ballattis' (see above, p. 30). The poet's inner state is correlated explicitly with that of the natural world: both are dark and gloomy. In Douglas's Seventh Prologue winter affects the poet's mind similarly, bringing before it 'Gousty schaddois of eild and grisly ded [death]' (46). Such ideas are perennial, yet it should be remembered how systematically medieval moralists drew parallels between the life of man and the seasons of the year. Lydgate, for instance, saw autumn as the messenger of old age, and called winter the 'orlogge' of death.[82]

Dunbar is melancholy, oppressed by 'havie thocht' (12), as at the beginning of other poems; 'thocht', as in *Schir, 3it remember as befoir* (K 42) and *Lucina schynnyng in silence of the nicht* (K 53), signifies a painful, obsessive brooding over one's problems. But in this poem the simple statement, 'I vexit am with havie thocht', is suddenly given dramatic embodiment. The poet is 'assayit'—the word means both 'approached' and 'attacked'—by personifications of his thought. This central section may remind us of a miniature morality play. It is even closer, in form, to introspective dream poems, such as Dunbar's own

---

[81] See Sister M. O. Connor, *The Art of Dying Well: The Development of the Ars Moriendi* (New York, 1942).

[82] Cf. J. A. Burrow, *The Ages of Man* (Oxford, 1986), 31–2. For the reading *lenth in*, cf. Bawcutt, 'The Text and Interpretation of Dunbar', *MÆ*, 50 (1981), 95.

'MORALITEE AND HOOLYNESSE'

This hinder nycht halff sleiping as I lay (K 51), where personified abstractions engage in talk around the sleeping poet. But this is not presented as a dream, and the action is simpler, briefer, and more symmetrically patterned than in the latter poem. There are five stanzas only, each of which is devoted to one personification. The series begins with Despair, who expresses not spiritual but materialistic fears; he speaks specifically of 'this court', and urges, 'get sum thing quhairon to leif' (18). He is succeeded by Patience and Prudence, whose advice is more conventionally moral, and finally by Age and Death:

> And than sayis Age, My freind, cum neir
> And be not strange, I the requeir;
> . . . .
> Syne Deid castis upe his ȝettis wyd
> Saying, Thir oppin sall the abyd;
> Albeid that thow wer never sa stout,
> Undir this lyntall sall thow lowt—
> Thair is nane uther way besyde. (31 ff.)

The presentation is dramatic: Age's first words imply a sinister over-intimacy, and 'be not strange' neatly implies the poet's reluctance to be on such close terms with old age. Death, like the others, has a stanza to himself, but there is a disturbing jolt in the pattern. In this case alone does a symbolic gesture precede the speech. Death's casting open of his 'ȝettis' is, ultimately, a Scriptural figure: 'Have the gates of death been opened unto thee' (Job 38: 17). But there is a hint of paradox in Dunbar's imagery. Death's gates are here so wide that no one can avoid passing through them—'Thair is nane uther way besyde'. But they are simultaneously so low that they force all to stoop—'Undir this lyntall sall thow lowt'. The physical smallness of the grave was a favourite topic for medieval moralists. Lazarus, in *The Towneley Plays*, turns to the audience, saying:

> Vinder the erthe ye shall / thus carefully then cowche;
> The royfe of youre hall / youre nakyd nose shall towche.[83]

Dunbar employs the same hortatory formula, 'undir . . . sall thow lowt', but replaces the usual image of the roof by the lintel appropriate to a gate or door. He presents a double image of death's inevitability and physical humiliation, yet his tone is dry and delicate. There are none of the gruesome details that occur in Lazarus's speech.
The poem ends:

---

[83] *The Towneley Plays*, ed. G. England and A. W. Pollard (EETS, ES 71, 1897, reprinted 1978), 391. See also *The Grave*; *CB XIII*, no. 29A; and Whiting, R. 187. Cf. Woolf, 83–4.

'MORALITEE AND HOOLYNESSE'

> For feir of this all day I drowp:
> No gold in kist nor wyne in cowp,
> No ladeis bewtie nor luiffis blys
> May lat me to remember this,
> How glaid that ever I dyne or sowp.
>
> 3it quhone the nycht begynnis to schort
> It dois my spreit sum pairt confort
> Off thocht oppressit with the schowris;
> Cum, lustie Symmer with thi flowris,
> That I may leif in sum disport.   (41–50)

The emphatic, repeated *this* (41, 44), echoing 'this lyntall', clearly alludes to Death, yet also sums up the poet's other anxieties. 'For feir of this' indeed recalls the refrain, *Timor mortis conturbat me*. Yet this poem does not end with an orthodox resolve to 'dispone' for the life hereafter, but with words that resemble the birds' joyful roundel at the end of *The Parliament of Fowls*: 'Now welcum, somer, with thy sonne softe'. There is anticipation of the delight that summer may bring, even though the tone is guarded and circumspect—*sum pairt* and *sum* clearly put limits to the pleasurable notions expressed in 'confort' and 'disport'.[84] The last stanza thus replies to the opening ones: the line '3it quhone the nycht begynnis to schort' echoes the temporal clauses in lines 2 and 6; and the rhyme between 'schouris' and 'flowris' is repeated. Yet this is repetition with a difference: there is an obvious antithesis between the verbs, *lenth* and *schort*, and the *schowris* of line 48 are symbolical—fusing the literal 'havy schouris' (7) with the poet's 'havie thocht' (12). The poet now eagerly summons the season whose absence he had earlier mourned. This carefully composed circular structure aptly mirrors the poet's preoccupation with the cycle of the year.

This is a poem about time, and different ways of responding to its passage—practical and prudential, as with Despair's 'in tyme provyde' (17), or homiletic, with Age's

> Remember thow hes compt to mak
> Off all thi tyme thow spendit heir.   (34–5)

Time is not personified, yet its familiar attribute, the hour-glass, is mentioned as the only check to Fortune (25). Time was a common topic for the moralist: it not only provoked proverbs and aphorisms—'Tyme gars all leir'—but was the subject of many rather undistinguished poems, such as the anonymous *Befoir the tyme is wisdome to prowyde* and Montgomerie's *A Description of Time*.[85] It is possible that

---

[84] Cf. the anonymous review-article in *TLS*, 18 Apr. 1958, 208.
[85] The motto occurs on the famous Lennox Jewel; for *Befoir the Tyme*, see *Bannatyne Manuscript*, fol. 75a; see also Montgomerie, *Poems*, 127.

the way in which Dunbar's poem ends may have shocked some of his more pious readers. But that does not mean that we must therefore find the ending 'ironic', as one critic suggested, and posit that the speaker is 'wrongheaded'.[86] Such a reading seems insensitive and perverse. Dunbar places the voices of orthodox morality at the very centre of this poem; he finds them disquieting, but does not deny their truth. Yet he also recognizes that the year, unlike man's life, is cyclical, and derives from this a partial 'confort'. His poem is striking for its bleak, truthful-sounding feeling, and for its awareness of the way in which Nature affects the human 'curage'. It is a precise statement of a perennial theme.

Quhome to sall I complene my wo (K 63) is extremely interesting, yet has received little discussion. It illustrates the folly of attaching simple labels to Dunbar's more complex poems. The editors, Schipper and Mackenzie, classed it as a petition, but Kinsley placed it among the 'Moralities'. Yet it is also a deeply-felt religious poem. Dunbar's contemporaries might well have called it a Complaint: there is a formulaic ring about the first line, which resembles the way another of Dunbar's poems begins—'Complane I wald, wist I quhome till' (K 45)—as well as the opening of Lindsay's *Complaint of Bagsche*, 'Allace, quhome to suld I complayne'.

The poem has two main sections. The first fifty lines treat a theme so common among medieval poets as to form a minor genre: a complaint on the evils of the time.[87] This first part has many familiar characteristics of moral poems, such as the proverbial refrain—'Into this warld may none assure'—and much generalization, often in negative form:

> Nane heir bot riche men hes renoun.   (16; cf. 18 and 33)

But such authoritative pronouncements are threaded with phrases like 'I knaw nocht' (3) and 'quhat to do I am in dowt' (14), and preceded by this questioning passage:

> Lord, how sall I my dayis dispone?
> For lang service rewarde is none,
> And schort my lyfe may heir indure
> And lossit is my tyme bygone.   (6–9)

This sounds like a petitioner's complaint, and other phrases also imply the viewpoint of a courtier or churchman in hope of a benefice. The tone of the stanza that begins, 'Vertew the court hes done dispyis' (21)

---

[86] Reiss, 134–5.
[87] On this type of writing, see J. Peter, *Complaint and Satire in Early English Literature* (Oxford, 1956), and S. Wenzel, *Preachers, Poets* (n. 7 above), 174–208.

certainly resembles Dunbar's petitions, yet it is phrased so circumspectly that it does not necessarily refer to his personal situation. The focus is less on mutability than on injustice—those who do evil prosper at the expense of the good. There is much latent personification, which becomes overt in

> Flattry weiris ane furrit goun
> And falsett with the lordis dois roun
> And trewth standis barrit at the dure
> And exul is honour of the toun.   (36-9)

This is highly visual, presented like a scene from everyday life. The vices have the attributes of material success, but the virtues are social rejects. This is followed by a startling change of perspective:

> Fra everilk mowth fair wirdis proceidis;
> In every hairt disceptioun breidis;
> Fra everylk e gois lukis demure
> Bot fra the handis gois few gud deidis:
> . . . .
> Toungis now ar maid of quhyte quhaill bone
> And hairtis ar maid of hard flynt stone
> And ene ar maid of blew asure
> And handis of adamant laith to dispone.   (41-4, 46-9)

The second of these stanzas is an amplification of the first, echoing it line by line. Its witty imagery transforms warm flesh and blood into insensate objects. A 'heart of stone' is a commonplace, but some of the other images are more complex—eyes are not only as blue but as hard as azure, or *lapis lazuli*, and the adamant has here a double significance. It was a type of hardness, and also mistakenly identified with the lodestone—'as hard as adamant' and 'as the adamant drawis iron' both appear in proverb lore.[88] The owners of the hands in line 49 are both stony-hearted and grasping. Personification bundles many individuals into a single class, but in these lines people are viewed differently, their bodies reduced to isolated fragments, almost as if they were dismembered.

This notion of physical disintegration enables Dunbar to make a neat transition to the second part of his poem:

> ȝit hairt with hand and body all
> Mon anser deth quhen he dois call
> To compt befoir the juge future.   (51-3)

(In *Henry V*, IV. i there is a similar turn from the *disiecta membra* on the battlefield to thoughts of their resurrection and judgement.) That this is the poem's turning-point is also suggested by the slight alteration of

[88] Whiting, A 40 and A 39.

the refrain; in this stanza alone is it interrogative, anticipating the many rhetorical questions to follow—

> O quha sall weild the wrang possesioun . . . (61)

or

> Quhat help is thair in lordschippis sevin . . . (66)

This section is wholly preoccupied with death and judgement. Whereas the first part speaks of the here and now, this looks to the future, and speaks of the resurrection of the body as imminent—a 'tyme sa sone to cum' (81). It contains apocalyptic imagery, of the trumpet-blowing angel (63) and the earth undergoing violent cataclysm:

> Than quho sall wirk for warldis wrak
> Quhen flude and fyre sall our it frak,
> And frely fruster feild and fure
> With tempest kene and hiddous crak? (76–9)

This draws upon the well-known legend of 'The Signs before Doomsday'.[89]

The contrast—in theme and tone—between these two sections is obvious, yet there is also continuity. A poem which seems, at the beginning, as if it might be a petition to an earthly ruler, ends unmistakably as a supplication to God. There is an interesting ambiguity in

> Lord, how sall I my dayis dispone? (6)

but no doubt at all as to who is the 'Lord' addressed in the last stanza:

> Lord, sen in tyme sa sone to cum
> *De terra surrectourus sum*,
> Reward me with non erdly cure—
> Bot me ressave in *regnum tuum*. (81–4)

This recalls the cry of the repentant sinner on the Cross, 'Lord, remember me, when thou comest into thy kingdom' (John 18: 36). The tone of the first part was world-weary and cynical, but the voice of one still concerned for his own advancement. The latter part, however, is dominated by *contemptus mundi*. The question, 'how sall I my dayis dispone?', is finally answered by a decisive rejection of worldly ambitions—'Reward me with non erdly cure'. The speaker is now clearly a churchman. The earlier preoccupation with the lack of justice in 'this warld' is succeeded by awed contemplation of divine

---

[89] Cf. W. Heist, *The Fifteen Signs before Doomsday* (East Lansing, 1952); the fullest Scottish treatment occurs in Lindsay's *Monarche*, 5254 ff.

justice in the next. Dunbar embeds in this passage some Latin lines (71 ff.), whose liturgical origin will be discussed later (p. 352). These and the echo (73) of Job's despairing cry, 'Let the day perish wherein I was born' (3: 3), contribute to the peculiar intensity of this part of the poem. It reads rather like a vernacular *Dies Irae*.

Three of Dunbar's poems, *Rorate celi desuper* (K 1), *Done is a battell on the dragon blak* (K 4), and *The Tabill of Confessioun* (K 6), are included in Bannatyne's 'ballatis of theoligie'. This phrase is perhaps misleading. These and other poems of Dunbar may take as their subjects the central tenets of Christianity—Christ's birth, death, and resurrection—but they are not theologically abstruse. Douglas's Tenth Prologue, also included in the 'ballatis of theoligie', expounds the mysteries of the Trinity, but no poem by Dunbar contains so learned an account of religious dogma. Dunbar's faith seems to have been secure and orthodox; but it would be impossible, on the evidence of these poems, to be more precise about how he viewed the intellectual and doctrinal movements of his time. One of his contemporaries was John Ireland, who wrote Latin commentaries on the *Sentences* of Peter Lombard and a vernacular treatise, *The Meroure of Wysdome*, termed 'a popular version of the current theology of the schools'.[90] Dunbar's religious poems are sometimes illuminated by Ireland's writings, but they should not be regarded as forming, like Ireland's *Meroure*, a carefully conceived programme of instruction in the Christian faith. They are chance survivals from what may once have been a much larger body of occasional devotional poetry.

In Scotland in the second half of the sixteenth century the great cataclysm of the Reformation swept away not only ancient forms of worship and the furnishings of churches but literary works that mentioned doctrines or practices offensive to Protestants. Dunbar's *Ballat of Our Lady* survives only in the pre-Reformation Asloan manuscript, and three of his other religious poems are extant only in single copies. If religious poems were copied in this period, they were often Protestantized.[91] The Bannatyne and Maitland versions of *The Tabill of Confessioun* are thus edited, somewhat clumsily, to make the work doctrinally acceptable. Both omit a stanza that lists the 'sevin commandis of the kirk' (81–8), presumably because of its obnoxious

---

[90] J. H. Burns, 'John Ireland: Theology and Public Affairs in the Late Fifteenth Century', *Innes Review*, 41 (1990), 151–81; and Br. Bonaventure, 'The Popular Theology of John Ireland', ibid. 13 (1962), 130–46.

[91] See A. A. MacDonald, 'Poetry, Politics and Reformation Censorship in Sixteenth-Century Scotland', *ES* 64 (1983), 410–21; and D. McRoberts, 'Material Destruction Caused by the Scottish Reformation', in *Essays on the Scottish Reformation 1513–1625*, ed. McRoberts (Glasgow, 1962), 415–62.

references to attending mass on Sunday and observing 'the festuall and the fasting day'. In another stanza the sinner confesses:

> Lord, I have done full litill reverence
> Unto the sacramentis sevin of gret renoun:
> To that hie eucarist moist of exellence,
> Baptasing, pennence, and confirmacioun,
> Matremony, ordour, and extreme uncioun.   (41–5)

In Maitland the first two lines were copied, then deleted, and the rest of the stanza omitted; in Bannatyne the stanza was awkwardly remodelled, so as to conform with Protestant dogma, which recognized not seven sacraments but two—the 'halye supper' and baptism. The version of the poem likely to be closest to Dunbar's own beliefs is preserved in Arundel 285 (c. 1540).[92] This devotional miscellany contains, in addition to three pieces by Dunbar, many poems and prayers, devotions to the Holy Name of Jesus, the Crown of Thorns, the Seven Wounds, and other commemorations of the Passion. It provides one of the best extant illustrations of late-medieval Scottish piety, and thus supplies an excellent context for all Dunbar's religious poems.[93]

These poems do not constitute an intimate spiritual autobiography, recording the unique relationship between one soul and God. They were intended for the use of others, chiefly pious laymen, who would read them along with books of hours and other devotional works in private meditation. Dunbar supplies no hint that they were designed, like Ireland's *Meroure*, specifically for the king, or even for other members of the court; the envisaged audience was probably similar to that for the moral poems. They fall, roughly, into two groups. The first, thoughtful and penitential in tone, have much in common with mortality poems such as *Quhome to sall I complene my wo*. The speaker is solitary, addressing God directly, as in *Salviour, suppois my sensualite* (K 7), or picturing himself in prayer before an image of the Crucifixion, in *The Passioun of Crist* (K 3). They are simultaneously personal and impersonal: the speaker is engaged in self-communing, but the 'self' is typical and representative. *Rorate celi desuper* and *Done is a battell* are very different; they are poems of celebration, triumphal in tone, and speak as if on behalf of persons gathered together in public worship. They have often been called 'hymns', although there is no evidence that they were sung. Yet such differences must not be

---

[92] For discussion, see Bawcutt, 'Text and Context in Middle Scots Poetry', in Blanchot and Graf, *Actes*, 31–2.
[93] See *Devotional Pieces in Verse and Prose*, ed. J. A. W. Bennett (STS, 1955); and Bennett, 'Scottish Pre-Reformation Devotion: Some Notes on British Library MS. Arundel 285', in *So Meny People Longages and Tonges*, ed. M. Benskin and M. L. Samuels (Edinburgh, 1981), 299–308.

exaggerated. The tone of *Ane Ballat of Our Lady* is public and communal—the Virgin is 'Our licht' (27) and 'Our wys pavys' (65)—but it is also a prayer, beseeching the Virgin's intercession on behalf of all sinners, and specifically of the speaker.

These overtly religious poems differ from the moral ones not only in their Christocentric subject-matter but in their emotionalism and, most strikingly, in their rich symbolic imagery. Such symbolism was not peculiar to Dunbar, but was a shared Christian language, inherited from the Bible and learned Bible-commentaries, and employed in sermons, the liturgy, Latin hymns, and much vernacular verse. Dunbar speaks of Christ as 'angell fude' (*Ballat of Our Lady*, 80) and 'the fude of angellis' (*The Passioun*, 54). This notion may be traced to the Scriptures—'Man did eat angels' food' (Psalm 78: 25)—and to scholastic interpretations, such as St Bruno's *Panis ergo angelorum bene dicitur Christus*. But Dunbar could have encountered it in many different places—in the Easter liturgy, for instance, or a prayer by Richard Rolle, or a fourteenth-century English poem, which likewise calls Christ 'the faire aungels fode' and 'aungels brede'.[94] Dunbar, unlike Douglas or Kennedy, rarely mentions his sources, nor does he usually expound the implications of such images. He seems to assume in readers the same easy familiarity with this symbolic language that he himself possesses. To many—particularly the devout—it was perhaps no stranger than the proverbs that form the chief embellishment of the moralities, and which are largely absent from these poems. No doubt some symbolic images were far more familiar than others—Christ the lamb, for instance, or Mary as 'ros of paradys' (*Ballat of Our Lady*, 40) and 'the ros Mary, flour of flouris' (*Rorate celi*, 4)—through their sheer ubiquity, in works of art as well as the liturgy. Some of Dunbar's readers may not have understood all the implications of this imagery; his fellow-clerics were clearly best equipped to perceive its full significance. None the less these poems are less learned and 'difficult' than some modern critics assume. This is true even of *Ane Ballat of Our Lady*; Dunbar could experiment so ingeniously with its form partly because of the very familiarity of its subject. Hundreds of medieval poems on the Virgin were composed; even within the scanty corpus of Scottish religious verse there survive many other 'ballatis of Our Lady', not only in the Asloan, Arundel, and Makculloch manuscripts, but embedded in secular works, like *The Howlat* (716–54) or *Lancelot of the Laik* (2085–2112).[95]

---

[94] See *Expositio Psalmorum*, in Migne, *Patrologia Latina*, cxlii. 294; J. A. W. Bennett, *Poetry of the Passion* (Oxford, 1982), 37–8 and 222 n. 10; *CB XIV*, no. 83.

[95] The *Ballat of Our Lady* is discussed more fully below, 354; cf. A. A. MacDonald, 'Religious Poetry in Middle Scots', *History of Scottish Literature I: Origins to 1660*, ed. R. D. S. Jack (Aberdeen, 1988), 91–102.

'MORALITEE AND HOOLYNESSE'

In *The Passioun of Crist* (K 3) Dunbar's theme is the central mystery of the Christian faith—a vast topic, matched by a vast literature, in Latin and the vernaculars, in prose and verse, and in many different modes, ranging from brief prayers to prolonged meditations, and dramatic enactment in the mystery cycles. How should Dunbar's poem be placed in relation to this great and complex tradition? It seems, in many respects, a highly characteristic product of late medieval piety, especially if it is compared with other pieces in Arundel 285: Kennedy's *The Passioun of Crist*, the Passion-section of the long treatise known as *The Contemplation of Sinners*, the prose *Remembrance of the Passion*, and the work there entitled *Ane Deuoit Remembrance of the Passioun of Crist*, which is a Scotticized version of part of Lydgate's *Testament*.[96] Dunbar's poem has much in common with the accounts of the Crucifixion in these other works, not only in its selection of events but also in emotive tone, language, and imagery. The ultimate source, for all, was the Gospel story, but many extra details and incidents were later incorporated; one of the most important of these later sources was the influential *Meditationes Vitae Christi*, then mistakenly linked with the name of St Bonaventura. Much of this extra material emphasized the cruelty of Christ's tormentors, who stretched his limbs to fit the cross, or let the cross fall deliberately, to increase his pain:

> To gar his cruell pane exceid
> Thay leit him fall doun with ane swak
> Quhill cors and corps and all did crak. (75–7)

Dunbar's phrasing and imagery are highly traditional. He describes the brutal tearing of Christ's clothing from his body:

> The clayth that claif to his cleir hyd
> Thay raif away with ruggis rude
> Quhill fersly followit flesche and blude. (59–61)

This closely resembles Kennedy's account of the same incident:

> The purpour claith, quhilk clewit to his hid
> With his awne blude, thai raif of him of force.
> His tender hid thai brak fra bak to syd. (680–2)

Dunbar compares Christ's persecutors to lions, who 'with awfull ruge ... hurlit him heir and thair' (19–20). Even such a small detail as this simile has behind it an ancient tradition: the lion, in some depictions of the Crucifixion, figured as a symbol of Christ's tormentors. It derived from the typological exegesis of certain Scriptural verses,

---

[96] See Bennett, Introduction to *Devotional Pieces*; line-references are to this edition.

particularly Psalms 21 (AV 22): 14—'as a lion ravening and roaring'—and 16: 12—'They have taken me, as a lion prepared for the prey'.[97]

Dunbar's purpose was as orthodox as his theme; he wrote not simply to instruct his readers, but to stir their emotions, to rouse the sorrow and pity that, as he says twice (22, 62), such a sight should provoke. The first stanza shows the poet entering an oratory in a friary, and praying:

> And kneling doun with ane pater noster
> Befoir the michtie king of glorie,
> Haveing his passioun in memorie,
> Syn to his mother I did inclyne,
> Hir halsing with ane gaude flore. (3–8)

Ireland recommended that one should pray in church, for several reasons. One was the presence of 'the ymage of Ihesu and his gracious passioun'; this caused 'memour' of Jesus and his mother, and this in turn instilled devotion.[98] The sequence of ideas recalls Walter Hilton's defence of images: looking at these images recalled to the memory the Passion of Our Lord, 'and thus slow and carnal minds may be stirred to compunction and devotion'.[99] *The Contemplation of Sinners* lays similar stress on the need for 'cotidiane fructfull rememorance' of Christ's Passion, 'as thow present his pane had hard and sene' (921, 930). Kennedy also repeatedly urges the reader to 'remember' the details of the Crucifixion, and to 'behald' them inwardly, 'as thow had present bene'; in return for contrition he promises divine grace.[100] Kennedy is characteristically diffuse; Dunbar's *Passioun of Crist* is far briefer, yet has essentially a very similar movement. It starts with memory—'Haveing his passioun in memorie'—and proceeds through the response of compassion to contrition and penance. This 'penitential conception' dominated much fifteenth-century Passion poetry.[101]

Dunbar's *Passioun of Crist* is orthodox in substance, but its form is novel, though not wholly unprecedented. After his prayers the poet falls asleep, and the rest of the poem consists of his dream. Such visionary experiences before a crucifix or sacred painting were not uncommon. The dream contains two parts, whose separation is formally signalled by the use of different refrains; each new stage is also marked by the same introductory formula, 'Methocht' (9 and 97).

---

[97] Dunbar's boar-simile (58) may also be traditional. Cf. J. Marrow, '*Circumdederunt me canes multi*: Christ's Tormentors in Northern European Art of the Late Middle Ages', *Art Bulletin*, 59 (1977), 169 and 172–4.
[98] *Asloan Manuscript*, i. 50.
[99] See Woolf, 184.
[100] *The Passioun*, 394, 465 ff., and 1700 ff.
[101] Woolf, 219.

'MORALITEE AND HOOLYNESSE'

The first and longer section describes the central events of the Passion, beginning with Judas's betrayal:

> Methocht Judas with mony ane Jow ...

and ending with the death upon the cross:

> Thus Jesus with his woundis wyde
> As martir sufferit for to de
> And tholit to be crucifyid,
> O mankynd, for the luif of the.   (93–6)

The narration is swift and selective. As J. A. W. Bennett noted, 'Judas at once merges with other Jews ... Herod is nowhere named, nor Pilate, nor Longinus'.[102] There is no mention of many other events that led up to the Crucifixion, nor of those that followed it. This has an emotional logic, since the dream 'befell on Gud Fryday' (143); the poem is a Good Friday meditation. Each stanza is devoted to a separate stage of the story, and the narrative style is simple. There is a succession of kinetic verbs, and a stark opposition, not between Jesus and named persecutors but between 'him' and 'thay':

> In tene thay tirvit him agane.   (33)
>
> Thay scurgit him bayth fut and hand.   (37)

The heroic aspect of Jesus the warrior is often implicit in the military phrasing:

> He baid in stour quhill he mycht stand.   (39)

Yet even this line, like many others, lays emphasis on Jesus's voluntary passivity—he 'baid', 'sufferit', and 'tholit' the Crucifixion.

The smooth narrative flow is interrupted only by the refrain: 'O mankynd, for the luif of the'. This apostrophe reminds the reader of his own close involvement in the action that is unfolding. Woolf called it a preacher's comment: 'not an expression of love, but the moral statement that you ought to love'.[103] But this does not take account of the syntactic ambiguity in the phrase, 'for the luif of the'. Dunbar's refrain is primarily a reminder of God's love for man, which contrasts shockingly with the human acts of hatred that, in each stanza, precede it. But it also calls upon the reader to show love in his turn. This stress upon reciprocity, upon love for love, was a common theme, particularly in those lyrics known as 'Appeals from the Cross':

> Behald my lufe, and gif me thin agane.[104]

---

[102] *Poetry of the Passion*, 122.
[103] Woolf, 234.
[104] Lydgate, *Testament*; quoted from Scottish version, in *Devotional Pieces*, 272. See also *CB XV*, no. 109: 'More ask I nott, but loue for loue agayne.'

Dunbar's refrain reads rather like a condensed version of some lines in a fourteenth-century rendering of *Iesu dulcis memoria*:

> Ihesu my loue, thou were so fre,
> Al that thou didest for loue of me
> . . . . . .
> Thou axist nouȝt but loue of me.[105]

The poem's second part grows logically out of the first, yet is strikingly different in mode. The dreamer is not merely a spectator, but becomes a participant in this psychic drama. In Kennedy's *Passioun of Crist* the reader is exhorted:

> Mak rowme to reuth, a place for piete dycht,
> Quhill that thi hert haue perfit compassioun.   (647–8)

But in Dunbar's poem the dreamer says that 'Reuth' whispered in his ear, Pity tugged at him, and Compassion 'straik' him painfully (97–101). Some of the words first used of Jesus's torment are reapplied to the dreamer's imaginative suffering:

> Than rudlie come Remembrance
> Ay rugging me withouttin rest.   (105–6)

Jesus's clothing had been torn away 'with ruggis rude' (60). The Passion is now re-enacted within the dreamer's heart; as he says, 'Pane with passioun me opprest' (109). But these painful images are followed by the 'sweit' and comforting words of Grace:

> Ordane for him ane resting place
> That is so werie wrocht for the,
> That schort within thir dayis thre
> Sall law undir thy lyntell bow;
> And in thy hous sall herbrit be
> Thy blissit salvatour, Chryst Jesu.   (115–20)

The phrase 'within thir dayis thre' pinpoints the mood, one of expectation and looking to the future, and the moment; Dunbar alludes not only to the Resurrection—as a historical event—but also to the reception of Christ's body at communion, which was then received by the laity only at Easter. The reference to God bowing low 'undir thy lyntell' echoes the Centurion's humble words, 'Lord, I am not worthy that thou shouldest come under my roof' (Matthew 8: 8; Luke 7: 6). These words were included in a prayer regularly said before communion.[106] The next two stanzas develop further the ancient image of the house of the soul. Penance is envisaged as a kind of spiritual spring-cleaning, so that 'the hous within' should be 'Ay

---

[105] *CB XIV*, no. 89.
[106] Cf. Kinsley, 234; Bennett, *Poetry of the Passion*, 126 and 223 n. 14.

reddie till our salvatour' (131). A new refrain is employed, which varies slightly yet always incorporates the name 'Jesu'; it alludes either to his redemptive role—'Thy blissit salvatour Jesu'—or echoes the earlier refrain—'Onlie for luif of sweit Jesu'. But whereas the first refrain—in some respects—ran counter to the sense of the stanzas in which it figured, in this last section refrain and stanza are wholly in unison. The dream and the poem end together. The poet, as in *The Thrissill and the Rois*, wakes 'halflingis in effray' (140), and resolves to record his experience. But the ending is far more sombre—he is awakened not by bird-song but by the earthquake that accompanied the Crucifixion.

Dunbar's poem has had few admirers, apart from J. A. W. Bennett. Scott found it 'brutal and crude in its insistence on the physical details of the Crucifixion'.[107] Woolf had a fine scholarly understanding of the poem's background, pointing out that Dunbar wrote in the same spirit as the authors of the mystery cycles; such details were intended to 'appal'. She, however, found *The Passioun* 'frigid', and criticized its allegorical section as too 'intellectual'.[108] Yet this is the most original part of the poem, and deeply moving. The words spoken by Grace have something of Herbert's tenderness in *The Sepulchre*:

> O blessed bodie! Whither art thou thrown?
> No lodging for thee, but a cold hard stone?
> So many hearts on earth, and yet not one
>   Receive thee?

Dunbar's subtle and ingenious use of the dream-form here enables him to interweave several different modes. The poem's structure is basically narrative, yet it verges on lyric in its brevity and its highly emotive refrains. At 144 lines it is shorter than several Passion lyrics included in Carleton' Brown's *Religious Lyrics of the XVth Century*.[109] Readers familiar with medieval dream poetry are unlikely to be disconcerted by the transition to personification allegory. The dream was a recognized medium for poetic introspection; here it provides an appropriate device both for re-enacting the historical events of the Crucifixion within a devout dreamer's mind and meditating on their significance.

The chief purpose of *The Tabill of Confessioun* (K 6) is practical and expository. It is an aid to penitential self-examination, in plan resembling Ireland's prose treatise with a similar title, whose opening sentence states: 'This buke and table of confessioun is ane myrrour in

---

[107] Scott, 286.
[108] Woolf, 234 and 308.
[109] Nos. 102 and 109. Woolf discusses Dunbar's poem but not Kennedy's, which is 'too leisurely' for lyric (237).

the quhilk thow may knaw thi conscience and thi stait and quharein thow has synnit'.[110] The layout of Dunbar's poem, however, finds parallels not only in Ireland's treatise but in many other similar works that survive from the late Middle Ages, both in verse and prose. It is schematic and arithmetical, with stanzas variously devoted to the five senses, the seven deadly sins, the seven deeds of corporal and spiritual mercy, the ten commandments, and the four cardinal virtues. The impetus for all such works can be traced to the Fourth Lateran Council, which in 1215 made confession mandatory for every Christian and so led to a proliferation of short penitential guides and manuals.[111] Elsewhere Dunbar reflects some new developments of the fifteenth century, notably the value placed on more frequent confession.[112] Yet the piety which recommended *The Tabill* to contemporaries tends to repel modern readers; within Dunbar's canon it holds a place similar to *The Parson's Tale* in Chaucer's.

Editors usually couple this poem with *The Maner of Passyng to Confessioun* (K 5). The resemblances between them are obvious. Both are designed for private reading, before the act of confession; and both envisage this as a Lenten preparation before reception of the eucharist at Easter (with the opening of *The Maner of Passyng* compare *The Tabill*, 151-2). Both voice concern as to the confessor's discretion (*Maner*, 29; *Tabill*, 91), and the need to make a full confession and to schrive oneself 'clene' (*Maner*, 10; *Tabill*, 4). But in other respects the poems could not be more different. *The Maner* is dry and admonitory, directed *at* the sinner; but the voice of *The Tabill* is that of the sinner himself. Any thought that Dunbar is speaking about himself in a peculiarly intimate way should be dismissed. Every possible sin is envisaged, including murder, and every kind of social context—'in court, in kirk, in tabill' (107), as well as 'At counsall, sessioun, and at perliament' (134). If Dunbar writes, 'I wrachit synnar vile and full of vice' (17), Ireland writes similarly, at the beginning of his *Table of Confessioun*, 'I synfull persone humilie confessis and schryvis me'.[113] The stance is the same, but Dunbar's tone is far more emotive. His *Tabill of Confessioun* has, in this respect, less in common with Ireland's treatise or the down-to-earth *Maner of Passyng* than with *The Passioun of Crist*. It is a supplication to God, as its refrain insists—'I cry the marcy and laser to repent'.

---

[110] *Asloan Manuscript*, i. 65.
[111] See Patterson, *Middle English Penitential Lyric*, no. 3; on the background, see L. E. Boyle, OP, 'The Fourth Lateran Council and Manuals of Popular Theology', in *The Popular Literature of Medieval England*, ed. T. J. Heffernan (Knoxville, Tenn., 1986), 30-43.
[112] See K 5. 57; and J. Bossy, *Christianity in the West 1400-1700* (Oxford, 1985), 49.
[113] *Asloan Manuscript*, i. 66.

'MORALITEE AND HOOLYNESSE'

The opening resembles that of *The Passioun*, picturing the speaker prostrate before the 'bludy figour dolorus' (3) of Christ. His contrition is made manifest by outward signs—'Falling on face full law' (7) before this image, and later gazing fixedly at it—'To the Crist Jesu casting up myn ee' (79). The personified figure of Contrition appears, in *The Passioun*, 'bathit in teiris' (99); in this poem Dunbar speaks literally of 'teris of sorrow fra myne ene distelling' (15). The theme reaches its climax in this passage:

> Thoucht I have nocht thi precius feit to kis
> As had the Magdalyn quhen scho did marcy craife,
> I sall as scho weipe teris for my mys
> And every morrow seik the at thi graife,
> That seis my hert; as thou hir forgaife,
> Thairfor forgife me as synner penitent.   (145–50)

In the Middle Ages Mary Magdalene became the object of an intense cult, and the many Latin hymns in her honour usually alluded to her copious tears. She witnessed the Crucifixion, and was one of the first to see the risen Christ; she was also identified with the woman, unnamed in the Gospels, who washed Jesus's feet with her tears and whose sins were forgiven. The seven devils said to have been cast out of her were sometimes equated with the seven sins.[114] Dunbar is wholly orthodox in presenting her as a model for the 'synner penitent', and also as a symbol of hope. She was exemplary, in her love of Christ and mourning for his death, and, above all, her contrition. She thus figures in the *Dies Irae*, along with the penitent thief on the cross, as a token of hope:

> Qui Mariam absolvisti
> Et latronem exaudisti
> Mihi quoque spem dedisti.[115]

The image of Jesus as the Man of Sorrows is not confined to the opening. There are other references to the Crucifixion, at first intermittent—'Rew on me, Jesu, for thy woundis fyve' (23)—but increasingly frequent in the last nine stanzas, where they form, together with the refrain, small self-contained prayers:

> O thow that deit for my redempcioun,
> I cry the marcy and laser to repent.   (119–20)[116]

---

[114] Luke 7 and 8; cf. J. Szöverffy, '*Peccatrix quondam femina*: A Survey of the Mary Magdalen Hymns', *Traditio*, 19 (1963), 79–146.
[115] *The Penguin Book of Latin Verse*, ed. F. Brittain (1962), 241.
[116] See also lines 111–12, 143–4.

Dunbar has essentially the same devotional purpose here as in *The Passioun of Crist*. There is similar stress on the role of memory, and a similar desire to share, imaginatively, in the Crucifixion:

> Thow mak me, Jesu, unto the to remember,
> I ask thy passioun in me so to abound
> Quhill nocht in me unmenȝit be a member
> Bot feiling wo with the of every wound.   (153–6)

Dunbar ends with a plea:

> Appelling fra thy justice court extreme
> Unto thi court of marcy exultive;
> Thou mak my schip in blissit port arrive
> That saillis heir in stormes violent.
> And saife me, Jesu, for thy woundis five ...   (163–7)

The legalism of lines 163–4 is not peculiar to Dunbar. Ireland, at the end of his *Table of Confessioun*, trusts not to God's 'extreme justice' but to his mercy; and in a treatise on penance he likewise distinguishes between God's two courts. The court of Justice is found in hell, and was used before Christ's birth; but the court of Mercy came into existence after the Incarnation and Passion, and may be appealed to only while the soul remains in the body, for God will use 'rigorus iustice' after death. As in Dunbar's poem, the truly penitent sinner must 'appele fra the court of Iustice rigorus to the court of mercy'.[117] The image of the soul as a storm-tossed ship was a medieval commonplace.[118] But the figure appealed to Dunbar—in *O wreche be war* (K 60) he exhorts, 'Bend up thy saill and win thy port of grace' (13), and in *Memento homo* (K 61) it is similarly associated with a final appeal to God as man's 'ransonner with woundis fyve' (45). These devotions to the Five Wounds and to the Name of Jesus were at their height in the fifteenth century.[119]

Rorate celi desuper celebrates the birth of Christ. The Nativity was immensely popular with medieval English poets, especially in the fifteenth century. It formed a theme not only for narrative, but for short epigrams—on the paradoxes of the Incarnation—and, above all, for carols and lullabies, which were designed to serve as a focus for the loving contemplation of the humanity of Christ as baby and of Mary as mother.[120] Dunbar's poem, however, belongs to a different kind—one that is today less familiar than the much-anthologized

---

[117] *Asloan Manuscript*, i. 80 and 58.
[118] Cf. Douglas, *Eneados*, Prol. 3.
[119] Arundel 285 contains two prayers to the Name of Jesus, and there were many Middle English prayers to the Five Wounds. See Gray, *Themes and Images*, 133 ff.
[120] Woolf, 143 ff. and 302–7.

'MORALITEE AND HOOLYNESSE'

carols and lullabies. It is a song of jubilation, and its tone is less tender than triumphant.

Most discussion has focused on the liturgical (and ultimately Scriptural) sources of the refrain and the imagery in the first stanza:[121]

> *Rorate celi desuper.*
> Hevins distill 3our balmy schouris
> For now is rissin the brycht day ster
> Fro the ros Mary, flour of flouris:
> The cleir sone quhome no clud devouris,
> Surminting Phebus in the est,
> Is cumin of his hevinly touris
> *Et nobis puer natus est.*

The poem's starting-point is a quotation from Isaiah (45: 8), employed in an Advent introit:

> Rorate, caeli, desuper et nubes pluant justum.
> Aperiatur terra et germinat Salvatorem.

[Heavens, let dew fall from above and may the clouds rain upon the just man. Let the earth open and bring forth the Saviour.]

The refrain originates in the office of the mass for Christmas Day: *Puer natus est nobis et filius datus est nobis* (A child is born to us and a son is given to us). Dunbar's reference to Christ as 'the cleir sone' recalls an Advent antiphon, *Orietur sicut sol Salvator mundi* (The Saviour of the world will arise as the sun), which derives from an Old Testament prophecy concerning the sun of righteousness (Malachi 4: 2). Dunbar puns on 'son' and 'sun', as does Milton, in *On the Morning of Christ's Nativity*: 'The sun himself withheld his wonted speed ... He saw a greater sun appear'.

Christ's birth was traditionally seen as the fulfilment of the words of Isaiah and other prophets. It is clearly important to recognize Dunbar's orthodoxy, and his sense of decorum in employing phrases associated with the services of Advent and Christmas. Yet we do not need to know the origin of his images to perceive their effect: *Rorate celi* is informed by a sense of renewal and the triumph of light over darkness. We should not, I think, overstress this poem's learning. Stylistically too it is extremely lucid. Many of the carols contain a similar interplay between Latin and the vernacular, and some have burdens very close to Dunbar's refrain:

> Now may we syngen as it is
> *Quod puer natus est nobis.*

or

---

[121] Cf. Kinsley, 223; Hughes and Ramson, *Poetry of the Stewart Court*, 55–7.

'MORALITEE AND HOOLYNESSE'

> Puer nobis natus est
> De virgine Maria.[122]

The *Rorate* introit, as Gray notes, 'must have been universally familiar, since it was repeated throughout the season of Advent'.[123] Its symbol for the Incarnation—the falling of dew—reached an audience far wider than churchmen; it figured in the York play of the Annunciation, and in one of the most famous of medieval lyrics:

> He cam also stylle ther his moder was
> As dew in Aprylle that fallyt on the gras.[124]

Dunbar's poem is accompanied, in Bannatyne, by six anonymous 'ballatis of the natiuitie', to which it has many interesting generic similarities. All employ an eight-line stanza, mostly with the same rhyme-pattern as Dunbar's (although the line has four beats in some, five beats in others); and all have a liturgical-sounding refrain, often in Latin—*Illuminare Ierusalem, Virgo peperit salvatorem*, or *Pro nobis christus homo factus est*.[125] But the resemblances between these poems and Dunbar's go further than metrical form; there is much shared imagery. In one Christ is 'the lamp of ioy that chasis all dirknes'; in another he is 'our dawing bricht', just as in Dunbar's poem he is 'Aurora' (38). In other poems Christ is 'the sterne of most bewte'; he descended 'as dew' upon the Virgin, and was 'her fruct that flurist fair'. There is in all of them, as in Dunbar, the same exultant rejoicing at Christ's birth, and in many the thought that man's best response is song:

> Quhairfoir sing all with confort and glaidnes.

or

> Sing, christin peple, with solace, joy and fest.[126]

Dunbar's 'ballat', however, stands out from those around it by sheer poetic skill. *Rorate celi* has a simple and easily perceived structure: a series of joyful commands—'To him gife loving [praise]' (14), 'Sing' (34), 'Be myrthfull and mak melody' (52)—which are far different from the stern injunctions of many moral poems. (Even line 17, which might seem an exception, lightens the reference to penance with the words 'be glaid'.) Each stanza contains a variation upon the same basic pattern, evident in the first stanza, with its coupling of command,

---

[122] Greene, *Carols*, nos. 19 and 36.
[123] Gray, *Themes and Images*, 105.
[124] *The York Plays*, ed. R. Beadle (1982), 113; *CB XV*, no. 81.
[125] *Bannatyne Manuscript*, fols. 27a–31a.
[126] Ibid., fols. 27a and 30b.

'MORALITEE AND HOOLYNESSE'

Rorate, and triumphant assertion, *Et nobis puer natus est*. This refrain provides the syntactic model for many lines—

> For now is rissin the brycht day ster. (3)
> The cleir sone...
> . . . . . .
> Is cumin of his hevinly touris. (5–7)
> To 30w is cumin full humly. (20)

These words fulfil the expectations of Christ's *coming* that run through the Advent services. The sequence of seven stanzas is orderly and hierarchic, but not rigidly so. The first two are addressed to the heavens, and to the 'hevinly operacionis', such as the angelic hosts. The next two stanzas are concerned with man, addressing first 'Synnaris', then singling out the clergy, as having a special role in 'observance devyne' (27). The next stanzas move lower in the chain of being, to birds and flowers, at the same time echoing themes stated in the first stanza. Birds are exhorted to sing and rejoice at night's passing and the rising of the spiritual sun; flowers, to spring up

> In honour of the blissit frute
> That rais up fro the rose Mary. (43–4)

There are other parallels between human and non-human forms of worship: the commandment to the clergy to 'Ensense his altar, reid and sing' (29), both looks forward, to the bird-song, and also recalls the 'balmy' showers distilled by the heavens (1–2).

The last stanza brings these themes together in a fine climax:

> Syng, hevin imperiall, most of hicht,
> Regions of air mak armony,
> All fishe in flud and foull of flicht
> Be myrthfull and mak melody:
> All *Gloria in excelsis* cry,
> Hevin, erd, se, man, bird and best;
> He that is crownit abone the sky
> *Pro nobis puer natus est*. (49–56)

There are several verbal echoes here; 'Syng' and 'Be myrthfull' had the same initial position in earlier lines (34 and 36). The crowded line, 'Hevin, erd, se, man, bird and best', sums up the poem's progression; *man* is almost at the mid-point of the line, a position similar to that he occupies in the poem itself. But the stanza does far more than recapitulate what has gone before; it is increasingly filled with song, which culminates with the *Gloria in excelsis*: an apt reference both to the angels' greeting to the shepherds (Luke 2: 14) and to human worship at mass. Music is a fit expression of joy and praise;

and is, of course, a symbol of cosmic harmony. Man here sings in concert with heaven and earth, bird and beast.

Dunbar's selectivity also distinguishes this poem from the surrounding ones. Some of these contain striking passages, but few, apart from *Ierusalem rejos for joy*, are wholly effective. Some are over-didactic or clumsily Latinate; others explore at length ideas that in Dunbar's poem are firmly subordinated to the central theme of praise and worship. Dunbar does no more than hint, for instance, at the contrast between God's omnipotence and the 'meik' manner of his Incarnation (15, 20), or the paradox of the 'barne benyng', the child who is also king of kings (26–8; 55–6). He refers very briefly to the Redemption—'ȝour saulis with his blud to by' (21)—but this poem is not, as are others, overshadowed by thoughts of the Crucifixion. *Rorate celi* is wholly given over to jubilant celebration.

Done is a battell on the dragon blak (K 4) is undoubtedly the most popular of Dunbar's religious poems, appealing alike to believers and non-believers. This may be due primarily to its forceful rhythms, which critics sometimes attempt to evoke in military metaphor: the first line is thus termed a 'cannonade', or the poem's 'thundering greatness' is said to have 'the ring of a steel gauntlet flung down'.[127] Another source of the poem's appeal must be its imagery—theologically orthodox yet deployed in such a way as to have the force of myth—bold, arresting, and mysterious. *Done is a battell* embodies an ancient view of the Redemption as a struggle between God and the devil: Christ is heroic and triumphant, a 'campioun' (2) and 'grit victour' (25). It is significant that he here receives the title Christ, which is 'pre-eminently his Resurrection name as against the Jesus of his suffering humanity'.[128] In *Done is a battell*, unlike *The Passioun*, the cross is not the instrument of shame and suffering, but a 'signe triumphall' (4), raised on high like a battle standard. Christ traditionally carried such a standard, when standing beside the empty tomb and when harrowing hell. (There are famous contemporary depictions of this in Piero della Francesca's *Resurrection* and Dürer's engraving of *Christ in Limbo*.) Dunbar shows us *Christus miles*, in the heroic rather than the chivalric sense. This conflict is vital to mankind—Christ is 'our' champion, and suffers for 'our' sake. But the figure is not elaborated in romance terms; Christ is not here the lover-knight, nor is the soul his lady, as in Henryson's *Bludy Serk*. Indeed man's part in this action seems small, subordinate to the clash of 'mighty opposites'. The poem abounds in polarities, not only between God

---

[127] Scott, 300; Lewis, *English Literature in the Sixteenth Century*, 96.
[128] Bennett, *Poetry of the Passion*, 77.

'MORALITEE AND HOOLYNESSE'

and the devil and life and death, but between faith and 'errour' (31), Christians and Jews, and light and darkness.

A further view of the Redemption is implicit in the poem. Hell is a prison, and the devils are gaolers (34). All human souls—not only those who figured in the 'Harrowing of hell' legend—have been liberated by payment of a ransom: 'Chryst with his blud our ransonis dois indoce' (7). This notion of the Redemption was archaic theologically—it had been superseded by the more complex doctrine of 'satisfaction' associated with St Anselm—but both the term *ransom* and the imagery associated with it persisted throughout the Middle Ages.[129] The Crucifixion was sometimes visualized as a document written with Christ's blood—'And with his precious blood he wrot the bille'.[130] Dunbar's verb *indoce*, 'endorse', stresses the transaction's legal validity, but the legal figure is not further developed. The poem's dominant image is more primitive and archetypal. Christ is a monster-slayer, and the dragon of the first line is recalled in the penultimate one—'Dispulit of the tresur that he 3emit'. The devil is a guardian of treasure, an ancient role for the dragon in classical and Germanic myth, but his treasure consists of human souls. There were many Scriptural sources for this figure of the dragon as the great foe of God and man, but the most important was the book of Revelation; there he is coupled with the serpent and identified with the devil: *draco, ille magnus, serpens antiquus, qui vocatur diabolus* (12: 9; also 20: 2–3).

Stanza two presents the devil in threefold form:

> Dungin is the deidly dragon Lucifer,
> The crewall serpent with the mortall stang,
> The auld kene tegir with his teith on char
> Quhilk in a wait hes lyne for us so lang
> Thinking to grip us in his clowis strang:
> The mercifull lord wald nocht that it wer so;
> He maid him for to fel3e of that fang:
> *Surrexit Dominus de sepulchro.*

Dragon, serpent, and tiger are frightening images that here reinforce one another, but do not receive equal weight. The treatment grows progressively more detailed: the serpent is described more fully than the dragon, and the tiger—introduced in a line whose structure parallels the preceding one—dominates the rest of the stanza. Medieval churchmen occasionally interpreted the tiger as a symbol of the devil: according to Hrabanus Maurus, *Tigris autem mystice significat astutiam [cunning] diaboli*, and according to Peter Damian, *quid hic*

---

[129] Woolf, 20–2, and her *Art and Doctrine: Essays on Medieval Literature*, ed. H. O'Donoghue (1986), 99–100.

[130] Chaucer, *An ABC*, 59.

*tigris nisi diabolus debet intellegi?*¹³¹ But this figure does not seem to have been as common as dragon and serpent. Perhaps because of this Dunbar felt imaginatively more free to develop the tiger's obvious natural symbolism. This he does very effectively, providing a vivid image not only of cruelty—the tiger's usual significance in proverbs and similes¹³²—but of latent menace. The tiger is shown not at a distance but close up, in terms of teeth and claws, which are ready to fasten upon a victim. (Devils were often pictured with bared teeth and with claws instead of fingers.) The tiger does not pursue his prey, but is 'in a wait', in ambush. The diction is plain, yet used with precision, and is rich in associations. The phrase *felȝe of that fang* means 'fail in an attempt to capture'; but *fang* had a range of senses, several of which are here relevant—an animal's prey, a thief's stolen goods, and war booty. At the end the devil is 'dispulit': deprived both of prey and spoils.

The central stanza presents Christ in a series of symbolic images that not only parallel but also surpass those for the devil. Christ is first compared to lamb, lion, and giant (17–20). Both the lamb and the lion were common types of Christ, familiar from the liturgy, and possessing a complex significance frequently expounded by preachers. Dunbar, however, points to those aspects that he wishes to stress: Christ is 'lyk a lamb in sacrifice' and like a lion 'rissin up agane'.¹³³ The third comparison,

> And as a gyane raxit him on hicht

needs more elucidation, because it has been mistakenly taken to refer to Samson, whose carrying off of the gates of Gaza was seen as a type of the Resurrection.¹³⁴ Dunbar's allusion can be traced to Psalm 18 (AV 19): 5: *Exultavit, ut gigas, ad currendam viam* (He has rejoiced, as a giant, to run his course). This psalm was commonly regarded as prophetic, and the giant, who was taken to be a figure of Christ, became the focus for much learned commentary. The term *gigas* was sometimes taken to refer to Christ's great strength, *quia fortis est et insuperabilis*; sometimes, and more importantly, it referred to his Incarnation.¹³⁵ The giants were said to be descended from gods and men; *Christus gigas* therefore alluded to Christ's double nature, divine

---

¹³¹ Migne, *Patrologia Latina*, cxi. 219 and cxlv. 775.
¹³² Whiting, T 284–97. In Scottish verse tigers are regularly 'cruel' and 'terne'.
¹³³ Kinsley, 236, notes that the bestiary story of the lion cub revivified by its father's breath was a type of the Resurrection.
¹³⁴ I am indebted to T. D. Hill, 'Dunbar's Giant: "On the Resurrection of Christ", 17–24', *Anglia*, 99 (1978), 451–6, and R. E. Kaske, '*Gigas* the Giant in *Piers Plowman*', *JEGP* 56 (1957), 177–85.
¹³⁵ Cf. E. H. Kantorowicz, *The King's Two Bodies* (Princeton, 1957), 50–1.

and human. St Ambrose's famous hymn, *Veni redemptor gentium*, uses this verse with reference to the Incarnation: 'Let him come forth from his chamber, from the royal hall of chastity, a giant of twofold substance, to run his course rejoicing' (*geminae gigas substantiae / Alacris ut currat viam*).[136] But the image of a giant Christ, who stretched from earth to the firmament, was also taken to allude to his Resurrection.[137] All three notions have relevance in this poem, but Dunbar's phrase 'raxit him on hicht' (stretched himself on high)—which parallels 'rissin up' (19) and 'Sprungin' (21)—suggests that it is the last one he wished to stress.

Dunbar then speaks of the risen Christ in more familiar imagery, as the dawn (Aurora), the sun (Apollo), and 'blisfull day' (21-3). This threefold symbolization of Christ as the light of the world counters the 'dirknes' (28) traditionally associated with evil, hell, devils, and ignorance; it is also opposed to the false radiance of *Lucifer* (9), once clad in light, now transformed into the 'blak' dragon. But the imagery of this stanza has a strange and riddling quality, even when its components are familiar—contraries are yoked together in the lamb and the lion, or the female Aurora and the male 'Appollo'. The transition from the first trio of similes to the second set of symbolic metaphors is briefly startling. The combined effect of these images, unlike those for the devil, is paradoxical. They are unified chiefly by the verbs—'rissin', 'raxit him on hicht', and climactically, '*Surrexit*'—all alike referring to the Resurrection.

Syntactically, *Done is a battell* is bold but simple. The first stanza establishes the pattern for the whole poem, with its explosive opening (that rivals Donne's 'Batter my heart' sonnet),[138] and succession of triumphant affirmations:

> Done is a battell on the dragon blak;
> Our campioun Chryst confoundit hes his force;
> The ȝettis of hell ar brokin with a crak;
> The signe triumphall rasit is of the croce ... (1-4)

The lines are end-stopped, and have the most basic kind of subject-predicate structure, with no dependent clauses. The tenses alternate between present and present perfect, implying both the eternal significance of Christ's act and its finality—something evident also in the lexical sense of 'Done' and 'confoundit'. The poem's very first word illustrates another striking feature of the syntax. 'Done' receives enormous prominence, from the dislocation of normal word-order; it may have been suggested by the initial position of *Surrexit* in the

---

[136] *Latin Verse*, ed. Brittain, 92.
[137] Kantorowicz, op. cit. 69-70.
[138] On alliterative patterning, see below, 373.

refrain. There are lesser inversions in 'confoundit hes' and 'rasit is'. The second stanza also opens with emphatic front-shifting of the participle:

> Dungin is the deidly dragon Lucifer.

This echoes both the syntax and the *d*-alliteration of the poem's opening line. Later, in the third stanza, the rhyme with 'Dungin' calls attention to a similar inversion:

> Sprungin is Aurora radius and bricht. (21)

This syntax, although forceful, might well have been monotonous, if unaltered. Thus in stanza two the first five lines contain but one verb; the compound subject hangs from the single predicate, 'Dungin is'. Stanzas three and four interweave dependent clauses with their central affirmation, that Christ is risen. But the final stanza is reminiscent, thematically and syntactically, of the first:

> The fo is chasit, the battell is done ceis,
> The presone brokin, the jevellouris fleit and flemit;
> The weir is gon, confermit is the peis,
> The fetteris lowsit and the dungeoun temit,
> The ransoun maid, the presoneris redemit;
> The feild is win, ourcumin is the fo,
> Dispulit of the tresur that he ӡemit:
> Surrexit Dominus de sepulchro. (33–40)

This syntax is equally paratactic, but there is a remarkable quickening of pace, like the *accelerando* of a musical climax; most lines make two statements instead of one. The rhetorical patterning is evident. Line 33 establishes the basic twofold norm, and lines 34, 36, and 37 repeat this with slight modifications. Lines 35 and 38 stand out, however, through their chiasmic arrangement of nouns and participles, which might be symbolized *abba* instead of *abab*. In them the final clauses thus have emphatic front-shifting of the verb: 'ourcumin is the fo'. The penultimate line slightly modifies the pattern: there is enjambment with the preceding one, yet 'Dispulit', in its initial position, has a prominence similar to the earlier 'Done' and 'Dungin'. But the poem's last words are not concerned with the devil; the refrain returns us to the risen Christ.

Critics usually treat *Done is a battell* as if it existed in splendid isolation. There are few medieval English lyrics devoted solely to the Resurrection, and the best-known both derive from Latin hymns—William Herebert's free rendering of *Iesu nostra redemptio*, and an anonymous version of the first verses of *Aurora lucis rutilat*.[139] But

---

[139] *CB XIV*, nos. 24 and 37; see Gray, *Themes and Images*, 146–8.

there survives a small cluster of Scottish poems on this theme, three of which accompany Dunbar's in Bannatyne's 'ballatis of theoligie'; a fourth is found in Arundel 285. *Done is a battell* is thus, quite literally, less isolated than sometimes appears. All these poems, Dunbar's included, have forty lines, and employ stanzas of the same pattern, *ababbcbc*.[140] Dunbar's refrain occurs as the first line of one of these poems, and there are many resemblances of imagery and phrasing, only a few of which are noted here:

> Our campioun chryst that to the feild him drest.
> [Cf. *Done is a battell*, 2.]
>
> Vpone the dragone a battel for to done.
> [Cf. *Done is a battell*, 1.]
>
> The sing triumphale of the croce
> Schew to confound the feindis feid.[141]
> [Cf. *Done is a battell*, 2 and 4.]

Neither Dunbar's poem nor the others can be dated, and it seems impossible to prove that any one of them is indebted to another. But *Done is a battell* stands out from the rest, rather as did *Rorate celi*, for its finer craftsmanship. It seems inherently most probable that Dunbar provided a vernacular model for these lesser poets.

What is incontrovertible, however, is that all these poets were profoundly influenced by the great Latin hymns and sequences of the medieval Church, some anonymous, some attributed to great figures, such as St Ambrose. These are the most likely sources for their shared phrasing and imagery. Christ figures as the Lion in the Easter sequence of Adam of St Victor:

> Sic de Juda leo fortis
> Fractis portis dirae mortis

and as *invictus leo*, crushing the dragon, in an Easter hymn by Fulbert of Chartres.[142] Christ the sacrificial Lamb appears again and again, as in this hymn for Easter eve:

> Iam pascha nostrum Christus est,
> Qui immolatus agnus est.[143]

In St Ambrose's hymn, *Splendor paternae gloriae*, Christ figures both as *Aurora* and as the true Sun.[144] Christ the Giant also appears repeatedly, often linked with the Lamb and Lion—

---

[140] Hill, 'Dunbar's Giant', 455–6, sees numerical symbolism, noting that Christ appeared to the Apostles for 40 days.
[141] *Bannatyne Manuscript*, fols. 37a and 34a.
[142] *Latin Verse*, ed. Brittain, 200 and 174.
[143] Ibid. 114.
[144] Ibid. 90–1.

> Fortis gigas, ille David . . .
> Gigas noster . . . agnus noster . . .
> Magnus leo . . . Christus, gigas orbiger.[145]

Although no precise source for *Done is a battell* is known, it undoubtedly belongs to the tradition of these Latin hymns. It shares not only their symbolic imagery but their martial and exultant tone.

[145] *Analecta Hymnica*, ed. G. M. Dreves and C. Blume (Leipzig, 1886–), viii, nos. 19 and 30; ibid. x, no. 25.

5
'Sportis and Jocositeis'

> A merry heart doeth good like a medicine.
> (Proverbs 17: 22)

MANY of Dunbar's readers, on turning from his serious poems to the comic ones, have experienced surprise, and indeed shock. Instead of spiritual orthodoxy we find cynicism and irreverence, and celebration of the pleasures of life. Instead of the idealistic and hierarchic world-view implicit in *The Thrissill and the Rois* we are shown a more topsy-turvy world, in which the laws of nature and society are apparently flouted or disregarded—a fox woos a lamb, craftsmen mimic gentlemen, an abbot tries to fly, a friar is a devil, or women dominate men. These poems often have structures that are not easy to categorize—many rouse expectations as to 'kind' and genre that are then subverted. Their tone and style are equally unpredictable. The language of the courtly and moral poems is refined and decorous; and, although not without imagery and symbolism, is largely unambiguous. But some of the comic poems employ low and vulgar diction; and many are replete with ambiguities, puns, double-meanings, and other word-play, that make their tone more complex and far more difficult to gauge.

One small illustration is *He that hes gold and grit riches* (K 70). Its first four stanzas catalogue the different ways in which men destroy their 'mirrynes' through their own folly. All four have a very similar structure, beginning with the indefinite 'He that hes' or 'He that may', and ending with the refrain—'He wirkis sorrow to him sell (self)'. This generalizing type of syntax is common in proverbs—a random selection includes 'He that lives best prays best', 'He that lives longest shall suffer most woe', or 'He that does evil hates the light'.[1] The poem is commonly treated as a morality, yet the tone is amused rather than indignant—it offers sardonic, even ribald, comments on human folly. It concludes,

> Now all this tyme lat us be mirry
> And sett nocht by this warld a chirry;
> Now quhill thair is gude wyne to sell,

---

[1] Whiting, L 405, L 407, E 184.

> He that dois on dry breid wirry
> I gif him to the Devill of hell. (21–5)

This is as morally unorthodox as the poem by 'Iohine Blyth', or another that begins 'Be mirry bretherene, ane and all'.[2] It treats its readers as boon companions, not sinners, and pours scorn on the rigours of the ascetic life—*wirry*, 'choke', nicely implies the discomfort of swallowing dry bread. This poem's notion of what it is to 'be mirry' is far from the virtuous merriness envisaged in moral ones, such as *Be mery man and tak nocht fer in mynd* (K 65). It is even further removed—disconcertingly so—from the end of another poem:

> Man, pleis thy makar and be mirry,
> And sett not by this warld a chirry ...   (K 68. 41–2)

In this pious setting the line 'And sett not by this warld a chirry' expresses *contemptus mundi*. Transferred to the new context of *He that hes gold* it becomes a mockery, and assumes a new sense—perhaps 'don't give a damn for what the world thinks'. The poem ends neatly, but explosively—'He that dois' (24) suggests a return to the poem's basic pattern, and leads one to expect the refrain's repetition. But Dunbar has a surprise in store—the violent, and indeed shocking curse.

Such poems, predictably, have met with a mixed response. There is no doubt that they have long been read with much enjoyment, and by many readers. Pinkerton, in the eighteenth century, expressed particular enthusiasm for Dunbar's comic poetry; and Speirs, in the present one, preferred it to what he called the 'ceremonial' poems, regarding it as the core of Dunbar's 'living achievement'.[3] Kinsley likewise singled out 'a wild comic fantasy' as the most distinctive aspect of Dunbar's genius.[4] Yet Kinsley also said that Dunbar lacked Henryson's 'humour' and 'humanity'; and others have charged him with 'bad taste', or termed his comedy 'coarse' and even blasphemous.[5] James Russell Lowell considered his humour nothing 'but the dullest vulgarity'.[6] Such adverse views are not confined to the past—the sensibilities of some present-day readers are offended by Dunbar's mockery of women or Highlanders. Ross finds the taste of two poems—*Lang heff I maed of ladyes quhytt* (K 33) and *In vice most vicius*

---

[2] See above, 144, and *Bannatyne Manuscript*, fol. 160a.
[3] *Ancient Scotish Poems* (1786), i, p. xi; *The Scots Literary Tradition* (1940), 36.
[4] *Dunbar: Poems* (Oxford, 1958), xix.
[5] 'The Mediaeval Makars', in *Scottish Poetry: A Critical Survey*, ed. Kinsley (1955), 32; see also Small, i, p. xcix; and *The Poems of William Dunbar*, ed. D. Laing (Edinburgh, 1834), i. 55–6.
[6] *Literary Essays* (1893), iv. 269.

he excellis (K 34)—'questionable by modern standards'.[7] A few critics have attempted to minimize the gulf between the different areas of Dunbar's writing: the most systematic is Reiss, who denies any 'real' difference beween 'Dunbar the court entertainer and Dunbar the moralist'; but others likewise view his comic poems 'in a moral perspective'.[8] Associated with this are remarkable new interpretations of Dunbar's poems, and profound disagreements as to which of them are genuinely funny: *The Dregy*, for instance, seems to some highly serious, whereas *The Goldyn Targe* is found comic.[9]

We should see this diversity of response as a small testimony to the continuing vitality of Dunbar's comic genius. Comedy tends to be divisive; it jolts, startles, disturbs, and enrages. Dunbar is likely to have angered some—though not all—of his first audience, since he exploited areas of social tension between Lowlanders and Highlanders, laymen and clerics, seculars and friars, men and women. His comic poems must also often have divided audiences into other groups: those who understood the Latin phrases, recognized the literary allusions, or perceived the ironies—and those who did not. Then, as now, he probably evoked conflicting responses even in the same mind—puzzlement and delighted comprehension, shock at his irreverence and amusement at his wit.

The comic traditions to which Dunbar was indebted are difficult to chart, and the attempts to analyse his relation to them are few and scattered. There was no single, largely coherent tradition, dominated by one master-work—such as *Le Roman de la Rose* in dream-allegory—but rather a body of extremely varied and miscellaneous comic writing, in Latin and the vernaculars, designed chiefly to entertain, and often somewhat low in literary esteem. Dunbar is not usually thought of as a story-teller, yet many of his poems contain lively dialogue and relate short anecdotes. He was clearly familiar with some of the many different types of medieval narrative—beast fables, fabliaux, the exempla and *jocosae narrationes* of the preachers, and the *facetiae*, which in their English form were commonly called 'merry tales' or 'jests'.[10] This is apparent in various ways: he uses animal stereotypes from the world of fable, especially the lamb and the fox; he makes fun of stock

---

[7] Ross, 181.

[8] Reiss, 68; Ross, 159–62; J. Hughes and W. S. Ramson, *Poetry of the Stewart Court* (Canberra, 1982), 103–21.

[9] Cf. W. Scheps, '*The Goldyn Targe*: Dunbar's Comic Psychomachia', *Papers on Language and Literature*, 11 (1975), 339–56.

[10] See D. Brewer, 'The International Medieval Popular Comic Tale in England', in *The Popular Literature of Medieval England*, ed. T. J. Heffernan (Knoxville, Tenn., 1986), 131–47; S. J. Kahrl, 'The Medieval Origins of the Sixteenth-Century English Jest-Books', *Studies in the Renaissance*, 13 (1966), 166–83; and B. White, 'Medieval Mirth', *Anglia*, 78 (1960), 284–301.

comic butts, such as deceitful friars or thieving tailors; he employs common story-telling motifs; and makes casual, passing allusions to a vast reservoir of jokes and witticisms, some of which probably circulated orally as well as in writing.

A good example occurs in *The Turnament* (K 52B), in the passage that describes the tailor:

> His baner born wes him befoir
> Quhairin wes clowttis ane hundreth scoir,
> Ilk ane of divers hew,
> And all stowin out of sindry webbis.   (133–6)

The tailor who steals from his customers is a common stereotype, but this banner, constructed out of stolen cloth, is less familiar and might well seem Dunbar's invention. Yet there was a popular story, first recounted in a *facetia* by Piovano Arlotto, of a dishonest tailor to whom the devil appeared, bearing a *bandiera* (banner) made from the cloth he had stolen for over fifty years; it was *di molte ragioni di colori*, like Dunbar's 'clowttis... of divers hew'. The terrified tailor vows to steal no more, but proves incorrigible in this and the later English versions of the tale, such as *The Wyll of the Devyll*, or a neat epigram by Sir John Harington.[11] Where Dunbar encountered the story is uncertain. In his poem the banner has a slightly different function, yet he retains the damning connection between tailor and devil. The texture of the passage is enriched by this small detail rather as the opening of *The Goldyn Targe* is enriched by allusions to Aurora and Phoebus. Unfortunately these popular tales and other witticisms have inevitably had a much shorter life than classical mythology. Some of Dunbar's comic poems contain allusions to topicalities or to jests once known to everyone that now mystify a modern reader. Comedy is liable to obsolescence, because it is so closely tied to the culture in which it originates.

Comedy is culture-bound in another way; it is highly sensitive to fluctuations in taste and standards of behaviour. Much medieval comedy seems alien, because it is predominantly harsh and derisive, and often provoked by physical discomfiture. Yet such comedy was far more common than the warm, sympathetic humour that we tend to associate with Chaucer.[12] Bursts of mocking laughter punctuate the fabliaux and *facetiae*; even in Henryson's *Fables* (1054) this is the

---

[11] See *Motti e Facezie del Piovano Arlotto*, ed. G. Folena (Milan, 1953), 103–5; *Jyl of Breyntford's Testament*, ed. F. J. Furnivall (1871), 22; Harington's *Epigrams* (1618), no. 20. A similar tale is also told in *The Pinder of Wakefield*, ed. A. E. Horsman (Liverpool, 1956), 21–2.

[12] Cf. K. Thomas, 'The Place of Laughter in Tudor and Stuart England', *TLS*, 21 Jan. 1977, 77–81.

response of bystanders to the Wolf's bloody brow. Dunbar's comedy is often of this type; the same derisive laughter greets the ungainly dancing of Dame Dounteboir:

> For lachtter nain mycht hald thair lippis   (K 28. 39)

and the scatological climax of *The Turnament*:

> Bot that sa gud ane bourd me thocht,
> Sic solace to my hairt it rocht,
> For lawchtir neir I brist.   (K 52B. 220–2)

In *O gracious princes* (K 30) Dunbar applies the word *bourde* to another poem (K 29), and there speaks of arousing not 'solace' but 'gam' in his audience. Some implications of this terminology have already been mentioned (p. 19), but it should also be noted how closely Dunbar's stance resembles that of the unknown authors of *John the Reeve*, *Sir Corneus*, and other popular, often vulgar tales. They too refer to their poem (or its subject) as a 'bourd'—'Off a bowrd I wyll 3ou schew'; they too speak of their intention to promote 'mirth', 'game and glee', or 'solace'—'Best is mirth of all solace.'[13]

There is an affinity between this poetry and other forms of medieval entertainment. *The Howlat* (665–845) contains a splendid account of a great feast, in which occurs a series of comic turns—the boisterous and often coarse buffoonery of juggler, bard, and two fools. At actual courts the festivities were sometimes of great magnificence, but sometimes surprisingly simple and crude. Most kings enjoyed watching performing animals, cock-fights, and bull-baiting, just as their subjects did. Edward II, on one occasion, paid a servant 'because he danced before the king on a table, and made him laugh very greatly'; on another day he rewarded a cook, 'because he rode before the king . . . and often fell from his horse, at which the king laughed greatly'.[14] In 1518 the Edinburgh records note that a man was chosen 'to be Litil John for to mak sportis and jocositeis in the toun'.[15] This innocent-sounding phrase covers not only pageantry but also the rowdy horseplay associated with the Robin Hood plays, the St

---

[13] These citations are from *John the Reeve*, 1–10, and *Sir Corneus*, 1–6, in *Ten Fifteenth-Century Comic Poems*, ed. M. Furrow (New York, 1985). Cf. G. H. McKnight, *Middle English Humorous Tales in Verse* (Boston, 1913), xvii, on 'bourdes'; and S. Wenzel, 'The Joyous Art of Preaching', *Anglia*, 97 (1979), 304–25, on preachers' use of the *burda*.

[14] See R. F. Green, *Poets and Princepleasers* (Toronto, 1980), 55 and *passim*. Similarly 'robust antics' are credited to Henry III, who threw one jester in the water and tore up another's clothes. Cf. E. Salter, *English and International: Studies in the Literature, Art and Patronage of Medieval England*, ed. D. Pearsall and N. Zeeman (Cambridge, 1988), 82.

[15] *Extracts from the Records of the Burgh of Edinburgh I: 1403–1528*, ed. J. D. Marwick (SBRS, 1869), 176.

Nicholas bishop and his attendant imps or 'deblatis', and the Abbot of Unreason—forcible ducking in the water of a mill-dam, for instance, or the 'spilling' of a house at Stirling, whose owner had to be recompensed by the king.[16] The authorities tolerated such unruly behaviour, along with occasional irreverence, as long as it did not go beyond certain limits and 'kept its place'. In 1527 the sacrist of Holy Trinity church, Edinburgh, was said to be *noctivagus goliator*, and to have assumed the garments *histrionum et fatuorum*; he was prohibited from doing this in the future, except, interestingly, *pro domini regis solacio aut inter tuos confratres et hoc moderate et discrete* (for the king's entertainment, or among thy brethren, and then moderately and with discretion).[17]

The comic buffoonery at the feast in *The Howlat* is immediately preceded by a devout hymn to the Virgin; in *The Canterbury Tales*, as is well known, 'cherles tales' mingle with courtly and pious ones. The conjunction of opposites that we find in Dunbar should not be regarded as peculiar or unique. Among his close contemporaries was Jean Molinet, who wrote, in addition to much courtly and religious verse, a mock-litany and the singularly salacious *sermon de Billouart*.[18] Poggio Bracciolini is remembered today chiefly as a distinguished humanist; but to Dunbar's contemporaries, such as Douglas and Skelton, he was equally famous for his scurrilous invectives and *Facetiae*.[19] Poggio traced their origin to the custom of *jocandi confabulandique* with his friends in the papal secretariat: 'nobody was spared, and whatever met with our disapprobation was freely censured; often the Pope himself was the first theme of our criticism, and many people attended our gatherings for fear of being ridiculed in their absence'.[20] It would be ridiculous to push comparison between these writers very far, and their respective milieux—the papal curia and the Scottish court—were very different. Yet Dunbar had something in common with Poggio, including his freedom of speech—'nobody was spared'.

Some of Dunbar's comic poems have a serious aspect, but we should not strain to find profound moral significance in *all* of them; nor should we go to the opposite extreme, and see them—in the modish sense of the term, at least—as 'carnivalesque'. They do not embody a struggle between 'folk culture' and the official Middle

[16] Cf. Mill, 28–9; and *TA* i. 270.
[17] Mill, 86–7.
[18] *Les Faictz et dictz*, ed. N. Dupire (SATF, 1936–9), ii. 548–54, and 558–66.
[19] See *Palice of Honour*, 1232–3, and *Garland of Laurel*, 372–3.
[20] See the apologia that concludes most of the many editions of *Liber facetiarum*; I owe this translation to F. P. Wilson, 'The English Jest-Books of the Sixteenth and Early Seventeenth Centuries', in *Shakespearian and Other Studies* (Oxford, 1969), 287.

Ages.[21] Despite their occasional indulgence in the verbal equivalent of dung-throwing, they cannot be construed as serious challenges to the social 'establishment' or the spiritual pieties of the age. Dunbar's usual stance is not radical, but deeply conservative. Although we have no firm evidence for his thinking about the nature of comedy, it seems most likely that he would have endorsed the common medieval belief that laughter and mirth were therapeutic. This notion was often conveyed in the simple yet suggestive figure of the relaxed bow, which V. A. Kolve called 'one of the central images' of the Middle Ages.[22] It was known to Henryson, who used it to justify the mixing of 'merrines' with serious matter in *The Fables*:

> ane bow that ay is bent
> Worthis vnsmart and dullis on the string;
> Sa dois the mynd that is ay diligent
> In ernistfull thochtis and in studying.   (22-5)

Dunbar's comic poems are essentially 'sportis and jocositeis', designed to provide 'solace' and 'gam'. Many of them originate as *bourds*; some remain little more than crude and ephemeral jests, but others are subtle and sophisticated poems. His comedy is deeply rooted in medieval culture and literary traditions; what makes it distinctive is his vivid imagination and verbal artistry. This chapter and the two that follow will consider those modes in which Dunbar particularly excels: parody and irony, flyting, and fantasy.

There is a remarkable degree of elasticity in the term *parody*. Some scholars sharply differentiate it from burlesque; others use the words almost interchangeably, or treat parody as a sub-member of burlesque.[23] Definitions range between the wide and the very narrow. At one extreme, parody is used so inclusively as to signify any form of humorous imitation: *Le Roman de Renart* has thus been called a parody of French feudal society.[24] At the other extreme, we are told that parody 'holds the mirror not up to nature but to another work of art', or that parody deals not with 'the world of things' but 'the world of

---

[21] Cf. M. Bakhtin, *Rabelais and his World*, trans. H. Iswolsky (1968), 437 and *passim*. More relevant to Dunbar seems the 'safety-valve' theory, associated with anthropologists like Max Gluckman and Victor Turner, that the temporary lifting of taboos reaffirms hierarchical principles.

[22] *The Play Called Corpus Christi* (Stanford, 1966), 128-9; cf. G. Olson, 'The Medieval Theory of Literature for Refreshment', *SP* 71 (1974), 303, and *Literature as Recreation*, 91 ff.

[23] Cf. N. Blake, *The English Language in Medieval Literature* (1977), 116; J. D. Jump, *Burlesque* (1972), 2.

[24] J. Flinn, *Le Roman de Renart... au moyen âge* (Toronto, 1963), 36.

words'.²⁵ I find the latter approach preferable: parody is intensely verbal, a composition that imitates another composition, or text, or literary genre. This imitation is undoubtedly humorous, but the nature of the comedy, its tone and direction, vary enormously. The verbs so often used of the relationship between a parody and its original— 'ridicules', 'attacks', 'mocks'—do not always seem accurate. Nor should that original necessarily be called, as it often is, a 'target'; 'subtext' seems a better, because more neutral, term. Parody is sometimes hostile, but it may also be affectionate and playful—a literary 'game'.

Parody-spotting is today very popular with medievalists. Indeed one scholar sarcastically remarks that parody has replaced the allegoric method 'comme source d'enrichissement des textes médiévaux'.²⁶ Chaucer's output is steadily increasing: first *Sir Thopas*, then the ballade *To Rosemounde*, somewhat more recently *The Tale of Melibee*.²⁷ The lyrics of MS Harley 2253 are also being subjected to parodic interpretation, and the critics are sometimes remarkably frank as to their motivation. If *Annot and John* is viewed as a parody of courtly love lyrics, says one, it 'is no longer singularly tedious but doubly impressive'; another says of *The Fair Maid of Ribblesdale*: 'An otherwise laborious and undistinguished poem turns into a glorious joke'.²⁸ This sounds like the criticism of last resort, the only way to rehabilitate a work that the reader apparently finds dull or unintelligible.

There is indeed a problem about identifying medieval parody, which largely springs from the difficulties of ascertaining what was comic many centuries ago, especially when we lack external evidence as to authorial intent or audience response. This is particularly true of parody, which presupposes that the work or author parodied is not only popular, but has stylistic individuality and a high degree of textual stability. These are notoriously rare in the medieval period. The great exception is the area of sacred writings: the Latin texts of the Scriptures, the liturgy, and certain hymns were comparatively stable and undoubtedly well known. This was by far the most fruitful source of medieval parody. There are comic versions of famous hymns, such as *Verbum bonum et suave*, *Iam lucis orto sidere* and the *Laetabundus* sequence, several versions of a Drunkards' Mass, and a Gospel

---

²⁵ G. D. Kiremidjian, 'The Aesthetics of Parody', *Journal of Aesthetics*, 28 (1969), 233; J. A. Dane, 'Parody and Satire in the Literature of 13th-Century Arras', *SP* 81 (1984), 8.
²⁶ T. Hunt, 'La Parodie médiévale: Le Cas d'*Aucassin et Nicolette*', *Romania*, 100 (1979), 341.
²⁷ Cf. A. C. and J. E. Spearing, *Poetry of the Age of Chaucer* (1974), 199–200; R. W. Elliott, *Chaucer's English* (1974), 179–80.
²⁸ D. J. Ransom, '"Annot and John" and the Ploys of Parody', *SP* 75 (1978), 140–1; T. L. Burton, 'The Fair Maid of Ribblesdale and the Problem of Parody', *EC* 31 (1981), 296.

according to the Mark of Silver.[29] The most solemn words of Christ were repeatedly perverted: in the *Apocalypse of Golias*, for instance, an abbot invites his monks to join him in drunken revelry by employing Christ's question to a disciple: 'Are ye able to drink of the cup that I shall drink of?[30] In late fifteenth-century France a particularly popular form was the mock-sermon, or *sermon joyeux*; these had such revealing titles as 'le sermon de Saint Jambon et Sainte Andouille' or 'le sermon de Frappe-cul', and celebrated, often crudely, the pleasures of food, wine, and sex.[31]

Many of Dunbar's poems might be termed 'parodic' in the wider sense: they invert solemn rituals, or subvert our expectations as to literary genre—as when a pious vision turns into a diabolic nightmare. But some of his poetry is parodic in the stricter sense, and springs directly from the central and largely clerical tradition of medieval parody—the finest examples are *The Testament of Maister Andro Kennedy* (K 38) and *The Dregy* (K 22). Two other poems, *Schir Thomas Norny* (K 27), and *The Turnament* (K 52B), have long been considered as burlesques of chivalric romance. I am not convinced, however, by all 'parodic' interpretations of Dunbar: by the common view that *My hartis tresure and swete assured fo* (K 12) parodies the typical love complaint, or by a more recent notion that *The Goldyn Targe* 'presents a parody of earlier love poetry'.[32]

There are parodic passages in some of Dunbar's longer poems. The Widow's speech, in *The Tua Mariit Wemen and the Wedo*, is a 'preching' (249), and might be regarded as a Scottish example of the *sermon joyeux*. *The Flyting* also contains a small, encapsulated parody:

> Thow Lazarus, thow laithly lene tramort,
> To all the warld thow may example be
> To luk upoun thy gryslie peteous port;
> For hiddowis, haw and holkit is thyne ee,
> Thy cheik bane bair, and blaiknit is thy ble;
> Thy choip, thy choll, garris men for to leif chest;
> Thy gane it garris us think that we mon de:
> I conjure the, thow hungert heland gaist!
>
> The larbar linkis of thy lang lene craig,
> Thy pure pynit thrott peilit and owt of ply,

---

[29] These hymns and their parodies are in *The Penguin Book of Latin Verse*, ed. F. Brittain (1962), 222 and 224; 112 and 225; for other texts and the general tradition, see P. Lehmann, *Die Parodie im Mittelalter* (2nd edn., Stuttgart, 1963).

[30] Ed. K. Strecker (Rome, 1928), st. 93; cf. J. Mann, 'Satiric Subject and Satiric Object in Goliardic Literature', *Mittellateinisches Jahrbuch*, 15 (1980), 74.

[31] See *Quatre Sermons joyeux*, ed. J. Koopmans (Geneva, 1984); and S. L. Gilman, *The Parodic Sermon in European Perspective* (Wiesbaden, 1974).

[32] See below, 300; and P. M. King, 'Dunbar's *The Golden Targe*: A Chaucerian Masque', *SSL* 19 (1984), 121.

'SPORTIS AND JOCOSITEIS'

> Thy skolderit skin hewd lyk ane saffrone bag
> Garris men dispyt thar flesche, thow spreit of Gy. (161–72)[33]

These lines are a mock *memento mori*: they purport to describe a living person, Walter Kennedy, but recall a class of late-medieval poems that sought to inspire piety through fear, dwelling on the repulsiveness of the dead body. There are many English variations on the theme, ranging from short poems and epitaphs to the grisly account of the ghost of Guinevere's mother in *The Awnteris of Arthur*.[34] A striking Scottish example, *The Thre Deid Pollis*, is attributed to Henryson.

Dunbar addresses Kennedy as if he were already a death's head, lingering on the fleshless bones and empty eye-sockets. His diction at times closely recalls Henryson—the epithets in Henryson's line 'Our holkit ene, our peilit pollis bair' (4) all figure in this passage (164, 165, and 170). Dunbar also adopts the same admonitory tone: Kennedy is an awful 'example' to the world (162), just as the *pollis*, or skulls, are an 'examplair' (7) or 'sair exampill' (15). Henryson exhorts the passer-by: 'haif mynd of deth, that thow mon dy' (14). Dunbar makes the point three times: Kennedy's face 'garris us think that we mon de', and inspires contempt for the pleasures of the flesh (166, 172). Kennedy's emaciation is such that he might well be a revivified corpse or ghost. Dunbar neatly signals this by the twin apostrophes to Lazarus and 'the spreit of Gy'. Both were then famous and evocative names. In Lazarus two biblical figures were confused: the man who lay at the rich man's gate, full of sores, who was believed to be a leper; and the Lazarus whom Christ raised from the dead. We should have in mind both sides of this 'composite figure':[35] earlier in *The Flyting* Kennedy was depicted as a beggar, living in a hovel 'that was the lippir menis' (154), but the primary reference is to the Lazarus who rose from the grave, who in medieval paintings is often portrayed in a horrific manner, and in the Towneley plays delivers a striking *memento mori* speech—'Let me be your boke, Youre sampill take by me'.[36] The *spreit* of Guy was the central figure of a didactic ghost tale, then very popular in Scotland (see below, p. 264). Dunbar here adapts a gruesome genre to make a grim joke at Kennedy's expense.

The Testament of Maister Andro Kennedy proclaims its clerical origins in a striking stylistic feature, the 'macaronic' alternation of Latin and Scots. Its fictional voice is clearly that of a clerk, who is also a drunkard. The question of Kennedy's actual identity has been discussed earlier (p. 51–2); here I am concerned chiefly with the poem's

---

[33] On *linkis* (Kinsley reads *lukis*), 'vertebrae', see Ch. 6. n. 36.
[34] On 'warnings from the dead', cf. Woolf, 312 ff.
[35] Henryson, ed. Fox, lxxxix.
[36] See above, 159, and Ch. 4, n. 83.

form. To say that the literary testament was a popular genre in the late Middle Ages is a considerable understatement. It seems sometimes as if anyone or any *thing* might make a testament: from Jesus to the devil; from asses and pigs to deer and parrots; from pining lovers to wise fools; from real persons, such as Lindsay's Squire Meldrum, to personified abstractions, such as Heart in *King Hart* or Death in Molinet's impressive *Testament de la Guerre*.[37] Critics of Dunbar regularly refer to Villon's *Grand Testament*, almost as if Villon invented the form single-handed. But the literary testament has a long and complex history; it was put to varied uses, pious, moral, and amatory. Yet the form's predominant purpose was comic and satiric: it was employed to ridicule both the testator and the legatees. *The Testament of Maister Andro Kennedy* is not the only poem to voice the self-incriminating confession of a drunkard: there are analogues, though no close resemblances, in the French *Testament de Tastevin* (*c.*1488) and the English *Testament of Colin Blowbol* (late fifteenth century).[38] The bequest-motif was frequently a vehicle for estate-satire, and this too is an element in Dunbar's poem.

Elizabeth Archibald has questioned whether *The Testament* should be termed parodic: 'there is no formal sub-text', she says, and 'the format of humorous bequests' does not constitute 'parody in the strict sense'.[39] But the real-life testament had enormous potential for parody. It was a written document that everyone of any social standing encountered sooner or later, as witness, executor, legatee or testator. It was not necessarily private and confidential, but usually made in public, before witnesses, often when the testator was dying. Even in a secular age to make one's will is a solemn task, since it forces the individual to contemplate his own death; in the past this was even more so, when the making of a testament was a duty required by the Church—Philippe Ariès called it a confession of faith and 'quasi-sacramental'.[40] The real-life testament also lent itself well to parody, because it had a comparatively fixed form and highly stereotyped phrasing, either in Latin or the vernacular, departures from which would be easily recognized.

It is instructive to compare *The Testament* with actual wills, particularly those of Scots, such as Sir James Douglas of Dalkeith (*c.*1390),

---

[37] On the subject generally, see W. H. Rice, *The European Ancestry of Villon's Satirical Testaments* (New York, 1941).

[38] For 'Tastevin', see *Recueil de poésies françaises des XVe et XVIe siècles*, ed. A. Montaiglon (Paris, 1865–78), iii. 77–83; for 'Blowbol', see edition by F. Lehmeyer (Erlangen, 1907).

[39] 'William Dunbar and the Medieval Tradition of Parody', in Lyall and Riddy, 337.

[40] *The Hour of our Death*, trans. H. Weaver (New York, 1981), 191; and 188 ff., on the 'function of the Will'.

'SPORTIS AND JOCOSITEIS'

Alexander of Sutherland (1456), Sir David Sinclair of 'Swynbrocht' (early sixteenth century), and Gavin Douglas (1522).[41] Structurally, *The Testament* follows the usual pattern closely. First there is the establishment of identity: 'I maister Andro Kennedy' may be compared with *Ego Jacobus de Douglas dominus de Dalketh* and *Ego Gawinus indignus episcopus Dounkeldensis*. Next, in stanza two, are the usual reflections on mortality. Stanzas three to five correspond to the so-called 'pious bequests': in these the soul is commended to God and the Virgin Mary, and there are instructions for the burial of the body. The main substance of the will is concerned with the disposition of property. Lastly, there are directions for the funeral procession and service. *The Testament* is also liberally sprinkled with the stereotyped legal phrases that appear regularly in contemporary wills—*condo testamentum meum* (17), *do et lego* (82), *residuum omnium bonorum* (89), and *in die mee sepulture* (97). One line—*Cum nichill sit certius morte* (9)—is the first half of a traditional formula, which customarily ends *Nec incertius hora mortis*, and usually figures at the beginning of a will.[42]

But this testament is, of course, far from traditional—it is, as the testator announces, *Non sicut more solito* (96). Modern readers have no difficulty in perceiving the poem's subversive drift, particularly in the comically inventive instructions for the funeral—a barrel borne on a pole, bagpipe playing a dance-tune, and four flagons of beer set crosswise on the grave:

> I will na preistis for me sing
> *Dies illa dies ire,*
> Na 3it na bellis for me ring
> *Sicut semper solet fieri;*
> Bot a bag pipe to play a spryng
> *Et unum* ail wosp *ante me.* (105–10)

Yet the parodic point is sharper, if we know the details of the sub-text, and recognize what has been altered, added, or omitted. Kennedy rejects what many wills explicitly stipulate—the singing of priests. Alexander of Sutherland thus left money 'til a prest to sing perpetualy for my saul'.[43] Another small but revealing example is

> *Licet eger in corpore*
> 3it wald my mouth be wet with drink. (15–16)

---

[41] Printed in *The Bannatyne Miscellany II*, ed. D. Laing (Bannatyne Club, 1836), 105–12; *Bannatyne Miscellany III*, ed. D. Laing (Bannatyne Club, 1855), 96–102, and 107–12; and Douglas, *Works*, ed. J. Small (Edinburgh, 1874), i, pp. cxix–cxxv.

[42] The notion may be traced to Seneca, but was a medieval commonplace: cf. Whiting, D 96; Woolf, 86; and Bawcutt, 'Text and Context in Middle Scots Poetry', in Blanchot and Graf, *Actes*, 35–7.

[43] *Bannatyne Miscellany III*, 96.

'SPORTIS AND JOCOSITEIS'

This quotes the first half of a testamentary formula: *eger corpore, sanus tamen mente.* Sir David Sinclair's will provides a gloss: 'seik in my body, nevir the les hail in to my mynd'.[44] But line 16 gives the formula a comic twist: 3*it*, like *tamen*, leads one to expect the customary declaration of sanity, but is replaced by the demand of the incorrigible drunkard.

In the third stanza Kennedy commends his soul to the wine cellar:

> I leiff my saull for evirmare
> *Per omnipotentum Deum*
> In to my lordis wyne cellar.   (18–20)

Per omnipotentum Deum seems to be an oath, but reminds one of the soul's more orthodox destination—at this stage Douglas entrusted his soul *Deo omnipotenti*. Kennedy's *Deum*, in this context, probably refers to the drinkers' god, Bacchus; indeed I suspect that the text may originally have read *Omnipotantem*, 'all-drinking', since this or a similar word was often substituted for *omnipotentem* in Latin parodies of the Creed.[45] Another line,

> *Bonum vinum ad bibendum*   (23)

may seem unremarkable, but occurs in several versions of the *Missa Potatorum*, or Drunkards' Mass, in this one of the Paternoster's petitions reads, not 'Give us this day our daily bread' but *Pater Bache . . . bonum vinum ad bibendum da nobis hodie.*[46] Kennedy later declares:

> *Corpus meum ebriosum*
> I leif on to the toune of Air;
> In a draf mydding for evir and ay . . .   (35–7)

Douglas requested that his body be buried—*corpus meum sepeliendum*—in the choir of St John's of Savoy, in London;[47] Kennedy, however, voluntarily chooses for his last resting-place not a kirk but a dunghill, the vile place to which were consigned the bodies of criminals and those excommunicated by the Church.[48] The line *corpus meum ebriosum* has the same structure as Douglas's phrase, with the significant substitution of *ebriosum*, 'sodden with drink'.

Dunbar's poem is better shaped than many literary testaments,

---

[44] Ibid. 107.
[45] Lehmann, *Parodie im Mittelalter*, 233 and 245.
[46] Ibid. 240 and 247.
[47] *Works*, ed. Small, i, p. cxxiii.
[48] Those who die under the cursing are to be buried in 'myddinis' and other vile places: *St Andrews Formulare 1514–1546*, ed. G. Donaldson and C. Macrae (Stair Society, 7, 1942) i. 271. On the throwing of Wallace's presumed corpse in 'a draf mydding', see A. A. Macdonald, 'William Dunbar . . . and Hary's Wallace', *Neophilologus*, 68 (1984), 471–7.

which often consist of an open-ended series of satiric bequests. This is as true of an ambitious work like Villon's *Grand Testament* as of a crude one like *Jill of Brentford's Testament*. But this poem is characterized by a strong beginning and a strong conclusion, and a pervasive sense of the sub-text. Throughout solemnity and lightheartedness are counterpoised. There is cheerful defiance, of testamentary custom and of death and judgement, symbolized strikingly in the rejection of *Dies illa, dies ire* (106). The poem probably split contemporary readers into those who relished its impiety, and those who were affronted. Yet the balance is not evenly maintained. The testator is a self-proclaimed fool (75), and the defiance collapses in the last line, with its request for the singing of *De terra plasmasti me*. This antiphon was usually sung at the point when the grave was covered with earth: 'Thou has created me from earth and covered me with flesh, O my redeemer, raise me on the last day'.[49]

The Testament, although inventive, belongs to a well-known genre. *The Dregy* is far more original, and I regard it as a small comic masterpiece. It displays great verbal and metrical virtuosity: Latin prose mixes with Scots verse, and the staple four-stress couplets are interspersed with triolets. The latter, termed 'roundels' by later poets, seem to have been introduced into Scotland by Dunbar.[50] The work produces a quasi-dramatic effect, as of different voices—now a solitary speaker, now a chorus, now conversational, now incantatory. The poem falls into two parts, to which Dunbar himself draws attention—first 'this epistell' (8), and later the *dregy*, or *dirige*, heralded in lines 23 and 28.

The opening is studded with epistolary formulae:

> We that ar heir in hevins glory
> To 3ow that ar in purgatory
> Commendis us on our hairtly wyis—
> I mene we folk in parradyis
> In Edinburcht, with all mirrines,
> To 3ow of Strivilling in distres ...   (1-6)

Dunbar does not, as is often stated, adopt the persona of an apostle;[51] the figure to whom he later compares himself (74) is the archangel Gabriel (74), divine messenger and bringer of good tidings, or 'consolatioun' (78), to a lower world. The poet is delivering a message on behalf of one group—'We that ar heir'—to another group, for much of the poem unambiguously also in the plural:

---

[49] See Ross, 165; cf. D. Sicard, *La Liturgie de la mort* (Munster, 1978), 124–5.
[50] Cf. Polwart, *Flyting*, 29, in Montgomerie, *Poems*, 60; on Maxwell's use of the form, see Bawcutt, 'The Commonplace Book of John Maxwell', in *A Day Estivall*, ed. A. Gardner-Medwin and J. H. Williams (Aberdeen, 1990), 59–68.
[51] Baxter, 58; Kinsley, 280.

'SPORTIS AND JOCOSITEIS'

> 3e heremeitis and hankersaidilis (anchorites)
> That takis 3our pennance at 3our tablis. (9–10)

(The plural reference to *famulos* (108) should also be noted.) The poem is addressed not solely to the king, but to the king and a number of his courtiers. Its precise occasion is not known, but Dunbar seems to be calling upon James IV and his household to return to Edinburgh from a penitential stay in Stirling, possibly (though not certainly) at the Franciscan house which he founded there.[52] Much of the comedy derives from the sort of local rivalry between two towns that is still familiar; indeed Asloan's title lays stress on this aspect of the poem— 'Dunbarris Derige of Edinburgh and Striuiling'.[53] Stirling is purgatorial, but Edinburgh is heaven, and Dunbar prays that they may return

> To eit swan, cran, pertrik and plever
> And every fische that swymis in rever;
> To drynk with us the new fresche wyne
> That grew upoun the rever of Ryne,
> Fresche fragrant clairettis out of France. (51–5)

Dunbar is unlikely to have known a curious thirteenth-century French work, *La Bataille d'enfer et de paradis*, yet it contains an interesting precedent for his poem—making a similarly audacious equation between Paris and Paradise, and Arras and Hell.[54]

Dirige, which is the ancestor of modern *dirge*, was a common shorthand title for part and sometimes the whole of the *Officium Mortuorum*, or Office of the Dead. This office had two parts: Vespers, said in the evening; and Matins, which together with Lauds constituted the night service. Vespers was commonly referred to as *Placebo*, from the first word of its opening antiphon; Matins was correspondingly known as *Dirige*, from its opening antiphon: *Dirige Domine Deus meus in conspectu tuo viam meam*. It is to this specific part of the Office of the Dead that Dunbar directs his audience's thoughts, when he announces

> We sall begyn ane cairfull soun,
> Ane dirige devoit and meik. (22–3)

---

[52] See Ch. 2 above, 72. James particularly favoured the Observant branch of the Franciscans. When in Stirling, however, he seems to have resided in the castle; the belief that he withdrew during Holy Week to do penance among the friars depends upon the unsupported testimony of John Hay (1586). See *TA* i, pp. cclxvi–cclxviii; ii, p. lxxx; W. Moir Bryce, *The Scottish Grey Friars* (Edinburgh, 1909), esp. ii. 177–8.

[53] The colophons to other copies say it is addressed 'to the king'; Bannatyne's title uniquely (and apparently erroneously) says, 'maid to king James the fyift' (fol. 102a).

[54] Ed. A. Guesnon, *Bulletin de la société de l'histoire de Paris*, 36 (1909), 45–57. Underlying this poem, it seems, are rivalries between the 'nations' at the University of Paris.

The Office of the Dead is not familiar to many today, and is sometimes confused with the Requiem Mass. But in Dunbar's time it was very well known, to the laity as well as clergy. It was primarily a service said in church over the coffin on the night before a burial, or a memorial service on behalf of the dead. In the later Middle Ages it became increasingly the custom to say the office daily, as an accretion to the usual 'hours'; it formed a regular section in books of hours, or primers, and devout laymen commonly read it in private.[55]

Critics have sometimes been puzzled as to the nature of the parody in this poem; one indeed says that it has 'little connection with the liturgy'.[56] But what Dunbar offers, in the first place, is parody of structure. The poem simulates the striking threefold pattern of Matins of the Dead. In its full form this consisted of three nocturns, each of which contained three lessons and three psalms; but a shortened form with only three lessons was usually said. Dunbar's pared-down *Dirige* has a similarly threefold structure, but does not imitate the content of the lessons, drawn from the Book of Job. Dunbar devises three *lectiones* of his own invention—prayers, or intercessions, for the release of those in the purgatory of Stirling—which are followed by three *responsiones*, of which the first is

> Tak consolatioun in ȝour pane,
> In tribulatioun   tak consolatioun
> Out of vexatioun cum hame agane,
> Tak consolatioun in ȝour pane. (39–42)

The triple repetition of the initial phrase may possibly be designed to recall the way verses are repeated in church services; it seems, in particular, to mimic the use of *repetenda*, or repeated shortened phrases, in responsories. This may be seen in the famous *Libera me* responsory from the Office of the Dead, with its repetition of *Dum veneris* and *Quando caeli movendi sunt et terra*.[57] The technique here resembles that of a short, anti-monastic piece, *De Monachis Carnalibus*, discussed by A. G. Rigg: this consists of couplets, 'each comprising a hexameter and a verse from the Psalms, producing a liturgical impression of Verse and Response'.[58]

The Dregy also contains a further threefold patterning, based on the liturgy, which has been obscured because the post-Reformation copyists slightly misplaced the Latin formulae, *Iube domine*, and *Tu*

---

[55] See G. Rowell, *The Liturgy of Christian Burial* (Alcuin Club, 59, 1977), 57–73; J. Harthan, *Books of Hours and their Owners* (1977), 17–18, 29–30.
[56] Archibald, 'Dunbar and the Medieval Tradition of Parody', 330.
[57] Quoted and discussed below, 352–3 and n. 21.
[58] '*Metra de monachis carnalibus*—the Three Versions', *Mittellateinisches Jahrbuch*, 15 (1980), 134–42.

autem, that should punctuate the work. Editors have never explained the significance of these abbreviated phrases. In the daily service of Matins each lesson is normally introduced by *Iube Domine benedicere* (said by the lector), and a Benediction, whose form varies (said by the priest). This authorizes the lector to begin, and asks for God's blessing on behalf of the listeners. Each lesson is followed by a prayer for mercy: *Tu autem Domine miserere nobis*. (The leader of the choir would say *Tu autem*, and the reader the rest.) The widespread understanding of these liturgical formulae, by clerks at least, is illustrated by the Archpoet's joking use of *Tu autem*:

> Brevem vero sermonem facio
> ne vos gravet longa narracio,
> ne dormitet lector pre tedio,
> et 'Tu autem' dicat in medio.

(I make my account short . . . lest the reader fall asleep from boredom, and say *Tu autem* before I have finished.)[59]

Yet the presence of these formulae in *The Dregy* poses a problem, since in Matins of the Dead they were (and are) customarily omitted.[60] It seems improbable that Dunbar introduced them either from ignorance or carelessness; I see this rather as another instance of his half-observing, half-flouting liturgical practice.

The end of *The Dregy*, in Latin, displays the most direct verbal parody in the poem. Yet recent comments produce a curious impression of random mimicry; the passage is said to contain 'a judicious mixture' of phrases from antiphons and responses, or 'witty distortions of sentences from various parts of the Office of the Dead'.[61] But Dunbar is wittier than this would suggest. His poem's conclusion is designed to recall a liturgical conclusion, that of Lauds, which was sung directly after Matins of the Dead. Here, after the Paternoster (cf. lines 97–8) and the psalm *Exaltabo te* occur the verses and responses that Dunbar comically perverts:

Lauds	The Dregy
Requiem aeternam dona eis Domine.	Requiem edinburgi dona eis, Domine.
Et lux perpetua luceat eis.	Et lux ipsius luceat eis.
A porta inferi	A porta tristitiae de Stirling

---

[59] *Die Gedichte des Archipoeta*, ed. H. Watenphul and H. Krefeld (Heidelberg, 1958), no. 1; and cf. L. Eisenhofer and J. Lehner, *The Liturgy of the Roman Rite* (1961), 453.

[60] Cf. *Breviarium Aberdonense*, introd. D. Laing (Bannatyne Club, 1854–5), ii, p. lxxxiii (v): 'non dicatur *Iube*', 'non dicatur *Tu autem*'.

[61] J. S. Norman, 'Thematic Implications of Parody in William Dunbar's "Dregy"', in Lyall and Riddy, 354; Archibald, op. cit. 330.

Erue Domine animas eorum.	Erue Domine animas etc corpora eorum.
Credo videre bona Domini	Credo gustare vinum Edinburgi
In terra viventium.⁶²	In villa viuentium.

I here quote the Maitland text of *The Dregy*, which is in many respects superior to that in Bannatyne. It also contains two lines, not in Bannatyne, which are likely to be original:

> Domine exaudi orationem meam
> Et clamor meus ad te veniat.

This is the opening of one of the penitential Psalms (102), but the verse figures in some versions of the Office of the Dead, and precisely at this point.[63] Dunbar, I think, is more audacious than is commonly realized. There is an ambiguity in *Domine* similar to that in its vernacular equivalent, 'Lord' (see above, p. 163). Dunbar uses words that the psalmist (and penitent sinner) addresses to God, to intercede with his own temporal lord to hear him and release the royal household from the austerities of Stirling. He concludes with a prayer, modelled on similar prayers in the final section of Lauds, exploiting an equally ambiguous word, *famulos* (servants, members of a household): 'libera famulos tuos apud villam de Stirling versantes ... Et ad Edinburgi gaudia feliciter perducas. Amen.'

Such comic audacity is not unparalleled. Skelton, in *Philip Sparrow*, not only parodied Scriptural verses but feminized *Domine* to *domina* (996, 1061, and 1114), speaking of a young girl as if she were the deity. The Archpoet, in his *Fama tuba dante sonum*, compared himself to the prophet Jonah, and thereby cast his patron, the Archchancellor of the Emperor Barbarossa, in the role of God. Indeed he went even further, reapplying to his patron and himself Christ's words, 'I am the Vine, ye are the branches' (John 15:5).[64] *The Dregy* also recalls the end of another poem addressed to James IV. In *Schir ʒit remember as befoir* (K 42) the equation between the miserable servitor and the soul in purgatory is quite unequivocal; the equation between the king and God, however, is unstated, but playfully implicit (see p. 126). *Schir ʒit remember* is a petition on behalf of the poet himself; *The Dregy* is also a petition, a witty *orationem* on behalf of the poem's fellow-courtiers.

This light-hearted poem has received heavy-handed treatment from

---

[62] *Sarum Breviary*, ed. F. Proctor and C. Wordsworth, 3 vols. (Cambridge, 1879–86), ii, col. 281; *Breviarium Aberdonense*, ii, p. lxxxv (v).

[63] See the Middle English version in *The Prymer or Lay Folks' Prayer Book*, ed. H. Littlehales (EETS, OS 105, 1895), 77: 'Lord, here thou my preier, / And my cry come to thee'.

[64] *Gedichte*, ed. Watenphul and Krefeld, no. 2.

some scholars. Lord Hailes did not include it in his *Ancient Scottish Poems* (1770), calling it a 'lewd and profane parody of the litanies of the Church of Rome'.[65] Some modern readers have also found Dunbar's joke difficult to accept, and sought ways to purge the poem of its irreverence. R. J. Lyall says that although Dunbar speaks with the 'voice of the courtly materialist' there is irony in his 'ostensible praise of the materialist life'; and Ross finds the speaker's viewpoint intentionally limited: 'indulgence in the pleasures of the body is a kind of death, suitably commemorated by an "office"'.[66] These moral interpretations seem strained and unconvincing. The poem's irony is very different: Dunbar calls his *Dirige* 'devoit' (23), when it is cheeky and irreverent, and speaks of its dancing, tripping verse as 'ane cairfull soun' (22), or sorrowful music. The poem undoubtedly makes humorous use of sacred things: it draws on the ritual of death to celebrate the good things of life, and employs one of the Church's most solemn services for a purpose that is trivial, when viewed from the standpoint of eternity. But Dunbar in no way ridicules the most serious parts of the service, the magnificent passages from Job. His poem is irreverent, but it is not obscene. The phrase 'lewd and profane' would be more accurately applied to the contemporary English carol, with the burden *Inducas, inducas / In temptationibus*, that parodies the Paternoster.[67]

The Dregy is not the only poem to make parodic use of the Office of the Dead—there are parallels in Skelton's *Philip Sparrow* and in a fifteenth-century poem on the death of the Duke of Suffolk.[68] It seems likely that the great increase in the performance of this Office in the late Middle Ages led to over-familiarity, and some lessening of its solemnity. In Dunbar's time it was 'constantly being celebrated in the burgh churches of Scotland'.[69] Lindsay later referred mockingly to 'daylie dolorous derigeis', and Alexander Scott criticized churchmen, who 'tyrit God with trifles . . . And daisit him with daily darigies'. It would be anachronistic to attribute to Dunbar the Reformers' contempt for 'the exorbitance of superstitious exiquies'; yet such phrases, coming from poets who lived close in time to him and were not avowed Protestants, are revealing in their lack of respect.[70]

* * *

---

[65] p. 243.
[66] 'Some Observations on the Dregy of Dunbar', *Parergon*, 9 (1974), 40–3; Ross, 163. For a less solemn 'Reappraisal', see J. Ting, in *SLJ* 14, no. 1 (1987), 19–36.
[67] Greene, *Carols*, no. 461.
[68] *Philip Sparrow*, 575–86; for the poem on Suffolk, see V. J. Scattergood, *Politics and Poetry in the Fifteenth Century* (1971), 164–8.
[69] D. McKay, 'Parish Life in Scotland', in *Essays on the Scottish Reformation 1513–1625*, ed. D. McRoberts (Glasgow, 1962), 110–11.
[70] *Monarche*, 4782; *Poems*, no. 1. 89–90. See *DOST*'s 16th-century citations for *dirige*; on the Protestant belief that burial should be reverent, but 'without the ceremony heretofore used', see Rowell, op. cit. 82.

'SPORTIS AND JOCOSITEIS'

Two of Dunbar's poems illustrate another type of comic mimicry that might best be termed 'mock-chivalric'. In *The Turnament* Dunbar takes a favourite romance theme, the single combat between two heroes, and gives it a bizarre twist. Tourneying was an aristocratic sport, which epitomized the skills and virtues of the knightly classes, especially horsemanship and courage. These combatants, however, are not knights but craftsmen, a tailor and a soutar—a pejorative term, like 'cobbler'. They do not display feats of prowess, but are clumsy and cowardly—the tailor falls from his horse, because he is 'nocht weill sittin', and both are so panic-stricken that they vomit and defecate. Critics have been most impressed by the tale's dirtiness, and rarely comment on its structural neatness and stylistic ingenuity. One reason for this may be that the poem is usually read in an inferior text, which mangles the syntax and sometimes modernizes the deliberate archaisms; the Asloan manuscript, from which I quote, preserves the best copy of the poem.[71] It is also likely that not all readers are familiar with the chivalric customs to which Dunbar alludes, and the literary vogue for describing *pas d'armes*, jousts, tournaments, and other ritualized forms of fighting. It is enlightening to place this poem beside Lindsay's description of the single combat in *Squyer Meldrum*, or the tournament in *The Knight's Tale*, or the countless (and extremely monotonous) battles in the Scottish romance *Clariodus*.

The action, from the start, is closely modelled on chivalric procedure. The tournament is 'cryit', or proclaimed, long in advance (121–2). The 'barras', or lists, is prepared, and each combatant makes a separate entry, 'conwoyit'—like Squire Meldrum—by his supporters. It is clear that this is a duel of chivalry, not of law, since the tailor and soutar fight on horseback, in full armour, and are served with spears. The combatants in the duel of law fought on foot, and usually attacked each other with batons tipped with horn which resembled small pickaxes.[72] Dunbar is punctilious in telling us also that the soutar

> was conwoyit out of the west,
> As a defendour stowt. (158–9)

This conforms to the tradition that the defender in such duels came from the west gate, and the challenger from the east.[73] (In *The Knight's Tale*, 2581 ff. likewise, Palamon and Arcite enter from opposite gates.) Other common chivalric themes are also glanced at—the proud boast

---

[71] *Asloan Manuscript*, ii. 89–92; Kinsley's line-numbering is retained, for ease of reference.
[72] Cf. G. Neilson, *Trial by Combat* (Glasgow, 1890).
[73] Ibid. 263.

'SPORTIS AND JOCOSITEIS'

or vow (145), and the bestowal of knighthood upon the field of battle (142, 176).

Yet such orthodoxy is again and again undermined. The knavish followers of the tailor and soutar are closer to craft processions than military retinues. It was stipulated that the Scottish crafts should regularly carry banners 'in all tymes of processioun', and on them were depicted the 'images, figures, and arms' of the respective trades.[74] But this tailor's banner does not carry a pair of shears, the customary 'taikin' of his craft; it is a 'taikin' rather of his dishonesty. The soutar's banner carries not the image of a real saint—one would expect Crispin and Crispianus—but the diabolic pseudo-saint, 'Girnega' (165). The tailor makes a proud vaunt, but it collapses ignominiously:

> For he in hart tuke sic a scunner
> A rak of fartis lyk ony thunner
> Went fra him blast for blast.   (154–6)

There is comic incongruity in this grandiose simile, which occurs more often in heroic contexts. In Douglas's *Eneados* a shaft flies 'like the blak thud of awfull thundris blast' (XII. xiiii. 90; *Aeneid*, xii. 923). In *Squyer Meldrum*, when two knights charged against each other, 'that meiting ... soundit lyke ane crak of thunder' (527–8). Chaucer, however, makes precisely the same jesting use of the simile in *The Miller's Tale* (3807). Even the syntax of 'blast for blast' seems to mimic a kind of phrase very common in battle poetry—'dint for dint', 'blow for blow', or (as in *Clariodus*) 'rap for rap'.[75]

Equally mock-chivalric are these lines on the soutar:

> Full sowtarlyk he was of laitis,
> For ay betwene the harnas platis
> The oyly bristit out.   (166–8)

Dunbar alludes primarily to the oil and grease associated with the cobbler's trade. But when heroes fought it was blood, not 'oyly', that burst from their armour, and only after they had striven long and valiantly:

> The blud owt at thar byrnys brest.

> Blud fra byrneis was bruschyt on the greyn.

---

[74] *Edinburgh Burgh Records*, ed. Marwick, 122; see also Mill, 124, on Aberdeen— 'Euery craft with thair awin baner with the Armes of thair craft thairin'; and ibid. 122–3, on the tailors' 'taikin'.
[75] *Clariodus, a Metrical Romance* (Maitland Club, Edinburgh, 1830), iii. 1142.

'SPORTIS AND JOCOSITEIS'

> Quhair euir thai hit thai persit ay the plait,
> Quhill that the blude burst out upon the grene.[76]

Dunbar's style is clearly modelled on such passages in *The Bruce* or other romance descriptions of battle. From their highly stereotyped diction he also chooses an archaic word like *birnes*, 'coat of mail', in

> His birnes brak and maid a bratill (193)

or formulaic and often alliterative phrases, 'speir and scheld', 'hors and man'. Some lines sound as if they were plucked, in their entirety, from such battle poetry:

> Thai spurrit apon athir syd,
> The hors attour the grene did glyd. (187-8)

When the soutar vomits 'blek' over the devil, Dunbar comments, 'So knychtlie he him quyt' (180). 'Sowtarlyk' behaviour is here neatly juxtaposed with 'knychtlie' pretensions. The chivalric notion of 'quyting' usually involved an exchange of blows—'a strok for another'—as in *Sir Gawain and the Green Knight* (287). There is little sword-play in *The Turnament*, but plenty of action, chiefly the undignified and involuntary action of the bowels—'In till his stomok was sic a steir' (172). The mock-chivalric mode is maintained to the tale's impudent conclusion; although no more than a 'bourd', the poet is obliged to record it and 'put in to rememberans' (224). Similar phrasing is applied, in *Squyer Meldrum*, with more decorum, to genuine heroes:

> Poetis, thair honour to auance,
> Hes put thame in rememberance. (11-12)

Dunbar's comic *Turnament* belongs to a minor literary genre that seems popular in sixteenth-century Scotland: later examples are Lindsay's *Justing betuix James Watsoun and Jhon Barbour*, Alexander Scott's *Justing and Debait up at the Drum*, and the anonymous *Sym and his Bruder*. Very much earlier is the English *Tournament of Tottenham* (before 1450).[77] The comedy of these pieces often derives from the ludicrous nature of the armour and weapons—buckets, hoes, rakes and flails—an element absent from Dunbar's poem. But all poke fun at rustics and artisans. There is evidence from various sources, chiefly German, that such grotesque combats, called *kübelturnier*, or 'bucket-jousts', were more than literary fiction, and were sometimes enacted,

---

[76] Barbour, *Bruce*, ii. 355; Hary, *Wallace*, xi. 28; William Stewart, *Croniclis of Scotland*, ed. W. B. Turnbull (Rolls series, 1858), i. 305.

[77] *Sym and his Bruder* and Scott's *Justing*, like *The Turnament*, are included in Bannatyne's 'balletis mirry'; *The Justing* is edited in *Longer Scottish Poems*, 269-78. On the genre, see G. F. Jones, 'The Tournaments of Tottenham and Lappenhausen', *PMLA* 66 (1951), 1123-40.

'SPORTIS AND JOCOSITEIS'

as entertainment for the upper classes. At Nuremberg, in 1491, the Emperor Maximilian held a chivalric tournament, in which princes participated; this was followed by a comic fight, in which the combatants were armed with straw helmets, straw shields, and blunt lances.[78] It should be recalled that the protagonists of Lindsay's *Justing* were actual 'servitouris' of James V—the one a barber-surgeon, the other a groom of the wardrobe. Their mock-joust may have taken place at St Andrews in 1539 or 1540.[79] Whether Dunbar likewise refers to some burlesque entertainment at the Scottish court is impossible now to document; but the poem is certainly written in a similar vein.

Schir Thomas Norny, although termed a 'burlesque romance', is better described as a mock-eulogy.[80] Thomas Norny was a member of 'this court' (10), like Dunbar himself, and apparently a fool or other entertainer (see above, p. 59). Dunbar, however, repeatedly calls him a knight, and sings his praises, with enthusiasm but mounting absurdity, as if he were a hero. Such commendations were a staple ingredient of romance, and tended to contain a stereotyped set of topics.[81] Dunbar conforms to the pattern very closely: he first names his hero, and mentions his mysterious parentage; he then refers to his martial exploits in distant regions—against Highlanders, however, not Saracens; he describes his rustic sports, and claims:

> Was never wyld Robein under bewch
> Nor ʒet Roger off Cleknyskleuch
>   So bauld a berne as he;
> Gy off Gysburne, na Allan Bell,
> Na Simonis sonnes off Quhynfell
>   At schot war never so slie.
>
> This anterous knycht quhar ever he went
> At justing and at tornament
>   Evermor he wan the gre;
> Was never off halff so gryt renowne
> Sir Bevis the knycht off Southe Hamptowne:
>   (I schrew him giff I le). (25–36)

This climactic passage, which is a comic version of the 'outdoing' topos, directs attention to the poem's literary context, thus functioning rather like the mention of Chaucer in *The Goldyn Targe*, or of 'haly legendis' in *This nycht befoir the dawing cleir*. The figures to whom Norny is compared came from the half-fictional world of song,

---

[78] Jones, op. cit. 1124–6.
[79] See Lindsay, ed. Hamer, iii. 140.
[80] Kinsley, 300.
[81] Cf. L. H. Loomis, 'Sir Thopas', in *Sources and Analogues of Chaucer's Canterbury Tales*, ed. W. F. Bryan and G. Dempster (Chicago, 1941), 504–59.

romance, and balladry. Some were rather dubious heroes—Robin Hood and several others were outlaws—but they were remarkably popular. Although *Bevis* was a fourteenth-century romance, it continued to be read throughout the sixteenth century.[82]

It is instructive to compare *Norny* with another of Dunbar's poems that celebrates a real knight and very distinguished soldier. Bernard Stewart, like Norny, is praised for his 'chevalry' and likewise termed 'aunterus', but he is compared to the far grander heroes of classical antiquity. *Bernard Stewart* is written in an elevated, even pompous, style; *Norny* is written in the minstrel manner, and its diction is studded with the stereotyped, frequently alliterative, phrases that abound in romance—'buklar nor brand', 'so bauld a berne', 'wyse and worthie', 'wys and wycht'. For *Bernard Stewart* Dunbar employs a slow-moving eight-line stanza; *Norny* is in the six-line form of tail-rhyme. This metre was still the medium for much popular narrative: it is employed for part (not the whole) of *Bevis*, for *John the Reeve* (which Dunbar mentions in K 42), and for one of the first works printed in Scotland, the romance *Eglamour*. The 'tail', in many tail-rhyme romances, was a feeble appendage, containing empty tags or asseverations—'I tell thee by my fay', or 'I tell you sickerly'.[83] But Dunbar's use is far from redundant: sometimes the 'tail' contains interesting details—'Gottin be sossery' (6); at other times it departs far from the romance norm, insinuating ironical doubts as to the veracity of the narrator or his hero—'This deid thocht na man kennis' (18), or 'He knawis gif this be leis' (24).

Many readers have perceived a resemblance between *Norny* and Chaucer's *Sir Thopas*. F. B. Snyder first noted 'the practical identity of the stanza' and some verbal similarities, and concluded that Dunbar was here 'consciously imitating *Sir Thopas*'.[84] Since then the relationship between the poems has been discussed and redefined. Elizabeth Eddy points out that Dunbar's poem is more 'localized' than Chaucer's, and 'more enclosed in the occasion for which it was written'.[85] Yet the comparison with *Sir Thopas* has proved unfortunate for Dunbar. It would seem to imply that his poem is merely second-hand and derivative; he is repeating Chaucer, well over a century later. Although the first seed for *Norny* was undoubtedly planted in Dunbar's mind by *Sir Thopas*, the resemblances between them should not be

---

[82] See above, 27.
[83] *John the Reeve*, 69 and 81; cf. A. M. Trounce, 'The English Tail-Rhyme Romances', *MÆ* 1 (1932), 176 ff.
[84] 'Sir Thomas Norray and Sir Thopas', *MLN* 25 (1910), 78–80.
[85] 'Sir Thopas and Sir Thomas Norny: Romance Parody in Chaucer and Dunbar', *RES*, NS 22 (1971), 409.

over-stressed. Dunbar's literary models were much closer to hand, as he himself indicated.

Norny opens:

> Now lythis off ane gentill knycht
> Schir Thomas Norny, wys and wycht,
> And full of chevelry,
> Quhais father was ane giand keyne—
> His mother was ane farie queyne
> Gottin be sossery.   (1–6)

This is regularly traced to *Sir Thopas*, which begins 'Listeth lordes in good entent'. Both Chaucer and Dunbar summon attention, in the peremptory manner of the minstrel. But Dunbar's northern verb *lythe* does not come from Chaucer, and has many parallels, in tail-rhyme romances, such as *Perceval of Galles*:

> Lef, lythes to me,

or the opening fitt of *The Gest of Robyn Hode*:

> Lythe and listin, gentilmen ...[86]

The giant and the fairy queen are also said to 'come from' *Sir Thopas*.[87] But giants and elf-queens play very different roles in that poem, and are hardly unique to Chaucer. One can find parallels to Norny's parentage elsewhere in romance, or in other Scottish poems—in *King Berdok* Mayok's father is 'the king of fary', and the speaker in *the Crying of ane Play* proclaims that he is 'generit ... of gyandis kynd'.[88] It should also be noted that there is no substance in the common critical belief that Dunbar makes a deliberate use of southern English in *Norny*, in order to remind his audience of *Sir Thopas* (see below, p. 360).

John Burrow has recently discussed the difficulty of determining the 'direction' of the comedy in poems that incongruously mix ingredients from contrasting worlds, one 'high' and the other 'low'. Although many critics of *Sir Thopas* view the jest as working both ways—against the high world of romance and the low bourgeois hero—he argues that, in practice, readers need to know which is the main target: 'It is as if the joke requires direction. Quite apart from any premeditated satirical intention on the author's part, such directedness must be taken as an internal or formal requirement of the

---

[86] Cf. Loomis, op. cit. 502, and *English and Scottish Popular Ballads*, ed. H. C. Sargent and G. L. Kittredge (Cambridge, Mass., 1904), no. 117.
[87] J. Burrow, 'Sir Thopas in the Sixteenth Century', in *Middle English Studies Presented to Norman Davis*, ed. D. Gray and E. G. Stanley (Oxford, 1983), 70.
[88] On *King Berdok* and *The Crying of ane Play*, see below, 258 (and n. 3).

genre: a principle of its ballistics.'[89] He himself regards the comedy of *Sir Thopas* as predominantly literary, directed against the contemporary romances. Dunbar's critics have been as ready as Chaucer's to find his mockery double-edged. We are thus told that in *The Turnament* 'knights are being laughed at under the guise of tradesmen', or that Dunbar derides not only the crafts but 'the grave and extravagant farce of the tournament itself.'[90] But I am not convinced that there exists such complexity in the poem.

Both in *Norny* and *The Turnament* Dunbar makes fun of persons low in the social hierarchy yet possessing pretensions to higher standing. In *Norny* it is an individual, apparently a fool and therefore of highly ambivalent status; in *The Turnament* it is a class, craftsmen aping gentlemen, and enacting roles that they cannot sustain. At the end they are stripped of the *style* (title)—of knights—to which they had aspired:

> The Devill gart thaim to dungeoun dryf
> And tham of knychthed to depryf,
>   Discharging tham all weir;
> And maid tham harlottis agane for euer,
> Quhilk style to kepe thai had fer levir
>   Na ony armes beir.   (211–16)

The poem voices a class antagonism towards two crafts that were despised, yet seem to have been growing more prosperous. The tailors, in particular, by the mid-sixteenth century formed 'a craft aristocracy', and were among the wealthiest citizens in Edinburgh.[91] The strife between the tailor and soutar may also allude to the quarrels then common between the crafts, particularly over precedence in processions.[92] Dunbar's other poetry does not support the idea that he was sympathetic to social mobility, or found chivalry farcical. *The Turnament* briefly presents a topsy-turvy world, but one that is rapidly righted. Its tone resembles that of a novella by Franco Sacchetti (d. 1401): in this an old peasant borrows a decrepit horse and goes off to a tournament, where he is 'hammered like a kettle at the kettle-maker's'. Everyone bursts into laughter, and his wife says, 'leave fighting to those who know how to do it'. This is endorsed by the narrator: 'the woman had much more sense than her husband, because she recognised her own and her husband's condition in life'.[93]

---

[89] 'Chaucer's *Sir Thopas* and *La Prise de Nuevile*', YES 14 (1984), 48.
[90] Scott, 236; Kinsley, 340.
[91] M. Lynch, *Edinburgh and the Reformation* (Edinburgh, 1981), 53.
[92] Mill, 64; cf. D. M. Palliser, 'The Trade Guilds of Tudor York', in *Crisis and Order in English Towns 1500–1700*, ed. P. Clark and P. Slack (1972), 104–6.
[93] See *Medieval Comic Tales*, ed. P. Rickard (Cambridge, 1972), 64–6.

'SPORTIS AND JOCOSITEIS'

It is more difficult to be sure of Dunbar's attitude towards his literary medium: tail-rhyme and the romance style. Burrow justly says that Dunbar 'does not seem concerned to ridicule such poetry in *Schir Thomas Norny*. Rather he accepts the minstrel manner, for the purposes of this poem, as establishing a norm against which the baseness of an absurd hero can be measured.'[94] The more complex forms of tail-rhyme are used for other accomplished poems—*The Dance of the Sevin Deidly Synnis* (K 52A) and *The Abbot of Tungland* (K 54). But Dunbar never puts this metre nor the romance style to 'straight' use; it is employed solely for comedy, usually of a grotesque type. He clearly distinguishes it from the more refined style of writing that *The Goldyn Targe* both celebrates and exemplifies. Dunbar enjoys experimenting with metre and diction; but there seems some ambivalence in his attitude towards the romance style—not 'ridicule', but perhaps amused affection.

Dunbar's parodic writing is often accompanied by irony. This is not surprising, since there are close affinities between parody and irony. Both are characterized by the presence of multiple layers of meaning. Classical rhetoricians commonly defined irony as the process of saying one thing and meaning the opposite (*contrarium*) or something different (*aliud*). Quintilian linked irony with moral duplicity, employing such terms as *simulatio* and *dissimulatio*.[95] Dunbar speaks, in *This waverand warldis wrechidnes*, of 'figurit speiche with faceis tua' (10); in context he is referring to flattery and hypocrisy, but the phrase well describes the rhetorically 'figured' and two-faced speech that he sometimes employs. Irony, like parody, is liable to divide an audience into two groups: those who see only the ostensible 'surface' meaning, and the initiates, who perceive the further or 'deeper' meaning. Hence it presents critics with similar problems of identification. Has an irony been missed, or has it been imported? Are we reading a specific word, line, or whole poem too simply and naïvely, or are we, conversely, torturing them into a false complexity?

Dunbar's readers have long recognized that many of his poems are, in some way or other, ironic. But new and startling ironies have been detected by Reiss. Not only does he regard *My hartis tresure* (K 12) as 'a study in irony', a view that is not wholly unfamiliar; he also considers Dunbar's finest love lyric, *Sweit rois of vertew and of gentilnes* (K 8) 'essentially ironic in its presentation of love'. He finds *Now of wemen this I say* (K 72) an exercise in 'heavy-handed irony', detects in *The*

---

[94] 'Sir Thopas in the Sixteenth Century', 74.
[95] For a survey, cf. B. Rowland in E. Birney, *Essays on Chaucerian Irony* (Toronto, 1985), xv–xxx.

Dregy a secondary layer of meaning that turns it into 'a lament for the court, the place of real death', and terms *In to thir dirk and drublie dayis* (K 69) one of Dunbar's 'most ironic' poems.[96] For Reiss Dunbar's whole view of life is marked by 'an ironic sense': this is no matter of 'surface effects', but reflects 'the essentially ironic world view of the Middle Ages'.[97] No one could deny that some of the finest medieval writers expressed a profound sense of man's blindness and ignorance *sub specie aeternitatis*. Its most famous illustration, for English readers, is probably Chaucer's image of Troilus, after his death, laughing as he contemplates those beneath who mourn for him. But irony of this 'cosmic' kind was by no means ubiquitous in medieval literature. Much of the 'irony' that Reiss discerns in Dunbar seems to me non-existent; it is conjured up to solve difficulties that result from ingenious but perverse readings of his poems. It springs from the fixed determination to find a moral significance in everything that Dunbar wrote.

Medieval irony, like medieval poetry, was not all of a piece. Its exponents were often far from solemn, and very few were as subtle as Chaucer; much medieval irony indeed was fairly simple and crude. We are often nudged into perceiving it by various devices. Poets—or their copyists—sometimes considered it advisable to insert the phrase *per antiphrasim* in rubrics or titles, lest anyone should miss the point.[98] Poets sometimes provided other clues—often remarkably explicit—that warned readers not to accept the literal meaning of their words. One favourite method was the use of a 'destroying refrain', such as Lydgate's 'Right [straight] as a rammes horne'; an obvious absurdity or discrepancy with factual reality contradicts the truth or the seriousness of what is said elsewhere.[99] A well-known example is the carol that purports to praise women, but has a burden that runs

> Of all creatures women be best,
> *Cuius contrarium verum est.*

This Latin tag, which seems to originate in scholastic disputation, accompanies other ironical commendations of women.[100]

Verbal irony is but one of many weapons in Dunbar's comic armoury. In *The Testament* the testator speaks of a certain William Gray:

---

[96] Reiss, 100, 102, 116, 68, and 135.
[97] 'The Ironic Art of William Dunbar', in *Fifteenth-Century Studies*, ed. R. F. Yeager (Hamden, Conn., 1984), 323. Cf. also 'Chaucer and Medieval Irony', *Studies in the Age of Chaucer*, 1 (1979), 67–82.
[98] See Utley, nos. 307 and 334. Both are attributed to Lydgate.
[99] *Minor Poems II*, ed. MacCracken, no. 18; cf. no. 19.
[100] Greene, *Carols*, no. 399. For discussion and other instances, see Greene's note, and Utley, no. 136.

'SPORTIS AND JOCOSITEIS'

> Myne awne deir cusing as I wene
> *Qui nunquam fabricat mendacia*
> Bot quhen the holyne growis grene (62–4)

The last line clearly undermines the approval voiced in the preceding ones, by making their truth conditional—not, as one might expect, on some form of the impossibility topos, but on its exact opposite. Holly is evergreen, and William Gray is thus an inveterate liar; he is Kennedy's cousin in a loaded sense.[101] In another poem that contains a wholly explicit attack on court parasites and hangers-on, Dunbar devotes one line to

> Monsouris of France (gud clarat cunnaris) (K 44. 42)

This simultaneously praises and dispraises. The French men are nobles, yet most sixteenth-century uses of 'monsour' (*mon sieur*) tend to be sarcastic. They are also 'gud'—not at any recognized craft, however, but as experts in tasting wine, and no doubt talking about it. Dunbar's phrase 'clarat cunnaris' mimics the term for those appointed to test the quality of ale—'ale cunners'.[102] These men, however, have no useful social role—they are little more than 'wine buffs'. Irony is also deployed in attacking the abbot of Tungland (K 54). His pretensions to medical learning are mockingly termed 'cunnyng' (26) and 'sciens' (28). They are preceded by this passage:

> Vane organis he full clenely carvit;
> Quhen of his straik so mony starvit,
> Dreid he had gottin that he desarvit
> He fled away gud speid. (21–4)

In isolation the phrase 'full clenely carvit' conveys bland approval. But the reference is not to the abbot's skills at the dinner table. He is engaged in blood-letting, and 'vane organis'—which a modern reader might well take to be superfluous bits of the body—is a learned term for the jugular veins. Dunbar says, in effect, that the abbot slit throats very neatly.

In these poems the irony is sporadic and intermittent, but elsewhere it is more sustained. In *This nycht in my sleip I wes agast* (K 56) there is strong dramatic irony; again and again words are uttered whose full truth is perceived only by the devil and not by those who speak them. *This nycht befoir the dawing cleir* (K 55) is a tissue of double-meanings, and has a highly equivocal narrator. The irony of some poems is much enhanced by the framework in which they are set. The finest example of this is *The Tua Mariit Wemen and the Wedo*, but it is also true of a

---

[101] On *adynata*, or 'ballatis of unpossibiliteis', see Ch. 7 below, n. 5.
[102] See *DOST*, *monsieur*, 2; and *ale cunner*.

less important poem, *Ane murlandis man of uplandis mak* (K 74). Its substance is essentially a complaint on the evils of the times; the *repetitio* on *sum* makes its catalogue-structure plain:

> Sum sweiris and forsaikis God;
> Sum in ane lambskin is ane tod;
> Sum in his toung his kyndnes tursis;
> Sum cuttis throttis, and sum pykis pursis. (36–9)

But most of the poem is placed in the mouth of a countryman, freshly returned from Edinburgh, and responding to the request of his neighbour—the 'man of uplandis mak'—for the latest news. There is thus a contrast between city corruption and rustic innocence, or naïvety. To this simple couple the abuses are not commonplace but novelties, as the refrain reminds us—

> Sic tydingis hard I at the sessioun.

The reference to the lawcourts suggests the poem's evident preoccupation with legal chicanery; yet 'the sessioun' is also the place where wrongdoing should be exposed, and where people gather to hear the latest news and scandal. The poem has several small verbal ironies. A proverb thus receives a perverse new intepretation: 'The ȝungar at the eldar leiris' (48).[103] But it is unchaste behaviour that the friars learn from their elders, 'And ar unmyndfull of thair professioun'. The last stanza is devoted to monks 'of devoit mynd'—

> Thay are so humill of intercessioun,
> All mercyfull wemen thair eirandis grantis. (50 ff.)

The pious-sounding phrases, 'devoit mynd' and 'humill of intercessioun', here have an amorous sense that is unfitting for churchmen. Dunbar uses *intercessioun* elsewhere in its more orthodox sense of 'prayer, entreaty, to God' (K 36. 26). The ironic application of *mercyfull* to women who are over-ready to comply with men's sexual demands resembles its use by the self-congratulatory Widow: 'I am so mercifull in mynd' (K 14. 501)

Rycht airlie on Ask Weddinsday (K 73) belongs to the genre of the gossips' meeting.[104] But Dunbar sharpens the satiric edge of this popular theme by the Lenten setting: these women are enjoying their drink precisely at the time when the Church requires abstinence:

> Rycht airlie on Ask Weddinsday
> Drynkand the wyne satt cumeris tway;
> The tane cowth to the tother complene:

---

[103] Not apparently in Whiting; but see note to *King Hart*, 656, in *The Shorter Poems of Gavin Douglas*, 235.
[104] See below, 338.

> Graneand and suppand cowd scho say,
> This lang Lentern makis me lene.   (1–5)

Yet Dunbar seems less interested in making a moral point than a comic one. The women's complaint, embodied in the refrain, is a flagrant contradiction of fact—'this lang Lentern' has only just begun, and the first cummer turns out to be not 'lene', but 'grit and fatt' (7). There is another explicit pointer to the narrator's stance in his comment on this same woman:

> 3it to be feble scho did hir fene [feign].   (8)

From the very beginning there is thus established a comic discrepancy between what the cummers say of themselves and what the poet says of them. The irony is obvious, but deft and amusing.

The first woman is comfortably ensconced 'On cowch besyd the fyre' (6), assuming an invalid's airs. The second woman encourages her to break the fast, and in one of the funnier passages asserts that the first has inherited from her mother both her 'megirnes' (12),[105] or slender figure, and her taste for wine of the best quality. This double compliment should clearly be read in reverse: frequent supping of malmesey has resulted in corpulence. It seems to have been a traditional motif in this genre for the drinkers to excuse their self-indulgence by saying that it was good for their health. In a convivial English carol the gossips thus gather, 'Ther seke bodyes to comforte'.[106] So too with Dunbar's cummers:

> Off droucht sic axis did thame strene.
> Be thane to mend thai hed gud hoip:
> That lang Lentrin suld nocht mak thaim lene.   (28–30)[107]

Their self-deception continues to the end. The poet speaks sarcastically of their 'droucht', or dryness, and its 'axis', a term for the onset or attack of an illness; he refers with similar irony to their hope 'to mend', to improve in bodily rather than spiritual health. The final line emphatically contradicts the earlier form of the refrain. It represents both the women's unvoiced 'hoip' and the poet's summing-up of the situation.

Several poems are examples of the mock-commendation, or 'blame-by-praise' type of irony. One, already discussed, is *Schir Thomas Norny*, which interweaves irony with parody. It incidentally provides a useful illustration of how an ironist's message sometimes fails to be

---

[105] This reading (from the copy in the Aberdeen Sasine Register) is preferable to Bannatyne's *nigirtnes*, 'miserliness'.
[106] Greene, *Carols*, no. 419.
[107] Quoted from the Aberdeen text.

received. The historian Sir James Balfour Paul took at their face value such laudatory phrases as 'ane gentill knycht' and 'this wyse and worthie knycht'; he thus called the piece 'a very eulogistic poem', written in Norny's 'honour'.[108] No reader, however, is likely to misinterpret *Thir ladyis fair* (K 71):

> Thir ladyis fair
> That makis repair
>   And in the court ar kend,
> Thre dayis thair
> Thay will do mair
>   Ane mater for till end
> Than thair gud men
> Will do in ten
>   For ony craft thay can.   (1–9)

It ends:

> Sic ladyis wyis
> Thay ar to pryis
>   To say the veretie,
> Swa can devyis
> And none suppryis
>   Thame nor thair honestie. (67–72)

The women are sent to court, to prosecute their husbands' legal business, and win 'remissioun' by granting sexual favours. The violation of orthodox morality leaves no doubt that the poet's praise of the women's wisdom is as ironical as his advice to other men (37–42) to emulate the 'gud'-ness of these husbands. But the tone is one of amused contempt rather than strong moral indignation—a contributory factor in this may be the poem's ingenious metrical pattern, and its light, tripping rhythms. It is impossible to say how far such a practice existed in contemporary Scotland, but other attempts to pervert justice, such as force or bribery, were common enough.[109] The poem belongs to a minor satirical genre: Bannatyne included it in a section entitled 'Schort Epegrammis aganis Women', and placed it next to another poem on the same theme, *The vse of court richt weill I knaw*.[110] But this is coarser and far more explicit. It speaks of the husbands as 'silly', something that Dunbar's readers are left to infer; and it ends with a laird finding 'His wyfe iaippit, his silver spendit'. Dunbar is far more veiled and equivocal. He refers to the women's *gud men*, which signifies both 'husbands' and 'virtuous men'. He

---

[108] *TA* iii, p. xcii.
[109] On the traffic in respites and remissions, see R. Nicholson, *Scotland: The Later Middle Ages* (Edinburgh, 1974), 569–70.
[110] Bannatyne, fols. 258a and 261b.

employs bawdy innuendoes, on *spend* (46) and *geir* (48), and puns on the legal sense of other words.[111] The double-speak continues throughout, and culminates in the final assertion of the poet's own 'veretie', or veracity, and the ladies' 'honestie'. This, the poem's very last word, sums up its ambivalence: women like this are good at preserving an outward appearance of *honesty*, in such senses as 'good fame', or 'respectability'; but they notably lack real moral excellence, above all, chastity.[112]

Another excellent mock-eulogy is *The Amendis to the Tel3ouris and Sowtaris* (K 52C). The poet dreams that he hears the voice of an angel, who lavishes praise on tailors and soutars, and prophesies their future glory in heaven; each stanza ends with the refrain,

> Tail3ouris and sowtaris, blist be 3e.

No one is likely to take this praise at face value. But what prompts our ironical reading? In the first place, most modern readers encounter the piece as a pendant to *The Turnament*, with its mockery of these craftsmen. (For discussion of the relation of these poems, see below, p. 288.) What is more, we may recall Dunbar's poem to the merchants of Edinburgh, which criticizes 'Tail3ouris, soutteris and craftis vyll' (K 75. 36). Dunbar draws upon a very long-established tradition of treating the humbler craftsmen—and tailors in particular—as targets for ridicule. It has not been noticed that there exists an analogue (not a source) for *The Amendis* in a Goliardic poem, which comically metamorphoses tailors into gods:

> Ego dixi: dii estis;
> Quae dicenda sunt in festis,
> Quare praetermitterem?
> Dii, revera, qui potestis
> In figuram novae vestis
> Transmutare veterem.[113]

[I have said: You are gods; why should I let pass the things which should be said at festivals? Gods indeed, who are able to transform an old garment into a new one.]

But the effect of Dunbar's poem does not depend on either its immediate context or our awareness of literary tradition. The very first line, with its topsy-turvy indication of time—'Betuix twell houris and ellevin'—hints at some absurdity to follow. The poet claims, like St

---

[111] Cf. L. Ebin, 'Dunbar's Bawdy', *Chau R* 14 (1979–80), 278–86.

[112] *OED* illustrates the sense-range better than *DOST*; cf. also W. Empson, *The Structure of Complex Words* (1951), 185 ff.

[113] Printed in *The Political Songs of England from the Reign of John to that of Edward II*, ed. Thomas Wright (Camden Soc., 1839), 51–6.

John, to be privileged, hearing an angel's revelations; but it is a mock-apocalypse that he narrates. What is striking, in the second stanza, is the sheer audacity of the angel's claim:

> In hevin hie ordand is 30ur place
> Aboif all sanctis, in grit solace,
> Nixt God grittest in dignitie . . .   (5-7)

Tailors and soutars are not merely guaranteed a place in heaven, among the blessed; they are promised the highest position, above the saints, and next to God himself. (Allan Ramsay, in the eighteenth century, was clearly disturbed by this, and must have found the poem blasphemous. He rewrote line 5 as 'High up for you is ordained a place', and line 7 as 'In Happynes and Dignity'. He also removed other references to God, and omitted lines 25-8 completely.[114]) Dunbar transforms the craftsmen's skill at disguising physical blemishes and deformities into a power to improve God's handiwork and even correct his mistakes:

> That God mismakkis, 3e do amend.   (10)

Those who have such miraculous powers—curing 'peple fra cruke and lame' (34)—must be saints; but this crazy logic is undermined by a destructive 'aside' in the penultimate line:

> In erd 3e kyth sic mirakillis heir,
> In hevin 3e salbe sanctis full cleir
> Thocht 3e be knavis in this cuntre;
> Tel3ouris and sowtaris, blist be 3ie.   (37-40)

Knavis provides a clue to the final assessment of these craftsmen; yet it should be remembered that this was also a word with 'faceis tua'. The tailors and soutars are 'servants, menials' (a low earthly status contrasts with their heavenly exaltation); but they are unmistakably also rogues, 'knaves' in its usual modern sense.[115] The poem contains other double-edged words, whose irony may be missed by some readers, since today the pejorative sense is most common. When Dunbar speaks of the tailor's 'craftis slie' (31), he simultaneously praises and dispraises. *Craft* signifies the tradesman's trade and his 'skill' at it, but also his trickery and deceit. *Slie* had a similarly wide semantic range: *I that in heill wes* illustrates both the eulogistic sense, 'skilled'—'Thame helpis no conclusionis sle' (39)—and the dyslogistic one, 'cunning'—'the Fend is sle' (7). Recent critics have read this poem very seriously; one terms it an attack on 'spiritual dissem-

---

[114] See W. Geddie, *A Bibliography of Middle Scots Poets* (STS, 1912), lxix.
[115] See *DOST*, *knave*, senses 2 and 5.

bling'.[116] But the deceptions it exposes seem trivial, and the 'cover-ups' are material and physical. Dunbar's tone is jesting and flippant; this ambivalent apology to the tailors resembles the poem addressed to James Dog (K 30). Dunbar is a subtle and playful ironist. His irony may be judged characteristically medieval in many respects—in targets and, to some extent, in techniques—but he is rarely ironic in the 'cosmic', or philosophic sense. Irony is frequent, indeed pervasive, in his comic poetry, but it takes many forms and serves different ends. Sometimes it undoubtedly promotes the cause of orthodox morality, as in *Thir ladyis fair* (K 71). More often the poet's stance is somewhat elusive; he seems to delight as much in the exploitation of equivocal and ambiguous language as in the exposure of human frailty and self-deception.

[116] Scott, 238; cf. Reiss, 83–4, and Ross, 176–7.

6

Flyting

DUNBAR often criticizes the manners and morals of his society, and demonstrates an easy familiarity with the multifarious traditions of medieval satire. In his poetry we meet favourite topics of 'estates' satire—the incompetent physician (K 54), dishonest craftsmen (K 56), and a crowd of idle and parasitical courtiers. The Church does not escape censure either: he repeatedly mentions the greed of pluralistic churchmen, who are more concerned with collecting benefices than the welfare of their parishioners (K 40, K 42, K 45, and K 51); he refers to the unchastity of monks (K 74), and the duplicity of friars (K 34, K 38, K 74), particularly the Franciscans (K 55). Occasionally there is acute observation of the local Scottish scene, as in the poem addressed to Edinburgh merchants (K 75), or this condemnation of landlords for extortionate increases in rents (*mailis*) and initial downpayments (*gersomes*):

> Barronis takis fra the tennentis peure
> All fruct that growis on the feure
> In mailis and gersomes rasit ouir hie,
> And garris thame beg fra dure to dure.   (K 80. 11–14)[1]

But Dunbar makes no mention of the most flagrant abuses in the contemporary Scottish Church, such as the appointment of laymen to lucrative offices, as 'commendators' of abbeys and monasteries.[2] What is most striking about his satiric stance is its conservatism and comparative conventionality. The wide dispersal of targets suggests that there was no one subject about which Dunbar felt particularly strongly. Often indeed the satiric element forms but one strand in a complex poem; sometimes it overlaps with 'complaint'—overtly moral denunciation of the vanity of 'this warld'—or with personal petitions on the poet's behalf. The tone varies widely, yet rarely reveals the strong sense of moral outrage that characterizes Henryson's *Fables* or

---

[1] Similar complaints occur in Henryson's Fable of The Wolf and the Lamb; cf. S. G. E. Lythe, 'Economic Life', in *Scottish Society in the Fifteenth Century*, ed. J. Brown (1977), 68–70.

[2] See I. B. Cowan, *The Scottish Reformation: Church and Society in Sixteenth-Century Scotland* (1982), 22 ff.; and L. Macfarlane, 'Was the Scottish Church Reformable by 1513?', in *Church, Politics and Society: Scotland 1408–1929*, ed. N. Macdougall (Edinburgh, 1983), 23–43.

Lindsay's attacks on the Scottish Church, a generation later; mockery and light amusement are more common in Dunbar than *saeva indignatio*.

According to some medieval theorists, the best satire was impersonal and impartial: it was directed against vice in general, not individuals. John of Garland said of a work that he termed a 'new satire':

> Nullus dente mali lacerabitur in speciali,
> Immo metro tali ludet stilus in generali. (3–4)

[No one specifically will be injured by the biting words of a spiteful man, rather in such a style my pen will sport in general terms.][3]

The same opposition was made by an English poet, who declared:

> Synglure persone I doo none name,
> But alle the world in generalle.[4]

Dunbar too alludes to this distinction, at the beginning of *The Flyting*. In a somewhat cryptic passage he speaks of a work—'ane thing'— written by his antagonist, Kennedy, apparently in collaboration with another poet, Quintin. Unfortunately we do not know the precise nature of this lost work, although it clearly angered Dunbar. If these poets wrote 'In generale' (2), it seems that he would tolerate their remarks; but if they write 'In speciall' (5) they will provoke him to fury and a terrible response in kind. Dunbar indeed displays most zest and originality precisely when he himself writes 'in speciall'. Many poems name 'synglure' persons, and constitute attacks on specific individuals. Their motivation is not particularly moral. Often it is retaliatory; as Dunbar says in *Schir, 3e have mony servitouris* (K 44. 82), 'with my pen I man me wreik'. These poems voice anger and aggression, but they also reveal delight in the creation of vivid, if caricatured, portraits. This is the branch of satire in which Dunbar most excels, that of lampoon, invective, and flyting.

The Flyting of Dunbar and Kennedie makes a considerable impact on most readers; like it or loathe it, few remain indifferent. From the eighteenth century onwards there has been disquiet at its 'unexampled' scurrility; and one modern critic called it 'the most repellent poem known to me in any language'.[5] Yet other readers have been more appreciative: Auden included two extracts from *The Flyting* in

---

[3] I owe this quotation to P. Miller, 'John Gower, Satiric Poet', in *Gower's Confessio Amantis: Responses and Reassessments*, ed. A. J. Minnis (Woodbridge, 1983), 85.
[4] *CB XV*, no. 173.
[5] Lord Hailes, *Ancient Scottish Poems* (Edinburgh, 1770), 274; Scott, 175.

his ill-fated *Oxford Book of Light Verse* (1938), and Eliot, in his essay on Byron, quoted a stanza with evident enjoyment.[6] We have, unfortunately, no sixteenth-century comment on the work, apart from Bannatyne's rubric: 'Jocound and mirrie'. But other evidence suggests that *The Flyting* was as popular as *The Goldyn Targe*, and possibly more influential. It was among the first Scottish poems to be printed; copies also exist in the Bannatyne, Maitland, and Reidpeth manuscripts, and Asloan contained a version, which no longer survives. What is more, Dunbar and Kennedy's *Flyting* seems to have been responsible for the later Scottish vogue of this kind of writing. It was succeeded by Stewart's *Flyting betuix the Soutar and the Tailʒeour*; by Lindsay's *Answer to the King's Flyting*; and by *The Flyting of Montgomerie and Polwart* (c.1580).[7] This latter work, which shows the stylistic influence of Dunbar and Kennedy, had a remarkably long-lived popularity. There were at least five editions and reprints in the seventeenth century, and it was included in James Watson's famous *Choice Collection of Comic and Serious Scots Poems* (1706-11). Flyting is thus one of the few poetic traditions that survived, unbroken, from the time of Dunbar to that of Allan Ramsay.

Flyting is a useful but slippery term. *OED* admirably defined reciprocal flyting as 'a kind of contest practised by the Scottish poets of the sixteenth century, in which two persons assailed each other alternately with tirades of abusive verse'. Today the term is chiefly employed by scholars and critics: sometimes in this restricted sense, of a literary genre, peculiarly Scottish and chronologically limited; sometimes in a vaguer sense, of fictional encounters as different in style and far apart in time as the quarrel between Unferth and Beowulf and the sophisticated wit-combats of Beatrice and Benedick.[8] Yet it is important to remember how comparatively recent are these literary-critical senses of the word. Throughout the medieval period, in England as well as in Scotland, the words *flyte*, *flyting*, and *flyter* were most common in non-literary uses and contexts. In Old English *flītan* meant 'to dispute or quarrel'. In later centuries *flyting* signified noisy quarrels and arguments, carried on chiefly by the lower orders, and—so it was insinuated—by women. A *flyter* was roughly synonymous

---

[6] *On Poetry and Poets* (1957), 206. For recent studies, see Bawcutt, 'The Art of Flyting', *SLJ* 10, no. 2 (1983), 5-24; R. J. Lyall, 'Complaint, Satire and Invective in Middle Scots Literature', in Macdougall, *Church, Politics and Society* (above, n. 2), 44-63; and D. Gray, 'Rough Music: Some Early Invectives and Flytings', *YES* 14 (1984), 21-43.

[7] Bannatyne includes Stewart's *Flyting*, Montgomerie's *Answer to ane Helandmannis invective*, and the anonymous *Answer to ane Inglis railler*. Other pieces—often entitled 'Answers'—are in *Satirical Poems of the Time of the Reformation*, ed. J. Cranstoun (STS, 1891-3).

[8] See *OED* and Supplement, *fliting*, *flyting*, 1b.

with a *scold* (Scots *scald*).⁹ *The Flyting of Dunbar and Kennedie* is the best-known of all poetic flytings, and may well have introduced the term into the vocabulary of literary criticism. (James VI, who equates flyting with invective, seems the first to speak of it unambiguously as a literary kind.¹⁰) But Dunbar was keenly aware of the word's everyday significance; he, like his contemporaries, coupled flyting with other forms of 'bad language', such as cursing and swearing, and he associated it with fishwives and 'carlingis' on the streets of Edinburgh (K 56. 76; K 75. 10–11).

Such noisy and public quarrels were then very common. The Scottish records, both of the Church courts and the burghs, contain numerous references to 'flytand on the Hie Gait' (Peebles, 1570) or 'publict flytting ... on the calsay' (Elgin, 1596). At Stirling in 1524 Jean and John Murray were fined for flyting and keeping their neighbours awake all night. At St Andrews in 1570 a baker's wife compounded the offence by flyting during 'the tyme of sermon on Sunday'.¹¹ Churchmen, it should be noted, could be equally culpable. In 1506 John Elphinstoun of Glasgow complained that a priest, Thomas Forsyth, had spoken injuriously of him *in lingua vernacula*— 'Iohne Elphinstoun is a defamit persone ... ane verray erratik and a low'.¹² In 1510 Master Andrew Birkmyre taunted another cleric: 'ӡe dow nocht to fessyn [fasten?] a scheip heid ... I sett nocht by ӡou a fert of ӡour ers'.¹³ In one case the king himself intervened. A letter of James IV defended Master Robert Forman from the charge that he had criticized 'the unchaste behaviour of Danish matrons'; the unnamed calumniator had either to defend his words, 'in person or at law', or make a public withdrawal.¹⁴ Defamation was taken very seriously indeed: 'A person who had been calumniated might hire a notary public to register a deed of protest and bring a charge before the court of the bishop or before the bailies'.¹⁵ Andrew Birkmyre was thus compelled to ask pardon, kneeling on the floor of the court, and

---

⁹ Cf. Bawcutt, 'Flyting', 6–7; and see the abundant evidence in *OED, MED, DOST*, and *SND*.

¹⁰ *Reulis and Cautelis...in Scottis Poesie*, in *Elizabethan Critical Essays*, ed. G. Gregory Smith (Oxford, 1904), i. 217.

¹¹ See *DOST*'s citations for *flyte, flytar*, and *flyting; Charters and Documents Relating to the Burgh of Peebles* (Edinburgh, 1872), 325; *Extracts from the Records of the Royal Burgh of Stirling*, ed. R. Renwick (Glasgow, 1887–9), 18; and *St Andrews Kirk Session Register*, ed. D. H. Fleming (SHS, 1889), 343.

¹² *Liber Protocollorum M. Cuthberti Simonis* (Grampian Club, 1875), ii. 155.

¹³ Ibid. 345–7. Cf. J. Durkan, 'The Early Scottish Notary', in *The Renaissance and Reformation in Scotland*, ed. I. B. Cowan and D. Shaw (1983), 39.

¹⁴ *The Letters of James the Fourth 1503–1513*, calendared R. K. Hannay and R. L. Mackie (SHS, ser. 3. 45, 1953), no. 182.

¹⁵ D. McKay, 'Parish Life in Scotland', in *Essays on the Scottish Reformation 1513–1625*, ed. D. McRoberts (Glasgow, 1962), 113.

instructed to *revocare verba injuriosa et contemptibilia*. Some of the potential punishments for flyting were horrifying. They included confinement in the *goif*, or pillory; wearing the *jougis*, a kind of iron collar that locked around the culprit's neck; and being placed in the cuckstool, and there pelted with eggs, dung, and mud.[16] These phenomena, it must be stressed, are not peculiar to Scotland; all are abundantly documented in the English records.[17]

It is important to be aware of the real-life context of literary flyting. Poets drew some of their *verba injuriosa* from what they heard around them, perhaps to a greater extent than we now realize; only occasionally do the court records cite peculiarly offensive phrases—'blay ribald missaell lipper huir', for instance, or 'cucold lowne, face to a pudden!'[18] Other motifs of poetic flyting are not fictional, but have contemporary parallels. Kennedy, for instance, admonishes Dunbar:

> Cum to the croce on kneis and mak a crya;
> Confesse thy crime, hald Kenydy the king,
> And wyth ane hauthorne scurge thy self and dyng.   (325–7)

Such public penance was regularly ordained by the courts. In 1523 a parishioner of St Giles, Edinburgh, who had committed slander, was commanded to appear in church before the altar at the time of high mass, and there beg forgiveness of the injured party on her knees.[19] Kennedy later vows,

> Cursit croapand craw, I sall ger crop thy tong
> And thou sall cry *cor mundum* on thy kneis;
> . . . .
> And thou sal lik thy lippis and suere thou leis.   (393 ff.)

Penitential doctrine stressed the importance of punishing the offending part of the body, in this case the tongue; even if the tongue was not mutilated, the offender was commonly instructed to pronounce in public some version of the phrase, 'Fals tung, thow leid'.[20] Kennedy's words, 'cry *cor mundum*', are also a much-used penitential formula. They are a shorthand reference to the verse, 'Create in me a clean heart, O God, and renew a right spirit within me' (Psalm 51: 10), and thus evoke one of the most contrite of the penitential psalms.[21]

---

[16] Cf. *Early Records of the Burgh of Aberdeen 1317, 1398–1407*, ed. W. C. Dickinson (SHS, ser. 3. 49, 1957), 21.

[17] Cf. J. A. Sharpe, *Defamation and Sexual Slander in Early Modern England: The Church Courts at York* (Borthwick Papers, 58; n.d.).

[18] See *DOST*, *hure, loun, cucold*; and *Stirling Burgh Records*, 43 and 83.

[19] McKay, 'Parish Life', 113.

[20] Cf. J. W. Spargo, *Juridical Folklore in England Illustrated by the Cucking-Stool* (Durham, NC, 1944), 106 ff. and Bawcutt, 'Flyting', 9.

[21] The phrase 'cry *cor mundum*' recurs in later flytings.

The Flyting poses many questions to which one can give only tentative answers. We cannot, with any confidence, treat it as a repository of biographical facts; yet we should not relegate it wholly to the realm of fiction. The truth, as so often, is more complicated: comic fantasy is built upon a substratum of fact (see above, pp. 7–8). It has been suggested that we should view *The Flyting* as the work solely of Dunbar: 'the product of a single writer creating two voices'.[22] But I see no reason to doubt Kennedy's authorship of those sections attributed to him; indeed Kennedy's contribution seems, stylistically, very different from Dunbar's. We do not know the date of *The Flyting* either, even though it is packed with allusions to contemporary persons and events. Suggestions have ranged widely, from the early 1490s to a much later period, 1500–5.[23] The print (*c*.1508) testifies only to the date of publication, not composition; but an allusion to the poet Stobo (d. 1505) seems to provide a more reliable *terminus ad quem*. What is most significant is that poets mentioned as dead or close to death in *I that in heill wes* are in this work very much alive—notably Kennedy himself, Stobo, and Sir John the Ross. We thus have not an absolute but a relative date for *The Flyting*; it certainly sounds the work of men who, even if they are not in extreme youth, are young and in high spirits. The warmth with which Dunbar speaks of Kennedy in *I that in heill wes* also suggests that by this time their quarrel, whatever its nature, was long past and forgotten.

The tone of *The Flyting* is difficult to assess. Although the two poets shower each other with abuse, few readers seem to have taken the anger seriously. Bannatyne's comment—'jocound and mirrie'—finds a counterpart, centuries later, in Auden's reference to flyting as 'sheer high-spirited fun'.[24] Most critics have concurred with Lord Hailes in believing that there 'was no real quarrel between the antagonists'.[25] A Preface attached to the 1621 print of Montgomerie and Polwart's *Flyting* explicitly says that these later poets were stirred by 'generous emulation' rather than 'malice'.[26] Dunbar and Kennedy are closer in tone to Montgomerie and Polwart than to the anonymous authors of the late-sixteenth-century invectives collected in Cranstoun's *Satirical Poems of the Reformation*. These are highly polemical, and inspired by political and religious fervour. Dunbar and Kennedy's *Flyting*, however, produces the impression of a ritualized, literary game, a contest in verbal and metrical ingenuity; Bannatyne twice asks the reader to

---

[22] Reiss, 55.
[23] For the earlier date, cf. M. P. McDiarmid, 'The Early William Dunbar and his Poems', *SHR* 59 (1980), 130–2; for the later, cf. Baxter, 74–84, and Kinsley, 285.
[24] *Ode to the Medieval Poets*.
[25] See above, n. 5.
[26] See Montgomerie, *Poems*, 57.

judge 'quha gat the war'—who got the worst of it. Yet games rouse powerful feelings, and some are both violent and dangerous. The beauties of football, according to the Scottish epigram, are 'brissit brawnis and brokin banis'.[27] *The Flyting* may be, in part, a collaborative game between two poets, but it also voices strong animosities, cultural and personal.

The tournament is a good contemporary example of such aggressive play. Both Dunbar and Kennedy often speak as if they are engaged in battle. Both picture themselves rather like champions engaged in single combat. Kennedy proclaims, 'I sall dyng the' (395), and at the end calls upon Dunbar to surrender his 'spere of were' and flee from the field (545–7). Dunbar angrily accepts the challenge to fight (65), but he rejects chivalric weapons and the notion of a contest between equals:

> With ane doig leich I schepe to gar the schowt,
> And nowther to the tak knyfe, swerd nor aix. (71–2)

More commonly the combat is envisaged as part of a judicial process, in which the contestants put their own veracity and their opponents' lies to the test of battle. Dunbar exclaims:

> Thow leis, tratour; quhilk I sall on the preif.
> Suppois thy heid war armit tymis ten
> Thow sall recryat, or thy croun sall cleif. (86–8)

Dunbar boasts that he will force Kennedy to become a recreant, and thus own himself both perjured and a coward. To another accusation Kennedy later replies:

> Quhare thou puttis poysoun to me, I appelle
> The in that part, preve it, pelour, wyth thy persone. (405–6)

This terminology—*preif on, recryat, puttis, appelle, preve . . . wyth thy persone*—derives from the 'law of armes'; it is simultaneously legal and chivalric.[28]

It is increasingly common to term *The Flyting* a verbal duel, in which Dunbar and Kennedy, the principals, are accompanied by other poets, who are their 'seconds'; but this latter notion is anachronistic.[29] Quintin is certainly called Kennedy's 'commissar' (34, 44, 131, 329);

---

[27] *Maitland Folio*, no. lxxvii. On the 'game' aspect, see D. Lampe, '"Flyting no Reason hath": The Inverted Rhetoric of Abuse', in *The Early Renaissance*, ed. A. S. Bernardo (New York, 1979), 101–20.

[28] Cf. 'I tak it apon me to preif it on the, body for body, as the law of armes schawis', cited from Loutfut by *DOST*, *preif*.

[29] Ross, 186; Reis, 54. 'Seconds' became associated with secret duels, at a later period, to safeguard against foul play; cf. V. G. Kiernan, *The Duel in European History* (Oxford, 1988), 63–4.

but this term was applied to a deputy for another person, and chiefly to the deputy appointed by an ecclesiastical dignitary to act for him in judicial matters. In the Official's Court, for instance, a commissar's duties would include pronouncing sentence on those convicted of slander and defamation.[30] Quintin seems to play this off-stage judicial role in *The Flyting*—Kennedy thus orders Dunbar,

> Pas to my commissare and be confest,
> Cour before him on kneis, and cum in will [be submissive].
>
> (329–30)

It is even more misleading to call Sir John the Ross Dunbar's 'second', or 'commissar'—this imposes a non-existent symmetry upon the work. Sir John the Ross is mentioned twice in *The Flyting*: in the first line Dunbar addresses him as a friend and confidant, and Kennedy later speaks of him as Dunbar's ally and fellow-poet (39–40). But at neither point is he called a *commissar*. What *The Flyting* vividly evokes is the existence of a coterie, a small group of friends, who know each other well but are—perhaps temporarily—split into opposing camps.

The Flyting is a quarrel, not a reasoned argument. It lacks the symmetry that characterizes many debate-poems, including Dunbar's own *Merle and the Nychtingall*. Yet its main outlines, at least in the form preserved by Bannatyne, are easy to perceive.[31] It has a four-part structure: two short, introductory passages, in which each poet challenges the other, are followed by the main invectives—Kennedy's being considerably longer than Dunbar's. *The Flyting* has often been accused of lacking 'logical coherence', or called 'merely a piling up of heterogeneous abuse'.[32] But this does the work an injustice. The undoubted obscurity of a few passages springs chiefly from their topicality and verbal audacity. The two poets do not call each other names in a wholly random fashion. Words and insults seem to tumble out, helter-skelter, but the disorder is simulated and the spontaneity calculated. There is remarkably little overlapping of abuse. Although each accuses the other of treachery, for instance, the charges have a different slant: Kennedy is disloyal to his lord, but Dunbar is too sympathetic to the English. *The Flyting* has a pattern less of argument than of accusation and rebuttal. Kennedy, in particular, retorts to Dunbar's charges in a highly characteristic manner:

---

[30] See S. Ollivant, Introd. to *The Court of the Official in Pre-Reformation Scotland* (Stair Soc. 34, 1982).

[31] The early print is fragmentary, and the Maitland and Reidpeth copies, although complete, are disordered. Schipper suggested a 6-part arrangement, but his arguments were rebutted by Baxter, 235–8, and Kinsley, 284.

[32] Mackenzie, 198.

Quhare thou writis Densmen dryit apon the rattis (355)
Quhare as thou said that I stall hennis and lammys. (361)

(For Dunbar's accusations, see *Flyting*, 51 ff., 149 ff., and 78 ff.) Real issues are at stake. At one level Dunbar and Kennedy speak as representatives of social groups, voicing the antagonisms of Lowlander and Highlander. At a more personal level they criticize each other's verbal artistry—their battle-cries are 'rethory' and 'eloquence' (97, 107, and 339). This is a poetic contest, and they vie in an obtrusive display of rhetorical skills. The metrical form of *The Flyting* is far from simple. Both poets employ an eight-line stanza, heavily enriched with alliteration. Dunbar disposes this in one pattern (*ababbccb*) for the first section of his *Flyting* and in another (*ababbcbc*) for the main invective. He concludes, as does Kennedy, with a remarkable volley of internal rhymes (233–48). As a device for providing a poem with a flamboyant finale, this was popular with other Scottish poets, not only those engaged in flyting.[33]

The 'coherence' of *The Flyting* is essentially imaginative. The taunts and insults that the two poets hurl at each other build up into contrasted portraits, or personae. Dunbar, the Lowlander, depicts Kennedy, the Highlander, as an 'Ersche katherene [thief]' (145), who cannot speak 'Inglis' correctly (110–12); Kennedy retorts that Erse was once 'the gud langage of this land' and should still be 'all trew Scottis mennis lede' (345–8). Dunbar presents a picture of Kennedy as a provincial, poverty-stricken, country-dweller:

Thow bringis the Carrik clay to Edinburgh cors. (211)

This is the tone not just of the Lowlander but of the city sophisticate, patronizing a rustic outsider. (The portrait seems a comical travesty of Kennedy's real social status, as property-owner, and churchman.[34]) Kennedy's picture of Dunbar has been discussed earlier (see pp. 7–8); but what should be noted here is how different is his approach. He concentrates on Dunbar's spiritual and intellectual shortcomings, and presents him as forever on the move—in England, Denmark, France, and on the road to Rome. For Kennedy Dunbar is an outsider of a different sort—a vagabond cleric, a rootless wanderer. Dunbar repeatedly calls Kennedy a 'baird' (49, 63, 96, 120, and *passim*)—a pejorative term in Scots usage for an idle entertainer. Kennedy likewise degrades Dunbar to a 'scald' (322), and even a minstrel—

Tak the a fidill or a floyte, and geste. (507)

---

[33] The most sustained example is the 64-line conclusion to Polwart's *Flyting*; see also Henryson, *Prayer for the Pest*, 65–88; Douglas, *Palice of Honour*, 2116–42; and Scott, *Poems*, no. 1.

[34] See Baxter, 62–3.

FLYTING

Dunbar is far more visual than Kennedy, who says little of Dunbar's physical appearance, except to imply his small stature—he calls him a dwarf (33, 395, 408) and threatens to serve him up, baked like 'a pullit hen' (516). But Dunbar lavishes his considerable descriptive powers on Kennedy's 'frawart phisnomy' (81), which—as some treatises on physiognomy maintained—betrayed his inner malice.[35] Dunbar sometimes concentrates on Kennedy's 'perrellus face' (150), viewing it in close-up and singling out different features for attention, such as the 'fowll front' (126) or the nose, which is variously termed 'snowt', 'grunʒe' and 'gruntill' (52, 123, 127), as if Kennedy were a pig. But Dunbar also brings other parts of the body before us: first displaying the 'skolderit' (tanned, sunburnt) skin (122, 171), and then removing it. He mercilessly dissects Kennedy, bone by bone, from the cheekbone, 'choip' and 'choll' (165–6), down through the 'larbar linkis' of his scraggy neck (169), to shoulders, hips, and other parts of the skeleton:

> Thy rigbane rattillis and thy ribbis on raw;
> Thy hanchis hirklis with hukebanis harth and haw,
> Thy laithly lymis ar lene as ony treis.   (180–2)

The diction has the precision of an anatomist—*linkis* refers to the cervical vertebrae, and in Middle English translates *spondilia*—or even of a butcher. The word *hukebanis* (huckbones, hucklebones) elsewhere occurs chiefly in household accounts—'For a heuck bone of beif'.[36] The overall effect is painfully gaunt: the ribs and spine are so uncushioned with flesh that they rattle; Kennedy's bones are said later to protrude through his skin (186).

Anatomists and butchers deal with dead bodies; again and again in *The Flyting* Kennedy is depicted as a corpse, 'carioun' (139), 'tramort' (161), or a Lazarus returned from the grave (above, p. 194). What is more, the corpse is often of a particularly shameful kind, that of a malefactor, a Danish criminal upon 'the rattis', or wheel (51), or a 'hangit man' (187). *The Flyting* is full of references to the gallows—some very brief, others more elaborate:

> Ay loungand lyk ane loikman on ane ledder;
> With hingit luik ay wallowand upone wry
> Lyk to ane stark theif glowrand in ane tedder.   (174–6)

There is here a double image of Kennedy—both as *loikman*, a term for the hangman, originating in fifteenth-century Edinburgh, and also

---

[35] Cf. Henryson's discussion in *Fables*, 2824 ff., which cites the proverb, *Distortum vultum sequitur distortio morum*. Most versions of the *Secreta Secretorum* contain a section on physiognomy.
[36] See Bawcutt, 'Dunbar: New Light', 87–8; and *DOST*, huke-bane, *OED*, huck-bone.

as the 'hingit' man, in a grotesque posture on the gallows. The hangman was himself likely to be a criminal; according to A. J. Aitken, the post was unpopular, and 'one method of recruitment was to offer the post to the next person due to be hanged'.[37]

Dunbar vividly establishes the poverty-stricken and essentially rural milieu to which Kennedy is said to belong. There are references to a host of small, everyday things—peasant food, such as 'ane haggeis' (128); clothing 'nocht worth ane pair of auld gray sox' (144); crops, such as peas, wheat, barley, oats; swine, oxen, and poultry; the mill at which Kennedy is said to beg for meal and husks of corn (147), or his 'luge' in a distant glen, once lived in by lepers (153–4). The imagery intermeshes with this world effectively: Kennedy is 'hippit as ane harrow' (179), his limbs are lean as 'ony treis' (182), and his complexion is sallow as 'ane leik' (102). He is addressed as 'tyke' or 'tykis face' (235, 238), or 'ugly averill' (an old horse); and his strange gait, 'hirpland' and 'hobland', resembles that of a 'hurcheoun', or hedgehog (179, 212). Elsewhere Kennedy is envisaged as a bird of prey—raven, 'raggit ruke' (57), and hungry *gled*, or kite (128, 237):

> Thow and thy quene, as gredy gleddis ȝe gang,
> With polkis to mylne and beggis baith meill and schilling.
> Thair is bot lys and lang nailis ȝow amang.
> Fowll heggirbald, for henis thus will ȝe hang;
> Thow hes ane perrellus face to play with lambis;
> Ane thowsand kiddis, wer thay in faldis full strang,
> Thy lymmerfull luke wald fle thame and thair damis.   (146–52)

Latent in the last four lines is the image of another predator, the fox, which reinforces that of the kites in line 146. (The same ironical application of the verb *play* to a fox's treatment of lambs occurs in *This hindir nycht in Dumfermeling*, 4.)

This passage illustrates the equivalence that Dunbar establishes in *The Flyting* between actual animals, such as hens, lambs, and even lice, and the metaphorical ones to which Kennedy is insultingly compared. Kennedy is often presented as thief, predator, parasite; but at times the tables are turned—he is, as here, a prey to lice, or his nose looks as if it has been devoured by kites (52), or he flees in terror, like a mobbed owl, 'ane howlat chest with crawis' (219). Kennedy, in another remarkable passage, is associated with the persecutors of saints:

> For he that rostit Lawarance had thy grunȝe,
> And he that hid sanct Johnis ene with ane wimple,
> And he that dang sanct Augustyne with ane rumple,

---

[37] See *ROSC* 3 (1987), 93–4; and *DOST, lokman*.

Thy fowll front had, and he that Bartilmo flaid;
The gallowis gaipis eftir thy graceles gruntill
As thow wald for ane haggeis, hungry gled.   (123–8)

Ostensibly the chief point of comparison is the ugly appearance of the persecutors, who were often depicted with long, hooked noses, and heavily lined foreheads. But words like 'rostit' and 'flaid' evoke the specific nature of St Lawrence and St Bartholomew's martyrdom, and the cruelty with which humans treat one another. In the last two lines Kennedy is grotesquely paralleled both with the gallows and a kite: all three are equally ravenous, gaping for food, a human nose, or 'gruntill', being of no more account than a haggis. Dunbar, in *The Flyting*, presents the natural world in a harsh, unattractive, and in some ways realistic, light—a cycle of eating and being eaten, a process of pursuit and flight. But human society is shown as similarly greedy and savage.

Kennedy is far more obtrusively a 'clerk' (in its double sense of scholar and churchman) than Dunbar. His *Flyting* is strewn with allusions to figures from the Bible or from ancient and recent history. He alludes to his authorities—'the writ makis me war' (258) or 'as the carnicle [chronicle] schawis' (272)—in the way that Douglas refers to Virgil or Boccaccio. He occasionally uses snatches of Latin—'Criant caritas at duris amore Dei' (383)—whereas Dunbar here confines himself to the vernacular. Kennedy speaks more obviously as a churchman, using the language of religious censure, and admonishing Dunbar, 'dree thy penaunce' (328). Dunbar calls Kennedy a heretic once (247), chiefly, it seems, because it furnishes a useful rhyme. But Kennedy, in a vivid passage, harps upon Dunbar's heresy, telling him to 'birn thy bill' (332), the phrase often used when commanding heretics to recant. He threatens Dunbar with the heretic's death:

> thou salbe brynt,
> Wyth pik, fire, ter, gun puldre or lynt
> On Arthuris Sete or on ane hyar hyll.   (334–6)

Dunbar is accused of Lollardry (524, 548), something for which there is no evidence in his poetry, and but scanty traces in contemporary Scotland. None the less the Scottish Church and Crown regarded Lollardry as 'a radical and politically dangerous sect'.[38] Kennedy's smear is consonant with the line he takes towards Lollards elsewhere in his poetry.[39]

One striking feature of Kennedy's *Flyting* is his obsession with

---

[38] L. J. Macfarlane, *William Elphinstone and the Kingdom of Scotland 1431–1514* (Aberdeen, 1985), 305.
[39] In the poem sometimes called 'The Praise of Age'; Bannatyne, fol. 52b.

kinship. It is studded with references to kin, the clan and the surname, ancestry and all kinds of family relationships—'fader', 'dame', 'eme', and 'nephew'. Such a preoccupation was by no means peculiar to the Highlander. In Scotland the Lowland 'surname' was as important as the Highland clan in engendering intense feelings of loyalty or hostility. Discussing the phenomenon, Jenny Wormald comments: 'It has long been axiomatic that Scottish society and politics were regularly dominated or bedevilled by considerations of kin even more than of rank and status, and certainly of principle.'[40] Kennedy's *Flyting* is informed by this sense of the importance of kin. When he wishes to boast, he speaks of his royal connections—'I am the kingis blude' (417)—or his family's loyalty to the Crown: 'My linage and forebearis war ay lele' (402). His attack on Dunbar is largely directed at his surname, and has two dimensions, historical and fantastic. He blackens Dunbar's name by alluding to the evil deeds of his alleged ancestors and 'elderis' (257, 311, 315); and he repeatedly mentions one notorious name, that of 'Corspatrik', Patrick Dunbar, first earl of March, who supported Edward I in the War of Independence. His story had recently been told in Hary's *Wallace*, a work to which Kennedy seems to allude (284 ff.). Simultaneously he dissociates the poet from the virtuous branches of the Dunbar family:

> The erl of Murray bure that surname ryght
> . . . .
> That successione is hardy, wyse and wycht. (386 ff.)

Dunbar cannot win: his 'curst kyn' (324) load him with infamy, but he himself brings shame upon his virtuous relatives:

> Thy kin that leivis may wary the and ban. (312)

But Kennedy also seeks to destroy Dunbar's good name by more fantastic means. He deforms his surname into *Dewlbeir*, devising a strained etymology and a monstrous origin for his branch of the Dunbar family—a conjunction of a devil (*dewl* or *deill*) and a she-bear (*beir*) (259–60). Such a jocular use of etymology and genealogy was not new;[41] and Dunbar himself calls Kennedy 'feyindis gett' (244). But Kennedy develops the topic in remarkable detail, inventing for Dunbar a bizarre and much-extended family of devils, pagans, persecutors of saints, and tormentors of Christ. Pluto himself is his 'hede of kyn' (535), and a chamber is awaiting him in hell (392). With such diabolic kin, how can Dunbar himself be other than a fiend?

---

[40] *Lords and Men in Scotland: Bonds of Manrent 1442–1603* (Edinburgh, 1985), 76–7.
[41] On medieval jesting with names, see E. R. Curtius, *European Literature and the Latin Tradition* (1953), 499–500.

This leads logically to Kennedy's taunt, *tu es dyabolus* (544), and the final consignment of Dunbar to hell:

> Spynk, sink with stynk *ad Tertara termagorum*. (552)

This is more forceful than Dunbar's last line:

> Rottin crok, dirtin dok—cry cok, or I sall quell the. (248)

One intriguing question posed by Dunbar and Kennedy's *Flyting* is whether it was ever 'performed', as if it were a dramatic spectacle. Scholars commonly speak of flyting as a 'court entertainment';[42] and a live audience would certainly enhance the pride of victory and the shame of defeat. But the evidence for some kind of public performance is scanty, and hardly conclusive. It chiefly concerns *The Flyting of Montgomerie and Polwart*, but might be interpreted as casting retrospective light on that between Dunbar and Kennedy. Allusions in the poems of Montgomerie, Polwart, and James VI suggest that verse flyting was carried on in public, on winter nights, in the presence of one's opponent and the king. Polwart jeers that he humiliated Montgomerie,

> As the last nicht did weill appeir,
> Quhill thow stuld fidging at the fyre ....[43]

Montgomerie and Polwart repeatedly refer in this way to the royal fireplace or chimney nook—as a place of special privilege, something to contend for or be banished from:

> Hellis ruik, with thy buik, leif the nuik,
> I command the![44]

Dunbar speaks of Kennedy's woebegone plight, 'now in winter' (118); and Kennedy interrupts his flyting with a direct appeal to James IV:

> Hye souverane lorde, lat nevir this synfull sot
> Do schame fra hame unto your nacioun. (481–2)

There is English evidence that associates mockery with feasting;[45] and the bard in Holland's *Howlat* threatens to 'ryme' those present at the feast unless they reward him (807).

Yet extant verse flytings are clearly too intricate to have been

---

[42] Reiss, 54; Lyall, 'Complaint, Satire and Invective', 45; G. Stevenson, in *Poems of Alexander Montgomerie: Supplementary Volume* (STS, 1910), xxv, calls it 'a contribution to the court amusements'.

[43] Montgomerie, *Poems*, ed. Stevenson, 144.

[44] Ibid. 184, and see Bawcutt, 'Flyting', 11–12.

[45] Udall notes the custom at English feasts of having some jesting fellow 'that maye scoff and iest vpon the geastes, as they sitten at the table'; see C. R. Baskervill, *The Elizabethan Jig* (Chicago, 1929), 22.

improvised. The poets, what is more, often call attention to their written nature: Lindsay, when addressing James V, says '3our ragment I haif *red*', and Kennedy both refers to Dunbar's 'skaldit skrowis [scrolls, writings]' (26) and speaks of sending him 'this cedull', or formal letter (48). When Kennedy wishes to refute a point, he sounds as if he were perusing a written document:

> Quhare thou writis Densemen dryit apon the rattis ... (355)

Invectives presumably first circulated by passing from hand to hand. But the usual method of getting publicity for written documents of any kind was to fix them in a place where they would be seen by many passers-by. Most commonly this was the door of a church, but in 1418 verses abusing the mayor of Cambridge were attached to his own gate; they too were characterized, in the terms employed by Kennedy, as a 'schedule' and a 'scrowe'.[46] In Scotland, in June 1452, a letter attacking the king and his privy council, describing the latter as traitors, was placed on the door of Parliament House.[47] The university debates, known as 'Quodlibet disputations', were sometimes a vehicle for personal antagonisms, and on one occasion a 'contumacious' scholar fixed a defamatory libel to the door of the new school at St Andrews. Life at this time was very communal; and, even though literacy was increasing, there were still many unable to read. Most important announcements would be both written and declaimed aloud: excommunications and cursings were read in church; denunciations, banishments, and proclamations of various kinds were made at the Market Cross—Buchanan thus speaks of a 'cartell' being both 'putt one the Mercat Croce of Edinburgh' and read aloud there.[48]

The Flyting between Dunbar and Kennedy is likely to have originated as separate invectives that circulated in manuscript among a small group of their intimates but undoubtedly reached a wider audience by some of the means just mentioned. Perhaps it may also, 'at least in its final form, have been recited before the king as a stylized duel in verse';[49] if so, it would be akin to the 'Quodlibet disputation' included in the entertainments for a royal visit to St Andrews in December 1508.[50] Yet the fact that *The Flyting* reached print in Dunbar's lifetime suggests that its appeal was not confined to courtiers or clerics.

---

[46] See R. M. Wilson, *The Lost Literature of Medieval England* (1952; 2nd edn. 1970), 191–4, and 194–5 (verses on the mayor). See also D. Gray, 'Rough Music', 31.
[47] Cf. N. Macdougall, *James III* (Edinburgh, 1982), 25.
[48] Cited by *DOST*, *cartell*, from *An Indictment of Mary Queen of Scots*, dated 1568.
[49] Kinsley, 284.
[50] See *Acta Facultatis Artium Sanctiandree*, ed. A. I. Dunlop (SHS, ser. 3. 54–5, 1964), cxxvi, cxxxv, and 132.

FLYTING

Whether or not *The Flyting* was performed, it is certainly quasi-dramatic. Imaginatively, it captures the effect of street-flyting or angry talk. This is particularly true of Dunbar's section of the work. It abounds in references to his own speech—'I cry the doun' (31)—and that of his interlocutor—'Thou speiris, dastard, gif I dar with the fecht' (65). He issues insulting commands, 'cry mercy' (184), 'cry grace' (235), and the last 'cry cok' (248). He fills *The Flyting* with the strident voices of other people, such as 'karlingis' (136) and fishwives (231), and incorporates snatches of what they say—

> All Karrik cryis, God gif this dowsy be drownd! (158)

It is full of noise of many kinds: from the 'clynk' of the town's warning bell (16) to the cry of a goose (159), the '3oule' of an owl (236), and the mocking 'bae and bleit' (204) of Kennedy's pursuers. This rises to a climax in the scene in which Kennedy is ejected from Edinburgh, dogs barking and citizens hurling abuse:

> Than carlingis cryis, Keip curches in the merk—
> Our gallowis gaipis—lo! quhair ane greceles gais!
> Ane uthir sayis, I se him want ane sark—
> I reid 3ow, cummer, tak in 3our lynning clais.
> Than rynis thow doun the gait with gild of boyis
> And all the toun tykis hingand in thy heilis;
> Of laidis and lownis thair rysis sic ane noyis
> Quhill runsyis rynis away with cairt and quheilis,
> And caiger aviris castis baith coillis and creilis
> For rerd of the and rattling of thy butis;
> Fische wyvis cryis, Fy! and castis doun skillis and skeilis,
> Sum claschis the, sum cloddis the on the cutis. (221–32)

The scene is one of near-anarchy, but above all of 'noyis' and 'gild' (clamour); dogs, fishwives, and even inanimate objects, like Kennedy's 'rattling' boots and the falling fish baskets and tubs (231), all contribute to the 'rough music'. In this effect Dunbar's alliteration plays a part, with the reiteration of the voiceless plosive /k/ in 'coillis and creilis', 'skillis and skeilis', and 'claschis ... cloddis ... cutis'. The incident constitutes a kind of charivari, a vivid expression of communal scorn and rejection. Dunbar enlists the community in his private quarrel—at one point switching significantly from the singular to the plural pronoun:

> We sall gar scale our sculis all the to scorne
> And stane the up the calsay quhair thow gais. (215–16)

The scene is uncomfortably close to a mob lynching.

Kennedy's *Flyting* is less noisy, but equally harsh. He speaks of Dunbar's noise as deafening—'thou devis the Devill thyne eme wyth dyn' (360). His stated objective is to 'put silence to' Dunbar (41, 254); this is not a peculiarly 'Gaelic idiom',[51] but a Scriptural one—Christ put the Sadducees to silence (Matthew 22: 34). He not only orders Dunbar to hold his tongue (359), but envisages its physical mutilation—either cropped (393) or devoured by ravens (374). Dunbar pictures the eviction of Kennedy from the urban community, but Kennedy goes much further. He expels Dunbar from Christendom—hell is the one place where he belongs, as 'induellar' (551), or rightful resident. Even if the overall effect of Kennedy's *Flyting* is somewhat long-winded, he none the less has the last word, and apparently reduces Dunbar to silence.

The literary antecedents of *The Flyting* have been much debated. Scholars have noted many analogues in earlier literature: the insulting verses and contests in abuse in Icelandic sagas, the *Edda* and Saxo Grammaticus; the Provençal *sirventes* and *tenso*; even 'Arabic slanging-matches on parallel themes'.[52] But these, though interesting, are extremely remote; it is unlikely that they were known to Dunbar and Kennedy. Far closer to hand, it is said, was the Gaelic poetic tradition. Kennedy came from Carrick, then a Gaelic-speaking area; and Dunbar repeatedly calls him a bard, mockingly associating flyting with 'Sic eloquence as thay in Erschry use' (107). Kinsley voices a common belief, when he says: 'the poetic mode of satire exemplified in the *Flyting* probably came into the Scottish court from Gaelic tradition before the time of Dunbar'.[53] Yet this view is remarkably difficult to substantiate. The power of early Irish poets to kill, maim, and blister the faces of their enemies was legendary—it was known to Shakespeare and many other sixteenth-century writers. But it is a legend that is curiously lacking in documentation. R. C. Elliott noted how few specimens of early Irish satire survive, and that most are 'incomprehensible'.[54] The evidence from medieval Scotland is even scantier. According to W. Gillies, although the Scottish *filidh* had a reputation for satire—the 'baird' in Holland's *Howlat* is a small testimony to this—none the less 'we do not possess many actual satires'. He also points out that, although there existed in Scottish Gaelic literature the notion of poetic combats, 'This did not become institutionalised as a literary genre in the way that flyting did in the Scots tradition'.[55]

The obsession with finding Gaelic antecedents for what is a striking

[51] Scott, 173, says it betrays his mind's 'Gaelic cast'.
[52] See Ross, 185, and J. M. Smith, *French Background of Middle Scots Literature* (1934), 51–7.
[53] Kinsley, 284; cf. Ross, 186.
[54] *The Power of Satire: Magic, Ritual, Art* (Princeton, 1960), 37.
[55] 'Gaelic: The Classical Tradition', in *The History of Scottish Literature, I: Origins to 1660*, ed. R. D. S. Jack (Aberdeen, 1988), 257.

phenomenon of Lowland Scots literature is often coupled with a failure even to mention the tradition of English invective and flyting, from the fourteenth century onwards: the poems of Lawrence Minot, for instance, and various anonymous pieces attacking the French, the Flemings, and also the Scots; attacks not only on groups but on hated individuals, such as the mayor of Cambridge, mentioned earlier, or the Duke of Suffolk (murdered in 1450)—'Now is the fox drevin to hole!'[56] Contemporary with Dunbar are the scurrilous lampoons on Henry VII's tax-gatherers, Empson and Dudley, preserved in *The Great Chronicle of London*.[57] Slightly later in time are the numerous invectives of Skelton, several of which are directed against the Scots. It is said that one of these works, *Against Garnesche* (c.1515), was modelled specifically on Scottish flytings; but the resemblances seem essentially generic.[58]

Dunbar and Kennedy received an education conducted largely in Latin. Kennedy's mother-tongue may have been Gaelic, but his extant verse is entirely in Scots, and mostly belongs to a learned, Latin tradition. In *The Flyting* he alludes to the *Eclogue* of Theodulus, a Latin poem then used as a school-text, which narrates the debate between Alithia, who represents the truth of Christianity, and Pseustis, who represents the falsehood of the pagans: Dunbar, damagingly, is said to be heir to 'false Eustase' (321–2).[59] Both poets would be familiar not only with such didactic debates but with a more popular tradition of Latin writing, that of invective. The notorious dispute between the Italian humanists, Poggio and Lorenzo Valla, was certainly known in Scotland, since it figures in *The Palice of Honour*:

> And Poggius stude with mony girne and grone
> On Laurence Valla spittand and cryand fy!   (1232–3)

Dunbar and Kennedy were as likely as Douglas to have known and relished this scurrilous quarrel. Even closer to them, in time and location, was the Anglo-French dispute (1489–90), conducted in Latin, between Robert Gaguin, the envoy of Charles VIII, and poets in the service of Henry VII—Bernard André, Giovanni Gigli, Pietro Carmeliano, and possibly Skelton.[60]

---

[56] Cf. Wilson, *Lost Literature*, 187–208; D. Gray, 'Rough Music', 30 ff.
[57] Ed. A. H. Thomas and I. D. Thornley (1938), 344–7 and 352.
[58] Cf. G. Kratzmann, *Anglo-Scottish Literary Relations 1430–1550* (Cambridge, 1980), 153–6.
[59] See G. L. Hamilton, 'Theodulus: A Medieval Textbook', *MP* 7 (1909–10), 169–85; and R. P. H. Green, 'The Genesis of a Medieval Textbook ... Ecloga Theoduli', *Viator*, 13 (1982), 49–106.
[60] Skelton's 'Recule ageinst Gaguyne' (*Garland of Laurel*, 1187) is not extant, but other contributions to the quarrel survive; cf. H. L. R. Edwards, 'Robert Gaguin and the English Poets 1489–90', *MLR* 32 (1937), 430–4. On these writers, see P. G. Bietenholz, *Contemporaries of Erasmus* (Toronto, 1985–7).

Abusive verse of all types was remarkably prevalent in the Middle Ages, not only in Latin but in most European vernaculars. The literary range was wide, spanning sophisticated invective, at one extreme, and songs, oral jingles, and popular snatches of verse, at the other. Ethnic and cultural rivalries formed a persistent theme. Some of the earliest English and Scottish examples, which are mostly preserved by chroniclers, such as Langtoft, Fabyan, and Wyntoun, are associated with the War of Independence. At the siege of Berwick (1296) the Scots were reported to have sung a song taunting Edward I 'with his longe shankes'; and after victory at Bannockburn they jeered, 'Maydenes of Engelande sare may ye morne'.[61] Most of the English responses are equally anonymous, apart from Minot's mockery of a Scotsman after the English victory at Halidon Hill (1333):

> Rughfute riveling, now kindels thi care![62]

The same taunts and insults continued in use for centuries: references to the well-known legend of the *anglicus caudatus*, or tailed Englishman, were regularly countered by the notion of the 'rough-footed' Scot, with his primitive *riveling*, or shoe of hairy, untanned leather.[63] Both were familiar to Skelton, who engaged in a flyting with a Scot called Dundas: 'Dundas / This Scottish as / He rymes and railes / That Englishmen have tailes'.[64] Both are employed in a short Scottish poem, which is possibly contemporary with Dunbar and Kennedy's *Flyting*: in it the Englishman's gibe, 'Rocht-futtit Scot, quhat sayis thow?', is answered by the Scot's threat, 'Talyt tyk, haue at the now!'[65] Dunbar and Kennedy certainly drew upon this widely diffused tradition for some of their taunts. Dunbar mocks Kennedy's Gaelic manner of dress—'with thy polk breik and rilling' (145), and later, exactly like Minot, metaphorically reduces him to the 'rilling' itself (243). Kennedy insults Dunbar by associating him with the infamous cause of 'Edward Langschankis' (270) and the 'Inglise rumplis' (351), or tailed Englishmen. But the cultural divide in *The Flyting*, interestingly, is not between English and Scots, but between the Lowlander, with his English sympathies, and the Highlander, who claims to be the true Scot.

Dunbar and Kennedy were surely acquainted not with one single tradition of flyting but with many: quarrels between individuals as well

---

[61] Many of these are collected by Wilson, *Lost Literature*, 200–8.

[62] *Poems of Minot*, ed. J. Hall (Oxford, 1914), no. 2.

[63] See further, Bawcutt, 'Flyting', 15–17; and G. Neilson, *Caudatus Anglicus: A Medieval Slander* (Edinburgh, 1896).

[64] *Against Dundas*, 7–10.

[65] Printed by Bawcutt, 'A Miniature Anglo-Scottish Flyting', *N&Q* 233 (1988), 441–4.

as national groups; conducted in Scots and English, and possibly Latin and Gaelic; and encountered not only in polished verse but upon the lips of clerics and fishwives in the 'Hie Gait' of Edinburgh.

Other poems of Dunbar have an affinity with *The Flyting*, even though, strictly speaking, some—such as *The wardraipper of Venus boure* (K 29) and *O gracius princes* (K 30)—are better classed as petitions. Many are attacks on specific individuals, which are conducted in the third person, not, as in *The Flyting*, face to face. They are full of comic anger, yet their tone ranges considerably—from the jocular to the savage and ferocious. They demonstrate, on a smaller scale, the skills evident in the portrait of Kennedy. Dunbar is interested in people, though not in the manner of Chaucer and Henryson. He is concerned neither with fairness nor with complex, three-dimensional characterization. His art is that of the caricaturist—he draws vivid, biased, and grotesque sketches. In *The Flyting* and elsewhere Dunbar repeatedly draws attention to physical imperfections—that which is 'mismaid' (*Flyting*, 53) and 'misfassonit' (K 52C. 25). He has a keen eye for deformity, disease, mutilation, and small bodily blemishes, such as corns and chilblains—'wyrok, Knowll tais ... mowlis' (K 52C. 18–19). His choice of imagery often dehumanizes people; they are compared to objects that have unpleasant associations or are used for menial tasks—overflowing 'gutaris' (K 14. 99), a 'saffrone bag' (K 23. 171), or a 'jurdane' (chamber-pot) (K 27. 38). The animal imagery in these poems is no less reductive: people are compared to animals low in social esteem, the tyke, the mastiff, and the 'aver', or cart-horse; what is more, these animals are often, as in *The Tua Mariit Wemen and the Wedo*, clumsy, diseased, or in some way humiliated, a baited bull (K 26. 27) or a hobbled horse, 'hopschackellt ... aboin the kne' (K 28. 11–12).

Dunbar ridicules people's physical appearance; and sometimes, as in *The Flyting*, places them in a particularly undignified position, farting, vomiting, and defecating. The scatological element in his poetry requires a brief digression, since many readers have found it offensive. How should we view 'this coarse comedy, to which'—it is said—'Dunbar seems to have been addicted'?[66] We should, firstly, not exaggerate its quantity; 'addicted' implies that references to excretion form the staple of Dunbar's comic writing. In fact they occur in eight of his poems, and are prominent only in two, *The Flyting* and *The Turnament of the Sowtar and the Tailȝour*. We should also recognize that Dunbar was by no means alone in finding the body's excretory functions comic: countless parallels exist in medieval drama, the jest

---

[66] Kinsley, 341.

books, *facetiae*, fabliaux, and Chaucer's 'cherles tales'. Yet dirty jokes are hardly peculiar to the Middle Ages. Fluctuations in taste through the centuries have at times confined them to the oral medium and all-male company, but in the permissive climate of the late twentieth century we are hardly entitled to congratulate ourselves (as did some nineteenth-century editors) on higher moral standards or greater delicacy of expression. What seems most important is the manner and purpose of such excretory allusions. The jest books rapidly produce an effect of mindless and monotonous crudity; few would say this of *The Miller's Tale*.

One scholar, discussing the grotesque marginal drawings in some medieval manuscripts, suggests that they have a moral purpose: 'they concretize commonplace Christian views about sin and the Devil'.[67] Others have argued likewise that medieval writers 'did not hesitate to use what we should call "obscenity" to illustrate a moral point'.[68] This seems true of one only of Dunbar's poems, *The Dance* (K 52A). Here the ugly appearance and activities of the Seven Deadly Sins undoubtedly correspond to their 'fowll' significance (14). *The Dance*, however, is immediately followed by *The Turnament*, one of the 'dirtiest' of Dunbar's poems, and one in which moral significance is minimal. For Dunbar the chief purpose of scatology is to debase and to degrade. Complex human beings are reduced to their lowest bodily functions. In *Sir Jhon Sinclair begowthe to dance*, hips, legs, and feet all betray their owners when they try to dance; in Dunbar's poems hips often behave inappropriately, crying, talking and coughing (see K 23. 110 and 200; K 28. 18 and 38). What is a small ingredient in some poems, however, is very prominent indeed in *The Flyting*, as much in Kennedy's contribution as in Dunbar's. References to loose bowels join other taunts about lice and fleas; all are manifestations of dirt, disease, and poverty. Kennedy's first words are 'Dirtin Dunbar'; and Dunbar's last line reduces Kennedy to a 'dirtin dok'. The adjective *dirtin* referred not just to 'dirt', in its modern general sense, but to excrement. The tone is not 'festive' (in the Bakhtinian sense), but derisive; such words are as insulting as the later phrase, 'dirt in your teeth!'[69]

Dunbar's wittiest and most inventive use of scatology occurs in *The Abbot of Tungland* (K 54). Here the flying abbot, attacked by birds, defecates:

---

[67] K. P. Wentersdorf, 'The Symbolical Significance of Figurae Scatologicae in Gothic Manuscripts', in *Word, Picture and Spectacle*, ed. C. Davidson (Kalamazoo, 1984), 1–19.
[68] D. W. Robertson, *Preface to Chaucer* (Princeton, 1962), 20.
[69] See citations in *DOST*, *dirt*.

> For feir uncunnandly he cawkit
> Quhill all his pennis war drownd and drawkit;
> He maid a hundreth nolt all hawkit
> Beneth him with a spowt.   (101–4)

There are elements here of psychological truth and, in context, poetic justice; also a Rabelaisian exaggeration: 'a *hundreth* . . . with *a* [one] spowt'. But there seems a further joke, not usually noticed, in the selection of the word *hawkit*, used by Scottish farmers to describe cattle whose coat is 'covered with white spots and streaks'.[70] Dunbar has devised a small aetiological myth, of a type found in many cultures, to explain how cattle came to look like this. He is writing in the same comic spirit as the unknown Scottish poet who described how a giantess 'spittit Loch Lomond with hir lippis' and 'pischit the mekle watter of Forth'.[71]

Many of these poems, like *The Flyting*, openly name names—Norny, Mure, Dog, Donald Owyr. But others produce a similar impression of attacking specific individuals, even though no names occur. *Complane I wald wist I quhome till* (K 45) at first seems a general complaint on the injustices of court life. It opens with a pell-mell catalogue of rogues; these prosper at the expense of nobles and men of learning, on whose behalf the poet claims to speak. But the most memorable passage occurs later, and is a portrait of one man. The focus narrows from the crowd of 'churllis, cuming of cart fillaris' (25) to a prelate, who is equally low-born. The point of view also shifts, from that of 'nobillis' and 'men off vertew and cuning' (10–11), in the plural, to that of 'the lerit sone off erll or lord' (41), presumably an impoverished younger son. It is through his eyes that we see the 'odius ignorance' of this upstart:

> Sa far above him set at tabell
> That wont was for to muk the stabell—
> Ane pykthank in a prelottis clais
> With his wavill feit and wirrok tais,
> With hoppir hippis and henches narrow
> And bausy handis to beir a barrow;
> With lut schulderis and luttard bak
> Quhilk natur maid to beir a pak;
> With gredy mynd and glaschane gane,
> Mell-hedit lyk ane mortar stane.   (51–60)

This is rancorous, but vivid. The prelate is as ugly and physically deformed as the 'mismad' mandrakes (21) mentioned earlier—he has bowed shoulders and bunioned toes. He is out of place in the

---

[70] See *DOST, hawkit*, and *OED, hawked*, a.2.
[71] *The Crying of ane Play*, in Mackenzie, 170–4.

aristocratic world, an impostor, 'Fenȝeing the feris [manners] off ane lord' (61). His physique reveals the class to which he belongs, and in which Nature placed him. Images from the farmyard—like the hopper to which his protuberant hips are compared—reinforce the notion of a man fit only for such low tasks as mucking out a stable or carrying a hand-barrow. In later dialect *mell-hedit* is applied to stupid people, like 'blockhead' today; Dunbar implies the cleric's stupidity as well as his large, oddly shaped head, resembling the hollowed stone used as a mortar for grinding herbs or barley. The figure may be imaginary, a type of the social climber for whom disdain was often voiced. Dunbar's language finds an interesting parallel in a comment, recorded by Pitscottie on James III's unworthy counsellors: they were better fitted 'to haue haldin the pleugh . . . or mokit cloissittis'.[72] Yet at the poem's end Dunbar avows personal knowledge of the cleric's iniquity—'I stand ford [guarantee it]' (62)—just as he identifies himself very closely with the 'auld servandis' (69), for whom he implores the king's favour.

Schir I complane of injuris (K 26) is an attack on a poet, apparently called Mure and otherwise unknown; his crimes include plagiarism and the addition to Dunbar's own 'indyting' of inferior 'versis of his awin hand wryting' (16). One phrase—'sen he ples with me to pleid' (5)—suggests that Mure himself engaged in flyting with Dunbar, but if so no trace of it survives. This poem testifies to Dunbar's pride in his own art (above, p. 34), but its form has received little discussion. Addressed to the king, it is a special kind of petition—a bill of complaint, itemizing grievances for which the refrain asks redress in a highly formulaic way:

> ȝour grace beseik I of remeid.

It was common for those in authority to receive such supplications. In 1483, for instance, the Hammermen made a complaint to the Edinburgh council, beseeching 'remeid of the greit injuris and skaythis done to thame'.[73] Dunbar contemptuously terms the other poet 'A refing sonne of rakyng Muris' (2), which might be rendered 'One of vagabond Mure's plundering sons'. He here speaks of Mure rather as if he were a Border reiver—a splendid vernacular excommunication, dated 1525, gives some idea of contemporary attitudes to the 'traitouris reyffaris theyffis murderizaris and men slayaris duelland within the sowth partis of this reaulme'.[74] Dunbar charges Mure not only with

---

[72] *The Historie and Cronicles of Scotland*, ed. Æ. J. G. Mackay (STS, 1899), i. 181.

[73] *Extracts from the Records of the Burgh of Edinburgh I: 1403–1528*, ed. J. D. Marwick (SBRS, 1869), 47.

[74] *St Andrews Formulare*, ed. G. Donaldson and C. Macrae (Stair Soc. 7, 1942), no. 229.

'refing' but with metaphorical murder, and with actual slander and treason. 'Lesing-making', or the utterance of calumnious sayings about the king or his 'lords, barons and other lieges', was the subject of repeated legislation in the fifteenth and sixteenth centuries; it was a crime that could be punished with the loss of life and goods.[75] Dunbar indeed envisages death as a possible punishment (12), and also speaks of public denunciation—'I sall him knawin mak hyne to Calis [Calais]' (6). But he finally urges the king to give Mure the dress and insignia of a fool:

> That ladis may bait him lyk a buill:
> For that to me war sum remeid. (27–8)

The language is extremely forceful. Dunbar claims that Mure has 'magellit' his own poetry (3), and later says:

> That fulle dismemberit hes my meter
> And poysonid it with strang salpeter,
> With rycht defamows speiche off lordis
> Quhilk with my collouris all discordis. (8–11)

Maggill was a verb with brutal senses: 'to hack, maim, mutilate'. It described corpses on a battlefield, or victims being tortured: 'Everie hour ... thay gaif him thre crewall straikis with ane dirk ... and maggillit him with threttie straikis'.[76] *Dismemberit* and *poysonid* were also most common in literal senses, and used of offences against the person. The vague notion of poison is intensified by the mention of *salpeter*, which does more than furnish a comic rhyme for *meter*. Saltpetre, or potassium nitrate, does not figure here because it was a preservative or 'was used medicinally'.[77] In Scotland at this time its chief uses were in alchemy and the making of gunpowder. It has an unpleasant taste, and in the Bible is a type of bitterness (Proverbs 25: 20). An English moralist, contemporary with Dunbar, used it similarly as a figure for malicious speech, and coupled it with arsenic as deadly poison—'Speke of salpeter arsnek or ony poyson mortall'.[78] Mure's speech 'discordis' with Dunbar's own 'collouris': saltpetre is certainly discordant with the notion of fine writing voiced in *The Goldyn Targe* (69, 263, 265)—sweet, 'suggurit', and 'mellifluate'.

The violence of Dunbar's language suggests wrath and indignation, and it has often been said that his tone 'is not that of one who jests'.[79] Yet the mood of this poem is difficult to gauge, particularly as we do

---

[75] Cf. Macdougall, *James III*, 279–80; and *DOST*, *lesing* and *lesing-makar*.
[76] Cited by *DOST*, *maggill*.
[77] So Small, iii. 293; Mackenzie, 197; Kinsley, 300.
[78] See *The Example of Euyll Tongues* (n.d., *STC* 10608), fol. A iiir.
[79] Baxter, 128; Reiss, 32.

not know either its precise cause or its consequences. It seems unlikely that Dunbar is literally asking the king to make Mure one of his fools. The poem itself is the punishment: it is what achieves the public humiliation of the other poet, making him 'knawin' (and known as a rogue and fool) not as far as Calais (the furthest extremity of England), but more cruelly and effectively, among his intimates, within the king's own 'palis'. Such public humiliation was Dunbar's declared aim in *The Flyting* also; there too, with similar comic hyperbole, he vowed to bring shame upon Kennedy and his allies,

> And throw all cuntreis and kinrikis thame proclame.   (24)

This poem seems to mix jest and earnest in the manner of *The Flyting*.

There is far less ambiguity about the tone of *The wardraipper of Venus boure* (K 29). Addressed to the queen, whom 'Venus' lightly compliments, it is a humorous complaint about the reluctance of her 'wardraipper', or officer of the wardrobe, 'To giff a doublett' to the poet. His name was James Dog, and this provided Dunbar not only with an irresistible pun but with the structure of his poem. It consists of a series of comic vignettes, in which Dog, when addressed, does not speak but 'barkis' (6) and 'girnis' (snarls) (10). One stanza pictures him 'wirriand ane hog' (7), or young sheep, another compares him to a tyke chasing cattle through a bog, and a third, climactically, identifies him with a mastiff:

> He is ane mastive, mekle of mycht,
> To keip ʒour wardroippe over nycht
> Fra the grytt Sowdane Gog ma Gog:
> Madam, ʒe heff a dangerous dog!   (17–20)

Because of its great size and ferocity the mastiff was considered a useful guard dog, but was not otherwise highly esteemed. Abraham Fleming, in his translation of John Caius' treatise on dogs, called it 'vaste, huge, stubborne, ougly and eager, of a heuy and burthensome body—terrible and frightfull to beholde'.[80] The mastiff was also known as a 'band-dog', from the chain or fetter used to restrain it; earlier in the poem Dunbar suggested that Dog needed 'ane havy clog' (11). A Dog of this size was a match not only for a courtier-poet (himself comically diminished to a 'hog') but for the 'Sowdane Gog ma Gog'; if so, he was perhaps indeed gigantic. Gogmagog (or Goemagot) was the name of a legendary British giant; but the term 'Sowdane' (a doublet of Sultan) suggests that Dunbar had in mind the

---

[80] *Of English Dogges* (1576); English Experience facs. 110 (1969), 25. J. Gilbert, *Hunting and Hunting Reserves in Medieval Scotland* (Edinburgh, 1979), 65 and 307, notes they were restrained by spiked collars and chains.

Saracen giants who often figure in medieval romance—one such, called 'Magog', is found in *Rauf Coilyear*.[81]

The poem is elegantly constructed. Stanzas two to four each open with a temporal clause, 'Quhen that I schawe ...', 'Quhen that I speik'; and each presents a scene in which the poet tries to ingratiate himself with a 'dangerous' Dog. *Dangerous* here has, in addition to its usual modern meaning, such senses as 'disobliging, unfriendly'. The syntactic pattern alters in the last two stanzas; each begins, 'He is ...', and the tone is one of confident assertion.

> He is ower mekle to be ȝour messan;
> Madam, I red ȝou get a less ane;
> His gang garris all ȝour chalmeris schog:
> Madam, ȝe heff a dangerous dog!   (21-4)

The canine imagery is sustained to the end: a *messan* was a small lapdog, and, contextually, a favourite. Dunbar implies that Dog is out of place in the feminine world of 'boure' and 'chalmeris', and too clumsy and bad-tempered to hold a position of privilege close to the queen. Dunbar's mastery of comic rhyme is particularly evident here: the name of his victim occurs in stressed final position at the end of each stanza, and each time it chimes with a different and usually damaging word, *clog, bog, Gog ma Gog.*

The wardraipper is immediately followed (in Maitland and Reidpeth) by *O gracious princes, guid and fair* (K 30). The link between the two poems has always been recognized: Maitland says of the first, 'Quod Dunbar of James Dog Kepair of the Quenis wardrop', and of the second, 'Quod Dunbar of the said James quhen he had plesett him'. But critics have paid little attention to *O gracious princes*, although it illustrates Dunbar's artistry in small things. It is less a sequel to *The wardraipper* than a comic palinode—a recantation, or 'singing again'. Dunbar once more addresses the queen, but retracts his previous criticism, adopting an ostensibly friendly tone towards Dog:

> In malice spack I nevir ane woord.   (6)

This second poem closely mirrors the form of the first; it has exactly the same number of lines, arranged in stanzas of the same pattern, and has a refrain that simultaneously alludes to the earlier one and contradicts it.

> Madam, ȝe heff ane dangerous dog

is replaced by

---

[81] On the name's varied significance, see *MED, gogmagog*, and Whiting, G 280.

> He is na dog; he is a lam.

The close relationship between the poems is evident also in the occasional echoing of phrases, such as 'to keip 3our wardrope' (10). But *O gracious princes* reverses the logical structure of *The wardraipper*, starting where the former poem ended—with advice to the queen—and ending where it began—with Dog's behaviour towards the poet. Both have altered:

> He hes sa weill doin me obey
> In till all thing, thairfoir I pray
> That nevir dolour mak him dram:
> He is na dog; he is a lam. (21–4)

The refrain is important; here, as in *The wardraipper*, an animal-image unifies the poem. Dunbar's technique is different, however—instead of richly embroidering the image, he allows its ironic implications to emerge without comment or amplification. It is just possible that 'he is a lam' makes a topical allusion, now lost to us. 'Lam', like 'Dog', was a common surname; indeed a 'James Lam' was a contemporary of Dunbar and Dog in the royal household, but his role—'of the pantry'—was lower in status, and comparison was perhaps insulting.[82] But this is not the primary point of the refrain. No reader could fail to be aware of the lamb's rich but multivalent significance—in religious iconography, fables, and proverb lore. At the poem's beginning the contrast with the large, 'dangerous' dog is all to the advantage of the lamb—a type of innocence, and proverbially meek and mild, 'tretable and benigne'.[83] But the lamb commonly symbolized not only Christ's innocence but his sacrifice; and in fables it was repeatedly a victim, unable to defend itself from more powerful animals. This implication becomes unmistakable in the latter half of the poem, in which Dog is depicted as feeble and in need of protection from his virago of a wife:

> The wyff that he had in his innis,
> That with the taingis wald braek his schinnis,
> I wald scho drownet war in a dam . . . (13–15)

The image of the lamb thus proves as damning as that of the dog. In this poem Dunbar's victim shrinks and dwindles, whereas in *The wardraipper*, although grotesque, he was an impressive and aggressive figure. His habitat likewise seems less colourful. In *The wardraipper* exotic figures like 'Venus' and the 'Sowdane' were comically juxta-

---

[82] He figures in entries close to those for James Dog; see *TA* i. 174, 193, and 231; ii. 52 and 308.
[83] For other uses by Dunbar, cf. K 4 and K 37. For the lamb's proverbial connotations, see Whiting, L 25–50, especially L 26, L 31–2.

posed with the midden and the bog. Here the milieu is domestic and rural, with a mill-dam, in which a shrew might well be ducked. Dunbar's poem is clearly an ironic compliment. But when he speaks of being Dog's friendly 'bruder' (3), the remark has some truth. The tone is that of brotherly 'ribbing' or joking among friends.

Sir Jhon Sinclair begowthe to dance (K 28) might be regarded as a group flyting. It makes fun of real persons, many of whom are named. There is no hint, however, that the poem was addressed to the queen, or—despite Maitland's colophon, 'Quod Dunbar of a dance in the quen[is] chalmer'—that she was present at the dance. The poem consists of a series of brief, malicious sketches of clumsy dancers, ludicrously lacking control of their limbs. The viewpoint, for the most part, is that of an amused onlooker; as the refrain comments,

> A mirrear dance mycht na man see.

We are reminded that this is a performance which has an audience by small asides, such as 'men tellis me' (26) and 'sum saed' (48); the fool too passes uncomplimentary remarks about a dignified official, 'the maister almaser' (19–20), and an unnamed bystander says, 'Tak up the Quenis knycht!' (6), when he has presumably fallen down. Yet we should not make too sharp a distinction between the dance and its audience. This is a court dance, in which the courtiers were presumably both participants and spectators.

This double vision, from the viewpoint of dancer as well as onlooker, is most strikingly evident in the poet himself. He appears in the third person, and then in the first:

> Than cam in Dunbar the mackar;
> On all the flure thair was nane frackar,
> . . . .
> Than cam in Maesteres Musgraeffe;
> Scho mycht heff lernit all the laeffe;
> Quhen I schau hir sa trimlye dance,
> Hir guid convoy and contenance,
> Than for hir saek I wissitt to be
> The grytast erle or duk in France . . . (22 ff.)

The device of including the poet himself in a sequence of comic portraits is not without precedent. There are parallels to Dunbar's self-mockery in the troubadours; a poem by Peire d'Alvernhe ridiculed poet after poet, and then said his own voice was like 'a frog singing in a well'.[84] What is striking here, however, is the syntactic discontinuity, which calls attention to this passage. Dunbar himself occupies the centre of the poem. He is agile—'nane frackar'—yet distinctly

---

[84] Cf. *Songs of the Troubadours*, trans. A. Bonner (1973), 77–8.

ludicrous, when he loses his slipper through over-energetic dancing. Mistress Musgrave embodies the ideal that the other dancers travesty: one of them had pretensions to teach the others (9), but only she 'mycht heff lernit all the laeffe'. The poem contains a clear compliment to this lady. Dunbar's half-jesting, half-romantic wish to be a French lord recalls the poem's opening, in which France itself is viewed, with a tinge of irony, as the source of all things new and fashionable.

The dancers may be ungainly, but the poem is put together ingeniously. It opens abruptly—'Sir Jhon Sinclair begowthe to dance'—yet *begowthe* implies that it is a beginning, of the dance as well as the poem. Stanza by stanza, each new performer is introduced by the same formal phrase, 'Than cam in'. Although presented as a series of individual turns, the dance is a group activity. Six dancers are mentioned—a point emphasized by 'fyve or sax' (43). Four are men, two women; but there is insufficient detail to indicate whether Dunbar is describing a specific dance, such as the morris or the base dance. In the seventh stanza the syntax alters:

> Quhen thair was cum in fyve or sax
> The Quenis Dog begowthe to rax,
> And of his band he maid a bred . . .   (43–5)

This last figure brings dance and poem to an ignominious end. He seems to interrupt the dance rather than to join it. He begins not to dance but to *rax*, or stretch himself after sleep. He is not the queen's knight, but her 'dog'—James Dog. Earlier dancers were compared to large, clumsy animals—a hobbled horse (12), or 'a stirk stackarand in the ry' (17)—but he *is* a dog, attempting to break away from his fetter, and moving like a mastiff (47). The word-play links this with the other poems on Dog, and suggests that all three were possibly composed at much the same time.

Dunbar may have found a model for *Sir Jhon Sinclair* in the burlesque dances that occur in other Scottish poems, notably *Colkelbie Sow* (309–467), *Peblis to the Play*, and *Christis Kirk on the Grene*.[85] The dances they describe are rustic, associated with village 'play' and festivity, and take place out of doors. The dancing is boisterous and unseemly, and there is much horseplay. In *Christis Kirk* one girl 'scornit Iok and scrippit at him / And morgeound him with mokkis' (21–2), and another high-leaping dancer 'hostit [coughed] at bayth the endis' (47). The diction is homely and alliterative, and popular

---

[85] None can be dated precisely, but their language suggests the late 15th century. See *Colkelbie Sow and the Talis of the Fyve Bestes*, ed. G. Kratzmann (New York, 1983); and *Maitland Folio*, nos. xliii and xlix. For an English example, see the dance that concludes *The Feast of Tottenham*, in *Ten Fifteenth-Century Comic Poems*, ed. M. Furrow (New York, 1985).

similes, often from the animal world, are used, to suggest the liveliness of the dancing:

> Ane ȝoung man stert in to that steid
> Als cant as ony colt. (*Peblis to the Play*, 51–2)

The viewpoint is not that of the participants but of 'an amused and superior onlooker'.[86] Peasants are trying vainly to imitate their social superiors or prestigious foreign models. In *Colkelbie Sow*, for instance, there is ridicule of the dancers' ignorance—they 'falit in futing' and later 'thay hard speik of men gud / And small thairof undirstud' (460–1); and in *Christis Kirk* the lute-player 'counterfutit France' (56). Dunbar's style resembles that of these poems, though his animal imagery is more original and more reductive. His tone is similarly derisive, but in this case it is courtiers, not peasants, who are viewed with amusement. In all these poems the dancers are ludicrous but not morally reprehensible. It has been suggested that Dunbar is here making a serious point, 'that sexual frenzy can reduce man to his baser self';[87] but I find no trace in the poem of such didacticism.

It is a pity that part of Maitland's colophon to another poem now regularly furnishes its title—*Ane Blak Moir* (K 33). Such advance information about the poem's theme largely destroys the ambiguities of its opening:

> Lang heff I maed of ladyes quhytt;
> Nou of ane blak I will indytt
> That landet furth of the last schippis;
> Quhou fain wald I descryve perfytt
> My ladye with the mekle lippis. (1–5)

The first two lines contain sharp antitheses: between Dunbar's practice in the past (*Lang* . . .) and his present purpose (*Nou*); between ladies in the plural and *ane* in particular; and, most pointedly, between *quhytt* and *blak*. Today we assume, from the start, that this contrast is one of race, and the assumption is, of course, borne out by the rest of the poem. But it should be remembered that this racial sense of *white* and its application chiefly to those of European stock was not common in Dunbar's time; *OED*'s first unambiguous use is dated 1604. In medieval English poetry *white* was a stock epithet for women, to be translated sometimes as 'fair-skinned'—'A wayle whyt as whalles

---

[86] A. H. Maclaine, 'The *Christis Kirk* Tradition: Its Evolution in Scots Poetry to Burns', *SSL* 2 (1964), 10. See also G. F. Jones, '"Christis Kirk", "Peblis to the Play" and the German Peasant-Brawl', *PMLA* 68 (1953), 1101–25.
[87] Ross, 208.

bone'[88]—sometimes more vaguely as 'beautiful'. When Henryson writes, in *The Thre Deid Pollis*, of 'ladeis quhyt, in claithis coruscant' (25), it is not to their race that he refers but their fragile beauty. (Dunbar's usage is similar in *The Tua Mariit Wemen and the Wedo*, 25, 28, 426, 499.) If *white* thus represented an ideal of fair-skinned beauty, *black* was applied to those who failed to fit the stereotype, those of any race, who were dark of skin and hair. The interesting medieval lyric that begins, 'Sum men sayon that y am blak', is not a poem about an African but a defence of brunettes.[89] The famous Agnes, Countess of March, was popularly known as 'blak Annas be ressone scho was blak skynnit'.[90] Dunbar's opening is blandly equivocal. His first readers may have been briefly uncertain whether he was about to describe a grand lady like 'blak Annas' or a 'blak moir'. Such uncertainties begin to be resolved in the third line, and by the fifth there is no doubt also as to the mockery.

Poems about ladies, even 'quhytt' ones, were not invariably complimentary. There existed a long tradition of describing ugly women, real or imaginary, some young but most old. Notorious Latin examples are found in Horace's coarse epodes VIII and XII and George Buchanan's cycle of poems about the prostitute Leonora. But a more appropriate context for Dunbar's poem is provided by medieval English verse: the ugly description of Dame Ragnell, or shorter pieces, such as Hoccleve's 'Of my lady wel me reiose I may', the anonymous 'O fresche floure, most plesant of pryse', and the verses once attributed to Chaucer, 'O mosy quince, hangyng by your stalke'.[91] These offer hideous catalogues of staring eyes, flat nose, wide mouth, yellow teeth, and figures shaped 'like a barelle' or a wine tun. Dunbar's piece, like several of these, has been termed a parody of the conventional eulogy of one's mistress.[92] But grotesque descriptions, even when they invite comparison (as Dunbar does) with the usual norms of beauty, are not necessarily parodic. In *Sir Gawain and the Green Knight* there is a carefully composed passage (943–69) in which the ugliness of Morgan le Fay is contrasted with the beauty of the castle's mistress—'vnlyke on to loke tho ladyes were' the poet, perhaps superfluously, tells us. Critics do not usually regard this as parody;

---

[88] *The Harley Lyrics*, ed. G. L. Brook (Manchester, 1948), no. 9; cf. B. Schmolke-Hasselmann, 'Middle English Lyrics and the French Tradition', in *The Spirit of the Court*, ed. G. Burgess and R. Taylor (Cambridge, 1985), 298–320.
[89] *SL*, no. 33.
[90] Pitscottie, quoted by R. Nicholson, *Scotland: The Later Middle Ages* (Edinburgh, 1974), 137.
[91] See *Dame Ragnell*, ed. L. Summer (Smith College Stud. 5, 1924); *SL*, no. 209; *Medieval English Love Lyrics*, ed T. Stemmler (Tübingen, 1970), no. 105.
[92] Utley, no. 161.

medieval rhetoricians would probably have classed it as *descriptio ad vituperium*. This is the mode to which Dunbar's poem belongs.

Dunbar's originality lies in choosing to describe a real black woman and in his attentive observation of her. The sketch is not flattering, but it is recognizable. The short English pieces mentioned earlier are feeble, metrically and descriptively; their portraits contain a random list of features, accompanied by a jumble of ugly but unrelated images. But Dunbar lavished care on this poem. Its five stanzas are neatly organized, largely in terms of *repetitio*, first on *Quhou*, which links the first and second stanzas; then on *Quhen* in the third, and on *Quhai* in the fourth and fifth. In the description there is similar art. Dunbar follows tradition in focusing chiefly on the face:

> Quhou schou is tute mowitt lyk ane aep
> And lyk a gangarell onto graep,
> And quhou hir schort catt nois up skippis,
> And quhou schou schynes lyk ony saep,
> My ladye with the mekle lippis.   (6–10)

The images are homely, sensuous, and visually precise. They interact effectively, reinforcing each other—the skin that gleams like oily black soap is later 'brycht as ane tar barrell' (12). The latter image is chosen primarily for its colour, yet hints also at the lady's ample figure. There is similar economy in the phrase 'schort catt nois'; it is instructive to contrast this with an earlier writer's clumsy attempt to ridicule not a female but a 'manly visage'—

> Youre forehed, mouth and nose so flatte,
> In short conclusyon, best lykened to an hare
> Of alle lyvyng thynges, saue only a catte.[93]

The purpose of Dunbar's three animal images—ape, toad (*gangarell*), and cat—is primarily descriptive, though we should recall that their symbolism is usually pejorative.

The first part of this poem contains a vignette that is unkind, but is neither coarse nor obscene. The tone changes in the last two stanzas, however, where the poem widens its scope, and ridicules those taking part in the Tournament of the Black Lady (see above, p. 54). Whoever wins, 'Sall kis and withe hir go in grippis' (18); but whoever is dishonoured in combat

> And tynis thair his knychtlie naem
> Sall cum behind and kis hir hippis.   (22–3)

This is derisive prediction—fantasy rather than fact. Dunbar is ridiculing the king himself (who jousted under the name of the Black

---

[93] *SL*, no. 208.

Knight) and his knights, and the conception of this tournament. But the insult to the black lady does not consist primarily in the coarseness of what is euphemistically termed 'the Misdirected Kiss'. In most instances of this theme, whether as a vulgar gibe—'Thy commissar Quintyne biddis the cum kis his ers' (*Flyting*, 131)—or as a folk-tale motif,[94] it is those who confer the kiss who are humiliated. In *The Miller's Tale* the joke is not at the expense of the beautiful and desirable Alison but of Absolon; indeed at its close Alison alone emerges unscathed. In one of the analogues to *The Miller's Tale*, a French fabliau, the misdirected kiss is the means by which a well-born lady punishes her 'vilain' husband, not just for his trickery but also for his cowardice. She jeers at him:

> J'ai non Berengier au lonc cul
> Qui à toz les coarz fait honte. (258–9)[95]

In Dunbar's poem the knights who will suffer the same indignity are likewise not simply defeated in battle, but disgraced—those who have received 'schaem' (21), the equivalent of *honte*, and lost their 'knychtlie naem'. What is far more offensive to the black woman, I think, is Dunbar's implication that to embrace her in a more orthodox fashion would be equally degrading to a knight.

The most polemical of Dunbar's flytings is *In vice most vicius he excellis* (K 34). It is closely involved with some of the most contentious issues of James IV's reign, the Lordship of the Isles and the uneasy relationship between the Lowlands and the Highlands. The gallows that in *The Flyting* furnished both poets with atmospheric similes here functions as literal reality (23). Alexander Myln, in an anecdote about Bishop Brown of Dunkeld, spoke casually of a Highlander 'dangling with beard unkempt on the gallows'; and after the 1494 rebellion many Highlanders were hanged in Edinburgh.[96] Dunbar's poem appears highly topical—'As in the ilis / Is *now* a preiff' (17–18)—yet it is not easy to ascertain the incident to which it alludes. The 'Donald Owyr' who is mentioned in line 19 is usually identified with Donald Dubh, bastard son of Angus Og. Angus's father John, fourth Lord of the Isles, had been forfeited in 1493; but between 1503 and 1506 there was a widespread rebellion, linked with an attempt to revive the

---

[94] Stith Thompson, *Motif-Index of Folk Literature* (Helsinki, 1955), K 1225.
[95] Printed in L. D. Benson and T. M. Anderson, *The Literary Context of Chaucer's Fabliaux: Texts and Translations* (New York, 1971), 10–25. This contains (70–1) a crude, later treatment, 'Old Hogyn's Adventure'.
[96] Cf. R. L. Mackie, *King James IV of Scotland* (Edinburgh, 1958), 198. See N. Macdougall, *James IV* (Edinburgh, 1989), 175–95; J. Bannerman, 'The Lordship of the Isles', in Brown, *Scottish Society*, 209–40; and J. Munro, 'The Lordship of the Isles', in *The Middle Ages in the Highlands* (Inverness, 1981), 33–5.

Lordship on Donald's behalf. According to modern historians, the revolt was crushed by October 1506; Donald was captured but not executed, and lived until 1545. The traditional identification of Dunbar's 'Donald Owyr' with Donald Dubh has not, however, been accepted by all scholars.[97] As the more candid historians admit, it is very difficult 'to put together a straight narrative' of events in the Highlands at this time, particularly those that concern the Lords of the Isles.[98] None the less, although other Highland risings occured during James IV's reign, the events of 1503–6 seem to have been the most serious challenge to his royal authority. What is more, Dunbar's acerbity towards 'The fell strong tratour Donald Owyr' implies that he was concerned not with some lesser Donald of the Isles (of whom there were several) but with the very focus of the revolt: 'Donald bastard and unlauchtfull sonne of umquhile Angus of the Ylis', for whose treasonable help and maintenance many Highland lords, such as Lauchlan Maclean and Torquil Macleod, were summoned to stand trial in Edinburgh.[99] The traditional identification, though not without problems, still seems the most plausible.

Dunbar's poem is far from being devoted solely to vilification of 'Donald Owyr', whose name occurs once, though in a central position, as a 'preiff' of his argument. The poem works at a high level of generality, opening with a sentenria and concluding with a proverb. Like Maitland's *Trason is the maist schamefull thing*, it is an attack on treason, or rather the figure of the traitor.[100] Where Dunbar differs from Maitland is in the sheer energy of his language. The diction of the first stanza is redolent of the lawcourts, learned and somewhat tautologous; but the metrical pattern squeezes the abstract nouns together, so that the sibilants hiss with contempt:

> In vice most vicius he excellis
> That with the vice of tressone mellis;
> Thocht he remissioun
> Haif for prodissioun,
> Schame and susspissioun
> Ay with him dwellis. (1–6)

---

[97] See Ross, 46 and 183; Nicholson, *Scotland: Later Middle Ages*, 545. The point at issue is whether 'Donald Owyr' is correctly identified with 'Donald Dubh' of the Gaelic sources and the 'Donald bastard' of the Acts of the Parliaments of Scotland (*APS*). *Owyr* is taken to represent Gaelic *odhar*, with the same sense as *dubh*, 'brown'. But the only references to a 'Donald Owyr', apart from Dunbar's, are dated 1494–7, and refer to an adult, clearly in favour with James IV; at that time the Donald of the 1503 rebellion was apparently a child (cf. Munro, 'Lordship of the Isles', 35).
[98] Munro, 'Lordship of the Isles', 23; Mackie, *James IV*, 188 ff.
[99] *APS* ii. 241; cited by Nicholson, *Scotland: Later Middle Ages*, 545.
[100] *Maitland Folio*, no. cxi.

The phrasing is often proverbial: 'Quha is a tratour or ane theif / Upoun himselff turnis the mischeif' (13-14).[101] The tone is one of intense moral indignation:

> God schawis the richt
> With soir vengence. (29-30)

When Henryson's Coppok similarly exclaimed, '3one wes ane verray vengeance from the heuin', she was compared to 'ane curate' (*Fables*, 530-1). Dunbar here speaks like a preacher or an Old Testament prophet.

There is no ridicule of Donald's physical appearance. The traitor is 'odious as ane owle' (7) and has a fox's 'kynd' (32), or nature, but both images are chosen for their adverse moral significance. The owl was regarded as *avis turpissima*, not only because it was ugly but because it shunned the light. According to a story in the fourteenth-century *Dialogus Creaturarum Moralizatus*, it was a type of the traitor. The owl conspired with other night birds to have lordship over all 'wild fowls', but was captured and brought before their true king, who—as in *The Thrissill and the Rois*—was the eagle:

he gaue this dredeful sentence agayne the traytowris, that euen forthwithe they shulde be drawyn through the cite and to be hangyd, and also that the owle and all her kynrede shulde haue perpetuall persecucyon, and be takyn for enymyes to all other byrdes, and to be banysshed from ther companye for euer.[102]

Dunbar does not develop this image, although there may be a subdued allusion to it in lines 27-8. The analogy between the traitor and the fox, however, dominates the last three stanzas, where affairs of state and the farmyard are juxtaposed in the manner of a beast fable. The fox's 'kynd', according to Henryson, is 'fen3eit, craftie and cawtelous' (*Fables*, 402). A traitor has the same propensity as the fox to cheat and dissemble. As long as a fox is alive, it poses a threat to hens; it is folly to grant to either fox or traitor a 'respyt' (33), or reprieve. The Scottish records, it should be noted, contain numerous such 'respitts' to Lauchlan Maclean and other Highland lords for various crimes, including their support of Donald Dubh.[103] Earlier in the poem Dunbar exulted in the failure of the risings; he also clearly opposes the policy of leniency towards the rebels.

Dunbar ends with an appeal to popular wisdom:

---

[101] Whiting, T 444 (from Ps. 7: 16).
[102] *The Dialogues of Creatures Moralysed*, ed. G. Kratzmann and E. Gee (Leiden, 1988), 180.
[103] *Register of the Privy Seal*, ed. M. Livingstone (Edinburgh, 1908), i, nos. 1083, 1163, 1174, 1197, 1203, and 1208. Cf. Nicholson, *Scotland: Later Middle Ages*, 569-70.

> The murtherer ay murthour mais,
> And evir quhill he be slane he slais;
> Wyvis thus makis mokkis.
> Spynnand on rokkis—
> Ay rynnis the fox
> Quhill he fute hais. (43–8)

The proverb 'So long runs the fox as he foot has' was later applied by John Knox to another 'crafty fox', the much-detested Cardinal Beaton.[104] Its sense seems to be that a villain will remain a villain until he dies. Dunbar argues, in effect, that foxes and traitors constitute a perpetual threat to good order, since their 'kynd' is unchanging. Implicit is the advice that the only method of dealing with both is to kill them.

It should be noted that the title by which this poem is usually known, *Epetaphe for Donald Oure*, is in accord neither with historical fact—Donald Dubh survived until 1545—nor with the poem's argument—that 'Donald' is still alive, but is better dead. Yet the title's appropriateness is rarely questioned; Baxter, one of the few to recognize the problem, suggested that 'the poet feigns that he is already writing Donald's epitaph'.[105] But the form of Dunbar's poem has little in common with contemporary epitaphs or mock-epitaphs: Skelton's treatise on 'two knaves somtyme of Dis', or this piece on Louis de Luxembourg, executed in 1475:

> Icy gist ce mechant et lourd
> Louis qui fut de Luxembourg,
> Le prodieur infame et faux...[106]

To call *In vice most vicius* an epitaph seems a misnomer. It originates in a colophon, 'quod Dunbar for donald ovre Epetaphe', found only in Bannatyne; the other witnesses, Maitland and Reidpeth, do not term the poem an epitaph. Here, as in other cases, Bannatyne seems to have misunderstood the poem's drift and misled later readers.[107]

Dunbar's tone has often been criticized. He has been accused, in a much-repeated passage, of being 'unnecessarily malignant towards one who had known no personal freedom save for the few years he was "out" against the Government'.[108] Considering how little is known of 'Donald Owyr', such a remark seems facile and over-romantic. In

---

[104] *History of the Reformation in Scotland*, ed. W. C. Dickinson (1949), i. 54–5; also Henryson, *Fables*, 827.
[105] Baxter, 141.
[106] Quoted in P. Champion, *Louis XI* (Paris, 1927), ii. 172. Cf. the verse epitaphs in *SL*, nos. 124 and 125.
[107] The poem seems to be a 'later addition'; see *Bannatyne Facsimile*, xi.
[108] Mackenzie, 211, is repeated by Scott, 262, and Kinsley, 309.

this poem Dunbar is not so much venting personal spite as voicing the received Lowland opinion of Highlanders: treacherous, thieving, and murderous; not domesticated (like hens), but wild (like foxes). Dunbar's contemporary, John Major, also distinguished between the two types of Scots, 'householding' and 'wild'. But the contrast can be traced back to the fourteenth century, to a well-known passage in Fordun, where Lowlanders are called 'domesticated and cultured, trustworthy, patient and urbane, decent in their attire, law-abiding and peaceful', but Highlanders are 'a wild and untamed people, rough and unbending, given to robbery ... comely in form, but unsightly in dress.[109] Dunbar, in this poem, accepts the stereotype, and does not subject it to analysis. His stance is strongly partisan, and is bound to provoke a hostile response from those, in any century, who take the opposite side (and express it no less forcefully). But Dunbar voices a legitimate viewpoint, that not only of the king and central government but of many ordinary 'householding' Scots, who felt themselves menaced by violent forays and raids, and desired, as parliament often stated, 'that the kingis lyeges may lif in quiete and peax'.[110]

[109] Cf. *Scottish Historical Documents*, ed. G. Donaldson (1970), 101–2; Nicholson, *Scotland: Later Middle Ages*, 206.
[110] *APS* ii. 228, cited by Munro, 'Lordship of the Isles', 33.

7
'Elrich Fantasyis'

THE term *eldritch* has been applied to a type or a tradition of comic writing. Referring specifically to Scottish poetry, C. S. Lewis used phrases like 'eldritch material' or 'eldritch humour', and spoke of 'the eldritch audacity which likes to play with ideas that would ordinarily excite fear or reverence'. A few years later Muriel Bradbrook placed *Dr Faustus* within a wider 'eldritch tradition' that she defined, in part, as 'horrific jesting'.[1] For Dunbar and his contemporaries the term *eldritch* principally indicated some supernatural phenomenon; the best modern equivalents are perhaps 'uncanny', 'weird', or 'spooky'. The word usually carried some implication of fear, as in Douglas's splendid line on the owl: 'Vgsum to heir was hir wild elrich screke' (Prol. 7. 108). Throughout the sixteenth century Scottish writers applied the word to 'browneis' and 'bogillis', to Pluto and the Cyclops and the 'weird sisteris', to angels and also elves, to the fairy queen and the desolate places inhabited by ghosts and demons.[2] Disapproving critics of Virgil, according to Douglas, found *Aeneid* VI pervaded by the 'elrich';

> Al is bot gaistis and elrich fantasyis,
> Of browneis and of bogillis ful this buke
> . . . .
> Lyke dremys or dotage in the monys cruke,
> Vayn superstitionys agaynst our richt beleve.   (Prol. 6. 17 ff.)

This passage nicely dramatizes the distrust felt by many Christians for unorthodox supernatural experience—'agaynst our richt beleve'— especially in the form of poetic fiction; and it combines this with a common-sense suspicion of dreams and 'fantasyis'.

I here apply the phrase 'elrich fantasyis' to a distinct and cohesive group of Dunbar's poems, the blackly comic dream-visions; but the term is also appropriate to other interesting yet neglected Scottish poems, some of which were almost certainly read by Dunbar. Two are attributed to poets of whom we know virtually nothing but their names—Lichtoun's *Dreme* and Rowll's *Cursing*. But most are anony-

---

[1] *English Literature in the Sixteenth Century* (Oxford, 1954), 71, 72-3; 'Marlowe's *Doctor Faustus* and the Eldritch Tradition', in *The Artist and Society in Shakespeare's England* (1982), 79-86.
[2] See *DOST*'s citations, s.v. *elrich*.

mous—*Fergus Gaist, The Crying of ane Play, Kynd Kittok, The Gyre Carling, King Berdok, The First Helandman,* and *Colkelbie Sow*.[3] Little is known definitely about the composition or date of these poems, but it is probable that they belong to the last decades of the fifteenth century or early years of the sixteenth. They seem popular in appeal, but not in origin. Metrically and linguistically inventive, they are the work of educated poets, some of whom were perhaps, like Dunbar, clerics. They should be distinguished from other comic Scottish poems, such as *The Freiris of Berwick* and *The Wife of Auchtermuchty*, which belong to a basically realistic mode and, despite comic exaggeration, deal with everyday life in a factual way. In the fantasies, however, although the setting is usually close to home—often in Fife or the Lothians—our sense of place is rapidly shattered. We are disorientated when familiar names are strangely coupled with remote or imaginary ones—'Peebles and Port Jaff' (*Dreme*, 33). We are transported to a dreamworld or an underworld, always to an otherworld.

In Lichtoun's *Dreme* the poet dreams that he is 'tane' by the 'king of farye' (6) and lost for seven years. Kittok finds an alehouse just outside the gates of heaven; her adventures start when she comes to 'ane elrich well' (8). Such magic wells are often found in folk-tales, and seem, in Scottish tradition, to function 'as the extreme limit of the known world'.[4] These poems are peopled with strange creatures: dwarfs, giants, elves, fairies, and demons. In one poem God and Saint Peter come to earth and take a walk in Argyle; in another the gyre carling, an ogress, marries Mahomet; and in a third the offspring of Fergus's ghost are Orpheus and queen 'Elpha'. Each of these poems narrates a series of bizarre events—'farleis' in the words of *The Dreme* (46) or a 'verray grit marvell', according to *Fergus Gaist* (2). They employ motifs from a remarkable variety of sources, from Arthurian romance to classical mythology, but their poets should not lose the credit for a vivid imagination. *The Dreme* pictures Enoch and Ely in paradise:

> Sittand on 3ule evin in ane fresch grene schaw
> Rostand straberries at ane fyre of snaw.   (41–2)

King Berdok lodges in summer in a cabbage 'stok', in winter in 'a cokkill schell' (6–8); and Kittok overtakes a newt, 'rydand on ane snaill' (10).

[3] These poems are most easily consulted in *The Bannatyne Manuscript*; for bibliographical information, see *Bannatyne Facsimile*, nos. 165, 168, 176, 182, 197, 199, 208, 230, and 401. Cf. Earl Guy, 'Some Comic and Burlesque Poems in Two Sixteenth-Century Manuscript Anthologies' (Ph.D. diss., Edinburgh, 1952).

[4] Cf. J. Wood, 'Lakes and Wells: Mediation Between the Real World and the Otherworld in Scottish Folklore', in Strauss and Drescher, 526.

'ELRICH FANTASYIS'

Most of these poems are included in Bannatyne's 'mirrie ballatis', and are undoubtedly humorous. Unlike some of the great ballads or *Sir Gawain and the Green Knight* they do not draw us far into an enchanted world, and invite us to suspend our disbelief. Lichtoun's *Dreme* voices the common-sense view: this 'fantasie' may spring from the consumption of too much ale. Although they are not strictly 'ballatis of unpossibiliteis'—a genre popular in Scotland that developed from the ancient topos of *adynata* or *impossibilia*—their comic method is similar: to pile up impossibilities, absurd juxtapositions and bizarre incongruities. In the *adynaton*, however, absurdity is purposeful, and in its late-medieval form anti-feminist.[5] But these fantasies delight in nonsense for its own sake. One is reminded of nursery rhymes, or, fleetingly, of Edward Lear. But we should not forget that there existed many medieval parallels: the marginal grotesques and *drôleries* in Gothic manuscripts, for instance, or humorous English poems, such as *The Land of Cokaygne* or a tale of 'marvels' that includes a church service conducted by fish, in which the salmon sings high mass and the herring is his clerk.[6] There is no doubt that some of the Scottish poems contain elements of parody or burlesque. *The Cursing* is a spoof-cursing upon those who stole five fat geese, 'With caponis henis and vthir fowlis' (14). *Fergus* is essentially a mock conjuration of a troublesome ghost—'With paternoster patter patter' (20). *The Gyre Carling* makes comic use of romance themes: its hero, who is strangely besotted with the monstrous ogress, bleeds not blood but 'ane quart of milk pottage', and besieges her tower with an army of moles—presumably they are good at tunnelling. *The First Helandman* makes a blasphemous allusion to Genesis, obscenely recalling the creation of Adam, the first man, from the dust of the earth. But such burlesque is mostly intermittent. With the exception of *Kittok* and *The First Helandman*, these poems ramble and drift in an inconsequential way. In the words of *Colkelbie Sow* they pile 'caisis upon caisis' (54), and we may well feel that their authors set out 'to bourd', but 'left it in a blondir' (46). What should also be stressed is their geniality; the humour is remarkably good-tempered. This is true not only of *Kittok* but also of *The First Helandman*; both play jocularly rather than caustically with stereotypes—woman as a drunkard, the Highlander as an incorrigible thief.

---

[5] For instances, see Bannatyne, fols. 155b, 249b, 265a, and 266a. On the figure of *adynaton*, see *American Journal of Philology*, 51 (1930), 32–41, and 86 (1965), 387–96; and cf. I. Linn, 'If all the Sky were Parchment', *PMLA* 53 (1938), 962–6.

[6] See L. M. C. Randall, *Images in the Margins of Gothic Manuscripts* (Berkeley, 1966); *Cokaygne*, in *Early Middle English Verse and Prose*, ed. J. A. W. Bennett and G. V. Smithers (2nd edn., Oxford, 1968); Greene, *Carols*, nos. 471–4; 'Herkyn to my tale' (*IMEV* 1116), in *Reliquiae Antiquae*, ed. T. Wright and J. O. Halliwell (1845), i. 81–6.

In the past several of these pieces were attributed to Dunbar, and included in editions of his poems. But there is no evidence that he wrote any of them—suggestions to this effect are sheer wishful thinking. Occasional similarities of phrasing are susceptible of several explanations; and any discussion of influence is impeded by the difficulty of dating all these poems, Dunbar's included. None the less I am sure that Dunbar was acquainted with some of these comic fantasies, or with others like them. A few were definitely circulating in his lifetime—*Kittok*, for instance, appeared in the early print that contains *The Tua Mariit Wemen and the Wedo*. What is more, there is evidence that he knew some version of *Colkelbie Sow*; he also refers to the 'Golk of Maryland', heroine of *King Berdok*, and mentions two poets by the name of 'Roull', one of whom is presumed to have been the author of *The Cursing*.[7] Dunbar shared the same imaginative heritage as these poets, and was at home in their strange world.

But Dunbar differs from them in two important respects. He is a dynamic poet, and his poems do not drift but drive onward, vigorously and purposefully, towards a climax, a disaster, or an epigrammatic 'point'. Whatever the absurdity, Dunbar seems in control; the eldritch is harnessed, and put to some purpose, though this is not always or primarily a moral one. But there is an even more striking difference. Dunbar's characteristic tone is not genial, but dark and sinister: we are told that God laughed 'his hairt sair' at Kittok's exploits and laughed also at the Highlander, but in Dunbar's poems the only laughter (apart from the poet's) is that of devils (K 52A. 29; K 56. 39). It is not faerie that predominates in his 'elrich fantasyis' but diablerie. (The closest parallel, in this respect, occurs in Rowll's *Cursing*.) Again and again in Dunbar 'the comic overlaps with the demoniac and the terrifying'.[8] There is a striking ambivalence in his response to the devil: the superficially flippant and irreverent tone of some poems coexists with a sombre and more fearful response. At the opening of *The Flyting* Dunbar threatens Kennedy with appalling consequences, and vows to raise the fiend—

> The erd sould trymbill, the firmament sould schaik,
> And all the air in vennaum suddane stink,
> And all the divillis of hell for redour quaik,
> To heir quhat I suld wryt with pen and ynk.   (9–12)

This is mock-apocalyptic, a vaunt far out of proportion to the ostensible subject. It is comic, yet has an intensity that derives from the very solemnity with which hell, damnation, and the devil were

---

[7] Cf. K 44. 65–6; K 13. 51; and K 62. 77–8. For discussion, see *Colkelbie Sow and the Talis of the Fyve Bestes*, ed. G. Kratzmann (New York, 1983), 3–5.

[8] Lewis, *English Literature*, 94.

spoken of on other occasions—and by Dunbar himself. No reader is disposed to laugh at the menacing figure of the devil in *Done is a battell*—dragon, cruel serpent, and 'auld kene tegir with his teith on char'.

Dunbar's ambivalence had deep and complex roots. He and his contemporaries combined intense interest in evil spirits with great uncertainty about their nature and mode of operation. At every level, learned and popular, they were supplied with abundant but conflicting information. When Robert Burton questioned, 'how far the power of spirits and devils doth extend', he drew much of his material from medieval philosophers and theologians.[9] At a more popular level the imagination was fed in a host of ways, visually and verbally: in wall paintings, sculptured capitals, or the woodcuts in prints of the *Ars Moriendi*, that showed fiends waiting by the bed to seize the soul of a dying man; and in sermons, saints' lives, such as *The Golden Legend*, or dramatic representations of the Fall of Lucifer and the Harrowing of Hell.[10] It is tantalizing to possess no more than the title of the *ludum de Bellyale*, performed in Aberdeen in 1471.[11] Devils were held to be incorporeal, yet could assume many forms. By the late-medieval period a demonic iconography had evolved that is still familiar today. Dunbar was not alone in speaking of 'devillis als blak as pik [pitch]' (K 56. 81)—blackness and deformity signified their spiritual ugliness. They were depicted with horns, and sometimes with feathers and wings—we should recall this when reading of the flying abbot of Tungland and the birds' belief that he might be 'the *hornit* howle' (K 54. 74). Devils could swell in size to giants, and shrink small enough to sit under a lettuce leaf. Devils could assume the shape of animals: Henryson gives the name 'Bawsy Broun' to a dog (*Fables*, 546), but Dunbar gives it to a fiend (K 52. 30). This produces a curiously double effect: it might seem reductive, yet it creates suspicion of everyday creatures; as the special sense of 'familiar' indicates, a devil might lurk in the shape of a domestic pet.

The multitudinousness of devils was stressed, along with their ubiquity. Picturesque similes were sought, in an effort to convey this. One medieval preacher said that they 'flye above in the eyer as thyke as motis in the sonne'. The same comparison was employed by Chaucer and Rowll, and Burton quoted learned authors to similar effect: 'the air is not so full of flies in summer as it is at all times of

---

[9] *The Anatomy of Melancholy*, ed. Holbrook Jackson (Everyman's Library, 1932), i. 180 ff.

[10] Late 15th-century French prints, such as *L'Art de bien mourir*, *Le Traicte des paines d'enfer et de purgatoire*, and *Le Traicte de l'advenement de l'antechrist*, were very popular, and versions were available in Scots and English.

[11] Mill, 117.

invisible devils'.¹² Dunbar writes within this tradition, when he speaks of devils 'Solistand ... as beis thik' (K 56. 82). The diabolic world bordered closely on that of ghosts and fairies, and also oddly paralleled that of the angelic hierarchies. Some believed that there existed nine orders of bad spirits, the first of which comprised the false gods of the Gentiles.¹³ Douglas thus equated Pluto with Satan, 'Prynce in that dolorous den of wo and pane' (Prol. 6. 151). Dunbar, however, in *The Goldyn Targe* (125), called Pluto an 'elrich incubus'. This seems to fuse god, demon, and fairy, recalling Pluto's rape of Proserpina as well as his medieval identification with the king of faerie. Although most devils were nameless, some acquired names and distinctive personalities. Rowll speaks of 'Devetinus the devill that maidd the dyce' (98), and his *Cursing* provides a useful compendium of the devil-lore likely to have been familiar to Dunbar. The 'Sanct Girnega' mentioned in *The Turnament* thus appears as a devil in *The Cursing* (95).¹⁴ Perhaps the most famous of medieval devils was Tutivillus, who figures in the Towneley Judgement play and *Mankind*, and is often depicted with a sack or in the act of writing, recording female gossip or evil speech of any kind.¹⁵ Kennedy included 'Tutivillus' among the clan of devilish relations that he devised for Dunbar at the end of *The Flyting* (513).

Plenty of medieval jokes exist about devils and hell. There is an excellent French fabliau about a minstrel who was carried to hell. One day he was left in charge of the damned souls and gambled them away in a game of dice with St Peter. Lucifer was so enraged that he threw the minstrel out—to heaven—and commanded his subordinates to bring no more minstrels and gamblers to hell. The tale ends: 'Now cheer up, all you minstrels, rogues, lechers and gamblers, for the one who lost those souls at dice has set you all free!'¹⁶ This is a specimen of a recurrent folk-joke: why are there no members of a given group (usually job or nationality) in hell? Why no weavers? Because the devils find their noise intolerable. Welshmen, for a similar reason, were

---

¹² See G. R. Owst, *Literature and Pulpit in Medieval England* (2nd edn., Oxford, 1961), 112; *Wife of Bath's Tale*, III. 868; *Cursing*, 106; *Anatomy of Melancholy*, i. 183 (cf. 188).
¹³ *Anatomy of Melancholy*, i. 187. But see 'The Ordering of the Bad Angels' in Aquinas, *Summa Theologica*, trans. by Fathers of the English Dominican Province (1922), I. cix.
¹⁴ Little is known of this figure, who perhaps survives in the rhyme 'Girnigo Gibbie, the cat's guid minnie'. *SND*, *Girnigo*, n. and adj.
¹⁵ See M. Jennings, 'Tutivillus: The Literary Career of the Recording Demon', *SP* 74 (1977), 1–95.
¹⁶ *Medieval Comic Tales*, trans. P. Rickard *et al.* (Cambridge, 1972), 19-25.

excluded from heaven.[17] A rather cryptic passage in *Fasternis Evin in Hell* (103 ff.) seems to allude to stories of this kind. Dunbar intends a double insult, I think, both in keeping minstrels out of hell—'For glemen thair wer haldin owt'—and consigning Highlanders, because of their ghastly yells, to its deepest abyss. Some saints' lives show reluctant admiration for the devil as a clever trickster, rather like the fox in beast fables. Devils were sometimes subtle and wily; at other times they dwindled into imps or the 'deblats' who attended upon the St Nicholas bishop;[18] or they degenerated into the clowns and buffoons who bluster and make coarse jokes in drama.[19] Medieval devils were by turns sinister and ridiculous, figures of fear and figures of fun. Hell itself was not immune from comic treatment. In Raoul de Houdenc's *Songe d'Enfer* the king of hell serves a ghastly banquet— the dishes are described with Gallic relish, and include the tongues of dishonest lawyers, fried 'en burre'. A similar infernal feast occurs in the anonymous and highly scurrilous *Salut d'Enfer*.[20] There is little likelihood that Dunbar knew either of these French poems, written in the thirteenth or early fourteenth century, yet they illustrate one of the traditions to which his *Fasternis Evin in Hell* belongs. Jean Frappier explained this pervasive late-medieval mockery as an unavowed means of escape from a real and otherwise almost unbearable fear: a defensive weapon against 'le terrorisme du Diable'. He drew a parallel with the behaviour of 'gens qui ont peur, la nuit, au coin d'un bois, et veulent se rassurer, cherchent à rendre leur crainte irréelle en plaisant, en prenant un petit ton guilleret, en se racontant des histoires drôles'.[21] Perhaps we should not seek one single explanation for such varied phenomena, nor find them astonishing. Black comedy is not confined to the Middle Ages, nor is it only children who enjoy what the Opies called 'ghoulism' and 'spookies'. The latent horror is what contributes a 'frisson' to many a joke.

Some of Dunbar's most potent comic imagery involves ghosts and evil spirits. The lover in *In secreit place* (K 13. 19) glowers and groans 'as ane gaist'. A striking passage in *The Flyting* (161–72) portrays Kennedy as a revivified corpse or revenant. Dunbar pretends to

[17] Cf. Stith Thompson, *Motif-Index of Folk Literature* (Helsinki, 1955), x. 251. 1; and *Medieval Comic Tales*, 55–6.
[18] See *DOST*, *deblat*, and Mill, 18.
[19] Cf. T. McAlindon, 'The Emergence of a Comic Type in Middle English Narrative: The Devil and Giant as Buffoon', *Anglia*, 81 (1963), 365–71.
[20] See *Le Songe d'enfer*, ed. P. Lebesgue (Paris, 1908; Geneva, 1974), 420 ff., and *Le Salut d'enfer*, in *Jongleurs et trouvères*, ed. A. Jubinal (Paris, 1835), 43–5, Cf. D. D. R. Owen, *The Vision of Hell: Infernal Journeys in Medieval French Literature* (Edinburgh, 1970), 158–61, 210–11.
[21] 'Châtiments infernaux et peur du diable', in *Histoire, mythe et symboles* (Geneva, 1976), 129–36.

exorcise him—'I conjure the, thow hungert heland gaist!'—and ends by comparing Kennedy to the 'spreit of Gy', the central figure in a popular ghost story, known all over Europe. The tale was highly didactic, purporting to give information about purgatory and the afterlife. Normally the ghost is invisible, manifesting itself only by speech and an uncanny sound, like that of a broom sweeping the pavement.[22] But Dunbar alludes to the ghost's appearance, which suggests that he may have seen some acted version. Lindsay claims, in *The Dreme* (16), to have amused the young James V by pretending to be 'the greislie gaist of gye'. In *The Tua Mariit Wemen and the Wedo* the Widow calls her last husband an 'evill spreit' (397), but earlier in the poem is a more extended development of the theme. The First Wife recalls her husband's love-making:

> Bot quhen that glowrand gaist grippis me about
> Than think I hiddowus Mahowne hes me in armes.
> Thair ma na sanyne me save fra that auld Sathane
> . . . . . .
> The luf blenkis of that bogill fra his blerde ene
> (As Bel3ebub had one me blent) abasit my spreit.   (100 ff.)

This husband is a shape-shifter: first a ghost, then different manifestations of the devil, lastly a 'bogill', whose amorous leers are alliteratively compared to those of Beelzebub. Dunbar implies the husband's ugliness and the wife's fear and repulsion; she speaks as if she were trying to ward off the embraces of an incubus. The eldritch and the comic are here deftly combined.

Several of Dunbar's poems are pervaded by diablerie: *This nycht in my sleip I wes agast* (K 56), *This nycht befoir the dawing cleir* (K 55), *The Abbot of Tungland* (K 54), *Lucina schynnyng in silence of the nicht* (K 53), and *Fasternis Evin in Hell* (K 52). All are bad dreams, or nightmares. A dream is an excellent frame for comic fantasy: the constraints of the waking world are absent, yet not totally abolished—they lurk on the margins of the experience. At the same time a dream's status is highly ambiguous; dreams provoked questions about their source, significance, and truth that were much discussed by writers in the Middle Ages. Some were aware of Macrobius's learned classification of different types of dream; still more were familiar with the complex Scriptural response, which included respect for the divine vision granted to St John, contempt for false, delusive dreams, and also the fearful words of Job: 'When I say, My bed shall comfort me . . . Then thou scarest me with dreams, and terrifiest me through visions' (7:

---

[22] Several English versions exist; two are printed in *Yorkshire Writers, Richard Rolle of Hampole*, ed. C. Horstman (1895–6), ii. 292–333.

13–14).[23] Doubts as to a dream's validity were commonly voiced by poets, including Dunbar:

> Thane thocht I thus, This is ane felloun phary,
> Or ellis my witt rycht woundrouslie dois varie;
> This seimes to me ane guidlie companie,
> And gif it be ane feindlie fantasie
> Defend me, Jhesu and his moder Marie! (K 51. 11–15)

Some dreams had spiritual significance, such as Dunbar's own vision of the Passion (K 3), but others might indeed be 'feindlie fantasie', or diabolic illusion. Pope Innocent III warned that dreams caused many to go astray, and Aquinas said that although demons could not directly sway man's reason they could incline his inferior faculties, such as imagination or the corporeal senses.[24] Other dreams might simply be nonsense—a common-sense attitude, voiced, somewhat ironically, by Douglas in Prologue 8: 'Thys was bot faynt [feigned] fantasy... Nevir word of verite' (175–6).

Despite some similarity of framework Dunbar's dream poems are characteristically varied. The prominence of the dreamer differs considerably: in *This nycht befoir the dawing cleir* he is at the centre of the poem; in *This nycht in my sleip I wes agast* he is marginal, simply an ironic spectator and recorder— his role curiously resembling that of Tutivillus. Our awareness of the poem as a dream also varies. It is strongly felt in *Fasternis Evin*, to which the solemn word *trance* is twice applied. In *Lucina schynnyng* phrases like 'ane dremyng and a fantesy' or 'my dreme it wes so nyce' direct us, very explicitly, to ponder how trustworthy this experience may be. But in *This nycht in my sleip I wes agast*, although opening lines imply that it is a dream, the dreamer almost fades from our consciousness, and at the end he is still apparently asleep. This is unusual, since most of Dunbar's dreams have abrupt, even explosive, endings. But the text of this poem poses many problems, and we should beware of finding deep significance in this failure to awake.

Criticism of *This nycht in my sleip I wes agast* has been scanty, and usually depreciative. It is often coupled with Dunbar's poem on Edinburgh (K 75), and regarded chiefly as a criticism of contemporary Scottish society. There is no doubt that the poem contains much social satire. Its form is that of a simple catalogue, each stanza being devoted to a single occupation; special attention is paid to the crafts, their corrupt practices, and the false claims they make for the quality

---

[23] Cf. A. C. Spearing, *Medieval Dream Poetry* (Cambridge, 1976), 1–16, and J. Le Goff, 'Le Christianisme et les rêves', in *L'Imaginaire médiéval* (Paris, 1985), 265–316.

[24] *De Miseria Condicionis Humanae*, ed. and trans. R. E. Lewis (Athens, Ga., 1978), 132–3; *Summa Theologica*, ed. cit. I. cxi.

of their wares. This is linked with an equally traditional and unifying theme: the misuse of oaths and asseverations. In sixteenth-century Scotland legislation was directed against such oaths; an Act of 1551 speaks of 'grevous and abominabill aithis, sweiring, execratiounis and blasphematioun of the name of God; sweirand in vane be his precius blude, body, passioun and woundis; Deuill stik, cummer, gor, roist or ryve thame'.[25] These same everyday oaths are uttered in Dunbar's poem: a minstrel exclaims, 'the Feind me *ryfe*' (61), and a gambler is heard to say, 'The Devill mot *stik* him with a knyfe / Bot he kest up fair syisis thre' (66–7). But such blasphemous references to God and the devil had long been of concern to preachers. Chaucer's Pardoner epitomizes medieval opinion on the subject:

> Gret sweryng is a thyng abhominable,
> And fals sweryng is yet more reprevable.
> . . . .
> But ydel sweryng is a cursednesse.[26]

Devotional writers were particularly appalled by casual references to God's body; an oath such as that of the courtier—'Be Chrystis windis [wounds] bludy and wyd' (12)—was regarded as a kind of second Crucifixion.[27] Preachers, long before Dunbar, singled out the market-place as the special haunt of such swearers. They also—in an effort to frighten them—told stories of terrible divine or diabolic retribution for swearing. One of these concerns a man whose favourite oath was 'the devel me adrenche'; it is no surprise to learn that he later fell into a ditch and was drowned.[28]

The figure of the devil is at the heart of Dunbar's poem. He is shown moving from one person to another, tempting and winning them to himself. The very refrain consists of his words, which shockingly invert the baptismal renunciation of the devil and all his works: 'Renunce thy God and cum to me'. The theme is very ancient. In the book of Job (1: 7) Satan goes to and fro in the earth, and in the New Testament Christians are warned that 'the devil, as a roaring lion, walketh about, seeking whom he may devour' (1 Peter 5: 8). In this poem the devil indeed walks about among men, seeking his prey; but he is no roaring lion nor a heroic figure like Milton's Satan. This is an intimate and familiar devil, passing 'throw the mercat' (4) and 'rownand', or whispering, in men's ears (84). The devil is said to be tempting men, but he rather appears to be listening gleefully as one after another damns himself: 'The Feind ressaif me gif I le' (23), or 'I

---

[25] Cited, more fully, by Baxter, 111.
[26] *CT* VI. 631 ff.
[27] Cf. Woolf, 395–400.
[28] Owst, *Literature and Pulpit*, 425.

gif me to the Feynd all fre' (28). The poem touches on the widespread fear that a moment's thoughtless oath might damn one forever. So in Webster's *White Devil* Lodovico envisaged poisoning his victim's tennis racket, 'That while he had been bandying at tennis / He might have sworn himself to hell' (v. i. 72–3). Almost every stanza divides into two sections, containing the words first of some human, then of the devil. But although two voices are heard it is not strictly a dialogue; the devil comments in mocking asides on what has just been said:

> Ane tail3our said, In all this toun
> Be thair ane better weilmaid goun
> I gif me to the Feynd all fre;
> Gramercy tel3our, said Mahoun,
> Renunce thy God and cum to me.
>
> Ane sowttar said, In gud effek,
> Nor I be hangit be the nek
> Gife bettir butis of leddir ma be;
> Fy, quod the Feynd, thow sairis of blek;
> Ga clenge the clene and cum to me.   (26–35)

Much of the pleasure of reading this poem derives from its execution of small variations upon a fixed pattern. We wonder what craft will come next, which oath will be uttered, and what will be the devil's riposte.

This nycht in my sleip I wes agast exists in two strikingly different versions, one containing thirteen stanzas, the other seventeen. There has been much discussion of the relationship between the texts, but no consensus has been reached.[29] Mackenzie preferred the shorter version, found in Maitland, calling it 'a self-contained little poem on a definite subject'; he argued that the fuller version, in Bannatyne, contains additions, made not by Dunbar but by his 'later admirers'. Baxter, however, considered that Bannatyne provided 'the only coherent text', and Kinsley similarly termed Bannatyne 'logical and well-ordered'. The differences between the two texts are so great that it would seem preferable, editorially, to print them both; certainly they should not be blended into a strange composite, as has been the practice of some editors—the poem thus has twenty-two stanzas in Mackenzie, eighteen in Schipper, and twenty-one in Small. Even in Kinsley's edition, for which Bannatyne provides the base-text, with Maitland's variants at the foot of the page, it is still difficult to appreciate the distinctive character of the two versions.

Yet these differences are often critically interesting. Maitland

---

[29] See Mackenzie, 238–9; Baxter, 111–12; Kinsley, 347–8. Reidpeth's text follows Maitland's closely.

regularly has *the* merchant, *the* tailor, etc., singling out socially representative figures in the same manner that Dunbar speaks of 'the campion' and 'the capitane' in *I that in heill wes*. But Bannatyne has the more indefinite phrasing—*ane* merchant, *ane* tailor. In the first stanza Maitland guides the reader's response to the oaths more explicitly than does Bannatyne, stressing their blasphemy:

> The commowne peiple bane and sueir,
> Blasfemiand Godis maiestie.

Bannatyne here has 'the peple', not 'the commowne peiple'; for most of its course the Maitland version seems directed specifically at the crafts. Only at the end appear two stanzas, on the thief and the courtier, which somewhat perfunctorily widen the indictment to all society. It seems true, on the whole, that the Bannatyne version is better structurally. The crafts, though prominent, are simply part of the busy throng likely to be found in any market. In Bannatyne the refrain occurs regularly instead of intermittently; and the use of the intimate form of the possessive—'*thy* God' rather than Maitland's '3*our* God'—is consistent with the usage elsewhere in both versions of the poem. Yet the Bannatyne version has defects. In one passage (46–60) the usual sardonic comment of the devil is missing. The Maitland text also often has more logical or wittier phrasing. The tailor's boast in Maitland—'Be thair ane better schappin gown' (12)—is grammatically preferable to Bannatyne's version, 'Be thair ane better weilmaid goun' (27). The devil's remark to the minstrel in Maitland—

> Exers that craft in all thy lyve
> Syn cum and play ane spring to me. (39–40)

is more amusing than Bannatyne's

> Exers that craft in all thy lyfe,
> Renunce thy God and cum to me. (64–5)

The two texts have different endings, yet each is effective. Maitland sums up:

> To bane and sweir na staittis stud a [had fear]
> Man or woman, grit or sma,
> Ryche and pwr nor the clargie.
> The dewill said than, Of commown la [law],
> All mensworne folk man cum to me.

The devil is personified as a wily lawyer; and the slight alteration of the refrain, as often in Dunbar, signals the poem's conclusion. Bannatyne has this stanza instead:

'ELRICH FANTASYIS'

> Me thocht the devillis als blak as pik
> Solistand wer as beis thik;
> Ay tempand folk with wayis sle,
> Rownand to Robene and to Dik,
> Renunce thy God and cum to me.

'Robene and ... Dik' seems the equivalent of modern 'Tom, Dick, and Harry'; it is more vivid than Maitland's similarly inclusive phrase, 'Man or woman, grit or sma'. This conclusion is startling, since the devil dissolves into a multitude of small devils—like a swarm of bees. The phrase 'me thocht' echoes the poem's opening lines (2 and 6); despite its conventionality it hints at the presence of the observing poet, who is absent from Maitland's conclusion.

Attempting to prove the superiority or the priority of one text of this poem to the other is clearly a difficult task. The hypothesis that I find most plausible is that Dunbar wrote a sardonic poem of this type, to which Bannatyne's version is probably the closer. But it seems likely that neither text represents Dunbar's original very faithfully; I suspect that his poem was so successful that it rapidly passed into the public domain, and was then reshaped fairly freely, as often happens with ballads or popular songs. It would be particularly easy to add or omit stanzas in a poem with this catalogue structure. The poem has some affinity with ballads. It brings together two folk-tale motifs, the rash or heedless oath—'the Feind ressaif me gif I le'—and the devil's visit to earth.[30] (Chaucer's *Friar's Tale* also combined these, though in a more subtle and complex form.) Long after Dunbar's time a similar theme was treated in the vulgar ballad. A. B. Friedman pointed out that 'A common seventeenth-century broadside, one which also made its way into the drolleries, was a satirical tale of the devil's ascent to earth and his encounter with a series of persons, usually the representatives of various occupations'.[31]

This nycht befoir the dawing cleir (K 55) also treats of an encounter between man and devil. Until fairly recently the poem was regarded as semi-autobiographical; Baxter, who devoted a whole chapter to its bearing on Dunbar's life, concluded that it showed him to have been 'a novice'—though not a friar—'of the Franciscan order'.[32] Yet there is no external evidence to support this; it is an inference from lines like these:

---

[30] Stith Thompson, *Motif-Index*, C. 12. 2 and C. 12. 5.
[31] *The Ballad Revival* (Chicago, 1931), 268. Cf. H. M. Belden, 'The Vulgar Ballad', *Sewanee Review*, 19 (1911), 220–1.
[32] Baxter, 26–40.

> In freiris weid full fairly haif I fleichit;
> In it haif I in pulpet gon and preichit
> In Derntoun kirk and eik in Canterberry. (36–8)

Today, despite the circumstantial local colour, this passage is regarded as fiction. A. G. Rigg challenged the use of the poem for 'biographical reconstruction', and demonstrated that there existed a medieval tradition of employing the self-incriminating confession to attack the venality and immorality of friars.[33] Dunbar's poem is now usually classified as satirical. Kinsley, who perceptively noted that its 'key symbol is the friar's habit', saw its leading theme as 'the falseness of the friars'.[34] *This nycht befoir the dawing cleir* is undoubtedly written within the long and flourishing tradition of anti-mendicant satire. Its identification of friar and devil is outrageous, yet familiar; it both recalls Chaucer's 'Freres and feendes been but lyte asonder',[35] and anticipates Faustus's command to Mephistophilis:

> Go and return an old Franciscan friar,
> That holy shape becomes a devil best.

Yet Dunbar's short poem makes no detailed or devastating indictment of the friars; to describe it as a 'satire' does not seem wholly adequate to the effect it produces in reading.

How does the poem work? The 'autobiographical' critics may have been mistaken in reading it too literally, but they testify, none the less, to the prominence of the poet-dreamer. The major interest lies in the relationship between the dreamer and his visitant, both of whom are exceedingly shifty figures, and in the enigmatic nature of the dream itself. In the hagiographic tradition—those same 'haly legendis' to which Dunbar himself draws attention (26)—dreams were a commonplace. Sometimes these concerned demons, who tempted or tormented the dreamer, and often assumed a fair-seeming shape. R. J. Lyall has discussed this type of vision, and noted that Rufino, one of St Francis's associates, was tempted by a devil in the guise of Christ.[36] But it was also common, especially, for men of great sanctity, to have visions of a very different kind. St Francis had several divine visitations, in one of which the painted image of Christ upon the cross spoke to him. In the tales and legends that multiplied after his death many miraculous apparitions of St Francis himself were narrated. Sometimes he came to convert the dreamers to a better way of life, sometimes to heal them from sickness, almost always to give instruc-

---

[33] 'William Dunbar: The "Fenyeit Freir"', *RES*, NS 14 (1963), 269–73.
[34] Kinsley, 346–7.
[35] *The Summoner's Tale*, III. 1674. Cf. A. Williams, 'Chaucer and the Friars', *Speculum*, 28 (1953), 499–513.
[36] 'Dunbar and the Franciscans', *MÆ* 46 (1977), 253–8.

tion. Thomas of Celano said: 'O how many did he admonish in dreams, ordering them what they were to do and forbidding what they were to avoid.'³⁷ Dunbar counts upon awareness of both types of dream, pious as well as demonic. At the outset we are uncertain as to the status either of his dream or of 'Sanct Francis'; only as it proceeds is the enigma resolved. As so often, Dunbar teases and puzzles his audience.

There is nothing inherently suspicious about the dream's beginning:

> This nycht befoir the dawing cleir
> Me thocht Sanct Francis did to me appeir
> With ane religious abbeit in his hand,
> And said, In this go cleith the my servand;
> Reffus the warld, for thow mon be a freir.   (1-5)

'Reffus the warld' is an appropriate command for a saint to utter. The poet's subsequent reluctance to assume the habit might be interpreted as human inadequacy, the response of a sinner unwilling to be saved. Franciscans told the story of a woman who was similarly recalcitrant:

> In the city of Narni was a woman who was a prey to a terrible frenzy ... At length blessed Francis appeared to her in a vision, saying 'Sign thyself with the cross', and on her answering, 'I cannot', the saint himself impressed the sign of the cross upon her, and drove out from her her madness and demoniacal fancies.³⁸

The diabolical nature of Dunbar's visitant is not exposed until the very last stanza:

> He vaneist away with stynk and fyrie smowk;
> With him me thocht all the hous end he towk,
> And I awoik as wy that wes in weir.   (48-50)

Discomfited devils traditionally left ruin in their wake. In a sermon, quoted by Owst, one similarly 'bare awey an ende of the howse'; and in a tale from the *Gesta Romanorum* two others 'bare away the hous rofe'.³⁹ Still closer to Dunbar are Hector Boece's tales of defeated demons, dated in 1486 and circumstantially located in Aberdeenshire: one flew away, accompanied by venomous odour and 'crak of fyre and reyk', and another carried off 'the bed and rufe of the hous'.⁴⁰

Dunbar's dreamer awakes, at the explosion, 'as wy that wes in weir'; *weir*, 'doubt, confusion', is appropriately the last word of a poem in

---

³⁷ *The Lives of St Francis of Assisi*, trans. A. G. F. Howell (1908), 48.
³⁸ Ibid. 134.
³⁹ *Literature and Pulpit*, 112; *Gesta Romanorum*, ed. S. J. Herrtage (EETS, ES 33, 1879), 421.
⁴⁰ *The Chronicles of Scotland*, trans. Bellenden, ed. R. W. Chambers and E. Batho (STS, 1938-41), i. 346-8.

which little is what it first appears. This Francis is but a pseudo-saint; the friar's habit is not a 'holy weid' (11) but a cover for 'gud cheir' (35) and an emblem of deceit; the call to a religious life is, paradoxically, a diabolic temptation; and the dream itself is a delusion. The poem is pervaded by the irony of false appearances. But much of the mockery is self-directed. In his *Daemonologie*, James VI said that, although the devil is permitted to assume the likeness of saints, God does not allow him 'so to deceive his own; but only such as first wilfully deceive themselves'.[41] This dreamer is a somewhat equivocal figure, who contradicts himself (at lines 24 and 35), and seems himself a pseudo-friar. In a comic touch he asks to be brought not the friar's habit but 'ane bischopis weid' (29), ostensibly because of bishops' greater sanctity; implicit is his desire for their higher status and wealth.

The poem is structurally neat. Its outer frame is the dream, its inner core a dialogue. The dream is briskly introduced, and ends equally rapidly. The last stanza is linked with the first by the repetition of some key words. The word *appeir* is clearly pejorative in

>This freir that did Sanct Francis thair appeir. (46)

In the light of this one notices the same word's ambiguity at its first occurrence:

>Me thocht Sanct Francis did to me appeir. (2)

Me thocht, with which Dunbar introduces most of his dream poems, is also neutral; only with hindsight does its ambiguity become suspicious. Within this frame is set the struggle for ascendancy between devil and man. The narrative has three stages, although this has unfortunately been obscured by the recent editorial practice of rearranging the sequence of stanzas.[42] The first is the most physical: the Franciscan habit is laid upon the bed, and the dreamer leaps away from it. Only in the second phase does the dreamer express his reluctance to become a friar in courteous but evasive speech. In the last stage this evasiveness is challenged by the visitant: 'All sircumstance put by and excusationis'. This is precisely what the dreamer now does; changing his tactics, he reveals first-hand knowledge of the friars.

>Als lang as I did beir the freiris style
>In me, God wait, wes mony wrink and wyle;
>In me wes falset with every wicht to flatter
>Quhilk mycht be flemit with na haly watter. (41–4)

---

[41] *Minor Prose Works of James VI*, ed. J. Craigie (STS, 1982), 3.
[42] See Bawcutt, 'Text and Context in Middle Scots Poetry', in Blanchot and Graf, *Actes*, 32–5.

It is this which defeats the devil. But why is this so? Was it the mention of God's name—a motif of many a folk-tale? Was it the reference to holy water, ritually used to exorcise evil spirits?[43] Neither seems sufficient. It is the dreamer's confession that forces the devil to show himself in his true form. Dunbar's poem is a wit-combat, with a structure resembling that of the riddle-poem *Diabolus et Virgo*, or the ballad *The Fause Knight upon the road*.[44] In all such pieces what is effective against the devil is bold argument and getting the last word.

It has long been accepted that this poem inspired George Buchanan's *Somnium* (*c*.1535); it possibly provided the first stimulus towards his series of anti-Franciscan poems that culminated in the *Franciscanus*. Buchanan said of the *Somnium* that he translated it from 'an old epigram written in the vernacular'—*epigramma vetus nostrate lingua scriptum in Latinos versus retuli*—and there is indeed a striking resemblance to *This nycht befoir the dawing cleir*.[45] Buchanan's forty-line poem is much the same length, and it too tells of a vision towards dawn (*sub auroram*), in which St Francis invites the dreamer to assume his habit and forsake the world:

> Et mihi subridens, 'Hanc protinus indue' dixit,
> 'Et mea dehinc mundi transfuga castra subi'. (9–10)

The rest of the poem consists of the dreamer's reply: he castigates the vices of the Franciscans, and his final topic develops a theme of Dunbar's, contrasting bishops with friars. Dunbar's

> Quhairfoir ga bring to me ane bischopis weid

is transferred from mid-position to the final epigrammatic riposte—

> At mihi da mitram, purpureamque togam.

Buchanan's poem is a free rehandling, not a close translation, of Dunbar's. Philip Ford has analysed some of the differences very interestingly, his object being 'to highlight Buchanan's poetic and satiric techniques'.[46] But comparison also throws light on Dunbar's poem. It lacks Buchanan's classical echoes (from Cicero, Lucan, and Martial) and his forceful rhetoric. Yet Dunbar tells a far better story—

---

[43] For parallels, see Stith Thompson, *Motif-Index*, G 303. 3. 1. 8; G 303. 16. 8; G 303. 16. 9; and G 303. 17. 2. 5. Cf. Whiting, D 208: To flee as the devil from holy water.

[44] *English and Scottish Popular Ballads*, ed. H. C. Sargent and G. L. Kittredge (Boston, Mass., 1904), nos. 1A and 3.

[45] See I. D. McFarlane, *George Buchanan* (1981), 52; also G. Neilson, 'The Franciscan: Some Footnotes', in *George Buchanan: Glasgow Quatercentenary Studies 1906* (Glasgow, 1907), 297–332.

[46] *George Buchanan, Prince of Poets* (Aberdeen, 1982), 48–54; this contains text and translation.

with mounting suspense as to its outcome, and lively dialogue. Buchanan's terse, one-line conclusion contrasts with the way Dunbar's poem ends—spread over a stanza, equally startling, but more complex. Dunbar's dreamer awakes in perplexity; Buchanan's dreamer is self-assured and plain-speaking, professing to bring out the truth from the beginning of his speech. Dunbar's dreamer is more compromised, and his poem is suffused with irony. There is a difference also in the poets' attitude to St Francis: Buchanan does not attempt, as Dunbar implicitly does, to distinguish between the true saint and the impostor. Dunbar's stance might be compared to that of Erasmus, who, in a letter to Charles Utenhove (1532), also recounted a vision of St Francis. In it the saint himself appeared—*nuper in somnis mihi post mediam noctem apparuit beatus Franciscus*—and thanked Erasmus for exposing the many vices of those who claimed to be his followers.[47] What Erasmus states explicitly, Dunbar lightly implies—the decline of the Franciscan order from its first principles.

Two of these poems concern a picturesque figure at James IV's court, John Damian. One has an unusually long title in Bannatyne, whose doggerel clumsiness seems to rule out Dunbar's authorship: 'Ane ballat of the fenʒeit freir of tungland / how he fell in the myre fleand to turkiland'. Damian was not a friar, but in 1504 became abbot of Tongland. I therefore prefer the title that the poem received in Asloan's contents-list: 'A ballat of the abbot of tungland'. Yet within the poem itself there is no such precise identification; the protagonist remains nameless throughout, in contrast with figures such as Mure, Dog, or Andro Kennedy. This lack of name does not seem accidental, but corresponds to his lack of a fixed identity: the unnamed 'he' slips through roles, or rather disguises, as easily as he passes through different countries. He is successively a 'waithman'—a term applied to outlaws—'a religious man', a 'leiche', a 'prelat', 'a new maid channoun', and an alchemist. This shape-shifting, like his vagrancy, is in keeping with his mysterious and diabolic origin: he is 'of Sathanis seid' (4), and comes from Tartary (5), land of the Tartars and commonly but erroneously associated with *Tartarus*, or hell. There is an interesting correlation also with the references to Damian in *The Treasurer's Accounts*, as 'leich', alchemist and 'new abbot' (see above, p. 56). Dunbar had no need to name names; he dropped hints, which (to judge from the titles given the poem) his audience picked up readily. Yet the absence both of a name and a location more specific than 'Scotland' (25) increases the potential for comic invention, and heightens the poem's universality. We shall never know the precise

---

[47] See *The Letters of Erasmus*, ed. P. S. Allen, x (1941), 79–83. Cf. J. A. Froude, *Life and Letters of Erasmus* (1894), 410–11.

relation of this tale to reality—far too much trust has been laid on Leslie's suspiciously varied accounts of the incident. Here, as so often, Dunbar is blending fact and fantasy.

The Abbot of Tungland has a clear-cut narrative structure, following the well-known pattern of the reversal of fortune, as line 95 briefly signals:

> And evir he cryit on Fortoun, Fy!

The first half of the poem outlines the abbot's picaresque career, which is largely successful, for him if not for his victims. Dunbar embroiders a common satirical theme—the greedy and incompetent doctor, who 'murdreist mony in medecyne' (30). Disaster comes when he turns alchemist, and fails to make the quintessence:

> And quhen he saw that nocht avail3eit
> A fedrem on he tuke
> And schupe in Turky for to fle;
> And quhen that he did mont on he
> All fowill ferleit quhat he sowld be
> . . . .
> The rukis him rent, the ravynis him druggit,
> The hudit crawis his hair furth ruggit:
> The hevin he micht not bruke.   (59 ff.)

The rise and fall in the abbot's fortunes are more than metaphor. He attempts to mount on high, and his downfall is equally literal—a tumble into a muddy pond, where he cowers panic-stricken among the ducks (119–20). The sense of comic retribution is strong; a rogue has come to the end which he long deserved and indeed feared—noted in the parenthetic 'dreid he had gottin that he desarvit' (23).

This poem has striking affinities with myth and folk-tale. Stories from many countries testify to the belief that flight is something forbidden—practised only by birds, spirits, and demons. Men who try to fly almost invariably come to disaster. Geoffrey of Monmouth tells how Bladud, father of King Lear, broke his neck in such an attempt.[48] Ranulph Higden tells a similar story of a monk, Oliver of Malmesbury, who attached feathers to his hands and feet, but fell after a short flight and was lame for ever after.[49] In the Stith Thompson classification of folk-tale motifs, attempts to fly are placed under the heading 'Overweening ambition is punished'.[50] Some unsuccessful flights are treated tragically, as in Virgil's handling of the legend of Daedalus and Icarus,

---

[48] *History of the Kings of Britain*, trans. L. Thorpe (1966), i. 10.
[49] *Polychronicon*, ed. H. C. Babington and J. R. Lumby (Rolls series, 1865–86), vii. 222.
[50] *Motif-Index*, L 421.

to which Dunbar refers (65). But mockery and derision are far more common.

Contemporary collections of jests include several tales about tricksters who announce to gullible crowds that they are going to fly. One is associated with the name of Scoggin:

> On a time Scoggin made the Frenchmen believe that he would fly into England, and did get him many goose-wings and tied them about his arms and legs, and went upon a high tower, and spread his arms abroad as though he would fly, and came down again, and said that all his feathers were not fit about him and that he would fly on the morrow ... On the morrow Scoggin got upon the tower and did shake his feathers, saying 'Go home, fools, go home. Trow you that I will break my neck for your pleasure?' ... There was a Frenchman had indignation at Scoggin, and he said, 'Tomorrow you shall see me fly to Paris'. And he got him wings, and went upon the tower, and spread his wings abroad, and would have flown, and fell down into the moat under the tower.[51]

This particular attempt to fly does not illustrate human daring and inventiveness, but folly and stupidity. Dunbar's poem is far funnier and his protagonist more depraved, yet embedded in it is a similar 'down to earth' view of man's capacities, which (with hindsight) we may find lacking in imagination. Yet Samuel Johnson displayed equal scepticism in his handling of the theme. In 'A Dissertation on the Art of Flying' (*Rasselas*, ch. 6), the Artist 'was every day more certain that he should leave vultures and eagles behind him'; but he ended, like Dunbar's abbot, in a lake, and 'the prince drew him to land, half-dead with terror and vexation'.

In Dunbar's poem there is one striking motif that is not present in most other versions; it is the birds who are responsible for the flight's failure. They take revenge for the invasion of their element, and expel the intruder. The abbot is not long allowed to go beyond man's earthbound limits—'the hevin he micht not bruke'. Drawing attention to his lack of identity, the birds wonder 'quhat he sowld be'. They learnedly speculate whether he might be the Minotaur or 'Martis blak smyth Vulcanus' (66–7). The flying abbot is as much a hybrid as the Minotaur, neither man nor bird; he assumes the 'fedrem', or feather coat, as earlier he had adopted the religious habit (11):

> The fowlis all at the fedrem dang
> As at a monster thame amang.   (109–10)

He resembles Vulcan both in his sooty labours at the alchemist's forge and in being thrown to earth from the heavens. There is poetic justice,

---

[51] See J. Wardroper, *Jest upon Jest: A Selection from the Jestbooks and Collections of Merry Tales* (1970), 93. For similar tricksters, see ibid. 82–3.

as critics have noted, in the way the punishment inflicted by the birds fits the abbot's crimes. The surgeon who let blood too freely (37) is now beaten 'with buffettis quhill he bled' (78); the man who 'full clenely carvit' his victims (21) is himself horribly mutilated; and, merciless in purging others (41 ff.), he now defecates from fear.

In this passage Dunbar also presents us with illustrations of *impossibilia*, or the 'World Upside-Down' topos. One disturbance of natural order is countered by another, or a reversal of what is assumed to be the normal relationship between birds and men. Birds attacking men are shown in some representations of the 'World Upside-Down', along with an ox cutting up a butcher or a fish eating a fisherman.[52] The poem derives some of its power from our response to such a reversal, the basic human fear of the sharp beaks of birds. Ross suggests that Dunbar was perhaps influenced by a much-illustrated passage in the Apocalypse (19: 17–21), in which an Angel summons the birds to destruction—'Come that ye may eat the flesh of kings . . . and of horses . . . and of all men'. Dunbar himself hints at another source:

> The myttane and Sanct Martynis fowle
> Wend he had bene the hornit howle;
> Thay set aupone him with a 30wle . . .   (73–5)

The mobbing of the owl by smaller birds also represents a reversal of accepted natural hierarchies.[53]

In this latter section of the poem Dunbar makes an original use of an ancient poetic topos, the catalogue of birds. The most famous medieval English example occurs in Chaucer's *Parliament of Fowls*, to which Dunbar clearly alludes in his characterization of the jay as scornful (97–8), and of the crows' 'cryis of cair' (115).[54] But Dunbar's reference to the owl and his highly alliterative style suggest that he also recalled Holland's *Buke of the Howlat*. This tells the fable of an owl who became discontented with his dull plumage, and was given a new 'fetherame'; but because of his pride the feathers were stripped from him by Nature's command. At least sixteen of Dunbar's birds also figure in Holland's witty catalogue of humanized birds (158 ff. and 313 ff.). What is more, an earlier passage in *The Abbot of Tungland* seems indebted to Holland's grotesque account of a fight between

---

[52] Cf. D. Kunzle, 'World Upside Down: The Iconography of a European Broadsheet Type', in *The Reversible World*, ed. B. Babcock (Ithaca, 1978), 39–94; P. Burke, *Popular Culture in Early Modern Europe* (1978), 188–9.

[53] Ross, 201–2; on 'the mobbing of the owl', see *The Owl and the Nightingale*, ed. E. G. Stanley (1960), 33 and 106.

[54] *Parliament of Fowls*, 346 and 363. For other uses of the topos, see Bawcutt, *Douglas*, 182–3.

two bird-fools and the rook-bard (820–6). The fools rush 'hiddy giddy' (hither and thither), and the bard is pulled about and begrimed, 'lyk a smaik smorit in a smedy' (a rascal smoke-blackened in a smithy). In his acount of the abbot's evil practices, Dunbar uses the same unusual compound, *hiddy giddy* (44), the same series of rhyme-words, and—literally rather than figuratively—a similar image of the alchemist, defiled 'For smowking of the smydy' (56).

Yet in most respects Dunbar is here very different from both Chaucer and Holland. His birds do not illustrate the variety and plenitude of Nature, as in *The Parliament of Fowls*, nor do they symbolize social classes and occupations, as in *The Howlat*. In this poem the emphasis is on the ferocity of the bird world. Although at least twenty-two are named, almost all are birds of prey; this is apt, since we are told in *Lucina schynnyng in silence of the nicht*, if not here, that the abbot's 'feddrame' was made from eagle feathers (23). Their song is not melodious, but a raucous series of 'ʒawmeris and ... ʒowlis' (122); and they engage in the violent activity characteristic of birds of prey. Dunbar's birds are warriors who have come to battle, and they are described in the phrasing of chivalric romance—'gaif him dynt for dynt' (76), or 'Als fers as fyre of flynt' (80), or 'The stork straik ay but stynt' (84). When the eagle strikes, Dunbar employs an alliterative formula favoured by Barbour—'rawcht him mony a rowt' (100).[55] The effect is mock-chivalric:

> Thik was the clud of kayis and crawis,
> . . . .
> That bikkrit at his berd with blawis
> In battell him abowt;
> Thay nybbillit him with noyis and cry ...   (89 ff.)

Again and again a single word, such as *berd* or *nybbillit*, reduces the scale and comically disrupts the military clichés.

The last scene is one of wild confusion: scattered feathers fly in the air; and the abbot lies 'at the plunge' (113), a term used elsewhere of diving birds, attacked by falcons, who immerse themselves in water.[56] He aspired, eagle-like, to fly on high, but now keeps company with ducks (119). The birds' strident cries awaken the dreamer, whose response is to 'curs that cankerit rowte' (127). Dream poems commonly end with bird-song; but the 'mirry' sound that wakes the dreamer in *The Thrissill and the Rois* is more typical than these 'hiddowis' shrieks. Why is the dreamer henceforth so hostile to the birds? 'Does part of him', so Ross suggests, 'secretly sympathize with

---

[55] See *Bruce*, ii. 423, and xii. 523.
[56] Cf. *Palice of Honour*, 1707. *Plunge* here means the act of diving, not—as it is often glossed—'deep pool'.

the would-be flyer?'[57] Such a generous response seems unlikely. The dreamer is more likely to have been angered because he failed to witness the tale's expected cruel climax; his dream is interrupted, rather than concluded, with the birds still threatening their victim and waiting to 'tak him in the tyde' (124). In *The Palice of Honour* the dreamer is equally annoyed, when told that he will not see the punishment of sinners—he 'desyris to se thair torment fane' (2059). Leslie, in his second account of the abbot's downfall, imputed a mixed response to the bystanders: they 'wist not quhither tha suld mair meine [lament] his dolour, or mervel of his dafrie . . . al war lyke to cleive of lauchtir'.[58] In Dunbar's poem there is a similar sense of the abbot's 'dafrie', but no hint of compassion for his 'dolour'; the response seems wholly derisive. If a further clue to the tone were needed, one should note that the jay 'skornit' the abbot 'as it was lyk [fitting]' (98).

One critic saw in this poem 'a retributive justice wholly in the manner of Dante', and considered that at its end 'order, both natural and divine', was reasserted.[59] The comparison to Dante seems out of place. This poem is a comic fantasy, and we should not seek in it profound significance. It is difficult to see the final cacophony as a serious reassertion of cosmic order. The poem's harsh justice seems closer to that of the fable, in which animal malefactors receive bloody heads or broken bones, or to that of the fabliau, in which rogues repeatedly end in ditches, dykes, and even less salubrious places.[60]

Lucina schynnyng in silence of the nicht is regularly treated as a companion to *The Abbot of Tungland*; yet in Bannatyne, the only manuscript to contain both poems, they are separated by many folios. Although they seem to have been sparked by the same incident, they are very different poems. In *The Abbot of Tungland* the dream element is minimal, serving chiefly to increase the scope for fantasy. In *Lucina schynnyng*, however, the nature of the dream and the dreamer's state of mind are both important. The two poems also differ in length and metrical form: *Lucina schynnyng* is only a third as long as *The Abbot of Tungland*, and has the same number of lines and stanza as *This nycht befoir the dawing cleir*. Within this short space Dunbar skilfully interweaves several poetic kinds—dream, complaint, petition, and mock-prophecy—and rouses varying expectations in his audience. The first two stanzas show the poet to be sleepless and unhappy:

---

[57] p. 200.
[58] *Historie of Scotland*, trans. Dalrymple, ed. E. G. Cody (STS. 1888–95), ii. 125.
[59] B. Hay, 'William Dunbar's Flying Abbot: Apocalypse Made to Order', *SSL* 11 (1973–4), 224–5.
[60] Cf. the end of *The Freiris of Berwick* (in Mackenzie, 195), where one friar ends in the mire, 'tap our taill'.

'With havy thocht I wes so soir opprest' (4). In the Middle Ages it was commonly love that kept poets awake, but this 'thocht' has other causes:

> Off Fortoun I complenit hevely
> That scho to me stude so contrariously. (6–7)

Dunbar here introduces a popular rhetorical topos, the Complaint of Fortune.[61] Medieval poets delighted to expatiate upon Fortune's inconstancy; Douglas, in *The Palice of Honour* (165–92), fills three stanzas with the stock antitheses—'Now wo, now weill, now firme, now friuolous'. But Dunbar does no more than allude to the theme, and passes rapidly to a vision of Fortune herself, who sternly addresses the dreamer 'with ane fremmit [unfriendly] cheir' (11). The most vivid earlier Scottish personification of Fortune occurs in *The Kingis Quair* (1105–55). But such an apparition, usually of a goddess or personified abstraction, who comes both to admonish and to comfort the dreamer, belongs to a very ancient tradition; it can be traced ultimately to Boethius's *Consolation of Philosophy*.

Dame Fortune's speech to the dreamer dominates *Lucina schynnyng*. It is a prediction, not a sermon, and contains in miniature several typical features of the medieval prophecy. A future event is said to depend upon the fulfilment of certain seemingly impossible signs, or 'taikinis' (20), which must be interpreted correctly. The dreamer's troubles will be 'at ane end' (19) only when an abbot flies in the air—

> He sall ascend as ane horreble grephoun;
> Him meit sall in the air ane scho dragoun;
> Thir terrible monsteris sall togidder thrist
> And in the cludis gett the Antechrist. (26–9)

Such bizarre events and such mysteriously symbolic creatures were the stuff of medieval prophecy, particularly of that type associated with Merlin and Thomas of Ercildoune, and first given currency by Geoffrey of Monmouth. Shakespeare's Glendower reputedly spoke likewise

> Of the dreamer Merlin and his prophecies,
> And of a dragon and a finless fish,
> A clip-winged griffin and a moulten raven...
> (*1 Henry IV*, III. i. 146–8)

Although Hotspur termed it 'skimble-skamble stuff', such prophecy was taken very seriously, not just by ignorant peasants but by kings

---

[61] Cf. H. R. Patch, *The Goddess Fortuna in Medieval Literature* (Cambridge, Mass., 1927); and F. P. Pickering, *Literature and the Arts in the Middle Ages* (1970), 206–22.

and their counsellors, in England and Scotland, well into the seventeenth century.[62]

Fortune's words are characteristic of the genre in their riddling and cryptic tone. What is more, her prophecy is apocalyptic, ending with a vision of Doomsday:

> And syne thay sall discend with reik and fyre
> And preiche in erth the Antechrystis impyre;
> Be than it salbe neir this warldis end. (36-8)

In his flight the abbot meets an eldritch company of witches, magicians, and evil spirits—Merlin was the reputed son of a devil; 'Mahoun' too was a pagan god and devil, and believed to have flown through the heavens on a winged horse; Simon Magus, according to the New Testament, was condemned for his traffic in holy things, but according to later legends he made an attempt to fly, aided by devils, and was dashed to the ground at the prayer of St Peter.[63] These figures are not chosen at random; they clearly offer parallels to various aspects of the abbot's nefarious career.

But it is the Antichrist who is the key figure in this poem. John Jewel, a Protestant, testifies to the enormous popular interest in the Antichrist, in the sixteenth century as throughout the Middle Ages, and to the amazing prophecies and 'fond tales' that circulated about what one Scottish writer called his 'curst procreacon, werst lyf, and most dampnable end':[64]

Some say he should be a Jew of the tribe of Dan; some, that he should be born in Babylon ... some, that Mahomet is Antichrist ... some, that he should be born of a friar and a nun; some, that he should continue but three years and a half ... and then should flee up into heaven, and fall down and break his neck.[65]

This attempt at flight was a central part of the Antichrist legend, and regarded as a blasphemous imitation of Christ: climbing the Mount of Olives he tries to ascend into heaven, and is killed, as Simon Magus had been. Such beliefs were partly founded upon Christ's own words, concerning the false Christs and prophets who would appear before his second coming at the end of the world (Matthew 24: 24). Antichrist

---

[62] See J. A. H. Murray's Introduction to *The Romance and Prophecies of Thomas of Erceldoune* (EETS, OS 61, 1875; 1973), and R. Taylor, *The Political Prophecy in England* (New York, 1911).

[63] Acts 8: 9-13, 18-24; *Acts of Peter and Paul*. Simon's fall was depicted by numerous artists, in manuscripts, frescos, and sculptures. Cf. J. A. W. Bennett, 'Dunbar's *Birth of Antichrist*, 31-2', *MÆ* 26 (1957), 196.

[64] See 'The Sex Werkdayis and Agis', *Asloan Manuscript*, i. 330.

[65] I owe this quotation to R. K. Emmerson's *Antichrist in the Middle Ages* (Seattle, 1981), 8.

was a pseudo-Christ, who would appear in human form at a climactic point in history, leading the forces of evil—he 'heads a body made up of pagans, unbelievers, false Christians, and all evil ecclesiastics'.[66] Writing of the Last Judgement, a Scottish contemporary of Dunbar's exclaimed, 'Greit taikin is the antechrist drawis neir', and said that his pursuivants, prophets, and preachers had already appeared.[67] In Dunbar's vision the abbot is unmistakably depicted as one of these harbingers of Antichrist, ready to preach his 'impyre' (37); and in his attempt to fly he joins Simon Magus as a diabolic prefiguration of Antichrist himself.

Yet despite the apocalyptic tone we do not take this prophecy seriously. What hangs upon its fulfilment is hardly momentous— neither the end of the world nor the fate of great kingdoms, merely the bestowal of a benefice (22). This is a spoof-prophecy, rendered comic by the triviality of its subject. It might be compared to the Enigma, or 'prophetical riddle' at the end of *Gargantua*, on which the Monk commented, 'it is in the style of the Prophet Merlin: make upon it as many grave allegories and glosses as you will ... for my part, I can conceive no other meaning to it, but a description of a set at tennis in dark and obscure terms'.[68] At the time of Rabelais, according to M. A. Screech, there was a taste for such 'amusing enigmas, which seem to be dealing with great matters but which turn out to be merely hidden ways of alluding to trivial, ordinary or obscene things'.[69] The mock-prophecy was closely akin to the mock-prognostication, for which there was also a vogue in the fifteenth and sixteenth centuries, especially in France. The most famous example of the kind was Rabelais' *Pantagrueline Prognostication* (1533), but it had many precursors.[70] The genre became popular in England, although the earliest surviving specimen is dated 1544; in Scotland also, at least in the later sixteenth century, there was a taste for 'Merry Prognostications'.[71]

At the end the dreamer awakes, and rejoices when he learns that an abbot is preparing to fly:

---

[66] Ibid. 20.
[67] *Contemplacioun of Synnaris*, 713–15; in *Devotional Pieces in Verse and Prose*, ed. J. A. W. Bennett (STS, 1955), 112.
[68] *Gargantua and Pantagruel*, trans. T. Urquhart (1921), i. 180.
[69] *Rabelais* (1979), 195.
[70] Ed. M. A. Screech *et al.* (Geneva, 1974). See Screech, op. cit. 195–200 and 195, and cf. Molinet's prose prognostications, in *Faictz et dictz*, ed. N. Dupire (SATF, 1936–9), ii. 888–914.
[71] See F. P. Wilson, 'Some English Mock-Prognostications', in his *Shakespearian and Other Studies* (Oxford, 1969), 251–84. For the Scottish evidence, see Gourlaw's Inventory, in *Bannatyne Miscellany II*, ed. D. Laing (Bannatyne Club, Edinburgh, 1836), 214, and M. A. Bald, 'Vernacular Books Imported into Scotland', *SHR* 23 (1926), 258.

'ELRICH FANTASYIS'

> Adew, quod I, My drery dayis ar done;
> Full weill I wist to me wald nevir cum thrift
> Quhill that twa monis wer sene up in the lift,
> Or quhill ane abbot flew aboif the mone.   (47–50)

But this ending is highly ambiguous. The presence of several moons in the sky was more commonly a portent of disaster than of 'thrift'. In *King John* (IV. ii. 186–7), when five moons are reported to have been seen, 'Old men and beldams . . . Do prophesy upon it dangerously'. Fortune is an unreliable goddess—Dunbar calls her a whore in *Quhome to sall I complene my wo* (K 63. 58). This dream is delusive, and the prophecy cheating. Dunbar's immediate audience would know that, whatever feats the abbot performed, he did not fly above the moon. If the dreamer feels 'confort' (46), he deludes himself, and he is still without his benefice. We should recall that serious prophecies were often intended to bring pressure upon a king or his counsellors. This poem makes fun both of the abbot and the poet himself, but it is also a veiled petition.

Lucina schynnyng is characteristic of Dunbar in its neat construction. Fortune's prophetic speech occupies a central block of six stanzas; it is preceded by two stanzas that constitute a prologue, and followed by two more that are devoted to the speech's effect upon the dreamer's mind. The sequence of bizarre events and grotesque images is designed to shock and puzzle, yet has an underlying logic. Many small details have a latent significance—the abbot ascends 'as ane horreble grephoun', because he is as much a monstrous hybrid as the griffin, half-eagle and half-lion. The verbal parallelism between two of Fortune's remarks—that the dreamer's 'truble' and the world are both near their end (19 and 38)—is comic, yet ominous. The poem's last word, *mone*, recalls the abbot's rendezvous at the moon with Merlin (33), but also circles back to the first line—

> Lucina schynnyng in silence of the nicht.

Critics have commented on the inapposite beauty of the poem's opening, but we should recall that Lucina, the moon, was a goddess as strange and unpredictable as Fortune, with whom Dunbar couples her in *The Goldyn Targe* (79). The moon was traditionally associated with sorcery and occult practices, and also with abnormal mental states—in *The Flyting* (53) Dunbar remarks that Kennedy is 'ilk mone' out of his mind. Despite the sky's brightness at the beginning, the poet longs for 'dayis licht' (5); there is an early hint that this moonlit dream is likely to be 'nyce' (41), or foolish, a specimen indeed of Douglas's 'dotage in the monys cruke'.

By far the most famous of Dunbar's diabolic visions is the poem that long received the title *The Dance of the Sevin Deidly Sinnis* (K 52).

'ELRICH FANTASYIS'

This combines one well-known theme, the allegorical description of the Seven Deadly Sins, with another that was equally rich and complex, the vision of hell.[72] The roots of this latter tradition have been traced both to accounts of the underworld by classical poets, such as Virgil, and to the Christian Apocrypha, particularly *The Apocalypse of St Peter* (*c.*135) and *The Apocalypse of St Paul* (whose oldest Latin version dates from the eighth century). It was these two works that were chiefly responsible for the horrific medieval notion of hell; they were enormously popular, and often translated into the vernaculars, and they influenced the depiction of hell found in later works, such as *The Vision of Tundal* and *St Patrick's Purgatory*. It is worth noting that the English version of *St Patrick's Purgatory* contained in the Auchinleck Manuscript is written, like Dunbar's poem, in tail-rhyme, though of the six-line type; it also displays a similar grim sarcasm, as in the reference to the 'ioie of helle' or the master fiend's invitation to Owein to join the dance:

> no haddestow neuer more meschaunce
> than thou schal haue in our daunce,
> when we schul play biginne.[73]

The seed for Dunbar's poem might lie in some such passing allusion to the 'dance' or 'play' of hell. But the motif of the evil soul being invited to dance with devils occurs elsewhere,[74] and the Auchinleck version of *St Patrick's Purgatory* has little else in common with *The Dance*. Dunbar here draws on popular and widely diffused notions of hell; his depiction is strikingly unlearned and unclassical. Unlike Henryson, in *Orpheus and Eurydice*, he makes no mention of figures like Cerberus, Ixion, or Tantalus. In his brief and suggestive way Dunbar evokes a shadowy location, from which emerge familiar details—smoke, flame, and scalding fire, and the notion of a deep pit or abyss (119).[75]

The torments are traditional, and one in particular has many parallels:

> Out of thair throttis thay schot on udder
> Hett moltin gold, me thocht a fudder,
> As fyreflawcht maist fervent;

---

[72] On the background, see M. W. Bloomfield, *The Seven Deadly Sins* (Michigan, 1952); D. D. R. Owen, *The Vision of Hell* (above, n. 20); E. J. Becker, *A Contribution to the Study of the Medieval Visions of Heaven and Hell* (Baltimore, 1899).
[73] Ed. E. Kölbing, *Englische Studien*, 1 (1887), 98–112; see stanzas 54 and 56.
[74] Cf. G. Bordman, *Motif-Index of the English Metrical Romances* (Helsinki, 1963), *E 752. 2. 1.
[75] The bottomless pit of Revelation (20: 1–3) was 'the common property of all mediaeval descriptions'. Cf. T. Spencer, 'Chaucer's Hell: A Study in Mediaeval Convention', *Speculum*, 2 (1927), 177–200.

'ELRICH FANTASYIS'

Ay as thay tomit thame of schot
Feyndis fild thame new up to the thrott
With gold of alkin prent. (61-6)

Force-feeding with molten metal was one of the stock torments of hell—Gluttony is also forced to lap hot lead (101)—but gold was peculiarly, as here, the punishment of the covetous. In one Flemish vision, Jehan de le Mote's *Voie d'Enfer et de Paradis*, the personified Avarice hopes to immure the dreamer's soul 'in a cellar, where sinners have molten gold poured down their throats'; a similar sight confronts the dreamer in Deguileville's *Pelerinage de l'Ame*.[76] Choking with boiling gold is still the usurer's punishment in Kyd's *The Spanish Tragedy* (I. i. 67) and Ford's *'Tis Pity She's a Whore* (III. vi. 8)—Dunbar includes 'ockeraris', or usurers, among the followers of 'Cuvatyce'. Henryson depicted 'Cresus' similarly in *Orpheus and Eurydice* (330), in what seems like a muddled memory of the legend of Crassus.[77] But Dunbar peculiarly intensifies the misery of the covetous by showing them as compelled not only to swallow the gold but to vomit it continually. Their cycle of torment is thus unending. The image is powerful and multivalent. The covetous, like all in this cruel dance, torture others as well as suffering themselves; and it also implies that covetousness is a moral disease. Most of the other Sins are deformed or diseased—the slothful are pathologically sleepy and 'slaw of feit' (76), the lecherous seem to be leprous, and the gluttons have huge 'wamis', or bellies.[78]

Dunbar's striking depiction of the Seven Deadly Sins rivals those of Langland and Spenser. He places the Sins, like Langland, in a penitential context: the vision is associated with 'Fasternis evin', or Shrove Tuesday, a time when Christians were about to acknowledge their sins in preparation for Lent; but these are unregenerate, 'schrewis that wer nevir schrevin' (7). In *Piers Plowman* (B V. 61 ff.) the setting is explicitly penitential; the sins are humanized, and the format is that of a series of confessions, made to the priest, Repentance. Comparison with Spenser's pageant of the Sins, in *The Faerie Queene* (I. iv), is more fruitful. Dunbar and Spenser inherited the same late-medieval iconographical traditions; both are often highly pictorial poets, and sometimes employ remarkably similar motifs. Spenser's Idleness is, like Dunbar's 'Sweirnes', or Sloth, 'still drownd in sleep'; in both spiritual languor is symbolized by physical slowness of movement, and is punished similarly. In Spenser Satan rode

---

[76] Owen, op. cit. 163 and 167.
[77] See Henryson, ed. Fox, 407-8.
[78] On 'the ubiquitous conception of sin as disease', cf. Bloomfield, op. cit. 111 and 232-3; on the association between lechery and leprosy, see ibid. 177 and 196.

>   with a smarting whip in hand,
> With which he forward lasht the laesie teme,
> So oft as *Slowth* still in the mire did stand.   (36)

In Dunbar it is Sloth's followers who are so lashed:

>   And Beliall with a brydill renʒie
>   Evir lascht thame on the lunʒie.   (74–5)

For both poets Gluttony is associated (though not identified) with one manifestation of the sin, drunkenness: in Spenser he bears 'a bouzing can' (22), in Dunbar

>   Him followit mony fowll drunckart
>   With can and collep, cop and quart.   (94–5)

The same expressive gesture is made by Spenser's Wrath:

>   And on his dagger still his hand he held   (33)

and Dunbar's Ire:

>   His hand wes ay upoun his knyfe.   (32)

Both poets are far more formal and symmetrical than Langland. Spenser regularly introduces the Sins with a similar phrase—'And by his side rode loathsome Gluttony', 'And next to him rode lustful Lechery'—and is equally formulaic in their dismissal. Dunbar is not so obviously schematic, yet he usually allots to each Sin one stanza, and observes the same basic pattern—first the sin, then its adherents, and the torments that they suffer. Spenser, however, is characteristically far more detailed and leisurely than Dunbar, devoting three stanzas to each Sin.

There are, not surprisingly, other differences of technique. Spenser, unlike Dunbar, often uses antique parallels—some details in his portrait of Gluttony evoke Bacchus or Silenus. They differ also in their use of animal symbolism. In Spenser the Sins are mounted on grotesquely symbolic 'brutall' beasts, but in Dunbar there are only occasional brief comparisons—Ire 'brandeist' like a bear (33), Sloth came 'lyk a sow out of a midding' (68), Lechery whinnied like a horse (80). These are apt similes, and some are highly traditional. In medieval didactic literature several members of the pig family symbolized sloth,[79] but the sow in particular was proverbially sleepy and sluttish. Other Scottish writers spoke of sinners as wallowing in sin, like a sow in a midden, or 'slepand in sleuth, as ony sow als sweir'.[80]

[79] See S. Wenzel, *The Sin of Sloth: Acedia in Medieval Thought and Literature* (Chapel Hill, NC, 1967), 106, and 140–1.
[80] See Whiting, S 539 and 541; S 966, 968, and 970; and Whiting, 'Scottish Proverbs', ii. 128.

'ELRICH FANTASYIS'

In *The Tua Mariit Wemen and the Wedo* (114) an old horse, signifies, as here, frustrated sexuality. Dunbar's choice of animal to symbolize libido may stem as much from inherited beliefs about the horse as from direct observation. It recalls, in particular, the diatribe against the lustful in Jeremiah (5: 8): 'They are become as amorous horses ... each one neighed after his neighbour's wife' (*Equi amatores ... facti sunt; unusquisque ad uxorem proximi sui hinniebat*).[81]

At the end the devil calls for 'a heland pad3ane'. Dunbar maliciously depicts Highlanders as half-devils, half-birds:

> Thae tarmegantis with tag and tatter
> Full lowd in Ersche begowth to clatter
> And rowp lyk revin and ruke.   (115-17)

The Scots knew of *Termagant* as the name for a mythical Saracen god—he appears, along with 'Mahoun', in *Rauf Coilyear* (850)—and in the plural the word commonly signified pagan idols or devils.[82] But Dunbar may here be making a punning reference to the *ptarmigan*, whose earliest recorded spellings (from the end of the sixteenth century) coincide with those of *termagant*.[83] The habitat of this bird is confined, appropriately, to the Scottish Highlands, and Dunbar's 'clatter and rowp' is not dissimilar to a modern naturalist's description of the ptarmigan's cry as 'a hoarse croak with a crackling note'.[84] This first image, of shrieking, birdlike devils, blends into the next one—the ravens and rooks, birds of prey that are equally raucous, and also ill-omened.[85]

Dunbar's poem is highly dynamic. The Sins do not form a static tableau; they are courtiers, commanded by the devil to perform both in a *gyis*, or masking, and a dance, whose modishness is stressed:

> He bad gallandis ga graith a gyis
> And kast up gamountis in the skyis
> That last came out of France.   (10-12)

This Dance of the Seven Sins is an original notion; there is no exact parallel, literary or pictorial.[86] The impression of a dance is strongest at the beginning, with Pride and his followers:

---

[81] Cf. Kinsley, 338-9; and V. A. Kolve, *Chaucer and the Imagery of Narrative* (1984), 237-48.
[82] See also Henryson, *Annunciation*, 68, and Kennedy, *Flyting*, 532.
[83] See the useful discussions of both words in *OED*.
[84] Cf. R. S. Fitter, *Guide to British Birds* (1952), 73-4.
[85] Ravens and rooks are paired in K 54. 70.
[86] J. Norman suggests a similarity to carvings in Roslin Chapel: 'Sources for the Grotesque in William Dunbar's "Dance of the Sevin Deidly Synnis"', *Scottish Studies*, 29 (1989), 55-75.

'ELRICH FANTASYIS'

> Mony prowd trumpour with him trippit—
> Throw skaldand fyre ay as thay skippit
> Thay gyrnd with hiddous granis. (22-4)

Trip, like *skip*, usually implies joyful dancing, as in Henryson's

> And all the trace he trippit on his tais;
> As he had hard ane pyper play he gais. (*Fables*, 2061-2)

But in this poem the context lends the two verbs ironic and painful connotations. Ire 'brandeist' like a bear (33). This economically suggests both the bellicose gestures of a man—Spenser's Wrath similarly 'brandisheth' a burning brand—and the lumbering movements of a performing bear. Bears in captivity, like these Sinners, performed 'dances' and were baited, or tormented. The impression of dancing seems weaker with Envy and Covetousness; but Sloth's followers are 'slaw of feit' in the dance, although the devils find painful means to make them 'quicker of coun3ie' (78). The word *coun3ie* has never been explained, but I take it to represent French *congé*, which in contemporary dance-manuals was equated with *branle*, a term for the final movement of the *basse daunce*.[87] All the Sins are engaged in action of some horrific kind, beating or tormenting one another. The dance is linear, and processional; the participants follow or lead one another, or—in a particularly suggestive phrase—are drawn 'furth in till a chen3ie' (73). Each Sin 'comes in', or enters the dance, in turn, like the real-life performers in *Sir Jhon Sinclair* (K 28). In both poems dancing represents a musical ideal that is travestied by the clumsy and ugly movements of the dancers. Music was regularly associated with heaven in medieval art and drama; but hell was a place without order or harmony.[88]

So far I have spoken of *The Dance*—as many critics do—as if it were a wholly independent poem. This is not so. It is associated with two other poems—*The Turnament of the Sowtar and the Tail3our* and *The Amendis to the Tel3ouris and Sowtaris*—to which Kinsley gave the collective title, *Fasternis Evin in Hell* (K 52).[89] In previous editions the poems have the same sequence as in Kinsley, but are numbered separately. All three are, in their different ways, skilful pieces of writing; they are clearly related to each other, yet the nature of the relationship poses problems for critics as well as editors. Should we

---

[87] Noted, for instance, in Robert Copland's *Maner of dauncynge of bace daunces after the use of Fraunce* (1521); cf. A. Michel, 'The Earliest Dance Manuals', *Medievalia et Humanistica*, 3 (1945), 129.

[88] Cf. J. Stevens, 'Music in Medieval Drama', *Proceedings of Royal Musical Association*, 84 (1957-8), 94-5; in hell there is *nullus ordo* (Job 10: 22).

[89] *The Turnament* and *The Amendis* are discussed separately, and more fully, above, 204 and 217-19.

regard them as one work or as three? The manuscripts that preserve the poems—the sole early testimony—implicitly give different answers to this question. Asloan contains only *The Turnament*, and there is no lacuna in this part of the manuscript to suggest that it was once accompanied by *The Dance* or *The Amendis*. Maitland preserves all three poems, not together, however, but in widely separate parts of the manuscript.[90] Bannatyne alone places the poems in the sequence that they have in most modern editions of Dunbar. We are entitled to wonder whether Bannatyne found the poems in this apparently orderly series, or whether he devised it himself. It was common for a long and complex work, particularly one composed of separable items, to be excerpted or anthologized; Bannatyne himself included three of the Prologues to Douglas's *Eneados*, and Asloan originally preserved a mere seven of Henryson's *Fables*. But the opposite procedure, of synthesizing poems into a new structure, seems far less common.[91] This is not the place for a full examination of the complex textual problems posed by these three poems. The balance of probabilities, however, suggests that Bannatyne has not imposed an orderly sequence upon them, but preserved an arrangement that corresponds to Dunbar's intentions. Yet it is still legitimate to consider how close is the interrelationship between the poems, and how far they form a structure which has, in Kinsley's words, 'essential unity'.[92]

The first two poems not only have much in common but are sharply contrasted with the third. *The Dance* and *The Turnament* are linked metrically and structurally. Both employ the same distinctive stanza—twelve-line tail-rhyme—and are enclosed within the same frame, the 'trance', mentioned in lines 3 and 223. This structural link is emphasized by the first line of *The Turnament*—'Nixt that a turnament wes tryid'—which uses the same connective word, *nixt*, employed earlier in *The Dance* (43, 55). They share the same location, hell, presided over by 'Mahoun'; and are informed by the same imaginative notion, a series of entertainments for 'Fasternis Evin'. (The date's symbolic significance has been discussed earlier, p. 70). To this *The Amendis* forms a striking contrast. Its metrical form is a quatrain, with refrain; and although it too is a dream, this is clearly a different one. Bannatyne, indeed, indicated both the identity of the first two poems and the separateness of *The Amendis*. *The Turnament* runs on from *The Dance* without a break, and its end is marked by a colophon: 'Heir endis the sowtar and tailȝouris war . . .'.[93] A rubric then marks the

---

[90] *Maitland Folio*, 12–16, 161–5, 317; see Kinsley's comment, 335.
[91] On the *Fables*' order and 'unity', see Henryson, ed. Fox, lxxv–lxxxi.
[92] p. 335.
[93] Fol. 112b. Bannatyne's Table of Contents also recognizes this unity: 'Off februar the xvtene nicht callit the turnament of the taillior and the the [*sic*] sowttar'.

beginning of a new poem: 'Followis the Amendis maid be him to the telʒouris and sowtaris for the turnament maid on thame'. This new vision is not located in hell, makes no reference to 'Fasternis Evin', and does not have a narrative structure.

The Amendis makes excellent sense as an autonomous poem, but is much enhanced by following *The Turnament*. Their relationship is analogous to that between *The wardraipper of Venus boure* (K 29) and *O gracius princes, guid and fair* (K 30): in each case an overt insult is followed by a mock-apology, and in each case the poems are related but distinct. Whether Dunbar intended, from the beginning, that *The Amendis* should be a sequel to *The Turnament* seems to me doubtful. Maitland's colophon to *The Amendis* gives it a rather different occasion: 'Quod Dunbar quhone he drank to the Dekynnis for amendis to the bodeis of thair craftis'. It is impossible to verify this assertion, yet the uncourtly and convivial setting of a craftsmen's feast suits this poem very well.[94] *The Turnament* is not the only poem in which Dunbar makes fun of tailors and soutars, and it is possible that he composed an ironical apology to them on another occasion, and at some later stage saw the appropriateness of linking it with *The Turnament*.

There is evidence that Dunbar liked to group poems on related subjects; but when he did so he often emphasized the links by some formal device or signal. Thus *O gracius princes* has the same metre and exactly the same length as *The wardraipper*. Two petitionary poems both employ the same key phrase—'the feist of benefice'—in their opening lines (K 40 and 41). And three moral poems (K 78-80) that form a series not only use the same stanza but call attention to their thematic parallelism by employing very similar refrains, all of which end with the identical phrase, 'sould discretioun be'. *The Dance* and *The Turnament* contain several formal indications, apart from those mentioned earlier, which confirm that they were designed as a two-part structure; *Fasternis Evin in Hell* seems an appropriate title for this work alone. The phrasing employed at the opening—'Mahoun gart cry ane dance' (6) recurs in the introduction of each new entertainment (109, and 122-4). *The Dance* and *The Turnament*, it should be noted, also have approximately the same number of lines. Indeed it seems possible that they once had exactly the same length, each consisting of 108 lines, disposed in nine twelve-line stanzas; only the two anomalous six-line stanzas in *The Dance* disturb this numerical symmetry. (The presence of these passages may be explained variously; although not strictly necessary to the action, they sound

---

[94] Bannatyne's text contains a reference to 'this fair' (17), which would tally with a craft feast. For an English poem possibly designed for such a craft 'drynkyng', see E. Wilson, 'The Debate of the Carpenter's Tools', *RES*, NS 38 (1987), 450-2.

authentic.[95]) There are other more significant parallels between the two poems: each is filled with violent and grotesquely ugly activity; each ends with Mahoun in person—not some lesser fiend—inflicting a similar punishment on those who have angered him: the Highlanders are consigned to 'the depest pot of hell' (119) and the craftsmen to a 'dungeoun' (211). Each poem may be seen as a diabolical travesty of two cherished courtly pastimes, the dance and the tournament.

Yet the differences between *The Dance* and *The Turnament* are striking. First and most obviously, *The Turnament* is coarser and more scatological: the protagonists, their horses, and even the devil are repeatedly befouled, 'beschittin'' (191, 218) and 'bespewit' (200). Combat is virtually replaced by vomiting and excreting; yet this has no profound moral significance—in contrast with *The Dance* (at lines 61 and 88–9)—only a kind of pyschological truth, in that the tailor and soutar are both terrified of each other. Secondly, *The Turnament* employs social stereotypes rather than personifications, and the mode is closer to satire than to moral allegory. I am not convinced by a suggestion that the tailor and soutar are 'clearly related to the Deadly Sins'.[96] The change of mode, of course, begins at the end of *The Dance*, with the stanzas devoted to minstrels and Highlanders. Yet this seems to me a rough rather than a 'smooth transition'.[97] In the course of reading one is conscious of a distinct change of tone: the work grows progressively less serious, and becomes the very 'bourd' that Dunbar proclaims it in line 220. The nature of the comedy alters—from something so horrific that it is hardly funny at all into a tall story or farce. The first poem embodies a horrifying idea, that human vice and its punishment are devised to amuse the devil—'Bot ȝit luche nevir Mahoun' (27). *The Turnament*, is simply a 'bourd', and provokes violent laughter in the poet himself. The two poems are indeed closely coupled—like participants in a three-legged race—but they are not united. Yet this effect—tonally jarring and discrepant—is perhaps precisely what Dunbar intended.

Several of the anonymous poems mentioned earlier in this chapter end flippantly, or address the audience in the convivial manner of minstrel verse: 'gar fill the cop' (*Dreme*) or 'Drynk with my guddame quhen ȝe gang by' (*Kittok*). But none can match Dunbar's throwaway ending:

> For this said justing it befell
> Befoir Mahoun, the air of hell:
> Now trow this, gif ȝe list.   (226–8)

---

[95] Reiss, 81, notes that they may be 'interpolations'; but stanzas originally of 12 lines might have been truncated by copyists.
[96] Reiss, 84.   [97] Kinsley, 339.

'ELRICH FANTASYIS'

In the last line *this* refers primarily to the 'justing' but also to all the other events of the 'trance' from which the poet has just awoken. If this is so in Bannatyne (which provides Kinsley's copy-text), the questioning of the whole dream-experience—'all this thing'—is even clearer in Asloan's version of the passage. Here the poet resolves

> To dyte how all this thing befell
> Befor Mahovne the heir of hell.
> Schirris, trow it gif ʒe list.

Dunbar ends other dreams with similar ambivalence. Even undoubtedly serious ones—*The Passioun* (K 3) and *The Thrissill and the Rois*—leave the dreamer 'halflingis in effray'. Among the comic visions one ends with a curse (K 54), another leaves the dreamer in perplexity (K 55), and a third incorporates the verdict that this is a 'nyce', or foolish, dream (K 53). If the dreamer himself is poised between conflicting emotions, readers are likewise left in uncertainty as to the exact mix of seriousness and amusement in the tone, and presented with questions rather than answers. Dunbar undoubtedly criticizes moral evils in several of these poems, but the way in which they conclude warns us against over-solemn readings and interpretations.

8
'Ladeis Bewtie ... Luiffis Blys'

CHAUCER, according to Gavin Douglas, was ever 'womanis frend';[1] no reader is likely to say this of Dunbar. Much of his poetry is not primarily concerned with women. It is 'man' who is repeatedly admonished in the moral poems, and 'the stait of man' (K 62. 9) that is their chief theme. *Man*, of course, like *homo*, signifies human beings of either sex, yet in many of these poems the 'man'—addressed as 'sone', for instance, in K 77—is explicitly or implicitly male. Few women, apart from 'the lady in bour', appear among the estates in *I that in heill wes*. Many of Dunbar's comic poems, such as *The Flyting* or *The Dregy*, have a strongly masculine ambience; the only women mentioned among the crafts in *This nycht in my sleip I wes agast* are the fishwives. None the less Dunbar's *œuvre* includes a small and extremely interesting group of poems in which women are prominent and figure variously—if predictably—as ladies, 'cummeris', 'carlingis', and 'coclinkis', or whores. Among them, as its title proclaims, is Dunbar's most ambitious poem, *The Tua Mariit Wemen and the Wedo*. These poems are as much concerned with men as with women: they treat of the relations between the sexes, love, sexuality, courtship, and marriage. Dunbar is not highly esteemed as a love poet, yet he was indifferent neither to 'ladeis bewtie nor luiffis blys' (K 69. 43). In context this line implies the delight of love as well as its transience; the alliterative interlace also suggests an inextricable alliance between love and 'ladeis', beauty and 'blys'.

Our knowledge of Scottish love poetry before Dunbar is fragmentary. There are many references to 'ballatis of lufe', but few that survive can be definitely dated before 1500. The responsibility for their disappearance can be attributed partly to changes in literary taste but chiefly to the hostility of the Reformers. One such poem, amazingly printed in the 1567 edition of *The Gude and Godlie Ballatis*, caused such scandal that it was denounced by the General Assembly and the offending page was deleted; the poem was so thoroughly suppressed that it remained unknown for centuries.[2] Some anonymous love poems

---
[1] *Eneados*, Prol. 1. 449.
[2] See A. A. MacDonald, 'Poetry, Politics and Reformation Censorship in Sixteenth-Century Scotland', *ES* 64 (1983), 415–6.

'LADEIS BEWTIE ... LUIFFIS BLYS'

in the Bannatyne Manuscript, such as the beautiful *Tayis Bank*, may be medieval, but most are impossible to date. The finest early Scottish love poem is undoubtedly *The Kingis Quair*: characterized by passionate yet idealistic feeling, it is also technically innovative, the first work by a Scot to be written in rhyme royal and to use the elevated style associated with Chaucer and Lydgate. How well known *The Kingis Quair* was to later poets is debatable; Dunbar and Douglas do not mention it, yet it was included in a manuscript anthology (Selden B. 24), compiled between 1488 and 1513, for Douglas's patron, Henry, Lord Sinclair.

This manuscript has great importance, not only because it preserves the sole copy of *The Kingis Quair* but because its other contents provide invaluable evidence as to the literary taste of a Scottish nobleman at the close of the fifteenth century. It illustrates the widespread admiration for Chaucer's love poetry, containing *Troilus and Criseyde*, *The Parliament of Fowls*, and *The Legend of Good Women*. But it also testifies to Scottish interest in other English poems about love—Sir John Clanvowe's debate, *The Boke of Cupide* (known also as *The Cuckoo and the Nightingale*), Hoccleve's *Letter of Cupid*, an adaptation of Christine de Pisan's *L'Epistre au Dieu d'Amours*; and Lydgate's *Complaint of a Lover's Life*. There is other evidence that the latter were popular in Scotland: Bannatyne contains *The Letter of Cupid*; and *The Complaint of a Lover's Life* occurs both in a print and the Asloan Manuscript. Their authors' names, however, were less well known, since Chaucer received the credit for both poems.[3] The Scots shared the late-medieval taste for love-complaints, poems lamenting the loss or treachery of a lover: this manuscript contains, in addition to Chaucer's *Complaint of Venus* and *Complaint of Mars*, pieces of a similar type—the Scottish *Quare of Jelusy*, and *The Lay of Sorrow* and *The Lufaris Complaynt*, whose exact provenance is doubtful.[4] Many of these poems are metrically elaborate—the nine-line stanza employed for *The Goldyn Targe* is found also in *The Lay of Sorrow*, together with another, even more ambitious, of sixteen lines.

Scottish courtiers enjoyed much the same songs and poems as their English contemporaries. Young's account of Margaret Tudor's reception in Scotland tells how the English knight, Sir Edward Stanley, and a Scottish gentleman sang 'ballades' together—'the wiche accorded varey well'. The incident supports John Stevens's view that love poetry often formed part of a courtly, social 'game'—it served as a pastime,

---

[3] See G. Kratzmann, *Anglo-Scottish Literary Relations 1430–1550* (Cambridge, 1980), 13–16; Bawcutt, *Douglas*, 38.

[4] See K. G. Wilson, '*The Lay of Sorrow* and *The Lufaris Complaynt*: An Edition', *Speculum*, 29 (1954), 708–26.

along with dancing, disguising, tale-telling, and other kinds of 'luftalkyng'.[5] What is also evident is the continued prestige of works originating in France and Burgundy, together with the remarkable conservatism of literary taste. Gerald Fitzgerald, whose youth was spent at the court of Henry VII, possessed numerous French books, among which were courtly lyrics, 'Launcelott du lake' and *Le Roman de la Rose*.[6] In Scotland there existed a similar liking for love allegory and dream poetry belonging to the tradition of *Le Roman de la Rose*, as also for large-scale narrative that combined 'amouris' with 'chevalry'. *The Avowis of Alexander* illustrates how long the taste persisted: this fifteenth-century Scottish rendering of *Les Vœux du Paon*, composed by Jacques de Longuyon in the fourteenth century, now survives only in a print, dated *c.*1580.[7]

Side by side with the refined and idealistic tradition of love poetry that is usually termed 'courtly' existed very different approaches to love. There were comic and bawdy poems, less concerned with emotions than with the physical mechanics of love-making. We tend to think of this as a vulgar tradition; songs and verses of this kind, such as the doggerel *A Talk of Ten Wives on their Husbands' Ware*, are often 'low' in style and diction. But we should not conclude that their audience or their authors were invariably different from those of courtly poems. The fifteenth-century miscellany known as *Les Adevineaux Amoureux* was devised to entertain polite society; but it contains obscene riddles as well as refined *demandes d'amour*.[8] The famous 'Henry VIII Songbook' includes several bawdy songs, among which are the highly suggestive 'forester' carols.[9] The pastance of courtiers could be as ribald as the jests and facetiae of clerics. But these poems were certainly popular in the sense that they were much enjoyed and widely diffused. There also existed another and far better documented tradition of writing about love, associated with the Church: serious, moralizing, often ascetic, the view of Troilus looking down upon the earth from the eighth sphere and despising human love as 'worldly vanyte'.[10] Modern readers may well be surprised to discover how many poems in Bannatyne's love section are 'Contemptis of lufe' and

---

[5] *Music and Poetry in the Early Tudor Court* (1961; Cambridge, 1979), 268–9, and 150–2. Cf. J. MacQueen, *Ballattis of Lufe* (Edinburgh, 1970), xi–lxix.

[6] See J. Boffey, *Manuscripts of English Courtly Love Lyrics in the Late Middle Ages* (Woodbridge, 1985), 140–1.

[7] This forms the second part of *The Buik of Alexander*, ed. R. G. Ritchie (STS, 1921–9).

[8] See J. W. Hassell, *Amorous Games: A Critical Edition of Les Adevineaux Amoureux* (Austin, Texas, 1974).

[9] Stevens, *Music and Poetry*, 388–426; also Greene, *Carols*, nos. 466 and 466.1.

[10] *Troilus and Criseyde*, v. 1809 ff. Cf. D. W. Robertson, *A Preface to Chaucer* (Princeton, 1962), *passim*.

'ballatis detesting of lufe and lichery'. Among the verse by Dunbar's contemporaries that it includes are Douglas's sober Fourth Prologue, and three pieces by Mersar, who 'did in luf so lifly write' (K 62). Mersar's poems are so didactic that few today are likely to find them lively.

The two traditions may seem far apart, yet overlap in one respect: in both women are usually denigrated, depicted as harlots, shrews, or drunkards. This is not the place to discuss the pervasive anti-feminism of medieval literature, whose roots and ramifications have been much studied.[11] It is more pertinent to consider which of the many writings about women were likely to be known to Dunbar and his readers. They certainly knew Chaucer's Wife of Bath, and probably, given the popularity of *Le Roman de la Rose*, Jean de Meun's 'La Vieille'. It is also probable that some Scots shared the contemporary taste for the amusing prose satire, *Les Quinze Joies de Mariage*: it was printed twice in France before the end of the fifteenth century, and available to English readers in a verse translation printed by Wynkyn de Worde in 1509.[12] The Asloan Manuscript contains one work strongly tinged with anti-feminism, the *Buke of the Sevin Sagis*, and another remarkable diatribe against women, *The Spectacle of Luf*. This prose treatise (*c*.1492) is a Scottish version of Jankin's book of wicked wives, narrating their nefarious deeds and the misery that befalls men 'throw that foull delectatioun of wemen quhilk thow callis luf'.[13] Five of the non-Gaelic verses in the Book of the Dean of Lismore are anti-feminist: they include a stanza from *The Testament of Cresseid* (561–7), and a witty version of some lines from Juvenal.[14] But these criticisms of women did not go unanswered. Notable defences of women were written; together with the attacks, they formed the complex tradition of *la querelle des dames*. The war between the sexes was itself a game, that was played sometimes lightheartedly, sometimes ferociously. Some Scots may have read Christine de Pisan's rebuttal of De Meun's slanders on women; many more must have known Hoccleve's *Letter of Cupid*.[15] A large section of Bannatyne's 'Ballatis of lufe' is devoted to the argument

---

[11] See J. Ferrante, *Woman as Image in Medieval Literature: From the Twelfth Century to Dante* (New York, 1975); and W. Matthews, 'The Wife of Bath and all her Sect', *Viator*, 5 (1974), 413–43. F. L. Utley's *The Crooked Rib: An Analytical Index to the Argument about Women in English and Scots Literature* (Columbus, Ohio, 1944) is particularly useful.

[12] See edn. by J. Rychner (Geneva, 1963); trans. B. A. Pitts (New York, 1985); and the Elizabethan *The Batchelars Banquet*, ed. F. P. Wilson (Oxford, 1929).

[13] *Asloan Manuscript*, i. 273.

[14] See NLS Catalogue of Gaelic Manuscripts (typescript), MS 72. 1. 37, for list of contents.

[15] Cf. Utley, especially 35 ff. On Hoccleve's rendering of *L'Epistre au Dieu d'Amours*, see J. Fleming, 'Hoccleve's "Letter of Cupid" and the "Quarrel" over the *Roman de la Rose*', *MÆ* 40 (1971), 21–40.

about women: first come epigrams and 'ballatis aganis evill wemen', then poems in their praise and 'to the reproche of vicius men'.

This rapid survey of a vast subject is designed to illustrate the context in which Dunbar wrote; it has called attention not to remote sources but to writings evidently popular and accessible. Dunbar's own poems about love display his characteristic variety, comprising lyrics and narratives, a beast fable and a dream allegory, poems about seduction as well as courtship. He writes of both the pain and the comedy of love, sometimes as if he were involved in the experience, sometimes from the viewpoint of the Christian moralist. Yet his most frequent role is neither as participant nor critic, but rather as the amused and ironic observer of the game of love. Dunbar is conversant with the social function of love poetry. In *The Goldyn Targe* (103, 129) he describes the singing of love ballats, in conjunction with dance and music: in *The Tua Mariit Wemen and the Wedo* (480) their reading is a vehicle for flirtation. Some poems purport to show Dunbar as having a reputation as a love poet. In one (K 55) there is no rebuttal of the assertion that the poet has long been a teacher of 'Venus lawis' (13); and another opens with the statement, 'Lang heff I maed of ladyes quhytt' (K 33). Yet contextually there is a humorous ambivalence about these phrases; both might covertly allude to the 'swan quhit' ladies of *The Tua Mariit Wemen and the Wedo*, and the 'lawis' they follow. There is similar obliquity in another poem that presents Dunbar himself as a lover. At the core of *Sir Jhon Sinclair begowthe to dance* (K 28) is lyrical delight in the graceful dancing of Mistress Musgrave:

> for hir saek I wissitt to be
> The grytast erle or duk in France. (33–4)

But this first-person response is preceded by a third-person glimpse of the poet as ludicrously over-energetic:

> For luff of Musgraeffe, men tellis me,
> He trippit quhill he tint his panton. (26–7)

We see Dunbar acting the lover, in order to pay a compliment, while simultaneously making fun of himself.

Two of Dunbar's poems belong to the very common type in which a lover beseeches the favour of his mistress. The epistolary form of such pieces was often quite explicit. An English one begins, 'This letter now I wryte', and another ends:

> Fare-wele, loue, tyl we mete
> For this tyme now my leve I take.[16]

---

[16] *SL*, nos. 195 and 197. Cf. Robbins, 'The Middle English Court Love Lyric', in *The Interpretation of Medieval Lyric Poetry*, ed. W. H. T. Jackson (Columbia, 1980), 205–32.

The diction and imagery of these poems were as stereotyped as their themes. Dunbar's *Sweit rois of vertew and of gentilnes* (K 8) draws on this tradition, yet is elegant and witty, and compact as a sonnet. Its fifteen lines are neatly deployed in three stanzas. The first is a compliment: the lady, addressed as rose and lily, is both beautiful and virtuous. But praise is tempered by a single reservation—

> Except onlie that 3e ar mercyles.

The second stanza parallels the first:

> In to 3our garthe this day I did persew;
> Thair saw I flowris that fresche were of hew—
> Baithe quhyte and rid [red] moist lusty were to seyne,
> And halsum herbis upone stalkis grene:
> 3it leif nor flour fynd could I nane of rew. (6–10)

Here four lines, praising the 'garthe' for its fresh flowers and 'halsum' (health-giving) herbs, are similarly qualified by a last one, deploring the absence of 'rew'. The poet concludes by lamenting the death of 'this gentill herbe', and resolves

> to plant his rute agane,
> So confortand his levis unto me bene. (14–15)

This garden hovers between the literal and the allegorical; but it is not difficult to read its *significatio*, since the parallels between the first and second stanza are more than syntactic. The rose and lily that symbolize the lady correspond to the flowers and herbs of her 'garthe'; both combine beauty with 'vertew' (4) or virtuous properties. There is an evident pun on the two sense of *rew*: firstly, the perennial shrub with strong-scented leaves (*OED*, *rue*, 2); and secondly, the emotion of pity (*OED*, *rue*, 1). Such figurative plants and gardens were common. Alain Chartier wrote a ballade that opens,

> J'ay ung arbre de la plante d'amours
> Enraciné en mon cuer proprement.[17]

Chartier's tree bore no fruit but sorrow, and its leaves were of 'ennuy'. A fragmentary poem of Dunbar's own time begins 'In all oure gardyn growis thare na flouris', and refers to a gardener with the ominous name of 'Dangere'.[18] One of Bannatyne's anonymous 'ballatis of lufe' likewise complains of a rose, growing in a garth, that once 'wes fresche and fair' and now is faded.[19] Dunbar, writing in this tradition, could

---

[17] *One Hundred Ballades, Rondeaux and Virelais from the Later Middle Ages*, ed. N. Wilkins (Cambridge, 1969), no. 77.
[18] See *The Chepman and Myllar Prints: A Facsimile*, ed. W. Beattie (Edinburgh, 1950), 88.
[19] Fol. 222b.

count on ready perception of the equation between the garden without rue and 'la belle dame sans merci'. There is an interesting precedent for his word-play in *The Lay of Sorrow*. In this poem a woman, complaining of her lover's unkindness, says,

> In my garding quhare I sewe
> All peiciencs, now fynd I nocht bot rewe. (51–2)

The garden symbolizes her mind: *peiciencs* signifies both 'patience' and a plant, the dock, and *rewe* signifies not only the herb but also 'grief, sadness'—in John Rolland's *Court of Venus* the personified figure of Despair likewise carries an emblematic 'bus of rew'.[20]

The wit, in *Sweit rois*, springs chiefly from this word-play. But a further 'irony' has been detected: 'In medieval herbals, rue (*ruta graveolens*) was especially effective in counteracting lust: it "wasteth the humour of Venus, and abateth in males the appetite of Venus" ... As a corrective to amorous desire, it is ironically included in the garden of love.'[21] Such irony, if it were present, would effectively destroy both the wit and the logic of this poem. It is true that amazing virtues were attributed to herbs, in both the learned and the popular tradition. But Dunbar and his readers, if aware of this particular item of herbal lore, would also know that rue's properties were many and varied. Speaking of the literal 'garthe', the poet might well desire the planting of rue, since its smell chases 'venemouse bestes out of gardyns'. But he is also speaking, figuratively, of his mistress's heart. According to Bartholomaeus Anglicus, there is a distinction between the effects of rue upon men and upon women: he notes that the herb indeed 'abateth in malis appetit [of] Venus', but also says that 'in wommen that beth colde and moyste [rue] worcheth the contrary by contrary cause'.[22] Although Bartholomaeus does not provide further details, these are spelt out clearly by Thomas Cogan: 'The second propertie is that Rue abateth carnall lust ... Yet *schola Salerni* in this point maketh a difference betweene men and women, for they say, *ruta viris coitum minuit, mulieribus auget*'.[23] Herbal lore would thus seem to confirm the lover's claim that he finds the presence of rue more 'confortand' than its absence.

My hartis tresure and swete assured fo (K 12) is also a lover's complaint. The poet repeatedly proclaims himself his lady's 'man', or feudal servant, but calls her a 'man slayar' (5), and says he will die

---

[20] *The Court of Venus*, ed. W. Gregor (STS, 1884), i. 172.
[21] Reiss, 101–2.
[22] *On the Properties of Things*, trans. Trevisa, ed. M. C. Seymour *et al.* (Oxford, 1975–88), book 17, cap. cxli.
[23] *The Haven of Health* (1584), 40.

unless she shows him favour. He concludes by protesting that he will
love her until his heart breaks asunder—

> And syne, fair weill, my hartis ladie deir! (49)

Troilus likewise called himself Criseyde's 'man' (i. 427), spoke of her
in the same oxymoron as his 'swete fo' (i. 873), and concluded a verse
letter:

> And far now wel, my owen swete herte. (v. 1421)

My hartis tresure, however, finds innumerable parallels to its epistolary
form, diction, imagery, and rhyme-royal stanza—not only in Chaucer
but in much contemporary love poetry. Longer than *Sweit rois of vertew*
and highly repetitious, it is in most respects a conventional and rather
dull poem.

This view, however, is not the accepted one. Whereas I regard *My
hartis tresure* as a typical love complaint, most critics concur with A. K.
Moore in viewing it rather as 'an effective parody of the typical
complaint'.[24] Yet what are the grounds for this reading? The language
is undoubtedly clichéd and conventional, yet conventionality in itself
is hardly proof of parody. Critics call the tone 'hysterical', and find the
rhetoric 'preposterous'.[25] But this seems a very modern response to

> O man slayar, quhill saule and life dissever
> Stynt of 3our slauchtir; allace, 3our man am I,
> A thousand tymes that dois 3ow mercy cry. (5–7)

This is 'going over the top'; but hyperbole and emotional extravagance
were the stuff of these love poems. Another Scot complains similarly
that his merciless mistress will slay him, and reflects

> Bot wo were me that it suld so betyd
> That scho thairthrow suld be cald ane homicyd
> . . . .
> A manslaar, and thairfoir ratefyd.

This was included in two recent anthologies, yet neither of its editors
regarded it as other than a straight love poem.[26] If Dunbar's piece was
intended as parodic, one would expect clearer signals to the reader—
reductive imagery for the lady, for instance, or a 'destroying refrain',
such as occurs in a humorous English complaint:

---

[24] *The Secular Lyric in Middle English* (Lexington, 1951), 204. Cf. also Scott, 59–60, Reiss, 100, Ross, 215, and Utley, no. 199.
[25] Kinsley, 255.
[26] Bannatyne, fol. 220a; MacQueen, *Ballattis of Luve*, no. 8; Hughes and Ramson, *Poetry of the Stewart Court*, no. 255.

'LADEIS BEWTIE ... LUIFFIS BLYS'

>   So your love changeth my chere,
>   That when I slepe I may not wake.²⁷

The one piece of evidence that might justify comic readings of this poem is its colophon: 'Quod Dunbar quhone he list to feyne'. Yet this is not necessarily the poet's own sarcastic postscript. The word 'feyne' may well imply the copyist's doubts as to Dunbar's heartfelt sincerity, but the colophon cannot, I think, be construed as 'when Dunbar chose to write a parody'. The usage seems closer to that of a scribal comment on Gower in a manuscript of *Confessio Amantis*: *fingens se auctor esse Amantem* (the author, feigning himself to be a lover ...).²⁸ The copyist of Dunbar's poem perhaps wished likewise to stress its fictional nature, or considered that Dunbar's characteristic response to love was more sardonic. However the colophon is interpreted, *My hartis tresure* does not seem particularly 'effective' either as straight love poem or as parody. Indeed, if intended as parodic, it is in a very different class from *The Dregy* or *The Testament of Maister Andro Kennedy*.

In secreit place this hindir nycht (K 13) is a short, comic poem about a courtship. The poet overhears an extremely intimate conversation:

>   In secreit place this hindir nycht
>   I hard ane bern say till a bricht:
>   My hunny, my houp, my hairt, my heill,
>   I haif bene lang ȝour lufar leill
>   And can of ȝow gett confort nane;
>   How lang will ȝe with denger deill?
>   Ȝe brek my hart, my bony ane.   (1–7)

We are introduced to the archetypal courtly lover, whose heart, as in *My hartis tresure*, is broken by his lady's coldness. His diction seems as refined as his sentiments: the lady is his 'heill', or salvation, and he speaks of his long 'leill' service; but she displays 'denger', the lover's implacable foe in *Le Roman de la Rose*. Yet this courtly impression is dispelled in the next stanza by undignified details in the lover's appearance and behaviour: his beard might be elegantly trimmed, 'bot all with kaill it wes bedroppit' (9), and his sexual desire is noted crudely—'he wald haif fukkit' (13).

The core of the poem consists of a formal dialogue, with stanzas allotted alternately to man and woman, and an alternating refrain. There is little attempt to characterize the speakers socially. Kinsley says of the couple that 'he is a backstairs fornicator ... she is a

---

²⁷ *Early English Lyrics*, ed. E. K. Chambers and F. Sidgwick (1907), 217. Cf. also Greene, *Carols*, no. 470.
²⁸ See J. Burrow, 'The Portrayal of *Amans* in *Confessio Amantis*', in *Gower's Confessio Amantis: Responses and Reassessments*, ed. A. J. Minnis (Woodbridge, 1983), 13.

giggling kitchen girl';[29] yet the poem itself is not so precise. The man is 'townsyche' (10), a word elsewhere applied to those from the town, as opposed to the country; although pejorative it does not necessarily mean 'uncourtly'.[30] Nothing is said of the woman's rank or occupation. What soon vividly emerge, however, are the differences between the speakers in personality and experience. The man says that he has never loved before:

> Sen that I born wes of my mynny
> I wowit nevir ane uder bot 3ow.   (16–17)

The woman, in reply, makes a similar claim, which is undercut by the last three words:

> My sweit swanky, saif 3ow allane
> Na leid I luvit all this owk [week].   (26–7)

Throughout the dialogue the woman has the ascendancy. Her first response to the man's suit is laughter. She is by turns affectionate and mocking, viewing the man as large and clumsy, yet also as infantile, still wet 'With muderis milk' (37), and a 'sucker', or young suckling (53). Both attitudes fuse comically in her image of him as an ungainly young bullock, recently weaned—'my strummill stirk 3it new to spane' (54). The woman is presented neither as the innocent victim of an experienced seducer nor as a mercenary harlot. She does not yield simply because the man gives her 'ane appill ruby' (57); the gift rather confirms her acceptance of his wooing (50–56), and her liking for him is evident in her comical refrain—'Fow leis me that graceles gane' (I'm very fond of that ugly mug).

What is the tone of this poem? It clearly makes fun of the lovers. The strain of farmyard imagery—calf, kid, 'strummill stirk'—implies that, despite the high-flown opening, human sexuality is little different from that of animals. The poem is reductive in another way. The man's refrain is '3e brek my hairt, my bony ane'; but such references to the heart, the traditional seat of elevated emotions, are far outweighed by references to other parts of the body, conventionally held in less esteem—'wame', 'bowk', 'belly', and the sexual organs, jocularly or euphemistically termed 'stang' or 'quhillyllillie'. Some critics regard In secret place as a satire, ridiculing 'amour courtois', or 'the high traditions of the love-lyric'.[31] Yet Dunbar's tone seems amused rather than contemptuous; there is a comic delight in the way lovers talk, the sheer absurdity of this particular 'luf-talkyng'.

The poem is often viewed in isolation, as if it were unique to

---

[29] Kinsley, 257.
[30] It corresponds to *townage* (K 9. 39); see *OED*, *townish*.
[31] Kinsley, 257; Ross, 166.

Dunbar. But the genre to which it belongs, the erotic dialogue, has a long history, ranging from the medieval *chansons d'aventure*, that told of encounters between knights or clerks and peasant girls, to the poems collected, centuries later, in Percy's Folio Manuscript and *The Merry Muses of Caledonia*. As this latter title suggests, the tradition was increasingly regarded as low and sub-literary. Yet humorous dialogues between lovers, with musical settings, are included in the Tudor song books, and placed next to refined love poems. One of these is located in a 'spence', and has a kitchen maid as its heroine.[32] The genre was also well known in Scotland, even if not particularly reputable. The Bannatyne manuscript contains several parallels to *In secreit place*: anonymous bawdy pieces, such as *In somer quhen flowris will smell*, *I met my lady weill arrayit*, and *I saw me thocht this hindir nicht*; and 'a more chaste and elegant' handling of the theme occurs in Henryson's *Robene and Makyne*.[33] The precise mix of ingredients varies—some poems tell of courtship, others of seduction; in some the poet (as here) is merely the unseen observer, in others he is himself the lover. But there is an evident tendency, in several Scottish poems, to present the man as a novice in the craft of love or as ineffectual, even impotent— 'his doingis were nocht wirth a leik'. In contrast the woman tends to be bold and self-assertive, taking the initiative, as in *Robene and Makyne*, or showing open contempt for her lover—'ȝe dow nocht, man!'[34] The depiction of the lovers in *In secreit place* derives, in part, from this tradition. Like many of these other pieces—*Robene and Makyne* excepted—*In secreit place* is characterized by bawdy imagery and *double entendres*. Where Dunbar's poem stands apart from the rest is in its sheer verbal exuberance: it contains a brilliant burlesque of the language of endearment (see below, p. 366). Although a slight doubt exists as to the authorship of *In secreit place*, the verve of its language constitutes a powerful argument in Dunbar's favour.

The affinity between *In secreit place* and *This hindir nycht in Dumfermeling* (K 37) has often been noted. Both poems employ the same seven-line stanza, a form that Dunbar uses only for humorous purposes; both contain bawdy double-talk; and both adopt a comic approach to sexuality. But the comedy of *This hindir nycht in Dumfermeling* is far blacker—the theme is seduction—and whereas *In secreit place* is threaded with animal imagery, in this poem the protagonists

---

[32] Stevens, *Music and Poetry*, 378–9, and 339–40; in the latter the girl exclaims, 'Be pes, ye make me spille my ale'. See also 'Walking in a meadowe greene' and 'When Phebus addrest himself to the west', in *Loose and Humorous Songs from Bishop Percy's Folio Manuscript*, ed. F. J. Furnivall (1868).

[33] Fols. 141a, 143a and 143b; Fox, *Poems of Henryson*, 470; Gray, *Henryson*, 264–5.

[34] *I met my lady*, 40.

themselves are animals—a 'tod', or fox, a lamb, and a wolf. The poem's opening tells us much about its tone and genre:

> This hindir nycht in Dumfermeling
> To me wes tawld ane windir thing:
> That lait ane tod wes with ane lame,
> And with hir playit and maid gud game,
> Syne till his breist did hir imbrace
> And wald haif riddin hir lyk ane rame:
> And that me thocht ane ferly cace. (1–7)

In anecdotal manner the poet relates something he has been told—not only a good story but a 'tall story', as is implicit in the phrases 'ane windir thing' and 'ane ferly cace'. Dunbar distances himself from his material here, rather as he does at the end:

> And this report I with my pen,
> How at Dumfermling fell the cace. (69–70)

The emphatic double mention of Dunfermline possibly pinpointed the tale's scandalous sub-text for contemporary readers; but it also pays oblique tribute to Henryson, the great Scottish master of beast fable, and thus announces the mode in which Dunbar proposes to write.

No source for this poem is known. Dunbar seems to be making a novel use of fable stereotypes—the lamb as a type of innocence, and the persistent enmity between fox and wolf. The fox is notorious for his cunning, but less familiar perhaps as a sexual predator; yet there is precedent for this in the stories belonging to the popular *Roman de Renard*. In one branch of this beast epic the fox attempts to rape Hersent, the wife of the wolf, Ysengrim, and in another episode he is put on trial for this offence.[35] Dunbar's phrasing occasionally recalls Henryson's *Fables*, in which the tod, wolf, and lamb are prominent. Dunbar calls the tod a 'lowry' (16), a nickname first recorded in Henryson.[36] He terms the lamb 'silly' (18, 40, 59); and although the epithet seems to be a stock one, it should be noted how frequently the phrase 'selie lamb' occurs in Henryson's *The Wolf and the Lamb*.[37] In this particular fable the wolf has 'girnand' teeth (2630); Dunbar applies the same epithet to the fox's jaws—'His girnand gamis hir nocht agast' (34). In Dunbar's poem the fox clasps the lamb by her throat:

> He held hir till him be the hals. (36)

---

[35] In Caxton's *History of Reynard the Fox*, ed. N. F. Blake (EETS, OS 263, 1970), Hersent's rape is narrated in ch. 33.
[36] Fox, *Poems of Henryson*, note to *Fables*, 429.
[37] *Fables*, 2620, 2625, and *passim*.

'LADEIS BEWTIE ... LUIFFIS BLYS'

The sinister implication of this embrace is evident, but is confirmed by the similar act of Henryson's wolf, before he devours the lamb:

> With that anone he hint him be the hals. (2699)

In another fable Henryson's fox is charged with having eaten a lamb, and hypocritically replies, 'My purpois wes with him for to haif playid' (1079); Dunbar ironically applies the same verb to the tod's handling of the lamb—'with hir playit and maid gud game'. Yet such details, although they reveal Dunbar's awareness of Henryson, are far outweighed by the differences between the poets. Dunbar's brief tale lacks the rich amplification that is so characteristic of Henryson. It also lacks Henryson's high seriousness; there is no *Moralitas*, and no clear moral point, except perhaps that any 'gud game' between tod and lamb is likely to be 'gud' for the fox, but disastrous for the lamb.

The poem has the usual ambivalence of the fable world, in which a tod behaves now like an animal, now like a gallant, asking his mistress for 'grace' (12). In the same anthropomorphic way the lamb prays to the Virgin for aid (13), and the tod swears 'be God' (38). But this tale is a 'ferly', and there are oddities to which the refrain insistently calls attention. The first is the tod's behaviour towards the lamb—he 'wald haif riddin hir lyk ane rame'. When men are compared to rams it usually implies extreme sexual rapacity. But for a tod to behave like a ram suggests, in addition, the mismating of species; there is perhaps a hint here of social disparity between the lovers. The refrain emphasizes, even more, the singular behaviour of the lamb. She does not run away, or show fear of the tod; still more strangely, she believes what he says:

> The lame gaif creddence to the tod:
> And that me thocht ane ferly cace. (41-2)

This lamb is doubly 'silly'—foolishly trusting as well as innocent. It is the fox's nature to devour lambs, as Dunbar implies, in a finely ambiguous passage:

> Scho wes ane morsall of delyte—
> He lovit na ʒowis auld, tuch, and sklender;
> Becaus this lame wes ʒung and tender
> He ran upoun hir with a race,
> And scho schup nevir for till defend hir. (23-7)

The primary sense of *morsall*, 'mouthful, small piece of food', needs no illustration; but Dunbar puns on its figurative, slangy application to a young woman—Hoccleve termed a prostitute 'a morsel of plesance' and Knox called Lady Erskine a 'morsall for the devillis mouth'.[38] The association of sexual activity with eating continues—old women are as unattractive as tough mutton—but is succeeded by the military terminology of 'race' (assault) and 'defend'.

Morton Bloomfield said that the world of fable 'is close to us, and we can easily orient ourselves ... we are given clear clues. We are not driven to discomfort by its strangeness.'[39] Dunbar's fable hardly meets these criteria; by its end the reader longs for clues to assist its interpretation. The tod apparently seduces the lamb—Dunbar feigns ignorance of the precise circumstances, using a favourite narrative ploy of Chaucer's—but the house is then besieged by the wolf. The tod lies low,

> And in the silly lambis skin
> He crap als far as he micht win,
> And hid him thair ane weill lang space.   (59–61)

The wolf thinks that all are asleep and returns to his den, 'Protestand for the secound place' (68). It is difficult to find a coherent explanation, on any level, of these events. Clearly the tod survives, and the wolf in some way is tricked, but the lamb's fate is unclear. As several critics have noted, the fox in a lamb's skin was a common Scottish figure for duplicity.[40] All, however, explain the ending differently: one says that the fox is 'covered in retreat by the lamb, who has to receive the wolf as a second suitor'; another that 'the skin's inhabitant is seduced rather than eaten'.[41] I find it more plausible that the lamb, last mentioned as cheeping in fear like a mouse (55), has finally been devoured by the tod.

Bannatyne gave this poem the heading, 'the wowing of the king quhen he wes in Dunfermeling'. His titles, however, are not always reliable, and no such heading is attached to the copies in Maitland and Reidpeth.[42] Bannatyne compiled his anthology at the beginning of the reign of James VI, great-grandson to James IV; he was almost as distant from that king as we are from Edward VII. Possibly he was aware of some floating rumour that identified the seducing tod with James IV, whose love affairs were common knowledge. The identification is not impossible, yet it raises questions that are rarely considered. Which of the king's mistresses does the lamb represent?

---

[38] *The Tale of Jonathas*, 159, in *Minor Works*, 221; see also Whiting, 'Scottish Proverbs', ii. 380.
[39] 'The Wisdom of the Nun's Priest's Tale', in *Chaucerian Problems and Perspectives*, ed. E. Vasta and Z. P. Thundy (Indiana, 1979), 70–82; this citation, 71.
[40] See Dunbar, K 14. 423, and K 74. 37; also Whiting, W 474.
[41] Kinsley, 313; R. J. Lyall, 'William Dunbar's Beast Fable', *SLJ* 1 (1974), 17–28.
[42] See Baxter, 51.

What contemporary figure is embodied in the wolf, whose hideous '3owling' so terrified the tod? James IV has been charged with many faults, but not with cowardice. Even if the tod's identification with James is accepted, I am unconvinced by critical attempts to find in the poem a highly moral purpose—'to awaken shame in the king . . . and encourage him to maintain a consciously rational existence'.[43] R. J. Lyall is right, I think, to say that the link between the poem and the king 'is not proven', and that it is not 'central to its theme or ironic structure'.[44] Dunbar probably alludes to some court scandal; despite his disclaimer (43-4) he here writes as a 'jangler', or purveyor of gossip. This poem is a tiny *roman à clef*, but it is one to which we have lost the key.

Two of Dunbar's poems are clearly indebted to the great tradition of allegorical poetry inspired by *Le Roman de la Rose*. *The Goldyn Targe* (K 10) is well known, and repeatedly discussed; *Sen that I am a presoneir* (K 9) has received far less critical attention.[45] Yet the two poems have much in common, and it is fruitful to compare them. Both are concise, containing, respectively, 279 and 112 lines. Dunbar differs from most medieval poets in his taste for short, pared-down allegories. Both employ the figure of love as warfare, and in both the lover is taken captive: in *The Goldyn Targe* (208-10) he is wounded and 'yoldyn as a wofull prisonnere' to Beauty; and the relationship between Beauty and her 'wofull presoneir' (32) forms the leading theme of *Sen that I am a presoneir*. Almost as prominent a role is allotted to Beauty in *The Goldyn Targe*, where she is 'first of all' (145) in the attack upon the lover. The poems share other personifications very common in love allegory; perhaps the most unusual is Comparison, who is merely mentioned in *The Goldyn Targe* (174) but in *Sen that I am a presoneir* seems to represent the lady's faculty for comparing one lover with others, usually to his disadvantage:

> The capitane, hecht Comparesone,
> To luke on me he thocht greit deyne. (27-8)

In both poems, as was traditional, it is the sense of sight that effects the lover's downfall: in *Sen that I am a presoneir* the lover is captured through 'luking' (5-14); and in *The Goldyn Targe* the dreamer is arrested

> All throu a luke quhilk I have boucht full dere. (135)

---

[43] Ross, 168.
[44] Lyall, op. cit. 25.
[45] One reason may be the slight doubt as to its authorship: Reidpeth's incomplete version is attributed to Dunbar, but the only complete text (in Bannatyne) is anonymous.

It might seem that in both poems Dunbar writes as if he himself were in love. Yet in each there is a curious ambiguity about the poet's role. *Sen that I am a presoneir* opens lyrically—

> Sen that I am a presoneir
> Till hir that farest is and best,
> I me commend fra ȝeir till ȝeir
> In till hir bandoun for to rest.   (1–4)

These lines are not separable from the eight-line stanza to which they belong; yet they stand apart from the main narrative, summing up its theme, rather like the burden of a carol. The poem opens in the first person—'I' occurs five times in the first stanza—yet after line 45 no more is heard of this 'I'-figure. The lover-as-speaker is absorbed into the third-person prisoner. The result is less inconsistency than increasing detachment in the presentation of the lover. The effect of *The Goldyn Targe* is also equivocal. It is narrated in the first person, and at its climax the poet exclaims passionately:

> Quhy was thou blyndit, Resoun? quhi, allace!
> And gert ane hell my paradise appere,
> And mercy seme quhare that I fand na grace.   (214–16)

Yet here too there is a disjunction between the poet's differing roles— now a lover and at the centre of the allegorical action, now a spectator, at a slight remove from the experience recounted.

The differences between these poems, however, are more striking than their similarities. Each treats a different aspect of love, and each selects different motifs from the allegorical repertoire—imprisonment and a siege in *Sen that I am a presoneir*, open battle in *The Goldyn Targe*. *Sen that I am a presoneir* is primarily concerned with courtship. The lover—or rather his heart—is imprisoned in the castle of 'pennance', or suffering; although at first scorned, he wins allies, among whom is the key figure of 'Petie'. These storm the castle, and free the prisoner—by implication the lady's resistance crumbles. A setback occurs, when Slander and Envy denounce the lover; but they are defeated by Matrimony, who

> The band of freindschip hes indost
> Betuix Bewty and the presoneir.   (103–4)

The allegoric plot, although reduced to its bare essentials, is coherent. It could indeed be a veiled account of a specific love affair, although the role of Matrimony implies that it is not extra-marital.

The imprisonment of the heart was a very common motif in love poetry—indeed there was a popular Scottish song called 'Lady, help your presoneir'.⁴⁶ But a particularly close parallel occurs in the homiletic allegory *King Hart*, whose hero is imprisoned in a castle with a scornful porter called 'Strangenes', just as in *Sen that I am a presoneir* (18). There are several other verbal similarities between these two poems, but their relationship is difficult to determine.⁴⁷ The love siege was also a popular medieval theme, in poetry and the visual arts; it figured on ivory caskets and mirror-cases as well as in tapestries.⁴⁸ Molinet's poem, *Le Hault Siege d'Amour*, is accompanied by a crude but vivid illustration, showing a tower attacked by figures armed with pikes and a small cannon; one of the defendants fires a crossbow.⁴⁹ In the late fifteenth century there was a vogue for the semi-dramatic treatment of the theme, in pageants and disguisings, particularly at courtly wedding festivities. At the marriage of Prince Arthur and Katharine of Aragon (1501) a siege furnished the subject for one of William Cornish's disguisings. This pageant clearly had a political dimension, and Gordon Kipling has plausibly interpreted it as a celebration of Tudor foreign policy: the dance that followed the storming of the castle symbolized 'the harmony of international peace as well as the concord of fulfilled romantic love'.⁵⁰ But many disguisings at the Tudor court were devised chiefly for recreation. One such was the siege of 'The Fortresse Dangerus' (1512); in another, on Shrove Tuesday 1522, Henry VIII and his knights, bearing names such as Ardent Desire, Nobleness, and Youth, stormed a castle of ladies; some were named Beauty, Bounty, and Pity, but others had such unpropitious names as Danger, Disdain, and Scorn, and defended the castle very stubbornly.⁵¹ Although it is impossible to demonstrate Dunbar's awareness of specific pageants, they provide a valuable context both for *Sen that I am a presoneir* and *The Goldyn Targe*; they illustrate the continuing popularity of such allegorical themes, and the ease with which they might be visualized by contemporaries.

A striking feature of the siege in *Sen that I am a presoneir* is its ferocity. In the 1522 disguising the ladies defended themselves 'with rose water and comfitttes, and the Lordes threw in dates and orenges and other fruites made for pleasure'.⁵² But there is no such pretty if

---

⁴⁶ *Complaynt of Scotland*, ed. A. M. Stewart (STS, 1979), 51.
⁴⁷ For discussion, see *Shorter Poems of Gavin Douglas*, ed. Bawcutt, lx. Neither poem is dated with certainty.
⁴⁸ Cf. R. S. Loomis, 'The Allegorical Siege in the Art of the Middle Ages', *American Journal of Archaeology*, 2nd ser. 23 (1919), 255–69.
⁴⁹ *Les Faictz et dictz*, ed. N. Dupire (SATF, 1936–9), ii. 567–83.
⁵⁰ *The Triumph of Honour* (Leiden, 1977), 105.
⁵¹ Edward Hall, *Henry VIII*, ed. C. Whibley (1904), i. 40 and 238–40.
⁵² Ibid. 239.

suggestive foolery in Dunbar. Cruel incidents occur—one figure is buried alive, another breaks his neck, and another is drowned in a sack. The siege has something of the violence of real warfare:

> Thai thairin schup for to defend,
> And thai thairfurth sail3eit ane hour;
> . . . .
> Thai fyrit the 3ettis deliverly
> With faggottis wer grit and huge . . .   (65 ff.)

This is much in the manner of Barbour, describing the siege of Berwick in 1318.[53] The narrative style of *Sen that I am a presoneir* is brisk and laconic. There is a high proportion of dialogue, and the refrain varies ingeniously, to fit in with this. Thought thus vows to free the lover—'I houp to lows the presoneir' (56)—whereas Comparison voices his opposition—'3e will nocht wyn the presoneir' (64). Perhaps the most interesting stylistic feature is the witty use of legal terminology. Envy 'blew out on' the prisoner (96), or outlawed him, to the blowing of a horn. 'Gud Fame' was succeeded by her heir, who 'gat ane confirmatioun' (109), a document confirming an inheritance. The union between Beauty and the Prisoner is a 'band of freindschip', endorsed by Matrimony (102–4). There is an evident word-play: *band* signifies both the marriage bond and, in a further sense, an alliance made between two parties for their mutual interest. Bonds of friendship were made between equals, and did not imply, like 'bonds of manrent', some kind of patron–client relationship.[54] Yet the lover retains the name of 'presoneir' till the poem's last line; although free, he is still as much in his lady's 'bandoun' as at the beginning. He resembles Arveragus in *The Franklin's Tale* (793), simultaneously 'servant in love and lord in marriage'; or the lover in *The Kingis Quair*, who becomes his lady's 'thrall,/For euer of fre wyll' (285–6). Such paradoxes were well established in the love tradition.

What is merely the starting-point for *Sen that I am a presoneir*—the initial process of falling in love—forms a major theme of *The Goldyn Targe*. In this erotic psychomachia the offensive is taken by Venus, 'lufis quene' (136), and by her agents, woman's attractive qualities, which are themselves personified as female—'dame' Beauty leads a troop of 'dameselis' (146–7), and Youth is accompanied by 'hir virgyns ying' (154). Against these forces the lover has one defence, Reason, personified as a knight, who wears plate and mail and bears a shield of gold (151–3). Reason's armour is solely protective, implying the lover's passivity; but the ladies, who are the aggressors, bear weapons, the darts and arrows traditionally employed by the god of love. The

[53] See *The Bruce*, xvii. 445–66.
[54] Cf. G. Donaldson, *Scottish Historical Documents* (Edinburgh, 1970), 97 and 140–3.

battle is brief, but has two stages. When the first attacks are parried by Reason, the forces of Venus retreat, 'reboytit of thair pray' (180). She, like a good commander, decides on a change of tactics, and brings up her best forces, 'the choise of Venus chevalry' (193). The new figure of 'Presence', perhaps to be interpreted as 'physical closeness', blinds Reason, casting 'a pulder in his ene' (203). The consequences are disastrous. 'Fair Calling'—who corresponds to Bel Accueil in *Le Roman de la Rose*—favours the lover only briefly, and is succeeded by Danger and 'Hevynesse' (218-28). This is the plight of the archetypal unhappy lover, whose mistress shows him no 'grace' (216).

The *Goldyn Targe* is far more complex than *Sen that I am a presoneir*. The allegorical action is but one of several elements—it is accompanied by reflections on the art of poetry (see above, pp. 21-3), preceded by the description of a beautiful May morning, and framed within a dream. These are familiar components in the tradition to which *The Goldyn Targe* belongs, yet they add to the intricacy of its structure; and its style, tone, and overall significance have provoked much debate among critics. C. S. Lewis found the allegorical story slight, and saw the poem's 'raison d'être' as 'pure decoration'. Denton Fox, in an influential article, argued that *The Goldyn Targe* was primarily 'a poem about poetry'. Many readers, however, take the love allegory more seriously: R. J. Lyall, for instance, sees the poem as embodying a strong and subtle 'moral argument'.[55] *The Goldyn Targe* certainly seems to me quite as much concerned with love as with poetry; it is also a work in which the goddess Nature is as important as Venus. Yet we should not attribute to this short and graceful poem a psychological complexity or ethical profundity that it does not possess. Its thought, for the most part, consists of commonplaces. It does not challenge prevailing orthodoxies, whether moral or literary. A sensitive reading of *The Goldyn Targe* must take account of its tone and also its small scale—it is, quite literally, a 'lytill quair'—as well as the proportions of its varied ingredients. The episode in which Reason is blinded resembles the criticism of human love in *The Merle and the Nychtingall*:

> Sic frustir luve it blindis men so far
> In to thair myndis it makis thame to vary. (90-1)

But this latter poem has a moral earnestness foreign to *The Goldyn Targe*, whose tone is far closer to the wry, mocking manner of *Quha will behald of luve the chance* (K 15). This short lyric elegantly dissects

[55] See *The Allegory of Love* (Oxford, 1936), 252; 'Dunbar's *The Golden Targe*', *ELH* 26 (1959), 311-34; 'Moral Allegory in Dunbar's "Goldyn Targe"', *SSL* 11 (1973-4), 47-65. These are three of the most distinctive critical approaches. Cf. also L. Ebin, 'The Theme of Poetry in Dunbar's "Goldyn Targe"', *Chau R* 7 (1972), 147-59.

love's 'schort plesance' and 'fair dissimulance'. *The Goldyn Targe* is not primarily concerned with inculcating moral lessons, and its final effect seems to me not sombre, but 'mirthfull'.

The 'dremes fantasy' (49) fills almost the whole poem, yet of the twenty-two stanzas allotted to it the love story occupies no more than twelve. The pace of narration is swift—'schortly for to speke' (136) is no mere line-filler. Dunbar often notes the speed with which events occur—'swift' (54, 237), 'sudaynly' (141, 207, 232), 'in a moment space' (210), 'in the space of a luke' (232), and 'in twynkling of ane eye' (235). The effect is twofold. It both evokes the fleeting evanescence of dreams, and suggests the nature of this love—hasty, frenetic, 'a short madness'. The boundary between waking and sleeping is at first blurred, not sharply demarcated. The 'real' yet highly idealized landscape of the opening turns into the backcloth for the dream itself. So too with the poet: at first he is not explicitly a lover but a pleased and insouciant spectator, exclaiming, 'joy was for to sene' (43); in the first stages of the dream his concern is likewise to 'discrive' and to 'compile' (64, 72) what he sees—as is evident in the extended *repetitio* on 'Thare saw I' (73-90) that follows. The transition from detached observer to engaged participant does not occur until well into the dream, when curiosity draws him too 'nere' (133); only then does the dreamer experience love for himself. The experience is characteristically paradoxical, and one in which the dreamer is increasingly 'affrayit' (134, 207, 242); he wakes with relief, as from a nightmare. His dream conveys a familiar truth—love is passionate, painful, and anti-rational—but it is viewed with a measure of irony and detachment. The poet-narrator is granted, very briefly, a glimpse of what it feels like to be a lover.

Stylistically, *The Goldyn Targe* far outshines *Sen that I am a presoneir*. The complex stanza is handled superbly. Sometimes the sense is disposed in symmetrically balanced units, as in the threefold patterning of the first stanza, where the rising of the poet parallels that of the sun and the lark. More commonly the sense is prolonged to the very end, with suspended clauses and phrases. Weaker poets of this time often flounder when attempting such a run-on style, but Dunbar is firmly in control of his syntax and his rhythms:

> Quhat throu the mery foulys armony
> And throu the ryveris soune rycht ran me by
> On Florais mantill I slepit as I lay;
> Quhare sone in to my dremes fantasy
> I saw approch agayn the orient sky
> A saill als quhite as blossum upon spray,
> With merse of gold brycht as the stern of day,

> Quhilk tendit to the land full lustily
> Als falcoune swift desyrouse of hir pray. (46-54)

This is vivid, sensuous, and highly visual, like much else in the poem. When the ladies disembark,

> Thair brycht hairis hang gletering on the strandis
> In tressis clere, wyppit with goldyn thredis;
> With pappis quhite and mydlis small as wandis. (61-3)

Despite a reference to 'wordis fair' (219), there is no dialogue in *The Goldyn Targe*. It unfolds like a pageant, and such details as the ship or the firing of a gun (238) may well have been suggested by some court disguising.[56] The poem is famous for the jewelled artifice of its dawn-description; yet the similes in lines 51-2 and 63, simple and semi-proverbial, illustrate that Dunbar's style is far more varied than is always recognized. The falcon-image is particularly compressed; it alludes primarily to the speed of the ship, but the reference to 'hir pray' is sinister and premonitory.

Dunbar interestingly describes the phenomenon of reflection:

> all the lake as lamp did leme of licht,
> Quhilk schadowit all about wyth twynkling glemis
> That bewis bathit war in secund bemys
> Throu the reflex of Phebus visage brycht. (30-3)

He also refers to the reverberation of sound—'The skyes rang for schoutyng of the larkis' (25; 108 and 240). The poem itself is full of verbal echoes, or 'secund bemys'. One line—'In mirthfull May, of eviry moneth quene' (252)—picks up earlier ones, 'In May in till a morow myrthfullest' (9), and 'May, of myrthfull monethis quene' (82). It has thus a recapitulatory quality, and in effect brings the narrative to a close. But the poem has a double ending, since its last three stanzas, though closely integrated, function as an envoi. The roses that are first mentioned, growing on the 'rosere' and in the 'rosy garth' (3, 22, 40), are real flowers. But in a later line—'Of all hir lusty rosis redolent' (275)—Dunbar speaks figuratively, of flowers of speech. The figure reaches its climax in the notion of Chaucer as 'ane flour imperiall' and 'rose of rethoris all' (253-4).

The poem abounds in such analogies between the natural and the human world. At the opening it is birds who sing 'full angellike' (10) and have 'hony throtis' (106); at the close it is poets who possess 'Angel mouthis most mellifluate' (265). The birds likewise serve Venus, as her 'chappell clerkis' (21). The same verb, *flete*, 'flow

---

[56] Cf. F. Shuffelton, 'An Imperial Flower: Dunbar's *The Golden Targe* and the Court Life of James IV of Scotland', *SP* 72 (1975), 193-207.

abundantly', is used of dew upon the branches (15) and of Cicero's verbal copiousness (70). Three striking words, drawn from the terminology of the visual arts—'anamalit', 'ourgilt', and 'enlumynit'— are applied first to the landscape (13, 27, 45), and later to the equally colourful and brilliant language of great poets (257–8, 266–7). The poem's dominant imagery is that of light. It opens with a reference to 'the stern of day', or the planet Venus; and its very last word is 'licht'. No reader can fail to notice how often the epithet 'bricht' occurs, or the many references to silver, gold, glittering gems, and 'bemes rede birnyng as ruby sperkis' (24). The ladies, with their 'brycht hairis' and flower-like beauty, also form part of this luminous landscape. In the natural world the source of all light is the sun, 'the goldyn candill matutyne' (4); in the world of poetry Chaucer is equally transcendent—'of our Inglisch all the lycht' (259).

Although 'affrayde' by his dream, the poet's awakening is tranquil and 'mirthfull':

> Suete war the vapouris, soft the morowing,
> Halesum the vale depaynt wyth flouris ying,
> The air attemperit, sobir and amene;
> In quhite and rede was all the felde besene
> Throu Naturis nobil fresch anamalyng
> In mirthfull May, of eviry moneth quene.   (247–52)

Dunbar inherited a tradition of viewing Nature as beneficent, a source of bodily and spiritual well-being. This notion of Nature is summed up in the term *Halesum*, 'health-giving', which was then something of a vogue-word among poets. It corresponds to Lydgate's 'holsum', which is repeatedly applied to the sights and scents of the garden in *The Complaint of the Lover's Life*; it is similarly employed by Douglas— 'richt hailsome was the sessoun of the 3eir'.[57] Nature sometimes provides a moral corrective to unhappy lovers; sometimes, as here, she brings them solace. Her role in this poem resembles that of Nature in *The Thrissill and the Rois*: she is coupled with Venus, 'quene and quene' (73), yet not identified with her.

This close yet not wholly harmonious relationship of Nature and Venus is one of the links that hold together the different parts of *The Goldyn Targe*. The network of metaphors and verbal echoes is more than mere decoration; it embodies a view of the world as pervaded by symbolical analogies, not only between flowers, birds, and young lovers, but also between the creative powers of Nature and the poet, who are both 'makaris', and whose artefacts are—in no pejorative

---

[57] Cf. *Complaint of the Lover's Life*, 14, 59, 85; *Palice of Honour*, 46; *Eneados*, Prol. 12. 226; *Tayis Bank*, 20.

sense—'enamelled'. *The Goldyn Targe* celebrates ideal beauty and 'myrth', yet it does not deny the existence of ugliness and sorrow. This kind of 'reality', paradoxically, is most evident in the dream, where the lover's final state is 'hevines'. Yet there is a foreshadowing of love's pain as early as the second stanza, which refers to Aurora's 'cristall teris', on parting from Phoebus (16–18). An acknowledgement of the less idyllic side of Nature runs throughout the poem: in the similes that mention hailstorms and rain-showers (178, 195), and the planetary-cum-mythological allusions to the baneful effects of 'crabbit Saturn' (114) or 'variant' Aeolus (122–3). So too with the world of poetry: it includes not only brilliant writers but 'rude' and 'imperfyte' ones, among whom Dunbar here modestly includes himself.

The thematic resemblance between *Now cumis aige* (K 17) and *The Merle and the Nychtingall* (K 16) was recognized by Bannatyne, who placed them together, and by Lord Hailes, who gave them confusingly similar titles—calling the former 'Of luve erdly and divine' and the latter 'The twa luves erdly and divine'.[58] Both are essentially religious poems, which condemn sexual love as 'feynit' (K 17. 4) and 'frustir [vain]' (K 16. 90). Both contrast this with the love of God, which alone is 'trew' and perfect (K 16. 79; K 17.14). Douglas, in his Fourth Prologue, provides a learned theological discussion of the 'twa luffis, perfyte and imperfyte', but in these poems the distinction between them is simple and absolute:

> No man hes curege for to wryte
> Quhat plesans is in lufe perfyte,
> That hes in fenʒeit lufe delyt—
> Thair kyndnes is so contrair clene.   (K 17. 13–16)

Both urge man to turn to Christ, whose love, shown by the Crucifixion, is more constant than any human lover's:

> Is nane sa trew a luve as He
> That for trew lufe of us did de.   (K 17. 79–80)
>
> O quhithir wes kythit thair trew lufe or none?
> He is most trew and steidfast paramour.   (K 16. 46–7)

The application to Christ of the strongly erotic 'paramour' may seem startling, but belongs to the same tradition as terming him the soul's 'leman'.[59] These themes are wholly orthodox—they figure in the palinode to *Troilus and Criseyde*, and countless religious lyrics. Neither poem expresses highly personal feeling. *The Merle and the*

---

[58] Bannatyne, fols. 283a–285b; *Ancient Scottish Poems* (1770), contents-page.
[59] See *DOST, paramour*, 2b; *CB XIV*, no. 52.

Nychtingall is a bird-debate, and the poet's function is largely that of a reporter. Only in the last stanza does he briefly adopt the role of the unrequited lover:

> Me to reconfort most it dois availl
> Agane for lufe quhen lufe I can find none,
> To think how song this merle and nychtingall. (117–19)

This speaker who now receives comfort is implicitly identified with the typical 'man', often mentioned (25, 43, 74, 101) and finally exhorted: 'Man, lufe God that the wrocht' (106 ff.). *Now cumis aige*, by contrast, is a first-person narrative, and ostensibly springs from direct experience of 'luvis court' (25–6). But here too the poet speaks on behalf of everyman, or rather that ideal man whom age has made wise.

The praise of old age, indeed, is quite as important a topic in this poem as love. In form it is a carol, and its burden couples the two themes:

> Now cumis aige quhair 3ewth hes bene,
> And trew lufe rysis fro the splene.

This is welcoming and affirmative, not mournful at youth's passing. Medieval writers often depicted the miseries of old age: there is a vivid portrait of 'Elde' in *The Parlement of the Thre Ages*, and a loathsome account of its 'propertes' in *The Prick of Conscience*.[60] But there also existed a didactic tradition of venerating age as a time that ideally brought experience and wisdom. Among Anglo-Saxon writers it was axiomatic that *gomol snoterost* (the old man is most sage).[61] Dunbar's contemporaries voiced similar thoughts. One anonymous Scottish piece has the refrain, 'Welcum eild, for 3outh is gone', and in a poem by Kennedy a man aged 60 says: 'blissit be God, my 3utheid is away'.[62] Henryson's *Praise of Age*, which also purports to be sung by an old man, has as its refrain, 'The more of age, the nerar hevynnis blisse'. All these poems, like Dunbar's, assert that age, whatever its disabilities, is to be valued for releasing one from youthful passions.

Dunbar's theme enjoyed a minor vogue among late-medieval courtly poets: the old man's farewell to love. It figures in Froissart's *Le Joli Buisson de Jonesce*, and Charles d'Orléans' *Songe en Complainte*.[63] But the closest English parallel is the end of *Confessio Amantis*, where

---

[60] *The Parlement of the Thre Ages*, ed. M. Y. Offord (EETS, OS 246, 1959), 153–63; *The Prick of Conscience*, ed. R. Morris (Berlin, 1863), i. 764–801.
[61] J. Burrow, *The Ages of Man: A Study in Medieval Writing and Thinking* (Oxford, 1986), 107.
[62] See *Maitland Folio*, 181, and Bannatyne, fol. 52b.
[63] See Burrow, 'The Portrayal of *Amans*' (n. 28 above), 18–21.

the ageing lover is dismissed from the court of Venus; Cupid withdraws the fiery dart, planted earlier in the lover's heart, and Reason returns, 'so that of thilke fyri peine / I was mad sobre'.[64] Gower's treatment, however, has a pathos and psychological insight that is lacking from this poem. The structure of *Now cumis aige* is neat but rather mechanical—each stanza, in turn, points the same simple contrast, between 'feynit' and true love, youth and age, and past and present. The well-known symptoms of courtly love, jealousy and obsessive secrecy, have been cured. He who loves God has no fear of rivals, and openness about this love damages no one's reputation but rather brings honour.

Apart from a reference to 'dame Venus brand' (3), the style of *Now cumis aige* is simple and unadorned. Its length—fifteen stanzas—may seem unusual for a carol, but is not unparalleled.[65] *The Merle and the Nychtingall* is far more ambitious, stylistically and metrically, as its opening proclaims:

> In May as that Aurora did upspring
> With cristall ene chasing the cluddis sable
> I hard a merle with mirry notis sing
> A sang of lufe with voce rycht comfortable
> Agane the orient bemis amiable
> Upone a blistull brenche of lawry grene;
> This wes hir sentens sueit and delectable:
> A lusty lyfe in luves service bene.
>
> Undir this brench ran doun a revir bricht
> Of balmy liquour cristallyne of hew
> Agane the hevinly aisur skyis licht,
> Quhair did upone the tother syd persew
> A nychtingall with suggurit notis new
> Quhois angell fedderis as the pacok schone;
> This wes hir song, and of a sentens trew:
> All luve is lost bot upone God allone.   (1–16)

This idealized spring scene resembles, on a much smaller scale, the beginning of *The Goldyn Targe* or Douglas's Twelfth Prologue. There is a similar taste for placing a noun between two modifiers—'balmy liquour cristallyne'—for heraldic colour terms—'sable', 'aisur'—and for mythological allusion. Aurora's 'chasing' away of night has a distant origin in the dawn descriptions of Ovid and Virgil.[66] Beginnings tend to be the most ornate parts of poems, and this heightened style

---

[64] *Confessio Amantis*, book VIII, 2868–9; in *Works*, ed. G. C. Macaulay (Oxford, 1899–1902).
[65] See Greene, *Carols*, nos. 149 and 314, which have thirty stanzas or more.
[66] On similar practice in the *Eneados*, see Bawcutt, *Douglas*, 138.

is not maintained throughout; yet there is much rhetorical patterning, including the sevenfold *repetitio* on 'Lufe' in lines 81–7.

These two antithetical stanzas state the poem's theme: the nightingale and the merle, or blackbird, both sing of love with equal sweetness, but the 'sentens' of their song is contrasted. The nightingale's song alone is 'trew'. The phrase 'upone the tother syd persew' stresses this opposition: it refers both to the nightingale's location, and to her adversarial stance—she appears 'on the other side' and 'pursues an action', as if in a lawcourt. The nightingale counters the song of the merle, until she capitulates—'Myn errour I confes' (97)— and the two birds sing in unison (105–12).

The poem belongs to a genre remarkably popular in the Middle Ages, first in Latin and later in the vernaculars. Debates were written on every conceivable subject, some frivolous, others serious; some, such as Lydgate's *Horse, Goose and Sheep*, involved several speakers, but it was most common, as here, to have two. The medieval vogue for the verse debate was allied to the educational use of formal disputation in schools and universities, and to its employment in the lawcourts. At the end of *The Merle and the Nychtingall* (115) the dispute is called a *pleid*, 'action at law, litigation'; this corresponds to Middle English 'plait', the term applied to the contest in *The Owl and the Nightingale*, a poem whose legal background has long been recognized.[67] The somewhat rigid structure of *The Merle and the Nychtingall*, in which the two speakers are allotted alternate stanzas, was common in debate poems. Slightly less common was another feature: the alternating refrains, which neatly, if mechanically, encapsulate the birds' contrasted viewpoints. (*In secreit place* employs the same device.) The closest Scottish parallels to the structure of *The Merle and the Nychtingall* are in Henryson's *Ressoning betuix Age and Youth* and Rolland's *Court of Venus*, where the narrator hears an unresolved dispute between two lovers. Esperance's refrain praises love—'I lufe ay leill, and that weill likis me'—but Disperance (Despair) says, 'I luifit to lang, and that forthinkis me'.[68] There is a fifteenth-century precedent for this form, however, in several English poems; Fox plausibly argued that there existed a sub-genre of 'debate poems which have stanzas rhymed *ababbcbc* with alternating refrains, and which often have the form of a *chanson d'aventure*'.[69]

English poets were fond of bird-debates, particularly those in which one speaker was the nightingale. The twelfth-century *Owl and the*

---

[67] *The Owl and the Nightingale*, ed. E. G. Stanley (1960), 5 and 1737.
[68] *The Court of Venus*, ed. Gregor, i. 313–640.
[69] *Poems of Henryson*, 458. Wyatt uses alternating refrains in a debate between a lover and his heart; *Poems*, ed K. Muir and P. Thomson (Liverpool, 1969), no. xci.

Nightingale is the earliest and most famous, but there also survive, as well as some fragments, the thirteenth-century *Thrush and Nightingale*, and Clanvowe's popular *Boke of Cupide*, in which a nightingale defends courtly love against the criticism of a 'leude' and churlish cuckoo.[70] As a genre the bird-debate overlaps with the fable and the bird-assembly, such as Chaucer's *Parliament of Fowls* and the anonymous *Parliament of Birds*. This latter ends with a 'sentens' similar to that of Dunbar's nightingale, stressing the superiority of divine to human love. The thrush advises all birds to sing, 'En dieu maffie sanz departer'.[71] No other debate seems to be known between a merle and a nightingale, but there existed a custom of pairing the two birds in medieval Latin poetry with which Dunbar may have been familiar. In several of the *Carmina Burana* the *merula* and *philomena* are linked, often in rivalry:

> dum garritus merule
> dulciter alludit,
> philomena carmine
> dulcia concludit.

[While it sweetly mocks the chattering of the blackbird, the nightingale concludes with sweet song.][72]

Poets often represented bird-song as competitive. In *The Romaunt of the Rose* the birds sing in order to 'sormounte' each other and 'to wynne hem prys' (666); and in *The Kingis Quair* the nightingale is questioned whether she fears that another bird may strive in song with her, 'the maistry to purchase' (409–10). Admonitory birds were not uncommon in love poems, where they tend to chide the lover for his sloth; and they were remarkably common in didactic verse. *Off Lentren in the first mornyng* (K 59), is placed in a bird's mouth; close to it in Bannatyne are three other moral pieces, all uttered by birds, one of which is later identified as Conscience. H. E. Sandison noted that 'moral and religious fowls' abound in the English *chansons d'aventure*.[73] Dunbar, like his contemporaries, would be familiar with a widely

---

[70] For the fragmentary nightingale-debates, see *SL*, nos. 179 and 180; *The Thrush and the Nightingale* is in *CB XIII*, no. 52; *The Boke of Cupide* is in *The Works of Sir John Clanvowe*, ed. V. J. Scattergood (Cambridge, 1965). Another 16th-century Scottish debate between a nightingale and a 'cheild' is incomplete; in it too the nightingale is highly moral. See *Miscellany of the Spalding Club* (Aberdeen, 1841–53), ii. xxvii–xxviii.

[71] For E. P. Hammond's edn. of *The Parliament of Birds*, see *JEGP* 7 (1907–8), 105–9.

[72] *Carmina Burana: Die Liebeslieder*, ed. A. Hilka and O. Schumann (Heidelberg, 1941), no. 59, st. 2; cf. also no. 58. 8–18, and no. 71, st. 2.

[73] Bannatyne, fols. 44a, 49a, and 53b; *The Chanson d'Aventure in Middle English* (Bryn Mawr, Penn., 1913), 39, and 82–7.

diffused tradition of talkative, admonitory, and often quarrelsome birds.

Dunbar displays no interest in the actual appearance or habitat of his birds. They are wholly symbolic: mouthpieces for opposing views. Since antiquity the nightingale had been famed for the beauty of its song. In the Middle Ages it was regarded as a harbinger of spring, but it was pre-eminently the bird of love, particularly love that was passionate, unhappy, or illicit. In poetry, the nightingale is often the lover's confidant or messenger; this theme is richly developed in *The Kingis Quair* (372 ff.). In *The Parliament of Birds* the nightingale is called 'Cupids bird', and in Jean de Condé's *Messe des Oiseaux* it is the priest of Venus.[74] For Dunbar to associate the bird with divine love might thus seem unorthodox. But the medieval symbolism of the nightingale was rich and complex. Its moral *significatio* was as varied as its song, which was sometimes termed sorrowful, sometimes—as in this poem—merry and joyful.[75] In *Ane Ballat of Our Lady* (34) Dunbar, like other poets, employs the nightingale as a figure for the surpassing excellence of the Virgin Mary. Two Latin poems by medieval English authors were called *Philomena*. One, by John of Howden (d. *c*.1275), treated the nightingale as the symbol of the meditative soul, singing praises to God.[76] But the spiritual interpretation of the nightingale found in the *Philomena* of John Peckham (d. 1292) was particularly famous; it was translated into English by Lydgate and by another anonymous poet. Peckham calls the nightingale *avis prudentissima*; her beautiful but anguished song commemorates Christ's Passion, and she signifies the virtuous soul filled with love of divine things (*animam virtutibus et amore plenam*).[77]

Neither of these 'Nightingale' poems constitutes Dunbar's source, but they illustrate the spiritual tradition in which he writes. Our first clue to the nightingale's significance is its plumage:

> Quhois angell fedderis as the pacok schone. (14)

This does more than suggest 'that Dunbar had not seen the nightingale'.[78] In medieval art and drama angels were commonly represented

---

[74] See *La Messe des oiseaux*, ed. J. Ribard (Geneva, 1970); trans. B. Windeatt in *Chaucer's Dream Poetry: Sources and Analogues* (Woodbridge, 1982), 104–19. Cf. W. Pfeffer, *The Change of Philomel: The Nightingale in Medieval Literature* (New York, 1985).

[75] Dunbar's nightingale is 'mirry' (26) as the merle (3); cf. Douglas, *Eneados*, Prol. 13. 61, and Whiting, N 110.

[76] See F. J. E. Raby, *A History of Christian-Latin Poetry from the Beginnings to the Close of the Middle Ages* (1953), 391–5.

[77] See Raby, *Christian-Latin Poetry*, 426–8; Pfeffer, *Change of Philomel*, 39 ff. For the English versions, see *Lydgate's Two Nightingale Poems*, ed. O. Glauning (EETS, ES 80, 1900).

[78] Kinsley, 275.

with wings of peacock feathers. This line, with its passing reference to *The Parliament of Fowls* (356), is designed to startle, and to indicate that this is no earthly bird. Its appearance is unnatural, and transfigured; and its song is equally transcendent: 'All luve is lost bot upone God allone'. The merle sings upon a branch of laurel; the nightingale is placed on the far side of a bright river, 'crystallyne of hew'. Both figure in the tradition of the *locus amoenus*; here, however, one location is natural, whereas the other sounds otherworldly, recalling the river of life, *splendidum tamquam crystallum*, in Revelation (22: 1). At the outset Dunbar briefly but effectively challenges the secular role of the nightingale, implicit in *The Kingis Quair* and explicit in *The Boke of Cupide*; in his poem it is not the nightingale but the merle that is the exponent of idealized passionate love.

The merle's first words are an exhortation to lovers (resembling the lark's in *The Thrissill and the Rois*): 'Awalk, 3e luvaris, o this May' (20). Her praise of love's ennobling power (81-8) finds a parallel in *The Boke of Cupide* (151-60), where love is likewise termed the source of 'al goodnesse'. Another short poem may be briefly mentioned here. *Be 3e ane lufar* (K 11) offers advice specifically to lovers, and its refrain lays orthodox stress on loyalty and discretion: 'Be secreit, trew, incressing of 3our name'. Human love here, as for the merle, is not inconsistent with virtue or morality. But despite the sustained *repetitio* on *Be* (which begins all 24 lines), the poem is clumsy, metrically and verbally; and the attribution to Dunbar is questionable.[79] Its main interest is generic: discussion of love's laws was a popular medieval theme, and may be traced to the instruction of the neophyte lover in *Le Roman de la Rose*. An 'ABC' of love figures in Henryson's *Robene and Makyne* (17-24), and immediately after *Be 3e ane lufar* Bannatyne placed Mersar's very similar poem, also termed an 'ABC'.[80]

The merle associates herself with the goddess Nature: her speeches appeal to the teaching (22) or promptings (52) of Nature, and explicitly invoke 'the law of kynd':

> Seis, quod the merle, thy preching, nychtingale;
> Sall folk thair 3ewth spend in to holines?
> Of 3ung sanctis growis auld feyndis but faill;
> Fy, ypocreit, in 3eiris tendirnes
> Agane the law of kynd thow gois expres
> That crukit aige makis on with 3ewth serene,
> Quhome Natur of conditionis maid dyvers.   (33-9)

The merle voices the popular notion that there was something both unnatural and hypocritical in youthful virtue. But her choice of proverb

---

[79] *Bannatyne Facsimile*, no. 241.
[80] Fol. 213a; a wittier example occurs on fol. 230a.

is revealing: 'young saint, old devil', as John Burrow has shown, was widely condemned by moralists.[81] It was termed sinful and *detestabile*, and 'the devil's own invention'. When employed in dramatic contexts, it was regularly placed in the mouths of devils or evil counsellors, such as Riot in the morality *Youth*, or Placebo in Lindsay's *Satire of the Three Estates*. Its self-incriminating use here is wholly traditional; so too is the nightingale's rejoinder, that to love God is not out of place at any age.

There is comic sophistry in the merle's later argument:

> God bad eik lufe thy nychtbour fro the splene,
> And quho than ladeis suetar nychtbouris be? (70–1)

The merle fails to distinguish the different senses of 'lufe', and also perverts the commandments. It is God whom one should love with all one's heart, or 'fro the splene'; the second and subsidiary commandment is to love one's neighbour as oneself (Matthew 22: 37 ff.). Rolland's Esperance also cites Scripture to prove that God 'ordanit lufe'; but his opponent comments, 'thow takis it in wrang kinde'.[82] The merle has something in common with the Widow in *The Tua Mariit Wemen and the Wedo*. Her speeches lack 'gud sentens', yet have a cheeky zest that enlivens the poem. Dunbar uses other devices to make the debate sound colloquial; he follows the common practice of strewing the discussion with scornful interjections—'fule', 'quhy dois thow raif?' (73), or 'Trew is the contrary' (89). The latter seems to have been a debater's stock retort: Dunbar put it in the nightingale's mouth, but Clanvowe gave it to the cuckoo:

> Nyghtyngale, thou spekest wonder faire,
> But, for al that, the sothe is the contreyre. (167–8)

The Merle and the Nychtingall is an undervalued poem. Its rigid pattern does not permit the development of a full or complex argument by either speaker. Yet some of the techniques, notably the bandying of proverbs, recall the lively debates conducted in Henryson's *Fables*. Dunbar here succeeds in giving succinct and lively expression to sharply contrasted views on love.

Women are at the foreground of a number of Dunbar's poems: these are remarkably different, ranging from explicit praise to veiled mockery. The first group is small, and includes the poems in honour of the Virgin (K 2) and the queen (K 31, K 50); although the first is religious and the latter secular, there are striking affinities between them in

---

[81] '"Young Saint, Old Devil": Reflections on a Medieval Proverb', *RES* NS 30 (1979), 385–96.
[82] *Court of Venus*, ed. Gregor, i. 442–51.

eulogistic diction, topoi, and imagery. Another member of this group is the poem that begins

> Now of wemen this I say for me,
> Off erthly thingis nane may bettir be.   (K 72. 1–2)

The words 'I say for me' have led some scholars to give this poem a personal interpretation: as 'a blatant piece of flattery', perhaps of the queen, or 'Dunbar's apology for former offences against the fair sex'.[83] It is rather Dunbar's one overt contribution to the debate about women, and deploys wholly traditional 'proofs' and arguments. Bannatyne conveniently assembled other 'ballattis of the prayis of wemen' close to this one—Stewart's *For to declair the he magnificens*, Weddirburn's *I think thir men ar verry fals and vane*, and two works that he mistakenly attributed to Chaucer, Hoccleve's *Letter of Cupid*, and the anonymous *All tho that list of wemen evill to speik*.[84] Dunbar's short poem is constructed from commonplaces. He praises women for their suffering in childbirth and tender care of children (13–18); the anonymous poet writes similarly,

> For we aucht first to think on quhat maner
> Thay bring ws furth and quhat pane thay indure
> First in our birth and syne fro 3eir to 3eir.   (8–10)

Another stock proof of women's excellence was the Virgin's surpassing virtue—in the carol's words, 'Wytnesse on Marie'[85]—and more particularly the choice of a woman to bear God. Theologians recognized this idea, which Dunbar expresses somewhat elliptically (27 ff.), as the *argumentum e conceptione*.[86] Stewart thus says, 'that only act savis thame all fra schame' (47), and Weddirburn remarks that God was born of woman, 'And nocht consaivit be menis polute seid' (13–14).

Another passage struck a modern critic as possessing 'a crudeness not uncommon in Dunbar':[87]

> Thay ar our verry nest of nurissing.
> In lak of thame quha can say ony thing,
> That fowll his nest he fylis, and for thy
> Exylit he suld be of all gud company.   (21–4)

But this saying, that a bird should not foul its own nest, was regularly used to make precisely the same point:

---

[83] Scott, 56; Schipper, 76.

[84] See respectively fols. 277a, 279a, 269a, and 275a. Utley, 50–2, lists other examples.

[85] Greene, *Carols*, no. 395.

[86] On the continuing use of this argument, cf. I. Maclean, *Woman Triumphant* (Oxford, 1977), 25–6.

[87] Scott, 57.

> Ane auld prowerb said is in inglische
> That bird or fowll is full dishonest
> . . . .
> That vsis to defoull his awin nest.
> Men to say weill of wemen it is best.[88]

Indeed, even at the end of the sixteenth century, the proverb was still being employed to chide those who spoke ill of women. Underlying Celia's criticism of Rosalind in *As You Like It* (IV. i. 194) is Lodge's 'what mettall are you made of that you are so satyricall against women? Is it not a foule bird defiles the owne nest?'[89]

Although this poem's attribution to Dunbar has never been questioned, it fits awkwardly into his canon. It is unusual in being the only one of his poems written in five-beat couplets; although short, it is repetitious, and rhythmically clumsy. Hoccleve and Hoccleve's source, Christine de Pisan, wrote very interestingly in women's defence; but this is a stock poem on a stock subject, and if indeed by Dunbar does him little credit.

Dunbar's humorous poems about women are no less indebted to literary tradition and female stereotypes than those that celebrate them—but they are distinctly more witty and subtle. This should not necessarily be attributed to Dunbar's personal animus against women, but rather to his greater talent for mockery and satire. *The Tua Mariit Wemen and the Wedo* has long fascinated readers, and provoked remarkably passionate and varied responses.[90] Yet its affinities with Dunbar's other poetry have been little explored. The theme of the 'wicket wyfe', for instance, who turns marriage into 'stryfe' figures briefly in *He that hes gold and grit riches* (K 70); and other short poems, such as *In secreit place* (K 13), *Thir ladyis fair* (K 71), and *Rycht airlie on Ask Weddinsday* (K 73), employ similar narrative techniques, imagery, and irony.

The structure of *The Tua Mariit Wemen and the Wedo* is deceptively simple: there is no complicated plot, merely three ladies talking in a 'grein arbeir' on Midsummer's Eve. Yet the poem moves far from these narrow confines—indoors and outdoors, disclosing the intimacies of bed and bower, as well as more public events, 'in kirk and in markat' (81). The ladies' husbands, although not present, are vividly evoked; so, to a lesser extent, are their servants, lovers, and kin. The poem eludes, somewhat similarly, critical attempts to define its bounds

---

[88] *Letter of Cupid*, 183 ff. For use of this proverb (Whiting, B 306) in a similar context, see also *CB XIV*, no. 110. 73–4.

[89] *Rosalynde*, in *Narrative and Dramatic Sources of Shakespeare*, ed. G. Bullough, ii (1968), 181.

[90] See the useful survey by E. Roth, 'Criticism and Taste: Readings of Dunbar's *Tretis*', *SLJ*, Supplement 15 (1981), 57–90.

too rigorously and to pin down its genre, significance, and tone. It largely consists of set speeches, yet these highly rhetorical orations contain anecdotes, descriptive vignettes, and snatches of conversation. It resounds with laughter, yet many critics (chiefly men) are unamused, and subject it to solemn and often hostile analysis. It is full of shocking contrasts: between beauty and ugliness, refinement and gross vulgarity; between the love that the ladies mention repeatedly, and the hatred and contempt that they feel. The poem has greater structural intricacy than first appears, and its verbal texture is rich, subtle, and allusive.

The substance of *The Tua Mariit Wemen and the Wedo* is talk: the poet overhears women talking about themselves and their husbands, and when they retire homewards, he too withdraws to an 'arber':

> And with my pene did report ther pastance most mery. (526)

A similar phrase—'this report I with my pen'—concludes *This hindir nycht in Dumfermeling*; in this poem, as in that, the poet has a strange story to tell, an 'uncouth aventur' (528). In its very much smaller way this, like *The Decameron*, is a framed tale-collection. The ladies form a rich, leisurely group, briefly isolated from the rest of society, who entertain themselves by talking 'of mony taill sindry' (38). Each member of the group is obliged to speak; at the Widow's turn, she exclaims, 'Now tydis me for to talk; my taill it is nixt' (246). Yet these stories purport to be truth rather than fiction, fragments of the women's life-history. Each 'taill' is greeted by laughter. The speeches are punctuated with brief, stylized references to feminine revelry:

> Than all thai leuch apon loft with latis full mery
> And raucht the cop round about full of riche wynis.
> (147–8; cf. 239–41, 505–10)

Yet the evident symmetry of this pattern is disturbed—as Chaucer interrupted the proposed plan of *The Canterbury Tales*—by the remarkable prominence of the Widow. Virtually half the poem is occupied by her speech, which much exceeds the total length of those allotted to the Wives.

Critics have termed the women's conversation a '*débat* on love and marriage', or an example of 'the inconclusive or balanced debate, in which, while neither side wins, there is a resolution [of the argument], stated or unstated'.[91] Yet this seems misleading. *The Tua Mariit Wemen and the Wedo* is not a debate-poem in the usual sense: its speakers, unlike those in *The Merle and the Nychtingall*, do not represent well-

---

[91] Kinsley, 259; N. Jacobs, 'The Typology of Debate and the Interpretation of *Wynnere and Wastoure*', *RES*, NS 36 (1985), 481.

defined and contrasted views. Although the women speak passionately about contentious issues, they do not take 'sides' nor do they argue with each other in an effort to 'win'. There is indeed a remarkable unanimity among them. Some have found fault with the poem precisely because they considered the women over-similar; others have called them two-dimensional, 'much less complete human beings than the Wife of Bath'.[92] But this lack of individuality seems wholly intentional. Chaucer often gives his characters names—Alisoun, Jankin, Nicholas—but Dunbar here speaks simply of 'the wedo' or 'the tothir wlonk' (150), rather as he speaks of 'the tane' and 'the tother' cummer in *Rycht airlie on Ask Weddinsday*. They are archetypes of feminity: they start as 'ladeis' (17), but increasingly speak on behalf of all women, irrespective of age and class—'we wemen', in the Widow's phrase (448). Much the same is true of the men—the husbands are nameless, and represent types, such as the *senex amans* and the impotent lecher. The basic antagonism is not between the women, but between male and female. Yet the women are not clones. The most important difference, as the title and the length of their speeches indicate, is in marital status. The speeches of the Wives are essentially complaints—unhappy and rebellious, they want to reject marriage; but the experienced and wily Widow accepts the status quo, and teaches them how to manipulate it for their own advantage.

The lack of dialectic in this poem was noted by Roy Pearcy, who suggested that it belonged to 'a previously unrecognised' genre, which he termed the *jugement*. The medieval French poems that, in his opinion, comprise this genre are usually known as fabliaux; all concern women who take part in some contest—who can best trick their husband, or provide the wittiest answer to an obscene riddle—and they end with the author passing judgement on the proceedings, or soliciting one from his audience:

> In all five French examples of the *jugement* genre, a game is played by three women, each of whom attempts to say or do something sexually more outrageous than the others... In all the instances where an explicit judgment is rendered, it favors the last of the three contestants, and the performances consequently arrange themselves in a climactic series.[93]

There are many differences between *The Tua Mariit Wemen and the Wedo* and these French poems, but the crucial one is that Dunbar's women are in no sense competitors or rivals. I would not myself classify this poem as a *jugement*, yet Pearcy is perceptive about its

---

[92] J. Speirs, 'A Survey of Medieval Verse', in *The Age of Chaucer*, ed. B. Ford (1954), 59.
[93] 'The Genre of William Dunbar's *Tretis of the Tua Mariit Wemen and the Wedo*', *Speculum*, 55 (1980), 58–74; this citation, 69.

'LADEIS BEWTIE ... LUIFFIS BLYS'

overall effect; the speeches do form a ritualized 'climactic series', and resemble a theatrical performance, or 'game'. But the game in which Dunbar's women take part belongs, I think, to the different tradition of the *demandes d'amour*.
The poem's chief structural pattern is that of question and answer. The Widow begins by firing questions at the wives, designed to elicit their views on love and marriage:

> Bewrie, said the wedo, ʒe woddit wemen ʒing,
> Quhat mirth ʒe fand in maryage sen ʒe war menis wyffis;
> Reveill gif ʒe rewit that rakles conditioun,
> . . . .
> Or gif ʒe think, had ʒe chois, that ʒe wald cheis better? (41 ff.)

Playful discussion of love, in the form of question and answer, was a courtly pastime that is often mentioned in medieval literature, and seems to have featured in real life. Boccaccio's *Il Filocolo* contains thirteen love questions, and there survive many French examples, some sentimental, some flippant, some obscene.[94] The practice is mentioned by Douglas in *The Palice of Honour* (1180 ff.), where 'mony fair demandis' figure among the entertainments at the Muses' feast. These *demandis* concerned both heroes—'quha best in thair times had bene'—and lovers—'quha traist louers in lustic ʒciris grene'. In the Scottish translation of *Les Vœux du Paon*, known as *The Avowis of Alexander*, there occurs an episode in which five young people indulge in 'play and gamyn':

> Thare was demandis and fare answeris,
> Enquestis, greting and prayers
> Of amouris and his worshep all
> . . . .
> Thay bourded and gamed fast
> . . . .
> To 'the king that suld nocht le'
> Thay cheisit Betys.[95]

This game of 'le roy qui ne ment' took different forms, but usually stipulated truthful answers to all questions, however embarrassing this might prove to the participants, including the 'king', or master of ceremonies.[96] In *The Avowis*, for instance, one young woman is instructed 'that sho the suth suld to him say', and another is similarly told, 'say me the suth'.[97]

---

[94] Cf. E. Ilvonen, 'Les Demandes d'amour dans la littérature française du Moyen Age', *Neuphil. Mitteil.* 14 (1912), 128–44.
[95] *Buik of Alexander*, ed. Ritchie (see n. 7), ii. 159, lines 2175 ff.
[96] Ilvonen, op. cit. 135. In Jean de Condé's fabliau *Le Sentier Battu* it is a *queen* who puts the questions.
[97] *Buik of Alexander*, 2192 and 2442.

In *The Tua Mariit Wemen and the Wedo* we find a similar combination of sport and truth-telling: Dunbar speaks repeatedly of the women's mirth, 'game' (241), and 'pastance most mery' (526). But the Widow exhorts the Second Wife to speak without feigning (151) and to confess the truth (153); in return she makes a compact that she herself will 'say furth the south [truth] dissymyland no word' (157). The Widow's role slightly resembles that of the 'king'. Yet there are obvious differences of tone and setting. In *The Avowis* young, unmarried men and women make flirtatious banter, and pose idealistic questions—'which gives greater joy, to see one's beloved, or to think of her?' In Dunbar's poem the group consists solely of married women, who speak bitterly of their married experience.

The Tua Mariit Wemen and the Wedo contains another and final question, that the poet puts to his 'auditoris':

> Of thir thre wantoun wiffis that I haif writtin heir,
> Quhilk wald 3e waill to 3our wif gif 3e suld wed one? (529–30)

There is a clear structural parallelism between the inner story and its frame: instead of a woman interrogating women, the poet addresses male listeners (actual or imaginary), and singles out one of the Widow's topics—'chois' of marriage partners—for renewed, sardonic consideration. It was not uncommon to end a medieval poem (or section of it) with a question. There are several examples in Chaucer, as at the end of *The Franklin's Tale*:

> Lordynges, this question, thanne, wol I aske now,
> Which was the mooste fre, as thynketh yow? (v. 1621–2)

But Chaucer usually, as here and in *The Knight's Tale*, invites the audience to ponder some ethical dilemma in a disinterested manner. Dunbar formulates his question differently—he asks, not 'what do you think of these women?', but 'which of them would you marry?' The question is highly equivocal, and Dunbar himself is playing an authorial 'game': concluding, yet in a most inconclusive way; implying that his audience is solely male, when it would probably be mixed; and playfully blurring any barrier between fictional 'wiffis' and actual 'auditoris'. The obvious response is likely to be a recent male critic's 'None of them'! But the poem as a whole poses more intractable questions, and is designed to be controversial. 'What thyng is it that wommen moost desiren?' It exposes not only women's desires but men's fears—concerning sexual satisfaction, material possessions, and, above all, power.

What is the role of the narrator? The practice of identifying him closely with Dunbar is remarkably persistent. Critics have repeatedly traced the poem's concern with female sexuality to the poet's own sexual repression. A. K. Moore suggested that only the 'warped' mind of a celibate 'could impugn the motives of women with such obvious pleasure'.[98] A. C. Spearing speculated similarly about the narrator:

he is a solitary male voyeur, hiding furtively to conceal his eagerness to see and hear what women say when they are by themselves. It seems likely that his solitariness and his confinement to the role of spectator where women are concerned should be related to Dunbar's real-life status as a priestly celibate, obsessed by what is forbidden to him.[99]

This seems fallacious, from both a literary and a historical standpoint. *The Tua Mariit Wemen and the Wedo* is a different sort of poem from the petitions; its narrator is a fiction, and to what extent he coincides with Dunbar is unclear. What is more, although nothing is known about the 'real-life' Dunbar's sexuality, there is abundant evidence as to other medieval churchmen. Celibacy may have been the priestly ideal, but we should not assume that all clergy were chaste and celibate. Bishop Elphinstone was the bastard son of a cleric, and before he himself could receive a living had to obtain papal and royal dispensations from his illegitimacy. This was by no means exceptional—Elphinstone's biographer speaks of 'the high incidence of illegitimate children fathered by the clergy in the later Middle Ages'.[100] It should be recalled that the Widow's sexual initiation started with 'the curat of our kirk' (306), and that her flirtatious looks were directed at clerks as well as knights (435).

Honourable people, however, do not eavesdrop on others, and the narrator, whatever his relation to Dunbar, seems unsympathetic to many readers. He is termed a 'peeping Tom' as well as a 'voyeur'.[101] Yet medieval poetry is full of poets who behave precisely in this way— Machaut and Deschamps, for instance,[102] and Lydgate, in *The Complaint of a Lover's Life*, who comes across a man lamenting in an arbour, and conceals himself 'priuely' among the bushes, with the object of hearing as much as possible:

> If that I myght in eny wise espye
> What was the cause of his dedely woo,
> Or why that he so pitously gan crie. (148–50)

---

[98] *Secular Lyric in Middle English*, 62. See Scott, 202, and K. M. Abenheimer, 'The Treatise of the Two Married Women and the Widow', *Psychoanalytic Review*, 31 (1944), 233–52.
[99] *Medieval to Renaissance in English Poetry* (Cambridge, 1985), 220.
[100] Macfarlane, *Elphinstone*, 16; and cf. 78.
[101] Scott, 204.
[102] Cf. the concealed dreamer in Machaut's *Jugement dou Roy de Behaingne*, or the poet in Deschamps' *Lay de Franchise*, who hides in a bush 'to observe' unseen; see Windeatt, *Chaucer's Dream Poetry*, 3–4; 152–5.

The narrator of *The Quare of Jelusy* likewise hides 'preuely' among the leaves (45–6), in order to hear a lady's lamentations; and Holland, in *The Howlat*, listens eagerly, and apparently in concealment, to the owl's complaint. The poet's role in *The Tua Mariit Wemen and the Wedo* would be very familiar to Dunbar's readers, and not necessarily reprehensible. The device of the concealed listener was a long-established convention, yet not an empty one. It served to establish a sense of intimacy and self-revelation: in *The Complaint of a Lover's Life* and *The Quare of Jelusy* lovers display their inmost feelings in a way that would not be likely in public. In these cases the poet shows sympathy and compassion. But self-revelation passes easily into self-betrayal, and the device clearly has comic potential. Theatrically, it is a staple of comedy, as in *Love's Labour's Lost*, where Berowne watches his fellow-lovers:

> Like a demigod here sit I in the sky,
> And wretched fools' secrets heedfully o'er-eye.   (IV. iii. 76–7)

For Dunbar too, as also in *In secreit place*, the device is principally a means of comic self-betrayal. It is a major source of dramatic irony: there is no hint that the women are aware of an observer, and they speak indiscreetly, because they think they are alone—the Second Wife exclaims, 'ther is no spy neir' (161), and the Widow boasts, 'no creatur kennis of our doingis' (454). All of them voice emotions normally hidden within their hearts (162 ff. and 333). The poet hears what men in general—and husbands specifically (271)—do not know. There is a comic parallelism between the core-story—women talking together about men—and its frame—the male poet reporting to male 'auditoris'. The narrator is privileged, but still a representative of the 'kin of Adam' (521), and hears disturbing things of his own sex. His presence thus reinforces our sense of the poem's male–female polarization.

The women, as line 161 implies, would regard the listener as a spy; he is bringing to light what the Wife of Bath called her 'privetee', intimate matters, such as the relations between wife and husband. According to another Wife, in *The Shipman's Tale*, it was unfitting to tell anyone of this 'privetee', 'Neither abedde, ne in noon other place'.[103] But all these wives, of course, cheerfully infringe such confidentiality themselves, when they talk to lovers or to female friends. Dunbar's poem testifies, on one level, to a perennial male curiosity as to what women are really like—'What are little girls made of?' Part of its appeal seems to lie in this. But to call the fictive narrator a 'voyeur' is misleading, since it implies a pathological desire

---

[103] *CT* III. 531; VII. 165.

to spy upon women. There is a prevalent impression that he sets out with the intention of spying, which results from an unfortunate misunderstanding of line 9:

> I drew in derne to the dyk to dirkin efter mirthis.

Dirkin efter is usually glossed as 'lie low in search of'; but *efter*, 'after', has this purposive sense only in conjunction with verbs like *seek* or *search*. *Dirkin* means 'lie still in the dark'. The poet is here depicted as a weary reveller, seeking rest after the Midsummer Eve merrymaking. He listens to the conversation out of curiosity, but the incident is shown, in the manner typical of *chansons d'aventure*, as wholly unexpected: 'this uncouth aventur quhilk airlie me happinnit' (528). One of the bawdy poems in Bannatyne has a similar frame: in the first stanza the poet 'wanderit' alone, and in its last his experience is termed 'this aventur'.[104]

The poem's irony, according to Spearing, is ultimately directed not against the characters within the fiction but against the 'complacently blind' narrator, who is 'as fatuously given to idealization of women at the end as he was at the beginning'.[105] But there seems little idealism in the first reference to the Widow as 'wantoun' (37), or in the mention of 'thir thre wantoun wiffis' in the penultimate line. The sense-range of *wantun* was wider then than today, but it was usually pejorative, and, when applied to women, indicated some degree of sexual laxity.[106] Such a word undercuts the bland commendation of the women as 'semely' and 'amyable' no less than their outrageous speeches. But the irony is variable and flickering. The narrator, as a man, shares to some extent in the husbands' blindness. Yet for most of the poem he is himself the ironist, the privileged observer, communicating his insights in a sardonic, deadpan manner that closely resembles that of Dunbar in *Thir ladyis fair*. The narrator is of interest, but he is not a richly developed or wholly consistent figure. Indeed through much of *The Tua Mariit Wemen and the Wedo* we are little aware of him, and his importance should not be exaggerated. If we do, we turn the poem's structure inside out, putting what is marginal and peripheral at its very centre.

The women converse in an idyllically beautiful garden. Such descriptive set-pieces are familiar preludes to medieval poems of many types, alliterative and non-alliterative alike. Yet here, as in *The Goldyn Targe*, the description seems to serve as more than a decorative

---

[104] Fol. 141a.
[105] *Medieval to Renaissance*, 223 and 220.
[106] Cf. Henryson's revealing collocation 'Wantoun, unwyse, without correctioun' (*Fables*, 1588).

framework or a mere device for getting the poem started. What then is its significance? John Speirs neatly illustrates two divergent responses. In 1938 he saw 'no essential contrast between the natural scene ... and the gossips, the beauty of nature and the ugliness of vice'. They are all filled with 'the same exuberance of life; they are equally on the plane simply of nature and instinct'.[107] In 1954 he took a more sober view: 'The descriptions ... produce an effect of midsummer opulence, rococo June with its festoons of flowers and leaves and its singing birds, and contrast sharply with the horrors exposed.'[108] Most critics subscribe to the latter view, seeing a shocking contrast (one of many) between the garden's ideal beauty and the ugly actuality of the women.[109] Yet the relationship between the women and their setting cannot, it seems to me, be reduced either to identity or stark opposition; it is teasing and enigmatic, like the association of Venus and Nature in *The Goldyn Targe*.

Dunbar dates the incident very precisely 'Apon the midsummer evin'. This was a time not only of great natural beauty but of human revelry and loosened inhibitions (above, p. 76). At the beginning the women blend into the garden; adorned with 'garlandis of fresche gudlie flouris', they are partially assimilated to their setting in a passage where the ambiguity of the syntax reinforces the sense of similes:

> All full of flurist fairheid as flouris in June—
> Quhyt, seimlie and soft as the sweit lillies,
> Now upspred upon spray as new spynist rose,
> Arrayit ryallie about with mony riche vardour
> That Nature full nobillie annamalit with flouris.   (27–31)[110]

At the end the women are still, metaphorically, flowers, or 'ryall rosis' (523). The poet is attracted to the garden not only by the women's high voices but by bird-song (5–7). The parallel, barely hinted here, becomes explicit later. The ladies are compared to birds remarkable for their beauty: the narrator calls them swan-white (243), and the Widow views herself as a peacock (379) and a 'papyngay' (382). This bird imagery links with a leading theme, voiced by the First Wife:

> Birdis hes ane better law na bernis be meikill,
> That ilk ȝeir, with new joy, joyis ane maik,
> And fangis thame ane fresche feyr ...   (60–2)

---

[107] 'William Dunbar', *Scrutiny*, 7 (1938), 61.
[108] 'Survey of Medieval Verse' (see n. 92), 59.
[109] Cf. Kinsley, 'The Tretis of the Tua Mariit Wemen and the Wedo', *MÆ* 23 (1954), 31–5; and J. Leyerle, 'The Two Voices of William Dunbar', *UTQ* 31 (1962), 333.
[110] My reading of the text differs from Kinsley's.

The Second Wife picks up the topic (205 ff.), and envies birds for their apparent freedom and joy. The 'law' of birds is contrasted with that of humans, and identified with 'the law of luf, of kynd and of nature' (58).

But what the women say either of nature or of love is not necessarily to be trusted. The 'law of kynd' was similarly invoked by the merle in *The Merle and the Nychtingall*. The Second Wife at one point reduces 'natur' (174) to the sexual drive, and the women's view of love is equally limited. 'Luf' is seen as the satisfaction of sexual appetite; it is not associated with affection, friendship, loyalty, or constancy, nor with any grand philosophical principle of cosmic harmony. Venus rules the poem—she is the only pagan deity to be mentioned—but her status is much degraded. She does not appear as planet nor as goddess, but is virtually no more than a common noun, a component in bawdy euphemisms, such as 'Venus werkis' (127) or 'Venus chalmer' (185). The women flagrantly reject the teachings of the Church that marriage was a *divinum vinculum*—as the Second Wife exclaims, 'chastite, adew!' (208).[111] Their views, however, infringe the code of courtly love more subtly yet no less shockingly. Yet it is left to the reader to draw such conclusions. This poem, unlike *The Merle and the Nychtingall*, contains no explicit moral, and, apart from the single epithet *wantoun*, there is no overt criticism of the women.

Dunbar leaves his audience similarly free to judge as to what constitutes 'the law of kynd'. According to modern naturalists, some birds pair for life, others do not. According to medieval bestiaries, not all birds lived as promiscuously as the First Wife claimed—the sparrow was lecherous, and termed 'Venus sone' by Chaucer; but the turtle-dove, mentioned by the Widow (262), was believed to be chaste and constant to her mate. The 'law of kynd' was a problematic concept. In Langland 'Kynd' instructed the dreamer, and informed him that all natural creatures, except man, were governed by reason— it 'reuled alle bestes, / Saue man and his make'.[112] Dunbar is not a philosophical poet, and is never as doctrinally explicit as Langland. Yet implicit in this poem is a view of Nature resembling that in *The Goldyn Targe*: she is both creative—her beautiful 'annamalit' works include women as well as flowers—and also re-creative, or 'sanative' (8). *The Tua Mariit Wemen and the Wedo* ends with a fine dawn-scene:

> berdis schoutit in schaw with ther schill notis.
> The goldin glitterand gleme so gladit ther hertis
> Thai maid a glorius gle amang the grene bewis.

---

[111] Cf. *William Hay's Lectures on Marriage*, trans. and ed. J. C. Barry (Stair Soc., Edinburgh, 1967), 10, 36–8, 114.
[112] Cf. *Piers Plowman*, B XI. 325 ff.

'LADEIS BEWTIE ... LUIFFIS BLYS'

> The soft sowch of the swyr and soune of the stremys,
> The sueit savour of the sward, singing of foulis,
> Myght confort ony creatur of the kyn of Adam
> And kindill agane his curage thoght it wer cald sloknyt. (519–22).

Here, as in *The Goldyn Targe*, Dunbar applies the epithets 'soft' and 'sueit' to the natural world, and speaks of it as bringing comfort. The phrasing recalls Nature's healing powers in *The Morte Arthure*:

> That whate swowynge of watyre, and syngynge of byrdez,
> It myghte salue hyme of sore, that sounde was neuere.[113]

But the stereotyped formula becomes humorously equivocal in Dunbar. Nature has power to revive the spirits (and the sexual desire) of 'ony creatur', but specifically of the narrator, whose 'curage' is chilled by what he has heard. Yet the ambiguity of *myght confort* should not be disregarded; Dunbar's shift from the simple past tense to the hypothetical mood leaves a slight doubt as to Nature's efficacy on this occasion.

Some of Dunbar's favourite comic modes are evident in this poem. Flyting was traditionally associated with women, particularly those of low social rank, such as fishwives and 'carlingis' (K 75). When the ladies abuse their husbands, their speech becomes more 'cummerlik' (510). Only the Widow uses the term 'flyte' (342), but she and the Second Wife acutely analyse the psychological origins of flyting; anger, when repressed, grows greater—'hepit so huge' (334)—and eventually explodes:

> Now sall the byle all out brist that beild has so lang. (164)

But it is the First Wife's wholly unrepressed outburst that is most memorable:

> I have ane wallidrag, ane worme, ane auld wobat carle,
> A waistit wolroun na wourth bot wourdis to clatter,
> Ane bumbart, ane drone bee, ane bag full of flewme. (89 ff.)

Here are features that recall *The Flyting*—degrading analogies—the man's eyes are later compared to stopped-up gutters—and reductive animal imagery, which includes insects and reptiles. But this flyting is more than a catalogue of abusive terms. At one point, when the wife recalls the husband's love-making, Dunbar shows his face in close-up, lingering on beard, bleary eyes, and 'hurcheone' skin. (The 'eldrich' aspect of this passage has already been noted.)

---

[113] *Morte Arthure*, ed. E. Brock (EETS, os 8, 1865), 931–2.

A strain of clerical parody runs through the Widow's speech, which concludes:

> This is the legeand of my lif, thought Latyne it be nane. (504)

Legend, in its general sense of 'story', fits aptly into the tale-telling theme, but it was specifically applied to the biographies of saints, such as those collected in Jacobus a Voragine's *Golden Legend*. Dunbar probably recalled Chaucer's humorous extension of the term, in *The Legend of Good Women*, to stories of women who had suffered martyrdom in love. But he seems to be echoing the Wife of *The Shipman's Tale*, who likewise proposes to tell 'a legende of my lyf/ what I have suffred sith I was a wyf'.[114] Dunbar's line neatly sums up the Widow's decorous façade—her assumption of 'a sanctis liknes' (254), and other pious features of 'the sanct' (444) and 'haly wif' (472).

The Widow, in her interrogation of the Wives, travesties the priestly role of confessor, urging them to 'reveill' (43) and later to confess (153) their inmost thoughts. In turn she too makes her confession, using an alliterative phrase, 'schaw ... in schrift' (251), that has a close parallel in a serious poem on penance (K 5. 19). But her speech belongs less to the confessional than to the pulpit. Like the Wife of Bath, she is a 'nobil prechoure':

> God my spreit now inspir and my speche quykkin
> And send me sentence to say substantious and noble,
> Sa that my preching may pers 3our perverst hertis. (247–9)

This prayer for divine inspiration might momentarily be taken at its face value.[115] But the Widow boldly contraverts the teachings of the Church, and her sermon is threaded with novel applications of Scriptural texts. Christ told his followers to beware of those who came in sheep's clothing, but inwardly were 'ravening wolves' (Matthew 7: 15). The Widow cheerfully applies to herself the Scottish equivalent: 'a fox in a lambis fleise' (423). Christ told the apostles to be wise as serpents and harmless as doves (Matthew 10: 16). The Widow gives her own version of this:

> Be dragonis baith and dowis ay in double forme
> And quhen it nedis 3ow onone note baith ther stranthis ...
> (263–4)

---

[114] *CT* VII. 145–6; cf. P. Strohm, '*Passioun, Lyf, Miracle, Legende*: Some Generic Terms in Hagiographical Narrative', *Chau R* 10 (1975–6), 71 ff.

[115] Cf. K. Bitterling, '*The Tretis* ... Words, Imagery and Genre', in Strauss and Drescher, 344–5.

The perverse new interpretation is clear—wives should assume the mild appearance of doves, but inwardly possess the ferocity of dragons. Another rewriting of the Scriptures has not always been perceived:

> Hutit be the halok lase a hundir ʒeir of eild!   (465)

[May the woman who reaches the age of a hundred, and is still a foolish girl, be ridiculed.]

This offers 'a boldly feminized version' of a much-glossed text from Isaiah (65: 20): *puer centum annorum morietur, et peccator centum annorum maledictus erit* (the child shall die a hundred years old, and the sinner being a hundred years old shall be accursed). This verse was interpreted, traditionally, as threatening the old but still childish sinner with damnation.[116] Dunbar transforms its significance, embedding it in the Widow's boast of her wisdom in matters of love. Contextually it means that the adult woman who cannot keep her love affairs secret deserves public scorn. The Widow earlier spoke of her sexual precocity:

> I wes apperand to be pert within perfit eild—
> Sa sais the curat of our kirk that knew me full ʒing.   (305–6)

Burrow plausibly suggested that *puer centum annorum* was regarded as an anti-type of the ideal *puer senex*: the latter 'virtuously anticipates the wisdom of old age in childhood, while the other viciously persists in the follies of childhood into extreme old age'.[117] If so, we should perhaps see lines 305–6 as an audacious rewriting of the *puer senex* topos.

The Widow emphasizes her didactic purpose: she orders the wives to listen to her 'lesson' (257), and to 'leir thir lessonis' (503), and they respond enthusiastically, saying they will 'exampill tak of her soverane teching' (507). Her speech has an interesting relationship with a minor branch of didactic literature, addressed to women, and usually labelled 'How the Good Wife Taught her Daughter'. The topic was extremely popular, and treatises with this or similar titles exist in English and many languages; there are two Scottish versions, *The Thewis of Gudwomen* and *Documenta Matris*.[118] The Widow's relationship to the wives is sisterly rather than maternal (cf. 251); yet her role resembles that of the Mother or Good Wife, passing on rules of conduct to those less wise and experienced than herself. The Good Wife treatises are not strictly parodied in the poem, but lurk in its background. They

---

[116] See Burrow, *Ages of Man*, 155–6; also Bawcutt and Riddy, *Longer Scottish Poems*, 387–8.
[117] *Ages of Man*, 153.
[118] See *The Good Wife Taught her Daughter*, ed. T. F. Mustanoja (Helsinki, 1948); and *Ratis Raving*, ed. R. Girvan (STS, 1939), 80–100.

provide a model of correct female behaviour—decorous and submissive to one's husband—that all three women subvert.

One small example is the beautiful yet amusing picture of the Widow in church; her white face, partly hidden by her mourning, is compared to the new moon emerging from black clouds—

> So keik [peep] I through my clokis and castis kynd lukis
> To knychtis and to cleirkis and cortly personis. (434–5)

Such flirtatious behaviour is singled out for disapproval in the *Documenta Matris*:

> And in the kirk kepe our all thing
> Fra smirking, keking, and bak luking.

Even the women's revelry—their loud laughter and heavy drinking—flouts the treatises, which repeatedly instruct, 'Laughe thou noght to lowde' and 'Sitte thou nought to longe on nyghtes by the cuppe'.[119]

The Widow is the chief focus for the poem's pervasive irony. It is not true that all the women speak alike. The Wives complain, but the Widow boasts, and her self-congratulatory speech is suffused with irony. Sometimes it takes the form of conscious sarcasm—her praise of marriage as 'the blist band that bindis so fast' (47) is immediately seen through by the First Wife. But the major irony in her long speech is not recognized by herself or by the others; it is of the self-betraying kind that informs the Wife of Bath's Prologue. The Widow rejoices in her own 'wit' (257, 288), sees herself as wise (294), and claims to speak on behalf of other 'wise wemen' (451). This self-appraisal is endorsed by the others, who regard her teaching as 'soverane' and herself as 'prudent' (507–8). There is a close precedent for this in the Wife of Bath, who likewise spoke of her own 'wit', and viewed herself, again and again, as a 'wys woman', proclaiming:

> This knoweth every womman that is wys.[120]

Judged by orthodox moral standards, this wisdom seems rather to be cunning duplicity, and even folly. Judged by the code of courtly love, the Widow is equally deluded, when she speaks of her 'honour' (284), and her 'mercy' in lines reminiscent of Chaucer:

> Bot mercy in to womanheid is a mekle vertu,
> For nevir bot in a gentill hert is generit ony ruth. (315–16)[121]

The irony is similar to that which Dunbar employs elsewhere. The Widow is as 'mercifull' (501) to her suitors as the women who grant

---

[119] *Documenta*, 207–8; *Good Wife*, stanzas 7 and 25.
[120] *CT* III. 400, 209, 524, and *passim*.
[121] *CT* I. 1761; for this notion's wide currency, cf. Whiting, P 243.

the 'eirandis' of young monks in *Ane murlandis man of uplandis mak* (K 74. 55). The wisdom that she commends is practised by 'the ladyis wyis' of *Thir ladyis fair* (K 71). The unhappy wife, who complains of her husband's unkindness or sexual inadequacy, is a stock theme both of the medieval French *chanson de mal mariée* and of later Scottish folk-song.[122] But the closest contemporary parallel to Dunbar's treatment is a short Scottish poem, attributed to Clapperton, with the revealing refrain, 'Wa worth maryage for euirmair!'[123] The speaker, like the First Wife, complains of being bound to a 'screw' (cf. 110, 116), 'quhilk dow nothing of chalmer glew' (27). She voices the same desire for untrammelled promiscuity—'I suld luif thame that wald luif me'—that is expressed by all three of Dunbar's women. It formed part of the tradition to be mutinous—the wife in one French *chanson* says, 'honis soit maris ki dure plus d'une mois'.[124] Clapperton's poem resembles Dunbar's in that the setting is a feast day, and the narrator listens, unperceived, to the complaint. But the woman is solitary, whereas Dunbar employs the slightly more naturalistic convention of a woman complaining to her female friends. An English example from the fifteenth century is *The Talk of Ten Wives*, in which each woman talks contemptuously of her husband's 'ware'. As in *The Tua Mariit Wemen and the Wedo* the wives are identified not by name but by number; and they too speak more freely, because they are drinking and on their own, 'no man hem a-monge'. Wife number six laments, like Dunbar's Second Wife,

> When I se that all is no3te,
> I thynke mony a thro tho3te,
> Bot Cryste wote my wyll.[125]

Dunbar's explicitness, and even his bawdy imagery, find parallels in this poem. Crude though it is, verbally and metrically, it provides—like Clapperton's—a useful illustration of a comic tradition that was clearly known to Dunbar.

This topic overlaps with another, sometimes called 'the gossips' meeting': women, often of the lower classes, gather together, talking and carousing. This was a very popular satiric theme. It forms the staple of *The Gospelles of Dystaves*, and figures as the 'third joy' in *Les Quinze Joies de Mariage*, where the wife and her 'commeres' meet and drink copiously. Skelton's *Tunning of Elinor Rumming* is probably the

---

[122] See Sandison, *Chanson d'Aventure*, 11–14 and T. Crawford, *Society and the Lyric* (1979), 110–12.
[123] *Maitland Folio*, no. lxxix.
[124] Quoted by Sandison, op. cit. 11.
[125] Printed in *Jyl of Breyntfords Testament*, ed. F. J. Furnivall (1871), 29; see Utley, no. 172.

'LADEIS BEWTIE ... LUIFFIS BLYS'

most famous English example, but there are others, such as an episode in the Chester play of the Deluge, and the convivial carol,

> How, gossip myne, gossip myn,
> Whan will we go to the wyne?[126]

Dunbar's relish for the theme is evident elsewhere, in the poem that opens

> Rycht airlie on Ask Weddinsday
> Drynkand the wyne satt cumeris tway.   (K 73)

Dunbar's boozy 'cumeris' are closely related to the friends of Noah's wife, whose drinking delayed them from entering the Ark. These gossips had a prodigious capacity—'for at one draughte thou drinke a quarte'—and proclaimed their preference for the best wine, in this case malmesey.[127] Dunbar's 'cumeris' drink equally heartily—

> Off wyne out of ane choppyne stowp
> Thay drank twa quartis sowp and sowp   (26–7)

and have the same taste for 'mavasy' (14). Although drinking was the major component in this genre, it was usually combined with subsidiary topics, such as hostility to husbands. One of Dunbar's 'cumeris' does everything possible to cause her husband 'tene', since 'In bed he is nocht wirth a bene' (23).

The Tua Mariit Wemen and the Wedo, from one angle, is a richly elaborated gossips' meeting. The ladies' enjoyment of wine is an insistent minor motif, if less important than their 'tene' (229) towards their husbands. Dunbar explicitly says that they 'carpit full cummerlik, with cop going round' (510), and the Widow refers to other female friends as 'cummaris' (353). There seems a tinge of social contempt in the Scottish use of this word, but it does not necessarily refer to the lower classes.[128] What Dunbar implies is that all women, whatever their rank, enjoy small intimate gatherings, from which men are excluded.

The Widow is a brilliant example of an ancient comic type: the dominant woman, or husband-tamer. The theme had many embodiments, of various degrees of literary sophistication, ranging from the wife of Auchtermuchty to the resourceful wife in *Les Quinze Joies*, who gets everything she wants, and reduces her husband to an abject,

---

[126] Greene, *Carols*, no. 419.
[127] *The Chester Miracle Cycle*, ed. R. M. Lumiansky and D. Mills (EETS, Supplementary Ser. 3, 1974), 52.
[128] *DOST, cummer*, n. 2, defines as 'godmother; female intimate; woman gossip'.

cuckolded slave.[129] The Widow gives a vivid account of her second husband's subjection:

> For as a best I broddit [goaded] him to all boyis laubour—
> I wald haif ridden him to Rome with raip in his heid.
> . . . .
> I wald na langer beir on bridill, bot braid up my heid;
> Thar myght na molet [bridle] mak me moy na hald my mouth in;
> I gert the ren3eis rak [break] and rif in to sondir;
> I maid that wif carll to werk all womenis werkis
> And laid all manly materis and mensk [honour] in this eird. (329 ff.)

Through this passage there runs a vein of powerful yet highly traditional imagery. For the Widow her husband is a beast to be goaded to menial activity. Another Scottish poet chooses the same image to commiserate with men who feel the 'brod' of 'evill wyvis':

> I can not tell the torment and the pyne
> Of thame that puttis thair nek this 3ok to draw.[130]

The husband in *Les Quinze Joies* is similarly pictured as an old mule, a worn-out nag, a docile ox, and a toothless, muzzled bear.[131]

Dunbar's leading image is that of the horse and rider. In its sexual applications, which were common, it was usual for men to be riders and women to be ridden. Riot, in Skelton's *Bowge of Court* (402), speaks pimp-like of his mistress: 'I lete her to hyre that men may on her ryde'. Dunbar himself elsewhere envisages the woman's role, sexually, as to be 'riddin' (K 37. 6; K 43. 48). But the tamed horse was an archetypal image of domination. When women rode men, it violated social norms, and implied a profound reversal of their usual roles. The medieval tale of Phyllis and Aristotle (to which Dunbar may refer in line 331) provided a popular illustration of the theme: in it the greatest sage of antiquity allowed himself to be ridden and scourged by a woman.[132] The Scots were familiar both with the tale and its twofold interpretation: for Douglas it signified the overwhelming power of love; for the author of *The Spectacle of Luf* it showed the power of evil women over men.[133] In *The Spectacle of Luf* the bridle is later an explicit symbol of 'maistrie', or dominance in marriage.[134] Powerful medieval wives regularly boast of taking the bit between their

---

[129] Cf. N. Davis, 'Women on Top: Symbolic Sexual Inversion and Political Disorder in Early Modern Europe', in *The Reversible World*, ed. B. A. Babcock (1978), 147–90.
[130] 'Aganis marriage of evill wyvis', Bannatyne, fol. 263b.
[131] The last is specifically the fate of the man who marries a widow; see edn. by Rychner, 100–1.
[132] Cf. G. Santon, 'Aristotle and Phyllis', *Isis*, 14 (1930), 8–19, and D. Gillam, 'Lovers and Riders in Chaucer's *Anelida and Arcite*', *ES* 63 (1982), 394–401.
[133] *Eneados*, Prol. 4. 31; *Asloan Manuscript*, i. 278.
[134] *Asloan Manuscript*, i. 296.

'LADEIS BEWTIE . . . LUIFFIS BLYS'

teeth—a gossip in *Les Quinze Joies* 'prins le frains aux dens'.[135] The Wife of Bath says, similarly, that her last husband 'yaf me al the bridel in myn hond' (III. 813). But Dunbar's Widow develops the image with particular relish. She speaks both of rebellion against male authority— 'I wald na langer beir on bridill'—and also of the husband's subjugation, himself forced to bear a 'kene brydill' (354). The reversal of sex-roles is explicit in lines 351–2, and summed up in the contemptuous 'wif carll'.

This notion of the tamed horse is interwoven with the other abundant animal imagery.[136] All three wives repeatedly compare their husbands to animals—a cat (120), a dog (273), and, above all, beasts of burden. The First Wife desires a new husband, who will be strong as an ox, 'forsy in draucht' (79, 85), and regards her old one as an 'aver', a pack-horse. The Widow similarly speaks of her husband not as a spirited courser but as a 'cappill', or draught-horse, fit only to bear panniers or pull a cart (355–7); later he too is an 'aver' (387). The intensity of the wives' repulsion is often conveyed through the epithets—the animals are ugly or diseased, 'that lene gib' (120), 'a farcy aver' (114), a 'dotit dog' (186). The bird imagery is similarly degrading. The Widow compares her husband to a plucked heron (382), and jeers:

> I crew abone that craudone as cok that wer victour.   (326)

This is rich in implications. The Widow envisages marriage as a cock-fight, and revealingly compares herself to a male bird, as elsewhere (379). The verb *crew* catches her tone of crowing boastfulness. The husband's degradation is a kind of castration: the Widow proclaims that she 'geldit' him 'of gudis and of natur' (392). She despised

> That superspendit evill spreit spul3eit of all vertu.   (397)

Dunbar seems to have been the first to use *geld* in this figurative sense, which links with the other cruel imagery of sick or mutilated animals. It suggests the husband's complete humiliation, sexually and financially—with an implicit connection between the two. He is now bankrupt, or 'superspendit' (perhaps with a sexual innuendo on 'spendit')—his resources 'spul3eit', or plundered, by his wife. The Widow's tone is very different from that of the Wife of Bath. The latter won psychological ascendancy over the husband who gave her 'the bridel'; but her speech is none the less full of affection. Dunbar's Widow delights in cruelty, and intensifies her husband's humiliation

---

[135] Ed. Rychner, 20.
[136] Cf. Bawcutt, 'Aspects of Dunbar's Imagery', in *Chaucer and Middle English Studies*, ed. B. Rowland (1974), 190–200.

by revealing it to her 'cummaris', adding to domestic 'scaith' public scorn (358).

The Widow boasts of success in marriage, but what she most enjoys is widowhood:

> Now done is my dolly nyght, my day is upsprungin;
> Adew dolour, adew; my daynte now begynis.
> Now am I a wedow, I wise, and weill am at ese;
> I weip as I wer woful, bot wel is me for evir. (412–15)

These antitheses, pointed by the alliteration, neatly establish two contrasted types that are wittily superimposed in Dunbar's portrait. The well-known collection of type-characters by Sir Thomas Overbury and others (1614) contains twin sketches of 'A Vertuous Widdow', a model of constancy, and 'An Ordinary Widdow', 'whose chiefest pride is in the multitude of her suitors'.[137] Both are witty embroideries upon ancient stereotypes. The social reality, in Dunbar's time as in Overbury's, was that remarriage was very common. But preachers and idealistic poets commended the woman who remained faithful to her dead husband forever, 'Soul as the turtle that lost hath hir make'.[138] The anti-type of this was 'the merry widow', liberated from the constraints of marriage, and a well-known figure in comic literature. *The Twelve Mery Jests of the Wyddow Edyth* (c.1525), which recounts the exploits of a kind of female Scoggin, became very popular in the sixteenth century, not only in England but in Scotland also.[139] But there is earlier evidence that the Scots were familiar with the theme of the easily consoled widow. When Henryson's hen Sprutok hears of the apparent death of Chantecleir, she is as joyful as Dunbar's Widow, and prepares to sing what may have been an actual song: 'Wes neuer wedow sa gay' (*Fables*, 509–15). *The Spectacle of Luf* devotes a chapter to widows' iniquities, and tells a particularly nasty version of the story, narrated by Petronius and very popular with medieval anti-feminists, of the Widow of Ephesus. In order to win her new suitor, she is prepared to lop off her dead husband's ears and strike out his teeth; this widow, as in many other medieval versions, adds callous brutality to unfaithfulness.[140]

Towards the end of Dunbar's poem occurs an interesting scene:

---

[137] *The Overburian Characters*, ed. W. J. Paylor (Oxford, 1936), 70–2.
[138] *CT* IV. 2080.
[139] See the copy printed in *Shakespeare Jest Books*, ed. W. Carew Hazlitt, iii (1864), 27–108. The work was stocked by the Edinburgh bookseller Robert Gourlaw: *Bannatyne Miscellany II* (Edinburgh, 1836), 214.
[140] *Asloan Manuscript*, i. 291–3; cf. the *vidua* theme in Rolland's *Sevin Seages*, ed. G. F. Black (STS, 1932), 7591–7950. See P. Ure, 'The Widow of Ephesus: Some Reflections on an International Comic Theme', *Durham University Journal*, 49 (1956), 1–9.

> Bot ȝit me think the best bourd quhen baronis and knychtis
> And othir bachilleris blith, blumyng in ȝouth,
> And all my luffaris lele, my lugeing persewis
> And fyllis me wyne wantonly with weilfair and joy:
> Sum rownis and sum ralȝeis and sum redis ballatis,
> Sum raiffis furght rudly with riatus speche;
> . . . .
> Bot with my fair calling I comfort thaim all;
> For he that sittis me nixt I nip on his finger;
> I serf him on the tothir syde on the samin fasson;
> And he that behind me sittis I hard on him lene,
> And him befor with my fut fast on his I strampt;
> And to the bernis far but sueit blenkis I cast;
> To every man in speciall speke I sum wordis
> So wisly and so womanly quhill warmys ther hertis.
>
> (476–81; 489–96)

The passage from which this comes is the comic climax—'the *best bourd*'—of the Widow's speech. It is highly rhetorical, falling into two, roughly equal, halves: the first describes the Widow's importunate suitors, or 'luffaris' (476–88); the second describes her response (489–500). The *repetitio* on *sum* in the first part breaks up the 'thik thrang' (488) into separate, representative figures—the same technique is used in *Be divers wyis and operatiounes* (K 20). It is matched by *repetitio* on *I* in the second section, although this, from its varying position in the lines, is less obtrusive. Each passage simultaneously suggests the presence of a crowd of suitors and 'every man in speciall' (495). Throughout refinement intermingles with crudity, in behaviour as in language. The orderly, ceremonial ritual of the feast—

> Sum kerffis to me curtasli, sum me the cop giffis   (484)

does not exclude the voicing of obscenities and dirty jokes—

> Sum raiffis furght rudly with riatus speche.   (481)

The courteous and the 'riatus' coexist.

Lines 490–4 are an amusing version of what seems to have been a well-known topos: the lady who manages to flirt with several men at once. Pearcy noted an analogue in a thirteenth-century Provençal poem, but there exist other parallels, far closer in time, one of which, a passage from the pseudo-Chaucerian *Remedy of Love*, was included in the Bannatyne manuscript.[141] In both the Provençal and English poems there are but three suitors; in Dunbar the sheer multitude of men brings the scene closer to farce. Pearcy notes that Dunbar's treatment has greater 'physicality' than that in the Provençal poem.

---

[141] Untitled note in *SSL* 16 (1981), 235–9; Bannatyne, fols. 258b–259b.

'LADEIS BEWTIE ... LUIFFIS BLYS'

But what particularly distinguishes Dunbar's version from the other two (apart from the very different contexts in which they occur) is the greater roughness, verging on cruelty, of his Widow. She says of one suitor, 'I *nip* on his finger', whereas the Provençal lady squeezes the man's hand 'doussamen'. Of another man the Widow says, 'with my fut fast on his I stramp [stamp, trample].' The lady in *The Remedy of Love*, by contrast, merely 'treads' upon her lover's foot, and the Provençal lady 'caussiga 'l pe' (presses it with her own). In these other poems the episode is associated with a question as to which lover received the greatest proof of his lady's favour. As *The Remedy of Love* puts it: 'Quhich of theis thre stoid now in grace?' (60). In fact a *demande d'amour*, with precisely the same shape, occurs in *Les Adevineaux Amoureux*: here too the lady has three suitors: 'Et comme celle qui moult est soubtille estraint l'un des troiz par le doy, l'aultre marche sur le piet, et au tiers cluigne de l'ueil'.[142] Dunbar, of course, presents the episode from the woman's viewpoint, and no question is posed. She deludes 'every man in speciall' into thinking that he receives favour, and manages to 'comfort thaim all'. The Widow is here triumphant, displaying her 'womanly' wisdom and rejoicing in the exercise of power—'maistrie', not merely over one man, husband or lover, but over a 'thik thrang'.

This episode has been interpreted very differently. Sibbald, in 1802, called it 'a most curious picture of a *route* in the reign of James IV'. Modern critics have questioned its social reality, seeing it rather as 'a fantasy of female power'. Some stress Dunbar's satiric purpose— 'the salon ... is exposed as a brothel ... [the Widow] satisfies her lust where she chooses'.[143] There is certainly an element of wish-fulfilment in the Widow's words; she displays no fear of pregnancy, no awareness that time will pass and beauty fade. Yet a wealthy widow was as likely to have a 'multitude' of suitors in Dunbar's time as in Overbury's; this is not just 'fantasy', but illustrates the exercise of real, if limited, female power. It should also be noted that the exposure is not solely of women: the Widow satisfies not only 'her lust' but that of men. Sibbald's remark is less naïve than it first appears—this scene, both ceremonial and licentious, catches the 'curious' reality of court life.

The Tua Mariit Wemen and the Wedo—like this small episode—has many facets. Readers have long recognized the elements of fantasy and satire; in this chapter I have been chiefly concerned with its literary artifice and use of comic stereotypes, both of which seem critically undervalued. Yet the poem also reflects social reality. The

---

[142] Hassell, *Amorous Games* (n. 8 above), 10.
[143] *Chronicle of Scottish Poetry* (Edinburgh, 1802), i. 231; Scott, 201; Kinsley, 273.

'LADEIS BEWTIE ... LUIFFIS BLYS'

First Wife bemoans the misery of marriage to an old, virtually senile man; and the Second Wife curses the 'wekit kyn' (214) who compelled her to marry in accord with their wishes rather than her own. Such disparity in the ages of wife and husband and such forced marriages were facts. Among the wealthy classes marriage was rarely the private choice of individuals, but 'a collective decision of family and kin'.[144] Young 'gentill' women had little choice as to marriage partners—it is hardly surprising that the Widow's reference to 'chois' (46) provokes such an explosive reaction. Yet there certainly existed strong women, who—like the fictional Widow or the real Margaret Paston and her mother-in-law, Agnes—possessed economic and social power, particularly in later life or as widows.[145] The legal status of widows was stronger than that of wives, in Scotland; and in late medieval England widowhood (with almost complete security in her dower) was the best time of a well-born woman's life.[146] There is no space to consider the distinctively *Scottish* nature of Dunbar's women, although the Widow shows a good grasp of Scottish law in her gradual appropriation of her husbands' property.[147] But there is a splendid real-life parallel to the Widow and her financial acumen in Marion Ogilvy, the long-time mistress of Cardinal Beaton; 'indomitable' and 'incorrigibly litigious', she was a very efficient business woman: 'She kept a firm grasp of her family's affairs throughout her life, taking charge of their business and legal papers and, at times, those of David Beaton himself'.[148] Both the Widow and Marion Ogilvy lend some credence to Pedro de Ayala's report that Scottish women were 'absolute mistresses of their houses, and even of their husbands, in all things concerning the administration of their property'.[149]

Dunbar's view of women in this poem is not wholly unsympathetic—the Wives, in particular, have genuine grievances, and there is occasional pathos in their depiction. The Widow is horrifying, yet undoubtedly abounds in the 'exuberance of life'—beside her the men seem puny. The husbands indeed are repellent, both physically and morally. One might well feel that such men get no more than

---

[144] L. Stone, *The Family, Sex and Marriage in England 1500–1800* (1977), 70.
[145] Cf. A. S. Haskell, 'The Paston Women on Marriage in the 15th Century', *Viator*, 4 (1973), 458–71.
[146] See R. K. Marshall, *Virgins and Viragos: A History of Women in Scotland from 1080 to 1980* (1983), 26–7; and R. E. Archer, 'Rich Old Ladies: The Problem of Late Medieval Dowagers', in *Property and Politics*, ed. T. Pollard (Gloucester, 1984), 15–35.
[147] Cf. E. Bentsen and S. L. Sanderlin, 'The Profits of Marriage in Late Medieval Scotland', *SLJ* 12(2) (1985), 5–18, but see correspondence in *SLJ* 13 (1986).
[148] M. H. B. Sanderson, *Cardinal of Scotland: David Beaton 1494–1546* (Edinburgh, 1986), 40–2.
[149] Quoted by G. Gregory Smith, *The Days of James IV* (1890), 65.

they deserve. The overall vision seems less misogynistic than misanthropic. The poem shows a world ruled not by love but by appetite—for sex, property, and, above all, power. It is comedy of the blackest type.

9
Language at Large

DUNBAR'S language has always fascinated his readers. Kennedy angrily called him a blabberer (*Flyting*, 344), but Lindsay, in his roll-call of great vernacular poets, spoke enthusiastically

> of Dunbar, quhilk language had at large,
> As maye be sene in tyll his golden targe. (*Papyngo*, 17–18)

This comment serves as a useful starting-point: written by a close contemporary, it expresses whole-hearted admiration, apparently for the copiousness of Dunbar's vocabulary, and singles out for special praise the poem whose style continues to be a focus for much modern debate. In the twentieth century many critics have commented on Dunbar's verbal 'brilliance', 'energy', and stylistic virtuosity.[1] Patrick Cruttwell voiced a fairly common response: 'Within it [Dunbar's writing] there are immediately apparent two styles, two dictions ... two poets. The one is ornate, artificial, and English; the other colloquial, natural, and Scottish.'[2] Cruttwell's hostility to the 'ornate' style—of which *The Goldyn Targe* and *The Thrissill and the Rois* are the chosen examples—contrasts amusingly with Lindsay's admiration. Both responses are rooted in different conceptions of good writing: Lindsay, like Dunbar, was happy to associate poets with rhetoricians; Cruttwell saw good poetry as something 'natural' and organic. This dichotomy—between art and nature, as also between English and Scottish—is theoretically naïve. It also over-simplifies the complex reality of Dunbar's own poems. It ignores the diversity of *The Goldyn Targe*, just as it ignores the high degree of artifice that characterizes many of the supposedly 'natural' poems, such as *The Flyting* and *The Tua Mariit Wemen and the Wedo*. That there exist extremes of style in Dunbar is undeniable, but it proves remarkably difficult to sort all eighty of his poems into one or other of these categories. In practice the critics who make such sharp distinctions tend to discuss the same poems again and again.

John Speirs praised Dunbar for 'his skilled command of the rich

---

[1] See E. Morgan, 'Dunbar and the Language of Poetry', *EC* 2 (1952), 138–58; and W. F. H. Nicolaisen, 'Line and Sentence in Dunbar's Poetry', in *Bards and Makars*, ed. A. J. Aitken *et al.* (Glasgow, 1977), 63.

[2] 'Two Scots Poets', in *The Age of Chaucer* (1954; 1963), 175. Cf. J. Leyerle, on 'two distinct dictions', in 'The Two Voices of William Dunbar', *UTQ* 31 (1962), 325.

and varied resources of language open to him'.[3] This is perceptive, but vague. What were these 'rich and varied resources'? We should recall that the languages of Scotland at this time included Latin and Gaelic: the former was the language of the Church and of education, as it was throughout Europe; the latter was spoken chiefly in the Highlands and Galloway. Dunbar was undoubtedly very much at home in Latin; there is no evidence that he spoke Gaelic, although *The Flyting* demonstrates that he was aware of the linguistic tensions and rivalries between Highlanders and Lowlanders.[4] His native tongue was Lowlands Scots—descended from Anglo-Saxon, and closely related to the northern dialects of Middle English, it none the less enjoyed national status as 'the langage of Scottis natioun' (Douglas, *Eneados*, Prol. 1. 103). It shared with English its basic grammatical structure and a common core of vocabulary, yet by 1500 had developed many distinctive features; in phonology, orthography, and a vocabulary rich in loans from Norse, Dutch, French, and Gaelic it differed considerably from southern English. Our knowledge of the linguistic resources available to Dunbar has been much extended by the progress of dictionaries such as *MED* and *DOST*, which provide precious evidence for contemporary usage both in England and Scotland. There have also appeared several illuminating articles by A. J. Aitken, former editor of *DOST*, on many aspects of the early Scottish language, ranging from pronunciation to the diction of poetry. What they show most clearly is the remarkable 'variation and variety in written Middle Scots'.[5] Poets, like other users of the language in sixteenth-century Scotland, had available to them not a simple choice between *two* styles, but a whole range of options.

Dunbar took full advantage of these options, and seems to have relished the challenge that they offered. To illustrate from one area, that of vocabulary, his words come from a wide variety of 'registers'— legal or liturgical, formal or vulgar, Latinate or Scots, poetic or everyday, archaic or newly coined. Among the poets of this time he is unrivalled not merely for the width of his vocabulary but for his sensitivity to the connotations of words and phrases. His poems abound in ironies, puns, and various kinds of word-play. To some

---

[3] *The Scots Literary Tradition* (1940), 35.
[4] Dunbar employs Gaelic words chiefly when referring to Highlanders, and usually depreciatively: *ingle, katherene, polk breik, glen, cabroch* (K 23); *caupe* (K 38); and *correnoch* (K 52). Cf. J. D. McClure, 'What Scots owes to Gaelic', *SLJ* Lang. Supplement, 5 (1986), 85–98.
[5] The title of his article in *Edinburgh Studies in English and Scots*, ed. A. J. Aitken, A. McIntosh, and H. Pálsson (1971), 177–209. See also 'Oral Narrative Style in Middle Scots', in Blanchot and Graf, *Actes*, 98–112; and 'The Language of Older Scots Poetry', in *Scotland and the Lowland Tongue*, ed. J. D. McClure (Aberdeen, 1983), 18–49.

extent his practice was affected by a sense of linguistic decorum. As *The Goldyn Targe* reveals, Dunbar was aware of contemporary views on diction, and the distinction between a high and a low style. But a substantial number of his poems can be classified neither as 'high' nor 'low'; plain, unostentatious, conversational yet not vulgar, they seem rather to belong to some 'middle' style. Yet even this degree of overall classification—into three rather than two styles—seems rigid and Procrustean. My study of Dunbar reveals that poems regularly classed as 'aureate' differ considerably; even within a single poem tone and style may change rapidly. One of the leading characteristics of Dunbar's language is its flexibility. Yet it must also be stressed that he is a poet for whom choice of diction and choice of metre are closely interrelated. In Dunbar verbal flamboyance, of any kind, is usually associated with a complex or unusual metrical form; by contrast, a simple stanza of four or five lines, often with a refrain—which appears his favourite form—is marked by a style that is far more plain and unobtrusive.

The Latin language was of absorbing interest to Dunbar's learned contemporaries. Erasmus and Lorenzo Valla, like other humanists, poured scorn on the barbarous Latin used by medieval schoolmen; several Scottish clerics possessed copies of Valla's influential *Elegantiae Linguae Latinae*, that came to be regarded as a textbook of correct Latinity.[6] Douglas was very conscious of the debate about Latin; in the Prologues to his translation of the *Aeneid* he praises the Latin of Virgil, calling it 'maist perfyte langage fyne' (Prol. 1. 382), and contrasts it with the poverty of his native tongue. This belief in the perfection of classical Latin and the comparative inferiority of the vernaculars was widespread throughout Europe, and by no means peculiar to Scotsmen. Many English writers spoke depreciatively of English as 'rude', 'rural', 'base', and 'vile'.[7] Dunbar, however, makes one passing reference to Latin (K 14. 504), and there is nothing extant to indicate that he shared Douglas's scholarly interest in that language. Only the envoi to *The Goldyn Targe*, with its revealing references to 'oure rude langage' and 'imperfyte' speech (266–7), shows his awareness of the low contemporary rating of the vernacular. Yet Dunbar makes effective, if scanty, use of Latin in his own poetry. He did not, as far as we know, write original Latin verse. He offers no parallel to Skelton, or to other Scots, such as Ireland, who included three Latin poems on the Virgin in *The Meroure of Wysdome*, and James Foullis, whose verses in various classical metres were printed at Paris

---

[6] Cf. Bawcutt, *Douglas*, 32–3.
[7] See R. F. Jones, *The Triumph of the English Language* (Stanford, 1953), 7 ff.

in 1512.⁸ Dunbar, writing in a long-established medieval tradition, incorporated Latin into his own poems, and seems to have been almost as much at ease in that language as in his own native Scots. For Dunbar Latin was certainly not dead, nor was it invariably lofty; it was a language in which one could jest as well as be serious.

The juxtaposition of Latin and Scots in *The Testament of Maister Andro Kennedy* is regularly termed 'macaronic', yet often with a hint of depreciation. Dunbar's technique is said to be 'not precisely macaronic', or it is noted that 'a more orthodox example is the *Polemo-Middinia* attributed to Drummond of Hawthornden'.⁹ But Dunbar was not setting out to write a work of the same kind as *Polemo-Middinia*, in which (as the very title indicates) two languages are jumbled together in a comic mish-mash:

> fechtam memorate bloodeam,
> Fechtam terribilem, quam marvellaverit omnis.¹⁰

The Testament belongs to an equally playful but more sophisticated tradition of mixing languages that might be better described as bilingual. In it the lines of verse are written alternately in Scots and Latin, a Latin that seems correct by medieval (if not classical) standards. Many of the poems belonging to this tradition were wholly serious, such as the thirteenth-century poem to the Virgin that opens:

> Of one that is so fayr and bri3t
> *velud maris stella*.¹¹

or a fifteenth-century version of the *Laetabundus* sequence:

> Glad and blithe mote 3e be,
> All that euer y here nowe se,
> *Alleluya*!
> Kynge of kyngys, lorde of alle,
> Borne he is in oxe stalle,
> *Res miranda*!¹²

There are also love poems written in two or more languages—one, addressed 'A celuy que pluys eyme en mounde', wittily mingles French, English, and Latin.¹³ Dunbar's use of this technique therefore did not,

---

⁸ See *The Meroure of Wysdome*, ed. C. Macpherson (STS, 1926), 171–86; J. Ijsewijn and D. F. S. Thomson, 'The Latin Poems of Jacobus Follisius or James Foullis of Edinburgh', *Humanistica Lovaniensia*, 24 (1975), 102–52.
⁹ Kinsley, 314; cf. Ross, 120, and Scott, 224.
¹⁰ For an extract, see *The Oxford Book of Scottish Verse*, ed. J. MacQueen and T. Scott (Oxford, 1966), 261–2.
¹¹ *CB XIII*, no. 17B.
¹² *CB XV*, no. 77B.
¹³ *Medieval English Lyrics*, ed. R. T. Davies (1963), no. 70.

in itself, necessarily imply 'the deflation of the dominant Latin by the rising vernaculars'.[14] It would seem rather to have grown out of the complex linguistic situation of medieval clerics; it was an ingenious display of skill in aligning languages. (Real-life testaments were written either in Latin or the vernacular; those in Latin often contain Scots phrases.[15]) Macaronic verse had many and varied uses. Yet there exists no full-scale study of the subject, despite its great significance for medieval culture and literature.[16] There was an ancient tradition, rooted in the jesting use of Latin itself, of using the technique for comic and satiric purposes. One example is the anti-mendicant 'Freeres, freeres, wo be 3e / *ministri malorum*'; another is the piece, quoted in Bower's *Scotichronicon* (xvi. 8), that begins, 'Lauch liis down our all, *fallax fraus regnat ubique*'.[17] Other examples are the bawdy carols that make derisive use of phrases from the liturgy.[18] Dunbar would certainly have known poems of this kind. But *The Testament* draws more specifically, I think, upon the tradition of convivial drinking-songs, some of which combine the macaronic technique with ecclesiastical parody. Particularly famous is a cluster of poems, modelled on the *Laetabundus* sequence, that extol the virtues of beer. One mixes Latin and German, another Latin and French:

> Or hi parra:
> La cerveyse nos chauntera
> *Alleluia*!
> Qui que en beyt
> Si tele seyt com estre deyt,
> *Res miranda*![19]

There are few surviving examples of such poems that mix English and Latin, but one from Richard Hill's Commonplace Book should be better known:

> The best tre, if 3e tak entent,
> *Inter ligna fructifera*,
> Is the vyne tre, by good argument,
> *Dulcia ferens pondera*.[20]

---

[14] Scott, 224.
[15] Sir James Douglas bequeathes 'unum anulum aureum in quo stat unum Ruby'; *Bannatyne Miscellany II*, ed. D. Laing (Bannatyne Club, 1836), 109.
[16] See, however, P. S. Diehl, *The Medieval European Religious Lyric* (1985), 110–13; Greene, *Carols*, ch. 3; and W. Wehrle, *The Macaronic Hymn Tradition in Medieval English Literature* (Washington, DC, 1933).
[17] See Wehrle, op. cit. 106; and Walter Bower, *Scotichronicon*, vol. 8, ed. D. E. R. Watt (Aberdeen, 1987), 218; *IMEV* 2787.
[18] Greene, *Carols*, nos. 457 and 461.
[19] Discussed by Greene, ibid. ciii.
[20] Ed. R. Dyboski (EETS, ES 101, 1908), 105.

In *The Testament* the Latin seems mostly, as one would expect, of legal origin (above, p. 196); but some phrases come from the Scriptures, such as this undignified use of Psalm 102: 9: *Potum meum cum fletu miscebam* (104). Yet it should not be assumed that the Latin component of *The Testament* is invariably dignified or pompous, in comic contrast with 'low' Scots words—'drink and draff' (39) or 'A barell bung ay at my bosum' (33). This is sometimes so, but not always; often it is the Latin that undercuts the vernacular:

> I callit my lord my heid, but hiddill,
> *Sed nulli alii hoc dixerunt.* (53–4)

In this poem two languages are in witty equilibrium; full enjoyment of the jest requires an understanding of both.

The Testament may have been designed chiefly to amuse Dunbar's fellow-clerks, but he put Latin to a more serious use in the moral or religious poems that were intended for a wider audience. Several contain Latin refrains that function in much the same way as the vernacular refrains; they state well-known truths but gain added authority from their liturgical or Scriptural origin. Devout laymen, even if they did not fully understand the literal sense, were likely to recognize the significance of such familiar, highly charged phrases as *Surrexit dominus de sepulchro* and *Timor mortis conturbat me*. Dunbar uses these snatches of Latin with tact and skill. In some poems, such as *Done is a battell*, the refrain is syntactically detached from the rest of the stanza and constitutes a formal, unchanging statement of the theme. In others, such as *Rorate celi desuper* or *Memento homo quod cinis es*, the wording varies in accordance with the syntax of the rest of the stanza. Such adjustments are slight, yet achieve a close integration of the Latin refrain within the vernacular poem.

An effective use of Latin occurs in *Quhome to sall I complene my wo* (K 63). Speaking of the Last Judgement, Dunbar imagines the horror of hell:

> *Ubi ardentes anime,*
> *Semper dicentes sunt, Ve, ve!*
> Sall cry Allace, that wemen thame bure,
> *O quante sunt iste tenebre!*
> Into this warld may none assure. (71–5)

Editors have not identified the exact source of this, but it has a sombre, highly relevant, liturgical origin in a passage associated with the *Libera me* responsory in the Office of the Dead:

> Libera me, domine, de morte aeterna,
> in die illa tremenda,
> quando caeli movendi sunt et terra
> . . . .
> Ardentes animae flent sine fine

> ambulantes per tenebras
> dicuntque singulae Vae Vae Vae;
> quantae sunt tenebrae.²¹

A Middle English primer contains this paraphrase of the lines:

> Brennynge soulis wepen with-outen ende; thei wepen withouten ende, walkynge bi derknessis; and ech of hem seien, wo! wo! wo! hou greet ben these derknessis.²²

Several English homilists also quote this passage in accounts of hell, one attributing it to St Chrysostom; it seems to have been well known.²³ Dunbar does not quote verbatim, but modifies the Latin to fit his verse; yet here, as in the poem's last stanza, he moves easily between the two languages. Awareness of the context of the Latin lines intensifies the solemnity of the vernacular passage in which they are embedded. It is possible that the liturgy may have supplied the stylistic model for this part of Dunbar's poem. His syntax is characterized by repeated rhetorical questions, from which trail temporal clauses:

> Than quho sall wirk for warldis wrak
> Quhen flude and fyre sall our it frak,
> And frely fruster feild and fure
> With tempest kene and hiddous crak?   (76-9)

Both sense and syntax seem to echo the much-repeated *Quando caeli movendi sunt et terra* of the liturgy.

Latin is usually regarded as a key element in the ornate style so often designated as 'aureate'. Despite its conceptual vagueness, 'aureate' seems an apt epithet for the style exemplified not only in the opening of *The Goldyn Targe* but in Douglas's Twelfth Prologue and *Palice of Honour* and many later Scottish poems. It is not a modern invention. Dunbar himself used 'aureate' to commend verbal excellence (*Goldyn Targe*, 71 and 263); Lydgate employed it almost interchangeably with 'eloquent'; and the phrase 'aureate terms' occurs elsewhere.²⁴ Gold is an obvious figure both for high value and a brilliant, highly refined style; Stephen Hawes thus envisaged ridding one's diction of the dross

---

[21] See *Sarum Breviary*, ed. F. Proctor and C. Wordsworth, 3 vols. (Cambridge, 1879-86), ii. 280.
[22] *The Prymer or Lay Folks' Prayer Book*, ed. H. Littlehales (EETS, os 105, 1895), 70.
[23] *Jacob's Well*, ed. A. Brandeis (EETS, os 115, 1900), 228-9; cf. G. R. Owst, *Preaching in Medieval England* (Cambridge, 1926), 337, and Hawes's *Conversion of Swearers*, 301-3, in *Minor Poems*, ed. F. W. Gluck and A. B. Morgan (EETS, os 271, 1974).
[24] Cf. J. Norton-Smith, in Lydgate's *Poems* (Oxford, 1966), 192-5; *Papyngo*, 16, and *Maitland Quarto*, no. lxix. 35.

of everyday—'As we do golde from coper puryfy'.[25] Today aureate terms tend to be identified with newly introduced Latin loanwords; C. S. Lewis, for instance, equates aureation with 'the use of polysyllabic coinages from Latin . . . as an ornament to style'.[26] It is certainly the Latinisms that arrest a modern reader's attention when starting to read *The Goldyn Targe*:

> Ryght as the stern of day begouth to schyne
> Quhen gone to bed war Vesper and Lucyne
> I raise and by a rosere did me rest;
> Up sprang the goldyn candill matutyne
> With clere depurit bemes cristallyne
> Glading the mery foulis in thair nest;
> Or Phebus was in purpur cape revest
> Up raise the lark, the hevyns menstrale fyne,
> In May in till a morrow myrthfullest.

Yet separate words, like *matutyne* and *cristallyne*, form only one element, though an important one, in this rich, complex, and elevated style. Quite as important are other factors: the demanding nine-line stanza; the mythological references to natural phenomena; the intricate patterning of the syntax; and the opening temporal clause, 'Ryght as . . .', which was almost a generic indicator of high-style descriptions of spring. The effect is leisured and idealistic—promoted by vaguely eulogistic epithets, such as *clere*, *fyne* and the superlative, *myrthfullest*. This is the style of eulogy: Dunbar employs it brilliantly here and in *The Thrissill and the Rois*, less successfully and perhaps more mechanically in the poems on Bernard Stewart. No more, however, will be said of *The Goldyn Targe*, since it has had attention earlier and received much scrutiny from critics.[27]

The supreme example of Dunbar's aureate style is *Ane Ballat of Our Lady* (K 2). It is famous, indeed notorious, for its 'half changed Latin':[28]

> Hale, sterne superne; hale, in eterne
> In Godis sicht to schyne;
> Lucerne in derne for to discerne
> Be glory and grace devyne;
> Hodiern, modern, sempitern,
> Angelicall regyne:

---

[25] *The Pastime of Pleasure*, ed. W. E. Mead (EETS, os 173, 1928), 916.
[26] *English Literature in the Sixteenth Century* (Oxford, 1954), 75.
[27] Cf. Aitken, 'Language of Scots Poetry', 21–2; A. Zettersten, 'On the Aureate Diction of William Dunbar', in *Essays Presented to Knud Schibsbye*, ed. M. Chesnutt *et al.* (Copenhagen, 1979), 51–68.
[28] Cf. B. Ellenberger, *The Latin Element in the Vocabulary of the Earlier Makars Henryson and Dunbar* (Lund, 1977), 14 and *passim*.

Our tern inferne for to dispern
Helpe, rialest rosyne.
Ave Maria, gracia plena:
Haile, fresche floure femynyne;
3erne us guberne, virgin matern
Of reuth baith rute and ryne.   (1-12)

Only the absence of grammatical inflections separates many of these words from their Latin etymons; some indeed have failed ever to become assimilated into the vernacular. Yet the diction of this poem, which produces an effect curiously different from that of *The Goldyn Targe*, has hardly been investigated. The traditional nature of the imagery has been shown;[29] what has not been explored is the extent to which the poem is modelled verbally upon late-medieval Latin hymns, sequences, and other verse addressed to the Virgin—not just in the choice of single words but in their patterning, and particularly their rhyme. The sheer quantity of these Marian hymns, written chiefly in accentual verse, their increasing ornateness, and their conventional, almost formulaic, diction, must be stressed.[30] It is this last factor which makes it difficult to trace specific sources for Dunbar's phrasing. It is as impossible to say where he encountered the Latin phrase, *virgo gloriosa*, that lies behind his own 'glorius virgin' (32) as to track the origins of the common alliterative formula in line 60: 'Thy name I sall ay nevyne'.[31] In each case, however, it is evident that Dunbar was familiar with two different but important poetic traditions.

The chain of internal rhymes in the first stanza is largely (if not entirely) Latinate: 'Hale, sterne *superne* ... in eterne ... *Lucerne* in derne ... 3erne us *guberne*, virgin matern'. The italicized words have a parallel in Henryson's line, addressed not to the Virgin but to God: 'Superne lucerne, guberne this pestilens'; and in another devout poem in MS Arundel 285.[32] Ringing in the ears of all three poets, I suspect, was a poem such as *Felix mater, ave*, which contains these lines:

Sacra pincerna veniae, regina superna,
Solis lucerna, precibus nos, virgo, guberna.[33]

---

[29] See Kinsley, 225-30, and I. Hyde, 'Primary Sources and Associations of Dunbar's Aureate Imagery', *MLR* 51 (1956), 481-92.

[30] See J. Szövérffy, *Marianische Motivik der Hymnen* (Leiden, 1985), and *A Concise History of Medieval Latin Hymnody* (Leiden, 1983), 70-1. Most of the illustrations that follow are drawn from *Analecta Hymnica Medii Aevi* (*AH*), ed. C. Blume and G. M. Dreves, vol. 32 (*De Beata Maria Virgine Pia dictamina*) (Leipzig, 1899; repr. 1961).

[31] *Ave virgo gloriosa* is the opening phrase of *AH* 32, nos. 35 and 36; for 'name ... nevyne', cf. *Howlat*, 33.

[32] *Prayer for the Pest*, 65; and *Devotional Pieces in Verse and Prose*, ed. J. A. W. Bennett (STS, 1955), 295.

[33] *AH* 32, no. 54.

Closely similar phrasing also occurs in the sequence *Ave, mundi spes Maria*:

> Ave, virginum lucerna,
> Per quam fulsit lux superna.

This was probably very well known, since it was used in the Sarum Mass of the Blessed Virgin.[34] Dunbar's second stanza contains a striking series of rhymes in the *b*-lines: *habitakle, tabernakle, signakle, umbrakle*. The first two words are commonly paired in Latin, with the same reference to the Virgin's womb:

> Orbis tabernaculum,
> In quo Dei virtus ei
> Fecit habitaculum.

or

> Ventris habitaculum Rex regum intravit,
> Cuius tabernaculum sibi dedicavit.[35]

The second pair of words also appears in Latin rhymes, for instance *pudoris signaculum* and *miseris umbraculum*.[36]

Stanza five opens, 'Haile, more decore than of before', and continues with a series of rhymes on *-ore* that include 'aurore' and 'Implore, adore, thow indeflore'. With this may be compared

> Ave, consurgens aurora,
> Fulgens et aurea hora,
> Virgo dulcis et decora,
> Pro nobis miseris ora;
> Ora semper, semper ora,
> Ora regem et implora
> . . . . .
> Dei genetrix Maria.[37]

Dei genetrix was a stock phrase for the Virgin, which occurs repeatedly in these hymns and also in a well-known antiphon, *Gaude Dei genetrix*.[38] It is the ultimate source of Dunbar's own phrase, 'Of Jhesu genitrice' (44 and 63-4). But Dunbar's further rhymes on *-trice*— 'imperatrice', 'victrice', 'Oratrice, mediatrice, salvatrice' (61-72)— also find parallels in the *-trix* rhymes of the Latin hymns: *imperatrix*

---

[34] Ibid., no. 24.
[35] Ibid., no. 4, stanza 12; the second comes from a *rhythmus* attributed to Peter Damian (LXIII. 41-2).
[36] *AH* 32, no. 38. 6.
[37] Ibid., no. 36. 1. 3; see also no. 49. 21.
[38] Cf. Woolf, 135.

atque datrix, salvatrix, interemtrix, donatrix, consolatrix, mediatrix, adiuvatrix, and many more.[39]

Dunbar was responsive not only to the sense of these hymns but to their sound-effects, their metrical *tune*. Sometimes he reproduced their rhymes almost verbatim; at other times he ingeniously found vernacular equivalents, playing off Latin against the vernacular, as in 'sterne superne'. It is mistaken to think that *Ane Ballat of Our Lady* contains only long, Latin-derived words. Some lines indeed consist solely of monosyllables (19, 27, 46, 82); nor is there anything Latinate about the cascade of *-icht* rhymes in stanza three:

> Haile, bricht be sicht in hevyn on hicht;
> Haile, day sterne orientale;
> Our licht most richt in clud of nycht
> Our dirknes for to scale ... (25–8)

No other poem by Dunbar has such an intricate metrical shape: 'each stanza ... built on the repeated module a_4b_3 round an *Ave Maria, gracia plena* anaphora, with triple internal rhyme and supplementary alliteration'.[40] Every stanza, it should be noted, requires fifteen rhyming words, for the *a*-lines alone. The rhyme-scheme largely determines the poem's structure—there is no logical progression of ideas, and the images for the Virgin, apart from one interesting cluster of architectural terms (73–8), are distributed almost at random. Words occur at particular points chiefly because they fit particular slots in the metrical pattern. Some readers may find this pattern a strait-jacket; Dunbar perhaps regarded it more as a trellis-work, a new and elegant support on which to display old, very familiar phrases.

Ane Ballat of Our Lady is far more ornate than Dunbar's other religious poems; indeed the end of *The Flyting* provides the closest metrical parallel. (Both are highly incantatory exercises in name-calling.) But such artifice was an increasingly common feature of *all* Marian lyrics in the late Middle Ages. Woolf, perhaps rightly, interprets this trend as 'a symptom of the decline of medieval devotion'.[41] Dunbar's contemporary, Molinet, combined an extreme feat of alliteration with an acrostic in his *Oroison sur Maria*. This contains five stanzas, which together form the name MARIA: each is devoted to a single letter, and 'chascun mot de chascun couplet [stanza] commence par la premiere lettre'.[42] An earlier poet, Hans von Cleve, used a twelve-line stanza, like Dunbar, for the Prologue to his

---

[39] *AH* 32, nos. 3. 2; 46. 11; 71. 5.
[40] Kinsley, 225.
[41] Woolf, 281.
[42] *Les Faictz et dictz*, ed. N. Dupire (SATF, 1936–9), ii. 455–6; also Woolf, 291–2.

Marienlieder (*c*.1400); he demonstrated his virtuosity by writing in German, French, English, and Latin:

> Ave alpha du stercher god!
> Je diroy volentiers un mot
> Of that swete ladi deer,
> Cuius venter te portavit...[43]

Dunbar seems to have sought the same 'bravura' effect as Molinet and Hans von Cleve; in all these poems, however, the interest of the external form outstrips that of its content.

The high style has been called 'Chaucerian' and, more recently, 'Lydgatian', but it might better be termed 'International Late Gothic'. It was widely fashionable in the late fifteenth century, and practised not only by English poets but by many French and Burgundian ones.[44] None the less, for Dunbar and his contemporaries the great exponents of the style were certainly Chaucer and Lydgate. The English of these poets was of the southern variety, and differed markedly from the northern dialects of English. The adoption of a refined 'Chaucerian' style thus seems to have become associated, for many Scottish poets at this time, with the adoption of certain features of southern English usage. This is not the place for a full discussion of the subject, which has received magisterial treatment from A. J. Aitken.[45] Some of these 'southern' or anglicized features, however, undoubtedly appear in Dunbar. One is the use of rhymes which require the English rather than the Scots pronunciation of words; *more* and *sore*, for instance, rhyme with *before* and *glore* in *Ane Ballat of Our Lady* (49–53). The usual Scots form of the first two words would have /a/ rather than /o/, and would have spellings such as ⟨mair, mare⟩ and ⟨sair, sare⟩. Another striking feature is the adoption of southern verbal forms, especially those which add the inflection -*n* to verbal stems, in the infinitive and plural present indicative. Several of these are present in *The Goldyn Targe*: *bene* corresponds to modern English 'are' in lines 71 and 264; it corresponds to 'is' in lines 77 and 89. In this poem Dunbar also uses infinitives such as *sene*, 'see' (43, 143), *sayn* 'say' (198), and *done*, 'do' (159). *The Goldyn Targe* contains other archaic or southern features, such as the present plural indicative *gladdeth* (85), and past participles with the prefix *y*-, which were then long obsolete in Scots—*ybent* (110 and 145). A third feature is the employment of

---

[43] *Bruder Hansens Marienlieder*, ed. M. S. Batts (Tübingen, 1963), 1; discussed by Diehl, *Medieval European Religious Lyric*, 110–11, and 295.

[44] Cf. P. Zumthor, *Le Masque et la lumière* (Paris, 1978); the fullest study is in H. Guy, *Histoire de la poésie française au XVe siècle* (Paris, 1910; 1968).

[45] Cf. Aitken, 'Language of Scots Poetry', 26 ff.

distinctively southern words or forms: *lyte* and *morowing* thus appear in *The Goldyn Targe* (71, 247) instead of their Scots equivalents *litill* and *morn*, or *morning*.

It is important, however, to see such anglicisms in perspective. They occur only in a small cluster of Dunbar's poems, being most obtrusive in *The Goldyn Targe* and also present, though to a lesser extent, in *The Thrissill and the Rois*, *Bewty and the Presoneir*, *Sweit Rois of Vertew*, *Ane Ballat of Our Lady*, and *The Merle and the Nychtingall*. They figure particularly in the love poems and dream visions, poetry of a type strongly associated with Chaucer and his English followers. They sometimes combine, not surprisingly, with specific echoes of Chaucer, as in the apostrophe to 'My lady Cleo that help of makaris *bene*' (*Goldyn Targe*, 77). Such anglicized forms are not found in all Dunbar's courtly verse—they seem, for instance, almost totally absent from the two poems on Stewart. One might query whether there is any correlation with the likely audience for particular poems. The southern pronoun *sche*—not the Scots *scho*—thus occurs in a petition, *Schir for 3our grace bayth nicht and day*, that was presumably delivered to the queen as well as the king. In *The Merle and and the Nychtingall* there is an amusing linguistic contrast between the refrains: the merle uses *bene*—'A lusty lyfe in luves service bene'—but the nightingale uses *is*—'All luve is lost bot upone God allone'. It is tempting, if dubious, to find a moral contrast here, between the courtly but decadent southern speech of the merle, and the plain, godly, Scots speech of the nightingale. But it must be remembered that later copyists often altered spellings and grammatical forms; at line 62 the nightingale employs the southern *bene* in Bannatyne, which appears as *is* in Maitland. Bannatyne also regularly spells the last word of the nightingale's refrain as *allone*, and throughout the poem the words with which it rhymes have spellings in ⟨o⟩. Yet these rhymes would be equally correct in the Scots pronunciation implied by ⟨a⟩ spellings. Indeed there is another interesting divergence at line 102: Maitland has *tane*, but Bannatyne has the hyper-anglicism, *tone*. It is arguable that Maitland here offers the better clue to Dunbar's intended pronunciation, since *tone* occurs nowhere else in his verse. For Dunbar, as for other Scottish poets, these southern forms were a metrical convenience—supplying an extra syllable or a handy rhyme. If one examines Dunbar's usage as a whole, what is most striking is the comparative sparseness of anglicisms; this contrasts with the remarkably profuse and eclectic use of such forms by Douglas.[46]

Obtrusive anglicization was avoided in humorous verse by most Scottish poets of this time. Yet some critics believe that the language

[46] See Bawcutt, *Douglas*, 143–5.

of one of Dunbar's comic poems, *Schir Thomas Norny* (K 27), displays 'touches' or 'elements' of southern English.⁴⁷ This stems from the long-held belief that he was here imitating Chaucer's *Sir Thopas*; there sometimes seems circularity in the thinking—thus it is suggested that Dunbar's supposed 'deviations from Middle Scots' were a means of 'consciously reminding his listeners of *Sir Thopas*'.⁴⁸ But the only southern features in *Schir Thomas Norny* are a few spellings, such as *non* and *evermor*, which were common in late sixteenth-century copies of Scottish texts. The poem contains no distinctively southern rhymes; indeed some, such as that between *chaist* and *gaist* (13–14), would be possible only in Scots or northern English. The vocabulary has no distinctive southern items—*lythis*, 'listen', in the opening line, was a northern and Scots verb, and its -*is* ending was a characteristic Scots form of the plural imperative. Perhaps the most plausible-sounding case for 'southern colouring' of the language concerns the use of *gane* in

> Ane fairar knycht nor he was ane
> On ground may nothair ryd nor gane. (7–8)

It is argued that the usual Scottish form would be *ga*, and that Dunbar is here using the 'southern infinitive ending', such as occurs in *Sir Thopas*:

> For in that contree was ther noon
> That to him durste ride or goon. (804–5)

But *gane*, 'go, walk', existed in Scottish usage, and seems to have had an identity quite separate from *ga*; it was used in prose as well as verse, and did not function solely as an infinitive. Precisely how it originated is obscure, but it seems to be 'a northernism and Scotticism, which conflates, coincidentally, with 'Chaucerian' -*n* ending verbs'.⁴⁹ What this phrase, *ryd nor gane*, illustrates is the strongly formulaic nature of the style; it and the equally stereotyped *buklar nor brand* (9) and *so bauld a berne* (27) abound in the romances and ballads that were still popular in Dunbar's day. Even the idiom in line 7, which has no precedent in *Sir Thopas* and today sounds somewhat illogical, may be paralleled in *A Gest of Robin Hode:*

---

⁴⁷ Cf. E. R. Eddy, 'Sir Thopas and Sir Thomas Norny: Romance Parody in Chaucer and Dunbar', *RES* NS 22 (1971), 401–9; also J. A. Burrow, '*Sir Thopas* in the Sixteenth Century', in *Middle English Studies Presented to Norman Davis*, ed. D. Gray and E. G. Stanley (Oxford, 1983), 69.
⁴⁸ Eddy, op. cit. 404–5.
⁴⁹ A. J. Aitken, in a private communication; see also *DOST, gane*, v.2, and *SND, gaun*.

LANGUAGE AT LARGE

> A soriar man than he was one
> Rode neuer in somer day.[50]

We know from *Schir Thomas Norny* itself that Dunbar was familiar with some Robin Hood tales.

The comic and low-life verse of Dunbar's contemporaries had a very distinctive diction; Aitken notes that it was 'much the most densely Scottish of any kind of writing in Older Scots'.[51] This diction might be defined negatively—by the absence of southernisms—and positively—by the presence of markedly Scottish or northern English words, idioms, and grammatical usages. Some of Dunbar's comic poems—notably *Sir Jhon Sinclair* (K 28), *In secreit place* (K 13), *The Flyting*, *The Abbot of Tungland*, and *Fasternis Evin in Hell*—owe much to this stylistic tradition. In his discussion of the topic Aitken draws many illustrations—*brat, derch, dreg, craig, carling, cute, choll, clod* are a small sample—from *The Flyting*. When Dunbar describes the abbot's ignominious fall, it is words of this type that he uses:

> And in a myre up to the ene
> Amang the glar did glyd.
> . . . .
> Thre dayis in dub amang the dukis
> He did with dirt him hyde. (107 ff.)

Dunbar's contemporaries would no doubt have termed this style 'rude' and 'rural'. But we should also note the precision with which Dunbar writes. The words *myre, glar, dub,* and *dirt* are not chosen mechanically, to fit some prescription for the 'low' style, but because of their sound and sense. They are by no means synonymous: the abbot lands in a marshy swamp, glides in its sticky slime, and, covered by dirt (which includes excreta), hides among ducks in a small pool.

In the comic poems Dunbar draws upon the lowest and most informal registers of the vocabulary. He uses catchphrases and fossilized jokes—'Johne Thomsounis man' (in the refrain of K 25); type-names and nicknames—'Johne Blunt' (K 14. 142), 'Jok Fule' (K 38. 73), 'Blak Belly and Bawsy Broun' (K 52. 30), 'Sanct Girnega' (K 52. 164)—the latter belongs to the category of mock-saints, also found in French tradition;[52] oaths and imprecations (notably in K 56); an abundance of abusive terms; and vulgarisms and obscenities— 'cuntbittin' (K 23. 50), 'ers' and 'kis his ers' (K 23. 56, 131), 'fukkit' (K 13. 13). Such expressions tend to be highly colloquial. Some are

---
[50] *English and Scottish Popular Ballads*, ed. H. C. Sargent and F. L. Kittredge (Boston, Mass., 1904), no. 117, st. 23.
[51] 'Language of Scots Poetry', 39.
[52] Cf. L. Réau, *Iconographie de l'art chrétien* (Paris, 1955), i. 321–2.

extremely ephemeral; when they go out of fashion, their sense is soon forgotten. It is likely that Dunbar's more puzzling and opaque words belong to this category, and died out of the spoken language before they could be caught by lexicographers. Almost the opposite is true of another component of his diction. Some words were in spoken use for centuries, but for one reason or another were not usually written down. The most notorious example is *fuck*; Dunbar was certainly not the first user of this verb, only its first recorded user. But it is likely that some of his other phrases were more colloquial than we realize. Aitken noted that the expression 'up to the ene' (in the passage quoted above) is not found again until the nineteenth century, except in another comic Scots poem, *The Wyf of Auchtermuchty*; he suggests that it was 'long transmitted only in popular currency'.[53] Such gaps between the first citation of a word or expression, in Dunbar, and its next occurrence, often centuries later, are not conclusive, but certainly point towards a currency in speech rather than writing. Another example is '3uillis 3ald'—apart from Dunbar's use (K 43) there is no record of this until the second half of the nineteenth century, in a work on Scottish superstitions and folklore.[54] Another interesting usage occurs in *The Flyting* (74): Kennedy is here called 'The fathir and moder of morthour and mischeif'. It was not uncommon for *father* or *mother*, separately, to have the figurative sense, 'source, origin'; but in combination the phrase is both intensive and richly comic. Dunbar perhaps did not necessarily invent the expression, which resembles one still in use today—as in 'it was the father and mother of all thunderstorms/rows'. Yet this slangy colloquialism, which was labelled Anglo-Irish by Eric Partridge, does not figure in the original edition of *OED*, and the present earliest citation is dated 1892.

Another feature of this popular style was an attempt to 'mimic in writing recent innovations in the pronunciation of spoken Scots'.[55] Dunbar, like other poets, thus sometimes uses the 'reduced', or shortened, forms of words, that seem to have been in circulation side by side with older, fuller forms. This often involves some kind of vocalization or loss of consonants. Thus the rhyme of *a*, 'all', with *Schau* (K 28. 9–10) implies vocalization of the final /l/; so too with the rhyme of *fow*, 'full', with *3ow* and *trow* (K 13. 17–21). Elsewhere in Dunbar there is some evidence for the loss of intervocalic or word-final /v/ or /f/. The best clues are provided by rhymes, such as that between *my sell*, 'myself', and *tell* (K 45. 71–2). Spellings unsupported by rhymes are not conclusive evidence that Dunbar wished these

---

[53] 'Oral Narrative Style', 105
[54] W. Gregor, *Notes on the Folklore of the North-East of Scotland* (1881), 157.
[55] Aitken, 'Language of Scots Poetry', 44.

forms to be used, yet they offer interesting hints as to the likely pronunciation. One instance is *twell*, 'twelve' (K 52C. 1); another is Bannatyne's version of the woman's refrain in *In secreit place*: 'Fow leis me that graceles gane'. Maitland's rendering, 'Full leif is me ȝour graceles gane', is probably easier for the modern reader to understand, but Bannatyne's spelling *Fow leis me* makes explicit the use of two contracted forms. In later Scots similar spellings, 'lese me' and 'leeze me', are recorded. Dunbar also uses, for rhyme purposes, another colloquial contraction—the reduced form of *it* to /d/ in 'I stand ford' (K 45. 62), which might be translated 'I vouch for it'.[56] The stylistic propriety of using such 'cuttit' words in flyting and invective was later noted by James VI.[57]

The *Flyting* is commonly held to illustrate a stylistic pole farthest from that of *The Goldyn Targe*—a prime example of Dunbar's use of the Scots vernacular. The truth of this is confirmed by the virtually total absence of southern features, whether in rhymes or grammar, and the corresponding density of words and phrases peculiarly characteristic of Scots and northern English. In addition, *The Flyting* is studded with oaths, vulgarisms, and 'dirty' words—Dunbar's final taunt is to call Kennedy 'dirtin dok', or 'dirty bum'. Dunbar incorporates many insults that are now unfamiliar but were probably the common currency of the streets, those *verba injuriosa* that the burgh records mention but rarely document. He speaks of Kennedy as 'Greitand in Galloway lyk to ane gallow breid' (141). No other poet seems to use the term *gallow breid*, but *DOST*'s one other citation usefully glosses both its sense and connotations: 'ȝe was angrie and called him gallow bread, quhilk is hangit man'. Some of these snatches of abusive speech, however, possibly had a wider geographical currency than is always recognized. One of the taunts hurled at Kennedy by the Edinburgh 'carlingis' is 'Our gallowis gaipis' (222; cf. 127). The sense is that the ravenous gallows must be constantly fed with criminals. There is evidence that this was a catchphrase current not only in Scotland but in England—Pistol remarks very similarly, 'Let gallows gape for dog', in *Henry V* (III. vi. 41). Earlier Dunbar said of Kennedy and his 'quene':

> Thair is bot lys and lang nailis ȝow amang. (148)

This taunt too may not have been Dunbar's invention, but a neat utilization of a semi-proverbial insult. *DOST* calls attention to a similarly alliterative Danish saying: *have intet andet end lus og lange*

---

[56] See *DOST*, *leis(e, lese me, 'd*, and *ford*.
[57] *Reulis and Cautelis*, in *Elizabethan Critical Essays*, ed. G. Gregory Smith, i. 217.

negle, 'to have nothing but lice and long nails'.[58] As for the 'cuttit' words, one can see some indications in *The Flyting*, such as the forms *mysell* (80), 'myself', *aw* (95), 'all', and *gaw* (183), 'gall'. Rhymes as well as spelling indicate that the vocalized pronunciation of these words is intended here. Possibly the shortened, monosyllabic form of *evin*, 'even', and *nevir*, 'never', is rhythmically implicit in the lines in which they occur (116, 209).

By such means Dunbar produces an effect of colloquial, even demotic, speech. But we should not over-simplify his artistry, nor reduce his technique to the systematic exclusion of formal words and inclusion of low ones. *The Flyting* is neither a string of dirty words nor a slice of actual speech; it would be exceedingly dull if this were so. Aitken has drawn attention to the groups of near-synonyms that existed in Scots, as in all languages, and the choice between different registers that they made possible.[59] Beside the neutral *face*, for instance, there existed the more dignified *visage* and *countenance*, and also the abusive *gane*, which might be rendered 'ugly mug'. Since Dunbar, in *The Flyting*, is much concerned with Kennedy's 'luik', or appearance, it is worth inspecting his usage. The term *face* occurs once or twice, but always with a pejorative modifier (150, 173, 235). Dunbar uses the contemptuous *gane* twice (167, 199), and obviously depreciative words for the nose, such as *snowt* (52) and *gruntill* (127), which were more commonly applied to animals. But he also uses the distinctly learned *phisnomy* (81), 'physiognomy', which comically implies his scientific interest in Kennedy's appearance. He also speaks of him grandiloquently as *wan-visaged* (101), 'livid-faced'. Neither *port* (163) nor *front* (84, 126, 173) are necessarily low or pejorative: *port* is applied to the queen's 'bearing' in *Gladethe thoue queyne* (K 31. 11); *front* is a neutral term for the forehead. In these usages it is the epithet that carries the insult. Dunbar also uses one very poetic word for the face or complexion, *ble*, embedded in the alliterative formula, 'blaiknit is thy ble' (165).

This tiny segment of Dunbar's diction in *The Flyting* is not, I think, untypical; the lexical range is wide. There are plenty of other words from the more formal or learned stratum of the vocabulary, and even a touch of mythology, when Dunbar refers not to stormy winds and sea but 'Eolus full woid and Neptunus' (91). Such words may in themselves be abusive, or they may be sarcastic, undermined by the context in which they occur. Again and again a comic effect results not from the dictionary sense of a word but from its deployment. *Giltin*, for instance, is a word that had a similar lexical status to *gilt*: for Ireland 'giltyn spurris' were a token of knighthood, and Haye

[58] See *DOST, lous*.   [59] 'Language of Scots Poetry', 45-6.

spoke likewise of a sword of honour, 'gilt' with gold.⁶⁰ Dunbar preserves the honorific sense of *gilt*, speaking of ladies' 'glorius gilt tressis' (K 14. 19; also K 50. 20). But when he mentions Kennedy's 'giltin hippis' (99), the epithet is grotesque and mocking; it presumably means 'yellow with excrement'. In isolation the phrase 'Haill, soverane senʒeour' sounds respectful; Dunbar uses the first two words in *Ane Ballat of Our Lady*. It is the context and, in particular, the bathetic second half-line that makes this use so derisive:

> Sen thow with wirschep wald sa fane be styld—
> Haill, soverane senʒeour! Thy bawis hingis throw thy breik!
>
> (103-4)

Dunbar often seems more innovative, verbally, in the comic poems than elsewhere. One instance is his use of compounding: based on long-established patterns of word-formation, it is witty and inventive, and usually pejorative. He employs compound epithets in descriptions of physical appearance—*gritheidit* (K 13. 41), *tute mowitt* (K 33. 6), 'with a projecting mouth', *pynhippit* (K 23. 185), *clubfacet* and *mell hedit* (K 45. 24, 60). In *The Flyting* Dunbar favours a type of nominal compound, in which a verb is combined with a noun that forms its grammatical object. A modern example is *pickpocket*, for which Dunbar's equivalent is *pykpuris* (114), 'pickpurse'. Several occur in the final stanzas, and seem to be Dunbar's own coinage—*clym ledder*, *fyle tedder* (240), and *lik schilling* (243). Although to modern readers these may seem obscure, they are compressed and dynamic: the first two depict Kennedy in the act of climbing the ladder (associated with the gallows) and then defiling the halter; the last implies that he is so impoverished that he does not simply steal grain but licks up the discarded husks. This type of compound is invariably pejorative when applied to persons.⁶¹ Another type, however, in which a noun is followed by an agent noun in -*er* has more neutral connotations, and often signifies someone's trade or occupation. But in Dunbar even innocent-seeming formations may be malicious, such as *ostir dregar* (K 23. 242), 'oyster-dredger', and *clarat cunnaris* (K 44. 42), an apt term for French wine connoisseurs. Others are straightforwardly abusive—Kennedy is *muttoun dryver* and *girnall ryver* (246), or a twofold thief, driving off sheep and breaking into granaries. At the opening of *The Turnament* is a cluster of these derisive compounds— *seme byttaris*, *beist knapparis*, *stomok steillaris*, *clayth takkaris*

---

⁶⁰ For these and other usages, see *DOST*, *giltin*, *gilt*.
⁶¹ Cf. H. Marchand, *The Categories and Types of Present-Day English Word-Formation* (Munich, 1969), 380-3.

(K 52. 130–1)—that succinctly evoke traditional stereotypes of the tailor as dirty and dishonest.[62]

Dunbar sometimes uses effective, probably *ad hoc*, combinations of two nouns, in which the first element is metaphorical: *catt nois* (K 33. 8) needs no explanation; *bledder cheikis* (K 45. 23) suggests cheeks that are fat, white, and swollen; *hurcheone scyne* (K 14. 107) refers to a man's face, prickly as a hedgehog. The line from which this comes—'And with his hard hurcheone scyne sa heklis he my chekis'—is remarkably compressed, far more than Dunbar's likely source, in *The Merchant's Tale* (IV. 1824–5):

> With thikke brustles of his berd unsofte
> Lyk to the skyn of houndfyssh, sharp as brere.

The Widow's term for her husband, *wif carll* (K 14. 351), is doubly opprobrious. It humiliates him both socially (a *carll* was a peasant) and sexually, seeing him as fit only for 'womenis werkis'. Another type of formation that Dunbar uses occasionally is the reduplicating compound—*hiddy giddy* (K 54. 44), or *quhillylillie, tirly mirly, towdy mowdy*, all bawdy, from *In secreit place*. Another example occurs in the description of a clumsy dancer as 'Ane hommiltye jommeltye juffler' (K 28. 16). *Hommiltye jommeltye* is recorded nowhere else, and may be Dunbar's invention. It is untranslatable, yet very effective rhythmically; the closest parallel is in nursery rhymes designed to accompany the bouncing of a child on one's knee—'Home again, home again, jiggety jig!' Like the other reduplicating expressions that Dunbar uses, it belongs to a playful and primarily oral area of language.

In secreit place consists largely of talk. The comedy springs partly from the gap between the courtly opening and the low-style conversation that follows. But what is most interesting, linguistically, about this poem is Dunbar's humorous and accurate use of terms of endearment. The lovers shower each other with the epithet *sweit* and such phrases as 'My hunny' (3), 'My hairt, sweit as the hunny' (15), and 'My hony soppis, my sweit possody' (30). Such endearments belong to an ancient tradition, and are not necessarily ludicrous. Nicholas, in *The Miller's Tale*, exclaimed:

> What do ye, hony-comb, sweete Alisoun,
> My faire bryd, my sweete cynamome?   (I. 3698–9)

And a seventeenth-century poet called his mistress, 'My dear pigeon, my pretty mop / My sweet pigsny, my honey sop'.[63] But Dunbar's coupling of 'hony soppis' with 'possody' inevitably accentuates the

---

[62] For fuller discussion, see Bawcutt, 'Dunbar: New Light', 92–3.
[63] See *Love and Drollery*, ed. J. Wardroper (1969), no. 100.

literal and culinary sense of both: the former a dish made of bread, honey, and water, the latter a posset, or drink made from hot, sweetened milk and ale or wine. Comparison of the loved one to plants and young animals also has a long history. But the flowers to which this man compares his girl are not the usual rose and lily (as in *Sweit rois of vertew*), but clover and 'curledoddy' (29), a name given to a weed, the ribwort plantain. The trite 'sweit as the hunny' is comically echoed by the disconcerting 'sweit as ony unȝeoun' (53). In *The Miller's Tale* Alisoun was compared to a kid and a calf; Dunbar's lovers also compare each other to farmyard animals—not only a kid and a calf but a clumsy young stirk. From a morphological point of view, the poem is striking for its use of diminutives, or pet-forms of words, ending in *-y* or *-ie*: *mynny* (16), 'mother', or *billie* (31), 'friend'. These overlap with the reduplicating compounds, already mentioned. Many of these are obscure and possible newly invented. All produce the effect of baby talk—it is appropriate that the man calls the girl 'My bony bab' (44)—and of a private language, designed to keep outsiders from entering an intimate, 'secreit' world.

Dunbar is making fun of the way lovers talk: pet names, diminutives, images, and bawdy *double entendres* jostle incongruously. He has registered some of the perennial characteristics of amorous language, which may still be observed in our own time. Much the same categories can be discerned in the Valentine messages that are placed each year in *The Times* and other newspapers: 'sweetie pie, honeybee, honey bun, honey bear, sweetpea, little pickled onion, pussy cat, little bear, my lamby, cutiepie, chickerbiddie, wiggsey woo, higgle huggle, wookie pookie, nicky wicky.' Even the deliberate rudeness of an expression like 'My belly huddroun' (38) may be paralleled by 'darling fishface' or 'fatsy'! Dunbar's lovers are not far removed from these modern senders of Valentines; their language too is 'affectionate, dotty, and richly soppy'.[64]

The style of many of Dunbar's poems, chiefly the moralities and petitions, is neither 'high' nor 'low'. The notion of a 'middle style' is hard to define. Extremes of any kind may be recognized easily, but the middle ground is usually as difficult to determine, linguistically, as it is in geography or politics. None the less this is the area to which belong poems otherwise very different—*My heid did ȝak* (K 21), or *This waverand warldis wretchidnes* (K 39), or *I that in heill wes* (K 62). The style in which they are written is unflamboyant and unobtrusive; it is a style that—unlike that of *The Goldyn Targe* and *The Flyting*—

---

[64] The modern expressions come from *The Times*, 13 Feb. 1988; cf. R. Burchfield, *Sunday Times*, 6 Mar. 1988.

does not call attention to itself. This way of writing was hardly peculiar to Dunbar. It resembles the comparatively unadorned style of some Tudor poets that Lewis termed 'Drab', and that the American poet Yvor Winters particularly admired, praising its 'plainness and directness' and the way it combined 'matter-of factness with passion'.[65] Yet this plain style did not originate in the sixteenth century; its roots lie in the practice of countless anonymous medieval poets. Some prominent features of this largely moral and didactic tradition, to which Dunbar owed much, have been discussed in an earlier chapter (pp. 134–8).

Dunbar's middle style is best defined negatively—by the absence of the conspicuous 'markers' of other styles, whether Latinisms or vulgarisms. The diction is largely drawn from the common core of the language; it includes a large number of words common to Scots and English, and many still remain in use today. The poems in this style tend to be the ones that modern readers find easiest to understand, without frequent consultation of the glossary. Syntactically, they avoid long, elaborate sentences or suspension of the sense. This is often coupled with the omission of conjunctions and relative pronouns, which produces a terse, clipped effect—

> I wald he had ane havye clog. (K 29. 11)

or

> He is na dog; he is a lam. (K 30, refrain)

It is noticeable that these poems are usually the ones in short stanzas, of four or five lines, often with a refrain. Within such a small space it would hardly be possible to construct sentences of any complexity.

Yet it would be mistaken to regard Dunbar's poems in this style as artless; almost all, even the most light-hearted, have some degree of discrete rhetorical patterning. This is evident in the two poems on James Dog, quoted above: in the first a *repetitio* on 'Quhen that I ...' links three of the central stanzas; in the second syntactic parallelism links the two stanzas devoted to Dog's wife—'The wyff that he had in his innis ...', 'The wyff that wald him kuckald mak ...'. The vocabulary and grammar of *I that in heill wes* could hardly be more basic; it is largely composed of such simple assertions as 'I am', 'I se that', and

---

[65] See *English Literature in the Sixteenth Century*, 64 and 223; and 'The 16th-Century Lyric in England: A Critical Reinterpretation', in *Elizabethan Poetry*, ed. P. J. Alpers (Oxford, 1967), 96 and 116. My terminology does not derive from the medieval notion of 'the three styles'; on this, cf. D. Burnley, *A Guide to Chaucer's Language* (1985), 183–200.

> The flesch is brukle, the Fend is sle . . .
> No stait in erd heir standis sickir . . .
> He takis the knychtis in to feild . . .

Yet the repetition of 'He takis', together with 'He has tane' and other variants, is carefully contrived, and—in context—remarkably chilling. In *This waverand warldis wretchidnes* a similar pattern of repetition with variation is put to very different use. An equally simple expression, 'It cumis', undergoes several comic metamorphoses—'It micht have cuming', and 'It is so lang in cuming'—until the indignation (over the long-awaited benefice) explodes:

> sa done tyrsum it is to byd it,
> It breikis my hairt and birstis my brane.   (82–3)

It, usually an insignificant pronoun, occurs fifteen times in seven stanzas. The referent, although clear at first, turns into some strangely vague object of universal desire:

> Quhen it dois cum, all men dois frane.   (79)

What these poems strikingly demonstrate is ease and flexibility. Some are hortatory, others intimate and reflective. Even the most serious are infused with a degree of humour or irony. The petitions are essentially verse-epistles, and the formulaic manner in which some begin or end resembles that of Cardinal Beaton's letters to James V: these 'show how a gentleman of Scotland wrote in the middle of the sixteenth century'.[66] Many display a mastery of *talking* in verse that finds a parallel in Douglas's Prologues. A small example of this occurs in an unpretentious complaint on the state of Dunbar's finances, *My lordis of chalker, pleis 30w to heir* (K 46). It is filled with the minutiae of accounting—paper, ink, and clinking 'countaris'—and the third stanza departs little from the word-order of prose:

I tuik fra my lord thesaurair/ane soume of money for to wair [expend]. / I cannot tell 30w how it is spendit, / bot weill I waitt that it is endit, / and that me think ane coumpt our sair [unpleasant reckoning].

This is chatty, conversational, and slightly impertinent. Several other poems contain effective modulations of tone and style. Bursts of anger, conveyed by flyting language, interrupt an otherwise calm and thoughtful poem, *Schir, 3e have mony servitouris* (K 44). The style of *I that in heill wes* is basically plain, yet has great dignity. It achieves heightening, largely through the Latin refrain, and striking inversions

---

[66] Cf. A. Lang, 'Letters of Cardinal Beaton 1537–1541', *SHR* 6 (1909), 150–8.

of word-order—'Victour he is at all melle' (23). This poem indeed fuses 'matter-of-factness with passion'.

One of the most powerful yet undervalued influences upon Dunbar was the tradition of alliterative poetry. The greatest poems of the alliterative revival in England—*Sir Gawain and the Green Knight*, *Piers Plowman*, *The Morte Arthure*—belong to the fourteenth century, and by the late fifteenth century the tradition was in decline, though not extinct. But in Scotland this period witnessed a remarkable flowering of alliterative poetry; one form in particular—the elaborate thirteen-line stanza with a wheel—was used by many poets, including Henryson, Holland, Douglas, and Montgomerie. What is more, alliteration is present in almost all Scottish poetry of this period, ranging from the lyrical *Tayis Bank* to the battle-scenes in Hary's *Wallace* and Douglas's *Eneados*. This variety of use perhaps needs stressing. In Scotland as in England the alliterative technique was not confined solely to one style or one kind of subject. Scottish poets used alliteration with ease and virtuosity: for story-telling as well as for landscape description. But there was a tendency, increasingly observable in the sixteenth century, to use it for humour and satire—as in the anonymous *Kynd Kittok* and Douglas's Eighth Prologue. There can be no doubt about Dunbar's familiarity with the tradition, but the highly conventional nature of the alliterative style makes it difficult to prove his knowledge of specific poems. The clearest pointers are Dunbar's own references to Holland (and presumably to *The Howlat*) and to *Rauf Coilyear*. We should also recall that *The Howlat* and the romance *Golagros and Gawane* were printed in Dunbar's own lifetime. This does not prove that he read these poems, but it increases the likelihood; it also confirms their contemporary popularity and availability.[67]

Almost all Dunbar's poems are characterized by the light ornamental alliteration then favoured by most Scottish poets. Sometimes it is highly obtrusive, as in the opening line of one petition—'Sanct salvatour, send silver sorrow!' (K 19). In the fine moral poems it tends to be more subtle, less obvious, yet surprisingly pervasive. Alliteration sometimes points an antithesis—'Now sound, now seik' (K 62. 10) or 'No gold in kist nor wyne in cowp' (K 69. 42)—but more often couples pairs of near-synonyms, like 'drug and draw' or 'firthe and fald' (K 43. 10, 12). Many of these rather stereotyped expressions did not necessarily originate in verse but were part of the diction of

---

[67] See F. Riddy, 'The Alliterative Revival', in *The History of Scottish Literature: Origins to 1660*, ed. R. D. S. Jack (Aberdeen, 1988), 39–54; Sir W. Craigie, 'The Scottish Alliterative Poems', *PBA* 28 (1942), 217–36; and T. Turville-Petre, *The Alliterative Revival* (Cambridge, 1977).

everyday life, along with proverbs and popular similes. Four of Dunbar's poems, however, stand out from the rest, through the density of their alliteration and their clear connection with the poetic tradition; yet only one, *The Tua Mariit Wemen and the Wedo*, is written in strict alliterative metre.

Dunbar's comic mimicry of romance motifs in *The Turnament* (K 52) has been discussed earlier. Battle-poetry of all kinds was pervaded by alliterative set phrases, and it is not surprising that they feature in this poem. Yet the sheer amount of alliteration in *The Turnament* is not always recognized, largely through the somewhat uncritical acceptance, by most editors, of Bannatyne's text. Asloan's version of the poem contains lines like these:

The *buthman* on the barras blent (139)

or

Wneis he mycht upsit (171)

or

His *birnes* brak and maid a bratill (193)

or

Sic solace to my hart *thar socht*. (221)

In Bannatyne these lines lack strong alliteration; instead of the italicized words he has, respectively, *tail3our, He mycht nocht rycht, harnas*, and *it rocht*. In each case there are good arguments for the superiority of Asloan's readings. *Buthman*, 'shopkeeper', was strongly pejorative, and the repetitive *tail3our* seems to have been introduced by eyeskip. *Wneis*, 'with difficulty', was an archaic word that Dunbar used elsewhere, also initially in the line (K 3. 45); the whole expression seems characteristic of alliterative romance—'He start up stoutly again, wneis micht he stand' (*Rauf Coilyear*, 155). *Birnes*, 'coat of mail', is an ancient and evocative word from heroic poetry; even the curious use here of the plural form with singular sense can be paralleled elsewhere, such as *Golagros and Gawane*, 843–4: 'That knight ... Braissit in birneis and basnet full bene'.[68] Bannatyne's *harnas*, 'armour', sacrifices both the heroic associations of *birnes* and its alliteration. In the last instance Bannatyne's *rocht* is usually explained as an error (or odd variant) for *wrocht*, 'worked', yet here too Asloan's reading makes good sense. The phrasal verb *seek to*, 'move towards', is well evidenced; indeed it occurs earlier in this poem (192), and in

---

[68] Ed. F. J. Amours in *Scottish Alliterative Poems* (STS, 1892–7). For other examples see *DOST, birny* 1b; and *MED, brinie*, n.

alliterative verse is applied, as here, to emotions reaching the *heart*—
'sorʒe soʒt to his hert'.[69] By the second half of the sixteenth century
alliterative poetry must have seemed old-fashioned; its diction was
certainly growing increasingly unfamiliar. The copyists of Douglas's
Eneados sometimes altered unusual words of alliterative provenance to
others that were presumably more commonplace.[70] In *The Turnament*
and other poems of Dunbar a similar practice also occurred; both
Bannatyne and Maitland made modernizing substitutions for words
that were becoming obscure, odd, or simply out-of-date.[71]

The Abbot of Tungland (K 54), like *The Turnament*, is written in tail-
rhyme; and it too is highly alliterative. In this poem Dunbar's
alliteration is notably witty and inventive. It juxtaposes notions that,
theoretically, should be far apart:

> In pottingry [pharmacy] he wrocht grit pyne;
> He murdreist mony in medecyne. (29–30)

Alliteration rises to a crescendo in the account of the birds' attack: it
guides their marshalling—'The golk, the gormaw and the gled' (77)—
and determines their characteristic activities:

> The stork straik ay but stynt. (84)

Dunbar couples 'kayis and crawis' (89), just as Holland did in *The
Howlat* (191); he seems to have learnt from Holland, in this and in
other respects. He brilliantly conveys the raucous cacophony of the
birds by various devices: the heavy use, especially in rhyme position,
of stressed monosyllables ending in voiceless plosives, especially /k/
—*dynt*, *straik*, *cluik*, *bruik*. Holland's owl complained of his persecution
by other birds:

> Sum skripe me with scorne, sum skrym at myn e. (67)

Dunbar, describing the 'mobbing' not of an owl but of the abbot,
employs alliteration on the same consonant clusters, /sk/ and /skr/—

> The ja him skrippit with a skryke
> And skornit him as it was lyk,
> . . . .
> The air was dirkit with the fowlis
> That come with ʒawmeris and with ʒowlis,
> With skryking, skrymming, and with scowlis
> To tak him in the tyde. (97 ff.)

This passage owes something to a more widely diffused alliterative
tradition. Douglas described the howls of Circe's wolves likewise:

---

[69] Cf. *Cleanness*, ed. J. J. Anderson (Manchester, 1977), 563.
[70] Cf. Bawcutt, *Douglas*, 154.
[71] See also Bawcutt, 'The Text and Interpretation of Dunbar', *MÆ* 50 (1981), 91 ff.

'ȝouland and ȝammerand, grislie for to heir' (*Eneados*, VI. xvi. 38). The ghost that appeared to Guinevere in *The Awntyrs of Arthure* came

> ȝauland ȝamerly, with many loude ȝelle.
> Hit ȝaules, hit ȝameres . . .[72]

Dunbar's *ȝawmeris* and *ȝowlis* belong to a small cluster of echoic words (modern equivalents are *yell, yowl, howl, bawl,* or *wawl*) which were often coupled in this way, and applied to the ghastly cries of owls, ghosts, or devils. Other poems by Dunbar suggest his awareness of the linguistic phenomenon that is termed sound-symbolism, or phonaesthesia: the regular association of a particular meaning with particular sounds or sequences of sounds. The stanza in *The Goldyn Targe* that describes the noisy end of the dream (235–43) is 'dominated', as Aitken notes, 'by voiceless plosives, notably /k/, in word-initial and word-final position, in rhyme and alliteration'.[73] Another dream, *This hinder nycht* (K 51), ends equally explosively with a stanza that contains the same rhymes as in *The Goldyn Targe—frak, rak, brak* (within the line) and *crak*. This is reinforced in both passages by alliteration on /r/, which in Scots is strongly trilled, not the feeble consonant used in modern standard English—'The rochis all resownyt with the rak'. A similar technique occurs in other passages concerned with noise and violence: the lines on the Last Judgement in *Quhome to sall I complene my wo* (76–80), the opening stanza of *Done is a battell*, and the last one of *The Dance* (K 52A).

James VI prescribed that flyting should be 'literall': 'the maist part of your lyne sall rynne vpon a [one] lettre'.[74] Alliteration is certainly prominent in Dunbar's *Flyting*. Line after line contains several alliterating syllables, usually three or four, sometimes five—

> Hell sould nocht hyd thair harnis fra harmis hynting. (8)

sometimes six—

> Lene larbar loungeour, baith lowsy in lisk and lonȝe. (121)

The density of alliteration in this poem, as in others, is obscured by the spelling, since it falls on any stressed syllable, whether at the beginning or in the middle of a word. Reading aloud brings out more clearly the consonantal pattern in 'the hurle behind' (194), or lines like

> Decrepit karlingis on Kennedy cryis owt. (136)

---

[72] Ed. R. Hanna III (Manchester, 1974), 86–7.
[73] 'Language of Scots Poetry', 48. See also M. Mackay, 'Structure and Style in Richard Holland's *Buke of the Howlat*', in Lyall and Riddy, 204–5.
[74] *Reulis and Cautelis*, in *Elizabethan Critical Essays*, ed. Smith, i. 218.

or
> Garris men dispyt thar flesche, thow spreit of Gy. (172)

Dunbar was by no means the first to find alliteration a 'powerful reinforcer' of insults. There is precedent in the short English poem attacking blacksmiths, both for his hyper-alliteration and his sound-symbolism:

> Swarte smekyd smethes, smatered with smoke ...
> . . . .
> Tik, tak, hic hac, tiket taket, tyk tak![75]

A marked increase in alliteration tends to coincide with catalogues of abuse, not only in *The Flyting* itself but in similar tirades in K 44 and K 45. Yet *The Flyting* is not technically in alliterative metre, and its diction is only rarely characterized by the special 'poetic' terms and formulae, such as 'sege' (13), 'berne' (210), and 'blaiknit is thy ble' (165).[76]

Dunbar's originality in choosing the unrhymed, alliterative line for *The Tua Mariit Wemen and the Wedo* has been obscured by its sheer antiquity. Although most English alliterative poets used the unrhymed form, Scottish poets preferred the stanzaic type of alliterative verse. (The cryptic prophecies, written on both sides of the Border, are only sporadically and irregularly alliterative.[77]) Dunbar's adoption of this metre thus goes against the prevailing trend in Scotland, and poses interesting questions as to his motives. It was not because of any incapacity for finding rhymes; Dunbar's mastery of different stanza-types is undisputed. It seems unlikely to have been a mere exercise in archaism, for its own sake. I would suggest that Dunbar was fascinated by the sheer difference of the metre from the stanzas that he used elsewhere, and that he relished the challenge posed by its peculiar combination of freedom and constraint. The freedom lay not merely in the absence of rhyme but in the longer line that was permitted—many lines in *The Tua Mariit Wemen and the Wedo* contain fourteen or fifteen syllables. Possibly Dunbar wished to experiment with a line of wholly different rhythmical structure, and the stress pattern of the alliterative line changes when it is combined with rhyme.[78] Perhaps even more important was the flexibility this metre permitted in

---

[75] See Turville-Petre, *Alliterative Revival*, 119; and 'A Complaint against Blacksmiths', in E. Salter, *English and International: Studies in the Literature, Art and Patronage of Medieval England* (Cambridge, 1988), 199–214.

[76] Cf. *Golagros and Gawane*, 1133: 'blakynnit thair ble'.

[77] Cf. Riddy, 'Alliterative Revival', 41; also C. Singh, 'The Alliterative Ancestry of Dunbar's "The Tretis of the Tua Mariit Wemen and the Wedo"', *Leeds Studies in English*, NS 7 (1974), 22–54.

[78] Cf. Turville-Petre, op. cit. 62.

arranging one's material; as in blank verse, paragraphs could be constructed of varying length, in accordance with the sense. The constraints were those common to all alliterative poets: the necessity to find for every line three or more alliterating syllables. This fostered the development of a characteristic poetic diction, highly conventional and formulaic, and often of great antiquity. The metre of *The Tua Mariit Wemen and the Wedo* put heavy demands on Dunbar; he has more recourse to this specialized diction here than in any other poem.

One of the most obvious characteristics of the alliterative style was the use of certain nouns and adjectives, found only or chiefly in poetry. Some of the well-known synonyms for a hero or warrior occur in *The Tua Mariit Wemen and the Wedo*—*freke* (210, 324), *leid* (283, 407, 497), or *sege* (469)—usually in their weakened, more general sense, 'man, person'. The reduction in their force is often carried further by Dunbar. The second husband is called 'that ald schaik' (105); the same term, *schalk*, has dignified connotations in *Sir Gawain* and *Golagros and Gawane*. Particularly interesting is a word that Dunbar twice applies to the wives: 'thir fair wlonkes' (36) and 'the tothir wlonk' (150). Dunbar is the last recorded user of *wlonk*, and to modern readers the word may well look outlandish. Yet it would have seemed familiar and apt to readers of *The Howlat* and many English alliterative poems, where it was applied to objects or persons that were exceptionally fine or beautiful.[79] 'Thir fair wlonkes' illustrates another striking feature of alliterative verse—the substantival use of the adjective. The Widow refers to her old husband as 'the ald' (286); the First Wife is introduced as 'ane lusty' (49) and dismissed as 'the semely' (146), and the Second Wife is similarly styled 'the plesand' (158) and 'this amyable' (239). Turville-Petre notes that there was an absence of poetic synonyms for women, and that the gap was filled, in part, by elevating these and similar epithets to the rank of nouns.[80] In much verse the alliterative pattern seems chiefly responsible for which of these epithets is chosen. In *Sir Gawain*, however, the use is often more subtle: when the mistress of the castle is called 'that cortays' (2411) it is singularly ironic. So too with Dunbar: we notice an ironic discrepancy between the commendatory terms for the ladies and the content of their speeches.

Another feature, common in alliterative verse, though not peculiar to it, was the use of set prepositional phrases, often denoting place. Dunbar's use of such tags may be seen at its simplest and most traditional in the descriptive passages at the beginning and end of *The Tua Mariit Wemen and the Wedo*: 'ane bird on ane bransche' (5), 'bird

---

[79] Cf. *Tayis Bank*, 118; *Howlat*, 553; *Awntyrs of Arthure*, 347 and 696.
[80] Turville-Petre, op. cit. 81.

... on the beuche' (6), 'upspred upon spray' (29), or 'schoutit in schaw' (516). All too often such tags served to fill slots in the alliterative pattern, or—in the stanzaic poems—to supply rhymes. But Dunbar is rarely redundant. In the central section of the poem tags like 'in bed' (128, 135, 385), 'in bour' (184), or 'in chalmer' (183, 194, 370) imply a location in suggestive contrast with that of the flowery garden. Elsewhere Dunbar often revitalizes an ancient formula. The Widow rejoices

> That undir Crist no creatur kennis of our doingis. (454)

The phrase *undir Crist* occurs in other alliterative verse, and there seems to mean 'anywhere' and to be roughly the equivalent of 'undir hevin' or 'in erd', also found in this poem (32, 168).[81] The line might be rendered, 'No creature anywhere knows of our doings'; yet in context the reference to Christ is almost as pointed as in the analogous phrase in *Sir Gawain*: 'The most kyd kny3tes vnder Krystes seluen' (51). Even if no human knows what these women get up to, God certainly does. A curiously common tag in Scottish verse of this period is *on raw*, literally 'in a row'. It appears in Henryson and Douglas, particularly in the phrase 'raik on raw'; and it occurs so often in *Golagros and Gawane*—'Before the riale on raw' (396) or 'Before the riale renkis richest on raw' (1277)—that the editor of this poem termed it 'meaningless'.[82] But the tag flashes into life in Dunbar. In *The Flyting* it neatly fits into the pattern of rhyme and alliteration:

> Thy rigbane rattillis and thy ribbis on raw. (180)

Yet it also contributes to the image of Kennedy's emaciation; one should not be able to see ribs well covered with flesh 'in a row'. In *The Tua Mariit Wemen and the Wedo* Dunbar pictures the women feasting:

> With ryalle cowpis apon rawis full of ryche wynis. (35)

Apon rawis here joins 'ryalle' and 'ryche' in a highly traditional collocation. But the plural implies a remarkable quantity of wine— 'rows upon rows'—and is the first humorous hint that the ladies are not wholly admirable.

The highly conventional nature of much alliterative verse is evident not only in the tags but in other patterns and arrangements of words, some fixed and formulaic, others more flexible. Dunbar does not disdain the traditional 'doublets', or pairs of words belonging to the same grammatical class. An instance occurs in 'Sum kissis me, sum clappis me' (483), which is analogous to the common Middle English

---

[81] Cf. *Sir Gawain and the Green Knight*, ed. N. Davis (Oxford, 1967), n. to line 51.
[82] Amours, *Alliterative Poems*, 448.

'clip and kiss', a phrase of great antiquity, found in the Anglo-Saxon *The Wanderer*. Dunbar's conformity to tradition is particularly evident in the two ornate passages of natural description:

> The dew donkit the daill and dynnit the feulis.
> I hard under ane holyn hevinlie grein hewit
> Ane hie speiche at my hand with hautand wourdis ... (10 ff.)

and

> the day did up daw and dew donkit flouris.
> . . . .
> Silver schouris doune schuke as the schene cristall
> And berdis schoutit in schaw with ther schill notis ... (512 ff.)

There are resemblances here to *Tayis Bank*, in which the poet hides under 'ane holene hewinlie hewit grene' and later hears how 'The schene birdis full schill couth schout / Into that semly schaw'.[83] But there are many parallels also in English verse—'donkande dewe', for instance, or 'The dewe appon dayses donkede full faire', or 'All donkyt the dales with the dym schowris'.[84] Dunbar's style is strongly reminiscent of other striking passages that occur—often as prologues—in *The Parlement of the Thre Ages*, *Wynnere and Wastoure*, *Death and Life*, and *The Morte Arthure*.

What is interesting is to see how Dunbar—particularly in the poem's central section—slightly modifies the traditional sense of a phrase, usually to humorous or ironic effect. He gives a bawdy application to the trite simile 'soft as silk' (96). He describes the reception of the First Wife's speech:

> Than all thai leuch apon loft with latis full mery
> And raucht the cop round about full of riche wynis. (147–8)

The phrase *leuch apon loft*, 'laughed loudly', was common, often with approving reference to male conviviality. In *Rauf Coilyear* (739) 'Thir lordis leuch upon loft'; so too in *The Howlat* (828) 'the lordis leuch apon loft'. The second line has similar connotations, as in Dunbar's own 'Lat anis the cop ga round about' (K 41. 14). But what is acceptable in lords is less decorous in ladies. The effect of displacing these phrases from men to women tallies with much else in the poem. Even more striking is the Second Wife's remark:

> Scho suld not stert for his straik a stray breid of erd. (234)

This line—'She would not flinch away, on account of his stroke, a straw's breadth of ground'—derives from the terminology of battle-

---

[83] *Tayis Bank*, 11 and 115–16.
[84] Quoted from *Sir Gawain*, 519; *Parlement of the Thre Ages*, 10; and *The Destruction of Troy*, 9639.

description. A close parallel, describing a real fight, occurs in *Golagros and Gawane*, 992: 'The sterne stakrit with the straik and stertis on stray'. But the subject of Dunbar's line is a woman, not a knight, and in context its sexual significance is clear. At the same time the military connotations are highly relevant in a poem so concerned with the war between the sexes. A somewhat similar effect is produced when the Widow says of her husband: 'he all stunyst throu the stound, as of a stele wappin' (340).

The existence of this strain in *The Tua Mariit Wemen and the Wedo*—archaic, inherited, 'poetic'—needs emphasis, because it gives the lie to any critic inclined to regard this poem as exemplifying a 'natural' mode of writing. In some respects *The Tua Mariit Wemen and the Wedo* is the most 'artificial' of Dunbar's poems. Yet it is unmistakably Scottish, and the obtrusive southernisms that figure in *The Goldyn Targe* are absent; this seems all of a piece, however, with its origins in a poetic tradition that belonged chiefly to the north and west of England. The poem certainly *sounds* colloquial. One measure of Dunbar's skill is the way that he works into the demanding alliterative pattern familiar everyday words, or prosaic legalisms, or *verba injuriosa*:

That hurtis 30w nought worth a hen; 30wr husband pays for all . . .
(269)

That his cheif chymys [dwelling] he had chevist to my sone . . .
(292)

I have ane wallidrag, ane worme, ane auld wobat [caterpillar] carle . . .
(89)

The poem, of course, purports to represent speech, and—specifically—women's speech. Dunbar provocatively challenges long-accepted notions about female linguistic inhibition and sense of decorum.[85] The speech of all three women is noteworthy for its physicality, sexual frankness, and breaking of verbal taboos. The Widow advises the other wives to be outwardly modest, and resemble 'turtoris in 3our talk' (262), but men and women alike here share a taste for the 'langage of lichory' (445). This poem abounds in comments on the way people talk; words and speech are 'hie' (12), frequently 'ryatus' (149, 193, 481), sweet (226), 'akword' (286), and—revealingly—'cummerlik' (510). Dunbar shows an awareness of the different social functions of language, particularly of its power to wound others, to release painful inhibitions, and—a major theme of the poem—to trick and dissemble.

---

[85] See E. Burness, 'Female Language in . . . *The Tua Mariit Wemen and the Wedo*', in Strauss and Drescher, *Scottish Language and Literature*, 359–68.

The Tua Mariit Wemen and the Wedo is characterized by a splendid verbal luxuriance. Dunbar reveals no sense of strain in achieving the alliterative pattern, but rather seeks out ways of making it richer. He uses double alliteration (*aabb*), and hyper-alliteration, and often links pairs of consecutive lines with the same alliterating sound. This device is particularly striking in the two set-pieces of description at beginning and end: in the first it is intermittent (lines 1–2, 5–6, 7–8, 9–10), but the last twenty lines of the poem (511–30) are arranged in alliterating couplets, many of which form sense-units. Sometimes the alliteration is mimetic, as with the repeated /sp/ cluster in

> And so I did him dispise; I spittit quhen I saw
> That superspendit evill spreit spulȝeit of all vertu.   (396–7)

At other times it reinforces more rhetorical patterning:

> Quhat throw the sugurat sound of hir sang glaid
> And throw the savour sanative of the sueit flouris . . .   (7–8)

Such balanced phrasing had long been a feature of the high alliterative style. Similar parallelism occurs in the First Wife's wish

> To schaw my renone royaly quhair preis was of folk—
> To manifest my makdome to multitude of pepill
> And blaw my bewtie on breid quhair bernis war mony,
> That I micht cheis and be chosin, and change quhen me lykit.
>
>   (72–5)

The expansion of line 72 in the following ones is highly symmetrical, and is capped by a similarly threefold pattern of infinitives in line 75. This is controlled and conscious amplification. Other forms of *repetitio* are also employed, along with much antithesis (as in 261 ff.). Yet this poem displays verbal opulence rather than verbosity; Dunbar's language is dense and packed with meaning. One small illustration is the way he uses the second half of his lines, which weaker poets tend to fill with empty phrases or formulae—*Golagros and Gawane* furnishes all too many examples, like 'suthly to sane' and 'teirfull to tell'.[86] There are few such 'fillers' in *The Tua Mariit Wemen and the Wedo*: only a solitary instance of 'the suth for to tell' (217) beside many strong phrases or exclamations, of which the most resounding is 'than chastite adew!' (208). It is striking indeed how often the last slot in lines is reserved for particularly pungent terms for the husbands— 'that auld sathane' (102) or 'that lene gib' (120) or 'that syphyr in bour' (184).

* * *

---

[86] See *Golagros and Gawane*, 5, 15, 39, and *passim*.

In conclusion, Dunbar's figurative language must be briefly mentioned. Its richness has frequently been noted in this book, but it is important to stress how largely imagery contributes to the visual brilliance, the wit, the structure, and the varying tone of Dunbar's poems. In this respect, as in others, he displays great versatility. He uses imagery both to enhance and to degrade; sometimes it is symbolic and wholly unnaturalistic, at others it embodies sensuous and exact observation of people and objects. Figures of every type—simile, metaphor, symbol, personification—abound in his poetry, and he draws on a variety of sources, ranging from the Scriptures, the liturgy, and the bestiary, to the homeliest objects in house and street.[87]

The brevity of Dunbar's images should be noted. There are no extended similes; the longest is the humorous analogy between the moon and the Widow (K 14. 432–5). Dunbar does not disdain short, semi-proverbial similes—swift as an arrow, green as grass, fresh as flowers, 'small as wandis', white as whalebone—the stock-in-trade of all medieval poets. Some well-worn comparisons receive an ironical twist, as when unfaithful wives are termed 'trest as the steill' (K 71. 28). Many of Dunbar's images are strikingly compressed: his succinct compounds, in which the first element carries the metaphor—*catt nois, bledder cheikis*—have already been mentioned, and he often uses verbs in a vigorous metaphorical way:

> sa *heklis* he my chekis   (K 14. 107)
> Quhen I that grome *geldit* had of gudis and of natur   (K 14. 392)
> My panefull purs so *priclis* me.   (K 19. 5)
> That fulle *dismemberit* hes my meter.   (K 26. 8)

Dunbar rarely uses an arresting image in isolation. Sometimes a single figure or analogy provides the organizing principle for the whole poem—the garden in *Sweit rois of vertew* (K 8), or the convivial feast in *Schir at this feist* (K 41). Sometimes it serves rather as the initial stimulus for rich metaphoric invention—the dog in *The wardraipper* (K 29), or the horse in *Schir lat it never in toune be tald* (K 43). In other poems several images are often grouped effectively, as in

> Sum that war ryatous as rammis
> Ar nou maid tame lyk ony lammis,
> And settin down lyk sarye crockis.   (K 32. 16–18)

These commonplace similes are juxtaposed in a witty and bathetic series. Lecherous courtiers dwindle from lusty rams into feeble lambs, and then—last indignity—are emasculated to *crockis*, 'old ewes'.

---

[87] See Bawcutt, 'Aspects of Dunbar's Imagery', in *Chaucer and Middle English Studies*, ed. B. Rowland (1974), 190–200.

Chains or clusters of imagery are likewise deployed in serious poems, very different from this one, such as *Done is a battell* (K 4) or *Quhome to sall I complene my wo* (K 63). Sometimes there is a sustained and complex interplay between a poem's theme and its recurrent imagery; the finest example of this is *The Tua Mariit Wemen and the Wedo*. But a smaller instance occurs in *The Dance of the Sevin Synnis*, where the faces of the lecherous glow 'Lyk turkas birnand reid' (87). The *turkas*, or smith's pincers, evokes not merely colour but torture. Hell was sometimes depicted as a forge, and devils carried pincers as well as pitchforks; in actual life the *turkas* might be employed to pull out eyes, teeth, or finger-nails.[88]

Idyllic imagery—particularly of colour and light—is not absent from Dunbar, but it cannot be denied that his most distinctive poems contain disturbing, painful, and often savage images. The animals to whom people are mockingly compared are often diseased, tormented, or mutilated. The beauty of bird-song is praised in *The Goldyn Targe* and *The Thrissill and the Rois*. Yet Dunbar's most vividly imagined birds are not those that sing 'thair houris' but those engaged in acts of aggression: from the figurative 'howlat chest with crawis' in *The Flyting* (219) to the 'cankerit' crowd that swoop destructively upon the Abbot of Tungland. The poem on the Crucifixion (K 3) is inevitably filled with physical violence—indicated by verbs such as 'tirvit', 'straik', 'birst', 'revin and scorde'. But the metaphoric use of similar words is common in Dunbar, and contributes to the peculiar intensity of his writing. In *The Passioun of Crist* we read of the Crown of Thorns

> Persing his heid with pykis grene. (44)

In *My heid did ȝak* (K 21) Dunbar speaks rather of a migraine

> Perseing my brow as ony ganȝie. (4)

In *The Passioun* the *pykis*, or thorns, are literal; in *Schir for ȝour grace* (K 25) they humorously yet painfully imply the pin-pricks caused by the royal Thistle (23). (The figurative use of 'geldit', 'priclis', 'magellit', and 'dismemberit' should also be recalled.)

Critics' favourite metaphor for Dunbar's language, stemming from his own reference to Chaucer's 'anamalit termes', is enamel. One hostile to *The Goldyn Targe* says, 'this diction *is* like enamel . . . fixed and prefabricated'; another speaks more sympathetically of 'the meticulously interlocked pattern' of Dunbar's words, that form 'a piece of

---

[88] Cf. *Wallace*, vi. 411; and *OED*, *turkis*.

enamelwork'.[89] But the hard fixity of enamel, although it well implies Dunbar's craftsmanship, totally fails to convey his dynamism as a poet. If pressed to supply a better image, I would prefer mercury, or quicksilver: tonally Dunbar is indeed mercurial, and his words are bright, supple, shifting, elusive, and almost as difficult to grasp for precise analysis as balls of quicksilver. Lindsay's phrase, 'at large', is significant. When used of language, it commonly meant 'at length' or 'in abundance'; but when used of people or animals, it meant 'at liberty'. This latter sense seems particularly apt: Dunbar is not merely a poet with a large vocabulary, but one who moves with freedom and immense confidence among words—'The complete consort dancing together.'

[89] Cruttwell (see n. 2), 176; D. Fox, 'Dunbar's *The Golden Targe*', *ELH* 26 (1959), 334; L. Ebin, 'Poetics and Style in Late Medieval Literature', in *Vernacular Poetics in the Late Middle Ages*, ed. Ebin (Kalamazoo, 1984), 276–7.

Select Bibliography

This is merely a guide—a complete bibliography would fill many pages—to some significant work on Dunbar and his background. For other books and articles, see also the bibliographies listed in section 1 and the footnotes to separate chapters. No place of publication is given for works published in London.

1. BIBLIOGRAPHIES

Geddie, William, *A Bibliography of Middle Scots Poets* (STS, 1912).
Ridley, Florence H., 'Middle Scots Writers', in *A Manual of the Writings in Middle English 1050-1500*, ed. A. E. Hartung, vol. 4 (New Haven, Conn., 1973), 1005-60.
Scheps, Walter, and Looney, J. A., *Middle Scots Poets: A Reference Guide to James I, Robert Henryson, William Dunbar and Gavin Douglas* (Boston, Mass., 1986).
Blanchot, Jean-Jacques, 'Dunbar and his Critics: A Critical Survey', in *Scottish Language and Literature, Medieval and Renaissance*, ed. D. Strauss and H. W. Drescher (Frankfurt, 1986), 303-36.

2. EDITIONS

The Poems of William Dunbar, ed. John Small, with W. Gregor and Æ. J. G. Mackay (STS, 1884-93).
The Poems of William Dunbar, ed. J. Schipper (Vienna, 1892-4).
The Poems of William Dunbar, ed. W. Mackay Mackenzie (1932; rev. edn. 1960).
The Poems of William Dunbar, ed. James Kinsley (Oxford, 1979).
Longer Scottish Poems I: 1375-1650, ed. Priscilla Bawcutt and Felicity Riddy (Edinburgh, 1987). (Contains *The Thrissill and the Rois*, *The Goldyn Targe*, and *The Tua Mariit Wemen and the Wedo*.)

3. STUDIES OF DUNBAR

Bawcutt, Priscilla, 'Aspects of Dunbar's Imagery', in *Chaucer and Middle English Studies*, ed. Beryl Rowland (1974), 190-200.
—— 'The Text and Interpretation of Dunbar', *MÆ* 50 (1981), 88-100.
—— 'The Art of Flyting', *SLJ* 10, no. 2 (1983), 5-21.
—— 'The Earliest Texts of Dunbar', in *Regionalism in Medieval Manuscripts and Texts*, ed. Felicity Riddy (Woodbridge, 1991), 183-98.
Baxter, J. W., *William Dunbar: A Biographical Study* (Edinburgh, 1952).

Fox, Denton, 'Dunbar's *The Golden Targe*', *ELH* 26 (1959), 311–34.
—— 'The Chronology of William Dunbar', *PQ* 39 (1960), 413–25.
Hope, A. D., *A Midsummer Eve's Dream: Variations on a Theme by William Dunbar* (Edinburgh, 1971).
Jack, R. D., 'Dunbar and Lydgate', *SSL* 8 (1970–1), 215–27.
Leyerle, J., 'The Two Voices of William Dunbar', *UTQ* 31 (1962), 316–38.
Lyall, R. J., 'Moral Allegory in Dunbar's "Goldyn Targe"', *SSL* 11 (1974), 47–65.
—— 'Dunbar and the Franciscans', *MÆ* 46 (1977), 253–8.
McDiarmid, M. P., 'The Early William Dunbar and his Poems', *SHR* 59 (1980), 126–39.
Morgan, Edwin, 'Dunbar and the Language of Poetry', *EC* 2 (1952), 138–58.
Pearcy, R., 'The Genre of Dunbar's *Tretis of the Tua Mariit Wemen and the Wedo*', *Speculum*, 55 (1980), 58–74.
Reiss, Edmund, *William Dunbar* (Boston, Mass., 1979).
Ross, Ian S., *William Dunbar* (Leiden, 1981).
Roth, Elizabeth, 'Criticism and Taste: Readings of Dunbar's *Tretis*', *SLJ* Supplement 15 (1981), 57–90.
Scott, Tom, *Dunbar: A Critical Exposition of the Poems* (Edinburgh, 1966).

4. THE LITERARY CONTEXT

Aitken, A. J., McDiarmid, M. P., and Thomson, D. S., ed., *Bards and Makars* (Glasgow, 1977).
Burrow, John, 'The Poet as Petitioner', *Studies in the Age of Chaucer*, 3 (1981), 61–75.
—— 'Autobiographical Poetry in the Middle Ages: The Case of Thomas Hoccleve', *PBA* 68 (1982), 389–412.
Curtius, E. R., *European Literature and the Latin Middle Ages*, trans. W. R. Trask (1953).
Fox, Denton, 'The Scottish Chaucerians', in *Chaucer and Chaucerians*, ed. D. S. Brewer (1966), 164–200.
Gray, Douglas, *Themes and Images in the Medieval English Religious Lyric* (1972).
—— 'Rough Music: Some Early Invectives and Flytings', *YES* 14 (1984), 21–43.
Green, Richard F., *Poets and Princepleasers* (Toronto, 1980).
Jack, R. D. S., ed., *The History of Scottish Literature I: Origins to 1660* (Aberdeen, 1988).
Kratzmann, Gregory, *Anglo-Scottish Literary Relations 1430–1550* (Cambridge, 1980).
Lehmann, Paul, *Die Parodie im Mittelalter* (2nd edn., Stuttgart, 1963).
Lewis, C. S., 'The Close of the Middle Ages in Scotland', in *English Literature in the Sixteenth Century* (Oxford, 1954), 66–119.
Lyall, R. J., 'Politics and Poetry in Fifteenth and Sixteenth Century Scotland', *SLJ* 3, no. 2 (1976), 5–29.

SELECT BIBLIOGRAPHY

—— and Riddy, F., ed. *Proceedings of the Third International Conference on Scottish Language and Literature* (Stirling, 1981).
McClure, J. D., and Spiller, M. R. G., ed., *Bryght Lanternis: Essays on the Language and Literature of Medieval and Renaissance Scotland* (Aberdeen, 1989).
Macdonald, A. A., 'Poetry, Politics and Reformation Censorship in Sixteenth-Century Scotland', *ES* 64 (1983), 410–21.
Olson, Glending, *Literature as Recreation in the Later Middle Ages* (Ithaca, New York, 1982).
Smith, Janet M., *The French Background of Middle Scots Literature* (Edinburgh, 1934).
Spearing, A. C., *Medieval to Renaissance in English Poetry* (Cambridge, 1985).
Stevens, John, *Music and Poetry in the Early Tudor Court* (1961; 1979).
Turville-Petre, Thorlac, *The Alliterative Revival* (Cambridge, 1977).
Utley, F. L., *The Crooked Rib: An Analytical Index to the Argument about Women* (New York, 1944; 1970).
Wittig, Kurt, *The Scottish Tradition in Literature* (Edinburgh, 1958).
Woolf, Rosemary, *The English Religious Lyric in the Middle Ages* (Oxford, 1968).

5. THE HISTORICAL CONTEXT

Lynch, Michael, Spearman, M., and Stell, G., ed., *The Scottish Medieval Town* (Edinburgh, 1988).
Macdougall, Norman, *James III: A Political Study* (Edinburgh, 1982).
—— *James IV* (Edinburgh, 1989).
Macfarlane, Leslie J., *William Elphinstone and the Kingdom of Scotland 1431–1514* (Aberdeen, 1985).
Mackie, R. L., *King James IV of Scotland* (Edinburgh, 1958).
McRoberts, David, ed., *Essays on the Scottish Reformation 1513–1625* (Glasgow, 1962).
Nicholson, Ranald, *Scotland: The Later Middle Ages* (Edinburgh, 1974).
Wormald, Jennifer, *Court, Kirk and Community: Scotland 1470–1625* (1981).

6. LANGUAGE

Aitken, A. J., 'Variation and Variety in Written Middle Scots', in *Edinburgh Studies in English and Scots*, ed. A. J. Aitken, A. McIntosh, and H. Pálsson (1971), 177–209.
—— 'The Language of Older Scots Poetry', in *Scotland and the Lowland Tongue*, ed. J. D. McClure (Aberdeen, 1983), 18–49.
—— 'A History of Scots', in *The Concise Scots Dictionary*, ed. Mairi Robinson *et al.* (Aberdeen, 1985).
—— and McArthur, T., *Languages of Scotland* (Edinburgh, 1979).
Macafee, Caroline, and Macleod, I., ed., *The Nuttis Schell: Essays on the Scots Language* (Aberdeen, 1987).

Index

Abell, Adam 43, 78
Aberdeen 40, 44, 89–92, 261
Aberdeen Sasine Register 8, 215
Adam of St Victor 183
Adevineaux Amoureux, Les 295, 344
adynata 213, 259
Agnes, Countess of March 250
Aitken, A. J. 230, 348, 358, 360, 361, 362, 364, 373
almoner, principal 50–1
Ambrose, St 181, 183
André, Bernard 81, 237
Anglo, S. 58, 78, 101
Annot and John 89, 192
Anselm, St 179
Antichrist 281–2
anti-feminism 259, 296–7
Aquinas 265
Arce, Antoine d' 50
Archibald, Elizabeth 195, 200, 201
Archpoet 104, 201, 202
Ariès, Philippe 195
Aristotle 35
Arlotto, Piovano 188
Arnold's Chronicle 75
Ars Moriendi, Craft of Deying 79, 138, 157–8, 261
Arthurian romance 26
Arundel 285, Manuscript 8, 16, 67, 165, 167, 183
Asloan, John 11
Asloan Manuscript 8, 11, 57, 71, 164, 199, 204, 222, 289, 292, 296, 371
Auchinleck Manuscript 284
Auden, W. H. 1–2, 3, 4, 5, 221, 225
Avowis of Alexander, The 295, 327–8
Awntyrs of Arthur, The 194, 373
Ayala, Pedro de 79, 345

Babington, Dr 50
Bakhtin, M. 71, 191, 240
Bale, John 15
ballat 29–33, 80, 125, 158
'ballatis of lufe' 132, 293–7
'ballatis, mirrie' 259
'ballatis of moralitie' 131–3
'ballatis of theoligie' 131, 164
Bannatyne Manuscript 9, 10, 11–13, 15, 39, 92, 131, 132, 134, 140, 144,
147, 150, 160, 164–5, 176, 183, 202, 222, 225, 227, 255, 259, 267–9, 274, 279, 289, 292, 294, 303, 306, 307, 315, 319, 323, 343, 359, 371
Barbour, John 26, 70, 206, 278, 310
Barclay, Alexander 84
Bartholomaeus Anglicus 299
Bataille d'enfer et de paradis 199
Baxter, J. W. 5, 6, 44, 49, 50, 56, 59, 69, 108, 128, 225, 243, 255, 266, 267, 269
Beaton, David 255, 345, 369
Bede 75
Bellenden, John 10, 14, 65
Bennett, J. A. W. 169, 171, 178
Birkmyre, Andrew 223
black people 53–5
blacksmiths, poem on 374
Blanchot, J.-J. 6, 25
Bloomfield, M. W. 284–5, 306
Boccaccio, Giovanni 25, 231, 325, 327
Boece, Hector 14, 65, 108–9, 271
Boethius 141, 280
Bower, Walter 351
Bradbrook, Muriel 257
Brantôme, Pierre 64
Brydges, Sir Egerton 92
Brown, A. L. 105
Brown, Carleton 9, 171
Buchan, David 28, 138
Buchanan, George 92, 234, 250, 273–4
Burel, John 91
Burgundy, dukes of 84, 85
Burns, Robert 1, 2
Burrow, John 4–5, 114–15, 158, 209, 211, 316, 322, 336, 360
Burton, Robert 118, 261–2
Bute, John 48, 59, 61

Calicut 41, 42
Carmeliano, Pietro 237
Carmina Burana 319
carols 15, 67–8, 72, 76, 107, 125, 126, 140, 154, 175–6, 203, 212, 295, 316–17
Cato 138
chanson de mal mariée 338

387

INDEX

chansons d'aventure 63, 134, 303, 318, 319, 331
Charles d'Orléans 77, 316
Charteris, Henry 29, 37
Chartier, Alain 298
Chastelain, G. 84, 87
Chaucer, Geoffrey 10, 19, 22, 23, 24, 26, 37, 122, 131, 156, 188, 190, 239, 261, 293, 294, 306, 313, 314, 325, 326, 333, 358; *ABC, An* 83, 179; *Adam, To* 34; *Anelida and Arcite* 9; *Book of the Duchess* 88; *Complaint of Mars* 77, 86, 294; *Complaint to his Purse* 104, 110–11; *Franklin's Tale* 37, 310, 328; *Friar's Tale* 269; *Knight's Tale* 25, 86, 204, 328; *Legend of Good Women* 93, 294, 335; *Melibee* 192; *Merchant's Tale* 25, 138, 366; *Miller's Tale* 205, 240, 252, 366–7; *Monk's Tale* 135; *Pardoner's Tale* 266; *Parson's Tale* 25, 172; *Physician's Tale* 88; *Rosemound* 29, 192; *Shipman's Tale* 330, 335; *Sir Thopas* 27, 192, 208–10, 360; *Summoner's Tale* 270; *Troilus and Criseyde* 9, 18, 33, 116, 212, 294, 295, 300, 315; *Truth* 134, 141; *Wife of Bath's Prologue* 25, 296, 326, 330, 337, 341
Chepman, Walter and Myllar, Andro 47; prints 8, 15
Chester Plays 339
Christis Kirk on the Grene 248–9
Cicero 22, 314
Clanvowe, Sir John 294, 319, 321, 322
Clapperton 338
Clariodus 204, 205
Clerk, John 39
Cleve, Hans von 357–8
Cogan, Thomas 299
Colkelbie Sow 27, 70, 248–9, 258, 259, 260
Colin Blowbol 53, 195
Columbus, Christopher 43
complaint 41, 85, 118, 161, 220
complaints, lovers' 294, 298–301
Complaynt of Scotland, The 27, 29, 130, 309
Contemplation of Sinners, The 73, 167, 168, 282
court life 6, 15, 17, 19, 36, 42, 47–75, 78–130, 307; entertainments 19, 26–9, 44, 54–62, 65–71, 75–7, 90, 101–2, 189–90, 207, 233–4, 309–10, 327
Craig, Alexander 100, 104

Craig, Thomas 92
Crathes Castle inscriptions 133
Crawford, T. 17
Crétin, Guillaume 104
Cruttwell, P. 347, 381–2
Crying of ane Play, The 47, 209, 241, 258
Curry 48, 50, 59
Curtius, E. R. 21, 83, 102, 125, 145

Dalkeith, Sir James Douglas of 133, 195
Damian, John 56–8, 81, 274–83
Damian, Peter 179
Dance of Death, the 154–5
Dante 18, 23, 279
Deguileville, Guillaume de 285
demandes d'amour 295, 327, 344
Demaundes Joyous, The 28
Deschamps, Eustache 85, 104, 127–8, 329
Devonshire Manuscript 9
Diabolus et Virgo 273
Dialogus Creaturarum Moralizatus 254
Dickinson, W. C. 150
Dies Irae 164, 173
Dog, James 51, 241, 244–7, 248, 274
Donald Dubh, *see* Owyr, Donald
Donne, John 73, 181
Dorsch, T. S. 104, 108, 110
Douglas, Gavin 7, 10, 19, 25, 34, 35, 36, 39, 46, 67, 105–6, 137, 166, 190, 196, 197, 231, 293, 294, 314, 359, 370; *Eneados* 9, 11, 13, 14, 15, 16, 18, 30, 205, 372, 373; Prologues to *Eneados* 74–5, 84, 158, 164, 257, 262, 265, 283, 289, 296, 315, 317, 348, 349, 353, 369; *Palice of Honour* 18, 22, 28, 29, 32, 33, 37, 41, 79–80, 147, 228, 237, 279, 280, 327, 353
Drummond of Hawthornden, William 33, 350
DUNBAR, WILLIAM
Life: 1–2, 4–8, 80–1, 103–9, 115, 225, 269–70, 328–9; *see also* court life
Topics:
allegory in 48, 92–103, 120–22, 158–9, 170–1, 284–8, 307–15
alliterative verse 26, 206, 208, 355, 357, 370–9
anglicisms 358–60
approach to poetry 16–36, 191
archaisms 204, 206, 371–2, 378
audience 13–16, 134, 165
aureate style 349, 353–4
canon 8–13, 150, 260, 324

INDEX

comic poems 185–292
critics' views of 1–5, 23–5, 37–8, 104, 131–2, 186–7, 221–2, 347–8, 381–2
dating of poems 8, 50–1, 54, 57, 62–77, 108–9, 225
debate poems 227, 237, 318–22, 325–6
dreams, visions 25, 32, 63, 92–103, 119–22, 168–71, 257–92, 311–12
flyting 36, 118, 220–56, 334
'game'-element in 5, 19–20, 67, 128, 191, 225–6, 326–8
genres, kinds 3–4, 5, 24, 25, 32, 104–5, 139, 141, 185, 198, 206, 214, 216, 222–3, 236–7, 255, 279, 303, 304, 318, 326; *see also* ballat; carols; *chansons d'aventure*; complaint; fables; fabliaux; gossips' meeting
imagery 23, 36, 88, 93–5, 98–100, 112–13, 117, 123–5, 127–30, 142, 146, 159, 162, 166, 174, 175, 178–81, 205, 229–31, 239, 242, 243, 244–5, 246, 249, 251, 252, 263, 283, 285–8, 298–9, 302, 313–14, 332–4, 340–1, 380–1
irony 77, 125, 155, 157, 161, 203, 211–19, 272, 274, 299, 330–1, 337–8
love poems 297–315
macaronic style 194, 350–2
makar, maker 3, 17–19
metrical forms 1, 12, 31–2, 82, 85, 103, 111, 135–6, 151, 178, 198, 208, 211, 228, 245, 284, 289, 290, 294, 312–13, 349, 357–8, 374–5, 379
moral poems 131–64
Nature, concept of 93–8, 311, 313–15, 321, 332–4
parody 3, 191–211, 259, 300–1, 335–7
petitions 103–30, 161–2
proverbs, use of 53, 110, 121, 125, 136–8, 145, 149, 160, 185, 254, 255, 321–2, 324
refrains 31, 65, 85, 91, 110, 119, 135–6, 150, 153–4, 246, 266, 305, 310, 318
religious poems 161–84, 315–22, 354–8
rhetoric, rhetorical topoi 21–3, 33–4, 82–4, 88, 146, 147–8, 151, 228, 251, 277, 280, 318, 343–4, 379
scatology 189, 191, 204, 239–41, 252, 291

Scriptural allusions 72, 89, 94, 102, 137, 138–9, 143, 145, 148, 159, 163–4, 166, 167–8, 175, 202, 224, 236, 264, 266, 277, 281, 321, 322, 335–6
style and language 3, 22–3, 97, 180, 181–2, 185, 198, 224, 229, 235–6, 253, 278, 303, 317, 347–82
women, poems on 3, 214–17, 249–52, 293–346
word-play 57, 88–9, 111–13, 119, 128–9, 217, 218, 244, 250, 299, 303, 305, 310
Poems:
Abbot of Tungland, The (K 54) 22, 25, 29, 31, 56–8, 211, 213, 240–1, 261, 264, 274–9, 361, 372–3, 381
Amendis to the Tel3ouris and Sowtaris, The (K 52C) 217–19, 239, 288–90, 363; *see also Fasternis Evin in Hell*
Ane Ballat of Our Lady (K 2) 11, 12, 29, 94, 164, 166, 320, 322, 354–8, 365
Ane murlandis man of uplandis mak (K 74) 43, 44, 45, 214, 220
Ballade of Bernard Stewart, The (K 35) 11, 12, 22, 29, 40, 51, 62, 64, 82 4, 107, 208, 359
Be divers wyis and operatiounes (K 20) 26, 57, 106, 114
Be mery man and tak nocht fer in mynd (K 65) 12, 142–3, 186
Be 3e ane lufar (K 11) 321
Bewty and the Presoneir, *see Sen that I am presoneir*
Blyth Aberdeane thow beriall of all tounis (K 48) 10, 44, 62, 89–92
Complane I wald wist I quhome till (K 45) 104, 114, 115, 117, 118, 161, 241–2, 363
Dance of the Sevin Deidly Sinnis, The (K 52A) 121, 211, 240, 260, 283–91, 373, 381; *see also Fasternis Evin in Hell*
Done is a battell on the dragon blak (K 4) 73, 131, 148, 164, 178–84, 261, 352, 373, 381
Dregy, The (K 22) 11, 12, 31, 40, 45, 72, 126, 187, 193, 198–203, 212, 293, 301
Eftir geving I speik of taking (K 80) 12, 44, 220
Fasternis Evin in Hell (K 52) 31, 40, 69–71, 263, 264, 265, 288–90, 361; *see also The Turnament*
Flyting of Dunbar and Kennedie, The

INDEX

DUNBAR, WILLIAM (cont.)
  (K 23) 7–8, 11, 12, 16, 20–1, 32,
  40, 43–4, 45, 50, 115, 141, 193–4,
  221–39, 244, 252, 260, 262, 263–4,
  283, 334, 347, 348, 357, 361,
  363–5, 373–4, 376, 381
Foure maner of men ar evill to pleis
  (K 83) 12, 66
Fredome, honour and nobilnes (K 68) 12,
  135–6
Full oft I mus and hes in thocht (K 64)
  149–50
Gladethe thoue queyne of Scottis regioun
  (K 31) 82, 87–9, 102, 322, 364
Goldyn Targe, The (K 10) 11, 12, 15,
  21–4, 27, 30, 32, 33, 44, 62, 74, 95,
  120, 187, 193, 211, 243, 262, 283,
  294, 297, 307–8, 310–15, 332,
  333–4, 347, 349, 353–4, 358–9,
  373, 381
He that hes gold and grit riches (K 70) 1,
  12, 144, 185–6, 324
How sould I rewill me or in quhat wys
  (K 82) 24, 136, 139–41
I seik about this warld unstabille (K 58)
  116, 148–9
I that in heill wes and gladnes (K 62) 5,
  11, 12, 17, 18, 24, 25–6, 31, 50,
  131, 146, 153–8, 218, 293, 296,
  367, 369–70
I thocht lang quhill sum lord come hame
  (K 47) 10, 29, 31, 103, 107–8, 109
*Illuster Lodovick of France most Cristin
  king* (K 36) 10, 14, 51, 62, 64, 84–7
In secreit place this hindir nycht (K 13)
  12, 63, 263, 301–3, 324, 361, 363,
  366–7
In to thir dirk and drublie dayis (K 69)
  30, 64, 117, 120, 122, 146, 158–61,
  212, 293, 370
In vice most vicius he excellis (K 34) 26,
  64, 186, 252–6
Lament for the Makars, see *I that in heill
  wes and gladnes*
Lang heff I maed of ladyes quhytt (K 33)
  8, 17, 53–5, 186, 249–52, 297
Lucina schynnyng in silence of the nicht
  (K 53) 22, 29, 57–8, 122, 264,
  278–83
Madam ʒour men said thai wald ryd
  (K 32) 69, 380–1
Man sen thy lyfe is ay in weir (K 67) 12,
  14, 132, 144–5
Maner of Passyng to Confessioun, The
  (K 5) 22, 71, 131, 139, 172

Memento homo quod cinis es (K 61) 12,
  72, 134, 146, 174, 352
Merle and the Nychtingall, The (K 16)
  22, 31, 95, 96, 97, 136, 227, 311,
  315–22, 325, 359
Musing allone this hinder nicht (K 81)
  12, 24, 63, 133, 136, 139–41
My hartis tresure and swete assured fo
  (K 12) 4, 193, 211, 299–301
My heid did ʒak ʒester nicht (K 21) 10,
  17, 31, 32, 64, 103, 114, 115–17,
  367, 381
My lordis of chalker pleis ʒow to heir
  (K 46) 10, 369
My prince in God gif the guid grace
  (K 18) 10, 20, 66, 109
Now cumis aige quhair ʒewth hes bene
  (K 17) 31, 315–17
Now of wemen this I say for me (K 72)
  211, 323–4
O gracious princes guid and fair (K 30)
  14, 19, 103, 108, 189, 239, 245–7,
  290, 368
*O wreche be war this warld will wend the
  fro* (K 60) 132, 135, 147–8, 174
Of discretioun (K 78–80) 136, 290
Off benefice sir at everie feist (K 40) 64,
  112–14, 124, 220
Off every asking followis nocht (K 78)
  12, 106, 136–8
Off lentren in the first mornyng (K 59)
  14, 44, 72, 134, 146, 147, 319
Passioun of Crist, The (K 3) 11, 12, 22,
  31, 32, 69, 73, 132, 165, 167–71,
  173, 174, 265, 292, 381
Quha will behald of luve the chance
  (K 15) 311–12
*Quhat is this lyfe bot ane straucht way to
  deid* (K 57) 12, 13, 31, 132, 145–6,
  147
Quho thinkis that he hes sufficence (K 66)
  134, 135, 142
Quhome to sall I complene my wo (K 63)
  161–4, 165, 352–3, 373, 381
Quhy will ʒe merchantis of renoun (K 75)
  10, 14, 26–7, 31, 40, 45–7, 150–3,
  217, 220, 265
Rorate celi desuper (K 1) 65, 164, 165,
  166, 174–8, 183
Rycht airlie on Ask Weddinsday (K 73)
  72–3, 214–15, 324, 326
Salviour suppois my sensualite (K 7) 31,
  132, 165
Sanct salvatour send silver sorrow (K 19)
  29, 45, 110–12, 117

390

INDEX

Schir at this feist of benefice (K 41) 14, 32, 112–13, 124, 380
Schir for 30ur grace bayth nicht and day (K 25) 103, 109–10, 359, 381
Schir I complane of injuris (K 26) 14, 17, 29, 33–4, 51, 59, 61–2, 242–4
Schir lat it never in toune be tald (K 43) 11, 12, 31, 40, 66–9, 103, 114, 123, 126–30, 370, 380
Schir Thomas Norny (K 27) 16, 27, 50, 59–60, 193, 207–11, 215–16, 360–1
Schir 3e have mony servitouris (K 44) 27, 31, 34–6, 45, 48, 62, 103, 108, 114, 117–18, 213, 221, 369
Schir 3it remember as befoir (K 42) 14, 27, 29, 32, 43, 103, 108, 114, 117, 122–6, 202
Sen that I am a presoneir (K 9) 12, 31, 61, 307–10, 312, 359
Sir Jhon Sinclair begowthe to dance (K 28) 17, 50–1, 52, 59, 61, 189, 239, 240, 247–9, 297, 361, 366
Sweit rois of vertew and of gentilnes (K 8) 31, 211, 298–9, 359, 380
Tabill of Confessioun, The (K 6) 4, 31, 71, 164–5, 171–4
Testament of Maister Andro Kennedy, The (K 38) 12, 13, 25, 31, 32, 44, 45, 51–3, 62, 193, 194–8, 212–13, 301, 350–2
The wardraippper of Venus boure (K 29) 14, 19, 51, 103, 108, 239, 244–6, 290, 368, 380
Thir ladyis fair (K 71) 216–17, 219, 324, 331, 338, 380
This hinder nycht halff sleiping as I lay (K 51) 10, 17, 31–2, 45, 63, 66, 114, 117, 119–22, 141, 159, 230, 265, 373
This hindir nycht in Dumfermeling (K 37) 39, 63, 303–7
This nycht befoir the dawing cleir (K 55) 4, 8, 22, 40, 63, 207, 213, 264, 269–74
This nycht in my sleip I wes agast (K 56) 63, 213, 260, 261, 264, 265–9, 293
This waverand warldis wretchidnes (K 39) 31, 40–3, 103, 114, 118–19, 211, 367, 369
Thrissill and the Rois, The (K 50) 8, 22, 25, 29, 30, 31, 62, 74–5, 92–103, 120, 123, 171, 185, 254, 278, 292, 314, 321, 347, 354, 359
To dwell in court my freind gife that thow list (K 77) 135, 141–2, 146–7, 293

To speik of gift or almous deidis (K 79) 12
To speik of science craft or sapience (K 76) 23, 44, 150–1
To the o marcifull salviour myn, see *Tabill of Confessioun*
Tua Mariit Wemen and the Wedo, The (K 14) 11, 12, 16, 25, 29, 30, 31, 44, 46, 63, 69, 75–7, 117, 193, 213–14, 239, 264, 287, 297, 324–46, 347, 366, 374–9, 381
Turnament, The (K 52B) 19, 188, 189, 193, 204–7, 210, 239–40, 262, 288–92, 365–6, 371–2; see also *Fasternis Evin in Hell*
dubious attributions 10, 12, 260; *Now fayre fayrest off every fayre* 31; *To London* 44, 82
Dunfermline 39
Durkan, J. 11, 15

Ebin, Lois 23–4, 382
Eddy, Elizabeth 59, 208, 360
Edinburgh 6, 40, 42, 45–7, 150–3, 198, 229, 234, 235
Edward I 238
Edward II 189
Eglamour 208
Eliot, T. S. 222, 382
Elliott, R. C. 236
Elphinstone, William 105, 329
Emmerson, R. K. 281–2
Erasmus 39, 138, 274, 349
Este, Isabella d' 60

fables 93, 129, 187, 188, 246, 254, 279, 297, 304–7, 319
fabliaux 187, 252, 262, 279, 326
facetiae 28, 187, 190, 276
Fair Maid of Ribbledale, The 192
Fasciculus Morum 144
Fause Knight, The 273
Fergus Gaist 258, 259
Fergusson, *Proverbs* 110
First Helandman, The 258–9
Fitzgerald, Gerald 295
Fleming, Abraham 244
Floure and the Leafe, The 10
fools 39, 50, 53, 58–62, 243–4
Ford, Philip 273
Fordun, John 256
Forman, Andrew 50, 54, 58
Foullis, James 349

Index

Fox, Denton 3, 4, 15, 23, 62, 132, 311, 318, 382
Francis, St 4, 270–4
Frappier, Jean 263
Freiris of Berwick, The 10, 258
Friedman, A. B. 15, 30, 269
Froissart, Jean 47, 316
Fryer, Peter 54

Gaelic 20–1, 37, 53, 236–9, 348
Gaguin, Robert 237
Galbraith, Thomas 49, 95
Garland, John of 221
Geoffrey of Monmouth 275, 280
Gesta Romanorum 271
Gigli, Giovanni 237
Gillies, W. 236
Goff, J. Le 265
Golagros and Gawane 370, 371, 375, 376, 378, 379
Golden Legend, The 261, 335
Goliardic clerks, verse 8, 22, 217
Golias, Apocalypse of 193
Good Wife treatises 138, 336–7
Gospelles of Dystaves 338
gossips' meeting 338–9
Gower, John 22, 26, 37, 77, 79, 301, 316–17
Gray, Douglas 2, 51, 133, 153, 155, 174, 176, 222
Graysteill 26
Great Chronicle of London, The 237
Green, R. F. 49, 80
Greene, R. L. 27, 67
Greene, Robert 112
Gringore, Pierre 101–2
Gude and Godlie Ballatis, The 30, 293
'Gy, spreit of' 27, 194, 264
Gyre Carling, The 258, 259

Hailes, Lord 18, 53, 153, 203, 221, 225, 315
Harington, Sir John 188
Harley 2253, Manuscript 192, 250
Hary, Blind 32, 80, 147, 232, 370
Hay, B. 279
Haye, Sir Gilbert 98, 101, 152, 364
Hawes, Stephen 14, 353
Henisch, B. A. 73
Henry VII 58, 79, 80, 81, 93, 101, 237, 295; elegy for 85, 87
Henry VIII 66, 79, 93, 106, 295, 309
Henryson, Robert 2, 15, 25, 26, 32, 39, 97, 186, 239, 370; *Abbey Walk* 133, 142; *Age and Youth* 318; *Bludy Serk* 178; *Fables* 10, 43, 93, 96, 99, 132, 134, 138, 142, 143, 147, 188–9, 191, 220, 254, 261, 288, 289, 304–5, 322, 342; *Orpheus and Eurydice* 146, 284, 285; *Praise of Age* 316; *Prayer for the Pest* 228, 355; *Robene and Makyne* 303, 321; *Testament of Cresseid* 29, 113, 118, 147, 296; *Thre Deid Pollis* 147, 194, 250
Herbert, George 171
Herebert, William 182
Higden, Ranulph 275
Highlands, Highlanders 20, 44, 78, 98, 228, 232, 238, 252–6, 287
Hill, Richard 351
Hilton, Walter 168
Hirsch, R. 43
Hoccleve, Thomas 4–5, 9, 10, 104, 106, 111, 136, 250, 305; *Letter of Cupid* 9, 294, 296, 323–4; *Regement of Princes* 107, 112, 122
Hogg, James 28
Holland, Richard 20, 26, 96, 122, 124, 166, 189, 190, 233, 236, 277–8, 330, 370, 372, 375, 377
Homer 22
Horace 22, 35, 250
Houdenc, Raoul de 263
Howden, John of 320
Howell, P. 127
Hunt, T. 192

Innocent III, pope 265
Ireland, John 72–3, 79–80, 164, 165, 168, 171–2, 174, 349, 364

Jacobs, N. 325
James I, of Scotland 85, 98; see also *Kingis Quair*
James III, of Scotland 49, 70, 78, 95, 242
James IV, of Scotland 1, 11, 14, 45, 49, 56–8, 59, 70, 74, 78–81, 84, 90, 95, 98, 100, 109–11, 121, 123, 165, 199, 223, 233, 251, 252, 274, 306–7, 344
James V, of Scotland 7, 14, 15, 47, 80, 81, 88, 128, 234, 264
James VI, of Scotland 65, 79, 90, 223, 233, 272, 306, 363, 373
Jewel, John 281
Jill of Brentford's Testament 198

INDEX

John, of Denmark 130
John the Reeve 27, 126, 189, 208
Johnson, Samuel 276
Johnston, Patrick 48, 49, 70
Jonson, Ben 32, 33, 105
Julius II, pope 56
Juvenal 296

Katharine of Aragon 80, 309
Kelly, James 53
Kennedy, Andro 48, 51–3, 77, 194–8, 274
Kennedy, Walter 5, 13, 49, 157, 166, 194, 263, 316; *Flyting* 7–8, 32, 37, 46, 62, 221–39, 347; *Passioun of Crist* 32, 167, 168, 170
King Berdok 209, 258, 260
King Hart 120, 195, 309
Kingis Quair, The 280, 294, 310, 319, 320, 321
Kinsley, James 7, 12, 13, 50, 51, 60, 122, 131, 142, 150, 161, 186, 210, 234, 236, 239, 255, 267, 270, 288, 289, 291, 300, 301, 302, 306, 325, 332, 344, 357
Kipling, Gordon 309
Knox, John 255, 306
Kolve, V. A. 191
Kratzmann, Gregory 24, 139
Kynd Kittok 258, 259, 260, 291, 370

Laing, David 77
Lam, James 246
Lancelot of the Laik 166
Land of Cokaygne, The 259
Langland, William 47, 121, 285–6, 333, 370
Latin 22, 192, 194–7, 237–8, 319, 320, 348, 349
Latin hymns 22, 173, 181, 182–4, 192–3, 355–7
Lay of Sorrow, The 294, 299
Lemaire, Jean 84
Leslie, John 54, 55, 57, 58, 75, 94, 275, 279
Lewis, C. S. 48, 104, 178, 257, 260, 311, 354, 368
Lichtoun 257–9
Lille, Alain de 96
Lindsay, Sir David 11, 15, 16, 80, 81, 128, 221, 222, 234, 322; *Bagsche* 161; *Dreme* 41, 152, 264; *Justing* 206–7; *Monarche* 126, 203; *Papyngo* 18, 37, 42, 78, 89, 113, 130, 347; *Squyer Meldrum* 195, 204–6
Lindsay, Robert, *see* Pitscottie
Lismore, Book of the Dean of 296
Liturgy 22, 72, 126, 153, 157, 175–7, 192, 198, 199–203, 350–3
Livy 14
Lollardry 231
London 44, 82, 153
Longuyon, Jacques de 295
Louis XII, of France 14, 79, 87, 101, 130
Loutfut, Adam 87, 124
Lowell, J. R. 186
Lufaris Complaynt, The 294
Lyall, R. J. 2, 152, 203, 222, 233, 270, 306–7, 311
Lydgate, John 9, 10, 22, 23, 37, 76, 77, 91, 121, 135, 143, 153, 158, 212, 294, 318, 320, 353; *Complaint of a Lover's Life* 294, 314, 329; *Fall of Princes, The* 9, 10, 84; *Letter to Gloucester* 104, 111; *Testament* 167; *Wicked Tunge, A* 24, 139

Mcbrek, Andrew 51
MacDiarmid, Hugh 24
McDiarmid, M. P. 5, 62
MacDonald, A. A. 41, 164
Macfarlane, L. 79, 105, 329
MacGregor, Duncan 53
Machaut, G. 116, 329
Mackenzie, W. M. 131, 161, 227, 255, 267
Mackie, R. L. 54, 108
Maclaine, A. H. 249
Maclean, Lauchlan 253–4
Macrobius 264
Maitland, John 140, 142
Maitland, Sir Richard 9, 12, 16, 88, 92, 113, 132, 141–2, 143–4, 253; Maitland Folio 9, 11–12, 31, 134, 137, 141, 149, 164–5, 202, 222, 245, 247, 249, 255, 267–9, 289, 290, 259
Maitland, William 142
Major, John 39, 47, 256
Malory, Sir Thomas 74
Mankind 262
Margaret, *dauphine* 85, 87
Margaret Tudor, Queen 14, 49, 62, 69, 74, 82, 87–94, 101, 105, 110, 244, 294
Martial 22, 34, 36, 99, 105, 125, 127, 273

INDEX

Martin, Florentine 15
Martineau-Génieys, C. 84, 85
Mary of Guise 90
Mary Magdalene 173
Mary Queen of Scots 66, 79, 88, 91, 92
Mary Tudor 101
Maximilian 207
Maxwell, John 10, 132
Maxwell, Robert 104
Melvill, James 16
Menologium 75
Mersar 26, 296, 321
Mery Tales of Gotham 73
Messe des oiseaux 320
Meun, Jean de 121
Miller, P. 221
Milton, John 42, 175, 266
Minot, Lawrence 237, 238
Molinet, Jean 81, 84, 85, 86, 190, 195, 282, 309, 357
Montgomerie, Alexander 31, 89, 104, 160, 222, 225, 233
Moore, A. K. 31, 300, 329
Morte Arthure, The 334, 370, 377
Mote, J. de 285
Munro, J. 252–3, 256
Mure 51, 61, 241, 242–4, 274
Musgrave, Mistress 50, 55, 66, 247–8, 297
Myllar, Andro, *see* Chepman, Walter
Myln, A. 252

Newton, Humfrey, 84
Norman, J. S. 201, 287
Norny, Thomas 48, 59–60, 207–11

Office of the Dead 153, 157, 199–203
Ogilvy, Marion 345
Ogilvy, Walter 80, 89
Oliver of Malmesbury 275
Olson, G. 2, 18
Overbury, Sir Thomas 342, 344
Ovid 3, 18, 22, 35, 41, 317
Owl and the Nightingale, The 318–19
Owst, G. R. 138, 139–40, 271
Owyr, Donald 241, 252–5

Paniter, Patrick 108
Parlement of the Thre Ages, The 316, 377
Parliament of Birds, The 319–20
Paston family 105, 345
patronage 105–7
Paul, Sir J. B. 216

Peacham, Henry 100
Pearcy, Roy 326, 343
Pearsall, D. 4, 24
Peblis to the Play 248–9
Peckham, John 320
Pecock, Reginald 75
Peire d'Alvernhe 2, 247
Persius 37, 125
Petrarch 18
Piers Plowman, *see* Langland
Pinkerton, J. 10, 131–2, 186
Pisan, Christine de 85, 87, 294, 296, 324
Pitscottie, Robert Lindsay of 54, 55, 58, 242, 250
Pliny 99
Poggio Bracciolini 28, 190, 237
Polemo-Middinia 350
Polwart, Patrick Hume of 222, 225, 228, 233
Prick of Conscience, The 316
prophetic writings 28, 29, 280–3, 374
Protestantism, Protestants 11, 65, 67, 68, 74, 164–5, 203, 293
Pseudo-Cato 141
Puttenham, George 18, 27, 36

Quare of Jelusy, The 74, 294, 350
Quinn, D. B. 41, 43
Quintilian 211
Quinze Joies de Mariage, Les 296, 338–41

Rabelais 241, 282
Ralegh, Sir Walter 142, 146
Ramsay, Allan 18, 92, 218, 222
Ramson, W. 132
Ratis Raving 138, 141, 143
Rauf Coilyear 27, 126, 245, 287, 370, 371, 377
Reformers, *see* Protestantism
Reidpeth Manuscript 9, 10, 12, 92, 115, 122, 128, 222, 255, 307
Reiss, Edmund 2, 13, 51, 103, 104, 116, 161, 187, 211–12, 219, 225, 226, 243, 291, 299, 300
Remedy of Love, The 343–4
René II, Duke of Lorraine 100
Rhétoriqueurs, Grands 84
Riddy, F. 370, 374
Rigg, A. G. 200, 270
Robertson, D. W. 2, 240
Robin Hood 27, 189, 208, 209, 360–1
Rolland, John 29, 110, 299, 318, 322
Rolle, Richard 166

INDEX

Rollins, H. 33
Roman de Renart, Le 191, 304
Roman de la Rose 47, 96, 187, 295, 296, 301, 307, 311, 321; English version 93, 319
romances 27–8, 204–10
Rosier des Guerres, Le 101
Ross, Ian 2, 51, 55, 59, 103, 116, 186, 187, 203, 219, 226, 249, 277, 278, 300, 302, 307
Ross, Sir John the 225, 227
Rowll 257, 260, 261, 262
Rug, Cuddy 59

Sacchetti, Franco 210
St Andrews 6, 45, 70, 234
St Patrick's Purgatory 284
Salut d'Enfer, Le 263
Sandison, H. 319
Schipper, J. 21, 161, 227, 267, 323
Scoggin 276, 342
Scott, Alexander 11, 31, 66, 141, 203, 206
Scott, Tom 4, 55, 56, 92, 99, 122, 132, 141, 157, 171, 178, 210, 219, 221, 255, 323, 329, 344, 351
Screech, M. A. 282
Selden B. 24, Manuscript 134, 294
Seneca 138, 143, 145, 196
Seven Deadly Sins 284–8
Sevin Sages, Buke of 296
Shippey, T. A. 138
Sibbald, J. 344
Sidney, Sir Philip 39, 116
Simon Magus 281–2
Sinclair, Henry, Lord 13, 294
Sinclair, Sir John 50, 51, 248–9
Sir Bevis 27, 207–8
Sir Corneus 189
Sir Gawain and the Green Knight 109, 206, 250, 259, 370, 375, 376
Skelton, John 10, 15, 25, 66, 93, 190, 238, 255, 349; *Bouge of Court* 120, 121, 128, 340; *Elinor Rumming* 338; *Garland of Laurel* 10, 22, 32, 89, 237; *Garnesche* 237; *Philip Sparrow* 202, 203
Smith, A. J. 115
Smith, Alexander 1, 5
Smith, Janet 25
Spearing, A. C. 99, 103, 329, 331
Spectacle of Luf, The 296, 340, 342
speculum principis tradition 92, 97, 101, 121
Speirs, John 2, 186, 326, 332, 347–8

Spenser, Edmund 19, 96, 128, 285–8
Statius 22, 96
Stevens, John 294–5
'Stewart' 12, 134
Stewart, Bernard 4, 14, 40, 50, 51, 62, 64, 81, 82–7, 208, 354
Stewart, William 15, 222, 323
Stobo 5, 49, 50, 225
Stone, L. 345
Suffolk, duke of 203, 237
Sutherland, Alexander of 196
Swynbrocht, Sir David Sinclair of 196, 197
Sylvius, Aeneas 64
Sym and his Bruder 206

Talk of Ten Wives, The 295, 338
Tastevin, Testament de 195
Tayis Bank 294, 370, 377
Taylor, Rachel 104
Theodulus, *Eclogue* of 237
Thomas of Celano 271
Thomas, Edward 68
Thompson, Stith 275
Thomson, D. 20
Thre Prestis of Peblis, The 61
Thrush and Nightingale, The 319
Thynne, William 10
Tongland, abbot of, *see* Damian, John
Tournament of Tottenham 206
Towneley Plays 159, 194, 262
Traill, Sandy 48
Treasurer 48–9
Tuck, J. A. 105
Turnbull, Alexander 106
Turville-Petre, T. 370, 374, 375
Tutivillus 262, 265
Twelve Mery Jests of the Wyddow Edyth 342

Udall, Nicholas 233
Utley, F. L. 92, 212, 250, 296, 338

Valentine, St 77
Valentines 367
Valla, Lorenzo 80, 237, 349
Villon, François 25, 32, 195, 198
Virgil 10, 18, 22, 35, 205, 257, 275, 284, 317
Vision of Tundal, The 284

INDEX

Walton, John 9, 10
Watson, James 222
Webbe, William 32
Weddirburn 323
Welsford, E. 59, 60
Wemyss, Sir John Wemyss of 6
Wife of Auchtermuchty, The 258, 339, 362
Wilson, F. P. 28, 190
Winters, Yvor 368
Wolsey, Cardinal 130
Woolf, R. 153, 154, 155, 157, 168, 169, 171, 357

Wordsworth, William 5, 97
'World Upside Down' 277
Wormald, J. 232
Wyatt, Sir Thomas 9, 31, 135, 318
Wynkyn de Worde 28, 296
Wyntoun, Andrew 26, 238

York Plays 94, 176
Young, Sir John 94, 102, 294
Youth 322